ECONOMETRIC METHODS

Third Edition

J. Johnston

University of California, Irvine

McGraw-Hill Book Company

New York St. Louis San Francisco Auckland Bogotá Hamburg
London Madrid Mexico Montreal New Delhi
Panama Paris São Paulo Singapore Sydney Tokyo Toronto

In memory of
B. and J.

This book was set in Times Roman by Science Typographers, Inc.
The editors were Patricia A. Mitchell and Scott Amerman;
the cover was designed by Nadja Furlan;
the production supervisor was Phil Galea.
The drawings were done by Burmar.
Halliday Lithograph Corporation was printer and binder.

ECONOMETRIC METHODS

6 7 8 9 0 HALHAL 8 9 8 7

ISBN 0-07-032685-1

Library of Congress Cataloging in Publication Data

Johnston, J. (John), date
Econometric methods.

Includes bibliographical references and index.
1. Econometrics. I. Title.
HB139.J65 1984 330'.028 83-14899
ISBN 0-07-032685-1

CONTENTS

PREFACE

This edition has been completely rewritten. The main features of the new edition are the following:

1. The mathematical, statistical threshold has been lowered in order to make the material more accessible to students with only an elementary prior knowledge of statistics. This has resulted in a somewhat larger proportion of words to symbols in the early chapters than would otherwise have been the case. A series of paragraphs on mathematical, statistical topics has also been provided in Appendix A. These are keyed into the early chapters to ease the transition into the heart of the book. For the same reason the chapter on matrix algebra has been retained and, indeed, expanded to include a geometric as well as an algebraic treatment of some topics.
2. All the inference procedures for the general linear model have been derived as special cases of a single basic procedure, namely, the testing of a set of linear restrictions on the parameters of the model (Chapter 5). This leads in turn to an exhaustive treatment of tests for structural change (Chapter 6). Chapter 6 also contains extended treatments of the use of dummy variables and of multicollinearity among the regressors.
3. Every effort has been made to cover both new and old topics on which substantial work has been done in recent years and which are thought to be significant and enduring rather than passing fancies. Such topics include the estimation of sets of equations with special reference to transcendental logarithmic approximations and applications in energy economics (Chapter 8), autocorrelated error terms (Chapter 8), time series techniques (Chapter 9) and, in *A Smorgasbord of Further Topics* (Chapter 10), the following "menu": recursive residuals, spline functions, pooling of time-series and cross-section data, variable-parameter models, qualitative dependent variables, and errors in variables. The author has also granted himself the indulgence of some personal comments on the present state of econometrics (Chapter 12).

4. The problem sets have been extended to become truly Anglo-American, with offerings from the Royal Statistical Society plus the universities of Cambridge, London, Manchester, and Oxford on one side of the pond, and Chicago, Michigan, Yale, and Washington on the other side. Grateful acknowledgment is made to various anonymous authorities for the first set, and to Arnold Zellner, Jan Kmenta, Peter Phillips, and Charles Nelson for the second. Appendix B also contains an extensive set of statistical, econometric tables, and grateful acknowledgment is made to the appropriate sources for permission to publish them.

My debts to many individuals can be warmly acknowledged but never fully recompensed. Craig Riddell (University of British Columbia) and Paul Ruud (University of California, Berkeley) read the entire manuscript and contributed many valuable comments. I am very grateful to both of them. My thanks also go to Ian McAvinchey (University of Aberdeen) and to my colleagues Ken Chomitz, Max Fry, and Charles Lave (University of California, Irvine) for comments on various chapters. Ken Chomitz has also produced a solutions manual for the problems in the text. This in some places is almost a supplementary text in that extended solutions have been written for various problems, outlining particular issues that could not be dealt with in the main text. Copies of the solutions manual are available to instructors on application to the publishers. Kathy Alberti and Barbara Sawyer did a magnificent job on a difficult manuscript. In addition, Barbara Sawyer did the preliminary artwork, prepared the tables in Appendix B, and proofread the entire manuscript. Finally, I gratefully acknowledge the questions and suggestions from teachers and students in many parts of the world during the two decades since the first publication of this book. I can only hope that this third edition will inspire a similar response.

J. Johnston

CHAPTER

ONE

THE NATURE OF ECONOMETRICS

Before asking the question, "What is econometrics?," one must pose the prior question, "What is economics?" The answer to the second question will indicate the role that econometrics can play in the development of economics. Although the focus of the exposition in this chapter will be on economic models, the methods that have been developed in econometrics can and do play an important role in other social sciences, where there is a concern with building and estimating models of the interconnections between various sets of variables in a predominantly nonexperimental situation.

1-1 ECONOMIC MODEL BUILDING

Economists seek to understand the nature and functioning of economic systems. Their concerns may relate to global aggregates, or *macro* quantities, such as the value of the gross national product (GNP), the level of employment, or the current level of the consumer price index. Alternatively, the focus of attention may be some sector or area of the economy, such as production and employment in the automobile industry or the price and volume of the peanut crop in Georgia. One objective of such an understanding is to be able to make conditional predictions of the likely future development of the system and hopefully enable economic agents, whether government, business, or consumers, to take action to control to some degree the evolution of the system. Another important objective is to test economic theories about the system.

The first step in seeking to understand the functioning of a system is to build a theoretical model. All models are inevitably simplifications of reality, and the model builder seeks to capture the fundamental features of the system being studied. The performance of an economy, or a sector of an economy, at any point in time will depend upon the decisions of various economic agents, taken in the context of the existing state of technology with given stocks of capital, labor, and other limited productive resources. Thus theoretical models typically contain *behavioral relations*, which describe the forces thought to determine the behavior of various groups of economic agents, and *technological relations*, which describe the restrictions imposed by the current technology and endowments of the system. Often technological relations, such as the production function, describing the maximum output achievable with various inputs of capital, labor, and other productive resources, may not appear explicitly in the model, but will have been used in the derivation of behavioral relations, such as the demand function for labor, and so on. In addition to behavioral and technological relations, economic models typically contain *identities* or *definitional relations*.

1-2 A NATIONAL INCOME MODEL

As an example of the model building process let us consider one of the simplest forms of the national income model, which is used as a pedagogic device in most elementary textbooks on economics. Such models begin with the national income identity. For a closed economy with no foreign trade, this identity in any period is

$$y \equiv c + i + g \tag{1-1}$$

where y = gross national product (GNP)
c = consumption expenditure
i = investment expenditure
g = government expenditure

all expenditure flows being measured in real terms. The construction of the model proceeds with the formulation of hypotheses about the determinants of the expenditure components of GNP.

Consumption expenditure might be hypothesized as dependent on disposable income, net of tax, and the rate of interest. Thus we write†

$$c = f((1-\tau)y, r) \tag{1-2}$$

where τ = tax rate (assumed constant across the economy)
r = rate of interest

The theoretical expectations about this relation are

$$0 < f_1 < 1, \qquad f_2 < 0 \tag{1-3}$$

where f_i indicates the partial derivative of the function with respect to the ith

† See App. A-1, Functions and Derivatives.

argument. The first assumption in Eq. (1-3) is that the marginal propensity to consume out of disposable income is a positive fraction less than unity. The second assumption is that a rise in the rate of interest will have a depressing effect on consumption since it raises the return on savings, increases the cost of financing consumer durables, and also reduces the nominal value of bonds, which are a part of wealth, which in turn might appear as an argument of the consumption function but has been omitted from Eq. (1-2) on grounds of simplicity.

The investment function may be specified as

$$i = f(\Delta y, r) \tag{1-4}$$

with

$$f_1 > 0, \qquad f_2 < 0 \tag{1-5}$$

The term Δy indicates the change in GNP. Investment is positively influenced by profit expectations, and the crude assumption here is that observed changes in real GNP serve as a proxy for these profit expectations. The rate of interest is again expected to be negatively related to this form of expenditure.

Collecting results, so far we have a three-equation model, namely,

$$y \equiv c + i + g$$
$$c = f((1 - \tau)y, r)$$
$$i = f(\Delta y, r)$$

supplemented by the expected signs on derivatives expressed in Eqs. (1-3) and (1-5). This model then constitutes a theory about the joint determination, or "explanation," of the three variables c, i, and y. Such an explanation is obviously *conditional* on the values assumed for g, r, and τ. The model builder now faces a decision on how to treat these remaining variables. Should one formulate theories to explain the determination of government expenditure, the rate of interest, and the tax rate, thus expanding the system to one of six equations? If one does, the new equations will almost certainly contain some explanatory variables on the right-hand side that have not previously appeared in the system, and these, in turn, raise the question of how they are to be treated. It might seem that economic models must become infinitely large, but there is not, of course, an infinite number of variables to be explained. In any case the behavior of model builders is very pragmatic. Everything is relative: all depends on the problem at hand. For some purposes a small model is sufficient and some variables, which in larger models would have explanatory equations, may be left "unexplained." In the present instance we make no pretense at economic realism, but only require a model for illustrative purposes, so we will restrict it to the three equations already specified.

The model contains only two behavioral relations, one for consumption and the other for investment. Economic theory has done two things. First, it has specified the list of explanatory variables on the right-hand side of each equation, and second, it has indicated the expected signs on the partial derivatives. This is usually as far as theory per se can go, but it still leaves a series of important questions unanswered.

1-3 UNANSWERED QUESTIONS

Functional form Theoretical considerations alone cannot usually specify the functional form connecting the variables in a relationship. Many functional forms are consistent with a priori signs on derivatives. Letting

$$z = (1 - \tau)y$$

denote disposable income and omitting the rate of interest variable, the following functional forms all give c as a monotonically increasing function of z and, with appropriate restrictions on parameters, could satisfy the condition that the marginal propensity to consume is a positive fraction:

$$c = \alpha_0 + \alpha_1 z$$

$$c = Az^{\alpha_1}$$

$$c = \alpha_0 - \alpha_1 z^{-1}$$

These functions, however, have different qualitative implications. In the first, an extra \$100 of income always produces the same absolute increase in consumption expenditure. The second and third functions both exhibit a declining marginal propensity to consume as income rises. However, the second function implies that consumption rises indefinitely with income, while the third shows consumption approaching a saturation or asymptotic level α_0 as income becomes very large. This is a typical example of the fact that the qualitative restrictions deriving from economic theory do not serve to delimit functional forms very closely.

Data definition and measurement Theory is sometimes precise and sometimes sloppy in the matter of definitions. In this model, for instance, should consumption be taken to mean expenditure, including actual expenditure on consumer durables, or should consumption of durables be treated as an implicit flow measured by the value of services from the existing stock of consumer durables? If the second definition is taken, is this consistent with the definition of the same variable in the national income identity? What is meant by income? Should it be adjusted for purely seasonal fluctuations or not? Is it to be taken as some recently observed level, or should it be interpreted as some kind of "permanent" or "long run" income? There are many different rates of interest. Should we select a "representative" rate or some combination of rates, and should this variable be treated the same way in both consumption and investment functions?

Lag structure Somewhat allied with problems of data definition are problems of lag structure. Should investment be specified as responding to the current interest rate or to some set of previous interest rates in view of the inevitable time lags involved in making and implementing investment decisions? Again, by the nature of things, economic theory cannot be specific about appropriate lag structures. Moreover, much of economic theorizing has necessarily been about *equilibrium* positions, as, for example, the equilibrium rate of consumption corresponding to some level of income, which has, in theory, remained constant long enough for consumers to become fully adjusted to it. In practice, the world is always staggering from one disequilibrium position to another, so actual data reflect adjustment processes rather than equilibrium positions. Equilibrium theory, by definition, says nothing about adjustment processes, and theories of adaptation and adjustment are still in a fairly primitive state.

Qualitative versus quantitative implications The theoretical model does yield unambiguous qualitative implications, such as that a rise in the rate of interest will depress GNP and a rise in government expenditures will increase it. In more complicated models qualitative conditions on the various equations may not lead to unambiguous predictions about the overall behavior of the model. If our simple model asserted that the rate of interest had a positive effect on consumption and a negative effect on investment, the direction of the rate of interest effect on GNP could not then be known without *quantitative* knowledge of the two separate effects and the magnitudes of consumption and investment. In practice, of course, policymakers are vitally concerned with the likely *magnitude* and *timing* of the effects of changes in the rate of interest, tax rates, or government expenditure. The expected signs of partial derivatives cannot provide this kind of information.

Choice between theories So far, in discussing the previous four problems, we have implicitly assumed that our theoretical model is "correct," but how can we tell whether a theory is sufficiently correct to be used as a valid tool of analysis? Perhaps there are as many theories as there are theorists. There is, in practice, a very important and very difficult problem involved in attempting to discriminate between competing theories. Some theoretical models differ in degree but not in kind. They might be regarded as variations on a theme. For example, another theorist might accept the general form of our consumption and investment functions but wish to add wealth as an additional explanatory variable to the first equation and capital stock to the second. At the other end of the spectrum would be a theorist who rejected the Keynesian flavor of our model and advanced instead a supply-determined theory of output or a model in which the fundamental driving force was the money supply.

1-4 ROLE OF ECONOMETRICS

Econometrics tackles all five questions. Its basic task is to put *empirical* flesh and blood on theoretical structures. This involves several crucial steps. First of all, the theory or model must be specified in explicit functional form. The econometrician does not have any special insights in this area that are denied to the economic theorist, so one usually starts with the simplest functional forms that are consistent with the a priori specifications. At the same time one makes an initial specification of the lag structure. As an example we might specify the three-equation national income model as

$$c_t = \alpha_0 + \alpha_1(1 - \tau)y_t + \alpha_2 r_t \tag{1-6}$$

$$i_t = \beta_0 + \beta_1(y_{t-1} - y_{t-2}) + \beta_2 r_{t-1} \tag{1-7}$$

$$y_t \equiv c_t + i_t + g_t \tag{1-8}$$

with a priori expectations

$$0 < \alpha_1 < 1, \qquad \alpha_2 < 0, \qquad \beta_1 > 0, \qquad \beta_2 < 0$$

The subscripts on the variables refer to time periods. The unit time period can be anything considered relevant by the econometrician, provided there exist appropriate data in terms of that unit. However, it is typically a quarter or a year, and the model is in discrete, not continuous, time.

The second task of the econometrician is to decide on the appropriate data definitions and assemble the relevant data series for the variables which enter the model. The third task is to perform a "marriage" of theory and data by means of statistical methods. The "offspring" of the marriage are various sets of statistics, which shed crucial light on the validity of the theoretical model that has been specified. The most important set consists of the numerical estimates of the parameters of the structural form. The Greek letters of Eqs. (1-6) and (1-7) are now replaced by numbers. There are further statistics which enable one to assess the reliability or precision with which these parameters have been estimated, which in turn helps us to check whether the model conforms to the theoretical expectations about signs of derivatives. There are still further statistics and diagnostic tests that help one to assess the performance of the model and decide whether or not to proceed sequentially by modifying the specification in certain directions and testing out the new variant of the model against the data.

Most of this book will be concerned with the statistical methods used by econometricians in estimating, testing, and evaluating economic models. Historically, econometrics started with the corpus of methods inherited from classical statistics. These methods, however, were mainly developed in the context of the experimental sciences. Special problems of statistical inference arise in economics, where the possibility of controlled experiments is the exception, not the rule, and these will be described in the chapters to follow. All that remains to be done in this introductory chapter is to indicate some of the possible applications of an econometric model, once it has been estimated. This will again be done with the simple model outlined above.

1-5 STRUCTURAL AND REDUCED FORMS

Equations (1-6) to (1-8) constitute the *structural* form of the model. The structural form may be regarded as a theoretical explanation, or hypothesis, about the determination of the three variables y_t, c_t, and i_t, *conditional* on the values currently assumed by g_t and r_t and also on the recent history of the system as represented by y_{t-1}, y_{t-2}, and r_{t-1}. This enables us to make the following classification of the variables in the system:

Current endogenous variables:	c_t, i_t, y_t
Lagged endogenous variables:	y_{t-1}, y_{t-2}
Current exogenous variables:	g_t, r_t
Lagged exogenous variables:	r_{t-1}

The crucial distinction is between endogenous and exogenous variables. The former are those variables whose current values are, in theory, explained by the functioning of the model. The model, however, has nothing to say about the determination of the exogenous variables. A second important distinction is that between the current time period t and previous periods, such as $t - 1$, $t - 2$, and so on. When we come to study the functioning of the model in period t, all lagged values, whether of endogenous or exogenous variables, are already given and cannot now assume new values. Once values are also fed in for the *current* exogenous variables g_t and r_t, the model then delivers the values of the current endogenous variables c_t, i_t, and y_t. This point may be expressed formally by recasting Eqs. (1-6) to (1-8) in an alternative form. Substituting Eqs. (1-6) and (1-7) in Eq. (1-8) and rearranging gives

$$y_t = (\alpha_0 + \beta_0)\delta + \alpha_2 \delta r_t + \beta_1 \delta(y_{t-1} - y_{t-2}) + \beta_2 \delta r_{t-1} + \delta g_t \qquad (1\text{-}9)$$

where

$$\delta = \frac{1}{1 - \alpha_1(1 - \tau)}$$

The important point about Eq. (1-9) is that only one current endogenous variable appears in the equation, namely, y_t on the left-hand side. The right-hand-side variables are a mixture of current exogenous variables and lagged variables, whether endogenous or exogenous. This collection of three sets of variables is labeled the class of *predetermined variables*, since, from the viewpoint of the model in period t, their values either are determined by the past history of the system or are set exogenously in the current period. The investment equation already has nothing but predetermined variables on the right-hand side, so we repeat it here:

$$i_t = \beta_0 + \beta_1(y_{t-1} - y_{t-2}) + \beta_2 r_{t-1} \qquad (1\text{-}10)$$

Finally, substituting Eq. (1-9) in the consumption function gives

$$c_t = [\alpha_0 + \alpha_1(1 - \tau)(\alpha_0 + \beta_0)\delta] + [\alpha_2 + \alpha_1(1 - \tau)\alpha_2\delta]r_t$$
$$+ \alpha_1(1 - \tau)\beta_1\delta(y_{t-1} - y_{t-2}) + \alpha_1(1 - \tau)\beta_2\delta r_{t-1} + \alpha_1(1 - \tau)\delta g_t \qquad (1\text{-}11)$$

The three Eqs. (1-9), (1-10), and (1-11) constitute the *reduced form* of the model. Each equation of the reduced form expresses a current endogenous variable as a function only of predetermined variables. The reduced form may be

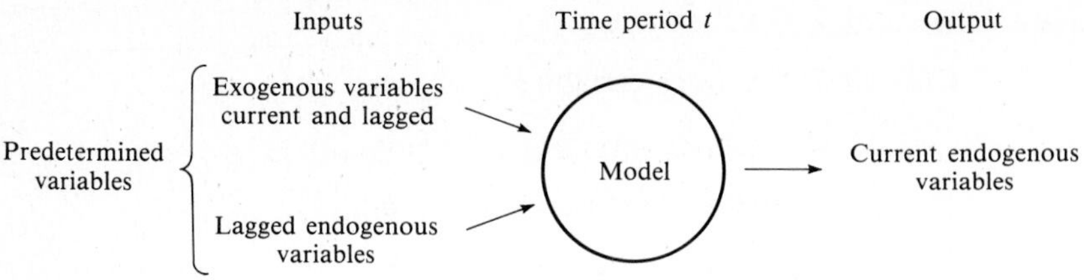

Figure 1-1

written compactly as

$$y_t = \pi_{10} + \pi_{11}g_t + \pi_{12}r_t + \pi_{13}r_{t-1} + \pi_{14}y_{t-1} + \pi_{15}y_{t-2} \tag{1-12}$$

$$c_t = \pi_{20} + \pi_{21}g_t + \pi_{22}r_t + \pi_{23}r_{t-1} + \pi_{24}y_{t-1} + \pi_{25}y_{t-2} \tag{1-13}$$

$$i_t = \pi_{30} + \pi_{33}r_{t-1} + \pi_{34}y_{t-1} + \pi_{35}y_{t-2} \tag{1-14}$$

where the π's are the functions of the structural parameters indicated in Eqs. (1-9) to (1-11). Schematically, the reduced form is indicated in Fig. 1-1.

The reduced form also indicates that there is one-way causation in the model in the sense that the exogenous variables influence the current endogenous variables, but there is no feedback in the opposite direction: current endogenous variables do not influence the exogenous variables.

1-6 MULTIPLIERS AND DYNAMIC PROPERTIES

The π's of the reduced-form equations are economically very important parameters. They measure the impact in the current period on each endogenous variable of a unit change in any predetermined variable. Consider, for example, a unit increase in the level of g_t. From Eq. (1-8) of the structural form there would be a simultaneous increase of one unit in GNP. But from the consumption function (1-6), increases in GNP will induce increases in consumption, which in turn, from Eq. (1-8), will induce further increases in GNP. The reduced-form coefficient

$$\frac{\partial y_t}{\partial g_t} = \pi_{11} = \frac{1}{1 - \alpha_1(1 - \tau)}$$

shows the end result of this process in period t. This is the national income multiplier of simple Keynesian theory. For example, if $\tau = 0.25$ and $\alpha_1 = 0.8$, $\pi_{11} = 2.5$, so that a unit increase in government expenditure, with tax rates and all other parameters unchanged, would raise national income in the same period by 2.5 units. Similarly, an inspection of

$$\pi_{10} = (\alpha_0 + \beta_0)\delta$$

shows that a unit increase (upward shift) in the intercept of either the consumption or the investment function would have equal multiplier effects on GNP. All the π's are multipliers, and they are termed *impact multipliers*, because they show the effect in the *current* period of changes in predetermined variables. Estimates of the structural coefficients can yield estimates of the reduced-form coefficients, and so these impact multipliers can be evaluated. Alternatively, the reduced-form equations may be estimated directly. These topics will be discussed in the chapter on simultaneous equation estimation later in the book.

The impact effects in period t are not the end of the story. Let us write Eq. (1-12) in first difference form,

$$\Delta y_t = \pi_{11}\Delta g_t + \pi_{12}\Delta r_t + \pi_{13}\Delta r_{t-1} + \pi_{14}\Delta y_{t-1} + \pi_{15}\Delta y_{t-2} \qquad (1\text{-}15)$$

where

$$\Delta y_t = y_t - y_{t-1}, \ldots$$

Let us suppose that g and r have been held constant sufficiently long for y to settle down at some constant equilibrium level. This involves the implicit assumption that equilibrium values exist and that the system is stable, and we will return to this point below. Equilibrium thus implies

$$\begin{aligned}
\Delta g_t &= \Delta g_{t-1} = \Delta g_{t-2} = \cdots = 0 \\
\Delta r_t &= \Delta r_{t-1} = \Delta r_{t-2} = \cdots = 0 \\
\Delta y_t &= \Delta y_{t-2} = \Delta y_{t-2} = \cdots = 0
\end{aligned}$$

Now suppose that the level of government expenditure in period $t + 1$ is raised by an amount d and then held constant at the new level indefinitely, that is,

$$\Delta g_{t+1} = d, \qquad \Delta g_{t+2} = \Delta g_{t+3} = \cdots = 0$$

From Eq. (1-15) the impact effect on national income in period $t + 1$ is

$$\Delta y_{t+1} = \pi_{11} d$$

In period $t + 2$, Eq. (1-15) reads

$$\Delta y_{t+2} = \pi_{14}\Delta y_{t+1} = \pi_{14}\pi_{11} d$$

In period $t + 3$, the equation reads

$$\begin{aligned}
\Delta y_{t+3} &= \pi_{14}\Delta y_{t+2} + \pi_{15}\Delta y_{t+1} \\
&= \pi_{14}^2\pi_{11} d + \pi_{15}\pi_{11} d
\end{aligned}$$

Thus the one-step change in g sets off a sequence of changes in y because of the lags in the system. There is thus a whole series of lagged multipliers, namely,

$$\frac{\partial y_{t+1}}{\partial g_{t+1}} = \pi_{11} \qquad \text{zero lag, or impact multipliers}$$

$$\frac{\partial y_{t+2}}{\partial g_{t+1}} = \pi_{14}\pi_{11} \qquad \text{one-period lag}$$

$$\frac{\partial y_{t+3}}{\partial g_{t+1}} = (\pi_{14}^2 + \pi_{15})\pi_{11} \qquad \text{two-period lag}$$

The estimated reduced form can be applied sequentially to trace out the dynamic effects of a postulated change in any exogenous variable. The multipliers at various lags are called *interim* multipliers, and if the impact and interim multipliers are summed over an infinite time horizon, assuming that the sum converges, we have a *total* multiplier giving the final effect on the equilibrium value of an endogenous variable of a one-step change in an exogenous variable.

Finally, we may look briefly at a third way of expressing the system, which casts light on the question of stability. Equation (1-12) may be rearranged as

$$y_t - \pi_{14}y_{t-1} - \pi_{15}y_{t-2} = \pi_{10} + \pi_{11}g_t + \pi_{12}r_t + \pi_{13}r_{t-1} \tag{1-16}$$

This is a second-order nonhomogeneous difference equation in y.† It is a fluke of this simple model that this reduced-form equation did not contain lagged values of any other endogenous variable, but it is always possible to derive a difference equation for each endogenous variable, which contains only exogenous variables on the right-hand side and does not contain any other endogenous variables, current or lagged. Equation (1-16) may be expressed more simply for present purposes as

$$y_t - \pi_{14}y_{t-1} - \pi_{15}y_{t-2} = f(g, r) \tag{1-17}$$

A remarkable feature of linear dynamic models is that each endogenous variable in the system can be described by a difference equation of the *same order* and with *identical* coefficients, but differing only in the linear combination of exogenous variables appearing on the right-hand side. To demonstrate this result in the present model, we take the investment function

$$i_t = \beta_0 + \beta_1(y_{t-1} - y_{t-2}) + \beta_2 r_{t-1}$$

Lag it one period and multiply by π_{14}, lag it two periods and multiply by π_{15}, and subtract both equations from the current equation. This gives

$$\begin{aligned} i_t - \pi_{14}i_{t-1} - \pi_{15}i_{t-2} = {} & \beta_1(y_{t-1} - \pi_{14}y_{t-2} - \pi_{15}y_{t-3}) \\ & -\beta_1(y_{t-2} - \pi_{14}y_{t-3} - \pi_{15}y_{t-4}) \\ & +\beta_0(1 - \pi_{14} - \pi_{15}) \\ & +\beta_2(r_{t-1} - \pi_{14}r_{t-2} - \pi_{15}r_{t-3}) \end{aligned}$$

The first two terms in parentheses on the right-hand side are seen from Eq. (1-17) to be functions only of exogenous variables. Thus

$$i_t - \pi_{14}i_{t-1} - \pi_{15}i_{t-2} = h(g, r) \tag{1-18}$$

Finally, applying the same treatment to the national income identity gives

$$\begin{aligned} c_t - \pi_{14}c_{t-1} - \pi_{15}c_{t-2} = {} & (y_t - \pi_{14}y_{t-1} - \pi_{15}y_{t-2}) \\ & -(i_t - \pi_{14}i_{t-1} - \pi_{15}i_{t-2}) \\ & -(g_t - \pi_{14}g_{t-1} - \pi_{15}g_{t-2}) \end{aligned}$$

and, using Eqs. (1-17) and (1-18), we have

$$c_t - \pi_{14}c_{t-1} - \pi_{15}c_{t-2} = k(g, r) \tag{1-19}$$

† For an introduction to difference equations, see A. C. Chiang, *Fundamental Methods of Mathematical Economics*, McGraw-Hill, New York, 1984.

Thus all three endogenous variables are characterized by a second-order difference equation with the same coefficients. The endogenous variables will therefore display the same dynamic behavior. The clue to this behavior comes from the roots of the common characteristic equation

$$\lambda^2 - \pi_{14}\lambda - \pi_{15} = 0$$

The structural and reduced-form equations show

$$\pi_{14} = -\pi_{15} = \frac{\beta_1}{1 - \alpha_1(1 - \tau)} > 0$$

Denoting this parameter by α, the characteristic equation becomes

$$\lambda^2 - \alpha\lambda + \alpha = 0$$

with roots

$$\lambda_1, \lambda_2 = \frac{\alpha \pm \sqrt{\alpha(\alpha - 4)}}{2}$$

If $\alpha < 4$, the roots are complex and the economic structure is inherently cyclical. The product of the roots is also α, and so if $\alpha < 1$, the cycles are damped, but if $1 < \alpha < 4$, the cycles are explosive. We see that α depends on

β_1, the acceleration coefficient of the investment equation
α_1, the marginal propensity to consume
τ, the tax rate

Thus, once again, empirical estimates of these parameters shed crucial light on the nature of the economic structure. The above model has been highly simplified for expository purposes, but these methods of analysis can be and are applied to large systems. We have attempted to illustrate the importance of econometric estimation and testing by reference only to a simplified aggregate system. Other varied illustrations of the power and range of econometrics will be given in the course of the book.

CHAPTER

TWO

THE TWO-VARIABLE LINEAR MODEL

The national income model of Chap. 1 has two complications that we do not wish to tackle right away. First of all, it is a simultaneous equation model with three equations to explain the determination of three endogenous variables. Second, each behavioral equation contains more than two variables. We will, however, begin our exposition of econometric methods by concentrating upon a *single equation* with just *two variables*. It is not claimed that a single two-variable equation is an adequate model of any economic process, but starting with it has the double advantage that certain fundamental ideas can be introduced in the simplest of all settings and that the tools and concepts developed for the two-variable model are essential building blocks for the more complicated cases which are treated in the rest of the book.

2-1 THE LINEAR SPECIFICATION

The relevant theory is now assumed to postulate

$$Y = f(X) \tag{2-1}$$

where Y indicates the dependent (explained) variable and X the independent (explanatory) variable. We may have theoretical expectations about the sign of $f'(X)$ or about the range of values in which it lies. In this chapter we will deal only with *linear* specifications.

A linear specification means that Y, or some transformation of Y, can be expressed as a linear function of X, or some transformation of X. In this sense,

$$Y = \alpha + \beta X \tag{2-2}$$

$$Y = \alpha X^{\beta} \tag{2-3}$$

and

$$Y = \exp\left\{\alpha + \beta\frac{1}{X}\right\} \tag{2-4}$$

are all linear specifications.† The first is already linear in Y and X. The second, on taking logarithms of both sides of the equation, may be written as

$$\log Y = \log\alpha + \beta\log X \tag{2-5}$$

which is linear in $\log Y$ and $\log X$. The third is

$$\log Y = \alpha + \beta\frac{1}{X} \tag{2-6}$$

which is linear in the logarithm of Y and the reciprocal of X. The function

$$Y = \alpha + \beta X + \gamma X^2$$

is linear in Y, X, and X^2, but it is not a *two*-variable linear function, and so its treatment will be postponed to Chap. 3. The function

$$Y = \alpha + \frac{\delta}{X - \beta}$$

however, where α, β, and δ are unknown parameters, cannot be reduced to a linear function of some transformations of Y and X, and so cannot be treated by the methods of this chapter.

The first step in the econometric investigation of the relationship between Y and X is to obtain a sample of n pairs of observations on the two variables. The sample data are thus indicated by

$$X_i, Y_i \qquad i = 1, 2, \ldots, n$$

Next we must make a choice between specifications such as Eqs. (2-2), (2-3), and (2-4). At this stage the choice is made by plotting the raw data or various transformations of them on two-dimensional scatter diagrams to see which, if any, yields an approximately linear scatter. Examples of various typical shapes and appropriate linearizing transformations will be given in Chap. 3. Here we will assume that Y and X denote appropriately transformed data, and so we postulate the linear relationship

$$Y = \alpha + \beta X$$

where α indicates the intercept made by the line on the vertical, Y, axis and β indicates the slope of the line.

The econometrician now faces the task of using the sample data to obtain numerical estimates of the unknown parameters α and β. If the postulated relationship were really true, one would have no problems at all; one would need

† See App. A-2, Exponential and Logarithmic Functions.

just two sample points and a ruler to join them. Further sample points would lie on the same straight line and would convey no additional information. However, *exact functional* relationships such as Eq. (2-2) are inadequate descriptions of economic behavior. Scatter diagrams do not yield points which all lie on a single straight line. Thus the specification of the linear relationship is expanded to

$$Y = \alpha + \beta X + u \tag{2-7}$$

where u denotes a stochastic variable with some specified probability distribution.† The purpose of the u term is to characterize the discrepancies that emerge between the actual, observed values of Y and the values that would be given by an exact functional relationship.

To fix these ideas let us suppose that we have data from a budget survey with X representing household disposable income and Y household consumption expenditure. Clearly, household expenditure will depend on some crucial factors in addition to income, such as household size and composition, so let us suppose that we are looking at the relationship between Y and X *within* a subset of households of a given size and composition. Nonetheless it would still be unrealistic to expect all households with a given income X_i to display exactly the same expenditure $\alpha + \beta X_i$. First of all, even among households of the same size and composition and with the same income, there will be variations in the precise ages of the parents and children, in the number of years since marriage, in whether the husband is a golfer, drinker, poker player, or bird-watcher, in whether the wife is addicted to spring hats, Paris fashions, swimming pools, or foreign sports cars, in whether the household income has been increasing or decreasing, in whether the parents are themselves the children of thrifty, cautious folks or carefree spendthrifts, and so forth. This list might be extended ad infinitum. Many factors may not even be quantifiable, and even if they are, it is not usually possible to obtain data on all of them. Even if it were, the number of variables would almost certainly exceed the feasible number of observations, so that no statistical means exist for estimating their influence. Moreover, many variables may have very slight effects so that, even with substantial quantities of data, the statistical estimation of their influence will be difficult and uncertain. We thus let the *net effect* of all these possible influences be represented by a single stochastic variable u.

A second reason for the addition of the stochastic term is that there may be a basic and unpredictable element of randomness in human responses. For purposes of practical statistics the distinction between these two reasons for variability does not matter since, for reasons of both theory and data, we hardly ever claim to have included all distinguishable and relevant factors in any relationship, so that the insertion of a stochastic term is required on the first count, and the second merely adds to its variance. Finally, we note that if there were measurement errors in Y so that the recorded values did not accurately reflect the values given by the theory, this would also be a component of the stochastic term and add to its variance.

† See App. A-4, Random Variables and Probability Distributions.

The variable u is often referred to as the *disturbance term* in the equation, or as the equation error. We cannot predict the specific value of u that will emerge in any single observation, but we can make propositions about the main features of its probability distribution. First of all, it is clear that the u's may take on positive or negative values, since the net effect of the many omitted and unmeasurable variables may push Y up or down from the value it would otherwise have had. However, there is usually no reason to expect a bias one way or the other, so the first assumption about u is that its average or expected value will be zero, that is,

$$E(u) = 0$$

Second, since u is the algebraic sum of many different positive and negative effects, we expect numerically small values of u to be much more frequent than very large values, so that the distribution will be unimodal around some fairly small value of u. If we add the assumption of symmetry, then the modal value will coincide with the expected value of zero. Third, we will often assume a specific form for the probability distribution, and an appeal to the central limit theorem suggests assuming a normal probability distribution for u.† Finally, we postulate that the various values of u will be distributed independently of one another. In terms of the budget data, that amounts to saying that if one household displays a positive disturbance, this does not make a positive (or a negative) disturbance more likely for neighboring or any other households. Each disturbance is conceived as drawn independently from some normal distribution

$$N(0, \sigma_u^2)$$

The assumption that the values of u are drawn independently from a normal distribution with zero mean and variance σ_u^2 is written compactly as

$$u \sim \text{NID}(0, \sigma_u^2)$$

where the symbol $\sim$ means "is distributed," and NID stands for "normally and independently distributed."

The specified model is illustrated graphically in Fig. 2-1. For a household with income X_i the average or expected expenditure is given by $\alpha + \beta X_i$. The actual expenditure will be $\alpha + \beta X_i + u_i$, where u_i is a random drawing from $N(0, \sigma_u^2)$. The complete mathematical specification of the model is

$$Y_i = \alpha + \beta X_i + u_i \qquad i = 1, 2, \ldots, n \qquad (2\text{-}8a)$$

$$E(u_i) = 0 \qquad \text{for all } i \qquad (2\text{-}8b)$$

$$E(u_i u_j) = \begin{cases} 0 & i \neq j, \text{ all } i, j \\ \sigma_u^2 & i = j, \text{ all } i, j \end{cases} \qquad (2\text{-}8c)$$

$$p(u_i) = N(0, \sigma_u^2) \qquad \text{for all } i \qquad (2\text{-}8d)$$

Assumptions (2-8b), (2-8c), and (2-8d) are a more extensive way of stating

$$u \sim \text{NID}(0, \sigma_u^2)$$

† See App. A-5, Normal Probability Distribution.

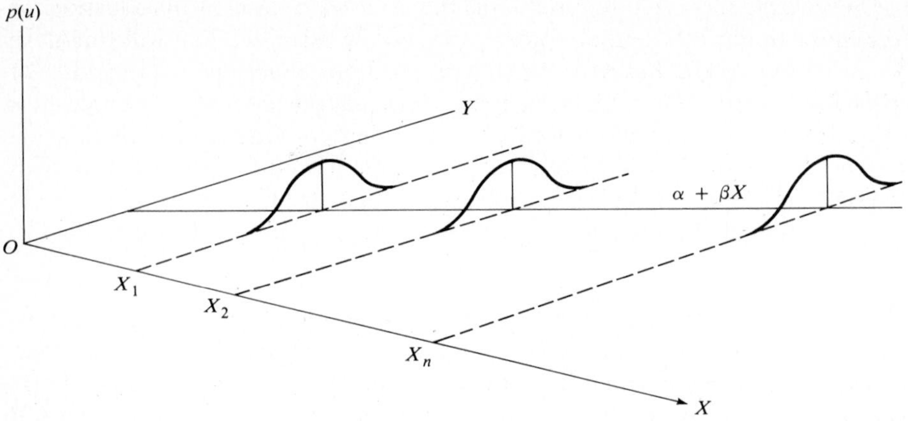

Figure 2-1

The reason for splitting them is that some of our subsequent derivations only require assumptions (2-8*b*) and (2-8*c*) and not the assumption of normality. The first part of assumption (2-8*c*) states that all possible covariances of the u's are zero, and the second part states that the variances of the u distributions at each point in Fig. 2-1 are the same.†

The three unknown parameters of the model are α, β, and σ_u^2. We now turn to methods by which these parameters may be estimated.

2-2 LEAST-SQUARES ESTIMATORS

An *estimator* is defined as a formula or method of estimating some unknown parameter, and an *estimate* as the numerical value resulting from the application of the formula to a specific set of sample data. We start with the n sample observations and plot them on a scatter diagram as in Fig. 2-2.

We typically plot scatter diagrams in the positive quadrant, but this is purely a matter of convenience since many economic variables, such as inventory investment, the balance of trade, the real rate of interest, and so forth, can take on both positive and negative values. Any straight line drawn through this scatter of points may be regarded as an estimate of the hypothesized relationship $Y = \alpha + \beta X + u$. A straight line is indicated by

$$\hat{Y} = a + bX \tag{2-9}$$

where $\hat{Y}$ indicates the height of the line at any given value of X. Once the numerical values a and b have been set, the line is determined, and one such line is shown in Fig. 2-2. If the line has been drawn through the scatter, some data

† If two variables are independently distributed, their covariance will be zero, but the reverse does not necessarily hold, except for normally distributed variables. See App. A-5, Normal Probability Distribution.

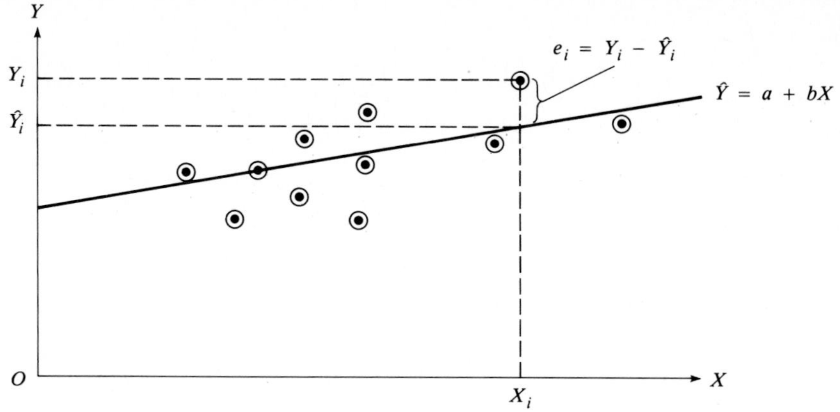

Figure 2-2

points will lie above the line and some below. We define the residuals from the line by

$$e_i = Y_i - \hat{Y}_i = Y_i - a - bX_i \qquad i = 1, 2, \ldots, n \tag{2-10}$$

so that any line generates a set of n sample residuals.

It would now seem sensible to choose the line, that is, to choose the values of a and b, to make the residuals "small." A possible criterion might be

$$\text{Select } a, b \text{ to make } \sum_{i=1}^{n} e_i = 0$$

Using Eq. (2-10), this criterion gives†

$$\Sigma e_i = \Sigma(Y_i - a - bX_i) = 0$$

which, on dividing through by n, gives‡

$$\bar{Y} = a + b\bar{X} \tag{2-11}$$

Equation (2-11) merely gives the condition that a and b should be chosen to make the line go through the point of means $(\bar{X}, \bar{Y})$. Thus we could pass a line with *any slope whatsoever* through $(\bar{X}, \bar{Y})$, and it would make the algebraic sum of the residuals zero. The criterion is thus inadequate to determine a specific line.

The least-squares criterion is stronger. If each residual is squared, negative signs disappear, and the sum of squared residuals is a nonnegative quantity. The least-squares principle is

$$\boxed{\text{Select } a, b \text{ to minimize } \Sigma e_i^2}$$

† Where there is no ambiguity about the range of summation, we will use Σe_i, or sometimes just Σe, instead of the more cumbersome $\Sigma_{i=1}^{n} e_i$, and similarly for other expressions.

‡ See App. A-3, Operations with Summation Signs.

From Eq. (2-10),

$$\Sigma e_i^2 = \Sigma(Y_i - a - bX_i)^2 \tag{2-12}$$

Thus

$$\Sigma e^2 = f(a, b)$$

since the sample data are given, so that passing different lines through the scatter (that is, choosing different values for a and b) produces variation in the residual sum of squares. The necessary conditions for a stationary value are

$$\frac{\partial(\Sigma e^2)}{\partial a} = \frac{\partial(\Sigma e^2)}{\partial b} = 0$$

Applying these conditions to Eq. (2-12) gives†

$$\begin{aligned} \Sigma Y &= na + b\Sigma X \\ \Sigma XY &= a\Sigma X + b\Sigma X^2 \end{aligned} \tag{2-13}$$

These are termed the *normal equations* for the straight line, for reasons that will become clear when we discuss the geometry of least squares in Chap. 4.

To estimate the line implied by Eq. (2-13) we first compute five quantities from the sample data, namely,

$$n, \quad \Sigma X, \quad \Sigma Y, \quad \Sigma XY, \quad \text{and} \quad \Sigma X^2$$

Substitution of the resultant numbers in Eq. (2-13) gives two simultaneous equations, which can then be solved for the two unknowns a and b. This gives the

†

$$\frac{\partial(\Sigma e^2)}{\partial a} = -2\Sigma(Y - a - bX) = -2\Sigma e = 0$$

gives $\Sigma Y = na + b\Sigma X$, and

$$\frac{\partial(\Sigma e^2)}{\partial b} = -2\Sigma X(Y - a - bX) = -2\Sigma Xe = 0$$

gives $\Sigma XY = a\Sigma X + b\Sigma X^2$. In obtaining the derivatives we leave the summation sign where it is, differentiate the typical term $(Y_i - a - bX_i)^2$ with respect to a and b in turn, and simply observe the rule that any constant can be moved in front of the summation sign but anything which varies from one sample point to another, such as X_i and Y_i, must be kept to the right of the summation sign. Finally, we have dropped the subscripts to leave the equations uncluttered, since there is no ambiguity about the range of summation. Strictly speaking, one should distinguish between the a and b which appear in the expression for the residual sum of squares

$$\Sigma e^2 = \Sigma(Y - a - bX)^2$$

and the solution values for a and b obtained by solving the equations

$$\frac{\partial(\Sigma e^2)}{\partial a} = \frac{\partial(\Sigma e^2)}{\partial b} = 0$$

but again no ambiguity is involved, and we have kept the expressions as simple as possible.

Table 2-1

	X	Y	XY	X^2	$\hat{Y}$	$e = Y - \hat{Y}$
	2	4	8	4	4.50	−0.50
	3	7	21	9	6.25	0.75
	1	3	3	1	2.75	0.25
	5	9	45	25	9.75	−0.75
	9	17	153	81	16.75	0.25
Sums	20	40	230	120	40.00	0

least-squares regression of Y on X, namely,

$$\hat{Y} = a + bX$$

or

$$Y = \hat{Y} + e = a + bX + e$$

The following example illustrates the application of these techniques to the X, Y data in Table 2-1.

Example 2-1 The normal equations are

$$40 = 5a + 20b$$
$$230 = 20a + 120b$$

with solution

$$a = 1, \qquad b = 1.75$$

The regression of Y on X is

$$\hat{Y} = 1 + 1.75X$$

Substituting each sample value of X in the regression equation gives the $\hat{Y}$ and e values shown in the last two columns of Table 2-1. Note that the $\hat{Y}$ values sum to the same total as the sample Y values, and the residuals, of course, sum to zero.

The linear regression has a number of important properties.

1. *The regression line passes through the point of means* $\bar{X}, \bar{Y}$ (*i.e., the sum of the residuals is zero*).

This follows directly from the first equation in Eqs. (2-13), which, on division by n, gives

$$\bar{Y} = a + b\bar{X}$$

and it is also shown in the footnote on page 18.

2. *The residuals have zero covariance with the sample* X *values and also with the predicted* $\hat{Y}$ *values.*

This also follows from the footnote on page 18 where $\partial(\Sigma e^2)/\partial b = 0$ gives $\Sigma Xe = 0$. The sample covariance between X and e, by definition, is

$$\begin{aligned}
\operatorname{cov}(X, e) &= \frac{1}{n}\Sigma(X - \bar{X})(e - \bar{e}) \\
&= \frac{1}{n}\Sigma(X - \bar{X})e \qquad \text{since } \bar{e} = 0 \\
&= \frac{1}{n}\Sigma Xe - \frac{1}{n}\bar{X}\Sigma e \\
&= \frac{1}{n}\Sigma Xe \qquad \text{since } \Sigma e = 0
\end{aligned}$$

Since $\hat{Y}$ is a linear function of X it follows directly that $\operatorname{cov}(\hat{Y}, e) = 0$.

3. *The regression coefficients may be computed sequentially from*

$$b = \frac{\Sigma xy}{\Sigma x^2} \tag{2-14a}$$

and

$$a = \bar{Y} - b\bar{X} \tag{2-14b}$$

where x *and* y *denote derivations from sample means,*

$$x = X - \bar{X}, \qquad y = Y - \bar{Y}$$

Equation (2-14b) is merely a rearrangement of the first equation in Eqs. (2-13), and Eq. (2-14a) follows from substituting Eq. (2-14b) into the second equation of Eqs. (2-13) to get

$$\Sigma XY = (\bar{Y} - b\bar{X})\Sigma X + b\Sigma X^2$$

giving

$$b\left[\Sigma X^2 - \frac{1}{n}(\Sigma X)^2\right] = \Sigma XY - \frac{1}{n}(\Sigma X)(\Sigma Y)$$

or

$$b\Sigma x^2 = \Sigma xy$$

Alternatively, since the least-squares line passes through the point of means, we may take $(\bar{X}, \bar{Y})$ as a new origin, as in Fig. 2-3. Consider a point P with coordinates (X_i, Y_i). The first coordinate can also be expressed as x_i, its distance from $\bar{X}$. The second coordinate can similarly be expressed as y_i and split into two components, namely,

$$y_i = \hat{y}_i + e_i$$

where

$$\hat{y}_i = \hat{Y}_i - \bar{Y}$$

which is also a proper deviation since Y and $\hat{Y}$ have the same mean value. The regression equation can now be written

$$\hat{y} = bx$$

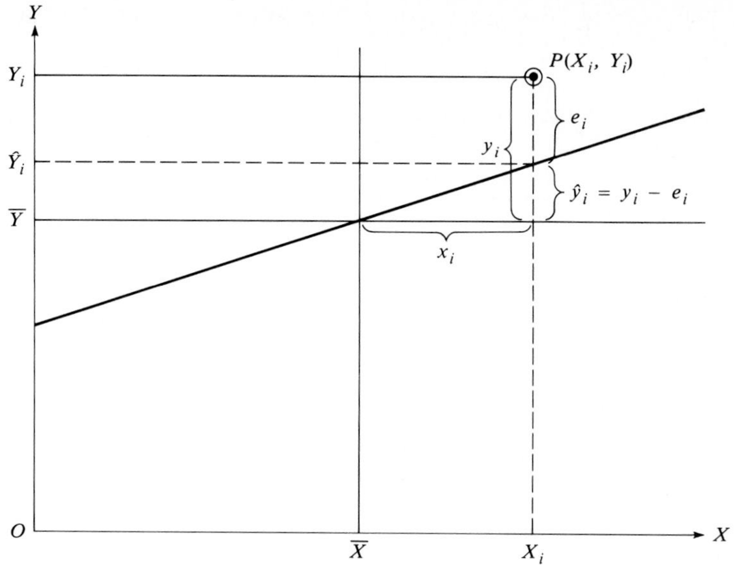

Figure 2-3

and the sum of squared residuals expressed as

$$\begin{aligned}\Sigma e^2 &= \Sigma(y - \hat{y})^2 \\ &= \Sigma(y - bx)^2 \\ &= \Sigma y^2 - 2b\Sigma xy + b^2\Sigma x^2\end{aligned}$$

which is only a function of b. Setting the derivative equal to zero gives

$$b = \frac{\Sigma xy}{\Sigma x^2}$$

The sum of squared residuals is seen to be a quadratic in b. The coefficient of b^2 is Σx^2, which is necessarily positive (unless all X values were identical). The quadratic is thus U-shaped, and the stationary point must give the *minimum* sum of squares.

4. *Decomposition of sum of squares*

The total variation in Y may be expressed as the sum of just two components, the variation "explained" by the linear regression and the variation "unexplained" by the regression. From property 3 we have

$$y_i = \hat{y}_i + e_i = bx_i + e_i$$

Squaring and summing over all n observations gives

$$\Sigma y^2 = \Sigma \hat{y}^2 + \Sigma e^2 + 2\Sigma \hat{y}e = b^2\Sigma x^2 + \Sigma e^2 + 2b\Sigma xe$$

or

$$\Sigma y^2 = \Sigma \hat{y}^2 + \Sigma e^2 = b^2\Sigma x^2 + \Sigma e^2 \tag{2-15}$$

since $\hat{y}$ and x each have zero covariance with e. The crucial quantities in Eq. (2-15) are

Σy^2 = total sum of squares in the dependent variable, measured about its mean (TSS)
Σe^2 = residual or unexplained sum of squares (RSS)
$\Sigma \hat{y}^2$ = explained sum of squares (ESS)

It follows from Eq. (2-15) that the explained sum of squares may be expressed in several alternative ways,

$$\text{ESS} = \Sigma\hat{y}^2 = b^2\Sigma x^2 = b\Sigma xy = \frac{(\Sigma xy)^2}{\Sigma x^2}$$

using Eq. (2-14a).

Example 2-2 The data of Table 2-1 may be expressed in deviation form, as in Table 2-2. Thus

$$b = \frac{\Sigma xy}{\Sigma x^2} = \frac{70}{40} = 1.75$$

and
$$a = \bar{Y} - b\bar{X} = 8 - 1.75(4) = 1$$

as before. The explained sum of squares may be calculated as

$$\text{ESS} = b\Sigma xy = 1.75(70) = 122.5$$

and the residual sum of squares may be obtained by subtraction as

$$\text{RSS} = \text{TSS} - \text{ESS} = 124 - 122.5 = 1.5$$

The proportion of the Y variation explained by the linear regression is

$$\frac{\text{ESS}}{\text{TSS}} = \frac{122.5}{124} = 0.988$$

The u values underlying the sample data are unknown and unobservable, for we could only measure them if we actually knew the true values α and β. Thus the variance of the disturbance distribution σ_u^2 cannot be estimated from a sample of

Table 2-2

	x	y	xy	x^2	y^2
	−2	−4	8	4	16
	−1	−1	1	1	1
	−3	−5	15	9	25
	1	1	1	1	1
	5	9	45	25	81
Sums	0	0	70	40	124

u values. We do, however, have the regression residuals $e_1, e_2, \ldots, e_n$, and it is plausible to base an estimate of the disturbance variance on them. Two alternative estimators are

$$\frac{\Sigma e^2}{n} \quad \text{or} \quad \frac{\Sigma e^2}{n-2}$$

Both are in use, but for reasons to be explained later in this chapter we typically use

$$s^2 = \frac{\Sigma e^2}{n-2} \tag{2-16}$$

2-3 THE CORRELATION COEFFICIENT

The regression estimated from Eq. (2-13) fixes a line which passes through the sample scatter of points in the X, Y space. The correlation coefficient indicates the "closeness" of the scatter about the fitted regression line. A visual inspection of the scatter cannot indicate the degree of closeness, since changes in the units of measurement for X and Y can stretch or contract scatters to give very different impressions of the relationship.

The correlation coefficient is defined as

$$r = \frac{\Sigma xy}{ns_x s_y} \tag{2-17}$$

where x and y denote deviations from sample means and s_x, s_y are the sample standard deviations,

$$s_x = \sqrt{\frac{\Sigma x^2}{n}} \qquad s_y = \sqrt{\frac{\Sigma y^2}{n}}$$

This is known as the Pearsonian (after the distinguished statistician Karl Pearson), or product moment, coefficient of correlation. Its rationale may be explained as follows. Referring to Fig. 2-3, the perpendiculars erected at $\bar{X}$ and $\bar{Y}$ divide the diagram into four quadrants. We pay particular attention to the sign of the product $x_i y_i$ in each quadrant.

NE quadrant	xy positive
NW quadrant	xy negative
SW quadrant	xy positive
SE quadrant	xy negative

Thus if we have a positive relationship, with sample points lying mainly in the NE and SW quadrants, Σxy tends to be a positive number. Conversely, a negative relationship will generate points mainly in the NW and SE quadrants, with Σxy tending to be a negative number. If there is little, if any, relationship between the two variables, sample points will be scattered in all four quadrants, and Σxy will tend to zero. Σxy, however, has two defects as a measure of association between X and Y. The first is that its numerical value may be increased by simply adding further observations. This is corrected by dividing by the sample size to give the sample covariance

$$\operatorname{cov}(X, Y) = \frac{\Sigma xy}{n}$$

Second, the covariance depends on the units in which X and Y are measured. Shifting from dollars to cents for each variable would increase the covariance by a factor of *ten thousand*. The covariance is standardized by dividing each deviation by the sample standard deviation of the variable in question. Defining

$$\text{variance of } X = \operatorname{var}(X) = s_x^2 = \frac{\Sigma x^2}{n}$$

and so on, and by some algebraic manipulation, we have a variety of ways of looking at and computing the correlation coefficient:

$$r = \frac{\operatorname{cov}(X, Y)}{\sqrt{\operatorname{var}(X)}\sqrt{\operatorname{var}(Y)}} \tag{2-18a}$$

$$= \frac{\Sigma xy}{n s_x s_y} \tag{2-18b}$$

$$= \frac{\Sigma xy}{\sqrt{\Sigma x^2}\sqrt{\Sigma y^2}} \tag{2-18c}$$

$$= \frac{n\Sigma XY - (\Sigma X)(\Sigma Y)}{\sqrt{n\Sigma X^2 - (\Sigma X)^2}\sqrt{n\Sigma Y^2 - (\Sigma Y)^2}} \tag{2-18d}$$

Looking at Eq. (2-18c) and rearranging gives

$$r = \left(\frac{\Sigma xy}{\Sigma x^2}\right)\frac{\sqrt{\Sigma x^2}}{\sqrt{\Sigma y^2}}$$

$$= b\frac{s_x}{s_y} \qquad \text{from Eq. (2-14}a\text{)}$$

or

$$b = r\frac{s_y}{s_x} \tag{2-19}$$

which shows the relationship between the regression slope and the correlation coefficient. Squaring Eq. (2-18c) gives

$$\begin{aligned} r^2 &= \frac{(\Sigma xy)^2}{(\Sigma x^2)(\Sigma y^2)} \\ &= \frac{b\Sigma xy}{\Sigma y^2} \\ &= \frac{\text{ESS}}{\text{TSS}} \\ &= 1 - \frac{\text{RSS}}{\text{TSS}} \\ &= 1 - \frac{\Sigma e^2/n}{\Sigma y^2/n} \end{aligned} \qquad (2\text{-}20)$$

Thus r^2 measures the proportion of the total sum of squares explained by the regression. The last two expressions in Eq. (2-20) show that the *limits of* r *are* ± 1. The residual sum of squares is nonnegative. It is only equal to zero if each and every residual e_i is zero, that is, if all the scatter points lie exactly on a straight line. A value of unity for r^2 thus corresponds to all points lying on the regression line. The sign of r depends upon the sign of the regression slope, that is, on the sign of the covariance term. The relationships in Eq. (2-20) also indicate why the correlation coefficient may be taken as a measure of the degree to which the scatter points lie close to the regression line. Note, finally, that r is a measure of the *linear* relation between X and Y; it is an inappropriate and misleading statistic if the relationship is nonlinear. Suppose, for example, that X indicates a firm's rate of output and Y the average variable cost per unit of output. Traditional theory postulates a U-shaped curve, which would generate points in all four quadrants of Fig. 2-3, with an r^2 tending toward zero.

2-4 PROPERTIES OF THE LEAST-SQUARES ESTIMATORS

Least squares is just one possible method of estimation. Other estimators may easily be defined. For instance, we might order the sample data by increasing size of X and pass a line through the first and last points. Or one might average the lowest two points and the highest two points and pass a line through these averages. Applying the first principle to the data of Table 2-1, we have

	X	Y
Lowest point	1	3
Highest point	9	17

giving an estimated slope of $14/8 = 1.75$, which happens to coincide with the least-squares slope. To make the line pass through the lowest point we have

$$3 = a + 1.75 \Rightarrow a = 1.25$$

This also ensures that the line passes through the upper point. The second principle gives

	X	Y
Average of two lowest points	1.5	3.5
Average of two highest points	7.0	13.0

giving an estimated slope of $9.5/5.5 = 1.727$ and an intercept of

$$a = 13 - 7(1.727) = 0.911$$

Recapitulating the least-squares regression, we now have three possible equations, namely,

$$\hat{Y} = 1 + 1.75X$$

$$\hat{Y} = 1.25 + 1.75X$$

$$\hat{Y} = 0.911 + 1.727X$$

In this example the scatter is almost perfectly linear, and so there is little difference between the equations yielded by the three methods. The more dispersed the scatter, the greater are likely to be the differences between the results.

The crucial question now is how to choose between equations or, equivalently, how to choose between estimating principles. The answer given in classical statistics is to choose on the basis of certain important properties of the various estimators. These properties refer to the behavior of the estimators in *repeated sampling*. At first sight this may seem a strange criterion. We usually have just one set of sample data, and we wish to do the best we can with that. Bayesian inference techniques, which are briefly discussed in Chap. 12, focus directly on that concern, but in this chapter we will outline the classical approach.

To fix ideas, let us return to the data of Table 2-1. We assume these data to have been generated by the model $Y = \alpha + \beta X + u$, and we now perform the conceptual experiment of imagining that repeated samples of five observations are drawn, but *with the* X *values fixed from sample to sample*. This is not to imply that economic variables are subject to experimental control and can actually be held constant as further samples are drawn. It is, rather, an assumption that substantially simplifies the derivation of the properties of the estimators, and it can be relaxed at a later stage. With the X's fixed, the only source of variation from sample to sample is in the u's, which in turn is reflected in the Y's. Suppose that, say, 10,000 samples were drawn, each consisting of five pairs of X, Y values. The application of the least-squares principle would thus yield 10,000 pairs of a, b values. These could be arranged in a bivariate frequency distribution. As the number of samples increases indefinitely, this distribution would tend to some smooth continuous function

$$f(a, b)$$

This is defined as the *joint sampling distribution* of a and b.

As with any bivariate distribution, we can integrate to obtain the marginal distributions $f(a)$ and $f(b)$, which are the sampling distributions of a and b, respectively. Concentrating on $f(b)$, we can imagine some distribution such as that shown in Fig. 2-4. This is a picture of the various sample values of b that would be obtained by the repeated application of the least-squares method to successive samples of n observations. The true parameter, β, that is being estimated is unknown, but it is reasonable to expect some sample estimates to be above β and others to be below.

There are three features of a sampling distribution that are crucial to the assessment of an estimator. These are the mean, the variance, and the mean-squared error. The mean value

$$E(b) = \int bf(b)\, db$$

indicates the average value that would be yielded by the estimator in repeated applications. The *bias* of the estimator is defined as

$$\text{bias}(b) = E(b) - \beta \tag{2-21}$$

If the bias is zero, the estimator is said to be *unbiased*. If the bias is nonzero, the estimator is said to be *biased*. The variance of the distribution

$$\text{var}(b) = \sigma_b^2 = \int [b - E(b)]^2 f(b)\, db \tag{2-22}$$

measures the spread of the distribution about its mean value. The standard deviation of the distribution σ_b is often referred to as the *standard error* of b. The

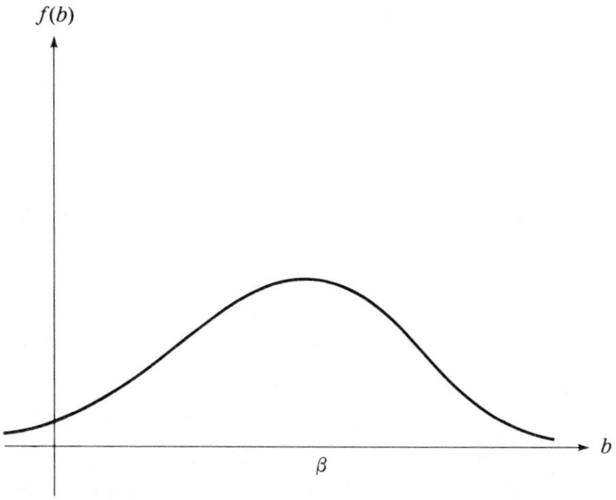

Figure 2-4

smaller the variance of the sampling distribution, the greater is the *precision* of the estimator, that is, the greater is the chance of a sample estimate lying within some specified interval about the true value. If we are comparing two estimators which are both unbiased but have different variances, one would naturally prefer the estimator with the smaller variance. If we consider the class of all unbiased estimators and can find one with a smaller variance than any other, it is said to be a *best unbiased* estimator.

A more difficult choice problem arises in comparing two estimators if both are biased and also have different variances. If one estimator has a larger bias but a smaller sampling variance than the other it is intuitively plausible to consider a tradeoff between the two characteristics. This notion is given formal expression in the mean-squared error,

$$\text{MSE}(b) = E\{(b-\beta)^2\} = \int (b-\beta)^2 f(b)\,db$$

Using Eqs. (2-21) and (2-22),

$$\begin{aligned}\text{MSE}(b) &= E\{[[b-E(b)] + [E(b)-\beta]]^2\}\\ &= E\{[b-E(b)]^2\} + E\{[E(b)-\beta]^2\}\\ &\quad +2E\{[b-E(b)][E(b)-\beta]\}\\ &= \text{var}(b) + [\text{bias}\,(b)]^2 \end{aligned} \tag{2-23}$$

as the cross-product term vanishes.† The mean-squared error measures the spread of the estimates around the true value β. Equation (2-23) shows that on the mean-squared-error criterion a biased estimator may be preferred to one with a smaller or zero bias if its variance is sufficiently small to offset the larger bias.

With this introduction we can return to the least-squares estimator and use assumptions (2-8*a*), (2-8*b*), and (2-8*c*) to derive the means and variances of their sampling distributions. Looking first at the least-squares slope, b may be expressed as

$$b = \frac{\Sigma x_i y_i}{\Sigma x_i^2} = \frac{\Sigma x_i Y_i}{\Sigma x_i^2} = \Sigma w_i Y_i \tag{2-24}$$

where

$$w_i = \frac{x_i}{\Sigma x_i^2} \tag{2-25}$$

It follows from Eq. (2-25) that

$$\Sigma w_i = 0, \qquad \Sigma w_i X_i = 1 \qquad \text{and} \qquad \Sigma w_i^2 = \frac{1}{\Sigma x_i^2} \tag{2-26}$$

† In evaluating $E\{[b-E(b)][E(b)-\beta]\}$ the rules are the same as for summations. Any factor which is a constant may be moved to the left and put as a multiplier in front of the expectation sign. The expectation of a constant is that same constant. Thus

$$\begin{aligned}E\{[b-E(b)][E(b)-\beta]\} &= [E(b)-\beta]\cdot E\{b-E(b)\}\\ &= [E(b)-\beta]\cdot[E(b)-E(b)]\\ &= 0\end{aligned}$$

To establish the properties of b in repeated sampling we need to express b in terms of the underlying stochastic variable u. Combining Eqs. (2-8a) and (2-24) gives

$$b = \Sigma w_i(\alpha + \beta X_i + u_i)$$
$$= \beta + \Sigma w_i u_i \qquad \text{using Eq. (2-26)}$$

Taking expectations,

$$E(b) = \beta \tag{2-27}$$

since $E(u_i) = 0$ for all i. Thus the least-squares slope is an unbiased estimator of the true slope. Its variance may be expressed as

$$\operatorname{var}(b) = E\{(b - \beta)^2\}$$
$$= E\{(\Sigma w_i u_i)^2\}$$

But

$$(\Sigma w_i u_i)^2 = \Sigma w_i^2 u_i^2 + 2\sum_{i<j} w_i w_j u_i u_j$$

Taking expectations and using Eq. (2-8c),

$$\operatorname{var}(b) = \sigma_u^2 \Sigma w_i^2 \tag{2-28}$$

which, on using Eq. (2-26), gives

$$\operatorname{var}(b) = \frac{\sigma_u^2}{\Sigma x^2} \tag{2-29}$$

Turning to the intercept,

$$a = \bar{Y} - b\bar{X}$$
$$= \alpha + \beta\bar{X} + \bar{u} - b\bar{X}$$
$$= \alpha - (b - \beta)\bar{X} + \bar{u}$$

Since $E(b) = \beta$ and $E(\bar{u}) = 0$, it then follows that

$$E(a) = \alpha \tag{2-30}$$

The variance of a is

$$\operatorname{var}(a) = E\{(a - \alpha)^2\}$$
$$= \bar{X}^2 E\{(b - \beta)^2\} + E\{\bar{u}^2\} - 2\bar{X}E\{(b - \beta)\bar{u}\}$$
$$= \bar{X}^2 \frac{\sigma_u^2}{\Sigma x^2} + \frac{\sigma_u^2}{n}$$
$$= \sigma_u^2 \left[\frac{1}{n} + \frac{\bar{X}^2}{\Sigma x^2}\right] \tag{2-31}$$

In this derivation $E\{\bar{u}^2\} = \sigma_u^2/n$ since $\bar{u}$ is the mean of a random sample of n

drawings from the u distribution which has zero mean and variance σ_u^2. The cross-product term vanishes since

$$E\{(b-\beta)\bar{u}\} = E\left\{(\Sigma w_i u_i)\left(\frac{1}{n}\Sigma u_i\right)\right\}$$

$$= E\left\{\frac{1}{n}\left[\Sigma w_i u_i^2 + \sum_{i \neq j}(w_i + w_j)u_i u_j\right]\right\}$$

$$= 0$$

The covariance between a and b is

$$\text{cov}(a, b) = E\{(a-\alpha)(b-\beta)\}$$

$$= E\{[\bar{u} - (b-\beta)\bar{X}](b-\beta)\}$$

$$= -\bar{X}E\{(b-\beta)^2\} \qquad \text{since} \qquad E\{(b-\beta)\bar{u}\} = 0$$

$$= -\frac{\bar{X}\sigma_u^2}{\Sigma x^2} \tag{2-32}$$

Formulas (2-29), (2-31), and (2-32) all involve the unknown σ_u^2. To make the formulas operational, this is replaced by its estimated value $s^2 = \Sigma e^2/(n-2)$.

Example 2-3 From the data in Table 2-2,

$$\Sigma x^2 = 40, \qquad \Sigma e^2 = 1.5, \qquad \text{and} \qquad n = 5$$

Thus

$$s^2 = 1.5/3 = 0.5$$

and

$$\text{var}(b) = \frac{0.5}{40} = \frac{1}{80} = 0.0125$$

$$\text{var}(a) = s^2\left[\frac{1}{n} + \frac{\bar{X}^2}{\Sigma x^2}\right]$$

$$= 0.5\left[\frac{1}{5} + \frac{16}{40}\right] = \frac{12}{40} = 0.3$$

We might use the same data to estimate the sampling variance of the slope estimated by passing a line through the lowest and highest points. Table 2-1 shows that the smallest X value occurs at the third observation and the largest at the fifth observation. Thus the alternative slope estimator is

$$b' = \frac{Y_5 - Y_3}{X_5 - X_3}$$

$$= \frac{1}{8}(Y_5 - Y_3)$$

$$= \frac{1}{8}[(\alpha + 9\beta + u_5) - (\alpha + \beta + u_3)]$$

$$= \beta + \frac{1}{8}(u_5 - u_3)$$

Hence $$E(b') = \beta$$

so that the alternative estimator is also unbiased. Its variance is

$$\begin{aligned}\text{var}(b') &= E\{(b' - \beta)^2\} \\ &= E\left\{\frac{1}{64}\left(u_5^2 + u_3^2 - 2u_5u_3\right)\right\} \\ &= \frac{\sigma_u^2}{32}\end{aligned}$$

Replacing σ_u^2 by the same estimate as in the least-squares case, the estimated sampling variance is

$$\text{var}(b') = \frac{1}{64} = 0.0156$$

which is about 25 percent greater than the variance of the least-squares estimate. If we form the ratio

$$\frac{\text{var}(b)}{\text{var}(b')} = \frac{0.0125}{0.0156} = 0.80$$

we have the *efficiency* of b' relative to b so that, by the least-squares criterion, b' is 80 percent efficient.†

This last example is an illustration of an important theorem, the Gauss-Markov theorem, that the least-squares estimators have minimum variance in the class of linear unbiased estimators. We will now prove this theorem just for the regression slope and give a proof of the general case in Chap. 5. We already know that b is an unbiased estimator. It is also said to be a linear estimator since its definition in Eq. (2-24) shows it to be a linear combination of the Y values, and hence it is also expressible as a linear combination of the stochastic u variables. Define a general linear estimator of β as

$$b_* = \Sigma c_i Y_i \tag{2-33}$$

where the c_i $(i = 1, 2, \ldots, n)$ are some set of weights. Substituting for Y_i from Eq. (2-8a) gives

$$b_* = \alpha\Sigma c_i + \beta\Sigma c_i X_i + \Sigma c_i u_i$$

† The alternative estimator does not provide any means of estimating σ_u^2, and we have only been able to estimate var(b') above by using the s^2 based on the least-squares residuals. However, this does not affect the calculation of the efficiency of b' since the proper definition is

$$\begin{aligned}\text{Efficiency of } b' &= \frac{\text{var}(b)}{\text{var}(b')} \\ &= \frac{\sigma_u^2/\Sigma x^2}{\sigma_u^2/32} \\ &= \frac{32}{40} = 0.8\end{aligned}$$

with $$E(b_*) = \alpha\Sigma c_i + \beta\Sigma c_i X_i$$

We require the weights to be such as to make b_* an unbiased estimator of β. This imposes the conditions

$$\Sigma c_i = 0 \qquad \text{and} \qquad \Sigma c_i X_i = \Sigma c_i x_i = 1 \tag{2-34}$$

Under these conditions the variance of b_* is

$$\text{var}(b_*) = \sigma_u^2 \Sigma c_i^2 \tag{2-35}$$

To compare this variance with that of the ordinary least squares (OLS) b, write

$$c_i = w_i + (c_i - w_i)$$

Thus

$$\Sigma c_i^2 = \Sigma w_i^2 + \Sigma(c_i - w_i)^2 + 2\Sigma w_i(c_i - w_i) \tag{2-36}$$

But

$$\begin{aligned} \Sigma w_i c_i &= \frac{\Sigma c_i x_i}{\Sigma x^2} \\ &= \frac{1}{\Sigma x^2} \qquad \text{using Eq. (2-34)} \end{aligned} \tag{2-37}$$

and, as already shown in Eq. (2-26),

$$\Sigma w_i^2 = \frac{1}{\Sigma x^2}$$

Thus

$$\Sigma w_i(c_i - w_i) = 0 \tag{2-38}$$

and so

$$\sigma_u^2 \Sigma c_i^2 = \sigma_u^2 \Sigma w_i^2 + \sigma_u^2 \Sigma(c_i - w_i)^2$$

which, using Eq. (2-28), gives

$$\text{var}(b_*) = \text{var}(b) + s_u^2 \Sigma(c_i - w_i)^2 \tag{2-39}$$

Since $\Sigma(c_i - w_i)^2 > 0$, unless $c_i = w_i$ for all i, this establishes that the OLS estimator has minimum variance in the class of linear unbiased estimators, and we write

b is a best linear unbiased estimator (b.l.u.e.) of β

The proof of the similar result for the intercept is left as an exercise for the reader.

This minimum variance property of least squares is the main reason for the widespread use of the technique. It rests on the assumption that the X's are fixed in repeated sampling, that the relationship has been correctly specified in Eq. (2-8a), and that the disturbances have zero mean, constant variance, and zero covariances. Notice that assumption (2-8d) on the normality of the u distribution has not been used so far. If we bring this assumption into play, the sampling distributions of a and b are fully determined. Since a and b are linear functions of the u's, they in turn are normally distributed variables. Once the mean and the variance are known, a normal distribution is completely specified. Thus

$$a \sim N\left(\alpha, \sigma_u^2\left[\frac{1}{n} + \frac{\bar{X}^2}{\Sigma x^2}\right]\right) \tag{2-40}$$

and

$$b \sim N\left(\beta, \frac{\sigma_u^2}{\Sigma x^2}\right) \tag{2-41}$$

It still remains to justify the expression given in Eq. (2-16) for the estimator of the disturbance variance. The ith residual is

$$\begin{aligned} e_i &= Y_i - \hat{Y}_i \\ &= \alpha + \beta X_i + u_i - a - bX_i \\ &= u_i - (a - \alpha) - (b - \beta)X_i \end{aligned}$$

From the expression for a just before Eq. (2-30),

$$a - \alpha = \bar{u} - (b - \beta)\bar{X}$$

Thus

$$e_i = (u_i - \bar{u}) - (b - \beta)x_i$$

Notice that $\bar{u}$, being a sample mean, cannot be set at zero, even though $E(u_i) = 0$. Squaring and summing,

$$\begin{aligned} \Sigma e_i^2 &= \Sigma(u_i - \bar{u})^2 + (b - \beta)^2\Sigma x_i^2 - 2(b - \beta)\Sigma(u_i - \bar{u})x_i \\ &= \Sigma u_i^2 - n\bar{u}^2 + (b - \beta)^2\Sigma x_i^2 - 2(b - \beta)\Sigma u_i x_i \end{aligned}$$

We note that

$$E(\Sigma u_i^2) = n\sigma_u^2$$

$$E(\bar{u}^2) = \text{var}(\bar{u}) = \frac{\sigma_u^2}{n}$$

$$E(b - \beta)^2 = \text{var}(b) = \frac{\sigma_u^2}{\Sigma x_i^2}$$

and

$$\begin{aligned} E\{(b - \beta)(\Sigma u_i x_i)\} &= E\{(\Sigma w_i u_i)(\Sigma u_i x_i)\} \\ &= \sigma_u^2 \Sigma w_i x_i \\ &= \sigma_u^2 \end{aligned}$$

Thus

$$E(\Sigma e_i^2) = (n - 2)\sigma_u^2$$

so

$$E\left(\frac{\Sigma e^2}{n - 2}\right) = \sigma_u^2$$

and the estimator proposed in Eq. (2-16) is unbiased. The distribution of this estimator will be established for the general case in Chap. 5.

2-5 INFERENCE IN THE LEAST-SQUARES MODEL

In the previous section we established the sampling distributions of a and b under assumptions (2-8a) to (2-8d). Results (2-40) and (2-41), however, involve the unknown σ_u^2, and so they are not operational as they stand. To derive the sampling distributions of a and b when σ_u^2 is replaced by its estimator s^2, we merely state here two results which will be proven later in Chap. 5, namely, that under the assumptions made so far,

$$\frac{\Sigma e^2}{\sigma_u^2} \sim \chi^2(n-2) \tag{2-42}$$

and

$$\Sigma e^2 \text{ is distributed independently of } f(a, b)$$

Concentrating first of all on inferences about β and recalling that the t distribution is given by the ratio of a standard normal variable to the square root of a χ^2 variable divided by its degrees of freedom,†

$$\frac{b-\beta}{\sigma_u/\sqrt{\Sigma x^2}} \sim N(0,1)$$

from Eq. (2-41) so

$$t = \frac{(b-\beta)\sqrt{\Sigma x^2}}{\sigma_u} \div \frac{\sqrt{\Sigma e^2}/\sigma_u}{\sqrt{(n-2)}}$$

giving

$$t = \frac{b-\beta}{s/\sqrt{\Sigma x^2}} \sim t(n-2) \tag{2-43}$$

Replacing σ_u^2 by its estimator s^2 shifts us from a normal distribution to a t distribution. As the sample size becomes very large, the t distribution tends toward the standard normal distribution, so for sample sizes in excess of 30 or so no great harm is done in treating $(b-\beta)\sqrt{\Sigma x^2}/s$ as if it were a standard normal variable.

The standard inference procedures based on Eq. (2-43) are then as follows. A 95 percent *confidence interval* for β is given by

$$b \pm t_{0.025} s/\sqrt{\Sigma x^2} \tag{2-44}$$

where $\sqrt{\Sigma x^2}$ is computed from the sample data, b from Eq. (2-14a), s from Eq.

† See App. A-7 on the χ^2, t, and F distributions.

(2-16), and $t_{0.025}$ is read off as the $2\frac{1}{2}$ percent point of the t distribution with $n - 2$ degrees of freedom. In general a $100(1 - \varepsilon)$ percent confidence interval for β is given by

$$b \pm t_{\varepsilon/2} s/\sqrt{\Sigma x^2} \tag{2-45}$$

To test the null hypothesis that β has some specified value β_0, that is,

$$H_0: \quad \beta = \beta_0$$

against the alternative hypothesis that β has some value other than β_0, that is,

$$H_1: \quad \beta \neq \beta_0$$

we insert β_0 in Eq. (2-43) and then have the conditional statement. If the null hypothesis is true,

$$\frac{b - \beta_0}{s/\sqrt{\Sigma x^2}} \sim t(n - 2)$$

This gives the sampling distribution of b under the null hypothesis, as shown in Fig. 2-5. If the null hypothesis were true, 95 percent of all sample values of b would lie within $t_{0.025}$ standard errors of β_0, that is, inside the symmetrical region about β_0 shown in the figure. If our sample b is found in either tail of the distribution, then either

1. The null hypothesis is true and an unlikely event has occurred

or

2. The null hypothesis is not true

In such a case we deliberately choose the second interpretation and thus follow this procedure. Reject H_0 at the 5 percent level of significance if

$$\left| \frac{b - \beta_0}{s/\sqrt{\Sigma x^2}} \right| > t_{0.025}$$

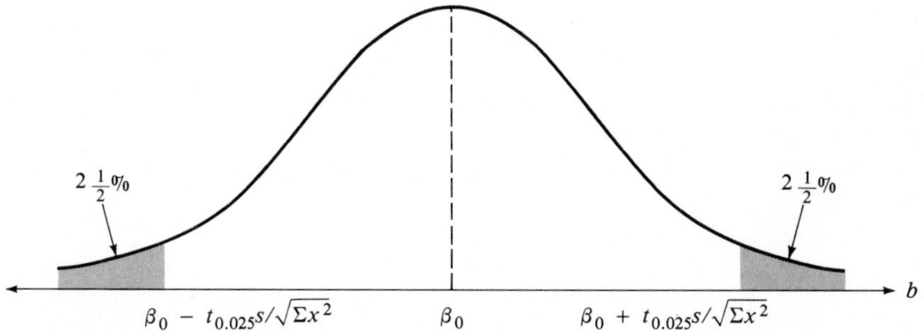

Figure 2-5 Sampling distribution of b under H_0: $\beta = \beta_0$.

Accept H_0 at the 5 percent level of significance if

$$\left|\frac{b-\beta_0}{s/\sqrt{\Sigma x^2}}\right| \leq t_{0.025}$$

In general the procedure is as follows. Reject H_0 at the 100ε percent level of significance if

$$\left|\frac{b-\beta_0}{s/\sqrt{\Sigma x^2}}\right| > t_{\varepsilon/2}$$

Accept H_0 at the 100ε percent level of significance if

$$\left|\frac{b-\beta_0}{s/\sqrt{\Sigma x^2}}\right| \leq t_{\varepsilon/2}$$

The null hypothesis most frequently tested is

$$H_0: \quad \beta = 0$$

This is referred to as *testing the significance* of X. If the hypothesis is true, the X variable plays no role in the determination of Y. Nonetheless when sample values of X and Y are drawn from such a population and the least-squares formula is applied, we will usually find nonzero values for b. These can arise from the fluctuations of random sampling even though the underlying β is truly zero. The appropriate significance test follows directly from replacing β_0 by zero in the results above. Thus reject H_0: $\beta = 0$ at the 100ε percent level of significance if

$$\left|\frac{b}{s/\sqrt{\Sigma x^2}}\right| > t_{\varepsilon/2}$$

The test statistic is now simply the ratio of b to its estimated standard error. Most computer programs for regression analysis print out the value of b and either its estimated standard error or else the ratio of b to its estimated standard error, and this is often referred to as the sample t statistic.† If the sample t statistic is numerically greater than the preselected critical value of t, we accept the alternative hypothesis and conclude that X plays a significant role in the determination of Y. The presentation of sample t statistics is thus directly useful for making significance tests. If, however, one wishes to test a null hypothesis that β has some value other than zero, one requires the standard error (s.e.) for substitution in the appropriate test statistic. This can be obtained from the computer printout as

$$\text{s.e.}\,(b) = \frac{b}{\text{sample } t \text{ statistic}}$$

† In the rest of the text we will normally drop the distinction between the *true* standard error and the *estimated* standard error, as it is usually clear from the context which concept is implied.

By a similar development, tests on the intercept are based on the t distribution:

$$t = \frac{a - \alpha}{s\sqrt{\left(\frac{1}{n} + \frac{\bar{X}^2}{\Sigma x^2}\right)}} \sim t(n-2) \tag{2-46}$$

Thus a $100(1 - \varepsilon)$ percent confidence interval for α is given by

$$a \pm t_{\varepsilon/2} s\sqrt{\left(\frac{1}{n} + \frac{\bar{X}^2}{\Sigma x^2}\right)} \tag{2-47}$$

and the hypothesis

$$H_0:\quad \alpha = \alpha_0$$

would be rejected at the 100ε percent level of significance if

$$\left| \frac{a - \alpha_0}{s\sqrt{\left(\frac{1}{n} + \frac{\bar{X}^2}{\Sigma x^2}\right)}} \right| > t_{\varepsilon/2}$$

Tests on σ_u^2 may be derived from the result stated in Eq. (2-42). Using that result one may, for example, write

$$\Pr\left\{ \chi^2_{0.025} < \frac{(n-2)s^2}{\sigma_u^2} < \chi^2_{0.975} \right\} = 0.95 \tag{2-48}$$

which merely states that 95 percent of the values of a χ^2 variable will lie between the values that cut off $2\frac{1}{2}$ percent in each tail of the distribution. This is illustrated in Fig. 2-6. The critical values are read off from the χ^2 distribution with $n - 2$

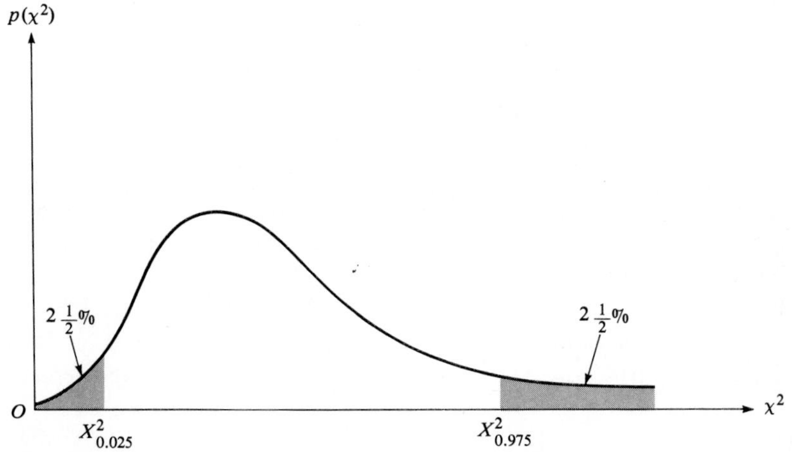

Figure 2-6

degrees of freedom. The only unknown in Eq. (2-48) is σ_u^2, and the contents of the probability statement may be rearranged to give a 95 percent confidence interval for σ_u^2 as

$$\frac{(n-2)s^2}{\chi^2_{0.975}} \quad \text{to} \quad \frac{(n-2)s^2}{\chi^2_{0.025}}$$

Example 2-4 From the data of Tables 2-1 and 2-2 we have already computed

$$a = 1 \qquad \text{var}(a) = 0.3$$
$$b = 1.75 \qquad \text{var}(b) = 0.0125$$

Thus

$$\text{s.e.}(a) = \sqrt{0.3} = 0.5477$$
$$\text{s.e.}(b) = \sqrt{0.0125} = 0.1118$$

Since $n = 5$, from the t distribution with 3 degrees of freedom,

$$t_{0.025} = 3.182$$

Thus a 95 percent confidence interval for α is

$$1 \pm 3.182(0.5477)$$

that is,

$$-0.74 \quad \text{to} \quad 2.74$$

and a 95 percent confidence interval for β is

$$1.75 \pm 3.182(0.1118)$$

that is,

$$1.39 \quad \text{to} \quad 2.11$$

The intercept is not significantly different from zero since

$$\frac{a}{\text{s.e.}(a)} = \frac{1}{0.5477} = 1.826 < 3.182$$

while the slope is strongly significant since

$$\frac{b}{\text{s.e.}(b)} = \frac{1.75}{0.1118} = 15.653 > 3.182$$

Once confidence intervals have been computed, there is no need to actually compute the significance tests, since a confidence interval which includes zero is equivalent to accepting the hypothesis that the true value of the parameter is zero, and an interval which does not embrace zero is equivalent to rejecting the null hypothesis.

From the χ^2 distribution with 3 degrees of freedom $\chi^2_{0.025} = 0.216$ and $\chi^2_{0.975} = 9.35$. We also have $\Sigma e^2 = (n-2)s^2 = 1.5$. Thus a 95 percent confidence interval for σ_u^2 is

$$\frac{1.5}{9.35} \quad \text{to} \quad \frac{1.5}{0.216}$$

that is,

$$0.16 \quad \text{to} \quad 6.94$$

2-6 ANALYSIS OF VARIANCE IN LEAST-SQUARES REGRESSION

The test for the significance of X (H_0: $\beta = 0$), derived in the previous section, may also be set out in an analysis of variance framework, and this alternative approach will be especially helpful when we treat problems of multiple regression in Chap. 5.

From Eq. (2-41) we have the result

$$\frac{b - \beta}{\sigma_u / \sqrt{\Sigma x^2}} \sim N(0, 1)$$

From the definition of the χ^2 variable in App. A-7 we then have

$$\frac{(b - \beta)^2}{\sigma_u^2 / \Sigma x^2} \sim \chi^2(1)$$

and since

$$\frac{\Sigma e^2}{\sigma_u^2} \sim \chi^2(n - 2)$$

independently of b

$$F = \frac{(b - \beta)^2 \Sigma x^2}{\Sigma e^2 / (n - 2)} \sim F(1, n - 2) \tag{2-49}$$

recalling that F is the ratio of two independent χ^2 variables, each divided by the number of its degrees of freedom. If $\beta = 0$,

$$F = \frac{b^2 \Sigma x^2}{\Sigma e^2 / (n - 2)} \sim F(1, n - 2) \tag{2-50}$$

Referring to the decomposition of the sum of squares in Eq. (2-15), the F statistic in Eq. (2-50) is seen to be

$$F = \frac{\text{ESS}/1}{\text{RSS}/(n - 2)} \tag{2-51}$$

Following this approach, the data are set out in an analysis of variance (ANOVA) table (Table 2-3). The entries in col. (ii) and (iii) of the table are additive. The mean squares in the final column are obtained by dividing the sum of squares in each row by the corresponding number of degrees of freedom. An intuitive explanation of the degrees of freedom concept is that it is equal to the number of values that may be set arbitrarily. Thus we may set $n - 1$ values of y at will, but the nth is then determined by the condition that $\Sigma y = 0$. Likewise, we may set $n - 2$ values of e at will, but the least-squares fit imposes two conditions on e,

Table 2-3 ANOVA for two-variable regression

Source of variation (i)	Sum of squares (ii)	Degrees of freedom (iii)	Mean square (iv)
X	$\text{ESS} = \Sigma\hat{y}^2 = b^2\Sigma x^2 = b\Sigma xy$	1	ESS/1
Residual	$\text{RSS} = \Sigma e^2$	$n-2$	$\text{RSS}/(n-2)$
Total	$\text{TSS} = \Sigma y^2$	$n-1$	

namely, $\Sigma e = \Sigma xe = 0$, and finally there is only 1 degree of freedom attached to the explained sum of squares since that depends only on a single parameter, β.

The F statistic in Eq. (2-51) is seen to be the ratio of the mean square due to X to the residual mean square. The latter may be regarded as a measure of the "noise" in the system, and thus an X effect is only detected if it is greater than the inherent noise level. The significance of X is thus tested by examining whether the sample F *exceeds* the appropriate critical value of F taken from the *upper tail* of the F distribution. Thus the test procedure is as follows. Reject H_0: $\beta = 0$ at the 5 percent level of significance if

$$F = \frac{\text{ESS}/1}{\text{RSS}/(n-2)} > F_{0.95}(1, n-2)$$

where $F_{0.95}$ indicates the value of F such that just 5 percent of the distribution lies to the right of the ordinate at $F_{0.95}$. Other levels of significance may be handled in a similar fashion.

Example 2-5 Table 2-4 shows the analysis of variance for the data of Table 2-2.

The sample F statistic is

$$\text{Sample } F = \frac{122.5}{0.5} = 245.0$$

and $F_{0.95}(1, 3) = 10.1$. Thus we reject H_0: $\beta = 0$.

The analysis of variance test is merely the significance test on β in another guise, but it is useful to have introduced the procedure here, as it will be applied

Table 2-4

Source of variation	Source of squares	Degrees of freedom	Mean square
X	122.5	1	122.5
Residual	1.5	3	0.5
Total	124	4	

extensively in later work. To establish the equivalence, recall that the t test for the significance of β is as follows. Reject H_0: $\beta = 0$ at the 5 percent level of significance if

$$\left| \frac{b}{s/\sqrt{\Sigma x^2}} \right| > t_{0.025}(n-2)$$

From Eq. (2-50) the F test procedure is as follows. Reject H_0: $\beta = 0$ at the 5 percent level of significance if

$$\frac{b^2 \Sigma x^2}{\Sigma e^2/(n-2)} > F_{0.95}(1, n-2)$$

The second test statistic is seen to be the square of the first. Thus

$$\text{Sample } F = (\text{sample } t)^2$$

It is also shown in App. A-7 that the F variable with $(1, r)$ degrees of freedom is the square of a t variable with r degrees of freedom. Thus

$$\text{Critical } F = (\text{critical } t)^2$$

and the two tests are completely equivalent.

Finally, there is another way of looking at the F test that will also be helpful later. It was shown in Eq. (2-20) that

$$\text{ESS} = r^2 \text{TSS} = r^2 \Sigma y^2$$

and

$$\text{RSS} = (1 - r^2)\text{TSS} = (1 - r^2)\Sigma y^2$$

Thus the sample F statistic may be written†

$$F = \frac{r^2/1}{(1 - r^2)/(n-2)} \tag{2-52}$$

Again, exploiting the relation between the t and F distributions, Eq. (2-52) gives

$$t = \frac{r\sqrt{(n-2)}}{\sqrt{(1 - r^2)}} \tag{2-53}$$

and this statistic may be referred to as the t distribution with $n - 2$ degrees of freedom to test the significance of the relationship between Y and X. From Example 2-2 we have

$$r^2 = \frac{\text{ESS}}{\text{TSS}} = \frac{122.5}{124.0} = 0.9879$$

† It is, of course, superfluous to insert unity as the divisor of the numerator in both Eqs. (2-51) and (2-52), but it maintains a correspondence between these expressions in models where there is only one explanatory variable to later models with several explanatory variables.

giving $r = 0.9939$. Substituting in Eq. (2-53) gives

$$t = \frac{0.9939\sqrt{3}}{\sqrt{(1 - 0.9879)}} = 15.65$$

From the data given in Examples 2-2 and 2-3

$$t = \frac{b}{\text{s.e.}(b)} = \frac{1.75}{\sqrt{0.0125}} = 15.65$$

and the square root of the sample F statistic in Example 2-5 is

$$t = \sqrt{F} = \sqrt{245.0} = 15.65$$

Thus all three tests are simply three versions of a single test. The test involving r may be regarded as a test of the significance of the correlation coefficient, that based on b as a test of the significance of the regression slope, and the analysis of variance formulation tests the significance of the explained sum of squares, but they are just three different ways of essentially asking the same question.

2-7 PREDICTION IN THE LEAST-SQUARES MODEL

Suppose we have a set of sample observations X_i, Y_i $(i = 1, \ldots, n)$ to which we have applied the least-squares techniques of the previous sections. In addition we suppose that our interest now focuses on some specific value of the independent variable X_0, and we are required to forecast, or predict, the value Y_0 likely to be associated with X_0. For instance, if Y denoted the consumption of gasoline and X the price of gasoline, we might be interested in predicting the demand for gasoline at some higher future price. The value of X_0 may lie within the range of sample X values, or, more frequently, we may be concerned with predicting Y for a value of X *outside* the sample observations. In either case the prediction involves the assumption that the relationship presumed to have generated the sample data still holds for the new observation, whether it relates to a future time period or to a unit that was not included in a sample cross section. Alternatively, we may have a new observation (X_0, Y_0), and the question arises whether this observation may be presumed to have come from the same population that generated the sample data. For example, an appeal might be made to motorists on grounds of patriotism to reduce their consumption of gasoline, and we may use the new observation to test whether the appeal is having any effect. Prediction theory enables us to perform both tasks. We may make two kinds of predictions, a *point* prediction or an *interval* prediction, in just the same way as we can give a point estimate or a confidence interval estimate of a parameter β. But in practice, a point estimate is of little use without some indication of its precision, so one should always provide an estimate of the prediction error. The point prediction is given by the regression value corresponding to X_0, that is,

$$\hat{Y}_0 = a + bX_0 \tag{2-54}$$

The true value of Y in the prediction period is given by

$$Y_0 = \alpha + \beta X_0 + u_0$$

where u_0 indicates the value that would be drawn from the disturbance distribution in the prediction period. The prediction error may then be defined as

$$\begin{aligned} e_0 &= Y_0 - \hat{Y}_0 \\ &= u_0 - (a - \alpha) - (b - \beta)X_0 \end{aligned} \tag{2-55}$$

Taking expectations

$$E(e_0) = 0$$

since $E(u_0) = 0$ and a and b are unbiased estimators of α and β. Thus the least-squares predictor, Eq. (2-54), is an unbiased predictor. The variance of the prediction error is then found by squaring Eq. (2-55) and taking expectations:

$$\begin{aligned} \text{var}(e_0) &= E(e_0^2) \\ &= \text{var}(u_0) + \text{var}(a) + X_0^2\,\text{var}(b) + 2X_0\,\text{cov}(a, b) \end{aligned}$$

since the other two covariances vanish.† On substitution from Eqs. (2-28), (2-31), and (2-32) this gives

$$\begin{aligned} \text{var}(e_0) &= \sigma_u^2\left[1 + \frac{1}{n} + \frac{\bar{X}^2}{\Sigma x^2} + \frac{X_0^2}{\Sigma x^2} - \frac{2X_0\bar{X}}{\Sigma x^2}\right] \\ &= \sigma_u^2\left[1 + \frac{1}{n} + \frac{(X_0 - \bar{X})^2}{\Sigma x^2}\right] \end{aligned} \tag{2-56}$$

The variance of the prediction error is thus at its minimum value when $X_0 = \bar{X}$ and increases nonlinearly as X_0 departs from $\bar{X}$. From Eq. (2-55) e_0 is seen to be a linear function of normal variables and so is itself distributed normally. Thus

$$\frac{e_0}{\sigma_u\sqrt{\left(1 + \dfrac{1}{n} + \dfrac{(X_0 - \bar{X})^2}{\Sigma x^2}\right)}} \sim N(0, 1)$$

Replacing the unknown σ_u by its estimate $s = \sqrt{\Sigma e^2/(n-2)}$ then gives

$$\frac{Y_0 - \hat{Y}_0}{s\sqrt{\left(1 + \dfrac{1}{n} + \dfrac{(X_0 - \bar{X})^2}{\Sigma x^2}\right)}} \sim t(n-2) \tag{2-57}$$

Everything in Eq. (2-57) is known except Y_0, and so, in the usual way, we derive a

† By assumption u_0 is independent of $u_1, u_2, \ldots, u_n$, and thus it has zero covariance with $(a - \alpha)$ and $(b - \beta)$, since these are each linear functions of $u_1, u_2, \ldots, u_n$.

95 percent confidence interval for Y_0 as

$$(a + bX_0) \pm t_{0.025}s\sqrt{\left(1 + \frac{1}{n} + \frac{(X_0 - \bar{X}^2)}{\Sigma x^2}\right)} \tag{2-58}$$

Sometimes interest centers on predicting the *mean* value of Y_0, that is,

$$E(Y_0) = \alpha + \beta X_0$$

rather than Y_0 itself, since there is, of course, no way of predicting the value of a single drawing from $p(u)$. The prediction error is now

$$\begin{aligned} e_0 &= E(Y_0) - \hat{Y}_0 \\ &= -(a - \alpha) - (b - \beta)X_0 \end{aligned}$$

which gives

$$\operatorname{var}(e_0) = \sigma_u^2\left[\frac{1}{n} + \frac{(X_0 - \bar{X})^2}{\Sigma x^2}\right]$$

and so a 95 percent confidence interval for $E(Y_0)$ is

$$a + bX_0 \pm t_{0.025}s\sqrt{\left(\frac{1}{n} + \frac{(X_0 - \bar{X})^2}{\Sigma x^2}\right)} \tag{2-59}$$

The width of the confidence interval in Eqs. (2-58) and (2-59) is seen to increase symmetrically the further X_0 is from the sample mean $\bar{X}$, as shown in Fig. 2-7.

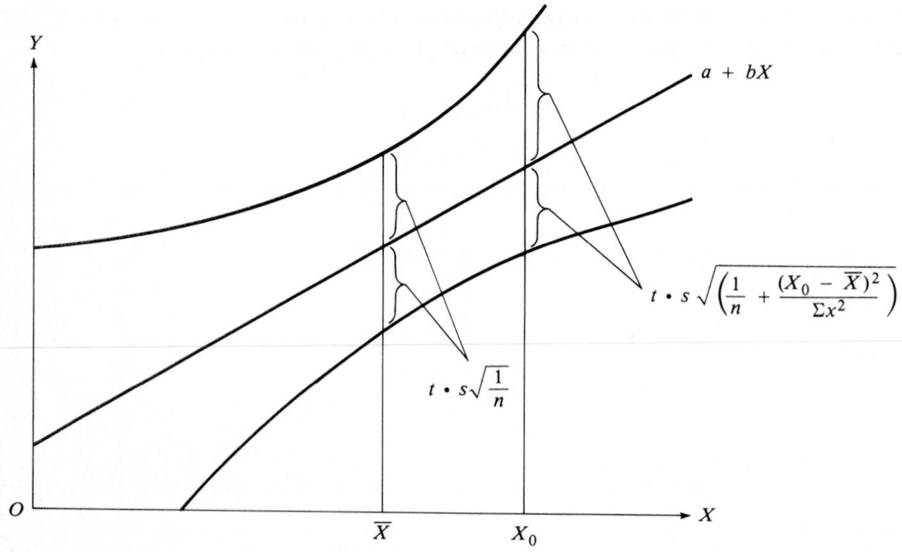

Figure 2-7

Example 2-6 Assembling relevant results for the data of Table 2-1,

$$\hat{Y} = 1 + 1.75X$$
$$n = 5$$
$$\bar{X} = 4$$
$$s^2 = \frac{\Sigma e^2}{n-2} = \frac{1.5}{3} = 0.5$$
$$\Sigma x^2 = 40$$

Suppose we require a 95 percent confidence interval for Y given $X = 10$. Applying Eq. (2-58) gives

$$1 + 1.75(10) \pm 3.182\sqrt{0.5}\sqrt{\left(1 + \frac{1}{5} + \frac{(10-4)^2}{40}\right)}$$

that is,

$$18.5 \pm 3.26$$

or $\qquad 15.24 \quad \text{to} \quad 21.76$

The 95 percent interval for $E(Y|X = 10)$ is

$$18.5 \pm 3.182\sqrt{0.5}\sqrt{\frac{1}{5} + \frac{(10-4)^2}{40}}$$

that is,

$$18.5 \pm 2.36$$

or $\qquad 16.14 \quad \text{to} \quad 20.86$

To test whether a new observation (X_0, Y_0) may be thought to come from the structure generating the sample data, one merely contrasts the observation with the confidence interval for Y_0. For example, the point (10, 25) gives a Y value which lies outside the interval 15.24 to 21.76, and one would conclude that it was unlikely to have been generated by the same structure as the sample data.

PROBLEMS

2-1 The least-squares estimate of α in $Y = \alpha + \beta X + u$ is $a = \Sigma(1/n - \bar{X}w_i)Y_i$, where $w_i = x_i/\Sigma x_i^2$ with $x_i = X_i - \bar{X}$ and

$$\operatorname{var}(a) = \sigma_u^2\left(\frac{1}{n} + \frac{\bar{X}^2}{\sum_{i=1}^{n} x_i^2}\right)$$

Show that no other linear unbiased estimate of α can be constructed with a smaller variance.

2-2 Show that if z_i are independent quantities from the same population, with variance σ^2, then the sampling variance of

$$b = \sum_{i=1}^{n} a_i z_i$$

is $\sigma^2\Sigma_{i=1}^{n}a_i^2$. Observations Y_i are related to fixed quantities X_i and the quantities z_i above by the relations $Y_i = \alpha + \beta X_i + z_i$ $(i = 1,\ldots, n)$. If the values of X_i are

X_1	X_2	X_3	X_4	X_5	X_6
1	2	3	4	5	6

an alternative estimate of β is

$$\tfrac{1}{8}(Y_6 + Y_5 - Y_2 - Y_1)$$

Deduce the sampling variance of this estimate and compare with it with the sampling variance of the least-squares estimate.

(Oxford University, 1958)

2-3 From a sample of 200 pairs of observations the following quantities were calculated:

$$\Sigma X = 11.34, \qquad \Sigma Y = 20.72, \qquad \Sigma X^2 = 12.16, \qquad \Sigma Y^2 = 84.96, \qquad \Sigma XY = 22.13$$

Estimate the regressions $Y = \hat{\alpha} + \hat{\beta}X$ and $X = \hat{\gamma} + \hat{\delta}Y$.

(R.S.S. Certificate, 1956)

2-4 Show that if r is the correlation coefficient between n pairs of values (X_i, Y_i), then the correlation coefficient between the n pairs $(\alpha X_i + b, cY_i + d)$, where a, b, c, and d are constants, is also r.

(R.S.S. Certificate, 1956)

2-5 The percentage of fat X and the percentage of nonfat solids Y are measured on milk samples of a number of dairy cows in two herds. A summary of the data is set out below. Calculate the linear regression of Y on X for each herd, and test whether the two lines differ in slope.

Herd A, number of cows = 16:

$$\Sigma X = 51.13, \qquad \Sigma Y = 117.25, \qquad \Sigma x^2 = 1.27, \qquad \Sigma y^2 = 4.78, \qquad \Sigma xy = 1.84$$

Herd B, number of cows = 10:

$$\Sigma X = 37.20, \qquad \Sigma Y = 78.75, \qquad \Sigma x^2 = 1.03, \qquad \Sigma y^2 = 2.48, \qquad \Sigma xy = 1.10$$

(R.S.S. Certificate, 1956)

[*Note:* If $\hat{\beta}_1$ is $N(\beta_1, \sigma_1^2/\Sigma x_1^2)$ and $\hat{\beta}_2$ is $N(\beta_2, \sigma_2^2/\Sigma x_2^2)$, where $\hat{\beta}_1$ and $\hat{\beta}_3$ are independent, then $\hat{\beta}_1 - \hat{\beta}_2$ is $N(\beta_1 - \beta_2, \sigma_1^2/\Sigma x_1^2 + \sigma_2^2/\Sigma x_2^2)$. If σ_1^2 and σ_2^2 are unknown, then a shift to the t distribution can be made if we assume $\sigma_1^2 = \sigma_2^2 = \sigma^2$ and pool the sum of squared residuals from each regression so that $(\Sigma e_1^2 + \Sigma e_2^2)/\sigma^2$ has a χ^2 distribution with $n_1 + n_2 - 4$ degrees of freedom.]

2-6 Data on aggregate income Y and consumption C yield the following regressions, expressed in deviation form:

$$\hat{y} = 1.2c$$

$$\hat{c} = 0.6y$$

If $Y \equiv C + Z$ (where Z is savings), compute the correlation between Y and Z, the correlation between C and Z, and the ratio of the standard deviations of Z and Y.

(R.S.S. Certificate, 1948)

2-7 The table below gives the means and the standard deviations of two variables X and Y and the correlation between them for each of two samples.

Sample	Number in sample	$\overline{X}$	$\overline{Y}$	s_x	s_y	r_{xy}
1	600	5	12	2	3	0.6
2	400	7	10	3	·4	0.7

Calculate the correlation between X and Y for the composite sample consisting of the two samples taken together. Comment on the fact that this correlation is lower than either of the two original values.

(R.S.S. Certificate, 1955)

2-8 An investigator is interested in the two following series:

	1935	'36	'37	'38	'39	'40	'41	'42	'43	'44	'45	'46
X, deaths of children under 1 year, thousands	60	62	61	55	53	60	63	53	52	48	49	43
Y, consumption of beer, bulk barrels	23	23	25	25	26	26	29	30	30	32	33	31

(*a*) Calculate the coefficient of correlation between X and Y.

(*b*) A linear *time trend* may be fitted to X (or Y) by calculating an OLS regression of X (or Y) on time t. This requires choosing an origin and a unit of measurement for time. For example, if the origin is set at mid-1935 and the unit of measurement is 1 year, then the year 1942 corresponds to $t = 7$. If the origin is set at end-1940 (beginning of 1941) and the unit of measurement is 6 months, then 1937 corresponds to $t = -7$. Show that any computed trend value $\hat{X}_t = a + bt$ is unaffected by the choice of origin and the unit of measurement.

(*c*) Let $\tilde{X}$ be X with any time trend removed; that is, $\tilde{X}_t = X_t - \hat{X}_t$. Calculate the correlation between $\tilde{X}$ and Y, and between $\tilde{X}$ and $\tilde{Y}$. Compare these values with that obtained in part (a), and comment on the difference.

(R.S.S. Certificate, 1954)

2-9 A sample of 20 observations corresponding to the regression model

$$Y = \alpha + \beta X + \varepsilon$$

where ε is normal with zero mean and unknown variance σ^2, gave the following data:

$$\Sigma Y = 21.9, \qquad \Sigma(Y - \bar{Y})^2 = 86.9, \qquad \Sigma(X - \bar{X})(Y - \bar{Y}) = 106.4,$$

$$\Sigma X = 186.2, \qquad \Sigma(X - \bar{X})^2 = 215.4$$

Estimate α and β and calculate estimates of variance of your estimates. Estimate the (conditional) mean value of Y corresponding to a value of X fixed at $X = 10$ and find a 95 percent confidence interval for this (conditional) mean.

(UL, 1958)

2-10 Consider the regression *without an intercept* $Y_i = \beta X_i + u_i$ $(i = 1, \ldots, n)$ for which all standard assumptions hold. Suppose we want to predict Y_0^2. Find a predictor $\tilde{Y}_0^2$ such that $E(\tilde{Y}_0^2) = E(Y_0^2)$.

(University of Michigan, 1981)

2-11 If the sample values of X in the linear model

$$Y_t = \alpha + \beta X_t + u_t$$

have zero mean, show that the covariance of the least-squares estimates of α and β is zero. Hence, or otherwise, prove that an unbiased estimator of β can be derived by estimating the equation

$$\hat{Y}_t = \hat{\beta} X_t$$

which is constrained to pass through the origin. What is the variance of this estimator of β?

(UL, 1973)

CHAPTER

THREE

EXTENSIONS OF THE TWO-VARIABLE LINEAR MODEL

The obvious limitations of the two-variable linear model are that it is linear and embraces only two variables. These restrictions limit the variety of statistical phenomena for which it provides an adequate description. In this chapter we describe some of the more important ways of extending the range of the model. First of all we discuss the case of replicated observations for various X values, which enables us to test the adequacy of the linear representation against the alternative hypothesis that the relationship of Y to X is *nonlinear*. Then we discuss various types of nonlinearity and the ways in which they may be handled. In some cases suitable *transformations* of the variables return the problem to a linear framework, in which case the simple techniques of Chap. 2 may be applied. In others, nonlinear relations have to be fitted directly, but the discussion of nonlinear estimation is beyond the scope of this book. Finally, an introduction to three-variable regression is provided, preparing the way for a general treatment of multiple regression in Chap 5.

3-1 REPEATED OBSERVATIONS AND A TEST OF LINEARITY

Suppose now that we have sample data which could be arranged in the form shown schematically in Table 3-1.

Here we have p distinct values of X and m observations on Y corresponding to each X observation, giving $n = mp$ sample observations altogether. This

Table 3-1 Sample data with replication

X	Y	Mean $\bar{Y}_i$
X_1	$Y_{11}Y_{12} \cdots Y_{1m}$	$\bar{Y}_1$
X_2	$Y_{21}Y_{22} \cdots Y_{2m}$	$\bar{Y}_2$
$\vdots$	$\vdots$	$\vdots$
X_i	$Y_{i1}Y_{i2} \cdots Y_{im}$	$\bar{Y}_i$
$\vdots$	$\vdots$	$\vdots$
X_p	$Y_{p1}Y_{p2} \cdots Y_{pm}$	$\bar{Y}_p$

situation is common in experimental design work: X, for example, might indicate the amount of fertilizer applied to standard sized plots and Y the yield per plot of some crop; or X might indicate drug dosage and Y the response of a patient. Since no two plots (or patients) are completely identical, they may be expected to display varied responses to any given level of X, and so repeated observations on Y are desirable. We have assumed in the layout of the table that we have the same number of replications m for each value of X. This is a simplification to keep the formulas as uncomplicated as possible. The various formulas can easily be amended to deal with the general case where there are m_i observations on Y corresponding to X_i and a total sample size of

$$n = \sum_{i=1}^{p} m_i$$

The first step in the analysis of replicated data is to compute the row means

$$\bar{Y}_i = \frac{1}{m} \sum_{j=1}^{m} Y_{ij} \tag{3-1}$$

where Y_{ij} denotes the jth observation in the ith row or class. The scatter diagram might look like Fig. 3-1 for the case of $m = 4$ and $p = 6$, with the circles indicating individual observations and the black squares the sample mean values of Y. Clearly, we can fit a least-squares regression to this scatter of 24 observations by the methods of Chap. 2. In this case, however, that turns out to be identical to the regression fitted to the six mean points shown on the scatter.† To see that this is so, consider the formula for the regression slope

$$b = \frac{\Sigma xy}{\Sigma x^2}$$

The deviations in this formula are measured from the overall sample means,

† This result does not hold when there are unequal numbers of observations in each class. See Eq. (3-6).

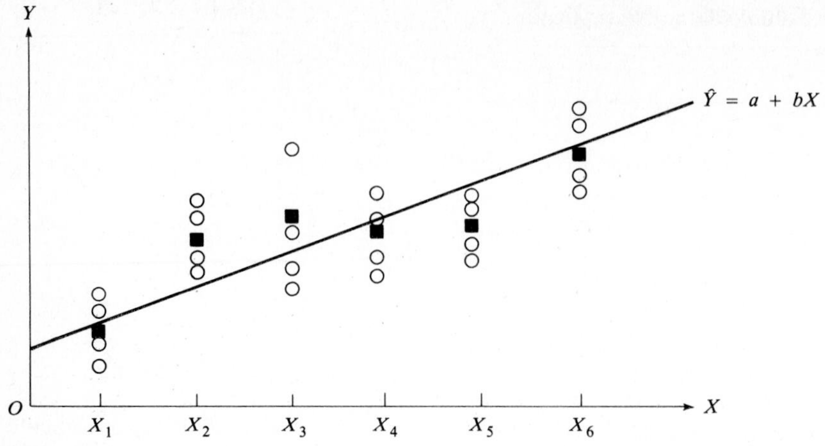

Figure 3-1

which we may now define as

$$\bar{Y} = \frac{1}{mp} \sum_{i=1}^{p} \sum_{j=1}^{m} Y_{ij}$$

or, using Eq. (3-1),

$$\bar{Y} = \frac{1}{p} \sum_{i=1}^{p} \bar{Y}_i \tag{3-2}$$

It is convenient to denote the X observations by X_{ij}, with the proviso that $X_{i1} = X_{i2} = \cdots = X_{im} = X_i$ for $i = 1, 2, \ldots, p$. Thus

$$\bar{X} = \frac{1}{mp} \sum_{i=1}^{p} \sum_{j=1}^{m} X_{ij} = \frac{1}{p} \sum_{i=1}^{p} X_i$$

Then

$$\Sigma x^2 = \sum_{i=1}^{p} \sum_{j=1}^{m} \left(X_{ij} - \bar{X}\right)^2$$

$$= m \sum_{i=1}^{p} \left(X_i - \bar{X}\right)^2$$

and

$$\Sigma xy = \sum_{i=1}^{p} \sum_{j=1}^{m} \left(X_{ij} - \bar{X}\right)\left(Y_{ij} - \bar{Y}\right)$$

$$= \sum_{i=1}^{p} \left(X_i - \bar{X}\right) \sum_{j=1}^{m} \left(Y_{ij} - \bar{Y}\right) \tag{3-3}$$

remembering that anything which is constant with respect to a particular summation sign can be moved leftward in front of that summation sign. But

$$\sum_{j=1}^{m} \left(Y_{ij} - \bar{Y}\right) = \sum_{j=1}^{m} \left[\left(Y_{ij} - \bar{Y}_i\right) + \left(\bar{Y}_i - \bar{Y}\right)\right] = m\left(\bar{Y}_i - \bar{Y}\right)$$

since the first term vanishes and the second is a constant with respect to summation over j. Thus

$$\Sigma xy = m \sum_{i=1}^{p} (X_i - \bar{X})(\bar{Y}_i - \bar{Y}) \tag{3-4}$$

Putting Eqs. (3-3) and (3-4) together, the regression slope is

$$b = \frac{\Sigma_{i=1}^{p}(X_i - \bar{X})(\bar{Y}_i - \bar{Y})}{\Sigma_{i=1}^{p}(X_i - \bar{X})^2} \tag{3-5}$$

but this is also the regression slope fitted *directly* to the X_i, $\bar{Y}_i$ points. The reason, of course, is that the m factor in Eqs. (3-3) and (3-4) cancels out and the class means are, in effect, each given a weight of unity in determining the regression slope. In the more general case of unequal numbers of observations, the regression slope would be given by

$$b = \frac{\Sigma_{i=1}^{p}\Sigma_{j=1}^{m_i}(X_{ij} - \bar{X})(Y_{ij} - \bar{Y})}{\Sigma_{i=1}^{p}\Sigma_{j=1}^{m_i}(X_{ij} - \bar{X})^2} = \frac{\Sigma_{i=1}^{p} m_i(X_i - \bar{X})(\bar{Y}_i - \bar{Y})}{\Sigma_{i=1}^{p} m_i(X_i - \bar{X})^2} \tag{3-6}$$

which can be regarded as a *weighted regression* applied to the class means, the weights being equal to the number of observations in each class.

In scatter diagrams such as that in Fig. 3-1, the class means will usually not lie exactly on the regression line, but will be spread around it in the same way as, but to a lesser degree than, the sample points are spread around the regression line. We are thus led to pose two related questions.

1. Is there any relationship between Y and X?
2. If so, is it a linear or a nonlinear relationship?

The problem may be modeled as follows. Set up the hypothesis

$$Y_{ij} = \mu_i + \varepsilon_{ij} \qquad \text{for } i = 1, 2, \ldots, p; j = 1, 2, \ldots, m \tag{3-7}$$

where the ε_{ij}'s are assumed to be independent normal variables with zero mean and variance σ^2. Thus

$$E(Y_i|X_i) = \mu_i \qquad \text{for } i = 1, 2, \ldots, p \tag{3-8}$$

The hypothesis embodied in Eq. (3-7) states that the m observations on Y in the ith class (corresponding to $X = X_i$) are random drawings from a normal population with mean μ_i and variance σ^2, and that a similar statement holds for the observations on Y in each of the p classes, the only systematic variation between classes being in the underlying mean values

$$\mu_1, \mu_2, \ldots, \mu_p$$

Note carefully the distinction between μ_i and $\bar{Y}_i$, the former being the true but unknown mean of the distribution from which the Y_i observations are drawn and the latter being the actual mean of those sample observations.

The variation hypothesized for the μ's allows a very flexible and general relationship between Y and X. In this context the null hypothesis of no relationship between Y and X could be set up as

$$H_0\colon\ \mu_1 = \mu_2 = \cdots = \mu_p = \mu \tag{3-9}$$

A test of H_0 can be based on a decomposition of the sum of squares in Y. We have

$$(Y_{ij} - \bar{Y}) = (Y_{ij} - \bar{Y}_i) + (\bar{Y}_i - \bar{Y}) \tag{3-10}$$

Squaring and summing over all sample observations gives†

$$\sum_{i,j}(Y_{ij} - \bar{Y})^2 = \sum_{i,j}(Y_{ij} - \bar{Y}_i)^2 + m\sum_i(\bar{Y}_i - \bar{Y})^2 \tag{3-11}$$

The decomposition of the sum of squares in Eq. (3-11) is similar to that given for the linear regression model in Chap. 2. The left-hand side again represents the sum of the squared deviations of Y, measured from the overall sample mean. The first term on the right-hand side is the sum of the squared deviations of the Y's, measured now about the relevant class means, and the second sum of squares is that due to the variation of the class means about the overall mean. We can thus describe Eq. (3-11) in the form

TSS	=	RSS	+	ESS
{Total sum of squares in Y}		{residual or error sum of squares "unexplained" by the class means}		{"explained" sum of squares due to the class means}

In conventional analysis of variance treatments the right-hand-side terms are described respectively as the *within* class and the *between* class sums of squares.

The assumption of normality for the Y's now enables us to derive the following test of H_0, based on RSS and ESS. From the results on the χ^2 distribution in App. A-7,

$$\frac{1}{\sigma^2}\sum_j(Y_{ij} - \bar{Y}_i)^2 \sim X^2(m-1) \qquad \text{for each } i = 1, 2, \ldots, p$$

Further, since the sum of independent χ^2 variables is also distributed as χ^2,

$$\frac{1}{\sigma^2}\sum_{i,j}(Y_{ij} - \bar{Y}_i)^2 \sim \chi^2(pm - p) \tag{3-12}$$

Since the mean of a χ^2 distribution is equal to its degrees of freedom, we have

$$E\left\{\frac{\Sigma_{i,j}(Y_{ij} - \bar{Y}_i)^2}{\sigma^2}\right\} = p(m-1)$$

† We now write the double summation $\Sigma_{i=1}^{p}\Sigma_{j=1}^{m}$ simply as $\Sigma_{i,j}$. Equation (3-11) is derived by noting that the cross-product term vanishes, that is,

$$\sum_{i,j}(Y_{ij} - \bar{Y}_i)(\bar{Y}_i - \bar{Y}) = \sum_i(\bar{Y}_i - \bar{Y})\sum_j(Y_{ij} - \bar{Y}_i) = 0$$

since $\Sigma_j(Y_{ij} - \bar{Y}_i) = 0$ for each $i = 1, 2, \ldots, p$.

or

$$E\left\{\frac{\Sigma_{i,j}(Y_{ij}-\bar{Y}_i)^2}{p(m-1)}\right\}=\sigma^2 \tag{3-13}$$

Under the null hypothesis the $\bar{Y}_i$ are independent normal variables with mean μ and variance σ^2/m. Thus

$$\frac{m\Sigma_i(\bar{Y}_i-\bar{Y})^2}{\sigma^2}\sim\chi^2(p-1) \tag{3-14}$$

and so

$$E\left\{\frac{m\Sigma_i(\bar{Y}_i-\bar{Y})^2}{p-1}\right\}=\sigma^2 \tag{3-15}$$

We state, without proof, that under the null hypothesis the sums of squares in Eqs. (3-12) and (3-14) are *independently* distributed. Thus since the F distribution is given by the ratio of two independent χ^2 quantities, each divided by its degrees of freedom, under H_0

$$F=\frac{m\Sigma_i(\bar{Y}_i-\bar{Y})^2/(p-1)}{\Sigma_{i,j}(Y_{ij}-\bar{Y}_i)^2/p(m-1)}=\frac{\text{ESS}/(p-1)}{\text{RSS}/p(m-1)}\sim F(p-1,p(m-1)) \tag{3-16}$$

The rationale of this test is easily seen from Eqs. (3-13) and (3-15). Under the null hypothesis the numerator and the denominator of F are independent estimates of σ^2, and thus we may expect F to vary randomly about unity. If, however, the null hypothesis is not true, the *between* class sum of squares in the numerator of F will reflect more than just the random variation of the class means about a common mean, and F will rise in value. The null hypothesis is then rejected if the computed value of F exceeds a preselected critical F value from the upper tail of the distribution.

The sums of squares in this F statistic may also be used to define the *correlation ratio* η as follows:

$$\eta^2=\frac{\text{ESS}}{\text{TSS}}=\frac{m\Sigma_{i=1}(\bar{Y}_i-\bar{Y})^2}{\Sigma_{i,j}(Y_{ij}-\bar{Y})^2}=1-\frac{\Sigma_{i,j}(Y_{ij}-\bar{Y}_i)^2}{\Sigma_{i,j}(Y_{ij}-\bar{Y})^2} \tag{3-17}$$

This is analogous to the definition of r^2 in Chap. 2, with the exception that the explained sum of squares is based on the variation of the sample means $\bar{Y}_i$, rather than the variation of the regression values $\hat{Y}_i$. The F statistic of Eq. (3-16) may then be stated equivalently

$$F=\frac{\eta^2/(p-1)}{(1-\eta^2)/p(m-1)}$$

which has the same structure as the expression involving r^2 in Eq. (2-52).

Table 3-2 One-way analysis of variance (ANOVA)

Source of variation	Sum of squares	Degrees of freedom	Mean square
Between classes	$m\sum_{i=1}^{p}(\bar{Y}_i - \bar{Y})^2 = \text{ESS}$	$p - 1$	$\text{ESS}/(p-1)$
Within classes	$\sum_{i,j}(Y_{ij} - \bar{Y}_i)^2 = \text{RSS}$	$p(m-1)$	$\text{RSS}/p(m-1)$
Total	$\sum_{i,j}(Y_{ij} - \bar{Y})^2 = \text{TSS}$	$mp - 1$	

The test defined in Eq. (3-16) is the standard one-way (or one factor) analysis of variance. It is based solely on the Y observations and is a test of the homogeneity of the p class means. The only role for the X variable has been to classify the Y's into classes associated with a common X value. Thus the X variables could have been *qualitative* variables, such as socioeconomic status or educational level. The data for the test are normally set out in an ANOVA table, such as Table 3-2.

The second and third columns of the table are additive, as usual. Thus, once any two of the sums of squares have been calculated, the third follows by using TSS = ESS + RSS.

We can now carry this analysis one step further and derive a test for the linearity of the relationship between Y and X. Figure 3-2 shows just one point (X_i, Y_{ij}) from the X, Y scatter, and $\hat{Y} = a + bX$ indicates the linear regression fitted to the data.

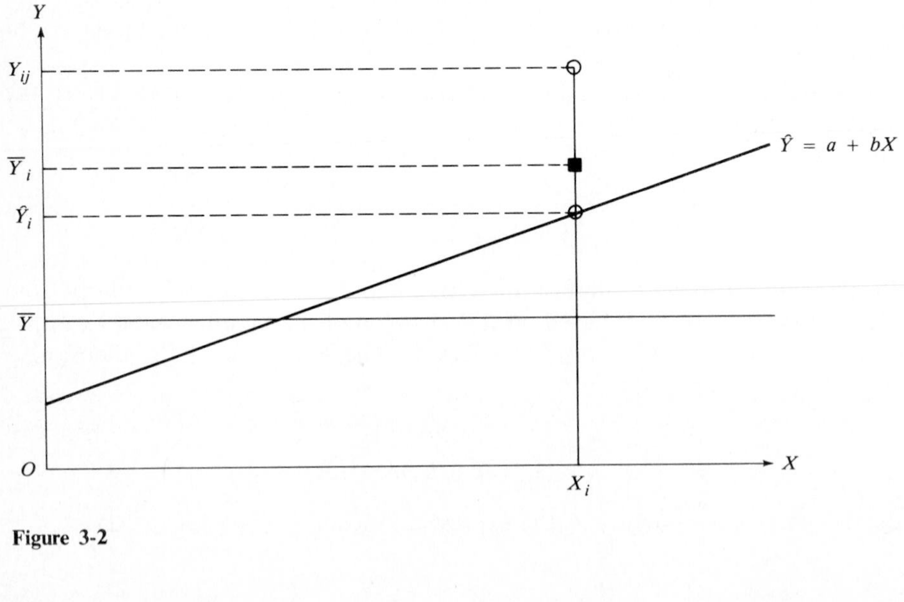

Figure 3-2

The deviation of Y_{ij} from the overall mean $\bar{Y}$ may be decomposed as follows†;

$$(Y_{ij} - \bar{Y}) = (Y_{ij} - \bar{Y}_i) + (\bar{Y}_i - \hat{Y}_i) + (\hat{Y}_i - \bar{Y}) \tag{3-18}$$

This decomposition embraces both the linear analysis of Chap. 2 and the analysis of class means in this section, as shown by the following groupings.

Linear analysis

$$(Y_{ij} - \bar{Y}) = \overbrace{(Y_{ij} - \bar{Y}_i) + (\bar{Y}_i - \hat{Y}_i)} + \overbrace{(\hat{Y}_i - \bar{Y})}$$

$$(Y_{ij} - \bar{Y}) = \underbrace{(Y_{ij} - \bar{Y}_i)} + \underbrace{(\bar{Y}_i - \hat{Y}_i) + (\hat{Y}_i - \bar{Y})}$$

Class mean analysis

Squaring Eq. (3-18) and summing over all the sample observations gives‡

$$\sum_{i,j} (Y_{ij} - \bar{Y})^2 = \sum_{i,j} (Y_{ij} - \bar{Y}_i)^2 + m\sum_i (\bar{Y}_i - \hat{Y}_i)^2 + m\sum_i (\hat{Y}_i - \bar{Y})^2 \tag{3-19}$$

In words, Eq. (3-19) states

$$\begin{Bmatrix}\text{Total sum}\\ \text{of squares}\\ \text{in } Y\end{Bmatrix} = \begin{Bmatrix}\text{sum of squares}\\ \text{about class}\\ \text{means}\end{Bmatrix} + \begin{Bmatrix}\text{sum of squares}\\ \text{due to variation}\\ \text{of class means}\\ \text{about linear}\\ \text{regression}\end{Bmatrix} + \begin{Bmatrix}\text{sum of squares}\\ \text{due to linear}\\ \text{regression}\end{Bmatrix}$$

We notice from Eq. (3-19) that r^2 is the ratio of the third term on the right-hand side to $\sum_{i,j}(Y_{ij} - \bar{Y})^2$, and η^2 is the ratio of the *sum* of the *second* and *third* terms to the same total sum of squares in Y. Thus

$$\eta^2 \geq r^2$$

The equality would only hold if all class means fell on the linear regression line. The middle term in Eq. (3-19) is thus proportional to the *excess* of η^2 over r^2 and is the basis of the linearity test set out in Table 3-3.

The sums of squares may be calculated in various ways. If r^2 and η^2 have already been calculated, the required quantities follow directly. If not, S_4 can be calculated first; S_1 is then the explained sum of squares due to the regression, to be calculated by the methods of Chap. 2; S_3 can be calculated directly; and S_2 then follows from the fact that

$$S_1 + S_2 + S_3 = S_4$$

If the class means deviate significantly from the linear regression, S_2 will tend to be large in relation to S_3, when appropriate allowance has been made for degrees

† In Fig. 3-2 we have shown, for simplicity, a case where Y_{ij} exceeds $\bar{Y}_i$, which in turn exceeds $\hat{Y}_i$, which again exceeds $\bar{Y}$, so that all the deviations on the right-hand side of Eq. (3-18) are positive. In general, of course, these deviations vary in sign.

‡ All three cross-product-terms vanish. Those involving $(Y_{ij} - \bar{Y}_i)$ vanish since $\sum_j(Y_{ij} - \bar{Y}_i)$ is zero for all i. The term involving $\sum_i(\bar{Y}_i - \hat{Y}_i)(\hat{Y}_i - \bar{Y})$ is simply proportional to the covariance between the regression values $\hat{Y}_i$ and the residuals $\bar{Y}_i - \hat{Y}_i$ about the regression line, and thus also vanishes.

Table 3-3 Test of linearity

Source of variation	Sum of squares	Degrees of freedom	Mean square
Regression	$m\sum_i(\hat{Y}_i - \bar{Y})^2 = r^2S_4 \quad = S_1$	1	
Class means about regression	$m\sum_i(\bar{Y}_i - \hat{Y}_i)^2 = (\eta^2 - r^2)S_4 = S_2$	$p - 2$	$S_2/(p-2)$
Within classes	$\sum_{i,j}(Y_{ij} - \bar{Y}_i)^2 = (1 - \eta^2)S_4 = S_3$	$p(m-1)$	$S_3/p(m-1)$
Total	$\sum_{i,j}(Y_{ij} - \bar{Y})^2 \quad = S_4$	$mp - 1$	

of freedom. The test for linearity is thus based on

$$F = \frac{S_2/(p-2)}{S_3/p(m-1)} \tag{3-20}$$

and the linear hypothesis is rejected in favor of a nonlinear alternative if the computed F exceeds a preselected critical value from $F(p-2, p(m-1))$.

Example 3-1 We have eight classes ($p = 8$), each class being defined by a particular value of X, and five observations ($m = 5$) in each class, giving 40 observed points on an X, Y scatter. The class means are shown in the final column of Table 3-4 and display a negative relationship with X, but the class means do not lie exactly on a straight line.

We now wish to build up the numerical equivalent of Table 3-3 for these data. The first step is to fit the linear regression of $\bar{Y}_i$ on X_i. The eight pairs of values yield the following numbers:

$$\sum_i X_i = 250 \qquad \sum_i X_i^2 = 9{,}500$$

$$\sum_i \bar{Y}_i = 165.6 \qquad \sum_i \bar{Y}_i^2 = 5{,}036.56 \qquad \sum_i X_i\bar{Y}_i = 3{,}585$$

Table 3-4 Replicated data

Class	X_i	Y_{ij}					$\bar{Y}_i$
$i = 1$	10	48	51	44	41	52	47.2
$i = 2$	15	33	32	37	42	41	37.0
$i = 3$	20	28	28	22	26	23	25.4
$i = 4$	30	22	17	26	14	19	19.6
$i = 5$	35	22	17	10	15	10	14.8
$i = 6$	40	10	10	11	11	10	10.4
$i = 7$	45	11	5	9	10	9	8.8
$i = 8$	55	2	0	0	6	4	2.4

from which

$$\sum_i (X_i - \bar{X})^2 = 9{,}500 - \frac{(250)^2}{8} = 1{,}687.50$$

$$\sum_i (X_i - \bar{X})(\bar{Y}_i - \bar{Y}) = 3{,}585 - \frac{250(165.6)}{8} = -1{,}590.00$$

$$\sum_i (\bar{Y}_i - \bar{Y})^2 = 5{,}036.56 - \frac{(165.6)^2}{8} = 1{,}608.64$$

so

$$b = -\frac{1590}{1687.5} = -0.9422$$

and

$$a = \frac{165.6}{8} + 0.9422\left(\frac{250}{8}\right) = 50.144$$

giving the regression equation

$$\hat{Y} = 50.144 - 0.9422X$$

Turning now to Table 3-3, we compute first of all the overall sum of squares:

$$S_4 = \sum_{i,j} (Y_{ij} - \bar{Y})^2$$

$$= \sum_{i,j} Y_{ij}^2 - \frac{1}{mp}\left(\sum_{i,j} Y_{ij}\right)^2$$

$$= 25{,}620 - \frac{1}{40}(828)^2 = 8.480.4$$

The sum of squares within classes, S_3, is obtained by calculating the sum of squared deviations within each class about the class mean and aggregating the result over all classes. For the ith class we have

$$\sum_j (Y_{ij} - \bar{Y}_i)^2 = \sum_j Y_{ij}^2 - \frac{1}{m}\left(\sum_j Y_{ij}\right)^2$$

For the first row in Table 3-4, this gives

$$(48)^2 + (51)^2 + \cdots + (52)^2 - \tfrac{1}{5}(48 + 51 + \cdots + 52)^2 = 86.8$$

Carrying out the same calculations for the remaining rows and aggregating gives

$$S_3 = 86.8 + 82.0 + 31.2 + 85.2 + 102.8 + 1.2 + 20.8 + 27.2 = 437.2$$

The square of the correlation ratio may now be computed from Eq. (3-17) as

$$\eta^2 = 1 - \frac{437.2}{8{,}480.4} = 0.948446$$

Table 3-5 Sums of squares from the data of Table 3-4

Source of variation	Sum of squares	Degrees of freedom	Mean square
Regression	$S_1 = 7{,}490.67$	1	
Class means about regression	$S_2 = 552.53$	6	92.09
Within classes	$S_3 = 437.20$	32	13.66
Total	$S_4 = 8{,}480.40$	39	

The next simplest quantity to compute is

$$S_1 = m\sum_i (\hat{Y}_i - \bar{Y})^2$$

From the regression of $\hat{Y}_i$ on X_i the explained sum of squares is

$$\sum_i (\hat{Y}_i - \bar{Y})^2 = \frac{(-1{,}590)^2}{1{,}687.50} = 1{,}498.133$$

Thus

$$S_1 = 5(1{,}498.133) = 7{,}490.67$$

The remaining sum of squares, S_2, can now be obtained by subtraction, and Table 3-5 is prepared.†

† There is a subtle point concerning the interpretation of r^2 in this example. We have seen that in the special case, where there is a constant number of observations per class, the regression slope may be calculated by considering *either* the 40 observations (X_{ij}, Y_{ij}) *or* the eight observations $(X_i, \bar{Y}_i)$. There are, however, two distinct r^2. One relates to the regression of $\bar{Y}_i$ on X_i and the other to the regression of Y_{ij} on X_{ij}. It is intuitively clear that the former r^2 must exceed the latter since the class means will lie closer to the regression line than the raw data. In Table 3-3 S_1 is expressed as $r^2 S_4$, and this r^2 is the one relating to the raw data. By definition, it is

$$r^2 = \frac{\left[\Sigma_{i,j}(X_{ij} - \bar{X})(Y_{ij} - \bar{Y})\right]^2}{\left[\Sigma_{i,j}(X_{ij} - \bar{X})^2\right]\left[\Sigma_{i,j}(Y_{ij} - \bar{Y})^2\right]}$$

Using Eqs. (3-3) and (3-4),

$$\sum_{i,j}(X_{ij} - \bar{X})^2 = 5(1{,}687.50) = 8{,}437.50$$

$$\sum_{i,j}(X_{ij} - \bar{X})(Y_{ij} - \bar{Y}) = 5(-1{,}590) = -7{,}950$$

and $\Sigma_{i,j}(Y_{ij} - Y)^2$ has already been calculated as 8,480.40. Thus

$$r^2 = 0.883292$$

Then

$$S_2 = (\eta^2 - r^2)S_4 = (0.948446 - 0.883292)8{,}480.4 = 552.53$$

which agrees with the value obtained by subtraction in Table 3-5.

The test statistic for the linear regression is

$$F = \frac{S_1/1}{(S_2 + S_3)/38} = \frac{7{,}490.67}{989.73/38} = 287.6$$

The 5 percent critical value from $F(1, 40)$ is 4.08, and the 1 percent value is 7.31, so this is a highly significant sample statistic, and the data would lead us to reject decisively the hypothesis of a zero coefficient for X. The test statistic

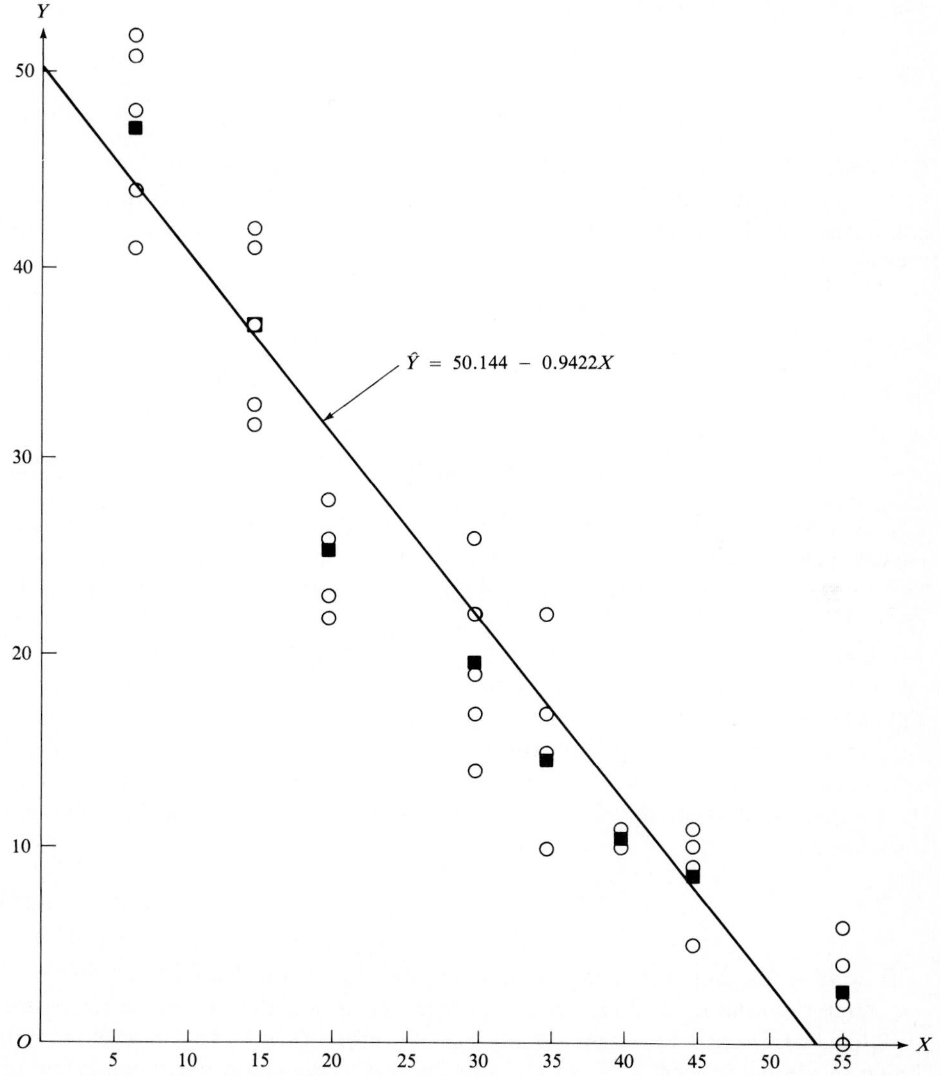

Figure 3-3

for the *linearity* of the relation is

$$F = \frac{S_2/6}{S_3/32} = \frac{92.09}{13.66} = 6.74$$

and the 1 percent critical value from $F(6, 30)$ is 3.47. This sample statistic is also significant, and we conclude that the true relationship is probably nonlinear. The scatter, regression line, and class means are shown in Fig. 3-3.

3-2 NONLINEAR RELATIONS

The relation

$$Y = \alpha + \beta X + u \tag{3-21}$$

is *linear* in the parameters α and β and also in the variables X and Y, and, as we have seen, application of the least-squares principle results in two simultaneous equations, which are linear in the estimates a and b and thus easy to solve. The relation

$$\log Y = \alpha + \beta X + u \tag{3-22}$$

may be written

$$Z = \alpha + \beta X + u \tag{3-23}$$

where

$$Z = \log Y \tag{3-24}$$

The scatter from Eq. (3-22) in the X, Y plane will be *nonlinear*. However, the transformation defined in Eq. (3-24) will yield a linear scatter in the X, Z plane, and so the techniques of Chap. 2 may be applied directly to Eq. (3-23). This is an example of a transformation of a variable, changing a relationship which is nonlinear in the original variables into one which is linear in the transformed variables. As will be seen below, simple transformations of one or both variables can deal with a wide variety of nonlinear relations.

Another approach is to introduce additional terms in X on the right-hand side of the relation. If Y denoted this average variable cost per unit of output and X the rate of output, the U-shaped cost curve of economic theory might be depicted as

$$Y = \alpha + \beta X + \gamma X^2 + u \tag{3-25}$$

The nonlinearity between Y and X here requires the introduction of an additional explanatory variable, X^2, and we are now involved in a three-variable regression problem, which will be taken up in Sec. 3-4. Relation (3-25), however, is still linear in the parameters α, β, and γ, and the least-squares principle can easily be extended to deal with three (and more) variables.

A more difficult relation is one such as

$$y = \alpha + \beta X^{\gamma} + u \tag{3-26}$$

If we attempted to apply least squares directly, we would have to choose values of a, b, and c to minimize

$$\sum_{i=1}^{n} e_i^2 = \sum_{i=1}^{n} (Y_i - a - bX_i^c)^2$$

The resultant normal equations are nonlinear in the unknowns and cannot be solved analytically. If, however, we consider a somewhat different relation,

$$Y = \beta X^{\gamma} u \tag{3-27}$$

taking logarithms of both sides gives

$$\log Y = \log \beta + \gamma \log X + \log u \tag{3-28}$$

There are *two* crucial differences between Eqs. (3-26) and (3-27): in the latter the intercept α is assumed to be zero and the disturbance term has also been entered multiplicatively rather than additively. The consequence of these assumptions is the linear relation in Eq. (3-28). If b and c denote the intercept and the slope, respectively, of the least-squares regression of $\log Y$ on $\log X$, we obtain estimates of β and γ as follows:

$$\text{Estimate of } \gamma = c$$
$$\text{Estimate of } \beta = \text{antilog } b$$

The quality of these estimates and the justification for the application of least squares to Eq. (3-28) depends, however, on $\log u$ having the properties postulated for the disturbance term in Chap. 2. The contrast between the treatment of the disturbance term in Eq. (3-26) and (3-27) illustrates one of the fundamental problems of the econometrician. Economic theory cannot yield precise propositions on the nature of the disturbance term, and so the econometrician proceeds somewhat pragmatically by first of all assuming the most convenient form for the disturbance term in any specific application and then attempting to test these assumptions as far as possible by the methods described in subsequent chapters.†

In principle the two main approaches to the fitting of nonlinear relations are either to seek transformations of some or all of the variables to reduce the problem to a linear form or else to fit the nonlinear form directly. The first approach is analyzed in more detail in the next section.

3-3 TRANSFORMATIONS OF VARIABLES

In very rare cases, economic theory may indicate the appropriate transformation of variables. As Zarembka has pointed out, the constant elasticity of substitution

† The late Sir Julian Huxley once defined God as a "personified symbol for man's residual ignorance." In a similar vein the disturbance term might be regarded as the econometrician's *stochastic* symbol for his residual ignorance, and then, as is sometimes done with God, the inscrutable and unknowable may be ascribed the properties most convenient for the current problem.

(CES) production function†

$$Y = \left(\alpha_1 K^\rho + \alpha_2 L^\rho\right)^{\nu/\rho}$$

gives

$$Y^{\rho/\nu} = \alpha_1 K^\rho + \alpha_2 L^\rho \tag{3-29}$$

Thus each observation on output should be raised to the power ρ/ν, and each observation on capital and labor inputs should be raised to the power ρ. This is an example of *power transformations* of the variables, and although Eq. (3-29) is linear in the transformed variables, it still poses difficult estimation problems. Some special cases of power transformations, however, yield simple estimating procedures, and we now turn to these.

Returning to two-variable relations, let us denote a transformation of the Y variable by $Y^{(\lambda_1)}$. This symbolism indicates that the transformation depends only on a single parameter λ_1. Likewise, let us indicate the transformation of the X variable by $X^{(\lambda_2)}$. A very general form of transformation has been proposed by Box and Cox, namely,‡

$$Y^{(\lambda_1)} = \begin{cases} \dfrac{Y^{\lambda_1} - 1}{\lambda_1} & \lambda_1 \neq 0 \\ \ln Y & \lambda_1 = 0 \end{cases} \tag{3-30}$$

and similarly,

$$X^{(\lambda_2)} = \begin{cases} \dfrac{X^{\lambda_2} - 1}{\lambda_2} & \lambda_2 \neq 0 \\ \ln X & \lambda_2 = 0 \end{cases} \tag{3-31}$$

At first sight these seem needlessly complicated transformations, and one might well ask, why not use the simple power transformation Y^{λ_1}, X^{λ_2}. An examination of Fig. 3-4 indicates the rationale behind the Box-Cox transformation. Fig. 3-4*a* shows the simple power transformation Y^λ for two illustrative values of Y, namely, 10 and $e = 2.84128$. The transformed variables cross at the (0, 1) point, and to the left and right of that point their ordering is reversed. The simple power transformation is thus unsatisfactory since different values of λ would not preserve the ordering of the data. Fig. 3-4*b* shows the graphs of Y^λ/λ for the same two values of Y, and now the ordering is the same for all values of λ, but a

† Chap. 3, "Transformation of Variables in Econometrics," in P. Zarembka (Ed.), *Frontiers in Econometrics*, Academic Press, New York and London, 1974. The constant elasticity of substitution (CES) production function was introduced by K. J. Arrow, H. B. Chenery, B. S. Minhas, and R. M. Solow, "Capital-Labor Substitution and Economic Efficiency," *Review of Economics and Statistics*, **43**, 1961, pp. 225–250. The elasticity of substitution is given by $1/(1-\rho)$ with $\rho < 1$, and ν denotes returns to scale.

‡ G. E. P. Box and D. R. Cox, "An Analysis of Transformations," *Journal of the Royal Statistical Society*, ser. B, 1964, pp. 211–252. From now on the symbols log and ln denote logarithms to base 10 and to base e (natural logarithms), respectively.

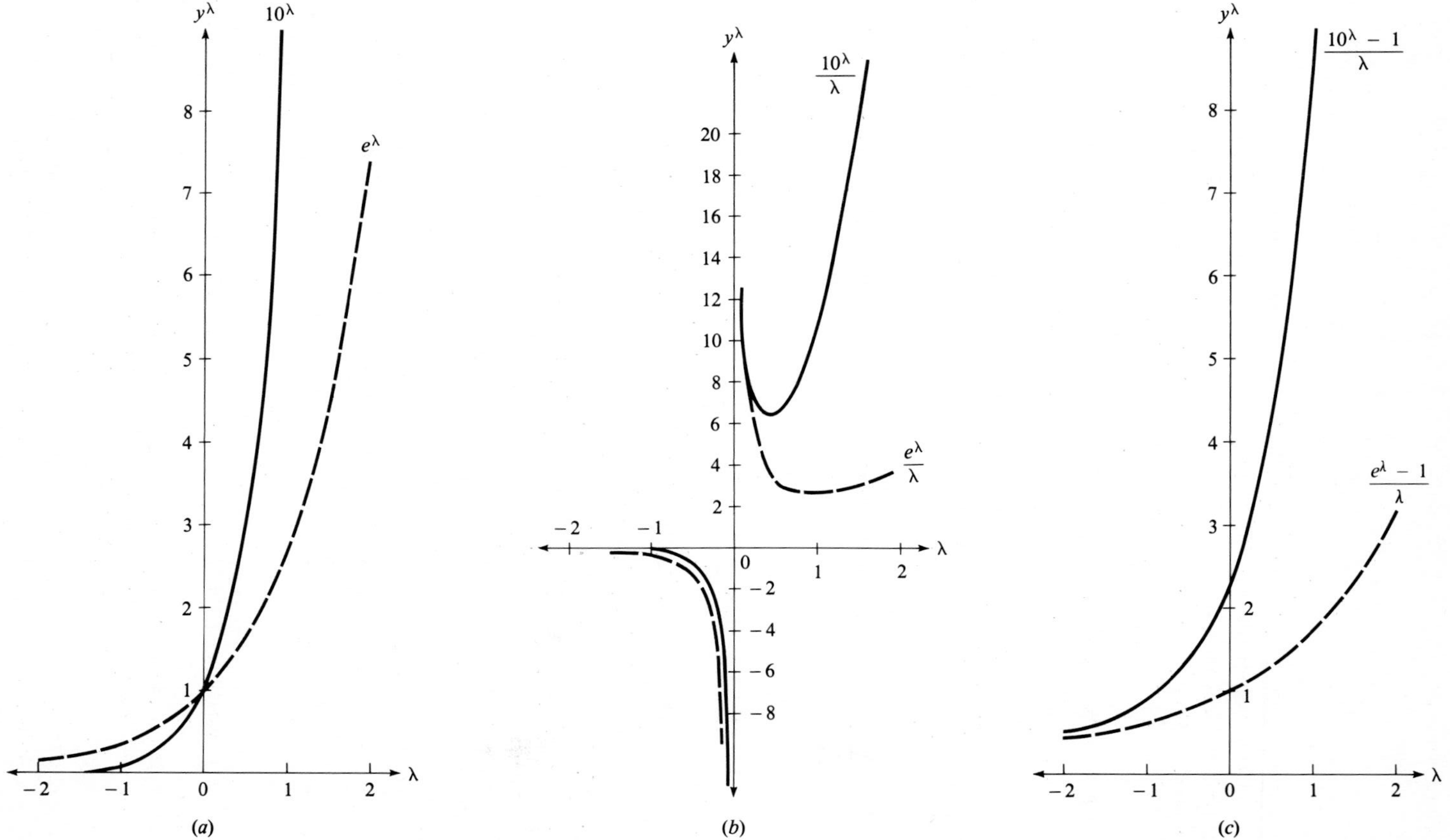

y^λ
10^λ
e^λ
(a)
$\frac{10^\lambda}{\lambda}$
$\frac{e^\lambda}{\lambda}$
(b)
$\frac{10^\lambda - 1}{\lambda}$
$\frac{e^\lambda - 1}{\lambda}$
(c)

Figure 3-4

discontinuity occurs at $\lambda = 0$. Finally, Fig. 3-4c shows the graph of the general transformation

$$\frac{Y^{\lambda} - 1}{\lambda}$$

and now the ordering is the same for all values of λ, and there is no discontinuity at $\lambda = 0$. If we substitute $\lambda_1 = 0$ in Eq. (3-30), we obtain $Y^{(\lambda_1)} = 0/0$, which is indeterminate. However, the application of L'Hôpital's rule shows that†

$$\lim_{\lambda_1 \to 0} Y^{(\lambda_1)} = \ln Y$$

Suppose now that the transformed variables fit the linear model, that is,

$$Y^{(\lambda_1)} = \alpha_0 + \beta X^{(\lambda_2)} + u \tag{3-32}$$

This model has five basic parameters, namely, α_0, β, λ_1, λ_2, and σ_u^2. In this section we will consider only some special cases corresponding to particular values of λ_1 and λ_2.

Case 3-1: $\lambda_1 = 1 = \lambda_2$ (Linear model). Combining Eqs. (3.30), (3-31), and (3-32) now gives

$$Y = \alpha + \beta X + u$$

where

$$\alpha = 1 + \alpha_0 - \beta$$

This is the simple linear model of Chap. 2.

† For a definition of L'Hôpital's rule see, for example, A. C. Chiang, *Fundamental Methods for Mathematical Economics*, 2d ed., McGraw-Hill, New York, 1974, p. 420. The application of the rule to $Y^{(\lambda_1)}$ states that

$$\begin{aligned}\lim_{\lambda_1 \to 0} Y^{(\lambda_1)} &= \lim_{\lambda_1 \to 0} \frac{(d/d\lambda_1)(Y^{\lambda_1} - 1)}{(d/d\lambda_1)(\lambda_1)} \\ &= \lim_{\lambda_1 \to 0} (Y^{\lambda_1} \ln Y) \\ &= \ln Y\end{aligned}$$

This development uses the result that $(d/d\lambda_1)(Y^{\lambda_1}) = Y^{\lambda_1} \ln Y$. To derive this from first principles, consider a general function

$$y = a^x$$

where a is some constant, and define

$$z = \ln y = x \ln a$$

Then $$\frac{dz}{dx} = \frac{dz}{dy}\frac{dy}{dx} = \frac{1}{y}\frac{dy}{dx}$$

But $$\frac{dz}{dx} = \ln a$$

Thus $$\frac{dy}{dx} = y \ln a = a^x \ln a$$

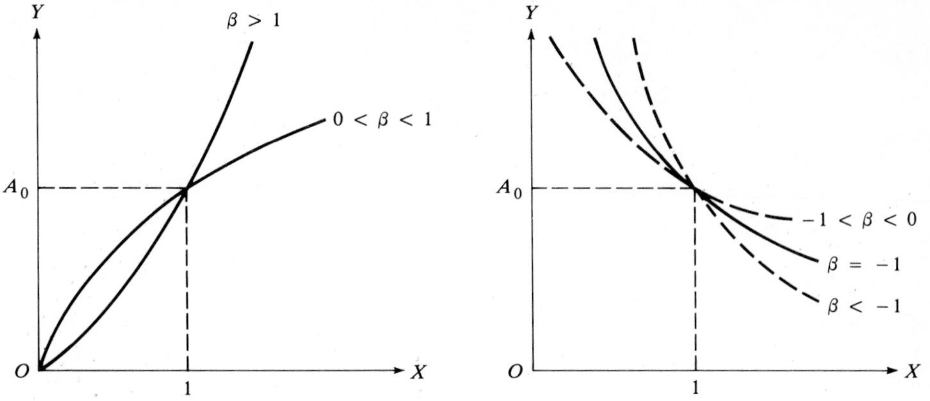

Figure 3-5 The log-log model.

Case 3-2: $\lambda_1 = 0 = \lambda_2$ (Log-log model). Combining Eqs. (3-30), (3-31), and (3-32) now gives

$$\ln Y = \alpha_0 + \beta \ln X + u \tag{3-33}$$

Again, all the techniques of Chap. 2 may be applied, *once the original data have been transformed to logarithmic form*. Notice that although Eq. (3-33) is specified in terms of logarithms to base e, one may take logarithms to base 10 in carrying out the empirical work. The estimate of α_0 will be affected by the choice of base, but that of β will not.†

Ignoring the disturbance term in Eq. (3-33), the relationship between Y and X is

$$Y = A_0 X^{\beta} \tag{3-34}$$

where

$$\ln A_0 = \alpha_0$$

From Eq. (3-34)

$$\frac{dY}{dX} = \beta A_0 X^{\beta - 1}$$

so that, if β is positive, the slope is always positive and Y tends to infinity as X tends to infinity. If β exceeds unity, the slope increases continually as X increases, while if $0 < \beta < 1$, the slope decreases continually, though always remaining positive. When β is negative, the slope is always negative. This gives the shapes pictured in Fig. 3-5. The relationship only exists for positive values of the variables.

The double logarithmic relationship has a very important characteristic. It is a *constant elasticity* function, and that elasticity is given by β.‡ Thus when Eq.

† If $\ln Y = N$, then $Y = e^N$,

$$\log_{10} Y = N \log_{10} e = \ln Y \log_{10} e$$

Thus Eq. (3-33) may be written

$$\log_{10} Y = (\alpha_0 \log_{10} e) + \beta \log_{10} X + (u \log_{10} e)$$

so that the intercept term being estimated is $\alpha_0 \log_{10} e$.

‡ See App. A-2, Exponential and Logarithmic Functions.

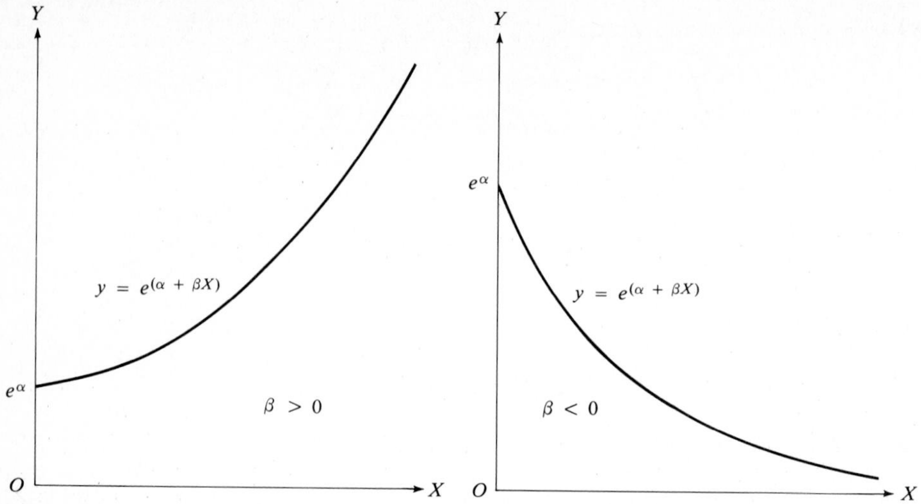

Figure 3-6

(3-33) is fitted to the data the regression slope is a point estimate of the elasticity. If $\beta = -1$, Eq. (3-34) gives

$$XY = A_0 \tag{3-35}$$

which is a rectangular hyperbola. If Y denoted the quantity purchased and X the price per unit of some commodity, then Eq. (3-35) would represent a demand curve with constant elasticity of -1 and a constant total expenditure on the commodity, whatever its price.

Case 3-3: $\lambda_1 = 0, \lambda_2 = 1$ (Semilog model). This combination of λ values gives†

$$\ln Y = \alpha + \beta X + u \tag{3-36}$$

where

$$\alpha = \alpha_0 - \beta$$

From Eq. (3-36),

$$\frac{1}{Y}\frac{dY}{dX} = \beta \tag{3-37}$$

Thus the *proportionate rate of change in* Y *per unit change in* X is a constant and equal to β. The function is only defined for positive values of Y. Ignoring the disturbance in Eq. (3-36), we may rewrite the function as

$$Y = e^{\alpha + \beta X} \tag{3-38}$$

and its general shape is shown in Fig. 3-6. The intercept is given by e^α, and the slope is positive or negative, depending on the sign of β.

† Equation (3-36) is a widely used specification in human capital models, where Y denotes earnings and X years of schooling. The specific functional form is derived from theoretical considerations by J. Mincer, *School, Experience and Earnings*, Columbia University Press, New York, 1974.

Table 3-6 Bituminous coal output in the United States, 1841–1910

Decade	Average annual output (1,000 net tons) Y	Log Y	$X = t$
1841–1850	1,837	3.2641	−3
1851–1860	4,868	3.6873	−2
1861–1870	12,411	4.0937	−1
1871–1880	32,617	4.5135	0
1881–1890	82,770	4.9179	1
1891–1900	148,457	5.1718	2
1901–1910	322,958	5.5092	3

A special case of Eq. (3-38) occurs when X denotes *time* and the function then describes a variable Y which displays a constant proportionate rate of growth ($\beta > 0$) or decay ($\beta < 0$).

Example 3-2 The first step in any empirical application of Eq. (3-36) is to check visually on whether the constant growth assumption seems warranted. This may be done either by plotting log Y against time or, equivalently, by plotting Y against time on commercial semilog paper. The first procedure applied to the data of Table 3-6 gives the scatter diagram shown in Fig. 3-7, and it is clear that the relationship is approximately linear.

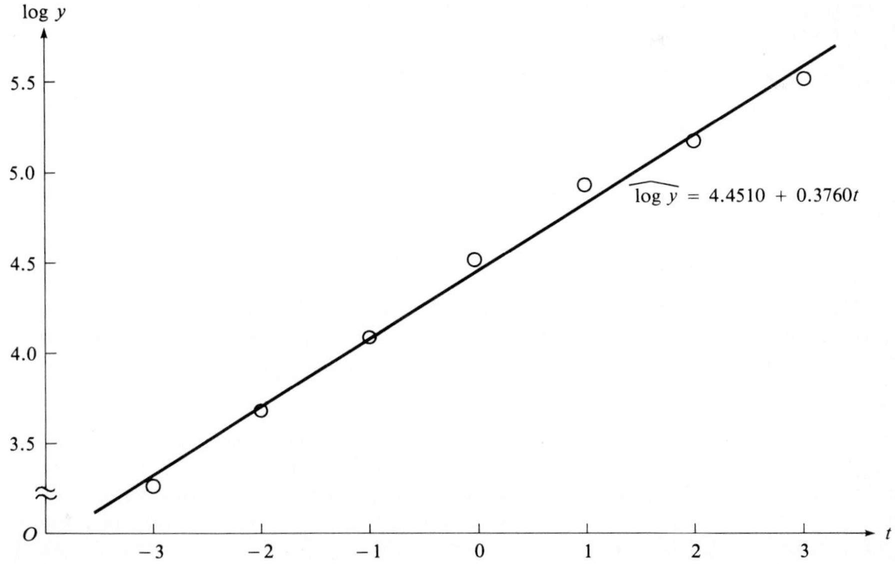

Figure 3-7

In fitting the constant growth curve

$$Y_t = e^{\alpha + \beta t} \tag{3-39}$$

to the data of Table 3-6, we have to be careful about the treatment of the time variable, about the base to which logarithms are taken, and about the way in which growth rates are expressed and measured. Equation (3-39) is a continuous time formulation. It may be expressed as

$$Y_t = Y_0 e^{\beta t} \tag{3-40}$$

where $Y_0 = \text{value of } Y \text{ at } t = 0$

and

$$\beta = \frac{1}{Y_t}\frac{dY_t}{dt} = \textit{instantaneous} \text{ rate of growth of } Y \text{ at time } t$$

When time is measured in discrete intervals, such as quarters or years, a constant growth series would be expressed as

$$Y_t = Y_0(1 + g)^t \tag{3-41}$$

where g = proportionate rate of growth in Y per unit of time

Taking logarithms of Eq. (3-41) to base 10 gives

$$\log Y_t = \log Y_0 + [\log(1 + g)]t \tag{3-42}$$

This is the equation estimated with actual data. Thus

$$\text{Intercept} = \text{estimate of } \log Y_0$$

$$\text{Slope} = \text{estimate of } \log(1 + g)$$

and so an estimate of g can be obtained. Taking logarithms of Eq. (3-40), also to base 10, gives

$$\log Y_t = \log Y_0 + (\beta \log e)t$$

Comparison with Eq. (3-42) shows that

$$\beta \log e = \log(1 + g)$$

or

$$\beta = \ln(1 + g) \tag{3-43}$$

which can be used to provide an estimate of β corresponding to any estimated g. The interpretation is that β is the rate which with continuous compounding would give the same result as a single increment at rate g.† We

† Suppose your friendly local bank manager offers interest of 10 percent per year on time deposits compounded annually. Then \$100 deposited now grows in successive years to \$110, \$121, \$133.1, and so on. In general, interest at $100r$ percent per year on an initial investment of \$100 will give a sum of $\$100(1 + r)^n$ after n years. Suppose further that the manager agrees to your suggestion that, instead of adding interest of 10 percent once a year, 5 percent should be added *twice* a year. After 2 years of graduate school your \$100 would now grow to $\$100(1.05)^4 = \$121.55$, so that your perspicacity has paid off to the tune of 55 cents. You now become greedy and suggest that 1 percent be added 10 times

can select the origin and the units of measurement for time at our convenience. In the final column of Table 3-6 we have chosen the midpoint of the 1871–1880 decade as the origin and measured time in units of 10 years. The normal equations for fitting a linear regression of log Y on t are

$$\Sigma \log Y = na + b\Sigma t$$

$$\Sigma t \log Y = a\Sigma t + b\Sigma t^2$$

Since the t's have been chosen so that $\Sigma t = 0$, these equations simplify to

$$a = \frac{\Sigma \log Y}{n}$$

$$b = \frac{\Sigma t \log Y}{\Sigma t^2}$$

For the data in the table, these equations give

$$a = 31.1575/7 = 4.4511$$

$$b = 10.5285/28 = 0.3760$$

Thus the regression estimate of Eq. (3-42) is

$$\widehat{\log Y} = 4.4511 + 0.3760t$$

The r^2 is 0.9945, which confirms the story of the scatter diagram that the constant growth curve fits this series very well. To find the estimated growth rate,

$$\log(1 + \hat{g}) = 0.3760$$

$$1 + \hat{g} = 2.3768$$

Thus

$$\hat{g} = 1.3768$$

Since t was measured in units of 10 years, this gives the estimated rate of growth *per decade* as 137.7 percent. The *annual* growth rate is found from

$$(1 + r)^{10} = 2.3768$$

---

a year, or perhaps $\frac{1}{2}$ percent 20 times a year. You have, in fact, discovered the principle that

$$(1 + r) < \left(1 + \frac{r}{2}\right)^2 < \left(1 + \frac{r}{3}\right)^3 < \cdots < \left(1 + \frac{r}{n}\right)^n < \cdots$$

Unfortunately it is no magic device for unlimited increases in your wealth. The sequence has a limit, namely,

$$\lim_{n \to \infty} \left(1 + \frac{r}{n}\right)^n = e^r$$

where

$$e = \lim_{n \to \infty} \left(1 + \frac{1}{n}\right)^n = 2.41828$$

For a 10 percent growth rate, $r = 0.10$ and $e^r = 1.1052$. Thus *continuous* compounding within a period at a rate of 10 percent is equivalent to a growth rate of just over $10\frac{1}{2}$ percent over the period.

giving

$$r = 0.0904$$

or just over 9 percent per annum. From Eq. (3-43) the corresponding continuous rate β is 0.0866.

Case 3-4: $\lambda_1 = 1, \lambda_2 = -1$ **(Reciprocal model).** These values give the relation

$$Y = \alpha + \beta\left(\frac{1}{X}\right) + u \tag{3-44}$$

The slope is $dY/dX = -\beta/X^2$. Thus if β is positive, the slope is everywhere negative, and conversely it is positive when β is negative. Since $1/X \to 0$ as $X \to \infty$, α denotes an asymptotic value for Y. The shape of this function is indicated in Fig. 3-8.

Fig. 3-8*a* indicates a typical shape of a Phillips curve, and many Phillips curves have been estimated by regressing the rate of wage change on the reciprocal of the unemployment rate. The estimate of α indicates the asymptotic floor for wage change; if it turns out negative, the Phillips curve cuts the unemployment axis. Fig. 3-8*b* has often been used to represent expenditure functions, where Y denotes expenditure on some specified commodity or service and X denotes total expenditure (or income), the data typically coming from a cross section of households. This particular application only makes sense when α is positive and β is negative, for α indicates the asymptotic level of expenditure. It follows that income or total expenditure has to reach some critical level $-\beta/\alpha$ before anything is spent on this commodity. Thus Eq. (3-44) cannot serve as a general model for all types of consumption since we need to allow for finite consumption of some commodities at values of X close to zero. This particular difficulty can be overcome by the choice of yet another pair of λ values.

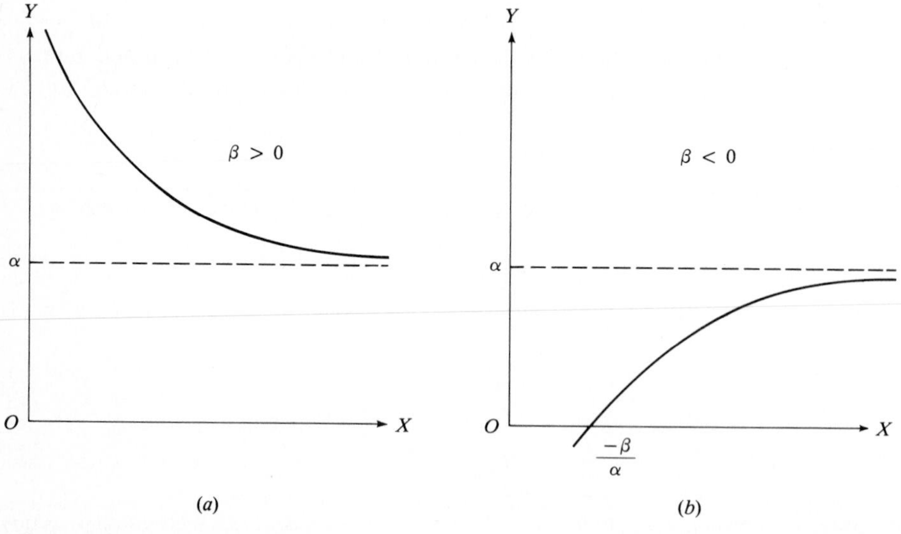

(*a*) (*b*)

Figure 3-8 The reciprocal model.

Case 3-5: $\lambda_1 = 0, \lambda_2 = -1$ (Logarithmic reciprocal model). This choice of parameters gives

$$\ln Y = \alpha - \beta\left(\frac{1}{X}\right) + u \tag{3-45}$$

Ignoring the disturbance term, we may write Eq. (3-45) as

$$Y = e^{\alpha - \beta/X} \tag{3-46}$$

Y is not defined for $X = 0$, but $Y \to 0$ as $X \to 0$, so we can define $Y(0)$ as zero, and we then have a function which is right-hand continuous at the origin. From Eq. (3-46)

$$\frac{dY}{dX} = \left(\frac{\beta}{X^2}\right)e^{\alpha - \beta/X} \tag{3-47}$$

Thus the slope is positive for positive β. The second derivative is

$$\frac{d^2Y}{dX^2} = \left(\frac{\beta^2}{X^4} - \frac{2\beta}{X^3}\right)e^{\alpha - \beta/X}$$

Hence there is a point of inflection where $X = \beta/2$. To the left of this point the slope increases with X; to the right of it the slope diminishes. As $X \to \infty$, $Y \to e^{\alpha}$. Substituting $X = \beta/2$ in Eq. (3-46) gives the value of Y at the point of inflection as $0.135e^{\alpha}$ or, in other words, about 13 percent of the asymptotic value of Y. The general shape of this function is shown in Fig. 3-9.

If X represents time, Eq. (3-46) then pictures a growth curve which starts at zero and approaches an asymptotic level. Rewriting Eq. (3-47) in an equivalent form gives

$$\frac{1}{Y}\frac{dY}{dX} = \frac{\beta}{X^2}$$

that is, the rate of growth in Y per unit change in X is inversely proportional to the square of X. Thus the rate of growth falls off sharply after low values of X, as

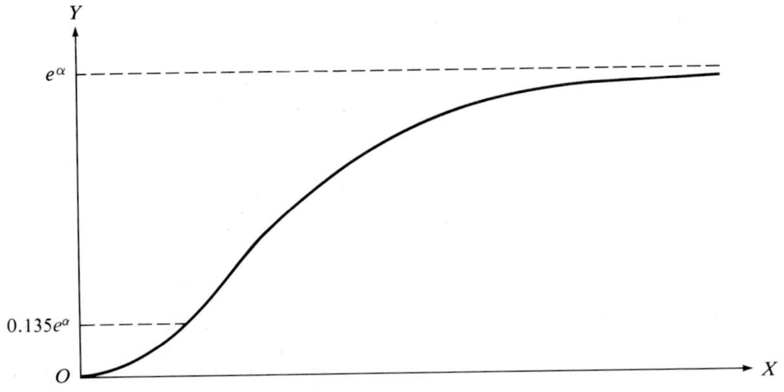

Figure 3-9 The logarithmic-reciprocal curve.

shown in Fig. 3-9. This can be a disadvantage of the curve, which may more than offset the ease of fitting.

A similar curve, which also has an upper asymptote at some finite level and a lower asymptote at zero, but has a more symmetrical shape between the two, is the *logistic*. This curve cannot be derived from the general linear relation (3-32) by a suitable choice of values for λ_1 and λ_2. Nonetheless it has been widely used in fitting growth trends, and so a brief account of it is given here. The logistic equation is

$$Y = \frac{k}{1 + be^{-at}} \tag{3-48}$$

where a, b, and k are parameters to be determined. We have written Y as a function of time t, as this is by far the most common practice, but in some applications it is quite feasible to replace t by some independent variable X.

From Eq. (3-48) it is clear that

$$Y \to k \quad \text{as} \quad t \to \infty$$

and

$$Y \to 0 \quad \text{as} \quad t \to -\infty$$

so that k is the upper asymptote and zero the lower asymptote. The first derivative of Eq. (3-48) is

$$\frac{dY}{dt} = \frac{a}{k} Y(k - Y) \tag{3-49}$$

Thus the rate of change of Y with respect to t is proportional to the current level Y and also to the distance still to travel to reach the saturation level k. The first derivative is positive for all values of t. The second derivative may be written

$$\frac{d^2Y}{dt^2} = \frac{a}{k}(k - 2Y)\frac{dY}{dt} \tag{3-50}$$

Setting this to zero gives a point of inflection at

$$t = \frac{1}{a}\ln b, \qquad Y = \frac{k}{2}$$

Thus when $Y < k/2$, the "large" value of $k - Y$ dominates the "small" value of Y in Eq. (3-49) and causes dY/dt to increase. As Y increases toward $k/2$, the relative balance of the two forces changes so that dY/dt reaches a maximum value when $Y = k/2$ and thereafter declines steadily as Y rises toward the saturation level k. The typical shape of the logistic curve is shown in Fig. 3-10, the main contrast with Fig. 3-9 being that the point of inflection occurs at half the saturation value rather than at a much lower level. The logistic curve is frequently used as a plausible approximation to the growth of any "population," whether bacterial, animal, human, or economic, where growth is thought to be *positively* related to the size of the existing population and *negatively* related to the current distance from a saturation level.

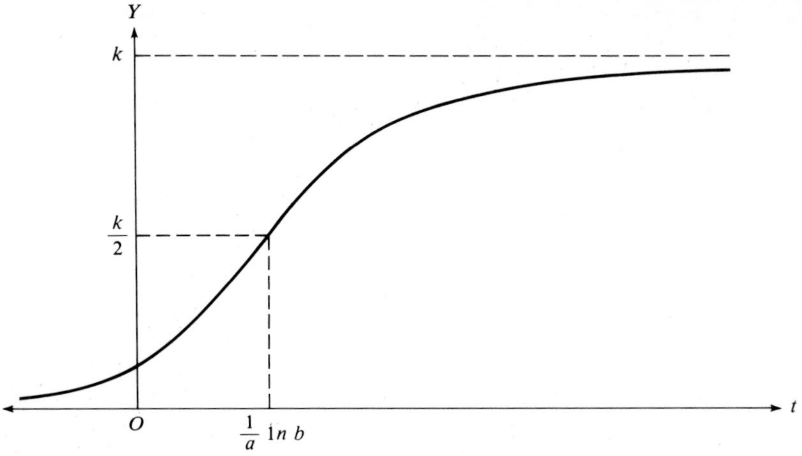

Figure 3-10 The logistic curve.

Estimation of all the parameters a, b, and k cannot be achieved by the simple methods that we have described so far. From Eq. (3-49) we can write

$$\frac{1}{Y}\frac{dY}{dt} = a - \left(\frac{a}{k}\right)Y$$

If time is measured in constant units, the left-hand side of this equation is approximately $\Delta Y/Y$, the proportionate rate of growth of Y. Thus one might fit the linear regression

$$\frac{Y_{t+1} - Y_t}{Y_t} = \hat{a} - \left(\frac{\hat{a}}{k}\right)Y_t + e_t \qquad (3\text{-}51)$$

which yields point estimates of a and k. To obtain an estimate of b, we note that Eq. (3-48) can be rearranged to give

$$b = \frac{k - Y}{Y}e^{at} \qquad (3\text{-}52)$$

Thus a value of b can be computed for each Y_t, given $\hat{a}$ and $\hat{k}$. An estimate b may then be obtained by averaging some or all of these computed b values, or alternatively by substituting $\bar{Y}$ and $\bar{t}$ in Eq. (3-52).

There are two main difficulties with this simple procedure for estimating the logistic function.† First of all we have point estimates of the parameters, but inference procedures are difficult, especially for b and k. Second, there is evidence that the procedure is unsatisfactory compared with a direct estimation by nonlinear methods.

† See F. R. Oliver, "Methods of Estimating the Logistic Growth Function," *Applied Statistics*, 1964, pp. 57–66. This paper describes an iterative program for computing the (nonlinear) least-squares estimates. A further paper, F. R. Oliver, "Notes on the Logistic Curve for Human Populations," *Journal of the Royal Statistical Society*, vol. 145, 1982, pp. 359–363, gives formulas for the asymptotic standard errors of the least-squares estimates.

Returning to the model

$$Y^{(\lambda_1)} = \alpha_0 + \beta X^{(\lambda_2)} + u$$

we have outlined five special cases, depending on particular choices of 1, 0, or -1 for the λ parameters. In each case a simple linear relation holds between the transformed variables, and the techniques of Chap. 2 may be applied, provided the assumptions about the disturbance term are fulfilled. However, the question immediately arises: Why restrict consideration to just three possible values for λ? If the λ's are free to take on any values, the approximation to linearity may well be improved, but we then have five parameters to be estimated, namely, α_0, β, λ_1, λ_2, and σ_u^2. If the λ's can be estimated and if we can test hypotheses about them, we may be able to discriminate between functional forms. This more general approach involves nonlinear estimation, which is beyond the scope of this book.

3-4 THREE-VARIABLE REGRESSION

As indicated in Sec. 3-2, some nonlinear relations may be represented by the use of several explanatory variables on the right-hand side of the relation. For example, the conventional total cost function of economic theory might be represented as

$$\text{TC} = \alpha + \beta Q + \gamma Q^2 + \delta Q^3 \tag{3-53}$$

where TC = total cost per period
Q = output per period

and α, β, γ, and δ are parameters. From Eq. (3-53), the average cost (AC) and the marginal cost (MC) are obtained, respectively, as

$$\text{AC} = \frac{\text{TC}}{Q} = \underbrace{\frac{\alpha}{Q}}_{\substack{\text{Average}\\ \text{fixed}\\ \text{cost}}} + \underbrace{(\beta + \gamma Q + \delta Q^2)}_{\substack{\text{Average}\\ \text{variable}\\ \text{cost}}} \tag{3-54}$$

and

$$\text{MC} = \frac{d(\text{TC})}{dQ} = \beta + 2\gamma Q + 3\delta Q^2 \tag{3-55}$$

With certain restrictions on the parameters, these functions will have the conventional shapes shown in Fig. 3-11.

Relation (3-54) shows AC as a *linear function* of the variables

$$Q, \qquad \frac{1}{Q}, \qquad \text{and} \qquad Q^2$$

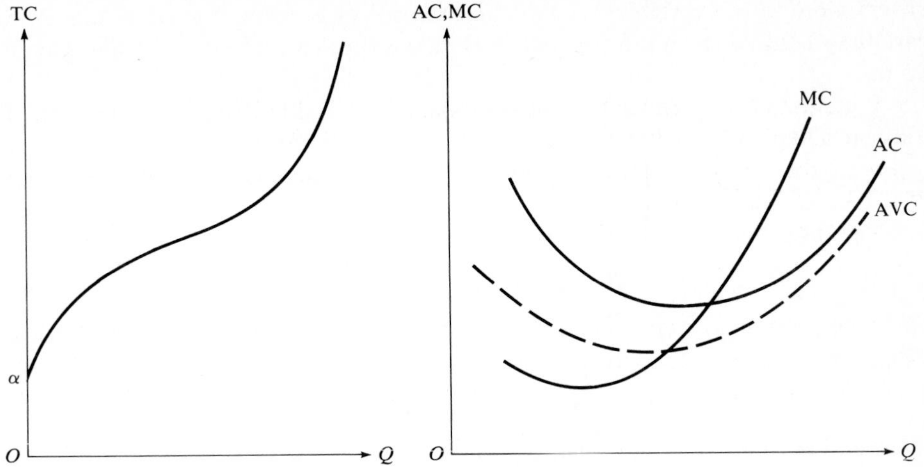

Figure 3-11

More generally the additional explanatory variables need not be restricted to transformations of a single variable but will be different variables. For example, an expectations-augmented Phillips curve may be written as

$$\dot{w}_t = \alpha + \beta\left(\frac{1}{u_t}\right) + \delta(\dot{p}_t^e)$$

where $\dot{w}_t$ = rate of wage change
u_t = unemployment rate
$\dot{p}_t^e$ = expected inflation rate

The statistical theory of relationships such as these may be more conveniently handled by using the following general notation:

$$Y = \beta_1 + \beta_2 X_2 + \beta_3 X_3 + \cdots + \beta_k X_k + u \tag{3-56}$$

This states that the dependent variable Y is determined by a linear combination of $k - 1$ explanatory variables $X_2, X_3, \ldots, X_k$ and a disturbance term. The subscripts on the X's indicate different explanatory variables. As the illustrations above show, some of these X's may well be transformations of other X's. The relation (3-56) is assumed to hold at each sample point. Thus we may write

$$Y_t = \beta_1 + \beta_2 X_{2t} + \beta_3 X_{3t} + \cdots + \beta_k X_{kt} + u_t \qquad t = 1, 2, \ldots, n \tag{3-57}$$

or, more compactly,

$$Y_t = \sum_{i=1}^{k} \beta_i X_{it} + u_t \qquad t = 1, 2, \ldots, n \tag{3-58}$$

where $$X_{1t} = 1 \qquad \text{for all } t$$

and the interpretation of the double subscript on X is that X_{ij} denotes the jth observation on the variable X_i. X_1 is an example of a *dummy* variable, that is, a variable which takes on a priori specified values (in this case unity) at the sample points.

Equation (3-57) defines the linear model in k variables, and it will be treated fully in Chap. 5. As an introduction we deal explicitly in this section with a three-variable model, but the concepts developed will facilitate our understanding of the k-variable model.

The three-variable model is specified as

$$Y_t = \beta_1 + \beta_2 X_{2t} + \beta_3 X_{3t} + u_t \qquad t = 1, 2, \ldots, n \tag{3-59}$$

Replacing the unknown β's in Eq. (3-59) by any arbitrary set of numerical coefficients b_1, b_2, and b_3 gives

$$Y_t = b_1 + b_2 X_{2t} + b_3 X_{3t} + e_t \tag{3-60}$$

The residual sum of squares in Eq. (3-60) is then

$$\begin{aligned} \text{RSS} = \sum_{t=1}^{n} e_t^2 &= \sum_{t=1}^{n} (Y_t - b_1 - b_2 X_{2t} - b_3 X_{3t})^2 \\ &= f(b_1, b_2, b_3) \end{aligned} \tag{3-61}$$

The least-squares principle states that b_1, b_2, and b_3 should be chosen to minimize the residual sum of squares defined in Eq. (3-61). The necessary condition is that

$$\frac{\partial(\text{RSS})}{\partial b_1} = \frac{\partial(\text{RSS})}{\partial b_2} = \frac{\partial(\text{RSS})}{\partial b_3} = 0$$

This gives the normal equations

$$\begin{aligned} \Sigma Y &= nb_1 + b_2 \Sigma X_2 + b_3 \Sigma X_3 \\ \Sigma X_2 Y &= b_1 \Sigma X_2 + b_2 \Sigma X_2^2 + b_3 \Sigma X_2 X_3 \\ \Sigma X_3 Y &= b_1 \Sigma X_3 + b_2 \Sigma X_2 X_3 + b_3 \Sigma X_3^2 \end{aligned} \tag{3-62}$$

All the summations merely involve the sample values of X_2, X_3, and Y, so Eq. (3-62) defines a set of three simultaneous equations which can be solved for the least-squares estimates b_1, b_2, and b_3.† These equations parallel those for the two-variable case in Eq. (2-13), and the derivation is the same as that shown in the footnote below Eq. (2-13). The resultant least-squares regression indicates a plane in three-dimensional space, and is written as

$$\hat{Y}_t = b_1 + b_2 X_{2t} + b_3 X_{3t} \qquad t = 1, 2, \ldots, n \tag{3-63}$$

or, equivalently,

$$Y_t = \hat{Y}_t + e_t \qquad t = 1, 2, \ldots, n \tag{3-64}$$

Dividing through the first equation in Eqs. (3-62) by the sample size n gives

$$\bar{Y} = b_1 + b_2 \bar{X}_2 + b_3 \bar{X}_3 \tag{3-65}$$

† Again, to keep the notation simple, we are not distinguishing between b_i as a variable parameter, as in Eq. (3-60), and b_i as the least-squares estimator, defined in Eq. (3-62).

Thus the regression plane passes through the point of means. Summing Eqs. (3-63) over the sample observations and dividing by n gives

$$\bar{\hat{Y}} = b_1 + b_2\bar{X}_2 + b_3\bar{X}_3$$

Comparison with Eq. (3-65) shows directly that

$$\bar{Y} = \bar{\hat{Y}}$$

and so from Eq. (3-64),

$$\bar{e} = 0 \tag{3-66}$$

Thus the mean of the regression values of Y is equal to the mean of the actual sample values or, in other words, the sum of the least-squares residuals is identically zero.

Result (3-66) may also be obtained directly from the condition

$$\frac{\partial(\text{RSS})}{\partial b_1} = 0$$

for

$$\frac{\partial(\text{RSS})}{\partial b_1} = -2\sum_{t=1}^{n}(Y_t - b_1 - b_2X_{2t} - b_3X_{3t}) = -2\sum_{t=1}^{n} e_t = 0$$

The equality of the other two partial derivatives to zero gives the important result that the least-squares residuals are uncorrelated with X_2, X_3, and $\hat{Y}$. For

$$\frac{\partial(\text{RSS})}{\partial b_2} = -2\sum_{t=1}^{n} X_{2t}e_t = 0 \tag{3-67}$$

and

$$\frac{\partial(\text{RSS})}{\partial b_3} = -2\Sigma X_{3t}e_t = 0 \tag{3-68}$$

Further

$$\Sigma e_t\hat{Y}_t = b_1\Sigma e_t + b_2\Sigma X_{2t}e_t + b_3\Sigma X_{3t}e_t = 0 \tag{3-69}$$

since each term on the right-hand side is zero.

Returning to Eq. (3-64) we can write it as

$$y_t = \hat{y}_t + e_t \tag{3-70}$$

where $y = Y - \bar{Y}$ and $\hat{y} = \hat{Y} - \bar{Y}$. Squaring and summing over all observations gives

$$\Sigma y^2 = \Sigma\hat{y}^2 + \Sigma e^2 \tag{3-71}$$

since from Eq. (3-69)

$$\Sigma e\hat{Y} = \Sigma e(\hat{y} + \bar{Y}) = \Sigma e\hat{y} = 0$$

Relation (3-71) is the familiar decomposition of the total sum of squares

$$\text{TSS} = \text{ESS} + \text{RSS}$$

and it suggests the definition of the *multiple correlation coefficient* R as

$$R^2 = \frac{\text{ESS}}{\text{TSS}} = \frac{\Sigma \hat{y}^2}{\Sigma y^2} = 1 - \frac{\Sigma e^2}{\Sigma y^2} \tag{3-72}$$

This coefficient is sometimes written as $R_{1.23}$, indicating that it relates to a regression where X_2 and X_3 are the explanatory variables. Similarly, for explanatory variables $X_2, X_3, \ldots, X_k$ it would be written $R_{1.23\ldots k}$, but in most cases there is no ambiguity and the subscripts are not inserted.

It is illuminating to note that R^2 is also equal to the square of the simple correlation coefficient between Y and $\hat{Y}$. From Eq. (2-20) the latter coefficient may be written

$$r_{y\hat{y}}^2 = \frac{(\Sigma y\hat{y})^2}{(\Sigma y^2)(\Sigma \hat{y}^2)}$$

But

$$\Sigma y\hat{y} = \Sigma \hat{y}(\hat{y} + e) = \Sigma \hat{y}^2$$

Thus

$$r_{y\hat{y}}^2 = \frac{\Sigma \hat{y}^2}{\Sigma y^2} = R^2$$

The normal equations in Eqs. (3-62) may also be simplified if expressed in deviation form. Substituting $\bar{Y} = b_1 + b_2\bar{X}_2 + b_3\bar{X}_3$ in the second and third equations gives

$$\begin{aligned} \Sigma x_2 y &= b_2 \Sigma x_2^2 + b_3 \Sigma x_2 x_3 \\ \Sigma x_3 y &= b_2 \Sigma x_2 x_3 + b_3 \Sigma x_3^2 \end{aligned} \tag{3-73}$$

The calculation of ESS, RSS, and R^2 is then easily made in terms of deviations:

$$\begin{aligned} \text{ESS} &= \Sigma \hat{y}^2 \\ &= \Sigma \hat{y}(b_2 x_2 + b_3 x_3) \\ &= b_2 \Sigma x_2 \hat{y} + b_3 \Sigma x_3 \hat{y} \\ &= b_2 \Sigma x_2 y + b_3 \Sigma x_3 y \end{aligned} \tag{3-74}$$

Thus once b_2 and b_3 have been obtained from Eqs. (3-73), ESS is easily computed from Eq. (3-74), and finally

$$\begin{aligned} \text{RSS} &= \Sigma e^2 \\ &= \Sigma y^2 - (b_2 \Sigma x_2 y + b_3 \Sigma x_3 y) \end{aligned} \tag{3-75}$$

and

$$R^2 = \frac{\Sigma \hat{y}^2}{\Sigma y^2}$$

The exposition so far has been slanted toward the calculation of estimates by hand or on a desk calculator. This may seem uncalled for in an era when there is

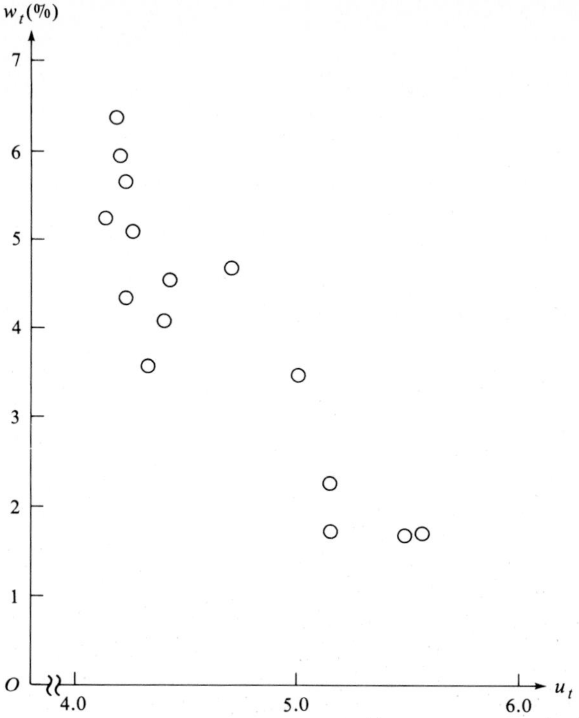

Figure 3-12

almost universal access to large-scale computers, but there is no one more dangerous than the unthinking user of a computer, who has no real understanding of the nature of the computations being processed inside the machine. The one sure way to that understanding is to process some fairly simple examples thoroughly and carefully.

Example 3-3 Figure 3-12 shows a scatter diagram of w_t versus u_t *for the first 16 quarters* of the data, that is, from 1954: 2 to 1958: 1. It is suggestive of a nonlinear negative relationship.† Fig. 3-13 shows the scatter of w_t plotted against the reciprocal of unemployment. The slope is now positive and the scatter approximately linear. The simple regression fitted to these data gives

$$\hat{w}_t = -9.7530 + 62.9490\left(\frac{1}{u_t}\right) \quad \text{with} \quad r^2 = 0.8229$$

Computing the same regression for all 26 quarters up to 1960: 3 gives

$$\hat{w}_t = -1.4486 + 26.2924\left(\frac{1}{u_t}\right) \quad \text{with} \quad r^2 = 0.4235$$

† The nonlinearity is, in fact, very slight. A linear regression of w_t on u_t has an $r^2 = 0.8192$, which is negligibly smaller than the r^2 of 0.8229 for the linear regression of w_t on $1/u_t$.

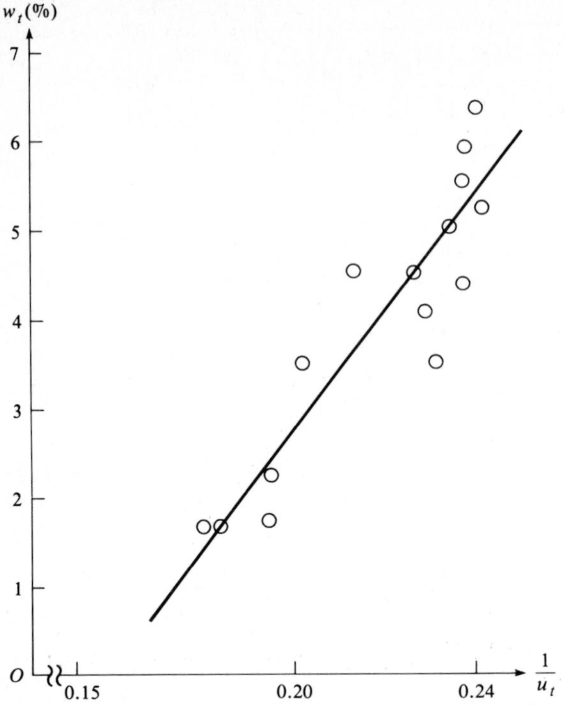

Figure 3-13

We see that the coefficients change substantially and the fit to the longer period is much worse than that to the shorter period. This is just the first example of how regressions can often change markedly when sample data are extended, and in Chap. 6 we will outline methods of analyzing such changes and testing for structural changes in the hypothesized relationship.

Perry introduced the lagged inflation rate as an additional explanatory variable, assuming it to be a good proxy for the expected rate of inflation. The resultant multiple regression for the early period 1954: 2 to 1958: 1 is

$$\hat{w}_t = -9.7396 + 62.9205\left(\frac{1}{u_t}\right) - 0.0054p_{t-1} \quad \text{with} \quad R^2 = 0.8230$$

and for the complete sample period it is

$$\hat{w}_t = -1.7220 + 25.3698\left(\frac{1}{u_t}\right) + 0.3069p_{t-1} \quad \text{with} \quad R^2 = 0.5197$$

We see that for the early period the addition of the lagged inflation rate gives no improvement in the regression: the square of the multiple correlation coefficient is identical to the third decimal place with the square of the simple correlation coefficient, and the coefficient of the inflation rate is negligible in size and perversely signed. For the complete period, the addition of the inflation rate yields some improvement in an initially rather unsatisfactory equation, and the coefficient of the lagged inflation rate is now correctly signed and no longer numerically negligible. We are not yet in a position to apply inference procedures to a multiple regression equation, but this example should alert us to the possibility of substantial variations in estimated relationships as a data base is expanded or contracted.

The b's are point estimates of the hypothetical β's, and all the usual inference questions arise, such as those discussed in Chap. 2. There is little point in working out these questions explicitly for the three-variable case, for in Chap. 5 we will develop all the required inference procedures for the general case of k variables. However, before leaving the three-variable case there are some additional algebraic relations to develop, which will also contribute to our understanding of more complicated relationships later.

With three interrelated variables Y, X_2, and X_3 there are three simple correlation coefficients denoted by

$$r_{12},\ r_{13},\ \text{and}\ r_{23}$$

where the subscript 1 refers to the Y variable. The techniques of Chap. 2 would also enable us to compute various regression slopes such as

$$\begin{aligned} b_{12} &= \text{slope of regression of } Y \text{ on } X_2 \\ b_{13} &= \text{slope of regression of } Y \text{ on } X_3 \\ b_{23} &= \text{slope of regression of } X_2 \text{ on } X_3 \end{aligned}$$

and there are, of course, three further regression slopes where the order of the subscripts on b is reversed.† The first question to explore is the connection between b_2 and b_3, the slopes of the regression plane, and the simple b's, the slopes of the various two-variable scatters. Solving Eq. (3-73) for b_2 gives

$$b_2 = \frac{\Sigma x_2 y \Sigma x_3^2 - \Sigma x_3 y \Sigma x_2 x_3}{\Sigma x_2^2 \Sigma x_3^2 - (\Sigma x_2 x_3)^2}$$

Dividing top and bottom by $\Sigma x_2^2 \Sigma x_3^2$ then gives‡

$$b_2 = \frac{b_{12} - b_{13} b_{32}}{1 - b_{23} b_{32}} = \frac{r_{12} - r_{13} r_{23}}{1 - r_{23}^2} \frac{s_1}{s_2} \tag{3-76}$$

Similarly,

$$b_3 = \frac{b_{13} - b_{12} b_{23}}{1 - b_{23} b_{32}} = \frac{r_{13} - r_{12} r_{23}}{1 - r_{23}^2} \frac{s_1}{s_3} \tag{3-77}$$

† In the regression X_2 on X_3 the residuals are measured in the X_2 direction, while in the regression of X_3 on X_2 the residuals are measured in the X_3 direction.

‡ This follows directly by applying Eqs. (2-14a) and (2-19), that is,

$$b_{12} = \frac{\Sigma y x_2}{\Sigma x_2^2}, \quad b_{32} = \frac{\Sigma x_3 x_2}{\Sigma x_2^2}, \quad b_{23} = \frac{\Sigma x_2 x_3}{\Sigma x_3^2}, \quad b_{12} = r_{12}\frac{s_1}{s_2}, \ldots$$

Thus the coefficient of X_2 in the multiple regression can be regarded as being based on the coefficient in the simple regression of Y on X_2, subject to a correction for the presence of X_3. If it should happen that X_2 and X_3 are uncorrelated in the sample, that is, $\Sigma x_2 x_3 = 0$, then $b_{23} = b_{32} = 0$, and the correction factor is zero, so that

$$b_2 = b_{12}, \qquad b_3 = b_{13}$$

The explanatory variables in this case are said to be *orthogonal*, and the multiple regression coefficients coincide with the simple regression coefficients. An older, but expressive notation for b_2 and b_3 is $b_{12.3}$ and $b_{13.2}$, respectively. A coefficient like b_{12} is then described as a *zero-order* coefficient and $b_{12.3}$ as a *first-order* coefficient, the number after the decimal point in the subscript indicating the one other explanatory variable present in this regression. Equations (3-76) and (3-77) thus indicate the connection between zero-order and first-order regression coefficients. It is natural to inquire if there is a similar hierarchy of correlation coefficients. The simple coefficients r_{12}, r_{13},... are defined as zero-order correlation coefficients. What then is the definition of a first-order correlation coefficient, and what meaning attaches to it?

This question may be approached in the following way. Suppose X_2 influences Y, but X_3 also influences Y. The simple correlation coefficient between Y and X_2 is by definition,

$$r_{12} = \frac{\Sigma y x_2}{\sqrt{\Sigma y^2}\sqrt{\Sigma x_2^2}}$$

Part of the variation in Y is really due to X_3, and so r_{12} will not correctly measure the correlation attributable to X_2. If one ran a linear regression of Y on X_3, the residuals are given by

$$y - b_{13}x_3$$

This series represents the variation in Y left over after the linear effect of X_3 has been removed. Correlating these residuals with X_2 gives

$$r'_{12} = \frac{\Sigma(y - b_{13}x_3)x_2}{\sqrt{\Sigma(y - b_{13}x_3)^2}\sqrt{\Sigma x_2^2}}$$

If X_2 and X_3 were uncorrelated in the sample, this coefficient simplifies to

$$r'_{12} = \frac{\Sigma y x_2}{\sqrt{\Sigma(y - b_{13}x_3)^2}\sqrt{\Sigma x_2^2}}$$

which will be numerically greater than the simple coefficient r_{12}. However, X_2 and X_3 are in general correlated, and the proper correction procedure is to remove the linear effect of X_3 from *both* X_2 and Y and then to correlate the resulting residuals. This gives

$$r_{12.3} = \frac{\Sigma(y - b_{13}x_3)(x_2 - b_{23}x_3)}{\sqrt{\Sigma(y - b_{13}x_3)^2}\sqrt{\Sigma(x_2 - b_{23}x_3)^2}} \tag{3-78}$$

Equation (3-78) defines a first-order correlation coefficient. It measures the correlation remaining between Y and X_2 after the linear effect of X_3 has been removed from each. It is more generally known as a *partial correlation coefficient*. Equation (3-78) simplifies to†

$$r_{12.3} = \frac{r_{12} - r_{13}r_{23}}{\sqrt{1 - r_{13}^2}\sqrt{1 - r_{23}^2}} \tag{3-79}$$

Similarly,

$$r_{13.2} = \frac{r_{13} - r_{12}r_{23}}{\sqrt{1 - r_{12}^2}\sqrt{1 - r_{23}^2}} \tag{3-80}$$

This latter expression may also be derived from first principles by finding the simple correlation between

$$(y - b_{12}x_2) \qquad \text{and} \qquad (x_3 - b_{32}x_2)$$

or, more simply, by interchanging subscripts 2 and 3 in Eq. (3-79). *A partial correlation coefficient between any two variables thus measures the correlation between the residuals left in each variable after the linear effect of all other explanatory variables has been removed.*

The multiple regression slopes b_2 and b_3, defined in Eq. (3-73), may also be interpreted in terms of these residuals. Regressing $(y - b_{13}x_3)$ on $(x_2 - b_{23}x_3)$ gives a regression slope of

$$\frac{\Sigma(y - b_{13}x_3)(x_2 - b_{23}x_3)}{\Sigma(x_2 - b_{23}x_3)^2} = \frac{\Sigma y(x_2 - b_{23}x_3)}{\Sigma(x_2 - b_{23}x_3)^2} \qquad \text{since } x_3 \text{ is uncorrelated with the residuals } (x_2 - b_{23}x_3)$$

$$= \frac{\Sigma yx_2\Sigma x_3^2 - \Sigma yx_3\Sigma x_2x_3}{\Sigma x_2^2\Sigma x_3^2 - (\Sigma x_2x_3)^2}$$

$$= b_2$$

† The explicit derivation is as follows. Using Eqs. (2-14*a*) and (2-20),

$$\text{numerator of } r_{12.3} = \Sigma yx_2 - b_{13}\Sigma x_2x_3 - b_{23}\Sigma yx_3 + b_{13}b_{23}\Sigma x_3^2$$

$$= nr_{12}s_1s_2 - r_{13}\frac{s_1}{s_3}nr_{23}s_2s_3 - r_{23}\frac{s_2}{s_3}nr_{13}s_1s_3$$

$$+ r_{13}r_{23}\frac{s_1s_2}{s_3^2}ns_3^2$$

$$= ns_1s_2(r_{12} - r_{13}r_{23})$$

where s_1 denotes the sample standard deviation of the Y values, s_2 the sample standard deviation of the X_2 values, and so on. In the denominator $\Sigma(y - b_{13}x_3)^2$ is the residual sum of squares in the regression of Y on X_3. From Eq. (2-20) this may be written as $ns_1^2(1 - r_{13}^2)$. Likewise $\Sigma(x_2 - b_{23}x_3)^2$ is the residual sum of squares in the regression of X_2 on X_3 and may be written as $ns_2^2(1 - r_{23}^2)$. Thus the denominator of Eq. (3-78) is $ns_1s_2\sqrt{1 - r_{13}^2}\sqrt{1 - r_{23}^2}$, and Eq. (3-79) follows.

from Eq. (3-73). Likewise, b_3 is just the simple regression slope obtained when the residuals $(y - b_{12}x_2)$ are regressed on the residuals $(x_3 - b_{32}x_2)$.

Finally, the multiple correlation coefficient $R_{1.23}$ is a second-order correlation coefficient, and it may also be expressed in various ways in terms of lower-order coefficients. For example, using Eq. (3-74) gives

$$R_{1.23}^2 = \frac{b_2 \Sigma x_2 y + b_3 \Sigma x_3 y}{\Sigma y^2}$$

Substituting for b_2 and b_3 from Eqs. (3-76) and (3-77) gives

$$R_{1.23}^2 = \frac{r_{12}^2 + r_{13}^2 - 2r_{12}r_{13}r_{23}}{1 - r_{23}^2} \tag{3-81}$$

The buildup of the explained sum of squares may also be looked at in *sequential* fashion, and this is illuminating for the analysis of variance treatment in Chap. 5. Suppose one first regressed Y on X_2. Then

$$r_{12}^2 \Sigma y^2 = \text{ESS due to the regression of } Y \text{ on } X_2$$

and

$$\Sigma y^2 (1 - r_{12}^2) = \text{RSS from the regression of } Y \text{ on } X_2$$

This latter quantity is the sum of squares still to be explained. Regressing the residuals $(y - b_{12}x_2)$ on the X_3 residuals, namely, $(x_3 - b_{32}x_2)$, then gives

$$r_{13.2}^2 \Sigma y^2 (1 - r_{12}^2) = \text{ESS in the regression of the } Y \text{ residuals on the } X_3 \text{ residuals}$$

and

$$(1 - r_{13.2}^2) \Sigma y^2 (1 - r_{12}^2) = \text{RSS in the regression of the } Y \text{ residuals on the } X_3 \text{ residuals}$$

Aggregating the ESS at each stage gives a *total* explained sum of squares in Y as

$$\Sigma y^2 \left[r_{12}^2 + r_{13.2}^2 (1 - r_{12}^2) \right] \tag{3-82}$$

Substituting for $r_{13.2}^2$ in Eq. (3-82) from Eq. (3-80) and using Eq. (3-81) gives

$$\Sigma y^2 \left[r_{12}^2 + r_{13.2}^2 (1 - r_{12}^2) \right] = \Sigma y^2 R_{1.23}^2 \tag{3-83}$$

But $\Sigma y^2 R_{1.23}^2$, by definition, indicates the sum of squares in Y explained by the *multiple regression* of Y on X_2 and X_3. Equation (3-83) thus shows that the multiple regression ESS can be regarded as built up in two steps, first the ESS due to the simple regression of Y on X_2 and second the ESS due to the simple regression of the Y residuals on the X_3 residuals. The *increment* in the ESS *due to adding* X_3 to the regression is

$$\Sigma y^2 (R_{1.23}^2 - r_{12}^2)$$

which, from Eq. (3-83), may be written

$$r_{13.2}^2 \Sigma y^2 (1 - r_{12}^2)$$

where $\Sigma y^2(1 - r_{12}^2)$ is the RSS after Y has been regressed on X_2. Thus $r_{13.2}^2$ indicates the proportion of the variation left after the simple regression on X_2, which is explained by adding X_3 to the set of explanatory variables. A similar development and interpretation may be made by starting with the simple regression of Y on X_3 and then adding X_2 to the explanatory variables.

Example 3-4 Denote the variables in Table 3-7 by

$$1 = w_t$$

$$2 = u_t^{-1}$$

$$3 = p_{t-1}$$

Table 3-7 Wage change, unemployment, and price change in the United States†

Year Quarter	w_t	u_t^{-1}	p_{t-1}
1954: 2	3.53	0.2312	1.229
3	1.74	0.1942	0.702
4	1.72	0.1794	0.000
1955: 1	1.71	0.1827	−0.522
2	2.27	0.1942	−0.260
3	4.57	0.2128	−0.173
4	4.52	0.2260	0.090
1956: 1	5.06	0.2353	0.699
2	5.56	0.2367	0.263
3	4.37	0.2367	1.048
4	5.95	0.2381	1.997
1957: 1	6.42	0.2395	2.507
2	5.26	0.2424	3.447
3	5.24	0.2410	3.589
4	4.08	0.2286	3.376
1958: 1	3.52	0.2010	3.023
2	3.50	0.1747	3.415
3	3.48	0.1544	3.221
4	2.94	0.1460	2.297
1959: 1	3.88	0.1487	1.966
2	4.35	0.1613	0.814
3	2.88	0.1747	0.404
4	3.33	0.1810	0.967
1960: 1	3.24	0.1878	1.367
2	2.78	0.1869	1.528
3	3.74	0.1869	1.762

† w = four-quarter percentage change in hourly earnings of production workers in all manufacturing

u = unemployment as a percentage of the civilian labor force

p = four-quarter percentage change in the consumer price index (CPI)

Source: G. Perry, *Unemployment, Money Wage Rates and Inflation*, MIT Press, Cambridge, MA, 1966.

For the complete sample period the zero-order correlation coefficients are

$$r_{12} = 0.6508 \qquad r_{13} = 0.3567 \qquad r_{23} = 0.0726$$

$$r_{12}^2 = 0.4235 \qquad r_{13}^2 = 0.1272$$

Thus

$$r_{12.3} = \frac{0.6508 - 0.3567(0.0726)}{\sqrt{\left[1 - (0.3567)^2\right]}\sqrt{\left[1 - (0.0726)^2\right]}} = 0.6707$$

$$r_{13.2} = \frac{0.3567 - 0.6508(0.0726)}{\sqrt{\left[1 - (0.6508)^2\right]}\sqrt{\left[1 - (0.0726)^2\right]}} = 0.4087$$

and $$r_{12.3}^2 = 0.4498 \qquad r_{13.2}^2 = 0.1670$$

and $R_{1.23}^2 = 0.5197$. In this example the two explanatory variables are practically uncorrelated, so there is little difference between the zero-order and the first-order correlation coefficients. Unemployment alone explains over 42 percent of the variation in wage change, price change alone accounts for about 13 percent, and the two variables jointly account for about 52 percent. Unemployment accounts for 45 percent of the variation unexplained by price, and price accounts for about 17 percent of the variation unexplained by unemployment.

PROBLEMS

3-1 Given five observations u_{-2}, u_{-1}, u_0, u_1, and u_2 at equally spaced points of time $t = -2, -1, 0, 1, 2$, show how to fit a parabola to the observations by least squares and show that the value given by the parabola at time $t = 0$ is

$$\tfrac{1}{35}(-3u_{-2} + 12u_{-1} + 17u_0 + 12u_1 - 3u_2)$$

(R.S.S. Certificate, 1955)

3-2 The "firmness" of cheese depends upon the time allowed for a certain process in the manufacture. In an experiment on this topic, 18 cheeses were taken, and at each of several times firmness was determined on samples from three of the cheeses. The results (on an arbitrary scale) are given below:

Time, h	Firmness		
$\frac{1}{2}$	102	105	115
1	110	120	115
$1\frac{1}{2}$	126	128	119
2	132	143	139
3	160	149	147
4	164	166	172

Estimate the parameters in a linear regression of firmness on time. Give standard errors of the estimates and test the adequacy of a linear regression to describe the results.

(R.S.S. Certificate, 1955)

3-3 Discuss briefly the advantages and disadvantages of the relation

$$v_i = \alpha + \beta \log v_0$$

as a representation of an Engel curve, where v_i is expenditure per person on commodity i and v_0 is income per person. Fit such a curve to the following data, and from your results estimate the income elasticity at an income of £5 per week.

Pounds per week								
v_i	0.8	1.2	1.5	1.8	2.2	2.3	2.6	3.1
v_0	1.7	2.7	3.6	4.6	5.7	6.7	8.1	12.0

Does it make any difference to your estimate of the income elasticity if the logarithms of v_0 are taken to base 10 or to base e? Explain carefully.

(Manchester University, 1956)

3-4 Response rates at various levels of ratable values.

Range of ratable value	A	B	C	D	E	F	G	H	I	J
Assumed central value X, £/annum	3	7	12	17	25	35	45	55	70	120
Response rate Y, percent	86	79	76	69	65	62	52	51	51	48

The data relate to a survey recently conducted in England. Estimate the constants in the regression equation

$$\frac{100}{100 - Y} = a + \frac{b}{X}$$

(Oxford University, 1955)

3-5 X_1, X_2, and X_3 are three correlated variables, where $s_1 = 1$, $s_2 = 1.3$, $s_3 = 1.9$ and $r_{12} = 0.370$, $r_{13} = -0.641$, and $r_{23} = -0.736$. Compute $r_{13.2}$. If $X_4 = X_1 + X_2$, obtain r_{42}, r_{43}, and $r_{43.2}$. Verify that the two partial coefficients are equal and explain this result.

(UL, 1952)

3-6 In the regression equation

$$y_t = \beta x_{1t} + \gamma x_{2t} + u_t \qquad t = 1, \ldots, n$$

all variables are expressed as deviations from their sample means. Consider the following alternative procedures for estimating β.

(a) Calculate the estimates $\hat{\beta}$ and $\hat{\gamma}$ in a regression of y on x_1 and x_2.

(b) Regress y on x_2 and calculate the regression residuals y_t^*; regress x_1 on x_2 and calculate the regression residuals x_{1t}^*; regress y^* on x_1^* to obtain an estimate b of β.

Show that the two procedures give the same result, that is, $\hat{\beta} = b$.

Show that the regression residuals given by each procedure, that is,

$$y_t - \hat{\beta} x_{1t} - \hat{\gamma} x_{2t} \qquad \text{and} \qquad y_t^* - b x_{1t}^*$$

are the same.

(UL, 1969)

3-7 Outline the properties of the following functions, and sketch their graphs:

(a) $y = \alpha + \beta \ln x$

(b) $y = \dfrac{x}{\alpha x - \beta}$

(c) $y = \dfrac{e^{\alpha + \beta x}}{1 + e^{\alpha + \beta x}}$

Find transformations which linearize functions (b) and (c), that is, for each function find a pair of transformations $f(x)$ and $g(y)$ such that $g(y)$ is a linear function of $f(x)$ and the α, β parameters may be estimated.

3-8 Your research assistant reports the following results in several different regression problems. In which cases could you be certain that an error had been committed? Explain.

(a) $R^2_{1.23} = 0.89$ and $R^2_{1.234} = 0.86$

(b) $r^2_{12} = 0.227$, $r^2_{13} = 0.126$, and $R^2_{1.23} = 0.701$

(c) $(\Sigma x^2)(\Sigma y^2) - (\Sigma xy)^2 = -1{,}732.86$

(University of Michigan, 1980)

3-9 Sometimes variables are *standardized* before the computation of regression and correlation coefficients. Standardization is achieved by dividing each observation on a variable by its standard deviation, so that the standard deviation of the transformed variable is unity. If the original relation is, say,

$$Y = \beta_1 + \beta_2 X_2 + \beta_3 X_3 + u$$

and the corresponding relation between the transformed variables is

$$Y^* = \beta_1' + \beta_2' X_2^* + \beta_3' X_3^* + u^*$$

where

$$Y^* = Y/s_y, \quad X_i^* = X_i/s_{x_i} \qquad i = 2, 3$$

what is the relationship between β_2', β_3', and β_2, β_3? Show that the partial correlation coefficients are unaffected by the transformation.

CHAPTER
FOUR

ELEMENTS OF MATRIX ALGEBRA

It is clear from the last section of Chap. 3 that it would be excessively tedious and complicated to build up to the general case of k-variable regression in a stepwise fashion. Fortunately, by the use of matrix algebra we have a compact and powerful way of treating the problem, and we shall see that the detailed results of the previous two chapters are merely special cases of a few simple matrix formulas. The rest of this chapter presents the elements of matrix algebra that are necessary for following the treatment in the remainder of the book. Most or all of this chapter may be skipped by those with adequate previous knowledge of matrices. For those whose knowledge is somewhat rusty it may hopefully serve as a useful review, but every attempt has been made to make the material accessible to a student with no prior knowledge of matrices, for the subject is so fundamental to modern econometrics (and economics) that no serious student can afford to be without it.†

Suppose our theory suggests that a dependent (explained) variable Y is a linear function of $k - 1$ independent (explanatory) variables $X_2, X_3, \ldots, X_k$.

† Nonetheless students with no prior knowledge of matrix algebra are likely to get indigestion if they attempt to work through all the material in this chapter before proceeding with the rest of the book. The topics are introduced approximately in the order in which they will appear in subsequent chapters. Thus the students should interact between this chapter and those that follow, learning enough from Chap. 4 to proceed with Chaps. 5, 6, and so on, and returning to Chap. 4 as necessary. Summaries of results have also been inserted at various stages in the chapter.

Allowing for a constant term, we would write the function as

$$Y = \beta_1 + \beta_2 X_2 + \beta_3 X_3 + \cdots + \beta_k X_k + u$$

If we have n sample observations, the model gives rise to the following set of n equations:

$$\begin{aligned} Y_1 &= \beta_1 + \beta_2 X_{21} + \beta_3 X_{31} + \cdots + \beta_k Y_{k1} + u_1 \\ Y_2 &= \beta_1 + \beta_2 X_{22} + \beta_3 X_{32} + \cdots + \beta_k X_{k2} + u_2 \\ &\cdots\cdots\cdots\cdots\cdots\cdots\cdots\cdots\cdots \\ Y_n &= \beta_1 + \beta_2 X_{2n} + \beta_3 X_{3n} + \cdots + \beta_k X_{kn} + u_n \end{aligned} \tag{4-1}$$

As a first step we rewrite these n equations in the form

$$\begin{bmatrix} Y_1 \\ Y_2 \\ \vdots \\ Y_n \end{bmatrix} = \begin{bmatrix} 1 & X_{21} & X_{31} & \cdots & X_{k1} \\ 1 & X_{22} & X_{32} & \cdots & X_{k2} \\ \cdots & \cdots & \cdots & \cdots & \cdots \\ 1 & X_{2n} & X_{3n} & \cdots & X_{kn} \end{bmatrix} \begin{bmatrix} \beta_1 \\ \beta_2 \\ \vdots \\ \beta_k \end{bmatrix} + \begin{bmatrix} u_1 \\ u_2 \\ \vdots \\ u_n \end{bmatrix} \tag{4-2}$$

or

$$\mathbf{y} = \mathbf{X}\boldsymbol{\beta} + \mathbf{u} \tag{4-3}$$

where the four boldface symbols correspond to the four sets of elements that have been enclosed in square brackets in Eq. (4-2). These symbols indicate *vectors* and *matrices*. For example,

$$\mathbf{y} = \begin{bmatrix} Y_1 \\ Y_2 \\ \vdots \\ Y_n \end{bmatrix}$$

is an n-element column vector, with the sample observations on Y arranged in a specific order in the form of a column. Likewise $\boldsymbol{\beta}$ is a k-element column vector, containing the coefficients of the hypothesized relation, and $\mathbf{u}$ is an n-element column vector, containing the n unknown disturbances.

$$\mathbf{X} = \begin{bmatrix} 1 & X_{21} & X_{31} & \cdots & X_{k1} \\ 1 & X_{22} & X_{32} & \cdots & X_{k2} \\ \cdots & \cdots & \cdots & \cdots & \cdots \\ 1 & X_{2t} & X_{3t} & \cdots & X_{kt} \\ \cdots & \cdots & \cdots & \cdots & \cdots \\ 1 & X_{2n} & X_{3n} & \cdots & X_{kn} \end{bmatrix}$$

is a *matrix* with n rows and k columns. A matrix is simply a *rectangular array* of elements, and we say that $\mathbf{X}$ is a matrix of order $n \times k$ to indicate that the rectangular array in $\mathbf{X}$ has n rows and k columns. In stating the order of a matrix, the number of rows is always given first and the number of columns second. Clearly, a column vector is merely a special case of a matrix, namely, a matrix with only one column. Likewise, a row vector such as

$$[1 \quad X_{21} \quad X_{31} \quad \cdots \quad X_{k1}]$$

is another special case, namely, a matrix with just one row.† We may thus look at the **X** matrix in two ways, as an ordered collection of column vectors or as an ordered collection of row vectors. Each column vector, apart from the first, denotes the sample observations on a particular explanatory variable. Thus, for example,

$$\mathbf{x}_3 = \begin{bmatrix} X_{31} \\ X_{32} \\ \vdots \\ X_{3n} \end{bmatrix}$$

denotes the sample observations on the variable X_3. The first column is a collection of units and, as we will see, is required in order to incorporate the intercept β_1 into the regression. Using this notation for the column vectors, we could express **X** as

$$\mathbf{X} = \begin{bmatrix} | & | & & | \\ \mathbf{x}_1 & \mathbf{x}_2 & \cdots & \mathbf{x}_k \\ | & | & & | \end{bmatrix} \tag{4-4}$$

where each $\mathbf{x}_i$ is an n-element column vector and $\mathbf{x}_1$ indicates a column of units. The rows of **X** indicate observations on all explanatory variables at a particular sample point plus a unit in the first position. Thus if the data are in time series form, the first row indicates the X values in the first time period, the second row the values in the second time period, and so forth. Thus using $\mathbf{s}_i$ to indicate the vector of observations at the ith sample point, the **X** matrix may also be expressed as‡

$$\mathbf{X} = \begin{bmatrix} - & \mathbf{s}_1 & - \\ - & \mathbf{s}_2 & - \\ & \vdots & \\ - & \mathbf{s}_n & - \end{bmatrix} \tag{4-5}$$

We have inserted vertical and horizontal lines in Eqs. (4-4) and (4-5) to emphasize that the first is a representation of **X** in terms of column vectors and the second a representation in terms of row vectors. In practice one usually writes these expressions more compactly as

$$\mathbf{X} = [\mathbf{x}_1 \quad \mathbf{x}_2 \quad \cdots \quad \mathbf{x}_k] = \begin{bmatrix} \mathbf{s}_1 \\ \mathbf{s}_2 \\ \vdots \\ \mathbf{s}_n \end{bmatrix}$$

it being clear from the context which are row and which are column vectors.

† We will adhere to the convention of indicating a matrix by an uppercase boldface letter and a vector by a lowercase boldface letter.

‡ We have indicated the row vectors by the letter **s** since they correspond to *sample* points. A more common notation is to let $\mathbf{x}_{i.}$ indicate the ith row of the **X** matrix and $\mathbf{x}_{.j}$ the jth column.

Equations (4-2) and (4-3) are equivalent ways of stating Eq. (4-1). For this to be so, operations on matrices must follow certain simple rules, which we will now describe.

4-1 OPERATIONS ON VECTORS AND MATRICES

The right-hand side of Eq. (4-3) indicates two elementary operations on matrices, namely, multiplication and addition.

Matrix Multiplication

Matrix multiplication is achieved by repeated applications of vector multiplication. The multiplication of an *n-element row* vector into an *n-element* column vector is defined as follows:

$$\begin{bmatrix} a_1 & a_2 & \cdots & a_n \end{bmatrix} \begin{bmatrix} b_1 \\ b_2 \\ \vdots \\ b_n \end{bmatrix} = a_1b_1 + a_2b_2 + \cdots + a_nb_n = \sum_{i=1}^{n} a_ib_i \qquad (4\text{-}6)$$

that is, corresponding elements are multiplied together and the results summed. As a numerical example,

$$\begin{bmatrix} 2 & 3 & -1 \end{bmatrix} \begin{bmatrix} 1 \\ 4 \\ 5 \end{bmatrix} = 2(1) + 3(4) + (-1)(5) = 9$$

As the definition and the example show, multiplying a $1 \times n$ vector into an $n \times 1$ vector produces a 1×1 vector, or a scalar quantity. Notice that the operation is not defined if the number of elements in the two vectors is not the same. It is also clear from the definition that

$$\begin{bmatrix} b_1 & b_2 & \cdots & b_n \end{bmatrix} \begin{bmatrix} a_1 \\ a_2 \\ \vdots \\ a_n \end{bmatrix} = \begin{bmatrix} a_1 & a_2 & \cdots & a_n \end{bmatrix} \begin{bmatrix} b_1 \\ b_2 \\ \vdots \\ b_n \end{bmatrix}$$

Suppose, however, we define the vectors **a** and **b** as column vectors, that is,

$$\mathbf{a} = \begin{bmatrix} a_1 \\ a_2 \\ \vdots \\ a_n \end{bmatrix} \qquad \mathbf{b} = \begin{bmatrix} b_1 \\ b_2 \\ \vdots \\ b_n \end{bmatrix} \qquad (4\text{-}7)$$

The above multiplication definition cannot apply directly to **a** and **b** since they are both column vectors. We thus define an operation of transposition, which turns column vectors into row vectors, and vice versa. Thus

$$\text{Transpose of } \mathbf{a} = \mathbf{a}' = [a_1 \quad a_2 \quad \cdots \quad a_n]$$

Transposition does not change any of the elements of the vector; they are merely written in the original order, but as a row instead of a column, or vice versa. It is also clear that transposing $\mathbf{a}'$ gets us back to the original column vector. Thus

$$(\mathbf{a}')' = \mathbf{a}$$

Some writers use a superscript T to indicate a transpose, that is, $\mathbf{a}^T = \mathbf{a}'$, but we will use a prime. We will also sometimes find it useful to take the transpose of a 1×1 vector, or scalar, and clearly, that leaves the scalar unchanged.

Scalar, Dot, or Inner Product

In general, unless we specifically state the contrary, a vector symbol will indicate a column vector, as in Eq. (4-7). The multiplication operation already defined in Eq. (4-6) then enables us to define the *scalar*, *dot*, or *inner* product of the two vectors $\mathbf{a}$ and $\mathbf{b}$ in Eq. (4-7) as

$$\mathbf{a}'\mathbf{b} = \mathbf{b}'\mathbf{a} = \sum_{i=1}^{n} a_i b_i \tag{4-8}$$

If we have two matrices $\mathbf{A}$ and $\mathbf{B}$, where $\mathbf{A}$ is of order $m \times n$ and $\mathbf{B}$ is of order $n \times p$, the product $\mathbf{AB}$ will be a matrix $\mathbf{C}$ of order $m \times p$, that is,

$$\underset{(m\times n)(n\times p)}{\mathbf{AB}} = \underset{(m\times p)}{\mathbf{C}} \tag{4-9}$$

If we indicate the rows of $\mathbf{A}$ by $\mathbf{a}_i$ ($i = 1, \ldots, m$) and the columns of $\mathbf{B}$ by $\mathbf{b}_j$ ($j = 1, \ldots, p$), each (scalar) element in $\mathbf{C}$ is the inner product of a row vector from $\mathbf{A}$ and a column vector from $\mathbf{B}$, namely,

$$\begin{bmatrix} - & \mathbf{a}_1 & - \\ - & \mathbf{a}_2 & - \\ & \vdots & \\ - & \mathbf{a}_m & - \end{bmatrix} \begin{bmatrix} | & | & & | \\ \mathbf{b}_1 & \mathbf{b}_2 & \cdots & \mathbf{b}_p \\ | & | & & | \end{bmatrix} = \begin{bmatrix} \mathbf{a}_1\mathbf{b}_1 & \mathbf{a}_1\mathbf{b}_2 & \cdots & \mathbf{a}_1\mathbf{b}_p \\ \mathbf{a}_2\mathbf{b}_1 & \mathbf{a}_2\mathbf{b}_2 & \cdots & \mathbf{a}_2\mathbf{b}_p \\ \cdots & \cdots & \cdots & \cdots \\ \mathbf{a}_m\mathbf{b}_1 & \mathbf{a}_m\mathbf{b}_2 & \cdots & \mathbf{a}_m\mathbf{b}_p \end{bmatrix} \tag{4-10}$$

The basic rule embodied in Eq. (4-10) is

Element in i, jth position in $\mathbf{AB}$ = inner product of *row* i of $\mathbf{A}$ and *column* j of $\mathbf{B}$

Example 4-1

$$\begin{bmatrix} 1 & 2 & 3 \\ 2 & 0 & 4 \end{bmatrix} \begin{bmatrix} 1 & 6 \\ 0 & 1 \\ 1 & 1 \end{bmatrix} = \begin{bmatrix} 1(1) + 2(0) + 3(1) & 1(6) + 2(1) + 3(1) \\ 2(1) + 0(0) + 4(1) & 2(6) + 0(1) + 4(1) \end{bmatrix}$$

$$\mathbf{AB} = \begin{bmatrix} 4 & 11 \\ 6 & 16 \end{bmatrix}$$

Example 4-2

$$\begin{bmatrix} 1 & 6 \\ 0 & 1 \\ 1 & 1 \end{bmatrix}\begin{bmatrix} 1 & 2 & 3 \\ 2 & 0 & 4 \end{bmatrix} = \begin{bmatrix} 1(1)+6(2) & 1(2)+6(0) & 1(3)+6(4) \\ 0(1)+1(2) & 0(2)+1(0) & 0(3)+1(4) \\ 1(1)+1(2) & 1(2)+1(0) & 1(3)+1(4) \end{bmatrix}$$

$$\mathbf{BA} = \begin{bmatrix} 13 & 2 & 27 \\ 2 & 0 & 4 \\ 3 & 2 & 7 \end{bmatrix}$$

As the examples and the definition in Eq. (4-10) make clear, the order in which matrices are multiplied is of crucial importance:

> **AB** *indicates that* **A** *is postmultiplied by* **B** *or, equivalently, that* **B** *is premultiplied by* **A**

This operation is only possible if the inner products of *rows* of **A** and *columns* of **B** exist, that is, if the number of columns in **A** is equal to the number of rows in **B**. In this event the matrices are said to be *conformable*. The simplest check is to write down the order of the two matrices to be multiplied, as in Eq. (4-9), and it is seen that the common index n disappears to give a product matrix of order $m \times p$. The product **BA** would only exist if $p = m$ so that the inner products of the *rows* of **B** and the *columns* of **A** could be formed. Note carefully that the definition of matrix multiplication involves the inner products of the *rows* of the *first* matrix and the *columns* of the *second*.

A special case of Eq. (4-10) occurs when one of the matrices is simply a vector. For example,

$$\begin{bmatrix} - & \mathbf{a}_1 & - \\ - & \mathbf{a}_2 & - \\ & \vdots & \\ - & \mathbf{a}_m & - \end{bmatrix}\begin{bmatrix} | \\ \mathbf{b} \\ | \end{bmatrix} = \begin{bmatrix} \mathbf{a}_1\mathbf{b} \\ \mathbf{a}_2\mathbf{b} \\ \vdots \\ \mathbf{a}_m\mathbf{b} \end{bmatrix} = \mathbf{c} \tag{4-11}$$

and $\mathbf{c}$ is an $m \times 1$ (column) vector.

Returning now to Eq. (4-2), the right-hand side incorporates the multiplication of a matrix by a vector, and applying the above rules gives

$$\mathbf{X\beta} = \begin{bmatrix} \beta_1 + \beta_2 X_{21} + \beta_3 X_{31} + \cdots + \beta_k X_{k1} \\ \cdots\cdots\cdots\cdots\cdots\cdots \\ \beta_1 + \beta_2 X_{2n} + \beta_3 X_{3n} + \cdots + \beta_k X_{kn} \end{bmatrix} \tag{4-12}$$

which is just an n-element column vector.

Matrix Addition

The right-hand side of Eq. (4-2) or Eq. (4-3) is now seen to consist of the *addition* of the two vectors $\mathbf{X\beta}$ and $\mathbf{u}$. This addition is simply achieved by *adding corresponding elements*. Thus the operation is only defined for vectors with the same number of elements. In general,

$$\mathbf{a} + \mathbf{b} = \begin{bmatrix} a_1 \\ a_2 \\ \vdots \\ a_n \end{bmatrix} + \begin{bmatrix} b_1 \\ b_2 \\ \vdots \\ b_n \end{bmatrix} = \begin{bmatrix} a_1 + b_1 \\ a_2 + b_2 \\ \vdots \\ a_n + b_n \end{bmatrix} \tag{4-13}$$

The definition in Eq. (4-13) is readily extended to the addition of matrices. Two matrices **A** and **B** can be added together only if they are of the same order $m \times n$. The sum matrix is also of the same order, and each element in it is simply the sum of the corresponding elements in **A** and **B**.

Applying Eq. (4-13), the right-hand side of Eq. (4-3) reduces to an n-element column vector,

$$\mathbf{X\beta} + \mathbf{u} = \begin{bmatrix} \beta_1 + \beta_2 X_{21} + \cdots + \beta_k X_{k1} + u_1 \\ \cdots\cdots\cdots\cdots\cdots\cdots\cdots\cdots \\ \beta_1 + \beta_2 X_{2n} + \cdots + \beta_k X_{kn} + u_n \end{bmatrix}$$

Equality of Matrices

Finally, Eq. (4-3) states an equality between **y** and $\mathbf{X\beta} + \mathbf{u}$. This simply means that the first element is **y**, equal to the first element in $\mathbf{X\beta} + \mathbf{u}$, and so on through all n elements, that is,

$$\begin{array}{c} Y_1 = \beta_1 + \beta_2 X_{21} + \cdots + \beta_k X_{k1} + u_1 \\ \cdots\cdots\cdots\cdots\cdots\cdots\cdots\cdots \\ Y_n = \beta_1 + \beta_2 X_{2n} + \cdots + \beta_k X_{kn} + u_n \end{array}$$

and so we are back to the n equations of Eq. (4-1) and have shown that the simple rules of matrix addition and multiplication enable us to write the system (4-1) in the compact form

$$\mathbf{y} = \mathbf{X\beta} + \mathbf{u}$$

Further Remarks on Matrices

Our primary purpose is to analyze the model $\mathbf{y} = \mathbf{X\beta} + \mathbf{u}$ by least-squares techniques, but in order to proceed with that we need to develop some further properties of matrices.

Transposition has already been defined for vectors. Since a matrix is a collection of vectors, we can define the transpose of a matrix. Let **A** be an $m \times n$ matrix, which we write in the form

$$\underset{(m \times n)}{\mathbf{A}} = \begin{bmatrix} | & | & & | \\ \mathbf{a}_1 & \mathbf{a}_2 & \cdots & \mathbf{a}_n \\ | & | & & | \end{bmatrix}$$

to indicate the m-element column vectors. The transpose **A**′ of **A** is defined as

$$\underset{(n \times m)}{\mathbf{A}'} = \begin{bmatrix} - & \mathbf{a}_1' & - \\ - & \mathbf{a}_2' & - \\ & \vdots & \\ - & \mathbf{a}_n' & - \end{bmatrix}$$

that is, the first row of **A** has become the first column of the transpose, the second row of **A** the second column of the transpose, and so forth. The definition might equally well have been stated in terms of the first column of **A** becoming the first row of **A**′, and so on. Clearly, **A**′ is of order $n \times m$.

Example 4-3

$$\mathbf{A} = \begin{bmatrix} 1 & 2 & 3 \\ 2 & 0 & 4 \end{bmatrix} \qquad \mathbf{A}' = \begin{bmatrix} 1 & 2 \\ 2 & 0 \\ 3 & 4 \end{bmatrix}$$

A symmetric matrix is defined to be one for which

$$\mathbf{A}' = \mathbf{A}$$

that is,

$$a_{ij} = a_{ji} \qquad \text{for } i \neq j$$

This property can only hold for *square* matrices ($m = n$), since otherwise **A**′ and **A** are not even of the same order.

Example 4-4

$$\mathbf{A} = \begin{bmatrix} 1 & -1 & 4 \\ -1 & 0 & 3 \\ 4 & 3 & 2 \end{bmatrix} = \mathbf{A}'$$

From the definition of a transpose it is immediately obvious that the following two properties hold:

$$(\mathbf{A}')' = \mathbf{A}$$

that is, the transpose of the transpose equals the original matrix, and

$$(\mathbf{A} + \mathbf{B})' = \mathbf{A}' + \mathbf{B}'$$

that is, the transpose of a sum is the sum of the transposes. Somewhat less obvious is the interpretation of (**AB**)′, the transpose of the product **AB**. Referring back to Eq. (4-10), we note again that the i, jth element in $\mathbf{C} = \mathbf{AB}$ is

$$c_{ij} = \mathbf{a}_i \mathbf{b}_j = \text{inner product of } i\text{th row of } \mathbf{A} \text{ into } j\text{th column of } \mathbf{B}$$

$$i = 1, \ldots, m; j = 1, \ldots, p$$

Transposition of **C** means that the i, jth element in **C**′ is the j, ith element in **C**. Using c'_{ij} to denote the i, jth element in **C**′ gives

$$c'_{ij} = c_{ji} = \mathbf{a}_j \mathbf{b}_i$$

But

$$\begin{bmatrix} - & \mathbf{a}_j & - \end{bmatrix} \begin{bmatrix} | \\ \mathbf{b}_i \\ | \end{bmatrix} = \begin{bmatrix} - & \mathbf{b}'_i & - \end{bmatrix} \begin{bmatrix} | \\ \mathbf{a}'_j \\ | \end{bmatrix}$$

from the definition of an inner product. Thus

$$c'_{ij} = \mathbf{b}'_i\mathbf{a}'_j = \text{inner product of } i\text{th row of } \mathbf{B}' \text{ and } j\text{th column of } \mathbf{A}'$$

and so, from the definition of matrix multiplication,

$$\mathbf{C}' = (\mathbf{AB})' = \mathbf{B}'\mathbf{A}' \tag{4-14}$$

This rule extends immediately to any number of matrices. Thus

$$(\mathbf{ABC})' = \mathbf{C}'\mathbf{B}'\mathbf{A}' \tag{4-15}$$

since

$$\begin{aligned}(\mathbf{ABC})' &= \mathbf{C}'(\mathbf{AB})' \\ &= \mathbf{C}'\mathbf{B}'\mathbf{A}'\end{aligned}$$

by repeated application of Eq. (4-14).

The associative law of addition holds for matrices, that is,

$$(\mathbf{A} + \mathbf{B}) + \mathbf{C} = \mathbf{A} + (\mathbf{B} + \mathbf{C}) \tag{4-16}$$

This result is obvious since matrix addition merely involves adding corresponding elements, and it does not matter in what order the additions are performed.

The associative law of multiplication also holds, that is,

$$(\mathbf{AB})\mathbf{C} = \mathbf{A}(\mathbf{BC}) \tag{4-17}$$

where **A**, **B**, and **C** are assumed to be of the appropriate order for multiplication. To prove this result, we will show that the i, jth elements on each side of Eq. (4-17) are the same. The ith row of the product **AB** is given by

$$[\mathbf{a}_i\mathbf{b}_1 \quad \mathbf{a}_i\mathbf{b}_2 \quad \cdots] = \mathbf{a}_i[\mathbf{b}_1 \quad \mathbf{b}_2 \quad \cdots] = \mathbf{a}_i\mathbf{B}$$

where $\mathbf{a}_i$ denotes the ith row of **A** and $\mathbf{b}_1, \mathbf{b}_2, \ldots$ denote the columns of **B**. Letting $\mathbf{c}_j$ denote the jth column of **C**, the i, jth element of (**AB**)**C** is then

$$\mathbf{a}_i\mathbf{B}\mathbf{c}_j$$

Similarly, the jth column of the product **BC** is

$$\mathbf{B}\mathbf{c}_j$$

and so the i, jth element of **A**(**BC**) is

$$\mathbf{a}_i\mathbf{B}\mathbf{c}_j$$

The distributive law also holds for matrices, that is,

$$\mathbf{A}(\mathbf{B} + \mathbf{C}) = \mathbf{AB} + \mathbf{AC} \tag{4-18}$$

To see this, let $\mathbf{a}_i$ denote the ith row of **A** and $\mathbf{b}_j$ and $\mathbf{c}_j$ the jth columns of **B** and **C**. The i, jth element on the right-hand side of Eq. (4-18) is then the scalar

$$\mathbf{a}_i\mathbf{b}_j + \mathbf{a}_i\mathbf{c}_j$$

and by the application of the distributive law for scalar algebra this is clearly equal to the inner product of $\mathbf{a}_i$ and the vector $\mathbf{b}_j + \mathbf{c}_j$, the jth column of $\mathbf{B} + \mathbf{C}$, which gives the i, jth element on the left-hand side of Eq. (4-18).

If a matrix is multiplied by a scalar, then every element in the matrix is multiplied by the scalar. For example,†

$$-2\begin{bmatrix} 1 & 2 & 3 \\ 2 & 0 & 4 \end{bmatrix} = \begin{bmatrix} -2 & -4 & -6 \\ -4 & 0 & -8 \end{bmatrix}$$

There are some square matrices of particular importance. First is the *unit* or *identity* matrix of order $n \times n$,

$$\mathbf{I}_n = \begin{bmatrix} 1 & 0 & 0 & \cdots & 0 \\ 0 & 1 & 0 & \cdots & 0 \\ \cdots & \cdots & \cdots & \cdots & \cdots \\ 0 & 0 & 0 & \cdots & 1 \end{bmatrix}$$

with units down the main, or principal, diagonal and zeros everywhere else. As we shall see, it plays in matrix algebra a role similar to that of unity in scalar algebra. As one illustration,

$$\mathbf{IA} = \mathbf{AI} = \mathbf{A}$$

that is, pre- or postmultiplication by $\mathbf{I}$ leaves any matrix unchanged, as may readily be verified by multiplying out $\mathbf{IA}$ and $\mathbf{AI}$. Thus the unit matrix may be entered or suppressed at will in matrix expressions. For instance,

$$\begin{aligned} \mathbf{y} - \mathbf{Py} &= \mathbf{Iy} - \mathbf{Py} \\ &= (\mathbf{I} - \mathbf{P})\mathbf{y} \end{aligned}$$

A diagonal matrix is like the identity matrix in that all off-diagonal terms are zero, but now the diagonal elements are scalar quantities, one of which at least is nonzero. The diagonal matrix may be written

$$\mathbf{\Lambda} = \begin{bmatrix} \lambda_1 & 0 & 0 & \cdots & 0 \\ 0 & \lambda_2 & 0 & \cdots & 0 \\ 0 & 0 & \lambda_3 & \cdots & 0 \\ \cdots & \cdots & \cdots & \cdots & \cdots \\ 0 & 0 & 0 & \cdots & \lambda_n \end{bmatrix} \tag{4-19}$$

or, more compactly, $\mathbf{\Lambda} = \text{diag}\{\lambda_1 \quad \lambda_2 \quad \cdots \quad \lambda_n\}$. Examples are

$$\begin{bmatrix} 1 & 0 \\ 0 & 0 \end{bmatrix}, \quad \text{and} \quad \begin{bmatrix} 2 & 0 & 0 \\ 0 & -4 & 0 \\ 0 & 0 & 5 \end{bmatrix}$$

A special case of Eq. (4-19) occurs when the λ's are all equal. This is termed a scalar matrix and may be written

$$\begin{bmatrix} \lambda & 0 & \cdots & 0 \\ 0 & \lambda & \cdots & 0 \\ \cdots & \cdots & \cdots & \cdots \\ 0 & 0 & \cdots & \lambda \end{bmatrix} = \lambda\mathbf{I}$$

† The scalar may be placed in front of or behind the matrix.

Another special case of a square matrix is an *idempotent* matrix. Let **A** be a square symmetric matrix, so that

$$\mathbf{A}' = \mathbf{A}$$

If **A** is idempotent, then

$$\mathbf{A} = \mathbf{A}^2 = \mathbf{A}^3 = \cdots$$

that is, multiplying **A** by itself, however many times, simply reproduces the original matrix.† As we will see later, idempotent matrices play an important role in statistical theory. An example of an idempotent matrix is

$$\mathbf{A} = \frac{1}{6}\begin{bmatrix} 1 & -2 & 1 \\ -2 & 4 & -2 \\ 1 & -2 & 1 \end{bmatrix}$$

as the reader can easily verify by multiplication.

Another important matrix is the *null matrix* **0** whose every element is zero. Obvious relations are

$$\mathbf{A} + \mathbf{0} = \mathbf{A}$$

and

$$\mathbf{A0} = \mathbf{0}$$

Similarly, we may have null row or column vectors.

Partitioned Matrices

Writing the matrix **X** in the form

$$\mathbf{X} = [\mathbf{x}_1 \quad \mathbf{x}_2 \quad \cdots \quad \mathbf{x}_k]$$

as in Eq. (4-4), is a special example of a partitioned matrix. The elements on the right-hand side are not scalars but vectors. In general a partitioned matrix contains submatrices as elements. The submatrices are obtained by partitions of the rows and columns of the original matrix. For example,

$$\mathbf{A} = \left[\begin{array}{ccc:c} 4 & 0 & 2 & -1 \\ 6 & 5 & 1 & 1 \\ \hdashline -3 & 2 & 0 & 5 \end{array}\right] = \begin{bmatrix} \mathbf{A}_{11} & \mathbf{A}_{12} \\ \mathbf{A}_{21} & \mathbf{A}_{22} \end{bmatrix} \tag{4-20}$$

where

$$\begin{aligned} \mathbf{A}_{11} &= \begin{bmatrix} 4 & 0 & 2 \\ 6 & 5 & 1 \end{bmatrix} \qquad \mathbf{A}_{12} = \begin{bmatrix} -1 \\ 1 \end{bmatrix} \\ \mathbf{A}_{21} &= [-3 \quad 2 \quad 0] \qquad \mathbf{A}_{22} = 5 \end{aligned} \tag{4-21}$$

The dashed lines indicate the partitioning, yielding the four submatrices defined in Eqs. (4-21).

† A square nonsymmetric matrix is idempotent if it satisfies $\mathbf{A}^2 = \mathbf{A}$, but we will only meet symmetric idempotent matrices in this book.

Our previous rules for the addition and multiplication of matrices apply directly to partitioned matrices *provided the submatrices are of appropriate dimension*. For example, if **A** and **B** are both written in partitioned form as

$$\mathbf{A} = \begin{bmatrix} \mathbf{A}_{11} & \mathbf{A}_{12} \\ \mathbf{A}_{21} & \mathbf{A}_{22} \end{bmatrix} \quad \text{and} \quad \mathbf{B} = \begin{bmatrix} \mathbf{B}_{11} & \mathbf{B}_{12} \\ \mathbf{B}_{21} & \mathbf{B}_{22} \end{bmatrix}$$

then

$$\mathbf{A} + \mathbf{B} = \begin{bmatrix} \mathbf{A}_{11} + \mathbf{B}_{11} & \mathbf{A}_{12} + \mathbf{B}_{12} \\ \mathbf{A}_{21} + \mathbf{B}_{21} & \mathbf{A}_{22} + \mathbf{B}_{22} \end{bmatrix}$$

provided **A** and **B** are of the same overall order (dimension) and each pair $\mathbf{A}_{ij}$, $\mathbf{B}_{ij}$ is of the same order. As an example of the multiplication of partitioned matrices,

$$\mathbf{AB} = \begin{bmatrix} \mathbf{A}_{11} & \mathbf{A}_{12} \\ \mathbf{A}_{21} & \mathbf{A}_{22} \\ \mathbf{A}_{31} & \mathbf{A}_{32} \end{bmatrix} \begin{bmatrix} \mathbf{B}_{11} & \mathbf{B}_{12} \\ \mathbf{B}_{21} & \mathbf{B}_{22} \end{bmatrix}$$

$$= \begin{bmatrix} \mathbf{A}_{11}\mathbf{B}_{11} + \mathbf{A}_{12}\mathbf{B}_{21} & \mathbf{A}_{11}\mathbf{B}_{12} + \mathbf{A}_{12}\mathbf{B}_{22} \\ \mathbf{A}_{21}\mathbf{B}_{11} + \mathbf{A}_{22}\mathbf{B}_{21} & \mathbf{A}_{21}\mathbf{B}_{12} + \mathbf{A}_{22}\mathbf{B}_{22} \\ \mathbf{A}_{31}\mathbf{B}_{11} + \mathbf{A}_{32}\mathbf{B}_{21} & \mathbf{A}_{31}\mathbf{B}_{12} + \mathbf{A}_{32}\mathbf{B}_{22} \end{bmatrix}$$

For the multiplication to be possible and for these equations to hold, the number of columns in **A** must equal the number of rows in **B** *and* the same partitioning must be applied to the columns of **A** as to the rows of **B**.

Summary on Matrix Operations

The main results of this section are summarized as follows:

1. The scalar, dot, or inner product of two n-element column vectors **a** and **b** is $\mathbf{a}'\mathbf{b} = \mathbf{b}'\mathbf{a} = \sum_{i=1}^{n} a_i b_i$.
2. The typical i, jth element in the product **AB**, where the matrices are conformable for multiplication, is $\sum_s a_{is} b_{sj}$.
3. The typical element in $\mathbf{A} + \mathbf{B}$ is $a_{ij} + b_{ij}$.
4. $\mathbf{A} = \mathbf{B}$ means $a_{ij} = b_{ij}$ for all i, j.
5. $(\mathbf{AB})' = \mathbf{B}'\mathbf{A}'$, $(\mathbf{ABC})' = \mathbf{C}'\mathbf{B}'\mathbf{A}'$.
6. $(\mathbf{A} + \mathbf{B}) + \mathbf{C} = \mathbf{A} + (\mathbf{B} + \mathbf{C})$.
7. $(\mathbf{AB})\mathbf{C} = \mathbf{A}(\mathbf{BC})$.
8. $\mathbf{A}(\mathbf{B} + \mathbf{C}) = \mathbf{AB} + \mathbf{AC}$.
9. $\mathbf{IA} = \mathbf{AI} = \mathbf{A}$.
10. The typical element in cA, where c is a scalar, is ca_{ij}.
11. $\mathbf{A} + \mathbf{0} = \mathbf{0}$.
12. $\mathbf{A0} = \mathbf{0A} = \mathbf{0}$.

11. A + 0 = A

4-2 MATRIX FORMULATION OF THE LEAST-SQUARES PROBLEM

Returning again to the linear model $\mathbf{y} = \mathbf{X}\boldsymbol{\beta} + \mathbf{u}$, this may be written in the form

$$\mathbf{y} = [\mathbf{x}_1 \quad \mathbf{x}_2 \quad \cdots \quad \mathbf{x}_k]\begin{bmatrix} \beta_1 \\ \beta_2 \\ \vdots \\ \beta_k \end{bmatrix} + \mathbf{u}$$

that is,

$$\mathbf{y} = \beta_1\mathbf{x}_1 + \beta_2\mathbf{x}_2 + \cdots + \beta_k\mathbf{x}_k + \mathbf{u} \tag{4-22}$$

Equation (4-22) states that the observed $\mathbf{y}$ vector is the sum of the disturbance vector $\mathbf{u}$ and a *linear combination* of the columns of $\mathbf{X}$. If we replace the unknown β's in Eq. (4-22) by guesses or estimates denoted by $b_1, b_2, \ldots, b_k$, then for the tth observation we have an observed value Y_t and a calculated value

$$b_1 X_{1t} + b_2 X_{2t} + \cdots + b_k X_{kt}$$

The difference between these two values defines a residual or error term,

$$e_t = Y_t - b_1 X_{1t} - \cdots - b_k X_{kt}$$

Repeating the procedure for all sample points gives

$$\mathbf{y} = b_1\mathbf{x}_1 + b_2\mathbf{x}_2 + \cdots + b_k\mathbf{x}_k + \mathbf{e} = \mathbf{X}\mathbf{b} + \mathbf{e} \tag{4-23}$$

where $\mathbf{b}$ is a k-element coefficient vector and $\mathbf{e}$ is an n-element vector of residuals.

The least-squares principle states that the b's in Eq. (4-23) should be chosen to minimize the sum of the squared residuals. This sum of squared residuals is

$$\mathbf{e}'\mathbf{e} = [e_1 \quad e_2 \quad \cdots \quad e_n]\begin{bmatrix} e_1 \\ e_2 \\ \vdots \\ e_n \end{bmatrix} = e_1^2 + e_2^2 + \cdots + e_n^2$$

From Eq. (4-23),

$$\mathbf{e} = \mathbf{y} - \mathbf{X}\mathbf{b}$$

Hence

$$\begin{aligned} \mathbf{e}'\mathbf{e} &= (\mathbf{y} - \mathbf{X}\mathbf{b})'(\mathbf{y} - \mathbf{X}\mathbf{b}) \\ &= (\mathbf{y}' - \mathbf{b}'\mathbf{X}')(\mathbf{y} - \mathbf{X}\mathbf{b}) \\ &= \mathbf{y}'\mathbf{y} - \mathbf{b}'\mathbf{X}'\mathbf{y} - \mathbf{y}'\mathbf{X}\mathbf{b} + \mathbf{b}'\mathbf{X}'\mathbf{X}\mathbf{b} \\ &= \mathbf{y}'\mathbf{y} - 2\mathbf{b}'\mathbf{X}'\mathbf{y} + \mathbf{b}'\mathbf{X}'\mathbf{X}\mathbf{b} \end{aligned} \tag{4-24}$$

since $\mathbf{y}'\mathbf{X}\mathbf{b}$ is a scalar and so is equal to its transpose $\mathbf{b}'\mathbf{X}'\mathbf{y}$. Once the sample data have been obtained, $\mathbf{y}$ and $\mathbf{X}$ consist of known numbers. Thus Eq. (4-24) expresses $\mathbf{e}'\mathbf{e}$ as a function of the unknown $\mathbf{b}$ vector,

$$\mathbf{e}'\mathbf{e} = f(\mathbf{b}) \tag{4-25}$$

and, treating the elements of **b** as *variables*, we have to minimize **e′e** with respect to **b**. This requires some elementary results on matrix differentiation.

Matrix Differentiation

If $f(\mathbf{b})$ contains, say, k different b's, then we may partially differentiate $f(\mathbf{b})$ with respect to each b_i in turn, obtaining k partial derivatives. Arranging these partial derivatives in the form of a column vector gives the general definition

$$\frac{\partial[f(\mathbf{b})]}{\partial \mathbf{b}} = \begin{bmatrix} \dfrac{\partial[f(\mathbf{b})]}{\partial b_1} \\ \dfrac{\partial[f(\mathbf{b})]}{\partial b_2} \\ \vdots \\ \dfrac{\partial[f(\mathbf{b})]}{\partial b_k} \end{bmatrix} \tag{4-26}$$

These derivatives might equally well have been arranged as a row vector. The important requirement is consistency of treatment and ensuring that vectors and matrices of derivatives that have to be added and multiplied are of appropriate order.

Suppose $f(\mathbf{b})$ is a linear function,

$$\begin{aligned} f(\mathbf{b}) &= \mathbf{a}'\mathbf{b} \\ &= a_1b_1 + a_2b_2 + \cdots + a_kb_k \end{aligned}$$

where the a's are given constants. Application of Eq. (4-26) then

$$\frac{\partial(\mathbf{a}'\mathbf{b})}{\partial \mathbf{b}} = \frac{\partial(\mathbf{b}'\mathbf{a})}{\partial \mathbf{b}} = \begin{bmatrix} a_1 \\ a_2 \\ \vdots \\ a_k \end{bmatrix} = \mathbf{a} \tag{4-27}$$

Suppose now that $f(\mathbf{b})$ is quadratic in the b's, that is,

$$f(\mathbf{b}) = \mathbf{b}'\mathbf{A}\mathbf{b}$$

This is a *quadratic form* in **b**, and we will develop the properties of quadratic forms later. Without any loss of generality we can suppose **A** to be a symmetric matrix denoted by†

$$\mathbf{A} = \begin{bmatrix} a_{11} & a_{12} & \cdots & a_{1k} \\ a_{12} & a_{22} & \cdots & a_{2k} \\ \cdots & \cdots & \cdots & \cdots \\ a_{1k} & a_{2k} & \cdots & a_{kk} \end{bmatrix}$$

† If **A** were not symmetric, define $\mathbf{A}^* = (\mathbf{A} + \mathbf{A}')/2$. Then $\mathbf{b}'\mathbf{A}\mathbf{b} = \mathbf{b}'\mathbf{A}\mathbf{b}/2 + \mathbf{b}'\mathbf{A}\mathbf{b}/2 = \mathbf{b}'\mathbf{A}\mathbf{b}/2 + \mathbf{b}'\mathbf{A}'\mathbf{b}/2$, on transposing the second $\mathbf{b}'\mathbf{A}\mathbf{b}$. Thus

$$\mathbf{b}'\mathbf{A}\mathbf{b} = \mathbf{b}'\frac{\mathbf{A} + \mathbf{A}'}{2}\mathbf{b} = \mathbf{b}'\mathbf{A}^*\mathbf{b}$$

Then

$$\begin{aligned}\mathbf{b'Ab} = a_{11}b_1^2 &+ 2a_{12}b_1b_2 + 2a_{13}b_1b_3 + \cdots + 2a_{1k}b_1b_k \\ &+ \quad a_{22}b_2^2 \quad + 2a_{23}b_2b_3 + \cdots + 2a_{2k}b_2b_k \\ &\qquad\qquad \ddots \qquad\qquad\qquad\qquad \vdots \\ &\qquad\qquad\qquad\qquad\qquad\qquad + \quad a_{kk}b_k^2\end{aligned}$$

Taking partial derivatives,

$$\frac{\partial(\mathbf{b'Ab})}{\partial b_1} = 2(a_{11}b_1 + a_{12}b_2 + \cdots + a_{1k}b_k) = 2\mathbf{a}_1\mathbf{b}$$

$$\cdots\cdots\cdots\cdots\cdots\cdots\cdots\cdots\cdots\cdots\cdots\cdots$$

$$\frac{\partial(\mathbf{b'Ab})}{\partial b_k} = 2(a_{1k}b_1 + a_{2k}b_2 + \cdots + a_{kk}b_k) = 2\mathbf{a}_k\mathbf{b}$$

where the **a**'s indicate the rows of **A**. Collecting these partial derivatives in a column vector,

$$\frac{\partial(\mathbf{b'Ab})}{\partial \mathbf{b}} = 2\begin{bmatrix}\mathbf{a}_1\mathbf{b} \\ \mathbf{a}_2\mathbf{b} \\ \vdots \\ \mathbf{a}_k\mathbf{b}\end{bmatrix} = 2\begin{bmatrix}\mathbf{a}_1 \\ \mathbf{a}_2 \\ \vdots \\ \mathbf{a}_k\end{bmatrix}\mathbf{b} = 2\mathbf{Ab} \tag{4-28}$$

Equations (4-27) and (4-28) give the standard results on the differentiation of linear and quadratic forms. Notice the parallel with the differentiation of scalar functions in that the power of the variable is reduced by 1 so that it disappears on differentiation of the linear form and appears linearly on differentiation of the quadratic form.

These two results may now be applied directly to minimize the residual sum of squares defined in Eq. (4-24).

$$\frac{\partial(\mathbf{b'X'y})}{\partial \mathbf{b}} = \mathbf{X'y}$$

using Eq. (4-27), since $\mathbf{X'y}$ is just a known k-element vector. Also

$$\frac{\partial(\mathbf{b'X'Xb})}{\partial \mathbf{b}} = 2(\mathbf{X'X})\mathbf{b}$$

using Eq. (4-28). Thus

$$\frac{\partial(\mathbf{e'e})}{\partial \mathbf{b}} = -2\mathbf{X'y} + 2\mathbf{X'Xb}$$

For a stationary value of the sum of squares all k partial derivatives must be zero, that is,

$$\frac{\partial(\mathbf{e'e})}{\partial \mathbf{b}} = \mathbf{0}$$

and so

$$(\mathbf{X}'\mathbf{X})\mathbf{b} = \mathbf{X}'\mathbf{y} \tag{4-29}$$

These are the *normal equations* for the least-squares regression, and include the equations for the two- and three-variable cases already derived in Chaps. 2 and 3.

Example 4-5 Two-variable regression For the two-variable regression the **X** matrix is

$$\mathbf{X} = \begin{bmatrix} 1 & X_1 \\ 1 & X_2 \\ \cdots & \cdots \\ 1 & X_n \end{bmatrix}$$

Thus

$$\mathbf{X}'\mathbf{X} = \begin{bmatrix} n & \Sigma X \\ \Sigma X & \Sigma X^2 \end{bmatrix} \quad \text{and} \quad \mathbf{X}'\mathbf{y} = \begin{bmatrix} \Sigma Y \\ \Sigma XY \end{bmatrix}$$

So Eq. (4-29) gives

$$nb_1 + b_2\Sigma X = \Sigma Y$$

$$b_1\Sigma X + b_2\Sigma X^2 = \Sigma XY$$

which are identical with Eqs. (2-13).

Example 4-6 Three-variable regression In this case

$$\mathbf{X}'\mathbf{X} = \begin{bmatrix} n & \Sigma X_2 & \Sigma X_3 \\ \Sigma X_2 & \Sigma X_2^2 & \Sigma X_2 X_3 \\ \Sigma X_3 & \Sigma X_2 X_3 & \Sigma X_3^2 \end{bmatrix}$$

and

$$\mathbf{X}'\mathbf{y} = \begin{bmatrix} \Sigma Y \\ \Sigma X_2 Y \\ \Sigma X_3 Y \end{bmatrix}$$

which, on substitution in Eq. (4-29), yield Eq. (3-62).

4-3 GEOMETRIC INTERPRETATION OF LEAST SQUARES

In many problems it is often helpful to have a geometric as well as an algebraic interpretation. We will thus introduce some basic notions on the geometry of vectors.

Consider a two-element vector

$$\mathbf{a} = \begin{bmatrix} 2 \\ 1 \end{bmatrix}$$

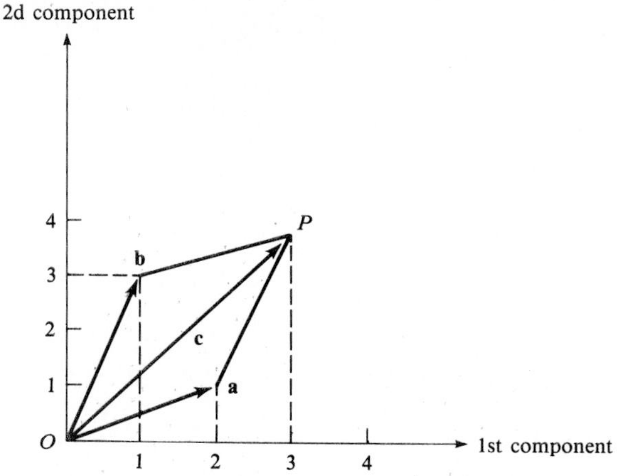

Figure 4-1

This may be pictured as a *directed line segment*, as shown in Fig. 4-1. The arrow denoting the segment starts at the origin and ends at the point with coordinates (2, 1). The vector **a** may also be indicated by the point at which the arrow terminates. If we have another vector, say, **b**,

$$\mathbf{b} = \begin{bmatrix} 1 \\ 3 \end{bmatrix}$$

the geometry of vector addition is conceived as follows. Start with **a** and then place the **b** vector at the terminal point of the **a** vector. This takes us to the point P in Fig. 4-1. This point defines the vector **c** as the sum of vectors **a** and **b**, and it is obviously also reached by starting with the **b** vector and placing the **a** vector at its terminal point. The process is referred to as completing the parallelogram, or as *the parallelogram law for the addition of vectors*. Clearly, the coordinates of P are (3, 4), and

$$\mathbf{c} = \mathbf{a} + \mathbf{b} = \begin{bmatrix} 2 \\ 1 \end{bmatrix} + \begin{bmatrix} 1 \\ 3 \end{bmatrix} = \begin{bmatrix} 3 \\ 4 \end{bmatrix}$$

so that there is an exact correspondence between the geometric and the algebraic treatments.

Now consider scalar multiplication of a vector. For example,

$$2\mathbf{a} = 2\begin{bmatrix} 2 \\ 1 \end{bmatrix} = \begin{bmatrix} 4 \\ 2 \end{bmatrix}$$

gives a vector in exactly the same direction as **a**, but of twice the length. The scalar multiplier may also be a negative number. For example,

$$-3\mathbf{a} = \begin{bmatrix} -6 \\ -3 \end{bmatrix}$$

These two vectors are shown along with **a** itself in Fig. 4-2. Clearly, all three terminal points lie on a single line through the origin, that line being uniquely defined by the vector **a**.

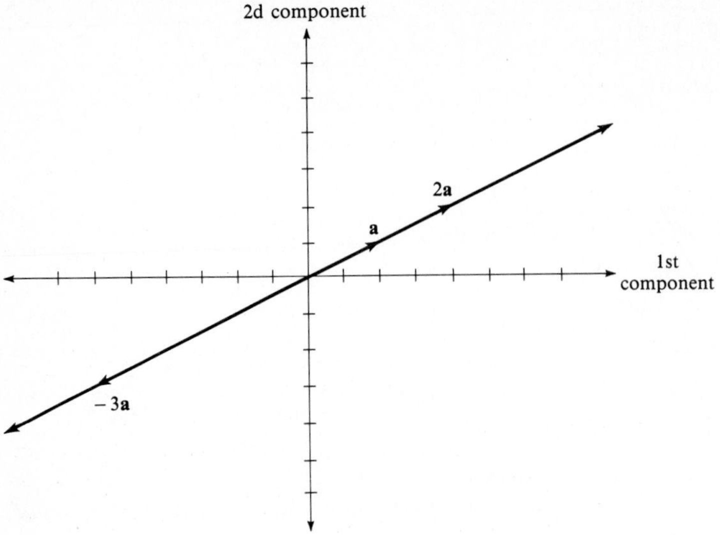

Figure 4-2

Combining the two operations of scalar multiplication and addition of vectors enables us to represent *any* two-element vector as a *linear combination* of the vectors **a** and **b**. If **c** denotes any arbitrary vector and it is to be represented as a linear combination of **a** and **b**, then we may write

$$\mathbf{c} = \lambda_1\mathbf{a} + \lambda_2\mathbf{b} \tag{4-30}$$

where λ_1 and λ_2 are appropriate scalars. As an illustration of Eq. (4-30) consider the following examples:

1. $\mathbf{c} = \begin{bmatrix} 4 \\ 0 \end{bmatrix}$

   may be expressed as

$$\mathbf{c} = 2\frac{2}{5}\begin{bmatrix} 2 \\ 1 \end{bmatrix} - \frac{4}{5}\begin{bmatrix} 1 \\ 3 \end{bmatrix}$$

   giving $\lambda_1 = 2\frac{2}{5}$ and $\lambda_2 = -\frac{4}{5}$. These values of λ_1 and λ_2 may be obtained graphically by sketching in the parallelogram whose main diagonal gives the **c** vector and then measuring the sides of the parallelogram in relation to **a** and **b**. Alternatively, one may solve the pair of simultaneous equations

$$\lambda_1\begin{bmatrix} 2 \\ 1 \end{bmatrix} + \lambda_2\begin{bmatrix} 1 \\ 3 \end{bmatrix} = \begin{bmatrix} 2\lambda_1 + \lambda_2 \\ \lambda_1 + 3\lambda_2 \end{bmatrix} = \begin{bmatrix} 4 \\ 0 \end{bmatrix}$$

2. $\mathbf{c} = \begin{bmatrix} 6 \\ 3 \end{bmatrix}$

   may be expressed as

$$\mathbf{c} = 3\begin{bmatrix} 2 \\ 1 \end{bmatrix} + 0\begin{bmatrix} 1 \\ 3 \end{bmatrix}$$

   giving $\lambda_1 = 3$ and $\lambda_2 = 0$.

3. $\mathbf{c} = \begin{bmatrix} 6 \\ 8 \end{bmatrix}$

   may be expressed as

$$\mathbf{c} = 2\begin{bmatrix} 2 \\ 1 \end{bmatrix} + 2\begin{bmatrix} 1 \\ 3 \end{bmatrix}$$

   giving $\lambda_1 = 2$ and $\lambda_2 = 2$.

We are now in a position to define a *vector space*. A vector space is a collection of vectors with the following properties:

1. If $\mathbf{v}_1$ and $\mathbf{v}_2$ are any two vectors in the space, then $\mathbf{v}_1 + \mathbf{v}_2$ is in the space.
2. If $\mathbf{v}$ is in the space and λ is a scalar constant, then $\lambda\mathbf{v}$ is in the space.

The set of vectors is said to be *closed* under addition and scalar multiplication, for these operations do not produce a vector outside the space.

Let us denote the two-dimensional space by the symbol $\mathcal{R}^2$. This vector space consists of all real two-element vectors. Clearly, any vector in the space can be expressed as a linear combination of the two vectors **a** and **b**. Our specification of **a** and **b**, however, was arbitrary. Consider another pair of vectors

$$\mathbf{e}_1 = \begin{bmatrix} 1 \\ 0 \end{bmatrix} \quad \text{and} \quad \mathbf{e}_2 = \begin{bmatrix} 0 \\ 1 \end{bmatrix}$$

These are usually described as unit vectors, and again any vector **c** in $\mathcal{R}^2$ may be expressed as a linear combination of these vectors, only now the determination of the λ's is particularly simple. The three previous numerical examples in this case give

1. $\begin{bmatrix} 4 \\ 0 \end{bmatrix} = 4\begin{bmatrix} 1 \\ 0 \end{bmatrix} + 0\begin{bmatrix} 0 \\ 1 \end{bmatrix}$ so $\lambda_1 = 4, \lambda_2 = 0$
2. $\begin{bmatrix} 6 \\ 3 \end{bmatrix} = 6\begin{bmatrix} 1 \\ 0 \end{bmatrix} + 3\begin{bmatrix} 0 \\ 1 \end{bmatrix}$ so $\lambda_1 = 6, \lambda_2 = 3$
3. $\begin{bmatrix} 6 \\ 8 \end{bmatrix} = 6\begin{bmatrix} 1 \\ 0 \end{bmatrix} + 8\begin{bmatrix} 0 \\ 1 \end{bmatrix}$ so $\lambda_1 = 6, \lambda_2 = 8$

so that the λ's are read off directly as the elements of the **c** vector.

Each pair of vectors in these examples, that is, **a**, **b**, and $\mathbf{e}_1$, $\mathbf{e}_2$, serves as a *basis* for the two-dimensional space $\mathcal{R}^2$. A basis is thus not unique. It is clear from the geometry that any two vectors can serve as a basis for $\mathcal{R}^2$ only if they *point in different directions*. If **a** and **b** point in the same direction, then one is simply a scalar multiple of the other, as in Fig. 4-2, and only further multiples of that vector can be expressed as linear combinations of **a** and **b**. The condition that the basis vectors point in different directions may also be expressed by stating that the vectors should be *linearly independent*. Two vectors **a** and **b** are said to be linearly independent if the only solution to

$$\lambda_1\mathbf{a} + \lambda_2\mathbf{b} = \mathbf{0} \tag{4-31}$$

is $\lambda_1 = 0 = \lambda_2$. If λ values can be found, at least one of which is nonzero, to satisfy Eq. (4-31), then the vectors are said to be *linearly dependent*.

As an illustration of these definitions, suppose

$$\mathbf{a} = \begin{bmatrix} 2 \\ 1 \end{bmatrix} \quad \text{and} \quad \mathbf{b} = \begin{bmatrix} 6 \\ 3 \end{bmatrix}$$

These vectors lie on the same ray through the origin, and the linear combination $3\mathbf{a} - \mathbf{b}$ yields the zero vector. However, if we revert to the original **a** and **b** vectors, namely,

$$\mathbf{a} = \begin{bmatrix} 2 \\ 1 \end{bmatrix} \quad \text{and} \quad \mathbf{b} = \begin{bmatrix} 1 \\ 3 \end{bmatrix}$$

it is impossible to find a pair of λ values, other than two zeros, such that

$$\lambda_1 \mathbf{a} + \lambda_2 \mathbf{b} = 0$$

We can easily find a pair of λ values to reduce the *first* element to zero, but the *same* combination will not reduce the second element to zero. A *basis* for $\mathcal{R}^2$ is thus defined to be any linearly independent pair of two-element vectors. It is clear from the geometry of the two-dimensional case that the representation of a given vector in terms of a given basis is *unique*, that is, there is one and only one pair of λ_1, λ_2 values which satisfy

$$\mathbf{c} = \lambda_1 \mathbf{a} + \lambda_2 \mathbf{b}$$

Given a basis $\mathbf{a}, \mathbf{b}$ for $\mathcal{R}^2$, we have seen that any vector **c** in $\mathcal{R}^2$ may be expressed as a unique linear combination of the basis vectors. Thus the vectors **a**, **b**, and **c** are linearly dependent, for the equation

$$\lambda_1 \mathbf{a} + \lambda_2 \mathbf{b} - \mathbf{c} = \mathbf{0}$$

holds for nonzero λ's. We might ask whether any arbitrary vector **v** in $\mathcal{R}^2$ may be expressed in terms of the expanded set of vectors **a**, **b**, and **c**. The answer is, of course, yes, but the coefficients will not be unique. For example, suppose that the **a**, **b**, and **c** vectors are

$$\mathbf{a} = \begin{bmatrix} 2 \\ 1 \end{bmatrix} \quad \mathbf{b} = \begin{bmatrix} 1 \\ 3 \end{bmatrix} \quad \mathbf{c} = \begin{bmatrix} 1 \\ 1 \end{bmatrix}$$

and we wish to express

$$\mathbf{v} = \begin{bmatrix} 6 \\ 8 \end{bmatrix}$$

as a linear combination of **a**, **b**, and **c**. One such combination is simply

$$\mathbf{v} = 2\mathbf{a} + 2\mathbf{b} + 0\mathbf{c}$$

but there are infinitely many others. Rewriting the general linear combination

$$\mathbf{v} = \lambda_1 \mathbf{a} + \lambda_2 \mathbf{b} + \lambda_3 \mathbf{c}$$

in the form

$$\mathbf{v} - \lambda_3 \mathbf{c} = \lambda_1 \mathbf{a} + \lambda_2 \mathbf{b}$$

any arbitrary value can be assigned to λ_3, and the left-hand side is then some specific two-element vector, which can be expressed as a linear combination of **a** and **b**. A set of vectors such as **a**, **b**, and **c** is called a *spanning set* since they span or generate the space $\mathfrak{R}^2$, that is, any vector in $\mathfrak{R}^2$ can be expressed as a linear combination of the spanning vectors. The distinction between a *basis* and a spanning set is that the basis consists of *linearly independent* vectors. A spanning set may be unnecessarily large, as in the case of the set **a**, **b**, and **c**. This spanning set can be reduced to a basis by dropping one vector.

Since linearly independent vectors point in different directions, there is then a nonzero angle between the vectors. This angle may be expressed in terms of the elements of the vectors.

Reverting to the two-dimensional **a**, **b** vectors in Fig. 4-3, let A denote the angle between the **a** vector and the horizontal axis and let B denote the angle between the **b** vector and the horizontal axis. The angle between the two vectors is

$$\theta = B - A$$

An elementary result in trigonometry states

$$\cos(B - A) = \cos B \cdot \cos A + \sin B \cdot \sin A \tag{4-32}$$

The length or *norm* of the vector **a** is, by Pythagoras's theorem, $\sqrt{a_1^2 + a_2^2}$. The length is often denoted by the symbol $\|\mathbf{a}\|$, and using the definition of the inner product in Eq. (4-8), we have

$$\|\mathbf{a}\|^2 = \mathbf{a}'\mathbf{a}$$

Likewise,

$$\|\mathbf{b}\|^2 = \mathbf{b}'\mathbf{b}$$

Substituting in Eq. (4-32) gives

$$\cos\theta = \frac{a_1 b_1}{\sqrt{\mathbf{a}'\mathbf{a}}\sqrt{\mathbf{b}'\mathbf{b}}} + \frac{a_2 b_2}{\sqrt{\mathbf{a}'\mathbf{a}}\sqrt{\mathbf{b}'\mathbf{b}}}$$

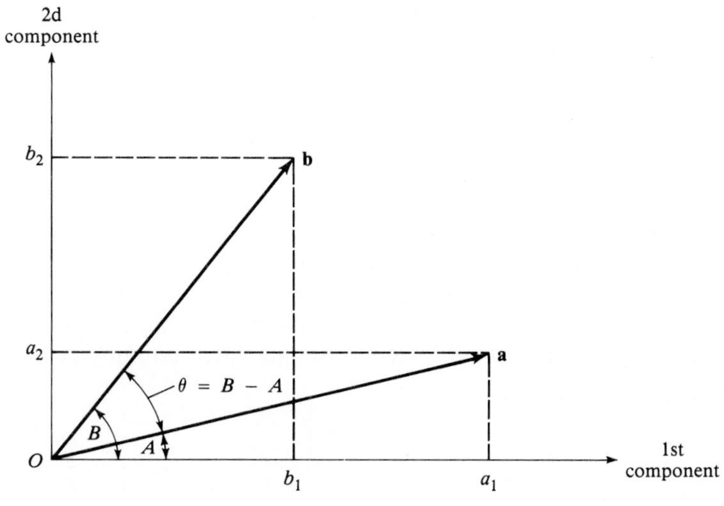

Figure 4-3

that is,

$$\cos\theta = \frac{\mathbf{a}'\mathbf{b}}{\sqrt{\mathbf{a}'\mathbf{a}}\,\sqrt{\mathbf{b}'\mathbf{b}}} \tag{4-33}$$

where it is understood that we take the positive square roots to indicate length.

There are two important special cases of Eq. (4-33). When **a** and **b** are linearly dependent, we may write

$$\mathbf{b} = \lambda\mathbf{a}$$

where λ is some appropriate scalar. The right-hand side of Eq. (4-33) then reduces to unity, giving $\theta = 0°$. When **a** and **b** are at right angles to each other, $\theta = 90°$ and $\cos\theta = 0$, giving $\mathbf{a}'\mathbf{b} = 0$. Conversely, when $\mathbf{a}'\mathbf{b} = 0$, $\theta = 90°$. Two vectors at right angles are said to be *orthogonal*. Thus two vectors are orthogonal if and only if

$$\mathbf{a}'\mathbf{b} = 0$$

Extensions to Three and Higher Dimensions

If we now consider real three-element vectors, then each vector corresponds to a point in the three-dimensional space $\mathcal{R}^3$. Any vector $\mathbf{v}$ in $\mathcal{R}^3$ may then be expressed as a unique linear combination of an appropriate set of three linearly independent vectors, which constitute a basis for $\mathcal{R}^3$. For instance, choosing

$$\mathbf{e}_1 = \begin{bmatrix} 1 \\ 0 \\ 0 \end{bmatrix} \qquad \mathbf{e}_2 = \begin{bmatrix} 0 \\ 1 \\ 0 \end{bmatrix} \qquad \mathbf{e}_3 = \begin{bmatrix} 0 \\ 0 \\ 1 \end{bmatrix}$$

as basis vectors, a vector $\mathbf{v}' = [3 \quad -2 \quad 5]$ may be written

$$\mathbf{v} = 3\mathbf{e}_1 - 2\mathbf{e}_2 + 5\mathbf{e}_3$$

If we take just two of these vectors, say, $\mathbf{e}_1$ and $\mathbf{e}_2$, then all linear combinations of $\mathbf{e}_1$ and $\mathbf{e}_2$ constitute a vector *subspace* in $\mathcal{R}^3$, namely, the horizontal plane, since the third component in each spanning vector is zero. More generally, any two three-element vectors, say,

$$\mathbf{a} = \begin{bmatrix} 1 \\ 2 \\ 3 \end{bmatrix} \qquad \text{and} \qquad \mathbf{b} = \begin{bmatrix} 5 \\ 1 \\ 1 \end{bmatrix}$$

span or generate a plane surface, as indicated in Fig. 4-4, by the plane containing $0ab$.

The set of all real n-element vectors constitutes the space $\mathcal{R}^n$. Each vector in $\mathcal{R}^n$ may be expressed as a unique linear combination of some appropriate set of n linearly independent vectors. To see that the linear combination must be unique, suppose that a vector $\mathbf{v}$ can be expressed as two different linear combinations of the basis vector $\mathbf{v}_1, \mathbf{v}_2, \ldots, \mathbf{v}_n$, namely,

$$\mathbf{v} = \lambda_1\mathbf{v}_1 + \lambda_2\mathbf{v}_2 + \cdots + \lambda_n\mathbf{v}_n$$

and

$$\mathbf{v} = \mu_1\mathbf{v}_1 + \mu_2\mathbf{v}_2 + \cdots + \mu_n\mathbf{v}_n$$

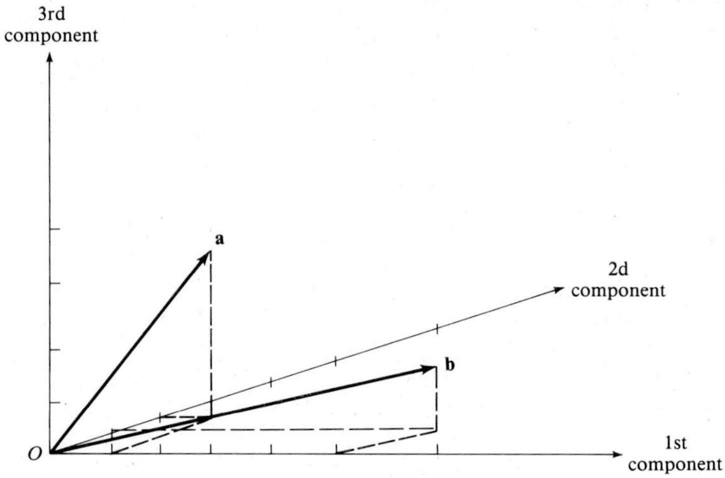

Figure 4-4

Subtracting one equation from the other gives

$$\mathbf{0} = (\lambda_1 - \mu_1)\mathbf{v}_1 + (\lambda_2 - \mu_2)\mathbf{v}_2 + \cdots + (\lambda_n - \mu_n)\mathbf{v}_n$$

But the basis vectors are linearly independent and so

$$\lambda_1 - \mu_1 = \lambda_2 - \mu_2 = \cdots = \lambda_n - \mu_n = 0$$

and the representation is unique. If we take a set of k $(< n)$ linearly independent n-element vectors, these generate a *subspace* of $\mathcal{R}^n$, which is termed a *hyperplane*. The *dimension* of this subspace is the number of linearly independent vectors spanning the subspace. The parallelogram law of addition and the cosine law of Eq. (4-33) apply to the general case of n-element vectors. We can thus conceive of a set of *mutually orthogonal* vectors $\mathbf{v}_1, \mathbf{v}_2, \ldots, \mathbf{v}_k$ if

$$\mathbf{v}_i'\mathbf{v}_j = 0 \qquad \text{for all } i, j, i \neq j$$

We are now in a position to complete the geometric treatment of the least-squares problem. The matrix

$$\mathbf{X} = [\mathbf{x}_1 \quad \mathbf{x}_2 \quad \cdots \quad \mathbf{x}_k]$$

consists of k n-element column vectors, where, by assumption, we have more observations than variables, so that $n > k$. The columns of $\mathbf{X}$ span a subspace in $\mathcal{R}^n$. The dimension of the subspace cannot exceed k and will only be equal to k if the columns of $\mathbf{X}$ are linearly independent. We refer to this subspace as the *column space* of $\mathbf{X}$. It is highly unlikely that the $\mathbf{y}$ vector lies in the column space of $\mathbf{X}$. If it did, $\mathbf{y}$ could then be expressed *exactly* as a linear combination of the $\mathbf{x}$ vectors, giving zero residuals at all sample observations. The general case is depicted in Fig. 4-5, where $\mathbf{y}$ lies outside the column space of $\mathbf{X}$.

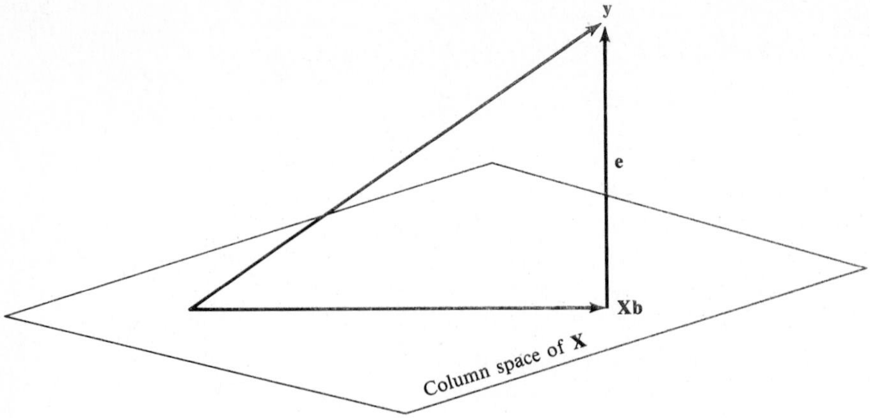

Figure 4-5

Assigning arbitrary b's to the $\mathbf{x}$ vectors gives

$$\mathbf{Xb} = [\mathbf{x}_1 \quad \mathbf{x}_2 \quad \cdots \quad \mathbf{x}_k] \begin{bmatrix} b_1 \\ b_2 \\ \vdots \\ b_k \end{bmatrix} = b_1\mathbf{x}_1 + b_2\mathbf{x}_2 + \cdots + b_k\mathbf{x}_k$$

which is then a vector that lies in the column space of $\mathbf{X}$. Choosing different $\mathbf{b}$ vectors gives, in turn, different $\mathbf{Xb}$ vectors. To each such $\mathbf{Xb}$ vector there corresponds a vector of residuals $\mathbf{e}$, so that the equation

$$\mathbf{Y} = \mathbf{Xb} + \mathbf{e}$$

as Fig. 4-5 shows, gives $\mathbf{y}$ as the sum of two vectors, of which one, $\mathbf{Xb}$, lies in the space spanned by the columns of $\mathbf{X}$ and the other, $\mathbf{e}$, lies outside that column space.

We wish to choose the $\mathbf{b}$ vector so as to make the point given by the tip of the $\mathbf{Xb}$ vector as close as possible to the tip of the $\mathbf{y}$ vector or, in other words, to minimize the length of the $\mathbf{e}$ vector. This is achieved by making the $\mathbf{e}$ vector perpendicular to the hyperplane generated by the columns of $\mathbf{X}$. Thus $\mathbf{e}$ must be orthogonal to any linear combination of the columns of $\mathbf{X}$. We have

$$\mathbf{e} = \mathbf{y} - \mathbf{Xb}$$

and $\mathbf{Xc}$ is any arbitrary linear combination of the columns of $\mathbf{X}$. Thus the orthogonality condition gives

$$\mathbf{c}'\mathbf{X}'(\mathbf{y} - \mathbf{Xb}) = \mathbf{c}'(\mathbf{X}'\mathbf{y} - \mathbf{X}'\mathbf{Xb}) = 0 \tag{4-34}$$

Since $\mathbf{c}$ is any arbitrary nonnull vector, this condition gives

$$\mathbf{X}'\mathbf{y} - \mathbf{X}'\mathbf{Xb} = \mathbf{0}$$

or

$$(\mathbf{X}'\mathbf{X})\mathbf{b} = \mathbf{X}'\mathbf{y} \tag{4-35}$$

which are the least-squares normal equations derived algebraically in Eq. (4.29).†

Summary on Vector Geometry

1. A vector space is a collection of vectors with the following properties:
   a. If $\mathbf{v}_1$ and $\mathbf{v}_2$ are any two vectors in the space, then $\mathbf{v}_1 + \mathbf{v}_2$ is in the space.
   b. If $\mathbf{v}$ is in the space and λ is a scalar, then $\lambda\mathbf{v}$ is in the space.
2. If the only solution to $\lambda_1\mathbf{a} + \lambda_2\mathbf{b} = \mathbf{0}$ is $\lambda_1 = 0 = \lambda_2$, then $\mathbf{a}$ and $\mathbf{b}$ are *linearly independent* vectors. Otherwise they are linearly dependent. In general if the only solution to $\lambda_1\mathbf{x}_1 + \lambda_2\mathbf{x}_2 + \cdots + \lambda_n\mathbf{x}_n = 0$ is $\lambda_1 = \lambda_2 = \cdots = \lambda_n = 0$, the n vectors are said to be linearly independent. If at least one λ is nonzero, they are linearly dependent.
3. A basis for $\mathcal{R}^2$ is any linearly independent pair of two-element vectors. Likewise, a basis for $\mathcal{R}^3$ is any three linearly independent three-element vectors.
4. Each vector in a space may be expressed as a unique linear combination of a set of basis vectors, and the minimum number in such a set is the *dimension* of the space.
5. The angle θ between vectors $\mathbf{a}$ and $\mathbf{b}$ is defined by

$$\cos\theta = \frac{\mathbf{a}'\mathbf{b}}{\sqrt{\mathbf{a}'\mathbf{a}}\sqrt{\mathbf{b}'\mathbf{b}}}$$

6. Two vectors are orthogonal when $\mathbf{a}'\mathbf{b} = 0$ ($\theta = 90°$).

4-4 SOLUTION OF SETS OF EQUATIONS

The next problem is how to solve Eq. (4-35) for the desired least-squares coefficients $\mathbf{b}$. From the original definitions the dimensions of Eq. (4-35) are as follows: $\mathbf{X}'\mathbf{X}$ is a square matrix of order $k \times k$, and $\mathbf{b}$ and $\mathbf{X}'\mathbf{y}$ are all k-element vectors. Thus Eq. (4-35) expresses the $\mathbf{X}'\mathbf{y}$ vector as a linear combination of the columns of $\mathbf{X}'\mathbf{X}$, and $\mathbf{b}$ indicates the coefficients of that linear combination. If the columns of $\mathbf{X}'\mathbf{X}$ are linearly independent, they constitute a basis for $\mathcal{R}^k$, and any k-element vector, such as $\mathbf{X}'\mathbf{y}$, may then be expressed *uniquely* in terms of the basis vectors. In other words, Eq. (4-35) has a unique solution for the $\mathbf{b}$ vector.

The solution of Eq. (4-35) for $\mathbf{b}$ may be expressed in terms of an *inverse matrix*. The meaning of an inverse matrix may be developed as follows. Let $\mathbf{A}$ be a square matrix of order n and let the n columns of $\mathbf{A}$ form a linearly independent set. Does a square matrix $\mathbf{B}$ of order n exist such that

$$\mathbf{AB} = \mathbf{I}? \tag{4-36}$$

† A vector such as $\mathbf{e}$, which is orthogonal to every vector on the hyperplane generated by the columns of $\mathbf{X}$, is said to be *normal* to the hyperplane—hence the term *normal equations*.

The answer is yes. Letting $\mathbf{b}_1$ denote the first column in $\mathbf{B}$ and equating first columns on both sides of Eq. (4-36) gives the vector equation

$$\mathbf{A}\mathbf{b}_1 = \mathbf{e}_1 \tag{4-37}$$

where $\mathbf{e}_1' = [1 \quad 0 \quad 0 \quad \cdots \quad 0]$. Since the columns of $\mathbf{A}$ are linearly independent, the vector $\mathbf{e}_1$ can be expressed as a *unique* linear combination of those columns. Thus $\mathbf{b}_1$ is uniquely determined. By a similar argument each column of $\mathbf{B}$ is uniquely determined, and so there is a matrix $\mathbf{B}$ satisfying Eq. (4-36).

We shall see later in this section that if the n columns of $\mathbf{A}$ are linearly independent, then so are the n rows. Then by a similar argument, a square matrix $\mathbf{C}$ of order n can be found such that

$$\mathbf{CA} = \mathbf{I} \tag{4-38}$$

for each row of $\mathbf{C}$ is uniquely determined as the coefficients of a linear combination of the rows of $\mathbf{A}$. Thus Eqs. (4-36) and (4-38) are both true. Postmultiplying Eq. (4-38) by $\mathbf{B}$ gives

$$\mathbf{CAB} = \mathbf{IB} = \mathbf{B}$$

But

$$\mathbf{CAB} = \mathbf{CI} = \mathbf{C}$$

using Eq. (4-36). Thus

$$\mathbf{C} = \mathbf{B}$$

Thus if the n columns (and rows) of $\mathbf{A}$ are linearly independent, a *unique* square matrix of order n exists, called the inverse of $\mathbf{A}$, and denoted by $\mathbf{A}^{-1}$, such that

$$\mathbf{AA}^{-1} = \mathbf{A}^{-1}\mathbf{A} = \mathbf{I} \tag{4-39}$$

If we assume that the k columns of $\mathbf{X'X}$ are linearly independent, then the inverse matrix $(\mathbf{X'X})^{-1}$ exists. Premultiplying both sides of Eq. (4-35) by this inverse gives

$$\mathbf{b} = (\mathbf{X'X})^{-1}\mathbf{X'y} \tag{4-40}$$

This expresses the least-squares vector $\mathbf{b}$ in terms of the sample data incorporated in $\mathbf{X}$ and $\mathbf{y}$. Equations (4-35) and (4-40) are two equivalent ways of expressing the vector of least-squares coefficients $\mathbf{b}$. Two distinct issues arise with respect to these equations. First, there is the *numerical*, or *computational*, question of how best to compute $\mathbf{b}$ for given $\mathbf{X}$ and $\mathbf{y}$. Second, there is a set of theoretical questions about inverse matrices like $(\mathbf{X'X})^{-1}$, such as, how are the elements of the inverse defined and what are the properties of inverse matrices? Our main interest lies with the second group of questions, though we will give some illustrations of numerical solution methods. We have defined the inverse $(\mathbf{X'X})^{-1}$ to exist when the columns of $\mathbf{X'X}$ are linearly independent. This concept is intimately related to the concept of the *rank* of a matrix, and it is to this topic that we now turn.

Rank of a Matrix

Consider any arbitrary matrix $\mathbf{A}$ of order $m \times n$. The columns of $\mathbf{A}$ define n vectors in $\mathcal{R}^m$. Likewise, the rows in $\mathbf{A}$ define m vectors in $\mathcal{R}^n$. Let r denote the maximum number of linearly independent rows in **A**, so that $r \leq m$. When r is strictly less than m, there may, of course, be more than one subset of row vectors which are linearly independent. For example, suppose we have a matrix with four rows ($m = 4$). It may be that rows 1, 2, and 4 form a linearly independent set and that rows 1, 3, and 4 also form a linearly independent set, but that all four rows are linearly dependent. In this case $r = 3$. Returning to the general matrix **A**, let us form a new matrix $\tilde{\mathbf{A}}$ by taking any set of r linearly independent rows and discarding the remaining $m - r$ rows. $\tilde{\mathbf{A}}$ is then of order $r \times n$. Let c indicate the maximum number of linearly independent columns in **A**. Then c must also indicate the maximum number of linearly independent columns in $\tilde{\mathbf{A}}$. Each column in $\tilde{\mathbf{A}}$ has r elements. Thus we have immediately that

$$c \leq r$$

for any vector in $\mathcal{R}^r$ may be expressed as a linear combination of r linearly independent vectors.

Reversing this argument we might form a matrix $\tilde{\tilde{\mathbf{A}}}$ of order $m \times c$ by retaining a subset of c linearly independent columns of **A** and discarding the remaining $n - c$ columns. Since r is defined as the maximum number of linearly independent rows in **A**, it also denotes the maximum number of linearly independent rows in $\tilde{\tilde{\mathbf{A}}}$. But since each row in $\tilde{\tilde{\mathbf{A}}}$ has just c elements, we have

$$r \leq c$$

Thus

$$r = c$$

that is, for any $m \times n$ matrix **A** *the maximum number of linearly independent rows is equal to the maximum number of linearly independent columns*. This number is defined to be the *rank* of the matrix, and we will denote the rank of **A** by the symbol

$$\rho(\mathbf{A})$$

Example 4-7 Consider

$$\mathbf{A} = \begin{bmatrix} 1 & 2 & 3 & 4 \\ 1 & 0 & 1 & 1 \\ 2 & 2 & 4 & 5 \end{bmatrix}$$

By inspection rows 1 and 2 are linearly independent; also rows 1 and 3 are linearly independent, but row 1 + row 2 − row 3 gives the zero vector, so all three rows are linearly dependent. Thus $r = 2$. Let us form a matrix $\tilde{\mathbf{A}}$ by discarding the third row of **A**. Thus

$$\tilde{\mathbf{A}} = \begin{bmatrix} 1 & 2 & 3 & 4 \\ 1 & 0 & 1 & 1 \end{bmatrix}$$

Clearly, all pairs of columns of $\tilde{\mathbf{A}}$ are linearly independent. Thus c is at least equal to 2. But it cannot exceed 2, for any column in $\tilde{\mathbf{A}}$ can be expressed as a linear combination of a pair of columns. For example,

$$\text{col } 3 = \text{col } 1 + \text{col } 2$$
$$\text{col } 4 = \text{col } 1 + 1.5 \text{ col } 2$$
$$\text{col } 1 = 3 \text{ col } 3 - 2 \text{ col } 4$$

and so on. Thus $r = c = 2 = \rho(\mathbf{A})$. Alternatively, if we commence with the columns of **A**, we cannot find a set of *three* linearly independent columns because the relations stated above for the columns of $\tilde{\mathbf{A}}$ also hold for the columns of the full matrix **A**, as readers should verify for themselves.

It is obvious that the rank of a matrix cannot exceed the number of columns or the number of rows, whichever is the smaller. That is,

$$\rho(\mathbf{A}) \leq \min(m, n) \tag{4-41}$$

When $\rho(\mathbf{A}) = m$, we say that the matrix has *full row rank*, and when $\rho(\mathbf{A}) = n$, that it has *full column rank*, but, of course, in any specific case, row rank and column rank are identical, and we speak unambiguously of the rank of the matrix.

Notice that it follows directly from the definition of rank that the rank of the transpose of **A** is equal to the rank of **A**, that is,

$$\rho(\mathbf{A}') = \rho(\mathbf{A}) \tag{4-42}$$

$$\begin{aligned} \text{for } \rho(\mathbf{A}') &= \text{number of linearly independent columns (rows) in } \mathbf{A}' \\ &= \text{number of linearly independent rows (columns) in } \mathbf{A} \\ &= \rho(\mathbf{A}) \end{aligned}$$

In the special case where **A** is a *square* matrix of order n and rank n, then **A** is said to be *nonsingular*, and a unique inverse $\mathbf{A}^{-1}$ exists, such that

$$\mathbf{A}\mathbf{A}^{-1} = \mathbf{A}^{-1}\mathbf{A} = \mathbf{I}_n$$

When the rank of **A** is less than n, **A** is said to be a *singular* matrix and its inverse does not exist.

Returning now to the general case of an $m \times n$ matrix **A**, let us suppose $\rho(\mathbf{A}) = r$. Thus there is *at least* one set of r linearly independent rows and at least one set of r linearly independent columns. If necessary, rows and columns may be interchanged so that the first r rows and the first r columns are linearly independent. The matrix may then be partitioned by the first r rows and columns:

$$\mathbf{A} = \left[\begin{array}{c|c} \mathbf{A}_{11} & \mathbf{A}_{12} \\ \hline \mathbf{A}_{21} & \mathbf{A}_{22} \end{array}\right] \begin{array}{l} \} \; r \text{ rows} \\ \} \; m - r \text{ rows} \end{array}$$

$$\underbrace{\phantom{\mathbf{A}_{11}}}_{r \text{ columns}} \quad \underbrace{\phantom{\mathbf{A}_{12}}}_{n - r \text{ columns}}$$

Thus $\mathbf{A}_{11}$ is a square nonsingular matrix of order r. Consider now the set of homogeneous equations

$$\mathbf{A}\mathbf{x} = \mathbf{0} \tag{4-43}$$

where **x** denotes a column vector of n unknowns. The equations are said to be homogeneous because of the **0** vector on the right-hand side of Eq. (4-43). If the equations read $\mathbf{A}\mathbf{x} = \mathbf{b}$, for $\mathbf{b} \neq 0$, they are said to be nonhomogeneous. Clearly,

if $\mathbf{x}_1$ *is a solution to Eq.* (4-43), *then so is* $c\mathbf{x}_1$ *for any scalar* c,

and

if $\mathbf{x}_1$ *and* $\mathbf{x}_2$ *are two distinct solutions to Eq.* (4-43), *then* $c_1\mathbf{x}_1 + c_2\mathbf{x}_2$ *is also a solution.*

Thus the set of solutions to Eq. (4-43) constitutes a vector space called the *nullspace* of **A**. Our immediate concern is to establish the *dimension* of this nullspace (that is, the number of linearly independent vectors which span the subspace). Let us drop the last $m - r$ rows from **A** and partition **x** conformably with the columns of **A**. This gives

$$[\mathbf{A}_{11} \quad \mathbf{A}_{12}]\begin{bmatrix}\mathbf{x}_1 \\ \mathbf{x}_2\end{bmatrix} = \mathbf{0} \tag{4-44}$$

where $\mathbf{x}_1$ contains r elements and $\mathbf{x}_2$ the remaining $n - r$ elements. This gives a set of r linearly independent equations in $n \geq r$ unknowns. Rewriting as

$$\mathbf{A}_{11}\mathbf{x}_1 + \mathbf{A}_{12}\mathbf{x}_2 = \mathbf{0}$$

and premultiplying by $\mathbf{A}_{11}^{-1}$, which exists since $\mathbf{A}_{11}$ is nonsingular, gives

$$\mathbf{x}_1 = -\mathbf{A}_{11}^{-1}\mathbf{A}_{12}\mathbf{x}_2 \tag{4-45}$$

The $\mathbf{x}_2$ subvector is arbitrary or "free" in the sense that we can specify the $n - r$ elements in $\mathbf{x}_2$ at will, but for any such specification the subvector $\mathbf{x}_1$ is determined by Eq. (4-45). Using Eq. (4-45), the general solution vector to Eq. (4-44) may be written

$$\mathbf{x} = \begin{bmatrix}\mathbf{x}_1 \\ \mathbf{x}_2\end{bmatrix} = \begin{bmatrix}-\mathbf{A}_{11}^{-1}\mathbf{A}_{12} \\ \mathbf{I}_{n-r}\end{bmatrix}\mathbf{x}_2 \tag{4-46}$$

The matrix in Eq. (4-46) has n rows and $n - r$ columns. The $n - r$ columns are linearly independent. This fact is guaranteed by the presence of the $\mathbf{I}_{n-r}$ submatrix, whose columns are necessarily linearly independent. Thus Eq. (4-46) expresses all solutions to Eq. (4-44) as linear combinations of $n - r$ linearly independent n-element vectors. But any solution to Eq. (4-44) is also a solution to Eq. (4-43), for the rows that have been discarded from **A** to arrive at Eq. (4-44) are linear combinations of the rows of $[\mathbf{A}_{11} \quad \mathbf{A}_{12}]$. Any discarded row may thus be expressed in the form

$$\mathbf{c}'[\mathbf{A}_{11} \quad \mathbf{A}_{12}]$$

where $\mathbf{c}'$ is some appropriate row vector of r elements. Postmultiplying by **x** gives

$$\mathbf{c}'[\mathbf{A}_{11} \quad \mathbf{A}_{12}]\,\mathbf{x} = 0$$

since **x** satisfies Eq. (4-44). Thus each solution **x** holds for the discarded rows, and Eq. (4-46) defines the solution vector for Eq. (4-43). Thus *the nullspace of* **A** *has dimension* $n - r$. This gives the important result that for an $m \times n$ matrix **A** with rank r

$$\text{Number of columns} = \text{rank} + \text{dimension of nullspace} \tag{4-47}$$

$$n = r + (n - r)$$

The nullspace is sometimes referred to as the *kernel* of **A** and its dimension as the *nullity*. Thus the result may also be stated as

$$\text{Number of columns} = \text{rank} + \text{nullity}$$

Example 4-8 Consider

$$\underset{\mathbf{A}}{\begin{bmatrix} 1 & 2 & 3 & 4 \\ 1 & 2 & 1 & 1 \\ 2 & 4 & 4 & 5 \end{bmatrix}} \underset{\mathbf{x}}{\begin{bmatrix} x_1 \\ x_2 \\ x_3 \\ x_4 \end{bmatrix}} = \underset{\mathbf{0}}{\begin{bmatrix} 0 \\ 0 \\ 0 \end{bmatrix}} \tag{4-48}$$

The rank of the matrix is seen to be 2 since rows 1 and 2 are clearly linearly independent, as are rows 1 and 3, but all three rows are not linearly independent, since

$$\text{row 1} + \text{row 2} - \text{row 3} = \mathbf{0}$$

Discarding the third row gives the set

$$\begin{bmatrix} 1 & 2 & 3 & 4 \\ 1 & 2 & 1 & 1 \end{bmatrix} \begin{bmatrix} x_1 \\ x_2 \\ x_3 \\ x_4 \end{bmatrix} = \begin{bmatrix} 0 \\ 0 \end{bmatrix} \tag{4-49}$$

Columns 1 and 3 are linearly independent, so we rewrite Eq. (4-49) as

$$\begin{bmatrix} 1 & 3 \\ 1 & 1 \end{bmatrix} \begin{bmatrix} x_1 \\ x_3 \end{bmatrix} = - \begin{bmatrix} 2 & 4 \\ 2 & 1 \end{bmatrix} \begin{bmatrix} x_2 \\ x_4 \end{bmatrix}$$

Solving this pair of equations for x_1 and x_3 gives

$$x_1 = -2x_2 + 1/2x_4$$

$$x_3 = \qquad - 3/2x_4$$

and the solution vector to Eq. (4-49) may be expressed as

$$\mathbf{x} = \begin{bmatrix} -2 & \frac{1}{2} \\ 1 & 0 \\ 0 & -\frac{3}{2} \\ 0 & 1 \end{bmatrix} \begin{bmatrix} x_2 \\ x_4 \end{bmatrix} \tag{4-50}$$

The matrix in Eq. (4-50) has two linearly independent columns, and so any solution to Eq. (4-49) may be expressed as a linear combination of two linearly independent four-element vectors. The solution vectors thus form a *two-dimensional subspace* in $\mathfrak{R}^4$. There are infinitely many solution vectors since the vector $\begin{bmatrix} x_2 \\ x_4 \end{bmatrix}$ on the right-hand side of Eq. (4-50) is arbitrary. Any solution defined by Eq. (4-50) is also a solution to the initial set of equations (4-48). This may be seen by noticing that each column vector in Eq. (4-50) satisfies the equation discarded from (4-48), that is,

$$[2 \quad 4 \quad 4 \quad 5]\begin{bmatrix} -2 \\ 1 \\ 0 \\ 0 \end{bmatrix} = 0$$

and

$$[2 \quad 4 \quad 4 \quad 5]\begin{bmatrix} \frac{1}{2} \\ 0 \\ -\frac{3}{2} \\ 1 \end{bmatrix} = 0$$

Since any solution vector **x** is a linear combination of these two column vectors, then **x** satisfies the third equation in Eqs. (4-48). Since it already satisfies the first two equations, it is a solution to Eq. (4-48). The nullspace of **A** thus has dimension 2, which is equal to the number of columns in **A** minus the rank of **A**. Each vector in the nullspace is orthogonal to each row in **A**.

There is a seeming element of arbitrariness in the partitioning that we applied to Eq. (4-49) and also in the choice of the row of **A** to be discarded. But this is apparent, not real. For example, suppose we partition Eq. (4-49) as

$$\begin{bmatrix} 3 & 4 \\ 1 & 1 \end{bmatrix}\begin{bmatrix} x_3 \\ x_4 \end{bmatrix} = -\begin{bmatrix} 1 & 2 \\ 1 & 2 \end{bmatrix}\begin{bmatrix} x_1 \\ x_2 \end{bmatrix}$$

which gives

$$\begin{aligned} x_3 &= -3x_1 - 6x_2 \\ x_4 &= \quad 2x_1 + 4x_2 \end{aligned}$$

with solution vector

$$\mathbf{x} = \begin{bmatrix} 1 & 0 \\ 0 & 1 \\ -3 & -6 \\ 2 & 4 \end{bmatrix}\begin{bmatrix} x_1 \\ x_2 \end{bmatrix} \tag{4-51}$$

Equation (4-51) again defines the nullspace of the matrix **A** in Eq. (4-48). It has dimension 2, and the columns in the matrix of Eq. (4-51) are linearly independent. This, however, is the same nullspace as defined by Eq. (4-50), for each column vector in Eq. (4-51) may be expressed as a linear combination of the column vectors in Eq. (4-50):

$$\begin{bmatrix} 1 \\ 0 \\ -3 \\ 2 \end{bmatrix} = \lambda_1\begin{bmatrix} -2 \\ 1 \\ 0 \\ 0 \end{bmatrix} + \lambda_2\begin{bmatrix} \frac{1}{2} \\ 0 \\ -\frac{3}{2} \\ 1 \end{bmatrix} \Rightarrow \lambda_1 = 0, \qquad \lambda_2 = 2$$

and

$$\begin{bmatrix} 0 \\ 1 \\ -6 \\ 4 \end{bmatrix} = \lambda_1\begin{bmatrix} -2 \\ 1 \\ 0 \\ 0 \end{bmatrix} + \lambda_2\begin{bmatrix} \frac{1}{2} \\ 0 \\ -\frac{3}{2} \\ 1 \end{bmatrix} \Rightarrow \lambda_1 = 1, \qquad \lambda_2 = 4$$

Thus the nullspaces are the same. Discarding the first or the second equation from **A** in the initial stage would also make no difference to the determination of the nullspace.

We may note here a particular application of Eq. (4-47), which will be very useful in the treatment of identification in Chap. 11. If **A** is $m \times n$ and has rank $n - 1$, then the dimension of the nullspace of **A** is 1, that is, *all solutions to*

$$\mathbf{Ax} = \mathbf{0}$$

lie on a single ray through the origin. Thus if

$$\mathbf{x}' = [x_1 \quad x_2 \quad \cdots \quad x_n]$$

is a solution, then so is

$$c\mathbf{x}' = [cx_1 \quad cx_2 \quad \cdots \quad cx_2]$$

for any constant c.

Result (4-47) also yields simple proofs of some important theorems on the ranks of various matrices. We notice that the crucial matrix for the least-squares vector in Eqs. (4-35) and (4-40) is $\mathbf{X}'\mathbf{X}$. The first important theorem states that

$$\rho(\mathbf{X}'\mathbf{X}) = \rho(\mathbf{XX}') = \rho(\mathbf{X}) \tag{4-52}$$

Let **X** be $n \times k$ with $\rho(\mathbf{X}) = r$. Then by Eq. (4-47) the nullspace of **X** has dimension $k - r$. If **m** denotes any vector in this nullspace,

$$\mathbf{Xm} = \mathbf{0}$$

Premultiplying by $\mathbf{X}'$ gives

$$\mathbf{X}'\mathbf{Xm} = \mathbf{0}$$

Thus **m** also lies in the nullspace of $\mathbf{X}'\mathbf{X}$. Let **s** be any vector in the nullspace of $\mathbf{X}'\mathbf{X}$. Then

$$\mathbf{X}'\mathbf{Xs} = \mathbf{0}$$

Premultiplying by $\mathbf{s}'$ gives

$$\mathbf{s}'\mathbf{X}'\mathbf{Xs} = (\mathbf{Xs})'(\mathbf{Xs}) = 0$$

Thus **Xs** is a vector with zero length and so must be the null vector, that is,

$$\mathbf{Xs} = \mathbf{0}$$

Thus **s** lies in the nullspace of **X**.

We have shown that **X** and $\mathbf{X}'\mathbf{X}$ have the same nullspace and hence the same nullity. Each matrix has k columns. Thus by Eq. (4-47) each matrix has rank r since

$$\text{Rank} = \text{number of columns} - \text{nullity}$$

For the least-squares case **X** is $n \times k$ with $k < n$. Provided there are no exact linear relations between the explanatory variables, **X** has full column rank, and so

$$\rho(\mathbf{X}'\mathbf{X}) = k$$

Since $\mathbf{X}'\mathbf{X}$ is a square matrix of order k, it is then nonsingular and the inverse $(\mathbf{X}'\mathbf{X})^{-1}$ exists.

To prove the rest of theorem (4-52) we merely note that $\rho(\mathbf{X}) = \rho(\mathbf{X}')$, and the above proof immediately gives

$$\rho(\mathbf{XX}') = \rho(\mathbf{X}') = \rho(\mathbf{X})$$

Notice that $\mathbf{XX}'$ is a square matrix of order n ($> k$) so that even if $\mathbf{X}$ has full column rank, $\mathbf{XX}'$ is still singular.

Another important theorem on rank may be stated as follows. If $\mathbf{A}$ is any $m \times n$ matrix with rank r, and $\mathbf{P}$ and $\mathbf{Q}$ are square nonsingular matrices of order m and n, respectively, then

$$\rho(\mathbf{PA}) = \rho(\mathbf{AQ}) = \rho(\mathbf{PAQ}) = \rho(\mathbf{A}) \tag{4-53}$$

that is, *pre- or postmultiplication of* **A** *by a nonsingular matrix does not change its rank.*

To prove $\rho(\mathbf{PA}) = \rho(\mathbf{A})$, let $\mathbf{m}$ be any vector in the nullspace of $\mathbf{A}$. Then

$$\mathbf{Am} = \mathbf{0}$$

Thus

$$\mathbf{PAm} = \mathbf{0}$$

and $\mathbf{m}$ also lies in the nullspace of $\mathbf{PA}$. Conversely, let $\mathbf{s}$ be any vector in the nullspace of $\mathbf{PA}$. Then

$$\mathbf{PAs} = \mathbf{0}$$

Since $\mathbf{P}$ is nonsingular, we may premultiply this equation by $\mathbf{P}^{-1}$ to obtain

$$\mathbf{As} = \mathbf{0}$$

Thus $\mathbf{s}$ also lies in the nullspace of $\mathbf{A}$, and $\mathbf{PA}$ and $\mathbf{A}$ have the same nullity and the same number of columns. Hence the ranks are the same.

To prove $\rho(\mathbf{AQ}) = \rho(\mathbf{A})$ we note that

$$\begin{aligned} \rho(\mathbf{AQ}) &= \rho(\mathbf{Q}'\mathbf{A}') \\ &= \rho(\mathbf{A}') \qquad \text{by the above proof} \\ &= \rho(\mathbf{A}) \end{aligned}$$

and finally

$$\rho(\mathbf{PAQ}) = \rho(\mathbf{A})$$

follows directly from the previous results.

Both previous theorems involve special cases of the multiplication of one matrix by another. In Eq. (4-52) a matrix was multiplied by its transpose. In Eq. (4-53) multiplication was by a nonsingular matrix. Our final theorem on rank relates to the perfectly general case of the multiplication of one rectangular matrix by another conformable rectangular matrix. Let $\mathbf{A}$ be $m \times n$ and let $\mathbf{B}$ be $n \times s$. Then

$$\rho(\mathbf{AB}) \leq \min[\rho(\mathbf{A}), \rho(\mathbf{B})] \tag{4-54}$$

that is, *the rank of the product* **AB** *is less than or equal to the smaller of the ranks of the constituent matrices.*

If $\mathbf{x}$ denotes any vector in the nullspace of $\mathbf{B}$, then

$$\mathbf{Bx} = \mathbf{0}$$

and so

$$\mathbf{ABx} = \mathbf{0}$$

Thus $\mathbf{x}$ also lies in the nullspace of $\mathbf{AB}$. But this time we cannot go in the opposite direction and prove that

$$\mathbf{ABy} = \mathbf{0} \qquad \text{implies} \qquad \mathbf{By} = \mathbf{0}$$

Thus all we can say is that the nullspace of $\mathbf{B}$ is contained in (or is a subspace of) the nullspace of $\mathbf{AB}$. Therefore, we have

$$\text{Dimension of nullspace of } \mathbf{B} \leq \text{dimension of nullspace of } \mathbf{AB}$$

Since $\mathbf{B}$ and $\mathbf{AB}$ have the same number of columns, it then follows from Eq. (4-47) that

$$\rho(\mathbf{AB}) \leq \rho(\mathbf{B})$$

By the usual trick with transposes,

$$\rho(\mathbf{AB}) = \rho(\mathbf{B'A'}) \leq \rho(\mathbf{A'}) = \rho(\mathbf{A})$$

and so Eq. (4-54) is proved.

Summary on the Rank of an $m \times n$ Matrix A

1. The maximum number of linearly independent rows is equal to the maximum number of linearly independent columns. This number is the rank of the matrix, denoted by $\rho(\mathbf{A})$.
2. $\rho(\mathbf{A}) \leq \min(m, n)$.
3. $\rho(\mathbf{A}) = \rho(\mathbf{A'})$.
4. If $\rho(\mathbf{A}) = m = n$, then $\mathbf{A}$ is nonsingular and a unique inverse $\mathbf{A}^{-1}$ exists.
5. $n = \rho(\mathbf{A}) +$ nullity of $\mathbf{A}$ where the nullity of $\mathbf{A}$ is the dimension of the subspace containing all vectors $\mathbf{x}$ which are solutions to $\mathbf{Ax} = \mathbf{0}$.
6. $\rho(\mathbf{X'X}) = \rho(\mathbf{XX'}) = \rho(\mathbf{X})$.
7. If $\mathbf{P}$ and $\mathbf{Q}$ are nonsingular matrices of orders m and n, respectively, then $\rho(\mathbf{PA}) = \rho(\mathbf{AQ}) = \rho(\mathbf{PAQ}) = \rho(\mathbf{A})$.
8. $\rho(\mathbf{AB}) \leq \min[\rho(\mathbf{A}), \rho(\mathbf{B})]$.

The Inverse Matrix

It is now time to return to the topic of matrix inversion and develop some of the properties of inverse matrices. We will also see how to compute inverse matrices, though this is a tedious and inefficient procedure for the *numerical* solution of equations. The procedure does, however, shed light on the theoretical properties of the inverse.

Let $\mathbf{A}$ denote a *square* matrix of order n. The condition for the inverse to exist may be stated in several equivalent ways:

1. $\mathbf{A}$ is nonsingular.
2. $\mathbf{A}$ has rank n.

3. The n rows of **A** are linearly independent.
4. The n columns of **A** are linearly independent.

To study the form of the inverse matrix let us begin with the 2×2 case. Denote **A** and $\mathbf{A}^{-1}$ as follows:

$$\mathbf{A} = \begin{bmatrix} a_{11} & a_{12} \\ a_{21} & a_{22} \end{bmatrix} \qquad \mathbf{A}^{-1} = \begin{bmatrix} \alpha_{11} & \alpha_{12} \\ \alpha_{21} & \alpha_{22} \end{bmatrix}$$

So far we have regarded matrices mostly as collections of vectors and paid little attention to the individual elements. The standard notation is to use the first subscript of an element to indicate the *row* in which that element appears and the second subscript to indicate the *column*. The definition of the inverse gives the general equation

$$\mathbf{A}\mathbf{A}^{-1} = \mathbf{I} \tag{4-55}$$

Specializing this equation to the 2×2 case and taking just the first column from each side of the equation gives

$$\begin{bmatrix} a_{11} & a_{12} \\ a_{21} & a_{22} \end{bmatrix} \begin{bmatrix} \alpha_{11} \\ \alpha_{21} \end{bmatrix} = \begin{bmatrix} 1 \\ 0 \end{bmatrix}$$

Treating the elements of the inverse as unknowns, the solution of this pair of equations gives

$$\alpha_{11} = \frac{a_{22}}{a_{11}a_{22} - a_{12}a_{21}}$$

$$\alpha_{21} = \frac{-a_{21}}{a_{11}a_{22} - a_{12}a_{21}}$$

Similarly, equating the second columns in Eq. (4-55) and solving gives

$$\alpha_{12} = \frac{-a_{12}}{a_{11}a_{22} - a_{12}a_{21}}$$

$$\alpha_{22} = \frac{a_{11}}{a_{11}a_{22} - a_{12}a_{21}}$$

Thus the inverse has been derived as

$$\mathbf{A}^{-1} = \frac{1}{a_{11}a_{22} - a_{12}a_{21}} \begin{bmatrix} a_{22} & -a_{12} \\ -a_{21} & a_{11} \end{bmatrix} \tag{4-56}$$

and it may readily be checked that indeed $\mathbf{A}\mathbf{A}^{-1} = \mathbf{A}\mathbf{A}^{-1} = \mathbf{I}$. Each element in $\mathbf{A}^{-1}$ is a function of the elements in **A**, and even for the 2×2 case certain important features of $\mathbf{A}^{-1}$ are apparent. First, each element in the inverse has a common divisor, namely, $a_{11}a_{22} - a_{12}a_{21}$. This is a function of *all* the elements in **A**. It is a scalar quantity and is defined as the *determinant* of **A**. For the 2×2 case we thus have

$$\det \mathbf{A} = |\mathbf{A}| = a_{11}a_{22} - a_{12}a_{21} = \sum_{\alpha, \beta} \pm\, a_{1\alpha}a_{2\beta} \tag{4-57}$$

The two expressions on the left of Eq. (4-57) are alternative ways of indicating the determinant. The final expression on the right means

$$\sum_{\alpha,\beta} \pm a_{1\alpha}a_{2\beta} =$$

> sum of all possible products of the elements of **A**, taken two at a time, with the first subscript in natural order 1, 2 and α, β indicating all possible permutations of 1, 2 for the second subscript, each product term being affixed with a positive (negative) sign as the number of inversions of the natural order in the second subscript is even (odd).

There are only two possible permutations of 1, 2, namely, 1, 2 itself and 2, 1. There is one inversion of the natural order in 2, 1 since 2 comes before 1. Thus the terms in the expansion are simply

$$a_{11}a_{22} - a_{12}a_{21}$$

The numerators of the elements in $\mathbf{A}^{-1}$ could have been produced by the following two rules:

1. For each element in **A**, strike out the row and column containing that element and write down the remaining element prefixed with a positive or negative sign in the pattern

$$\begin{bmatrix} + & - \\ - & + \end{bmatrix}$$

This gives the matrix

$$\begin{bmatrix} a_{22} & -a_{21} \\ -a_{12} & a_{11} \end{bmatrix}$$

2. Transpose the matrix obtained in rule 1 to get

$$\begin{bmatrix} a_{22} & -a_{12} \\ -a_{21} & a_{11} \end{bmatrix}$$

Let us try to apply these rules to the 3 × 3 case. Now we have

$$\mathbf{A} = \begin{bmatrix} a_{11} & a_{12} & a_{13} \\ a_{21} & a_{22} & a_{23} \\ a_{31} & a_{32} & a_{33} \end{bmatrix}$$

By extension of Eq. (4-57) we define the determinant of **A** as

$$\det \mathbf{A} = |\mathbf{A}| = \sum_{\alpha,\beta,\gamma} \pm a_{1\alpha}a_{2\beta}a_{3\gamma} \tag{4-58}$$

There will be $3! = 6$ terms in the expansion, since that is the number of possible permutations of 1, 2, 3. Half will have a positive sign and half a negative sign. The explicit expression is

$$|\mathbf{A}| = a_{11}a_{22}a_{33} + a_{12}a_{23}a_{31} + a_{13}a_{21}a_{32} - a_{11}a_{23}a_{32} - a_{12}a_{21}a_{33} - a_{13}a_{22}a_{31} \tag{4-59}$$

As a check on the signs we may notice, for instance, that in the third term in Eq.

(4-59) the order of the second subscripts is

$$3, 1, 2$$

which contains two inversions since 3 comes in front of both 1 and 2. The final term

$$3, 2, 1$$

yields *three* inversions (3 before 2 and 1 and 2 before 1).

Expressions (4-58) and (4-59) correctly define the determinant of a third-order matrix. The expression is already so cumbersome that the generalization to the nth-order case would be unpleasant. However, we shall derive below a more tractable expression for the determinant.

The numerator rule for the second-order case, however, does not extend to the third-order case without modifications. If we strike out the row and column containing, say, a_{11}, we are now left with the 2×2 submatrix

$$\begin{bmatrix} a_{22} & a_{23} \\ a_{32} & a_{33} \end{bmatrix}$$

rather than a scalar element. We, in fact, replace a_{11} with the *determinant* of this submatrix, appropriately signed, and similarly for the other elements. The general rules for determining the elements of $\mathbf{A}^{-1}$ in the 3×3 case may now be stated.

Let M_{ij} be the determinant of the 2×2 submatrix obtained when row i and column j are deleted from $\mathbf{A}$. M_{ij} is termed a *minor*. Further define

$$C_{ij} = (-1)^{i+j} M_{ij}$$

C_{ij} denotes a cofactor and is simply a *signed minor*. Thus the sign of M_{ij} does not change if $i + j$ is an even number and does change if that sum is odd.

The rules then become as follows:

1. Form a matrix in which each element (a_{ij}) is replaced by the corresponding cofactor (C_{ij}).
2. Transpose this matrix. The result is sometimes referred to as the *adjugate* or *adjoint* matrix.
3. Divide each element in rule 2 by $|\mathbf{A}|$. The result is $\mathbf{A}^{-1}$.

For the third-order case

$$C_{11} = \begin{vmatrix} a_{22} & a_{23} \\ a_{32} & a_{33} \end{vmatrix} = a_{22}a_{33} - a_{23}a_{32}$$

$$C_{23} = -\begin{vmatrix} a_{11} & a_{12} \\ a_{31} & a_{32} \end{vmatrix} = -(a_{11}a_{32} - a_{12}a_{31})$$

and so on, and

$$\mathbf{A}^{-1} = \frac{1}{|\mathbf{A}|} \begin{bmatrix} C_{11} & C_{21} & C_{31} \\ C_{12} & C_{22} & C_{32} \\ C_{13} & C_{23} & C_{33} \end{bmatrix} \tag{4-60}$$

Finally, we may note an alternative expression for the determinant of **A**. Returning to Eq. (4-59) and collecting terms in the elements of the first row gives

$$|\mathbf{A}| = a_{11}(a_{22}a_{33} - a_{23}a_{32}) + a_{12}(-a_{21}a_{33} + a_{23}a_{31}) + a_{13}(a_{21}a_{32} - a_{22}a_{31})$$

Using the definitions of cofactors just given, we then have

$$|\mathbf{A}| = a_{11}C_{11} + a_{12}C_{12} + a_{13}C_{13} \tag{4-61}$$

This defines $|\mathbf{A}|$ as a linear combination of the elements in the first row, each element being multiplied by its cofactor. This definition is clearly not unique. $|\mathbf{A}|$ may be expressed in terms of the elements of any row (or column), provided that in each case the elements are multiplied by the corresponding cofactors. Readers should satisfy themselves by direct substitution that any other similar expansion gives the same result as Eq. (4-59).

These rules for the 3×3 case have been rather plucked out of the air. Let us check that they work for a numerical example before continuing to the nth-order case.

Example 4-9

$$\mathbf{A} = \begin{bmatrix} 1 & 3 & 4 \\ 1 & 2 & 1 \\ 2 & 4 & 5 \end{bmatrix}$$

Replacing each element by its minor gives the matrix

$$\begin{bmatrix} \begin{vmatrix} 2 & 1 \\ 4 & 5 \end{vmatrix} & \begin{vmatrix} 1 & 1 \\ 2 & 5 \end{vmatrix} & \begin{vmatrix} 1 & 2 \\ 2 & 4 \end{vmatrix} \\ \begin{vmatrix} 3 & 4 \\ 4 & 5 \end{vmatrix} & \begin{vmatrix} 1 & 4 \\ 2 & 5 \end{vmatrix} & \begin{vmatrix} 1 & 3 \\ 2 & 4 \end{vmatrix} \\ \begin{vmatrix} 3 & 4 \\ 2 & 1 \end{vmatrix} & \begin{vmatrix} 1 & 4 \\ 1 & 1 \end{vmatrix} & \begin{vmatrix} 1 & 3 \\ 1 & 2 \end{vmatrix} \end{bmatrix} = \begin{bmatrix} 6 & 3 & 0 \\ -1 & -3 & -2 \\ -5 & -3 & -1 \end{bmatrix}$$

Signing the minors gives the matrix of cofactors as

$$\begin{bmatrix} 6 & -3 & 0 \\ 1 & -3 & 2 \\ -5 & 3 & -1 \end{bmatrix}$$

Transposing gives the adjugate matrix

$$\begin{bmatrix} 6 & 1 & -5 \\ -3 & -3 & 3 \\ 0 & 2 & -1 \end{bmatrix}$$

Expressing the determinant of **A** in terms of the elements in the first row gives

$$|\mathbf{A}| = a_{11}C_{11} + a_{12}C_{12} + a_{13}C_{13} = 1(6) + 3(-3) + 4(0) = -3$$

Thus the inverse matrix is

$$\mathbf{A}^{-1} = \begin{bmatrix} -2 & -\frac{1}{3} & 1\frac{2}{3} \\ 1 & 1 & -1 \\ 0 & -\frac{2}{3} & \frac{1}{3} \end{bmatrix}$$

It is easily checked that $\mathbf{A}\mathbf{A}^{-1} = \mathbf{A}^{-1}\mathbf{A} = \mathbf{I}$.

For the nth-order case the rules for obtaining $\mathbf{A}^{-1}$ are essentially those already stated for the third-order case. The determinant is defined as

$$|\mathbf{A}| = \sum_{\alpha, \beta, \ldots, \nu} \pm a_{1\alpha} a_{2\beta} \cdots a_{n\nu} \tag{4-62}$$

or alternatively

$$|\mathbf{A}| = a_{i1}C_{i1} + a_{i2}C_{i2} + \cdots + a_{in}C_{in} \qquad \text{for any } i = 1, \ldots, n$$

or (4-63)

$$|\mathbf{A}| = a_{1j}C_{1j} + a_{2j}C_{2j} + \cdots + a_{nj}C_{nj} \qquad \text{for any } j = 1, \ldots, n$$

The cofactors are now the signed minors of matrices of order $n - 1$, and the inverse matrix is

$$\mathbf{A}^{-1} = \frac{1}{|\mathbf{A}|} \begin{bmatrix} C_{11} & C_{21} & \cdots & C_{n1} \\ C_{12} & C_{22} & \cdots & C_{n2} \\ \cdots & \cdots & \cdots & \cdots \\ C_{1n} & C_{2n} & \cdots & C_{nn} \end{bmatrix} \tag{4-64}$$

Properties of Determinants

The following properties are stated for the determinants of nth-order matrices, but they will often be illustrated for the 2×2 case. To economize on space, proofs will not always be given.

1. $|\mathbf{A}'| = |\mathbf{A}|$ *even if* $\mathbf{A}$ *is not symmetric.*

$$\begin{vmatrix} a & b \\ c & d \end{vmatrix} = ad - bc = \begin{vmatrix} a & c \\ b & d \end{vmatrix}$$

2. *If* $\mathbf{B}$ *is obtained from* $\mathbf{A}$ *by interchanging any two rows (or columns) of* $\mathbf{A}$, $|\mathbf{B}| = -|\mathbf{A}|$.

$$|\mathbf{B}| = \begin{vmatrix} c & d \\ a & b \end{vmatrix} = cb - ad = -\begin{vmatrix} a & b \\ c & d \end{vmatrix} = -|\mathbf{A}|$$

Suppose in an $n \times n$ matrix we interchange the first two rows. Let a_{ij} denote the i, jth element in the original matrix and b_{ij} the i, jth element in the new matrix. A term such as

$$a_{1\alpha} a_{2\beta} a_{3\gamma} \cdots a_{n\nu}$$

in the expansion of $|\mathbf{A}|$ thus becomes

$$b_{2\alpha} b_{1\beta} b_{3\gamma} \cdots b_{n\nu}$$

in the expansion of $|\mathbf{B}|$, where

$$\left.\begin{aligned} b_{1j} &= a_{2j} \\ b_{2j} &= a_{1j} \end{aligned}\right\} \quad j = 1, 2, \ldots, n$$

$$b_{ij} = a_{ij} \qquad \text{for all } j;\ i = 3, 4, \ldots, n$$

The numerical values of these two terms are identical; the crucial question is the sign. To determine the sign of the second term, the first subscripts must be put in natural order and the number of inversions in the second subscript determined. This gives

$$b_{1\beta}b_{2\alpha}b_{3\gamma} \cdots b_{n\nu}$$

and, compared with the corresponding term in $|\mathbf{A}|$, *one* inversion has been introduced or removed, so that this term (and each and every term) changes sign in $|\mathbf{B}|$ as compared with $|\mathbf{A}|$. If we interchange rows i and j, which are separated by, say, r rows, reordering the b elements in any term to put the first subscripts in natural order will involve $2r + 1$ changes, where each change introduces a new inversion in the second subscript or removes an existing inversion. This is illustrated below, where only the first subscripts on the b's are shown.

$$b_i \underbrace{b_{i+1} b_{i+2} \cdots b_{j-1}}_{r \text{ elements}} b_j$$

Since $2r + 1$ is an odd number, the sign of the term changes, and so $|\mathbf{B}| = -|\mathbf{A}|$. Property 1 then ensures that interchanging any two columns will also change the sign of the determinant.

3. *If a matrix has two or more identical rows (or columns), its determinant is zero.*

$$\begin{vmatrix} a & b \\ a & b \end{vmatrix} = ab - ab = a$$

From property 2, interchanging identical rows would change the sign of the determinant. But the new matrix is identical with the old, and so its determinant is unchanged. This gives

$$|\mathbf{A}| = -|\mathbf{A}|$$

so that

$$|\mathbf{A}| = 0$$

4. *Expansions in terms of* alien *cofactors vanish. By this is meant an expression such as*

$$a_{j1}C_{i1} + a_{j2}C_{i2} + \cdots + a_{jn}C_{in}$$

where the elements of row j *are multiplied by the cofactors of the elements of row* i.

This is exactly the expression we would obtain for the determinant of a matrix whose rows i and j are identical. By property 3, that determinant is zero.

5. *If* **B** *is formed from* **A** *by adding a multiple of one row (or column) to another row (or column), the value of the determinant is unchanged.*

$$\begin{aligned} |\mathbf{B}| &= \begin{vmatrix} a + \lambda c & b + \lambda d \\ c & d \end{vmatrix} = (a + \lambda c)d - (b + \lambda d)c \\ &= ad - bc + \lambda(cd - cd) \\ &= \begin{vmatrix} a & b \\ c & d \end{vmatrix} = |\mathbf{A}| \end{aligned}$$

Suppose row i of $\mathbf{B}$ = row i of $\mathbf{A} + \lambda \cdot$ row j of $\mathbf{A}$. Expanding $|\mathbf{B}|$ in terms of its ith row gives

$$\begin{aligned}|\mathbf{B}| &= (a_{i1} + \lambda a_{j1})C_{i1} + (a_{i2} + \lambda a_{j2})C_{i2} + \cdots + (a_{in} + \lambda a_{jn})C_{in} \\ &= (a_{i1}C_{i1} + a_{i2}C_{i2} + \cdots + a_{in}C_{in}) + \lambda(a_{j1}C_{i1} + a_{j2}C_{i2} + \cdots + a_{jn}C_{in}) \\ &= |\mathbf{A}|\end{aligned}$$

since the coefficient of λ is an expansion in terms of alien cofactors, which vanishes.

6. *If the rows (or columns) of* $\mathbf{A}$ *are linearly dependent,* $|\mathbf{A}| = 0$*, and if they are linearly independent,* $|\mathbf{A}| \neq 0$*. If the rows of*

$$\mathbf{A} = \begin{bmatrix} a & b \\ c & d \end{bmatrix}$$

are linearly dependent, there exist nonzero scalars λ_1, λ_2 *such that*

$$\lambda_1 a + \lambda_2 c = 0$$
$$\lambda_1 b + \lambda_2 d = 0$$

Thus

$$c = -\frac{\lambda_1}{\lambda_2}a \quad \text{and} \quad d = -\frac{\lambda_1}{\lambda_2}b$$

and $\mathbf{A}$ *may be written*

$$\mathbf{A} = \begin{bmatrix} a & b \\ \lambda a & \lambda b \end{bmatrix}$$

where $\lambda = -\lambda_1/\lambda_2$*, and so* $|\mathbf{A}| = \lambda(\mathrm{ab} - \mathrm{ab}) = 0$.

In the general case if row i is a linear combination of certain other rows, subtracting that linear combination from row i will produce a zero row. Subtracting the linear combination is merely a repeated application of property 5 and so leaves the determinant unchanged, but that determinant is zero since the process has ended with a matrix containing a zero row.

If the rows (columns) of $\mathbf{A}$ are linearly independent, there is no way to produce a zero row (column) and $|\mathbf{A}| \neq 0$. Thus *nonsingular matrices have nonzero determinants*. If this were not so, the inverse matrix defined in Eq. (4-64) would not exist, since each element is divided by $|\mathbf{A}|$. Conversely, *singular matrices have zero determinants.*

This result also provides a means of checking on the rank of low-order matrices. If $\mathbf{A}$ is $m \times n$ and has rank r, then there must be *at least one* square submatrix of order r, which is nonsingular and thus has a nonzero determinant, and all square matrices of order $r + 1, r + 2, \ldots,$ have zero determinants. Thus we have the following alternative definition of rank:

Rank of $m \times n$ matrix = order of largest nonvanishing determinant

Example 4-10

$$\mathbf{A} = \begin{bmatrix} 1 & 2 & 3 & 4 \\ 1 & 2 & 1 & 1 \\ 2 & 4 & -6 & -10 \end{bmatrix}$$

The rank must be at least 2, since although

$$\begin{vmatrix} 1 & 2 \\ 1 & 2 \end{vmatrix} = 0$$

there are plenty of nonvanishing second-order determinants that can be formed from the elements of **A**. For example,

$$\begin{vmatrix} 1 & 3 \\ 2 & -6 \end{vmatrix} = -12 \qquad \begin{vmatrix} 2 & 1 \\ 4 & -10 \end{vmatrix} = -24$$

and so on. Notice that these are the determinants of second-order submatrices obtained by deleting any one row and any two columns from **A**. There are four possible third-order determinants to evaluate. Deleting the fourth column,

$$\begin{vmatrix} 1 & 2 & 3 \\ 1 & 2 & 1 \\ 2 & 4 & -6 \end{vmatrix} = \begin{vmatrix} 0 & 0 & 2 \\ 1 & 2 & 1 \\ 2 & 4 & -6 \end{vmatrix} = 2\begin{vmatrix} 1 & 2 \\ 2 & 4 \end{vmatrix} = 0$$

The first step in this evaluation has been to subtract row 2 from row 1, which by property 5 does not alter the value of the determinant. This gives an expansion, using Eq. (4-63), in terms of the first row, which now contains just a single term. To evaluate

$$\begin{vmatrix} 1 & 3 & 4 \\ 1 & 1 & 1 \\ 2 & -6 & -10 \end{vmatrix}$$

we might subtract row 1 from row 2 and we also subtract twice row 1 from row 3 to get

$$\begin{vmatrix} 1 & 3 & 4 \\ 0 & -2 & -3 \\ 0 & -12 & -18 \end{vmatrix} = \begin{vmatrix} -2 & -3 \\ -12 & -18 \end{vmatrix} = 0$$

The two other third-order determinants may similarly be seen to be zero, so that $\rho(\mathbf{A}) = 2$. Alternatively, we might have spotted that

$$\text{row } 3 = 6 \cdot \text{row } 2 - 4 \cdot \text{row } 1$$

which establishes that the rank cannot be 3, without a need of evaluating third-order determinants. This matrix also illustrates another important point. Looking at the square submatrix formed from the first three columns of **A**, we have already shown that its determinant is zero, and inspection of the second-order determinants within it shows that its rank is 2. Its three rows are connected by the relationship stated above, but the same relationship does not hold between the three columns. The linear dependence between the *three* columns is expressed by

$$2 \cdot \text{column } 1 - 1 \cdot \text{column } 2 = \mathbf{0}$$

or

$$2 \cdot \text{column } 1 - 1 \cdot \text{column } 2 + 0 \cdot \text{column } 3 = \mathbf{0}$$

The important point is that a set of vectors is linearly dependent even if some (but not all) of the coefficients in the linear combination are zero.

7. *The determinant of a triangular matrix is equal to the products of the diagonal elements.*

$$\begin{vmatrix} a & 0 \\ c & d \end{vmatrix} = \begin{vmatrix} a & b \\ 0 & d \end{vmatrix} = ad$$

A triangular matrix may be *lower triangular*, as in

$$\mathbf{A} = \begin{bmatrix} a_{11} & 0 & 0 & \cdots & 0 \\ a_{21} & a_{22} & 0 & \cdots & 0 \\ a_{31} & a_{32} & a_{33} & \cdots & 0 \\ \cdots & \cdots & \cdots & \cdots & \cdots \\ a_{n1} & a_{n2} & a_{n3} & \cdots & a_{nn} \end{bmatrix}$$

or upper triangular, as in

$$\mathbf{A}^* = \begin{bmatrix} a_{11} & a_{12} & a_{13} & \cdots & a_{1n} \\ 0 & a_{22} & a_{23} & \cdots & a_{2n} \\ 0 & 0 & a_{33} & \cdots & a_{3n} \\ \cdots & \cdots & \cdots & \cdots & \cdots \\ 0 & 0 & 0 & \cdots & a_{nn} \end{bmatrix}$$

Expanding **A** by the first row gives

$$|\mathbf{A}| = a_{11} \begin{vmatrix} a_{22} & 0 & \cdots & 0 \\ a_{32} & a_{33} & \cdots & 0 \\ \cdots & \cdots & \cdots & \cdots \\ a_{n2} & a_{n3} & \cdots & a_{nn} \end{vmatrix}$$

Expanding the new determinant by its first row and repeating the process n times gives

$$|\mathbf{A}| = a_{11}a_{22} \cdots a_{nn}$$

Expanding $|\mathbf{A}^*|$ successively by the first column similarly gives

$$|\mathbf{A}^*| = a_{11}a_{22} \cdots a_{nn}$$

Two special cases of this result follow directly:

- The determinant of a diagonal matrix is simply the product of the diagonal elements:

- The determinant of the unit or identity matrix is unity:

$$|\mathbf{A}| = \begin{vmatrix} a_{11} & 0 & \cdots & 0 \\ 0 & a_{22} & \cdots & 0 \\ \cdots & \cdots & \cdots & \cdots \\ 0 & 0 & \cdots & a_{nn} \end{vmatrix} = a_{11}a_{22} \cdots a_{nn}$$

$$|\mathbf{A}| = \begin{vmatrix} 1 & 0 & \cdots & 0 \\ 0 & 1 & \cdots & 0 \\ \cdots & \cdots & \cdots & \cdots \\ 0 & 0 & \cdots & 1 \end{vmatrix} = 1$$

8. *Multiplying any row (column) of a matrix by a constant λ multiplies the determinant by λ. Multiplying every element in a matrix by λ multiplies the determinant by λ^n.*

These properties follow directly from the definition of the determinant in Eq. (4-62), where it is seen that each term in the expansion is the product of n elements, one and only one from each row and column of the matrix.

9. *The determinant of the product of two square matrices is the product of the determinants.*

$$|\mathbf{AB}| = |\mathbf{A}| \cdot |\mathbf{B}|$$

This rule is only of interest when **A** and **B** are both nonsingular. If either is singular, **AB** is singular and both sides of the equation are zero. If **A** is nonsingular, repeated applications of property 5, that is, additions of multiples of rows and columns, can produce a diagonal matrix **D**, such that $|\mathbf{D}| = |\mathbf{A}|$.

Example 4-11

$$\mathbf{A} = \begin{bmatrix} 1 & 2 \\ 3 & 4 \end{bmatrix} \qquad \text{with } |\mathbf{A}| = -2$$

Subtract 3 · row 1 from row 2 to get

$$\begin{bmatrix} 1 & 2 \\ 0 & -2 \end{bmatrix}$$

Then add row 2 to row 1 to get

$$\mathbf{D} = \begin{bmatrix} 1 & 0 \\ 0 & -2 \end{bmatrix} \qquad \text{with } |\mathbf{D}| = -2 = |\mathbf{A}|$$

If these steps are performed on the matrix **AB**, the result is a matrix **DB** with $|\mathbf{AB}| = |\mathbf{DB}|$ by property 5. This statement in general requires that only row operations have been performed on **A** to obtain the diagonal matrix **D**. This is always possible. The first step in the example is equivalent to premultiplying **A** by

$$\mathbf{F}_1 = \begin{bmatrix} 1 & 0 \\ -3 & 1 \end{bmatrix}$$

and the second step to a further premultiplication by

$$\mathbf{F}_2 = \begin{bmatrix} 1 & 1 \\ 0 & 1 \end{bmatrix}$$

The sequence of operations is then described by premultiplication by a single matrix

$$\mathbf{F} = \mathbf{F}_2\mathbf{F}_1 = \begin{bmatrix} -2 & 1 \\ -3 & 1 \end{bmatrix}$$

so that **FA** = **D**, as the reader may verify. By property 8,

$$\begin{aligned} |\mathbf{DB}| &= d_{11}d_{22} \cdots d_{nn}|\mathbf{B}| \\ &= |\mathbf{D}| \cdot |\mathbf{B}| \\ &= |\mathbf{A}| \cdot |\mathbf{B}| \end{aligned}$$

Thus

$$|\mathbf{AB}| = |\mathbf{A}| \cdot |\mathbf{B}|$$

Properties of Inverse Matrices

1. $(\mathbf{AB})^{-1} = \mathbf{B}^{-1}\mathbf{A}^{-1}$ *provided* **A** *and* **B** *are each nonsingular.*

The simplest proof is to multiply **AB** by the suggested inverse and see that the unit matrix results, since we already know that the inverse matrix is unique:

$$\mathbf{ABB}^{-1}\mathbf{A}^{-1} = \mathbf{AIA}^{-1} = \mathbf{I}$$

and similarly,

$$\mathbf{B}^{-1}\mathbf{A}^{-1}\mathbf{AB} = \mathbf{I}$$

This technique is sometimes useful in deriving inverse matrices, namely, guess at a plausible inverse and check by multiplication to see whether it works. The above result extends readily to products of three or more matrices. Thus

$$(\mathbf{ABC})^{-1} = \mathbf{C}^{-1}\mathbf{B}^{-1}\mathbf{A}^{-1}$$

The warning must again be inserted that this result only holds when the constituent matrices are nonsingular. Students occasionally produce "miraculous" proofs by applying this theorem to *rectangular* matrices.

2. $(\mathbf{A}^{-1})^{-1} = \mathbf{A}$

   that is, *taking the inverse of the inverse reproduces the original matrix.*

   From the definition of an inverse,

$$(\mathbf{A}^{-1})(\mathbf{A}^{-1})^{-1} = \mathbf{I}$$

Premultiplying by **A** gives the required result.

3. $(\mathbf{A}')^{-1} = (\mathbf{A}^{-1})'$

   that is, *the inverse of the transpose equals the transpose of the inverse.*

We have

$$\mathbf{AA}^{-1} = \mathbf{I}$$

Transposing,

$$(\mathbf{A}^{-1})'\mathbf{A}' = \mathbf{I}$$

Postmultiplying by $(\mathbf{A}')^{-1}$,

$$(\mathbf{A}^{-1})'\mathbf{A}'(\mathbf{A}')^{-1} = (\mathbf{A}')^{-1}$$

Thus

$$(\mathbf{A}^{-1})' = (\mathbf{A}')^{-1}$$

4. $|\mathbf{A}^{-1}| = \dfrac{1}{|\mathbf{A}|}$

   that is, *the determinant of* $\mathbf{A}^{-1}$ *is the reciprocal of the determinant of* $\mathbf{A}$.

   This follows directly from properties 7 and 9 of determinants, for

$$\mathbf{AA}^{-1} = \mathbf{I}$$

gives

$$|\mathbf{A}| \cdot |\mathbf{A}^{-1}| = 1$$

5. *The inverse of an upper (lower) triangular matrix is also an upper (lower) triangular matrix.*

   We merely illustrate this result for a lower triangular 3×3 matrix:

$$\mathbf{A} = \begin{bmatrix} a_{11} & 0 & 0 \\ a_{21} & a_{22} & 0 \\ a_{31} & a_{32} & a_{33} \end{bmatrix}$$

By inspection it is seen that three cofactors are zero, namely,

$$C_{21} = -\begin{vmatrix} 0 & 0 \\ a_{32} & a_{33} \end{vmatrix}, \qquad C_{31} = \begin{vmatrix} 0 & 0 \\ a_{22} & 0 \end{vmatrix}, \qquad C_{32} = -\begin{vmatrix} a_{11} & 0 \\ a_{21} & 0 \end{vmatrix}$$

Thus

$$\mathbf{A}^{-1} = \frac{1}{|\mathbf{A}|}\begin{bmatrix} C_{11} & 0 & 0 \\ C_{12} & C_{22} & 0 \\ C_{13} & C_{23} & C_{33} \end{bmatrix}$$

6. *The inverse of a partitioned matrix: If*

$$\mathbf{A} = \begin{bmatrix} \mathbf{A}_{11} & \mathbf{A}_{12} \\ \mathbf{A}_{21} & \mathbf{A}_{22} \end{bmatrix}$$

where $\mathbf{A}_{11}$ *and* $\mathbf{A}_{22}$ *are* square nonsingular *matrices*,

$$\mathbf{A}^{-1} = \begin{bmatrix} \mathbf{B}_{11} & -\mathbf{B}_{11}\mathbf{A}_{12}\mathbf{A}_{22}^{-1} \\ -\mathbf{A}_{22}^{-1}\mathbf{A}_{21}\mathbf{B}_{11} & \mathbf{A}_{22}^{-1} + \mathbf{A}_{22}^{-1}\mathbf{A}_{21}\mathbf{B}_{11}\mathbf{A}_{12}\mathbf{A}_{22}^{-1} \end{bmatrix} \tag{4-65}$$

where $\mathbf{B}_{11} = (\mathbf{A}_{11} - \mathbf{A}_{12}\mathbf{A}_{22}^{-1}\mathbf{A}_{21})^{-1}$, *or alternatively*,

$$\mathbf{A}^{-1} = \begin{bmatrix} \mathbf{A}_{11}^{-1} + \mathbf{A}_{11}^{-1}\mathbf{A}_{12}\mathbf{B}_{22}\mathbf{A}_{21}\mathbf{A}_{11}^{-1} & -\mathbf{A}_{11}^{-1}\mathbf{A}_{12}\mathbf{B}_{22} \\ -\mathbf{B}_{22}\mathbf{A}_{21}\mathbf{A}_{11}^{-1} & \mathbf{B}_{22} \end{bmatrix} \tag{4-66}$$

where

$$\mathbf{B}_{22} = \left(\mathbf{A}_{22} - \mathbf{A}_{21}\mathbf{A}_{11}^{-1}\mathbf{A}_{12}\right)^{-1}$$

These formulas are frequently used. The first form, Eq. (4-65), is the simpler if we are interested in an expression that involves just the first row of the inverse. Conversely, Eq. (4-66) is the simpler for expressions involving the second row. The derivation of the formulas is straightforward but tedious. Let

$$\mathbf{A}^{-1} = \begin{bmatrix} \mathbf{B}_{11} & \mathbf{B}_{12} \\ \mathbf{B}_{21} & \mathbf{B}_{22} \end{bmatrix}$$

where the $\mathbf{B}_{ij}$ submatrices have the same dimensions as the corresponding $\mathbf{A}_{ij}$ submatrices. Postmultiplying $\mathbf{A}$ by $\mathbf{A}^{-1}$ gives the matrix equations

$$\begin{aligned} \mathbf{A}_{11}\mathbf{B}_{11} + \mathbf{A}_{12}\mathbf{B}_{21} &= \mathbf{I} \\ \mathbf{A}_{11}\mathbf{B}_{12} + \mathbf{A}_{12}\mathbf{B}_{22} &= \mathbf{0} \\ \mathbf{A}_{21}\mathbf{B}_{11} + \mathbf{A}_{22}\mathbf{B}_{21} &= \mathbf{0} \\ \mathbf{A}_{21}\mathbf{B}_{12} + \mathbf{A}_{22}\mathbf{B}_{22} &= \mathbf{I} \end{aligned}$$

where the unit matrix has been partitioned conformably with $\mathbf{A}$. The third equation in this set gives

$$\mathbf{B}_{21} = -\mathbf{A}_{22}^{-1}\mathbf{A}_{21}\mathbf{B}_{11} \tag{4-67}$$

Substituting this in the first and solving for $\mathbf{B}_{11}$ gives

$$\mathbf{B}_{11} = \left(\mathbf{A}_{11} - \mathbf{A}_{12}\mathbf{A}_{22}^{-1}\mathbf{A}_{21}\right)^{-1} \tag{4-68}$$

A similar treatment of the second and fourth equations yields

$$\mathbf{B}_{12} = -\mathbf{A}_{11}^{-1}\mathbf{A}_{12}\mathbf{B}_{22} \tag{4-69}$$

and

$$\mathbf{B}_{22} = \left(\mathbf{A}_{22} - \mathbf{A}_{21}\mathbf{A}_{11}^{-1}\mathbf{A}_{12}\right)^{-1} \tag{4-70}$$

These four expressions are seen to constitute, respectively, the first and second columns in the two alternative formulations of $\mathbf{A}^{-1}$.

To derive the remaining columns in Eqs. (4-65) and (4-66) we multiply out $\mathbf{A}^{-1}\mathbf{A} = \mathbf{I}$ to obtain

$$\begin{aligned} \mathbf{B}_{11}\mathbf{A}_{11} + \mathbf{B}_{12}\mathbf{A}_{21} &= \mathbf{I} \\ \mathbf{B}_{11}\mathbf{A}_{12} + \mathbf{B}_{12}\mathbf{A}_{22} &= \mathbf{0} \\ \mathbf{B}_{21}\mathbf{A}_{11} + \mathbf{B}_{22}\mathbf{A}_{21} &= \mathbf{0} \\ \mathbf{B}_{21}\mathbf{A}_{12} + \mathbf{B}_{22}\mathbf{A}_{22} &= \mathbf{I} \end{aligned}$$

The second equation in this set gives

$$\mathbf{B}_{12} = -\mathbf{B}_{11}\mathbf{A}_{12}\mathbf{A}_{22}^{-1} \tag{4-71}$$

Substituting this and Eq. (4-67) in the fourth equation of the first set above and solving for $\mathbf{B}_{22}$ gives

$$\mathbf{B}_{22} = \mathbf{A}_{22}^{-1} + \mathbf{A}_{22}^{-1}\mathbf{A}_{21}\mathbf{B}_{11}\mathbf{A}_{12}\mathbf{A}_{22}^{-1} \tag{4-72}$$

These two expressions complete the second column in the definition of $\mathbf{A}^{-1}$ in Eq. (4-65). The third equation of this set and the first equation of the previous set yield

$$\mathbf{B}_{21} = -\mathbf{B}_{22}\mathbf{A}_{21}\mathbf{A}_{11}^{-1} \tag{4-73}$$

and

$$\mathbf{B}_{11} = \mathbf{A}_{11}^{-1} + \mathbf{A}_{11}^{-1}\mathbf{A}_{12}\mathbf{B}_{22}\mathbf{A}_{21}\mathbf{A}_{11}^{-1} \tag{4-74}$$

which completes the first column in Eq. (4-66).

7. *The inverse of a block diagonal matrix: Let* $\mathbf{A}$ *be*

$$\mathbf{A} = \begin{bmatrix} \mathbf{A}_{11} & \mathbf{0} \\ \mathbf{0} & \mathbf{A}_{22} \end{bmatrix}$$

where $\mathbf{A}$, $\mathbf{A}_{11}$, *and* $\mathbf{A}_{22}$ *are all square matrices. If* $\mathbf{A}$ *is nonsingular, then so are* $\mathbf{A}_{11}$ *and* $\mathbf{A}_{22}$ *since each has linearly independent columns (rows). Then*

$$\mathbf{A}^{-1} = \begin{bmatrix} \mathbf{A}_{11}^{-1} & \mathbf{0} \\ \mathbf{0} & \mathbf{A}_{22}^{-1} \end{bmatrix} \tag{4-75}$$

This is merely a special case of property 6 or, alternatively, it may be seen directly as the inverse since $\mathbf{AA}^{-1}$ is clearly $\mathbf{I}$. A special case of this result is the inverse of a diagonal matrix. If

$$\mathbf{A} = \begin{bmatrix} a_{11} & 0 & \cdots & 0 \\ 0 & a_{22} & \cdots & 0 \\ \cdots & \cdots & \cdots & \cdots \\ 0 & 0 & \cdots & a_{nn} \end{bmatrix}$$

$$\mathbf{A}^{-1} = \begin{bmatrix} \frac{1}{a_{11}} & 0 & \cdots & 0 \\ 0 & \frac{1}{a_{22}} & \cdots & 0 \\ \cdots & \cdots & \cdots & \cdots \\ 0 & 0 & \cdots & \frac{1}{a_{nn}} \end{bmatrix}$$

8. *The inverse of a Kronecker product: The* direct *or Kronecker product of two matrices* $\mathbf{A}$ *and* $\mathbf{B}$ *is defined as*

$$\mathbf{A} \otimes \mathbf{B} = \begin{bmatrix} a_{11}\mathbf{B} & a_{12}\mathbf{B} & \cdots & a_{1n}\mathbf{B} \\ a_{21}\mathbf{B} & a_{22}\mathbf{B} & \cdots & a_{2n}\mathbf{B} \\ \cdots & \cdots & \cdots & \cdots \\ a_{m1}\mathbf{B} & a_{m2}\mathbf{B} & \cdots & a_{mn}\mathbf{B} \end{bmatrix} \tag{4-76}$$

In this definition **A** is a general matrix of order $m \times n$, and likewise **B** can be a rectangular matrix of any order, say, $p \times q$. In this case $\mathbf{A} \otimes \mathbf{B}$ is of order $mp \times nq$. Suppose **A** is square of order m and nonsingular and that **B** is square of order p and nonsingular. The Kronecker product $\mathbf{A} \otimes \mathbf{B}$ is square of order mp and nonsingular. Its inverse is given by

$$(\mathbf{A} \otimes \mathbf{B})^{-1} = \mathbf{A}^{-1} \otimes \mathbf{B}^{-1} \tag{4-77}$$

The proof may be obtained by multiplying out. The right-hand side of Eq. (4-77) is

$$\mathbf{A}^{-1} \otimes \mathbf{B}^{-1} = \frac{1}{|\mathbf{A}|}\begin{bmatrix} C_{11}\mathbf{B}^{-1} & C_{21}\mathbf{B}^{-1} & \cdots & C_{m1}\mathbf{B}^{-1} \\ C_{12}\mathbf{B}^{-1} & C_{22}\mathbf{B}^{-1} & \cdots & C_{m2}\mathbf{B}^{-1} \\ \cdots & \cdots & \cdots & \cdots \\ C_{1m}\mathbf{B}^{-1} & C_{2m}\mathbf{B}^{-1} & & C_{mm}\mathbf{B}^{-1} \end{bmatrix}$$

Multiplication by Eq. (4-76) yields the identity matrix.

9. *Determinants of partitioned matrices: We sometimes need to express the determinant of* **A** *in terms of the determinants of submatrices. We begin by noting that*

$$\begin{vmatrix} \mathbf{A}_{11} & \mathbf{0} \\ \mathbf{0} & \mathbf{I} \end{vmatrix} = |\mathbf{A}_{11}| \tag{4-78}$$

for if we evaluate the determinant on the left-hand side by expanding in terms of the elements of the last row, the only nonzero term is the last one, which is unity multiplied by a determinant of the same form, except that the order of **I** *has been reduced by* 1. *Proceeding in this way the result follows.*

A block diagonal matrix may be expressed as the product of two simpler block diagonal matrices, namely,

$$\mathbf{A} = \begin{bmatrix} \mathbf{A}_{11} & \mathbf{0} \\ \mathbf{0} & \mathbf{A}_{22} \end{bmatrix} = \begin{bmatrix} \mathbf{A}_{11} & \mathbf{0} \\ \mathbf{0} & \mathbf{I} \end{bmatrix}\begin{bmatrix} \mathbf{I} & \mathbf{0} \\ \mathbf{0} & \mathbf{A}_{22} \end{bmatrix}$$

Applying property 9 of determinants and also Eq. (4-78) gives

$$|\mathbf{A}| = |\mathbf{A}_{11}| \cdot |\mathbf{A}_{22}| \tag{4-79}$$

Now consider

$$\begin{vmatrix} \mathbf{A}_{11} & \mathbf{A}_{12} \\ \mathbf{0} & \mathbf{I} \end{vmatrix} = |\mathbf{A}_{11}| \tag{4-80}$$

This follows from the same argument used to establish Eq. (4-78). We can now find the determinant of a block-triangular matrix.

$$\mathbf{A} = \begin{bmatrix} \mathbf{A}_{11} & \mathbf{A}_{12} \\ \mathbf{0} & \mathbf{A}_{22} \end{bmatrix} = \begin{bmatrix} \mathbf{I} & \mathbf{0} \\ \mathbf{0} & \mathbf{A}_{22} \end{bmatrix}\begin{bmatrix} \mathbf{A}_{11} & \mathbf{A}_{12} \\ \mathbf{0} & \mathbf{I} \end{bmatrix}$$

Thus

$$|\mathbf{A}| = |\mathbf{A}_{11}| \cdot |\mathbf{A}_{22}| \tag{4-81}$$

This is a matrix generalization of property 7 of determinants, namely, that the determinant of a triangular matrix is the product of the diagonal elements. The final step is to establish the determinant of a general partitioned matrix

$$\mathbf{A} = \begin{bmatrix} \mathbf{A}_{11} & \mathbf{A}_{12} \\ \mathbf{A}_{21} & \mathbf{A}_{22} \end{bmatrix}$$

where $\mathbf{A}_{11}$ and $\mathbf{A}_{22}$ are square and nonsingular. Define

$$\mathbf{B}_1 = \begin{bmatrix} \mathbf{I} & -\mathbf{A}_{12}\mathbf{A}_{22}^{-1} \\ \mathbf{0} & \mathbf{I} \end{bmatrix} \qquad \text{and} \qquad \mathbf{B}_2 = \begin{bmatrix} \mathbf{I} & \mathbf{0} \\ -\mathbf{A}_{22}^{-1}\mathbf{A}_{21} & \mathbf{I} \end{bmatrix}$$

Then

$$\mathbf{B}_1\mathbf{A}\mathbf{B}_2 = \begin{bmatrix} \mathbf{A}_{11} - \mathbf{A}_{12}\mathbf{A}_{22}^{-1}\mathbf{A}_{21} & \mathbf{0} \\ \mathbf{0} & \mathbf{A}_{22} \end{bmatrix}$$

and since $|\mathbf{B}_1| = |\mathbf{B}_2| = 1$,

$$|\mathbf{A}| = |\mathbf{A}_{22}| \cdot |\mathbf{A}_{11} - \mathbf{A}_{12}\mathbf{A}_{22}^{-1}\mathbf{A}_{21}| \qquad (4\text{-}82)$$

An alternative expression may be derived in a similar fashion as

$$|\mathbf{A}| = |\mathbf{A}_{11}| \cdot |\mathbf{A}_{22} - \mathbf{A}_{21}\mathbf{A}_{11}^{-1}\mathbf{A}_{12}| \qquad (4\text{-}83)$$

Cramer's Rule

This inordinately long section on the solution of equations may be rounded off by the derivation of Cramer's rule for the solution of a set of n nonhomogeneous equations in n unknowns. The set of equations may be written

$$\mathbf{A}\mathbf{x} = \mathbf{b} \qquad (4\text{-}84)$$

where, by assumption, $\mathbf{A}$ is a square known matrix of order n and nonsingular, $\mathbf{x}$ is a vector of n unknowns, and $\mathbf{b}$ is a known n-element vector. There is an unfortunate clash of notation between conventions in algebra and conventions in statistics. The normal equations for the least-squares vector are

$$(\mathbf{X}'\mathbf{X})\mathbf{b} = \mathbf{X}'\mathbf{y}$$

Here $(\mathbf{X}'\mathbf{X})$ is a known matrix and $\mathbf{X}'\mathbf{y}$ a known vector, each depending on the empirical data in a given problem, and $\mathbf{b}$ denotes a vector of unknown coefficients. It is too late in the day to resolve this conflict; the student must maintain sufficient intellectual agility to interpret the symbols according to the context.

Returning to Eq. (4-84), the solution vector is written

$$\mathbf{x} = \mathbf{A}^{-1}\mathbf{b}$$

Substitution for $\mathbf{A}^{-1}$ from Eq. (4-64) gives

$$\mathbf{x} = \frac{1}{|\mathbf{A}|}\begin{bmatrix} C_{11} & C_{21} & \cdots & C_{n1} \\ C_{12} & C_{22} & \cdots & C_{n2} \\ \cdots & \cdots & \cdots & \cdots \\ C_{1n} & C_{2n} & \cdots & C_{nn} \end{bmatrix}\begin{bmatrix} b_1 \\ b_2 \\ \vdots \\ b_n \end{bmatrix}$$

Thus

$$x_1 = \frac{1}{|\mathbf{A}|}(b_1C_{11} + b_2C_{21} + \cdots + b_nC_{n1})$$

The expression in parentheses is seen to be the evaluation of the following determinant by the elements in the first column:

$$b_1C_{11} + b_2C_{21} + \cdots + b_nC_{n1} = \begin{vmatrix} b_1 & a_{12} & a_{13} & \cdots & a_{1n} \\ b_2 & a_{22} & a_{23} & \cdots & a_{2n} \\ \cdots & \cdots & \cdots & \cdots & \cdots \\ b_n & a_{n2} & a_{n3} & \cdots & a_{nn} \end{vmatrix}$$

Similar results hold for each element in $\mathbf{x}$. The ith element is thus the *ratio of two determinants*, the denominator being the determinant of $\mathbf{A}$ and the numerator the determinant of the matrix obtained from $\mathbf{A}$ by replacing the ith column of $\mathbf{A}$ by $\mathbf{b}$ and leaving the other $n - 1$ columns unchanged.

Example 4-12 Solve the system

$$\begin{aligned} 2x_1 + 4x_2 - x_3 &= 15 \\ x_1 - 3x_2 + 2x_3 &= -5 \\ 6x_1 + 5x_2 + x_3 &= 28 \end{aligned}$$

This may be accomplished by several methods.

(*a*) *Cramer's rule* First calculate $|\mathbf{A}|$, and it is helpful to expand in terms of the elements of a column, say, the first. Thus

$$|\mathbf{A}| = \begin{vmatrix} 2 & 4 & -1 \\ 1 & -3 & 2 \\ 6 & 5 & 1 \end{vmatrix} = 2\begin{vmatrix} -3 & 2 \\ 5 & 1 \end{vmatrix} - 1\begin{vmatrix} 4 & -1 \\ 5 & 1 \end{vmatrix} + 6\begin{vmatrix} 4 & -1 \\ -3 & 2 \end{vmatrix}$$

$$= 2(-13) - 9 + 6(5) = -5$$

Then

$$-5x_1 = \begin{vmatrix} 15 & 4 & -1 \\ -5 & -3 & 2 \\ 28 & 5 & 1 \end{vmatrix} = 15(-13) + 5(9) + 28(5) = -10$$

so that $\qquad x_1 = 2$

$$-5x_2 = \begin{vmatrix} 2 & 15 & -1 \\ 1 & -5 & 2 \\ 6 & 28 & 1 \end{vmatrix} = -15\begin{vmatrix} 1 & 2 \\ 6 & 1 \end{vmatrix} - 5\begin{vmatrix} 2 & -1 \\ 6 & 1 \end{vmatrix} - 28\begin{vmatrix} 2 & -1 \\ 1 & 2 \end{vmatrix}$$

$$= -15(-11) - 5(8) - 28(5) = -15$$

so that $\qquad x_2 = 3$

and

$$-5x_3 = \begin{vmatrix} 2 & 4 & 15 \\ 1 & -3 & -5 \\ 6 & 5 & 28 \end{vmatrix} = 15\begin{vmatrix} 1 & -3 \\ 6 & 5 \end{vmatrix} + 5\begin{vmatrix} 2 & 4 \\ 6 & 5 \end{vmatrix} + 28\begin{vmatrix} 2 & 4 \\ 1 & -3 \end{vmatrix}$$

$$= 15(23) + 5(-14) + 28(-10) = -5$$

giving

$$x_3 = 1$$

Thus the solution vector is $\mathbf{x}' = [2 \quad 3 \quad 1]$.

(*b*) *Calculation of* $\mathbf{A}^{-1}$ From the calculations already completed in (*a*),

$$\mathbf{A}^{-1} = -\frac{1}{5}\begin{bmatrix} -13 & -9 & 5 \\ 11 & 8 & -5 \\ 23 & 14 & -10 \end{bmatrix}$$

Thus

$$\mathbf{x} = -\frac{1}{5}\begin{bmatrix} -13 & -9 & 5 \\ 11 & 8 & -5 \\ 23 & 14 & -10 \end{bmatrix}\begin{bmatrix} 15 \\ -5 \\ 28 \end{bmatrix} = -\frac{1}{5}\begin{bmatrix} -10 \\ -15 \\ -5 \end{bmatrix} = \begin{bmatrix} 2 \\ 3 \\ 1 \end{bmatrix}$$

Methods (*a*) and (*b*) are essentially slightly different ways of laying out the same set of tedious calculations. A computationally much more efficient method, not just for small systems but more especially for large systems, is the *elimination method.*

(*c*) *Elimination method* Lay out the system in matrix form as

$$\begin{bmatrix} 2 & 4 & -1 \\ 1 & -3 & 2 \\ 6 & 5 & 1 \end{bmatrix}\begin{bmatrix} x_1 \\ x_2 \\ x_3 \end{bmatrix} = \begin{bmatrix} 15 \\ -5 \\ 28 \end{bmatrix}$$

In the first step we produce zeros in the second and third positions of the first column by subtracting one-half the *first equation* from the *second* and three times the *first* from the *third*. This gives

$$\begin{bmatrix} 2 & 4 & -1 \\ 0 & -5 & 2.5 \\ 0 & -7 & 4 \end{bmatrix}\begin{bmatrix} x_1 \\ x_2 \\ x_3 \end{bmatrix} = \begin{bmatrix} 15 \\ -12.5 \\ -17 \end{bmatrix}$$

Next we produce a zero in the third position of the second column by subtracting $\frac{7}{5}$ times the second equation from the third.

$$\begin{bmatrix} 2 & 4 & -1 \\ 0 & -5 & 2.5 \\ 0 & 0 & 0.5 \end{bmatrix}\begin{bmatrix} x_1 \\ x_2 \\ x_3 \end{bmatrix} = \begin{bmatrix} 15 \\ -12.5 \\ 0.5 \end{bmatrix}$$

This gives an upper triangular system, which is solved for the x's by *back substitution*. The third equation gives directly

$$x_3 = 1$$

The second equation

$$-5x_2 + 2.5x_3 = -12.5 \qquad \text{or} \qquad -5x_2 = -15$$

then gives

$$x_2 = 3$$

and the first equation

$$2x_1 + 4x_2 - x_3 = 15 \qquad \text{or} \qquad 2x_1 = 4$$

gives

$$x_1 = 2$$

In the elimination method the inverse $\mathbf{A}^{-1}$ is never calculated at all. The calculations are fast and simple compared with the first two methods, but it does not shed light on the theoretical properties of the inverse.

4-5 THE EIGENVALUE PROBLEM

The previous section was concerned with the solution of the set of equations

$$\mathbf{Ax} = \mathbf{b} \tag{4-84}$$

This section is concerned with solutions of

$$\mathbf{Ax} = \lambda\mathbf{x} \tag{4-85}$$

where $\mathbf{A}$ is a known square matrix of order n, $\mathbf{x}$ is an unknown n-element column vector, and λ is an unknown scalar. This problem will arise in a number of places later in the book. It is known as the eigenvalue problem. In contrast with Eq. (4-84) there are now two unknowns, a vector and a scalar. Solutions will come in pairs; to each λ there will correspond an $\mathbf{x}$ vector. The λ's are known as *eigenvalues*, *latent roots*, or *characteristic roots* and the $\mathbf{x}$'s as *eigenvectors*, *latent vectors*, or *characteristic vectors*.

For $n = 2$, Eq. (4-85), written out in full, becomes

$$(a_{11} - \lambda)x_1 + a_{12}x_2 = 0$$
$$a_{21}x_1 + (a_{22} - \lambda)x_2 = 0$$

which may be put back in matrix form as

$$(\mathbf{A} - \lambda\mathbf{I})\mathbf{x} = \mathbf{0} \tag{4-86}$$

Equation (4-86) is equivalent to Eq. (4-85) for any n. If the matrix $\mathbf{A} - \lambda\mathbf{I}$ is nonsingular, the *only* solution to Eq. (4-86) is the trivial $\mathbf{x} = \mathbf{0}$. Thus for a nontrivial solution to exist, the matrix must be singular or, in other words, have a zero determinant. This condition gives

$$|\mathbf{A} - \lambda\mathbf{I}| = 0 \tag{4-87}$$

which is known as the *characteristic equation* for the matrix $\mathbf{A}$. This gives a polynomial equation in the unknown λ. Each root or eigenvalue λ_i may be substituted back into Eq. (4-86) and the corresponding eigenvector $\mathbf{x}_i$ obtained.

For the 2×2 case it is easily seen that the characteristic equation is

$$\lambda^2 - (a_{11} + a_{22})\lambda + (a_{11}a_{22} - a_{12}a_{21}) = 0 \tag{4-88}$$

with roots

$$\lambda_1 = \frac{1}{2}\left[(a_{11} + a_{22}) + \sqrt{(a_{11} + a_{22})^2 - 4(a_{11}a_{22} - a_{12}a_{21})}\right]$$

$$\lambda_2 = \frac{1}{2}\left[(a_{11} + a_{22}) - \sqrt{(a_{11} + a_{22})^2 - 4(a_{11}a_{22} - a_{12}a_{21})}\right]$$

In the special case of a 2 × 2 *symmetric* matrix, $a_{12} = a_{21}$, the roots become

$$\lambda = \frac{1}{2}\left[(a_{11} + a_{22}) \pm \sqrt{(a_{11} - a_{22})^2 + 4a_{12}^2}\right]$$

and since the content of the square root sign is the sum of two squares, *the roots are necessarily real for a real symmetric matrix.* Notice also that the characteristic equation may be written

$$(\lambda_1 - \lambda)(\lambda_2 - \lambda) = \lambda^2 - (\lambda_1 + \lambda_2)\lambda + \lambda_1\lambda_2 = 0$$

Comparison with Eq. (4-88) shows that

$$\text{Sum of roots} = \lambda_1 + \lambda_2 = a_{11} + a_{22}$$

$$= \text{trace (sum of diagonal elements of } \mathbf{A}) \tag{4-89}$$

$$\text{Product of roots} = \lambda_1\lambda_2 = a_{11}a_{22} - a_{12}a_{21} = |\mathbf{A}| \tag{4-90}$$

These two properties hold true in the general nth-order case, as does the previous result on real roots for a real symmetric matrix.

Example 4-13

$$\mathbf{A} = \begin{bmatrix} 4 & 2 \\ 2 & 1 \end{bmatrix}$$

Thus

$$(\mathbf{A} - \lambda\mathbf{I}) = \begin{bmatrix} 4 - \lambda & 2 \\ 2 & 1 - \lambda \end{bmatrix}$$

and the characteristic equation is

$$\lambda^2 - 5\lambda = 0$$

with roots

$$\lambda_1 = 5 \quad \text{and} \quad \lambda_2 = 0$$

For $\lambda_1 = 5$, substitution in Eq. (4-86) gives

$$\begin{bmatrix} -1 & 2 \\ 2 & -4 \end{bmatrix}\begin{bmatrix} x_1 \\ x_2 \end{bmatrix} = \mathbf{0} \Rightarrow x_1 = 2x_2$$

Thus one element in the eigenvector is arbitrary, and so if $\mathbf{x}$ satisfies Eq. (4-86) for some λ, then so does $c\mathbf{x}$, where c is an arbitrary constant. It is conventional to *normalize* the vector by setting its length at unity, that is, making

$$x_1^2 + x_2^2 = 1$$

which, with $x_1 = 2x_2$, gives

$$\mathbf{x}_1 = \begin{bmatrix} \dfrac{2}{\sqrt{5}} \\ \dfrac{1}{\sqrt{5}} \end{bmatrix} \quad \text{corresponding to } \lambda_1 = 5$$

Similarly, it may be shown that

$$\mathbf{x}_2 = \begin{bmatrix} \dfrac{1}{\sqrt{5}} \\ -\dfrac{2}{\sqrt{5}} \end{bmatrix}$$

is the eigenvector corresponding to $\lambda_2 = 0$.

It is seen that the eigenvectors are *orthogonal*, $\mathbf{x}_1'\mathbf{x}_2 = 0$. If we assemble the eigenvectors in a matrix X,

$$\mathbf{X} = [\mathbf{x}_1 \quad \mathbf{x}_2] = \begin{bmatrix} \dfrac{2}{\sqrt{5}} & \dfrac{1}{\sqrt{5}} \\ \dfrac{1}{\sqrt{5}} & -\dfrac{2}{\sqrt{5}} \end{bmatrix}$$

and then form $\mathbf{X}'\mathbf{X}$, we obtain the result that

$$\mathbf{X}'\mathbf{X} = \mathbf{X}\mathbf{X}' = \begin{bmatrix} 1 & 0 \\ 0 & 1 \end{bmatrix} \tag{4-91}$$

We will derive this result for the general case below. Forming the matrix product $\mathbf{X}'\mathbf{A}\mathbf{X}$ gives

$$\begin{bmatrix} \dfrac{2}{\sqrt{5}} & \dfrac{1}{\sqrt{5}} \\ \dfrac{1}{\sqrt{5}} & -\dfrac{2}{\sqrt{5}} \end{bmatrix} \begin{bmatrix} 4 & 2 \\ 2 & 1 \end{bmatrix} \begin{bmatrix} \dfrac{2}{\sqrt{5}} & \dfrac{1}{\sqrt{5}} \\ \dfrac{1}{\sqrt{5}} & -\dfrac{2}{\sqrt{5}} \end{bmatrix} = \begin{bmatrix} 5 & 0 \\ 0 & 0 \end{bmatrix} \tag{4-92}$$

The diagonal matrix on the right-hand side of Eq. (4-92) displays the eigenvalues 5 and 0 on the main diagonal.

Properties of Eigenvectors and Eigenvalues of a Real Symmetric Matrix of Order *n*

In statistical applications we are mainly concerned with symmetric real matrices. Properties with an asterisk apply specifically to real symmetric matrices; those without an asterisk apply to real nonsymmetric as well as to symmetric matrices.

1.* *The eigenvalues are real.*

Suppose we have a complex eigenvalue $\lambda + i\mu$, where i denotes $\sqrt{-1}$, and a corresponding complex eigenvector $\mathbf{x} + i\mathbf{y}$. Then

$$\mathbf{A}(\mathbf{x} + i\mathbf{y}) = (\lambda + i\mu)(\mathbf{x} + i\mathbf{y})$$

Multiplying out and equating real and imaginary parts gives

$$\mathbf{A}\mathbf{x} = \lambda\mathbf{x} - \mu\mathbf{y}$$

and
$$\mathbf{Ay} = \mu\mathbf{x} + \lambda\mathbf{y}$$

Premultiplying the first equation by $\mathbf{y}'$ and the second by $\mathbf{x}'$ gives

$$\mathbf{y}'\mathbf{Ax} = \lambda\mathbf{x}'\mathbf{y} - \mu\mathbf{y}'\mathbf{y}$$
$$\mathbf{x}'\mathbf{Ay} = \mu\mathbf{x}'\mathbf{x} + \lambda\mathbf{x}'\mathbf{y}$$

When $\mathbf{A}$ is symmetric, $\mathbf{y}'\mathbf{Ax} = \mathbf{x}'\mathbf{Ay}$ (a scalar equals its transpose). Subtracting the first equation from the second then yields

$$0 = \mu(\mathbf{x}'\mathbf{x} + \mathbf{y}'\mathbf{y})$$

Since the eigenvectors must be nontrivial, $\mathbf{x}'\mathbf{x} > 0$ or $\mathbf{y}'\mathbf{y} > 0$ (or both), so

$$\mu = 0$$

that is, there cannot be a complex eigenvalue. Real eigenvalues in turn generate real eigenvectors, that is, $\mathbf{y} = \mathbf{0}$.

2.* *Eigenvectors corresponding to distinct eigenvalues are pairwise orthogonal.*

If $\mathbf{x}_1, \mathbf{x}_2$ denote the eigenvectors corresponding to λ_1, λ_2, then

$$\mathbf{Ax}_1 = \lambda_1\mathbf{x}_1 \Rightarrow \mathbf{x}_2'\mathbf{Ax}_1 = \lambda_1\mathbf{x}_2'\mathbf{x}_1$$

and
$$\mathbf{Ax}_2 = \lambda_2\mathbf{x}_2 \Rightarrow \mathbf{x}_1'\mathbf{Ax}_2 = \lambda_2\mathbf{x}_1'\mathbf{x}_2$$

The symmetry of $\mathbf{A}$ gives

$$\mathbf{x}_1'\mathbf{Ax}_2 = \mathbf{x}_2'\mathbf{Ax}_1$$

Thus

$$\lambda_1\mathbf{x}_2'\mathbf{x}_1 = \lambda_2\mathbf{x}_1'\mathbf{x}_2$$

If $\lambda_1 \neq \lambda_2$, this last equation gives

$$\mathbf{x}_1'\mathbf{x}_2 = 0$$

3.* *If an eigenvalue* λ *has multiplicity* k (*that is, is repeated* k *times*), *there will be* k *orthogonal vectors corresponding to this root.*†

As an illustration of this result consider the diagonal matrix

$$\mathbf{A} = \begin{bmatrix} 1 & 0 & 0 \\ 0 & 2 & 0 \\ 0 & 0 & 1 \end{bmatrix}$$

The characteristic equation is

$$(1 - \lambda)^2(2 - \lambda) = 0$$

with roots

$$\lambda_1 = 1 \qquad \text{with multiplicity 2}$$
$$\lambda_2 = 2$$

† For a proof, see G. Hadley, *Linear Algebra*, Addison Wesley, Reading, MA, 1961, pp. 243–245.

For $\lambda_2 = 2$, $(\mathbf{A} - \lambda\mathbf{I})\mathbf{x} = \mathbf{0}$ gives

$$\begin{bmatrix} -1 & 0 & 0 \\ 0 & 0 & 0 \\ 0 & 0 & -1 \end{bmatrix} \begin{bmatrix} x_1 \\ x_2 \\ x_3 \end{bmatrix} = \mathbf{0} \Rightarrow \mathbf{x}_2 = x_2 \begin{bmatrix} 0 \\ 1 \\ 0 \end{bmatrix}$$

The multiple root gives

$$\begin{bmatrix} 0 & 0 & 0 \\ 0 & 1 & 0 \\ 0 & 0 & 0 \end{bmatrix} \begin{bmatrix} x_1 \\ x_2 \\ x_3 \end{bmatrix} = \mathbf{0} \Rightarrow \mathbf{x}_1 = x_1 \begin{bmatrix} 1 \\ 0 \\ 0 \end{bmatrix} + x_3 \begin{bmatrix} 0 \\ 0 \\ 1 \end{bmatrix}$$

The root with multiplicity 2 thus yields two orthogonal eigenvectors $\mathbf{e}_1$ and $\mathbf{e}_3$.

4.* *The* n*th-order symmetric matrix* **A** *has eigenvalues* $\lambda_1, \lambda_2, \ldots, \lambda_n$, *possibly not all distinct.*† *Properties* 2 *and* 3 *then guarantee a set of* n *orthogonal eigenvectors* $\mathbf{x}_1, \mathbf{x}_2, \ldots, \mathbf{x}_n$, *such that*

$$\mathbf{x}_i'\mathbf{x}_j = 0 \qquad i \neq j;\ i, j = 1, 2, \ldots, n \tag{4-93}$$

As we have seen, any eigenvector is arbitrary up to a scale factor,

$$\mathbf{A}\mathbf{x}_i = \lambda_i \mathbf{x}_i \qquad \mathbf{A}(c\mathbf{x}_i) = \lambda_i(c\mathbf{x}_i)$$

where c is any constant. The arbitrariness may be removed by *normalizing* the **x** vectors, and the most common normalization is to set the length of each vector at unity, that is,

$$\mathbf{x}_i'\mathbf{x}_i = 1 \qquad i = 1, 2, \ldots, n \tag{4-94}$$

Conditions (4-93) and (4-94) define an *orthonormal* set of vectors. The conditions may be combined in a single statement,

$$\mathbf{x}_i'\mathbf{x}_j = \delta_{ij}, \qquad \delta_{ij} = \begin{cases} 0 & i \neq j \\ 1 & i = j \end{cases} \tag{4-95}$$

where δ_{ij} is known as the Kronecker delta. Define **X** to be an nth-order matrix whose columns are the vectors $\mathbf{x}_1, \mathbf{x}_2, \ldots, \mathbf{x}_n$. Condition (4-95) may then be written in the alternative form

$$\mathbf{X}'\mathbf{X} = \mathbf{I} \tag{4-96}$$

From the definition and uniqueness of the inverse matrix it then follows that

$$\mathbf{X}' = \mathbf{X}^{-1} \tag{4-97}$$

The matrix **X** is then said to be an *orthogonal matrix*, that is, a matrix such that *its inverse is simply its transpose*. It would be more appropriate to call it an orthonormal matrix, since Eq. (4-96) requires all the columns to have unit length as well as being orthogonal, but the former designation is the one established in the literature. A remarkable property of orthogonal matrices follows immediately from Eq. (4-97). Since the inverse is unique,

$$\mathbf{X}\mathbf{X}' = \mathbf{I} \tag{4-98}$$

† See G. Hadley, op. cit., p. 245.

that is, although **X** was constructed as a matrix with orthogonal *columns*, its *row vectors are also orthogonal*. Thus an orthogonal matrix is defined by

$$\mathbf{X}'\mathbf{X}' = \mathbf{X}\mathbf{X} = \mathbf{I} \tag{4-99}$$

Example 4-14

$$\mathbf{A} = \begin{bmatrix} 1 & 2 & 0 \\ 2 & 2 & \sqrt{2} \\ 0 & \sqrt{2} & 1 \end{bmatrix}$$

The characteristic equation is then

$$\begin{vmatrix} 1-\lambda & 2 & 0 \\ 2 & 2-\lambda & \sqrt{2} \\ 0 & \sqrt{2} & 1-\lambda \end{vmatrix} = 0$$

that is,

$$(1-\lambda)(1+\lambda)(-4+\lambda) = 0$$

with roots

$$\lambda_1 = 1 \qquad \lambda_2 = -1 \qquad \lambda_3 = 4$$

$$\lambda_1 = 1: \qquad (\mathbf{A} - \mathbf{I})\mathbf{x} = \begin{bmatrix} 0 & 2 & 0 \\ 2 & 1 & \sqrt{2} \\ 0 & \sqrt{2} & 0 \end{bmatrix} \begin{bmatrix} x_1 \\ x_2 \\ x_3 \end{bmatrix} = \begin{bmatrix} 0 \\ 0 \\ 0 \end{bmatrix} \Rightarrow \mathbf{x}_1 = \begin{bmatrix} \dfrac{-1}{\sqrt{3}} \\ 0 \\ \dfrac{\sqrt{2}}{\sqrt{3}} \end{bmatrix}$$

$$\lambda_2 = -1: \qquad (\mathbf{A} + \mathbf{I})\mathbf{x} = \begin{bmatrix} 2 & 2 & 0 \\ 2 & 3 & \sqrt{2} \\ 0 & \sqrt{2} & 2 \end{bmatrix} \begin{bmatrix} x_1 \\ x_2 \\ x_3 \end{bmatrix} = \begin{bmatrix} 0 \\ 0 \\ 0 \end{bmatrix} \Rightarrow \mathbf{x}_2 = \begin{bmatrix} \dfrac{2}{\sqrt{10}} \\ \dfrac{-2}{\sqrt{10}} \\ \dfrac{1}{\sqrt{5}} \end{bmatrix}$$

$$\lambda_3 = 4: \qquad (\mathbf{A} - 4\mathbf{I})\mathbf{x} = \begin{bmatrix} -3 & 2 & 0 \\ 2 & -2 & \sqrt{2} \\ 0 & \sqrt{2} & -3 \end{bmatrix} \begin{bmatrix} x_1 \\ x_2 \\ x_3 \end{bmatrix} = \begin{bmatrix} 0 \\ 0 \\ 0 \end{bmatrix} \Rightarrow \mathbf{x}_3 = \begin{bmatrix} \dfrac{2}{\sqrt{15}} \\ \dfrac{3}{\sqrt{15}} \\ \dfrac{\sqrt{2}}{\sqrt{15}} \end{bmatrix}$$

Thus

$$\mathbf{X} = \begin{bmatrix} -\dfrac{1}{\sqrt{3}} & \dfrac{2}{\sqrt{10}} & \dfrac{2}{\sqrt{15}} \\ 0 & -\dfrac{2}{\sqrt{10}} & \dfrac{3}{\sqrt{15}} \\ \dfrac{\sqrt{2}}{\sqrt{3}} & \dfrac{1}{\sqrt{5}} & \dfrac{\sqrt{2}}{\sqrt{15}} \end{bmatrix}$$

The reader can check numerically that the rows of **x** all have unit length and are pairwise orthogonal (as, of course, are the columns).

5.* *The orthogonal matrix of eigenvectors diagonalizes* **A**, *that is,*

$$\mathbf{X}'\mathbf{A}\mathbf{X} = \mathbf{\Lambda} \tag{4-100}$$

where $\mathbf{\Lambda} = \text{diag}\{\lambda_1, \lambda_2, \ldots, \lambda_n\}$.

For λ_j and $\mathbf{x}_j$ we have

$$\mathbf{A}\mathbf{x}_j = \lambda_j \mathbf{x}_j$$

Premultiplying by $\mathbf{x}_i'$,

$$\mathbf{x}_i'\mathbf{A}\mathbf{x}_j = \lambda_j \mathbf{x}_i'\mathbf{x}_j = \lambda_j \delta_{ij} \qquad \text{using Eq. (4-95)} \tag{4-101}$$

Equation (4-101) displays the i, jth element in **X′AX**, and collecting for all i, j gives Eq. (4-100). An alternative proof illustrates a useful exercise in matrix manipulation.

$$\mathbf{A}\mathbf{X} = \begin{bmatrix} | & | & & | \\ \lambda_1\mathbf{x}_1 & \lambda_2\mathbf{x}_2 & \cdots & \lambda_n\mathbf{x}_n \\ | & | & & | \end{bmatrix}$$

$$= \begin{bmatrix} | & | & & | \\ \mathbf{x}_1 & \mathbf{x}_2 & \cdots & \mathbf{x}_n \\ | & | & & | \end{bmatrix} \begin{bmatrix} \lambda_1 & & & \\ & \lambda_2 & & \\ & & \ddots & \\ & & & \lambda_n \end{bmatrix}$$

$$= \mathbf{X}\mathbf{\Lambda}$$

Premultiplying by **X′** then gives Eq. (4-100). We should not conclude from this result that only symmetric matrices can be diagonalized. If for any matrix **A** there are *n linearly independent eigenvectors* and we arrange them as the columns of a matrix **X**, then

$$\mathbf{X}^{-1}\mathbf{A}\mathbf{X} = \mathbf{\Lambda} \tag{4-102}$$

The contrast with Eq. (4-100) is that the columns of **X** are not necessarily of unit length, nor are they necessarily orthogonal.

6. *The sum of the eigenvalues is equal to the sum of the diagonal elements* (*trace*) *of* **A**.

This property is true for any matrix, but the proof is particularly simple for symmetric matrices. Denote the trace of a (square) matrix **A** by

$$\text{tr}(\mathbf{A}) = a_{11} + a_{22} + \cdots + a_{nn}$$

For two matrices, **A** of order $m \times n$ and **B** of order $n \times m$,

$$\text{tr}(\mathbf{AB}) = \text{tr}(\mathbf{BA}) \tag{4-103}$$

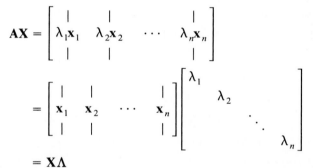

AB is of order $m \times m$. Its ith diagonal element is

$$c_{ii} = \sum_{j=1}^{n} a_{ij} b_{ji}$$

Thus

$$\operatorname{tr}(\mathbf{AB}) = \sum_{i=1}^{m} \sum_{j=1}^{n} a_{ij} b_{ji}$$

BA is of order $n \times n$. Its jth diagonal element is

$$d_{ii} = \sum_{i=1}^{m} b_{ji} a_{ij}$$

Thus

$$\operatorname{tr}(\mathbf{BA}) = \sum_{j=1}^{n} \sum_{i=1}^{m} b_{ji} a_{ij} = \operatorname{tr}(\mathbf{AB})$$

This result extends simply to

$$\operatorname{tr}(\mathbf{ABC}) = \operatorname{tr}(\mathbf{BCA}) = \operatorname{tr}(\mathbf{CAB}) \tag{4-104}$$

Turning now to

$$\mathbf{X'AX} = \boldsymbol{\Lambda}$$

$$\operatorname{tr} \boldsymbol{\Lambda} = \operatorname{tr}(\mathbf{X'AX})$$

$$= \operatorname{tr}(\mathbf{AXX'}) \qquad \text{using Eq. (4-104)}$$

Thus

$$\operatorname{tr} \boldsymbol{\Lambda} = \operatorname{tr}(\mathbf{A}) \tag{4-105}$$

or

$$\lambda_1 + \lambda_2 + \cdots + \lambda_n = a_{11} + a_{22} + \cdots + a_{nn}$$

7. *The product of the eigenvalues is equal to the determinant of* **A**.

This result is again true for any matrix, but the proof is very simple for symmetric matrices. We note first that when **X** is an orthogonal matrix,

$$|\mathbf{X}| = \pm 1 \tag{4-106}$$

for

$$\mathbf{X'X} = \mathbf{I} \Rightarrow |\mathbf{X'}| \cdot |\mathbf{X}| = 1$$

but

$$|\mathbf{X}| = |\mathbf{X'}|$$

Thus

$$|\mathbf{X}| = \pm 1$$

Returning again to

$$\mathbf{X'AX} = \boldsymbol{\Lambda}$$

$$|\mathbf{X'}| \cdot |\mathbf{A}| \cdot |\mathbf{X}| = |\boldsymbol{\Lambda}|$$

Thus

$$|\mathbf{A}| = \lambda_1 \lambda_2 \cdots \lambda_n \tag{4-107}$$

8. *The rank of* **A** *is equal to the number of nonzero eigenvalues.*

We established in Eq. (4-53) that pre- or postmultiplication of any matrix by nonsingular matrices does not change its rank. Thus, again from Eq. (4-102),

$$\rho(\mathbf{\Lambda}) = \rho(\mathbf{A}) \tag{4-108}$$

and the easiest way to establish the rank of $\mathbf{\Lambda}$ is to determine the order of the largest nonvanishing determinant that can be formed from its elements. This is simply equal to the number of nonvanishing eigenvalues.

9. *The eigenvalues of* $\mathbf{A}^2$ *are the squares of the eigenvalues of* **A**, *but the eigenvectors of both matrices are the same.*

$$\mathbf{Ax} = \lambda\mathbf{x}$$

Premultiplying by **A**,

$$\mathbf{A}^2\mathbf{x} = \lambda\mathbf{Ax} = \lambda^2\mathbf{x}$$

which establishes the result. We may note, in passing, a very useful application of this result in analyzing the stability of dynamic systems. Suppose $\mathbf{y}_t$ denotes a vector of the values taken by a number of economic variables in time period t, and suppose $\mathbf{y}_t$ can be expressed in terms of the previous values by the system of equations

$$\mathbf{y}_t = \mathbf{Ay}_{t-1} \tag{4-109}$$

Even if the original specification of the system involves lags of more than one period, an appropriate definition of new variables can produce a derived system of the type of Eq. (4-109).† Successive substitution in Eq. (4-109) gives

$$\mathbf{y}_t = \mathbf{A}^t\mathbf{y}_0$$

where $\mathbf{y}_0$ denotes initial values of the variables. Provided **A** has a linearly independent set of eigenvectors,

$$\mathbf{X}^{-1}\mathbf{AX} = \mathbf{\Lambda}$$

or

$$\mathbf{A} = \mathbf{X\Lambda X}^{-1}$$

Thus

$$\mathbf{A}^2 = \mathbf{X\Lambda X}^{-1}\mathbf{X\Lambda X}^{-1} = \mathbf{X\Lambda}^2\mathbf{X}^{-1}$$

So

$$\mathbf{A}^t = \mathbf{X\Lambda}^t\mathbf{X}^{-1}$$

and the elements of $\mathbf{y}_t$ are seen to be linear combinations of the *tth powers* of the eigenvalues of **A**. Thus if the system is to be stable, we need

$$|\lambda_i| \leq 1, \qquad i = 1, \ldots, n$$

10. *The eigenvalues of* $\mathbf{A}^{-1}$ *are the reciprocals of the eigenvalues of* **A**, *but the eigenvectors of both matrices are the same.*

$$\mathbf{Ax} = \lambda\mathbf{x}$$

† See G. Chow, *Analysis and Control of Dynamic Economic Systems*, Wiley, New York, 1975, pp. 21–35.

Premultiply by $\mathbf{A}^{-1}$,

$$\mathbf{x} = \lambda \mathbf{A}^{-1}\mathbf{x}$$

or

$$\mathbf{A}^{-1}\mathbf{x} = \left(\frac{1}{\lambda}\right)\mathbf{x}$$

which establishes the result.

11. *Each eigenvalue of an idempotent matrix is either zero or unity.*

By property 9

$$\mathbf{A}^2\mathbf{x} = \lambda^2\mathbf{x}$$

But when $\mathbf{A}$ is idempotent,

$$\mathbf{A}^2\mathbf{x} = \mathbf{A}\mathbf{x} = \lambda\mathbf{x}$$

Thus

$$\lambda(\lambda - 1)\mathbf{x} = \mathbf{0}$$

and since any eigenvector $\mathbf{x}$ is not the null vector,

$$\lambda = 0 \qquad \text{or} \qquad \lambda = 1$$

12. *The rank of an idempotent matrix is equal to its trace.*

This follows from properties 6, 8, and 11,

$$\begin{aligned} \rho(\mathbf{A}) &= \rho(\boldsymbol{\Lambda}) && \text{from property 8} \\ &= \text{number of nonzero eigenvalues} \\ &= \operatorname{tr}(\boldsymbol{\Lambda}) && \text{from property 11} \\ &= \operatorname{tr}(\mathbf{A}) && \text{from property 6} \end{aligned}$$

4-6 QUADRATIC FORMS AND POSITIVE DEFINITE MATRICES

We have already introduced quadratic forms briefly in Sec. 4-2 and have seen that there is no loss of generality in considering only symmetric matrices. For a 2×2 symmetric matrix $\mathbf{A}$ and a two-element column vector $\mathbf{x}$, the quadratic form is

$$\mathbf{x}'\mathbf{A}\mathbf{x} = a_{11}x_1^2 + 2a_{12}x_1x_2 + a_{22}x_2^2$$

For a third-order matrix

$$\begin{aligned} \mathbf{x}'\mathbf{A}\mathbf{x} = a_{11}x_1^2 &+ 2a_{12}x_1x_2 + 2a_{13}x_1x_3 \\ &+ \quad a_{22}x_2^2 \quad + 2a_{23}x_2x_3 \\ &\qquad\qquad\qquad + \quad a_{33}x_3^2 \end{aligned}$$

For the general nth-order case

$$\begin{aligned}\mathbf{x}'\mathbf{A}\mathbf{x} = a_{11}x_1^2 &+ 2a_{12}x_1x_2 + 2a_{13}x_1x_3 + \cdots + 2a_{1n}x_1x_n \\ &+ a_{22}x_2^2 + 2a_{23}x_2x_3 + \cdots + 2a_{2n}x_2x_n \\ &+ a_{33}x_3^2 + \cdots + 2a_{3n}x_3x_n \\ &\ddots \\ &+ a_{nn}x_n^2\end{aligned}$$

Definitions

If $\mathbf{x}'\mathbf{A}\mathbf{x} > 0$ for all $\mathbf{x} \neq 0$, the quadratic form is said to be *positive definite* and $\mathbf{A}$ is said to be a *positive definite matrix.*

If $\mathbf{x}'\mathbf{A}\mathbf{x} \geq 0$ for all $\mathbf{x} \neq 0$, the form and matrix are *positive semidefinite.*

Reversing the above inequality signs defines negative definite and negative semidefinite matrices, respectively. If a form is positive for some $\mathbf{x}$ vectors and negative for others, it is said to be *indefinite.*

It is important to have tests for positive definite matrices.

1. *A necessary and sufficient condition for the real symmetric matrix* $\mathbf{A}$ *to be positive definite is that all the eigenvalues of* $\mathbf{A}$ *be positive.*

To prove the necessary condition assume $\mathbf{x}'\mathbf{A}\mathbf{x} > 0$. For any eigenvalue λ_i

$$\mathbf{A}\mathbf{x}_i = \lambda_i\mathbf{x}_i$$

Premultiplying by $\mathbf{x}_i'$ gives

$$\mathbf{x}_i'\mathbf{A}\mathbf{x}_i = \lambda_i\mathbf{x}_i'\mathbf{x}_i = \lambda_i$$

Since $\mathbf{x}'\mathbf{A}\mathbf{x} > 0$ holds for any $\mathbf{x} \neq 0$, it holds for each eigenvector, and so $\lambda_i > 0$ for all i. To prove sufficiency we assume all $\lambda_i > 0$ and show that $\mathbf{x}'\mathbf{A}\mathbf{x} > 0$. Since a symmetric matrix has a full set of n orthogonal eigenvectors $\mathbf{x}_1, \mathbf{x}_2, \ldots, \mathbf{x}_n$, any nonnull vector $\mathbf{x}$ may be expressed as a linear combination of the eigenvectors

$$\mathbf{x} = c_1\mathbf{x}_1 + c_2\mathbf{x}_2 + \cdots + c_n\mathbf{x}_n$$

Thus

$$\begin{aligned}\mathbf{A}\mathbf{x} &= c_1\mathbf{A}\mathbf{x}_1 + c_2\mathbf{A}\mathbf{x}_2 + \cdots + c_n\mathbf{A}\mathbf{x}_n \\ &= c_1\lambda_1\mathbf{x}_1 + c_2\lambda_2\mathbf{x}_2 + \cdots + c_n\lambda_n\mathbf{x}_n\end{aligned}$$

$$\begin{aligned}\mathbf{x}'\mathbf{A}\mathbf{x} &= (c_1\mathbf{x}_1 + c_2\mathbf{x}_2 + \cdots + c_n\mathbf{x}_n)'(c_1\lambda_1\mathbf{x}_1 + c_2\lambda_2\mathbf{x}_2 + \cdots + c_n\lambda_n\mathbf{x}_n) \\ &= c_1^2\lambda_1 + c_2^2\lambda_2 + \cdots + c_n^2\lambda_n\end{aligned}$$

since

$$\mathbf{x}_i'\mathbf{x}_j = \delta_{ij} = \begin{cases} 0 & i \neq j \\ 1 & i = j \end{cases} \qquad i, j = 1, 2, \ldots, n$$

Since all λ_i are assumed to be positive, $\mathbf{x}'\mathbf{A}\mathbf{x} > 0$.

2. *A necessary and sufficient condition for a real symmetric matrix* $\mathbf{A}$ *to be positive definite is that the determinant of every principal submatrix be positive.*

The principal submatrices of **A** are a set of n submatrices such as

$$\mathbf{a}_{ii}, \quad \begin{bmatrix} a_{ii} & a_{ij} \\ a_{ji} & a_{jj} \end{bmatrix}, \quad \begin{bmatrix} a_{ii} & a_{ij} & a_{ik} \\ a_{ji} & a_{jj} & a_{jk} \\ a_{ki} & a_{kj} & a_{kk} \end{bmatrix}, \ldots, \mathbf{A}$$

More conventionally one takes the upper submatrices

$$\mathbf{A}_1 = [a_{11}] \quad \mathbf{A}_2 = \begin{bmatrix} a_{11} & a_{12} \\ a_{21} & a_{22} \end{bmatrix} \quad \mathbf{A}_3 = \begin{bmatrix} a_{11} & a_{12} & a_{13} \\ a_{21} & a_{22} & a_{23} \\ a_{31} & a_{32} & a_{33} \end{bmatrix} \quad , \ldots, \quad \mathbf{A}_n = \mathbf{A}$$

When **A** is positive definite, $\mathbf{x}'\mathbf{A}\mathbf{x} > 0$ for any nonzero **x**. Thus we may consider an **x** vector whose first r elements are nonzero and whose last $n - r$ elements are zero, that is,

$$\mathbf{x}' = [\mathbf{x}'_r \quad \mathbf{0}']$$

Then

$$\mathbf{x}'\mathbf{A}\mathbf{x} = [\mathbf{x}'_r \quad \mathbf{0}'] \begin{bmatrix} \mathbf{A}_r & * \\ * & * \end{bmatrix} \begin{bmatrix} \mathbf{x}_r \\ \mathbf{0} \end{bmatrix} = \mathbf{x}'_r \mathbf{A}_r \mathbf{x}_r$$

where **A** has been partitioned by the first r and the last $n - r$ rows and columns and the asterisks denote the remaining submatrices in **A**, which get wiped out by the zero subvector in **x**. Since

$$\mathbf{x}'\mathbf{A}\mathbf{x} > 0$$

it follows that

$$\mathbf{x}'_r \mathbf{A}_r \mathbf{x}_r > 0$$

Thus by the previous condition all the roots of $\mathbf{A}_r$ are positive, and so

$$|\mathbf{A}_r| > 0$$

A suitable choice of **x** vectors then gives the necessary and sufficient condition for **A** to be positive definite as

$$|\mathbf{A}_1| > 0, \; |\mathbf{A}_2| > 0, \; |\mathbf{A}_3| > 0, \ldots, \; |\mathbf{A}| > 0 \tag{4-110}$$

Finally we state a number of useful theorems on positive definite matrices.

1. *If* **A** *is symmetric and positive definite, a nonsingular matrix* **P** *can be found such that*

$$\mathbf{A} = \mathbf{P}\mathbf{P}' \tag{4-111}$$

We know that the matrix of eigenvectors of **A** can be used to diagonalize **A**, that is, from Eq. (4-100),

$$\mathbf{X}'\mathbf{A}\mathbf{X} = \mathbf{\Lambda}$$

which gives

$$\mathbf{A} = \mathbf{X}\mathbf{\Lambda}\mathbf{X}' \tag{4-112}$$

When **A** is positive definite, all its eigenvalues are positive. Thus $\mathbf{\Lambda}$ may be factored into

$$\Lambda = \Lambda^{1/2}\Lambda^{1/2}$$

where
$$\Lambda^{1/2} = \begin{bmatrix} \sqrt{\lambda_1} & & & \\ & \sqrt{\lambda_2} & & \\ & & \ddots & \\ & & & \sqrt{\lambda_n} \end{bmatrix}$$

Substitution in Eq. (4-112) gives

$$\mathbf{A} = \mathbf{X}\Lambda^{1/2}\Lambda^{1/2}\mathbf{X}' = (\mathbf{X}\Lambda^{1/2})(\mathbf{X}\Lambda^{1/2})'$$

which gives Eq. (4-111) with

$$\mathbf{P} = \mathbf{X}\Lambda^{1/2}$$

and $\mathbf{P}$ is nonsingular since it is the product of nonsingular matrices.

2. *If* $\mathbf{A}$ *is* $n \times n$ *and positive definite and if* $\mathbf{P}$ *is* $n \times m$ *with* $\rho(\mathbf{P}) = m$, *then* $\mathbf{P'AP}$ *is positive definite.*

Clearly, $\mathbf{P'AP}$ is an $m \times m$ symmetric matrix, and for any m-element vector $\mathbf{y}$,

$$\mathbf{y}'(\mathbf{P'AP})\mathbf{y} = \mathbf{x}'\mathbf{A}\mathbf{x}$$

where $\mathbf{x} = \mathbf{Py}$. Thus $\mathbf{x}$ is seen to be a linear combination of the m linearly independent columns of $\mathbf{P}$, and so $\mathbf{x} = \mathbf{0}$ if and only if $\mathbf{y} = \mathbf{0}$. Thus $\mathbf{P'AP}$ is positive definite.

The final three results are stated without proof.

3. *If* $\mathbf{A}$ *is* $n \times m$ *with rank* $m < n$, *then* $\mathbf{A'A}$ *is positive definite and* $\mathbf{AA'}$ *is positive semidefinite.*
4. *If* $\mathbf{A}$ *is* $n \times m$ *with rank* $k < \min(m, n)$, *then* $\mathbf{A'A}$ *and* $\mathbf{AA'}$ *are each positive semidefinite.*
5. *If* $\mathbf{A}$ *and* $\mathbf{B}$ *are positive definite matrices and* $\mathbf{A} - \mathbf{B}$ *is also positive definite, then* $\mathbf{B}^{-1} - \mathbf{A}^{-1}$ *is positive definite.*†

4-7 MAXIMUM AND MINIMUM VALUES

It is convenient to express the main results on maxima and minima in matrix terms. Consider a scalar variable y defined as a function of n independent variables,

$$y = f(x_1, x_2, \ldots, x_n)$$

† A proof of this result is given in P. Dhrymes, *Introductory Econometrics*, Springer-Verlag, New York, 1978, App. A2.13.

which may also be written

$$y = f(\mathbf{x})$$

The first-order or total differential of the function is defined as

$$dy = f_1\,dx_1 + f_2\,dx_2 + \cdots + f_n\,dx_n \tag{4-113}$$

where

$$f_i = \frac{\partial y}{\partial x_i} \qquad i = 1, 2, \ldots, n$$

and the dx_i indicate arbitrary changes in the x_i. For small dx_i the first-order differential gives the approximate value of the resultant change in y. Denoting the vector of partial derivatives by $\mathbf{f}$ and the vector of differentials by $\mathbf{dx}$,

$$\mathbf{f} = \frac{\partial y}{\partial \mathbf{x}} = \begin{bmatrix} f_1 \\ f_2 \\ \vdots \\ f_n \end{bmatrix} \qquad \mathbf{dx} = \begin{bmatrix} dx_1 \\ dx_2 \\ \vdots \\ dx_n \end{bmatrix}$$

the first-order differential of y is simply

$$dy = \mathbf{f}'\,\mathbf{dx} \tag{4-114}$$

If y has a stationary value at a point

$$\mathbf{x}^* = [x_1^* x_2^* \;\cdots\; x_n^*]$$

then $dy = 0$ for all points in the neighborhood of $\mathbf{x}^*$. For such points $\mathbf{dx} \neq 0$, and so from Eq. (4-114) the necessary condition for a stationary value is

$$\mathbf{f} = \mathbf{0}$$

that is, all partial derivatives are zero at the stationary point.

A stationary point may be a maximum, where the value of the function is less at all points in the neighborhood of $\mathbf{x}^*$; a minimum, where the value of the function is greater at all points in the neighborhood of $\mathbf{x}^*$; or a saddle point, where the value of the function increases in some directions from $\mathbf{x}^*$ and diminishes in others. One may distinguish between these possibilities by means of the second-order differential d^2y. The second-order differential may be found by totally differentiating the first-order differential. It is an approximation to the change in dy as we move away from the point $\mathbf{x}^*$. Clearly, for a maximum value dy will decrease from zero to some negative value, so d^2y will be negative, and conversely for a minimum value d^2y will be positive. For a saddle point d^2y will be positive for some $\mathbf{dx}$ and negative for other $\mathbf{dx}$.† Totally differentiating Eq.

† It is possible, but extremely rare, to have $d^2y = 0$ for some $\mathbf{dx}$. Such complexities are ignored here.

(4-113) gives

$$
\begin{aligned}
d^2y &= \frac{\partial}{\partial x_1}[f_1\,dx_1 + f_2\,dx_2 + \cdots + f_n\,dx_n]\,dx_1 \\
&\quad + \frac{\partial}{\partial x_2}[f_1\,dx_1 + f_2\,dx_2 + \cdots + f_n\,dx_n]\,dx_2 \\
&\quad + \cdots + \frac{\partial}{\partial x_n}[f_1\,dx_1 + f_2\,dx_2 + \cdots + f_n\,dx_n]\,dx_n \\
&= f_{11}\,dx_1^2 + 2f_{12}\,dx_1\,dx_2 + 2f_{13}\,dx_1\,dx_3 + \cdots + 2f_{1n}\,dx_1\,dx_n \\
&\qquad + f_{22}\,dx_2^2 + 2f_{23}\,dx_2\,dx_3 + \cdots + 2f_{2n}\,dx_2\,dx_n \\
&\qquad\qquad \ddots \\
&\qquad\qquad\qquad + f_{nn}\,dx_n^2
\end{aligned}
$$

where

$$f_{ij} = f_{ji} = \frac{\partial^2 y}{\partial x_i \partial x_j} \qquad \text{for } i \neq j, \text{ all } i, j$$

and dx_i^2 indicates the square of the differential dx_i. The second-order differential is thus seen to be a quadratic form in $\mathbf{dx}$. The matrix of the quadratic form is the symmetric Hessian matrix of second-order partial derivatives, which we will denote by

$$\mathbf{F} = \frac{\partial^2 y}{\partial \mathbf{x}^2} = \begin{bmatrix} f_{11} & f_{12} & \cdots & f_{1n} \\ f_{12} & f_{22} & \cdots & f_{2n} \\ \cdots & \cdots & \cdots & \cdots \\ f_{1n} & f_{2n} & \cdots & f_{nn} \end{bmatrix}$$

and we may write

$$d^2y = \mathbf{dx}'\mathbf{F}\,\mathbf{dx} \tag{4-115}$$

Thus d^2y is positive or negative as $\mathbf{F}$ is positive definite or negative definite. To summarize, the conditions for a maximum or a minimum at a point $\mathbf{x}^*$ are as follows:

	First-order condition	Second-order condition
Maximum	$\mathbf{f} = \dfrac{\partial y}{\partial \mathbf{x}} = 0$	$\mathbf{F} = \dfrac{\partial^2 y}{\partial \mathbf{x}^2}$ is negative definite
Minimum	$\mathbf{f} = \dfrac{\partial y}{\partial \mathbf{x}} = 0$	$\mathbf{F} = \dfrac{\partial^2 y}{\partial \mathbf{x}^2}$ is positive definite

where $\mathbf{f}$ and $\mathbf{F}$ are evaluated at $\mathbf{x}^*$.

Constrained Extrema

In finding stationary values of $y = f(x_1, x_2, \ldots, x_n)$ the x's were assumed to be independent variables. Thus we could specify n arbitrary differentials $dx_1, dx_2, \ldots, dx_n$. In some problems, however, the x's may be subject to one or more constraints, and we have to find a maximum or minimum value of y subject to the constraints. We will assume for the moment that the function has a single maximum or minimum value and state the problem formally as follows:

Find the $\mathbf{x}^*$ *vector which maximizes (minimizes)* y *subject to the* $m < n$ *constraints*

$$g_j(\mathbf{x}) = 0 \qquad j = 1, 2, \ldots, m, m < n$$

Define the column vector

$$\mathbf{g}(\mathbf{x}) = \begin{bmatrix} g_1(\mathbf{x}) \\ g_2(\mathbf{x}) \\ \vdots \\ g_m(\mathbf{x}) \end{bmatrix}$$

and a column vector of m Lagrange multipliers,

$$\boldsymbol{\lambda} = \begin{bmatrix} \lambda_1 \\ \lambda_2 \\ \vdots \\ \lambda_m \end{bmatrix}$$

Using these we define a new objective function as

$$\varphi = f(\mathbf{x}) - \boldsymbol{\lambda}'\mathbf{g}(\mathbf{x}) \tag{4-116}$$

Thus φ is a scalar quantity, which is a function of the $m + n$ variables in $\boldsymbol{\lambda}$ and $\mathbf{x}$. The first-order condition for a stationary value of φ is that all $m + n$ first-order partial derivatives should vanish, that is,

$$\begin{bmatrix} \dfrac{\partial \varphi}{\partial \mathbf{x}} \\ \dfrac{\partial \varphi}{\partial \boldsymbol{\lambda}} \end{bmatrix} = \begin{bmatrix} \dfrac{\partial f}{\partial \mathbf{x}} - \dfrac{\partial}{\partial \mathbf{x}}(\boldsymbol{\lambda}'\mathbf{g}(\mathbf{x})) \\ \mathbf{g}(\mathbf{x}) \end{bmatrix} = \mathbf{0} \tag{4-117}$$

Some care is required in the interpretation of

$$\frac{\partial}{\partial \mathbf{x}}(\boldsymbol{\lambda}'\mathbf{g}(\mathbf{x}))$$

Since

$$\boldsymbol{\lambda}'\mathbf{g}(\mathbf{x}) = \lambda_1 g_1(x_1, x_2, \ldots, x_n) + \lambda_2 g_2(x_1, x_2, \ldots, x_n) + \cdots + \lambda_m g_m(x_1, x_2, \ldots, x_n)$$

we have

$$\frac{\partial(\boldsymbol{\lambda}'\mathbf{g}(\mathbf{x}))}{\partial x_1} = \lambda_1\frac{\partial g_1}{\partial x_1} + \lambda_2\frac{\partial g_2}{\partial x_1} + \cdots + \lambda_m\frac{\partial g_m}{\partial x_1} = \boldsymbol{\lambda}'\frac{\partial \mathbf{g}}{\partial x_1}$$

$$\cdots\cdots\cdots\cdots\cdots\cdots\cdots\cdots\cdots\cdots\cdots\cdots$$

$$\frac{\partial(\boldsymbol{\lambda}'\mathbf{g}(\mathbf{x}))}{\partial x_n} = \lambda_1\frac{\partial g_1}{\partial x_n} + \lambda_2\frac{\partial g_2}{\partial x_n} + \cdots + \lambda_m\frac{\partial g_m}{\partial x_n} = \boldsymbol{\lambda}'\frac{\partial \mathbf{g}}{\partial x_n}$$

where

$$\frac{\partial \mathbf{g}}{\partial x_i} = \begin{bmatrix} \dfrac{\partial g_1}{\partial x_i} \\ \dfrac{\partial g_2}{\partial x_i} \\ \vdots \\ \dfrac{\partial g_m}{\partial g_i} \end{bmatrix} \qquad i = 1, 2, \ldots, n$$

Since $\partial f/\partial \mathbf{x}$ is an $n \times 1$ vector, we need to arrange for $(\partial/\partial\mathbf{x})(\boldsymbol{\lambda}'\mathbf{g}(\mathbf{x}))$ to have n rows. Defining $\mathbf{G}$ as the $n \times m$ matrix of partial derivatives,

$$\mathbf{G} = \begin{bmatrix} \dfrac{\partial g_1}{\partial x_1} & \dfrac{\partial g_2}{\partial x_1} & \cdots & \dfrac{\partial g_m}{\partial x_1} \\ \dfrac{\partial g_1}{\partial x_2} & \dfrac{\partial g_2}{\partial x_2} & \cdots & \dfrac{\partial g_m}{\partial x_2} \\ \cdots & \cdots & \cdots & \cdots \\ \dfrac{\partial g_1}{\partial x_n} & \dfrac{\partial g_2}{\partial x_n} & \cdots & \dfrac{\partial g_m}{\partial x_n} \end{bmatrix} = \begin{bmatrix} \dfrac{\partial \mathbf{g}}{\partial x_1} & \dfrac{\partial \mathbf{g}}{\partial x_2} & \cdots & \dfrac{\partial \mathbf{g}}{\partial x_n} \end{bmatrix}$$

we have

$$\frac{\partial \varphi}{\partial \mathbf{x}} = \frac{\partial f}{\partial \mathbf{x}} - \mathbf{G}\boldsymbol{\lambda}$$

and the first-order conditions for a stationary point are

$$\frac{\partial f}{\partial \mathbf{x}} - \mathbf{G}\boldsymbol{\lambda} = \mathbf{0}$$
$$\mathbf{g}(\mathbf{x}) = \mathbf{0} \qquad (4\text{-}118)$$

The second equation in Eqs. (4-118) ensures that the stationary value satisfies the constraints. To distinguish between maxima and minima, we must still examine whether the quadratic form in Eq. (4-115) is negative definite or positive definite, but now only for **dx** vectors which do not violate the constraints. Totally differentiating the jth constraint

$$g_j(x_1, x_2, \ldots, x_n) = 0$$

gives

$$0 = dg_j = \frac{\partial g_j}{\partial x_1}dx_1 + \frac{\partial g_j}{\partial x_2}dx_2 + \cdots + \frac{\partial g_j}{\partial x_n}dx_n$$

There is a similar condition for each constraint. Thus the **dx** vectors which do not violate the constraints are given by

$$\mathbf{G}'\,d\mathbf{x} = \mathbf{0} \tag{4-119}$$

In many cases the **F** matrix consists only of constants, and so its definiteness can be established independently of any **x** values.

PROBLEMS

4-1 Expand (**A** + **B**)(**A** − **B**) and (**A** − **B**)(**A** + **B**). Are these expansions the same? If not, why not? How many terms are in each?

4-2 Given

$$\mathbf{A} = \begin{bmatrix} 1 & 0 & 3 \\ 2 & -1 & 1 \end{bmatrix} \qquad \mathbf{B} = \begin{bmatrix} 3 & 4 & 1 \\ 0 & -1 & 5 \\ 1 & 2 & -2 \end{bmatrix} \qquad \mathbf{C} = \begin{bmatrix} 2 \\ -1 \\ 4 \end{bmatrix}$$

Calculate (**AB**)′, **B**′**A**′, (**AC**)′, and **C**′**A**′.

4-3 Find all matrices **B** obeying the equation

$$\begin{bmatrix} 0 & 1 \\ 0 & 2 \end{bmatrix} \mathbf{B} = \begin{bmatrix} 0 & 0 & 1 \\ 0 & 0 & 2 \end{bmatrix}$$

4-4 Find all matrices **B** which commute with

$$\mathbf{A} = \begin{bmatrix} 0 & 1 \\ 0 & 2 \end{bmatrix}$$

to give **AB** = **BA**.

4-5 Write down a few matrices of order 3 × 3 with numerical elements. Find first their squares and then their cubes, checking the latter by using the two processes $\mathbf{A}(\mathbf{A}^2)$ and $\mathbf{A}^2(\mathbf{A})$.

4-6 Prove that diagonal matrices of the same order are commutative in multiplication with each other.

4-7 Let

$$\mathbf{J} = \begin{bmatrix} 0 & 0 & 1 \\ 0 & 1 & 0 \\ 1 & 0 & 0 \end{bmatrix}$$

Write out in full some products **JA**, where **A** is a rectangular matrix. Describe in words the effect on **A**. Do the same with products of type **AJ**. Find $\mathbf{J}^2$.

4-8 If

$$\mathbf{V} = \begin{bmatrix} 0 & 1 & 0 \\ 0 & 0 & 1 \\ 0 & 0 & 0 \end{bmatrix}$$

find $\mathbf{V}^2$ and $\mathbf{V}^3$. Examine some products of the type **VA**, $\mathbf{V}^2\mathbf{A}$, and **V**′**A**.

4-9 Given

$$\mathbf{A} = \begin{bmatrix} 1 & 3 & 2 \\ 2 & 6 & 9 \\ 7 & 6 & 1 \end{bmatrix} \qquad \text{and} \qquad \mathbf{E} = \begin{bmatrix} 0 & 1 & 0 \\ 1 & 0 & 0 \\ 0 & 0 & 1 \end{bmatrix}$$

Calculate $|\mathbf{A}|$, $|\mathbf{E}|$, and $|\mathbf{B}|$, where **B** = **EA**. Verify that $|\mathbf{B}| = |\mathbf{E}|\,|\mathbf{A}|$.

4-10 Show that

$$\begin{vmatrix} 1 & 1 & 1 \\ a & b & c \\ a^2 & b^2 & c^2 \end{vmatrix} = (c-b)(c-a)(b-a)$$

4-11 If (x_1, y_1) and (x_2, y_2) are points on the x, y plane, show that the equation

$$\begin{vmatrix} x & y & 1 \\ x_1 & y_1 & 1 \\ x_2 & y_2 & 1 \end{vmatrix} = 0$$

represents a straight line through the two points.

4-12 Prove that the determinant of a skew-symmetric matrix of odd order vanishes identically. (If **A** is a skew-symmetric matrix, then $\mathbf{A}' = -\mathbf{A}$.)

4-13 Show that the matrix

$$\mathbf{Q} = \begin{bmatrix} \frac{1}{\sqrt{6}} & \frac{-2}{\sqrt{5}} & \frac{1}{\sqrt{30}} \\ \frac{-2}{\sqrt{6}} & \frac{1}{\sqrt{5}} & \frac{-2}{\sqrt{30}} \\ \frac{1}{\sqrt{6}} & 0 & \frac{-5}{\sqrt{30}} \end{bmatrix}$$

is orthogonal, that is, that $\mathbf{Q}' = \mathbf{Q}^{-1}$.

4-14 If the u_i are normal variables with

$$E(u_i) = 0 \qquad l = 1, \ldots, n$$

$$E(u_i^2) = \sigma^2 \qquad i = 1, \ldots, n$$

$$E(u_i u_j) = 0 \qquad i \neq j$$

show that $E(\mathbf{u}'\mathbf{A}\mathbf{u}) = \sigma^2 \operatorname{tr}(\mathbf{A})$.

4-15 Given

$$\mathbf{X} = \begin{bmatrix} 1 & 1 \\ 1 & 2 \\ 1 & 1 \\ 1 & 3 \end{bmatrix}$$

Compute

$$\mathbf{A} = \left(\mathbf{I}_4 - \mathbf{X}(\mathbf{X}'\mathbf{X})^{-1}\mathbf{X}'\right)$$

Show that **A** is idempotent and determine its rank. Find the characteristic roots and the associated characteristic vectors of **A**, and hence obtain the orthogonal matrix which diagonalizes **A**.

4-16 **A** and **B** are nonsingular matrices of the same order. Prove that **AB** and **BA** possess identical characteristic roots. Show also that no such matrices can be found to satisfy the equation

$$\mathbf{AB} - \mathbf{BA} = \mathbf{I}$$

(Cambridge Economics Tripos, 1967)

4-17 Evaluate the characteristic roots and vectors of

$$\mathbf{A} = \begin{bmatrix} 5 & -6 & -6 \\ -1 & 4 & 2 \\ 3 & -6 & -4 \end{bmatrix}$$

4-18 Examine the following quadratic forms for positive definiteness:

(*a*) $6x_1^2 + 49x_2^2 + 51x_3^2 - 82x_2x_3 + 20x_1x_3 - 4x_1x_2$
(*b*) $4x_1^2 + 9x_2^2 + 2x_3^2 + 8x_2x_3 + 6x_3x_1 + 6x_1x_2$

(Cambridge Economics Tripos, 1968)

4-19 (*a*) Given that

$$\mathbf{A} = \begin{bmatrix} 2 & 2 & 2 \\ 2 & 2 & 2 \\ 2 & 2 & 2 \end{bmatrix} \qquad \mathbf{B} = \begin{bmatrix} 1 & 0 & 1 \\ 0 & -1 & 0 \\ 1 & 0 & 1 \end{bmatrix}$$

find $\mathbf{A}^n$ for $n > 1$ and $\mathbf{B}^n$ for $n > 1$.

(*b*) If **A** is defined as

$$\mathbf{A} = \begin{bmatrix} \frac{1}{3} & \frac{2}{3} & \frac{2}{3} \\ \frac{2}{3} & \frac{1}{3} & -\frac{2}{3} \\ \frac{2}{3} & -\frac{2}{3} & \frac{1}{3} \end{bmatrix}$$

show that **A** is orthogonal.

Prove that the product of two orthogonal matrices of the same order is also an orthogonal matrix.

(UL, 1967)

4-20 **X** is a square matrix of order n and **a** is an $n \times 1$ vector. Find

$$\frac{\partial(\mathbf{a}'\mathbf{X}\mathbf{a})}{\partial \mathbf{X}}$$

(*a*) When the elements of **X** are independent.

(*b*) When **X** is symmetric.

Note: If **X** is a matrix whose elements are variables x_{ij} and $f(\mathbf{X})$ is a scalar function, then

$$\mathbf{Z} = \frac{\partial f(\mathbf{X})}{\partial \mathbf{X}}$$

is a matrix of the same order as **X** such that

$$z_{ij} = \frac{\partial f(\mathbf{X})}{\partial x_{ij}}$$

CHAPTER
FIVE

THE k-VARIABLE LINEAR MODEL

Chapter 2 contains a fairly complete treatment of the two-variable ($k = 2$) model. Some of the algebra of the three-variable ($k = 3$) model was developed in Sec. 4 of Chap. 3. Section 1 of Chap. 4 indicated the power of matrix algebra to give a compact representation of the general k-variable model. It is now time to give a complete statistical treatment of the k-variable model. To facilitate this treatment we first provide a review of some basic statistical results in matrix form. These results are extensions of the material on matrix algebra in Chap. 4 and the statistical material in various sections of App. A.

5-1 PRELIMINARY STATISTICAL RESULTS

Let $\mathbf{x}$ denote a vector of random variables $X_1, X_2, \ldots, X_n$. Each variable has an expected value

$$\mu_i = E(X_i) \qquad i = 1, 2, \ldots, n$$

Collecting these expected values in a vector $\boldsymbol{\mu}$, gives

$$\boldsymbol{\mu} = E(\mathbf{x}) = \begin{bmatrix} E(X_1) \\ E(X_2) \\ \vdots \\ E(X_n) \end{bmatrix} = \begin{bmatrix} \mu_1 \\ \mu_2 \\ \vdots \\ \mu_n \end{bmatrix} \tag{5-1}$$

The application of the operator E to the vector $\mathbf{x}$ means that E is applied to each element of $\mathbf{x}$. The variance of X_i, by definition, is

$$\operatorname{var}(X_i) = E\{(X_i - \mu_i)^2\}$$

and the covariance between X_i and X_j is

$$\operatorname{cov}(X_i, X_j) = E\{(X_i - \mu_i)(X_j - \mu_j)\}$$

If we define the vector $\mathbf{x} - \boldsymbol{\mu}$ and then form

$$E\{(\mathbf{x} - \boldsymbol{\mu})(\mathbf{x} - \boldsymbol{\mu})'\} = E\left\{\begin{bmatrix} (X_1 - \mu_1) \\ (X_2 - \mu_2) \\ \vdots \\ (X_n - \mu_n) \end{bmatrix} [(X_1 - \mu_1)(X_2 - \mu_2) \cdots (X_n - \mu_n)]\right\}$$

$$= \begin{bmatrix} E(X_1 - \mu_1)^2 & E(X_1 - \mu_1)(X_2 - \mu_2) & \cdots & E(X_1 - \mu_1)(X_n - \mu_n) \\ E(X_2 - \mu_2)(X_1 - \mu_1) & E(X_2 - \mu_2)^2 & \cdots & E(X_2 - \mu_2)(X_n - \mu_n) \\ \cdots & \cdots & \cdots & \cdots \\ E(X_n - \mu_n)(X_1 - \mu_1) & E(X_n - \mu_n)(X_2 - \mu_2) & \cdots & E(X_n - \mu_n)^2 \end{bmatrix}$$

we see that the elements of this matrix are the variances and covariances of the X variables, the variances being displayed on the main diagonal and the covariances in the off-diagonal positions. The matrix is known as a variance-covariance matrix or, more simply, as a variance matrix or a covariance matrix.† We will generally refer to it as a variance matrix, denote it by var($\mathbf{x}$), and

$$\operatorname{var}(\mathbf{x}) = E\{(\mathbf{x} - \boldsymbol{\mu})(\mathbf{x} - \boldsymbol{\mu})'\} = \boldsymbol{\Sigma} \tag{5-2}$$

The variance matrix $\boldsymbol{\Sigma}$ is clearly symmetric. It is important to determine whether $\boldsymbol{\Sigma}$ is positive definite or not. Define a scalar variable Y as a linear combination of the X's, that is,

$$Y = (\mathbf{x} - \boldsymbol{\mu})'\mathbf{c} \tag{5-3}$$

where $\mathbf{c}$ is any arbitrary n-element column vector. Squaring Eq. (5-3) and taking expectations gives

$$\begin{aligned} E(Y^2) &= E\{\mathbf{c}'(\mathbf{x} - \boldsymbol{\mu})(\mathbf{x} - \boldsymbol{\mu})'\mathbf{c}\} \\ &= \mathbf{c}'E\{(\mathbf{x} - \boldsymbol{\mu})(\mathbf{x} - \boldsymbol{\mu})'\}\mathbf{c} \\ &= \mathbf{c}'\boldsymbol{\Sigma}\mathbf{c} \end{aligned}$$

There are two useful points to notice about this development. First of all, $(\mathbf{x} - \boldsymbol{\mu})'\mathbf{c}$ is a scalar, thus its square may be found by multiplying it by its transpose. Second, whenever we have to take the expectation of a complicated matrix expression, the E operator may be moved to the right past any vectors or matrices consisting only of constants, but it must stop in front of any expression

† Alternative expressions for the variance-covariance matrix are cov($\mathbf{x}$) and $V(\mathbf{x})$.

involving random variables. Since Y is a scalar random variable, $E(Y^2) \geq 0$. Thus

$$\mathbf{c}'\mathbf{\Sigma}\mathbf{c} \geq 0$$

and $\mathbf{\Sigma}$ is positive semidefinite. But

$$E(Y^2) = 0 \Rightarrow Y = 0$$

which, from Eq. (5-3), means that the X deviations $(X_1 - \mu_1), (X_2 - \mu_2), \ldots, (X_n - \mu_n)$ are linearly dependent. Thus

$\mathbf{\Sigma}$ *is positive definite, provided no linear dependence exists among the* X'*s*.

The n random variables will have some *multivariate probability density function* (pdf) written

$$p(\mathbf{x}) = p(X_1, X_2, \ldots, X_n)$$

which is simply some formula or rule giving the likelihood of various combinations of X values. The most important multivariate pdf is the multivariate normal. The univariate normal distribution is specified once its mean μ and its variance σ^2 are given. The multivariate normal is similarly specified in terms of its mean vector $\boldsymbol{\mu}$ and its variance matrix $\mathbf{\Sigma}$. The formula is

$$p(\mathbf{x}) = \frac{1}{(2\pi)^{n/2}|\mathbf{\Sigma}|^{1/2}} \exp\left[-\frac{1}{2}(\mathbf{x} - \boldsymbol{\mu})'\mathbf{\Sigma}^{-1}(\mathbf{x} - \boldsymbol{\mu})\right] \tag{5-4}$$

A compact shorthand statement of Eq. (5-4) is

$$\mathbf{x} \sim N(\boldsymbol{\mu}, \mathbf{\Sigma})$$

to be read, "the variables in $\mathbf{x}$ are distributed according to the multivariate normal law with mean vector $\boldsymbol{\mu}$ and variance matrix $\mathbf{\Sigma}$." When $n = 1$, $\mathbf{\Sigma} = \sigma^2$ and Eq. (5-4) becomes

$$p(X) = \frac{1}{\sqrt{2\pi}\,\sigma} \exp\left[-\frac{1}{2\sigma^2}(X - \mu)^2\right]$$

which is the familiar univariate normal density. When $n = 2$, if we use ρ to denote the correlation between X_1 and X_2, the variance matrix becomes

$$\mathbf{\Sigma} = \begin{bmatrix} \sigma_1^2 & \rho\sigma_1\sigma_2 \\ \rho\sigma_1\sigma_2 & \sigma_2^2 \end{bmatrix} \qquad \text{with } |\mathbf{\Sigma}| = \sigma_1^2\sigma_2^2(1 - \rho^2)$$

Notice that $|\mathbf{\Sigma}| > 0$ unless $\rho^2 = 1$, so that the variance matrix is positive definite unless there is perfect linear correlation between the two variables, in agreement with the general result above. Substitution in Eq. (5-4) gives

$$p(X_1, X_2) = \frac{1}{2\pi\sigma_1\sigma_2\sqrt{1 - \rho^2}} \exp\left\{-\frac{1}{2(1 - \rho^2)}\left[\left(\frac{X_1 - \mu_1}{\sigma_1}\right)^2 - 2\rho\left(\frac{X_1 - \mu_1}{\sigma_1}\right)\left(\frac{X_2 - \mu_2}{\sigma_2}\right) + \left(\frac{X_2 - \mu_2}{\sigma_2}\right)^2\right]\right\}$$

An especially important case of Eq. (5-4) occurs when all the X's have the same variance σ^2 and are all pairwise uncorrelated.† Then

$$\mathbf{\Sigma} = \sigma^2\mathbf{I}$$

with

$$|\mathbf{\Sigma}| = \sigma^{2n}, \qquad \mathbf{\Sigma}^{-1} = \frac{1}{\sigma^2}\mathbf{I}$$

and
$$p(\mathbf{x}) = \frac{1}{(2\pi\sigma^2)^{n/2}}\exp\left[-\frac{1}{2\sigma^2}(\mathbf{x}-\boldsymbol{\mu})'(\mathbf{x}-\boldsymbol{\mu})\right] \tag{5-5}$$

Equation (5-5) thus factorizes into

$$\begin{aligned} p(X_1, X_2, \ldots, X_n) &= \prod_{i=1}^{n}\left\{\frac{1}{\sqrt{2\pi}}\exp\left[-\frac{1}{2\sigma^2}(X_i-\mu_i)^2\right]\right\} \\ &= p(X_1)p(X_2)\cdots p(X_n) \end{aligned}$$

so that the multivariate density is the product of the separate *marginal* densities, that is, the X's are *distributed independently* of one another. This is an extremely important result. *Zero correlations between normally distributed variables imply statistical independence.* This result does not necessarily hold for variables which are not normally distributed. Notice carefully that these results depend on zero correlations in the *population* and not on zero sample correlations.

A more general case of this result may be derived from Eq. (5-4). Suppose $\mathbf{\Sigma}$ has the form

$$\mathbf{\Sigma} = \begin{bmatrix} \mathbf{\Sigma}_{11} & \mathbf{0} \\ \mathbf{0} & \mathbf{\Sigma}_{22} \end{bmatrix} \tag{5-6}$$

where $\mathbf{\Sigma}_{11}$ is square of order r and $\mathbf{\Sigma}_{22}$ is square of order $n-r$. The form of Eq. (5-6) means that each and every variable in the set $X_1, X_2, \ldots, X_r$ is uncorrelated with each and every variable in the set $X_{r+1}, X_{r+2}, \ldots, X_n$. Applying a similar partitioning to $\mathbf{x}$ and $\boldsymbol{\mu}$,

$$(\mathbf{x}-\boldsymbol{\mu})'\mathbf{\Sigma}^{-1}(\mathbf{x}-\boldsymbol{\mu}) = (\mathbf{x}_1-\boldsymbol{\mu}_1)'\mathbf{\Sigma}_{11}^{-1}(\mathbf{x}_1-\boldsymbol{\mu}_1) + (\mathbf{x}_2-\boldsymbol{\mu}_2)'\mathbf{\Sigma}_{22}^{-1}(\mathbf{x}_2-\boldsymbol{\mu}_2)$$

using Eq. (4-75) for $\mathbf{\Sigma}^{-1}$. Also from Eq. (4-79)

$$|\mathbf{\Sigma}| = |\mathbf{\Sigma}_{11}||\mathbf{\Sigma}_{22}|$$

Making these substitutions in Eq. (5-4) gives

$$\begin{aligned} p(\mathbf{x}) &= \left\{\frac{1}{(2\pi)^{r/2}|\mathbf{\Sigma}_{11}|^{1/2}}\exp\left[-\frac{1}{2}(\mathbf{x}_1-\boldsymbol{\mu}_1)'\mathbf{\Sigma}_{11}^{-1}(\mathbf{x}_1-\boldsymbol{\mu}_1)\right]\right\} \\ &\quad\times\left\{\frac{1}{(2\pi)^{(n-r)/2}|\mathbf{\Sigma}_{22}|^{1/2}}\exp\left[-\frac{1}{2}(\mathbf{x}_2-\boldsymbol{\mu}_2)'\mathbf{\Sigma}_{22}^{-1}(\mathbf{x}_2-\boldsymbol{\mu}_2)\right]\right\} \end{aligned}$$

† The assumption of a common variance is only made for simplicity. All that is required for the result is that the $\mathbf{\Sigma}$ matrix be diagonal.

that is,

$$p(\mathbf{x}) = p(\mathbf{x}_1)p(\mathbf{x}_2)$$

so that the first r variables are distributed independently of the remaining $n - r$ variables.

Distributions of Quadratic Forms

Suppose

$$\mathbf{x} \sim N(\mathbf{0}, \mathbf{I})$$

that is, the n variables in $\mathbf{x}$ have independent normal distributions, each with zero mean and unit variance. In other terminology, the X's are independent standardized normal variables. The sum of squares $\mathbf{x}'\mathbf{x}$ is a particularly simple example of a quadratic form with matrix $\mathbf{I}$. From the definition of the χ^2 variable,

$$\mathbf{x}'\mathbf{x} \sim \chi^2(n)$$

for $\chi^2(n)$ is the sum of the squares of n independent standardized normal variables.

Suppose now that

$$\mathbf{x} \sim N(0, \sigma^2\mathbf{I}) \tag{5-7}$$

The variables are still independent and have zero means, but each X has to be divided by σ to yield a variable with unit variance. Thus

$$\frac{X_1^2}{\sigma^2} + \frac{X_2^2}{\sigma^2} + \cdots + \frac{X_n^2}{\sigma^2} \sim \chi^2(n)$$

that is,

$$\frac{1}{\sigma^2}\mathbf{x}'\mathbf{x} \sim \chi^2(n) \tag{5-8}$$

or

$$\mathbf{x}'(\sigma^2\mathbf{I})^{-1}\mathbf{x} \sim \chi^2(n) \tag{5-9}$$

Equation (5-9) shows explicitly that the matrix of the quadratic form is the inverse of the variance matrix.

Suppose now that

$$\mathbf{x} \sim N(\mathbf{0}, \mathbf{\Sigma}) \tag{5-10}$$

where $\mathbf{\Sigma}$ is a positive definite matrix. The equivalent expression to Eq. (5-9) would now be

$$\mathbf{x}'\mathbf{\Sigma}^{-1}\mathbf{x} \sim \chi^2(n) \tag{5-11}$$

This result does in fact hold, but the proof is no longer direct since the X variables are no longer statistically independent. The trick is to transform X's into Y's, which will be independent standardized normal variables. Since $\mathbf{\Sigma}$ is positive definite, by Eq. (4-111) there exists a nonsingular matrix $\mathbf{P}$ such that

$$\mathbf{\Sigma} = \mathbf{P}\mathbf{P}'$$

which gives

$$\mathbf{\Sigma}^{-1} = (\mathbf{P}^{-1})'\mathbf{P}^{-1} \qquad \text{and} \qquad \mathbf{P}^{-1}\mathbf{\Sigma}(\mathbf{P}^{-1})' = \mathbf{I} \tag{5-12}$$

Define an n-element $\mathbf{y}$ vector as

$$\mathbf{y} = \mathbf{P}^{-1}\mathbf{x}$$

The Y variables are multivariate normal since they are linear combinations of the X's,

$$E(\mathbf{y}) = \mathbf{P}^{-1}E(\mathbf{x}) = \mathbf{P}^{-1}\mathbf{0} = \mathbf{0}$$

and

$$\begin{aligned}\text{var}(\mathbf{y}) &= E\{\mathbf{P}^{-1}\mathbf{x}\mathbf{x}'(\mathbf{P}^{-1})'\} \\ &= \mathbf{P}^{-1}\mathbf{\Sigma}(\mathbf{P}^{-1})' \\ &= \mathbf{I}\end{aligned}$$

from Eq. (5-12). Thus the Y's are standardized normal variables and

$$\mathbf{y}'\mathbf{y} \sim \chi^2(n)$$

But

$$\mathbf{y}'\mathbf{y} = \mathbf{x}'(\mathbf{P}^{-1})'\mathbf{P}^{-1}\mathbf{x} = \mathbf{x}'\mathbf{\Sigma}^{-1}\mathbf{x}$$

from Eq. (5-12). So

$$\mathbf{x}'\mathbf{\Sigma}^{-1}\mathbf{x} \sim \chi^2(n)$$

which is the result anticipated in Eq. (5-11).

Assume again

$$\mathbf{x} \sim N(\mathbf{0}, \mathbf{I})$$

and now consider the quadratic form $\mathbf{x}'\mathbf{A}\mathbf{x}$ where $\mathbf{A}$ is idempotent with rank $r \leq n$. If we denote the matrix of eigenvectors of $\mathbf{A}$ by $\mathbf{Q}$, then

$$\mathbf{Q}'\mathbf{A}\mathbf{Q} = \mathbf{\Lambda} = \begin{bmatrix} 1 & & & & & \\ & 1 & & & & \\ & & \ddots & & & \\ & & & 1 & & \\ & & & & 0 & \\ & & & & & \ddots \\ & & & & & & 0 \end{bmatrix} \begin{matrix} \} \; r \text{ terms} \\ \} \; n - r \text{ terms} \end{matrix} \tag{5-13}$$

where $\mathbf{\Lambda}$ will have r units and $n - r$ zeros on the main diagonal. Define

$$\mathbf{y} = \mathbf{Q}'\mathbf{x}$$

Thus

$$\mathbf{x} = \mathbf{Q}\mathbf{y}$$

since $\mathbf{Q}$ is orthogonal. Then

$$E(\mathbf{y}) = \mathbf{0}$$

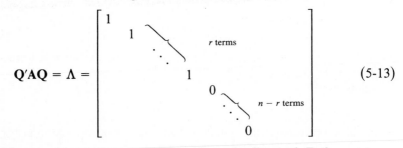

and
$$\begin{aligned}\text{var}(\mathbf{y}) &= E\{\mathbf{yy}'\} \\ &= E\{\mathbf{Q}'\mathbf{xx}'\mathbf{Q}\} \\ &= \mathbf{Q}'\mathbf{IQ} \\ &= \mathbf{I}\end{aligned}$$

since $\mathbf{Q}'\mathbf{Q} = \mathbf{I}$. Thus the Y's are independent standardized normal variables. The quadratic form may now be expressed as

$$\begin{aligned}\mathbf{x}'\mathbf{Ax} &= \mathbf{y}'\mathbf{Q}'\mathbf{AQy} \\ &= Y_1^2 + Y_2^2 + \cdots + Y_r^2\end{aligned}$$

using Eq. (5-13). Thus

$$\mathbf{x}'\mathbf{Ax} \sim \chi^2(r)$$

The general result is

If $\mathbf{x} \sim N(\mathbf{0}, \sigma^2\mathbf{I})$ *and* $\mathbf{A}$ *is idempotent of rank* r, $\dfrac{1}{\sigma^2}\mathbf{x}'\mathbf{Ax} \sim \chi^2(r)$

Independence of Quadratic Forms

Suppose $\mathbf{x} \sim N(\mathbf{0}, \sigma^2\mathbf{I})$ and we have two quadratic forms

$$\mathbf{x}'\mathbf{Ax} \qquad \text{and} \qquad \mathbf{x}'\mathbf{Bx}$$

where $\mathbf{A}$ and $\mathbf{B}$ are *symmetric idempotent* matrices of the same order. We seek the condition for the two forms to be independently distributed. Because the matrices are symmetric idempotent,

$$\mathbf{x}'\mathbf{Ax} = (\mathbf{Ax})'(\mathbf{Ax})$$

and
$$\mathbf{x}'\mathbf{Bx} = (\mathbf{Bx})'(\mathbf{Bx})$$

If each of the variables in the vector $\mathbf{Ax}$ has zero correlation with each variable in $\mathbf{Bx}$, they will be distributed independently of one another, and hence any function of the one set of variables, such as $\mathbf{x}'\mathbf{Ax}$, will be distributed independently of any function of the other set, such as $\mathbf{x}'\mathbf{Bx}$. The covariances between the variables in $\mathbf{Ax}$ and those in $\mathbf{Bx}$ are given by

$$\begin{aligned}E\{(\mathbf{Ax})(\mathbf{Bx})'\} &= E\{\mathbf{Axx}'\mathbf{B}\} \\ &= \sigma^2\mathbf{AB}\end{aligned}$$

These covariances (and hence the correlations) are all zero if and only if

$$\mathbf{AB} = \mathbf{0} \tag{5-14}$$

Since $\mathbf{A}$ and $\mathbf{B}$ are symmetric, the condition may be equivalently stated as $\mathbf{BA} = \mathbf{0}$; the one implies the other. Thus *two quadratic forms with idempotent matrices will be distributed independently if the product of the idempotent matrices is the null matrix.*

Independence of a Quadratic Form and a Linear Function

Assume $\mathbf{x} \sim N(\mathbf{0}, \sigma^2\mathbf{I})$. Let $\mathbf{x}'\mathbf{Ax}$ be a quadratic form with $\mathbf{A}$ a symmetric idempotent matrix of order n and let $\mathbf{Lx}$ be an m-element vector, each element being a linear combination of the X's. Thus $\mathbf{L}$ is of order $m \times n$, and we note that it need not be square or symmetric. If the variables in **Ax** and **Lx** are to have zero covariances, we require

$$E\{\mathbf{Axx'L'}\} = \sigma^2\mathbf{AL'} = \mathbf{0}$$

or equivalently

$$\mathbf{LA} = \mathbf{0} \tag{5-15}$$

5-2 ASSUMPTIONS OF THE LINEAR MODEL

The first basic assumption of the model is that the vector of sample observations on Y may be expressed as a linear combination of the sample observations on the explanatory X variables plus a disturbance vector, that is,

1. $\mathbf{y} = \beta_1\mathbf{x}_1 + \beta_2\mathbf{x}_2 + \cdots + \beta_k\mathbf{x}_k + \mathbf{u}$ (5-16)

where each vector is a column vector of n elements. The $\mathbf{x}_1$ vector is a column of units to allow for an intercept term. Each of the remaining $\mathbf{x}_i$ vectors ($i = 2, 3, \ldots, k$) denotes the sample observations on a specific explanatory variable. The β's are unknown population (model) parameters, but even if we knew their values, the linear combination ($\beta_1\mathbf{x}_1 + \cdots + \beta_k\mathbf{x}_k$) would not determine the **y** vector *exactly*, for economic relations are stochastic, not exact. Thus **u** is a disturbance vector measuring the discrepancies between the linear combination and any actual sample realization of Y values.†

Equation (5-15) may be expressed in matrix form as

$$\mathbf{y} = \mathbf{X}\boldsymbol{\beta} + \mathbf{u} \tag{5-17}$$

where

$$\mathbf{y} = \begin{bmatrix} Y_1 \\ Y_2 \\ \vdots \\ Y_n \end{bmatrix} \qquad \mathbf{X} = \begin{bmatrix} | & | & & | \\ \mathbf{x}_1 & \mathbf{x}_2 & \cdots & \mathbf{x}_k \\ | & | & & | \end{bmatrix} \qquad \boldsymbol{\beta} = \begin{bmatrix} \beta_1 \\ \beta_2 \\ \vdots \\ \beta_k \end{bmatrix} \qquad \mathbf{u} = \begin{bmatrix} u_1 \\ u_2 \\ \vdots \\ u_n \end{bmatrix}$$

The central problem is to obtain an estimate of the unknown $\boldsymbol{\beta}$ vector. To make any progress with this we need to make some further assumptions about how the observations on Y have been generated.

2. $E(\mathbf{u}) = \mathbf{0}$, that is, $E(\mathbf{y}) = \mathbf{X}\boldsymbol{\beta}$

To illustrate the meaning of this assumption, let us assume that the X variables measure family income and various other family characteristics and Y denotes family expenditure on, say, travel. The first *row* of the **X** matrix is some

† An outline of the various reasons for the introduction of the disturbance term has already been given in Sec. 1 of Chap. 2.

specific set of numbers for family income, size, and composition. Let $\mathbf{s}_1$ denote a row vector consisting of these numbers. Then

$$E(Y_1) = \mathbf{s}_1\beta$$

is the average, or expected, level of travel expenditure for this type of family. However, if we observe the *actual* travel expenditure of a family with these characteristics, it may be greater than the expected level, and the expenditure of another family with the same characteristics may well be less than the expected value. Or if we observe the travel expenditures of the same family in different periods of time, these may be expected to fluctuate around the mean value. However, if the theorist has done a good job in specifying all the significant explanatory variables to be included in $\mathbf{X}$, it is reasonable to assume that both positive and negative discrepancies from the expected value will occur and that, on balance, they will average out at zero, that is,

$$E(u_1) = 0$$

Similar considerations apply to each row of $\mathbf{X}$, and so we have

$$E(\mathbf{u}) = \begin{bmatrix} E(u_1) \\ E(u_2) \\ \vdots \\ E(u_n) \end{bmatrix} = \begin{bmatrix} 0 \\ 0 \\ \vdots \\ 0 \end{bmatrix}$$

3. $E(\mathbf{uu}') = \sigma^2\mathbf{I}$

Since $E(\mathbf{u}) = \mathbf{0}$, $E(\mathbf{uu}')$ is a variance matrix. This assumption gives

$$\begin{bmatrix} \text{var}(u_1) & \text{cov}(u_1, u_2) & \cdots & \text{cov}(u_1, u_n) \\ \text{cov}(u_2, u_1) & \text{var}(u_2) & \cdots & \text{cov}(u_2, u_n) \\ \cdots & \cdots & \cdots & \cdots \\ \text{cov}(u_n, u_1) & \text{cov}(u_n, u_2) & \cdots & \text{var}(u_n) \end{bmatrix} = \begin{bmatrix} \sigma^2 & 0 & \cdots & 0 \\ 0 & \sigma^2 & \cdots & 0 \\ \cdots & \cdots & \cdots & \cdots \\ 0 & 0 & \cdots & \sigma^2 \end{bmatrix}$$

This is a double assumption, namely:

- Each u distribution has the same variance.
- All disturbances are pairwise uncorrelated.

The first property is referred to as *homoscedasticity* (or homogeneous variances) and its opposite as *heteroscedasticity*. If the sample observations related to travel expenditures of a cross section of households, the assumption of homoscedasticity would probably not be a reasonable one, since low income families will almost certainly have low average expenditures on travel *and* also a low variance of actual travel expenditure about the average, while high income families will tend to display both higher mean levels of expenditure and greater variance about the mean. The second part of this assumption—all disturbances being pairwise uncorrelated—is a very strong assumption indeed. Again, in the context of the travel example it means that the size and sign of the disturbance for any one family has no influence on the size and sign of the disturbance for any other family. This is not to deny the possibility of "keeping up with the Joneses" as an important economic and sociological fact. If such a phenomenon does exist, it would be more appropriately characterized in the specification of the X variables. If the sample data related, say, to aggregate travel expenditure over a period of years, the same assumption means, for example, that unusually heavy expenditure in one year does not tend to be associated with unusually low (or high) expenditures in the next year or indeed in any subsequent year.

4. $\rho(\mathbf{X}) = k$

This assumption states that the explanatory variables do not form a linearly dependent set. For example, if we had just two explanatory variables, X_2 and X_3, and this assumption was not fulfilled, there would then exist an exact relationship

$$X_3 = c_1 + c_2 X_2 \tag{5-18}$$

which, combined with the hypothesized

$$Y = \beta_1 + \beta_2 X_2 + \beta_3 X_3 + u \tag{5-19}$$

gives

$$Y = (\beta_1 + \beta_3 c_1) + (\beta_2 + \beta_3 c_2) X_2 + u \tag{5-20}$$

The constants c_1 and c_2 can be determined exactly, and we can estimate the intercept and slope of Eq. (5-20), but there is no way to obtain estimates of the three β parameters.

5. **X** *is a nonstochastic matrix.*

This assumption at first sight seems incongruous. It means that if we take another sample of n observations, the **X** matrix of explanatory variables remains unchanged, the only source of variation then being in the **u** vector and hence in the **y** vector. However, the social sciences are notoriously difficult for being *observational* and *nonexperimental* so that in general the X variables are not subject to experimental control by the social scientist. There are three main points to be made about this assumption. First of all, in spite of the remarks above, there are cases where the X data can be controlled. In a cross-section survey, the sample design may call for the inclusion of certain numbers of families with specific characteristics, and sampling is continued until these specifications are met. Second, even if it is not in fact feasible to control the X data precisely, it is still useful to be able to make statistical inferences which are *conditional* on the X values actually present in the sample. In this light it is very much an assumption of convenience in that it simplifies dramatically the derivation of several basic statistical results. Third, once these simple results have been derived, it is possible to weaken the assumption to allow the X variables to be *stochastic, but distributed* *independently of the disturbance term*, and then see what modifications of the earlier results are required.

6. *The* **u** *vector has a multivariate normal distribution.*

Assumptions 2, 3, and 6 may then be combined in the single statement:

$$\mathbf{u} \sim N(\mathbf{0}, \sigma^2\mathbf{I}) \tag{5-21}$$

5-3 ORDINARY LEAST-SQUARES (OLS) ESTIMATES

The most frequently used estimating technique for the model outlined in Sec. 5-2 is least squares. The hypothesized model is

$$\mathbf{y} = \mathbf{X}\boldsymbol{\beta} + \mathbf{u} \tag{5-22}$$

Let $\mathbf{b}_*$ denote any arbitrary k-element vector. This in turn serves to define a vector of errors, or residuals,

$$\mathbf{e}_* = \mathbf{y} - \mathbf{X}\mathbf{b}_* \tag{5-23}$$

The least-squares principle for choosing $\mathbf{b}_*$ is to *minimize the sum of the squared residuals* $\mathbf{e}_*'\mathbf{e}_*$. From Eq. (5-23)

$$\begin{aligned}\mathbf{e}_*'\mathbf{e}_* &= (\mathbf{y} - \mathbf{X}\mathbf{b}_*)'(\mathbf{y} - \mathbf{X}\mathbf{b}_*)\\ &= \mathbf{y}'\mathbf{y} - 2\mathbf{b}_*'\mathbf{X}'\mathbf{y} + \mathbf{b}_*'\mathbf{X}'\mathbf{X}\mathbf{b}_*\end{aligned}$$

Thus

$$\frac{\partial(\mathbf{e}_*'\mathbf{e}_*)}{\partial\mathbf{b}_*} = -2\mathbf{X}'\mathbf{y} + 2\mathbf{X}'\mathbf{X}\mathbf{b}_* \tag{5-24}$$

The necessary condition for a stationary point requires that we set Eq. (5-24) equal to the **0** vector. Denoting the resultant OLS *solution* for $\mathbf{b}_*$ simply by **b** gives

$$(\mathbf{X}'\mathbf{X})\mathbf{b} = \mathbf{X}'\mathbf{y} \tag{5-25}$$

These are referred to as the OLS *normal equations*. Assumption 4 ensures that $\mathbf{X}'\mathbf{X}$ is nonsingular. Thus an equivalent expression for **b** is

$$\mathbf{b} = (\mathbf{X}'\mathbf{X})^{-1}\mathbf{X}'\mathbf{y} \tag{5-26}$$

The vector of OLS residuals is likewise denoted by **e**, where

$$\mathbf{e} = \mathbf{y} - \mathbf{X}\mathbf{b} \tag{5-27}$$

Using this expression to substitute for **y** in Eq. (5-25) gives

$$(\mathbf{X}'\mathbf{X})\mathbf{b} = (\mathbf{X}'\mathbf{X})\mathbf{b} + \mathbf{X}'\mathbf{e}$$

Thus

$$\mathbf{X}'\mathbf{e} = \begin{bmatrix}\mathbf{x}_1'\mathbf{e}\\ \mathbf{x}_2'\mathbf{e}\\ \vdots\\ \mathbf{x}_k'\mathbf{e}\end{bmatrix} = \begin{bmatrix}0\\0\\ \vdots\\ 0\end{bmatrix} = \mathbf{0} \tag{5-28}$$

This is a fundamental OLS result. The first element in this equation gives

$$\bar{e} = 0$$

that is, the residuals from the OLS regression always have zero mean, provided that the equation contains a constant term. The remaining elements in Eq. (5-28) state that the residual has *zero sample correlation with each* X *variable.*

To establish that the stationary point does indeed correspond to a *minimum* of the sum of squares, differentiate Eq. (5-24) once again with respect to $\mathbf{b}$ to obtain

$$\frac{\partial^2(\mathbf{e}_*'\mathbf{e}_*)}{\partial \mathbf{b}_*^2} = 2(\mathbf{X}'\mathbf{X}) \tag{5-29}$$

From Sec. 4-7 this gives a minimum provided $\mathbf{X}'\mathbf{X}$ is positive definite. To establish this, let $\mathbf{d}$ be any nonnull k-element vector, and consequently define an n-element vector $\mathbf{c}$ as

$$\mathbf{c} = \mathbf{X}\mathbf{d} \tag{5-30}$$

The assumption that $\mathbf{X}$ has full column rank ensures that $\mathbf{c}$ is nonnull; otherwise Eq. (5-30) would express a linear dependence between the columns of $\mathbf{X}$. Thus

$$\mathbf{c}'\mathbf{c} = \mathbf{d}'\mathbf{X}'\mathbf{X}\mathbf{d} > 0$$

and $\mathbf{X}'\mathbf{X}$ is positive definite.

Returning to Eq. (5-26),

$$\mathbf{b} = (\mathbf{X}'\mathbf{X})^{-1}\mathbf{X}'\mathbf{y}$$

and substituting

$$\mathbf{y} = \mathbf{X}\boldsymbol{\beta} + \mathbf{u}$$

gives

$$\mathbf{b} = \boldsymbol{\beta} + (\mathbf{X}'\mathbf{X})^{-1}\mathbf{X}'\mathbf{u} \tag{5-31}$$

Taking expectations gives

$$E(\mathbf{b}) = \boldsymbol{\beta} \tag{5-32}$$

since

$$E\{(\mathbf{X}'\mathbf{X})^{-1}\mathbf{X}'\mathbf{u}\} = (\mathbf{X}'\mathbf{X})^{-1}\mathbf{X}'E(\mathbf{u}) = \mathbf{0}$$

by assumptions 2 and 5. The OLS estimator is thus a *linear unbiased* estimator. The linearity property refers to linearity in $\mathbf{y}$ (or $\mathbf{u}$) as is seen in Eq. (5-26) or Eq. (5-31), for each element in $\mathbf{b}$ is a linear combination of the elements of $\mathbf{y}$ (or $\mathbf{u}$), the weights being functions of the $\mathbf{X}$ data which are nonstochastic. The unbiasedness is established in Eq. (5-32).

Next we derive the variance-covariance matrix of the OLS estimators. From Eqs. (5-31) and (5-32),

$$\mathbf{b} - E(\mathbf{b}) = \mathbf{b} - \boldsymbol{\beta} = (\mathbf{X}'\mathbf{X})^{-1}\mathbf{X}'\mathbf{u}$$

Thus

$$\begin{aligned}\text{var}(\mathbf{b}) &= E\{(\mathbf{X'X})^{-1}\mathbf{X'uu'X}(\mathbf{X'X})^{-1}\}\\ &= (\mathbf{X'X})^{-1}\mathbf{X'}\sigma^2\mathbf{IX}(\mathbf{X'X})^{-1} \qquad \text{from assumptions 3 and 4}\\ &= \sigma^2(\mathbf{X'X})^{-1} \qquad (5\text{-}33)\end{aligned}$$

since $\mathbf{I}$ may be suppressed at will and the scalar σ^2 moved in front or behind matrices. The elements on the main diagonal of Eq. (5-33) give the sampling variances of the corresponding elements of $\mathbf{b}$, and the off-diagonal terms give the sampling covariances. The most important result in least-squares theory is that no other linear unbiased estimator can have smaller sampling variances than those of the OLS estimator in Eq. (5-33). OLS estimators are thus said to be *best linear unbiased estimators* (b.l.u.e.), that is, to have minimum variance within the class of linear unbiased estimators. This result is known as the Gauss-Markov theorem.

The following proof is somewhat roundabout, but it has the advantage of establishing a further important result at the same time. Let $\mathbf{c}$ denote an arbitrary k-element column vector of known constants and define a scalar quantity μ as

$$\mu = \mathbf{c}'\boldsymbol{\beta} \qquad (5\text{-}34)$$

If we choose $\mathbf{c}' = [0 \quad 1 \quad 0 \quad \cdots \quad 0]$, then $\mu = \beta_2$. Thus we can use Eq. (5-34) to pick out any single element in $\boldsymbol{\beta}$. Or if we choose

$$\mathbf{c}' = [1 \quad X_{2,n+1} \quad X_{3,n+1} \quad \cdots \quad X_{k,n+1}]$$

then

$$\mu = E(Y_{n+1})$$

which is the *expected value* of the dependent variable Y in period $n + 1$, conditional on the X values in that period.

We wish to consider the class of linear unbiased estimators of μ. Thus define a scalar m which will serve as a linear estimator of μ, such that

$$m = \mathbf{a'y} = \mathbf{a'X}\boldsymbol{\beta} + \mathbf{a'u} \qquad (5\text{-}35)$$

where $\mathbf{a}$ is some n-element column vector. The definition ensures linearity. To ensure unbiasedness we have

$$\begin{aligned}E(m) &= \mathbf{a'X}\boldsymbol{\beta} + \mathbf{a'}E(\mathbf{u})\\ &= \mathbf{a'X}\boldsymbol{\beta}\\ &= \mathbf{c}'\boldsymbol{\beta}\end{aligned}$$

only if

$$\mathbf{a'X} = \mathbf{c}' \qquad (5\text{-}36)$$

From Eqs. (5-35) and (5-36),

$$\begin{aligned}\text{var}(\mathbf{m}) &= E\{\mathbf{a'uu'a}\}\\ &= \sigma^2\mathbf{a'a}\end{aligned}$$

which derivation uses the fact that since $\mathbf{a'u}$ is a scalar, its square can be written as the product of its transpose and itself. The problem is thus to choose $\mathbf{a}$ to minimize $\mathbf{a}'\mathbf{a}$ subject to the k side conditions $\mathbf{a}'\mathbf{X} = \mathbf{c}'$. Define

$$\phi = \mathbf{a}'\mathbf{a} - 2\boldsymbol{\lambda}'(\mathbf{X}'\mathbf{a} - \mathbf{c}) \tag{5-37}$$

Here $\boldsymbol{\lambda}$ is a column vector of k Lagrange multipliers, and the side conditions (5-36) have been transposed to make the multiplications in Eq. (5-37) conformable. Differentiating

$$\frac{\partial \phi}{\partial \mathbf{a}} = 2\mathbf{a} - 2\mathbf{X}\boldsymbol{\lambda} = \mathbf{0} \tag{5-38}$$

and

$$\frac{\partial \phi}{\partial \boldsymbol{\lambda}} = 2(\mathbf{X}'\mathbf{a} - \mathbf{c}) = \mathbf{0} \tag{5-39}$$

Premultiplying Eq. (5-38) by $\mathbf{X}'$ and using Eq. (5-39) gives

$$\mathbf{c} = \mathbf{X}'\mathbf{a} = \mathbf{X}'\mathbf{X}\boldsymbol{\lambda}$$

Thus

$$\boldsymbol{\lambda} = (\mathbf{X}'\mathbf{X})^{-1}\mathbf{c}$$

Substituting back in Eq. (5-38) gives

$$\mathbf{a} = \mathbf{X}\boldsymbol{\lambda} = \mathbf{X}(\mathbf{X}'\mathbf{X})^{-1}\mathbf{c}$$

and so the desired minimum variance linear unbiased estimator of $\mathbf{c}'\boldsymbol{\beta}$ is

$$\begin{aligned} m &= \mathbf{a}'\mathbf{y} \\ &= \mathbf{c}'(\mathbf{X}'\mathbf{X})^{-1}\mathbf{X}'\mathbf{y} \\ &= \mathbf{c}'\mathbf{b} \end{aligned} \tag{5-40}$$

that is, the unknown $\boldsymbol{\beta}$ is replaced by the OLS $\mathbf{b}$. It follows directly that †

1. Each OLS coefficient b_i is a best linear unbiased estimator of the corresponding population coefficient β_i.
2. The b.l.u.e. of any linear combination of β's is that same linear combination of the b's.
3. The b.l.u.e. of $E(Y_s)$ is

$$b_1 + b_2 X_{2,s} + b_3 X_{3,s} + \cdots + b_k X_{k,s}$$

The Model in Deviation Form

In Chaps. 2 and 3 it was seen that the two- and three-variable regression models could also be treated in deviation form. The essence of the approach was to first of all express all data in terms of deviations from sample means and then estimate the regression parameters in two stages, the first stage dealing with the slope coefficients and the second stage with the intercept term. The same treatment may

† As far as the disturbance u is concerned, the derivation of the Gauss-Markov result has only required the assumptions of zero mean and zero covariances and has not required the assumption of normality.

be applied to the k-variable model by use of the following transformation matrix:

$$\mathbf{A} = \mathbf{I} - \frac{1}{n}\mathbf{ii}' \tag{5-41}$$

where $\mathbf{i}$ denotes a column vector of n units. Thus

$$\mathbf{A} = \begin{bmatrix} 1 & & & \\ & 1 & & \\ & & \ddots & \\ & & & 1 \end{bmatrix} - \frac{1}{n}\begin{bmatrix} 1 & 1 & \cdots & 1 \\ 1 & 1 & \cdots & 1 \\ \cdots & \cdots & \cdots & \cdots \\ 1 & 1 & \cdots & 1 \end{bmatrix}$$

If $\mathbf{y}' = [Y_1 \quad Y_2 \quad \cdots \quad Y_n]$ then

$$\frac{1}{n}\mathbf{i}'\mathbf{y} = \bar{Y}$$

and

$$\mathbf{Ay} = \mathbf{y} - \mathbf{i}\bar{Y} = \begin{bmatrix} Y_1 - \bar{Y} \\ Y_2 - \bar{Y} \\ \vdots \\ Y_n - \bar{Y} \end{bmatrix}$$

Thus premultiplying any column vector of observations by $\mathbf{A}$ produces a vector showing those observations in deviation form. Two special cases are

$$\mathbf{Ai} = \mathbf{0} \tag{5-42}$$

or, more generally, premultiplying any vector of identical elements by $\mathbf{A}$ gives the zero vector. Second,

$$\mathbf{Ae} = \mathbf{e} \tag{5-43}$$

for the residuals have zero mean, and are thus already in deviation form. It is easily verified that the $\mathbf{A}$ matrix is symmetric idempotent.

The OLS estimator $\mathbf{b}$ and residual vector $\mathbf{e}$ are connected by

$$\mathbf{y} = \mathbf{Xb} + \mathbf{e} \tag{5-44}$$

If we partition the $\mathbf{X}$ matrix as

$$\mathbf{X} = [\mathbf{x}_1 \quad \mathbf{X}_2]$$

where $\mathbf{x}_1(= \mathbf{i})$ is the usual column of units and $\mathbf{X}_2$ the $n \times (k-1)$ matrix of observations on the variables $X_2, X_3, \ldots, X_k$, we can rewrite Eq. (5-44) as

$$\mathbf{y} = \mathbf{x}_1 b_1 + \mathbf{X}_2\mathbf{b}_2 + \mathbf{e} \tag{5-45}$$

where $\mathbf{b}' = [b_1 \quad \mathbf{b}_2']$ indicates a conformable partitioning of the $\mathbf{b}$ vector into the intercept b_1 and the subvector $\mathbf{b}_2$ of slope coefficients. Premultiplying Eq. (5-45) by $\mathbf{A}$ gives

$$\mathbf{Ay} = \mathbf{AX}_2\mathbf{b}_2 + \mathbf{e}$$

using Eqs. (5-42) and (5-43). Premultiplying this by $\mathbf{X}_2'$ yields

$$\mathbf{X}_2'\mathbf{Ay} = \mathbf{X}_2'\mathbf{AX}_2\mathbf{b}_2 \tag{5-46}$$

for $\mathbf{X}_2'\mathbf{e} = \mathbf{0}$ from Eq. (5-28). Finally, using the symmetric idempotency of $\mathbf{A}$ means that Eq. (5-46) is equivalent to

$$(\mathbf{AX}_2)'(\mathbf{Ay}) = (\mathbf{AX}_2)'(\mathbf{AX}_2)\mathbf{b}_2 \tag{5-47}$$

The interpretation of Eq. (5-47) is as follows:

- $\mathbf{b}_2$ is the subvector of OLS slope coefficients.
- $\mathbf{Ay}$ is the $\mathbf{y}$ vector expressed in deviation form.
- $\mathbf{AX}_2$ is the matrix of explanatory variables in deviation form.
- Equation (5-47) is a set of normal equations [compare with Eq. (5-25)] in terms of deviations, whose solution yields the OLS slope coefficients.
- The remaining coefficient, which is the intercept term, is obtained by premultiplying $\mathbf{y} = \mathbf{Xb} + \mathbf{e}$ by $\mathbf{i}'/n$ to yield

$$\bar{Y} = \begin{bmatrix} 1 & \bar{X}_2 & \bar{X}_3 & \cdots & \bar{X}_k \end{bmatrix} \begin{bmatrix} b_1 \\ b_2 \\ b_3 \\ \vdots \\ b_k \end{bmatrix}$$

or

$$b_1 = \bar{Y} - b_2\bar{X}_2 - b_3\bar{X}_3 - \cdots - b_k\bar{X}_k \tag{5-48}$$

The sum of squared deviations in the dependent variable, denoted by TSS, is

$$\text{TSS} = \mathbf{y}'\mathbf{Ay}$$

This may be decomposed into an explained sum of squares (ESS) and a residual sum of squares (RSS) in the manner of Chaps. 2 and 3. Return to

$$\mathbf{Ay} = \mathbf{AX}_2\mathbf{b}_2 + \mathbf{e}$$

Transposing and multiplying,

$$\underset{\text{(TSS)}}{\mathbf{y}'\mathbf{Ay}} = \underset{\text{(ESS)}}{\mathbf{b}_2'\mathbf{X}_2'\mathbf{AX}_2\mathbf{b}_2} + \underset{\text{(RSS)}}{\mathbf{e}'\mathbf{e}} \tag{5-49}$$

since the cross-product term vanishes in view of $\mathbf{X}'\mathbf{e} = \mathbf{0}$. The multiple correlation coefficient $R_{1.23\cdots k}$ for the k-variable case may then be defined in a number of alternative ways. The basic definition is

$$R^2_{1.23\cdots k} = \frac{\text{ESS}}{\text{TSS}} = 1 - \frac{\mathbf{e}'\mathbf{e}}{\mathbf{y}'\mathbf{Ay}} \tag{5-50}$$

In view of Eq. (5-49) this is equivalent to

$$R^2 = \frac{\mathbf{b}_2'\mathbf{X}_2'\mathbf{AX}_2\mathbf{b}_2}{\mathbf{y}'\mathbf{Ay}} = \frac{\mathbf{b}_2'\mathbf{X}_2'\mathbf{Ay}}{\mathbf{y}'\mathbf{Ay}} \tag{5-51}$$

where the second expression follows from Eq. (5-46). Alternatively, we may start with the complete OLS regression

$$\mathbf{y} = \mathbf{Xb} + \mathbf{e}$$

Transposing, multiplying, and again using $\mathbf{X}'\mathbf{e} = \mathbf{0}$ gives

$$\mathbf{y}'\mathbf{y} = \mathbf{b}'\mathbf{X}'\mathbf{X}\mathbf{b} + \mathbf{e}'\mathbf{e} \tag{5-52}$$

Using $\mathbf{b} = (\mathbf{X}'\mathbf{X})^{-1}\mathbf{X}'\mathbf{y}$, equivalent expressions for Eq. (5-52) are

$$\mathbf{y}'\mathbf{y} = \mathbf{b}'\mathbf{X}'\mathbf{y} + \mathbf{e}'\mathbf{e} = \mathbf{y}'\mathbf{X}(\mathbf{X}'\mathbf{X})^{-1}\mathbf{X}'\mathbf{y} + \mathbf{e}'\mathbf{e} \tag{5-53}$$

Comparing Eq. (5-52) with Eq. (5-49), the residual sum of squares, $\mathbf{e}'\mathbf{e}$ is the same in each equation, since the OLS regression is unique and it makes no difference whether we fit the complete regression directly to the original data or transform the data into deviation form and compute the slope coefficients followed by the intercept. The left-hand sides differ only in that

$$\mathbf{y}'\mathbf{y} = \Sigma Y_i^2$$

and

$$\begin{aligned} \mathbf{y}'\mathbf{A}\mathbf{y} &= \Sigma(Y_i - \bar{Y})^2 \\ &= \Sigma Y_i^2 - n\bar{Y}^2 \\ &= \mathbf{y}'\mathbf{y} - n\bar{Y}^2 \end{aligned}$$

Subtracting the correction for the mean $n\bar{Y}^2$ from both sides of Eq. (5-52) gives

$$\underset{\text{(TSS)}}{(\mathbf{y}'\mathbf{y} - n\bar{Y}^2)} = \underset{\text{(ESS)}}{(\mathbf{b}'\mathbf{X}'\mathbf{X}\mathbf{b}' - n\bar{Y}^2)} + \underset{\text{(RSS)}}{\mathbf{e}'\mathbf{e}}$$

Thus the previous expressions for R^2 in terms of sums of squares may all be computed in terms of the original data, provided only that the correction for the mean is subtracted from any total or explained sum of squares (but not from the residual sum of squares).

It is sometimes useful to compute an R^2, adjusted for degrees of freedom, especially when comparing the explanatory power of different numbers of explanatory variables. Adding any extra explanatory variable can never increase the residual sum of squares and thus can never decrease the R^2 defined in Eq. (5-50), since that expression takes no account of the *number* of explanatory variables employed. It may be rewritten as

$$R^2_{1.23\cdots k} = 1 - \frac{\mathbf{e}'\mathbf{e}/n}{\mathbf{y}'\mathbf{A}\mathbf{y}/n}$$

The adjusted R^2 is defined as

$$\bar{R}^2_{1.23\cdots k} = 1 - \frac{\mathbf{e}'\mathbf{e}/(n-k)}{\mathbf{y}'\mathbf{A}\mathbf{y}/(n-1)}$$

The rationale behind the adjustment is that k parameters have been used in fitting the regression plane from which the residual sum of squares is measured, and one parameter, the sample mean, has been estimated in computing TSS. As will be seen later, these provide unbiased estimators of the disturbance variance and the Y variance. Equivalent expressions for the adjusted coefficient are

$$\begin{aligned} \bar{R}^2_{1.23\cdots k} &= 1 - \frac{n-1}{n-k}\left(1 - R^2_{1.23\cdots k}\right) \\ &= \frac{1-k}{n-k} + \frac{n-1}{n-k}R^2_{1.23\cdots k} \end{aligned}$$

It is thus possible for the adjusted coefficient to decline if an additional variable produces too small a reduction in $1 - R^2$ to compensate for the increase in $(n - 1)/(n - k)$.

Example 5-1 To help fix some of these concepts, here is a brief numerical example. The numbers have been kept artificially simple so as not to obscure the nature of the operations with cumbersome arithmetic. The sample data are

$$\mathbf{y} = \begin{bmatrix} 3 \\ 1 \\ 8 \\ 3 \\ 5 \end{bmatrix} \qquad \text{and} \qquad \mathbf{X} = \begin{bmatrix} 1 & 3 & 5 \\ 1 & 1 & 4 \\ 1 & 5 & 6 \\ 1 & 2 & 4 \\ 1 & 4 & 6 \end{bmatrix}$$

where we have already inserted a column of units in the first column of **X**. From these data we readily compute

$$\mathbf{X'X} = \begin{bmatrix} 5 & 15 & 25 \\ 15 & 55 & 81 \\ 25 & 81 & 129 \end{bmatrix} \qquad \text{and} \qquad \mathbf{X'y} = \begin{bmatrix} 20 \\ 76 \\ 109 \end{bmatrix}$$

The normal equations of Eq. (5-25) are then

$$\begin{bmatrix} 5 & 15 & 25 \\ 15 & 55 & 81 \\ 25 & 81 & 129 \end{bmatrix} \begin{bmatrix} b_1 \\ b_2 \\ b_3 \end{bmatrix} = \begin{bmatrix} 20 \\ 76 \\ 109 \end{bmatrix}$$

Rather than invert $(\mathbf{X'X})$ we will solve these equations by the elimination method. In the first step subtract three times the first row from the second and five times the first row from the third. This gives the revised system

$$\begin{bmatrix} 5 & 15 & 25 \\ 0 & 10 & 6 \\ 0 & 6 & 4 \end{bmatrix} \begin{bmatrix} b_1 \\ b_2 \\ b_3 \end{bmatrix} = \begin{bmatrix} 20 \\ 16 \\ 9 \end{bmatrix}$$

Next subtract six-tenths of row 2 from row 3 to get

$$\begin{bmatrix} 5 & 15 & 25 \\ 0 & 10 & 6 \\ 0 & 0 & 0.4 \end{bmatrix} \begin{bmatrix} b_1 \\ b_2 \\ b_3 \end{bmatrix} = \begin{bmatrix} 20 \\ 16 \\ -0.6 \end{bmatrix}$$

The third equation gives $0.4b_3 = -0.6$, that is,

$$\boxed{b_3 = -1.5}$$

Substituting for b_3 in the second equation,

$$10b_2 + 6b_3 = 16$$

gives

$$\boxed{b_2 = 2.5}$$

Finally, the first equation

$$5b_1 + 15b_2 + 25b_3 = 20$$

gives

$$\boxed{b_1 = 4}$$

The regression equation is thus

$$\hat{Y} = 4 + 2.5X_2 - 1.5X_3$$

Alternatively, transforming the data into deviation form gives

$$\mathbf{Ay} = \begin{bmatrix} -1 \\ -3 \\ 4 \\ -1 \\ 1 \end{bmatrix} \qquad \text{and} \qquad \mathbf{AX} = \begin{bmatrix} 0 & 0 \\ -2 & -1 \\ 2 & 1 \\ -1 & -1 \\ 1 & 1 \end{bmatrix}$$

The normal Eqs. (5-46) now become

$$\begin{bmatrix} 10 & 6 \\ 6 & 4 \end{bmatrix} \begin{bmatrix} b_2 \\ b_3 \end{bmatrix} = \begin{bmatrix} 16 \\ 9 \end{bmatrix}$$

The observant reader will notice that these are the second and third equations obtained in the first step of the elimination method above.†

Thus the solutions for b_2 and b_3 will coincide with those already obtained. Likewise, b_1 will be the same as before, for the final equation in the back substitution above is readily seen to be

$$b_1 = \bar{Y} - b_2\bar{X}_2 - b_3\bar{X}_3$$

Thus the elimination process applied to $(\mathbf{X'X})\mathbf{b} = \mathbf{X'y}$ is, in fact, equivalent to transforming the data into deviation form and proceeding in two-step fashion.

To calculate R^2 we note from the $\mathbf{Ay}$ vector that

$$\text{TSS} = \mathbf{y'Ay} = 28$$

† The reason why may be seen as follows:

$$\mathbf{X'X} = \begin{bmatrix} n & \Sigma X_2 & \Sigma X_3 \\ \Sigma X_2 & \Sigma X_2^2 & \Sigma X_2 X_3 \\ \Sigma X_3 & \Sigma X_2 X_3 & \Sigma X_3^2 \end{bmatrix}$$

To produce a zero in the (2, 1) position, we must subtract $\Sigma X_2/n$ ($= \bar{X}_2$) times the first row from the second. In the (2, 2) position this gives $\Sigma X_2^2 - n\bar{X}_2^2 = \Sigma(X_2 - \bar{X}_2)^2$, and in the (2, 3) position it gives $\Sigma X_2 X_3 - n\bar{X}_2\bar{X}_3 = \Sigma(X_2 - \bar{X}_2)(X_3 - \bar{X}_3)$. A similar argument applies to the transformed third row.

Calculating the explained sum of squares from $\mathbf{b}_2'\mathbf{X}_2'\mathbf{A}\mathbf{y}$ gives

$$\text{ESS} = [2.5 \quad -1.5]\begin{bmatrix} 16 \\ 9 \end{bmatrix} = 26.5$$

Thus

$$\text{RSS} = 28 - 26.5 = 1.5$$

and
$$R^2 = \frac{26.5}{28} = 0.9464$$

so that the regression has accounted for almost 95 percent of the variance of Y. As a check we may calculate the explained sum of squares from $\mathbf{b}'\mathbf{X}'\mathbf{y}$ by subtracting the correction for the mean,

$$\mathbf{b}'\mathbf{X}'\mathbf{y} = [4 \quad 2.5 \quad -1.5]\begin{bmatrix} 20 \\ 76 \\ 109 \end{bmatrix} = 106.5$$

$$n\bar{Y}^2 = 5(4)^2 = 80$$

Thus
$$\text{ESS} = \mathbf{b}'\mathbf{X}'\mathbf{y} - n\bar{Y}^2 = 26.5$$

in agreement with the previous calculation.

Estimation of σ^2

Finally in this section we derive an estimator of σ^2, the variance of the disturbance term. As the values of u are not directly observable, it seems plausible to base an estimate of σ^2 on the residual sum of squares $\mathbf{e}'\mathbf{e}$. The only question is what should the divisor be, and this can be settled by requiring the estimator to be unbiased. We have

$$\begin{aligned} \mathbf{e} &= \mathbf{y} - \mathbf{X}\mathbf{b} \\ &= \mathbf{y} - \mathbf{X}(\mathbf{X}'\mathbf{X})^{-1}\mathbf{X}\mathbf{y} \\ &= \left[\mathbf{I} - \mathbf{X}(\mathbf{X}'\mathbf{X})^{-1}\mathbf{X}'\right]\mathbf{y} \\ &= \mathbf{M}\mathbf{y} \end{aligned} \tag{5-54}$$

where

$$\mathbf{M} = \mathbf{I} - \mathbf{X}(\mathbf{X}'\mathbf{X})^{-1}\mathbf{X}' \tag{5-55}$$

$\mathbf{M}$ is a very important matrix. It is easily verified that it is symmetric idempotent. It also follows directly by multiplying out that

$$\mathbf{M}\mathbf{X} = \mathbf{0} \tag{5-56}$$

Returning to Eq. (5-54),

$$\mathbf{e} = \mathbf{M}(\mathbf{X}\boldsymbol{\beta} + \mathbf{u})$$

that is,
$$\mathbf{e} = \mathbf{M}\mathbf{u}$$

in view of Eq. (5-56). From the symmetric idempotency of $\mathbf{M}$,

$$\mathbf{e}'\mathbf{e} = \mathbf{u}'\mathbf{M}\mathbf{u}$$

Taking expectations

$$\begin{aligned} E(\mathbf{e}'\mathbf{e}) &= E(\mathbf{u}'\mathbf{M}\mathbf{u}) \\ &= E\{\mathrm{tr}(\mathbf{u}'\mathbf{M}\mathbf{u})\} && \text{since } \mathbf{u}'\mathbf{M}\mathbf{u} \text{ is a scalar} \\ &= E\{\mathrm{tr}(\mathbf{M}\mathbf{u}\mathbf{u}')\} && \text{from Eq. (4-15)} \\ &= \sigma^2 \,\mathrm{tr}\,\mathbf{M} && \text{by assumption 3} \end{aligned}$$

From Eq. (5-55)

$$\begin{aligned} \mathrm{tr}(\mathbf{M}) &= \mathrm{tr}(\mathbf{I}) - \mathrm{tr}\left[\mathbf{X}(\mathbf{X}'\mathbf{X})^{-1}\mathbf{X}'\right] \\ &= \mathrm{tr}(\mathbf{I}) - \mathrm{tr}\left[(\mathbf{X}'\mathbf{X})^{-1}\mathbf{X}'\mathbf{X}\right] \\ &= n - k \end{aligned}$$

Thus if we define

$$s^2 = \frac{\mathbf{e}'\mathbf{e}}{n-k} \tag{5-57}$$

it follows that

$$E(s^2) = \sigma^2$$

and we have found the desired unbiased estimator. The square root s is often referred to as the *standard error of the estimate*, and may be regarded as the standard deviation of the Y values about the regression plane.

5-4 INFERENCE IN THE OLS MODEL

So far we have not used the assumption that the u's are multivariate normal, but this now becomes necessary. We now make the twin assumptions

$$\mathbf{u} \sim N(\mathbf{0}, \sigma^2\mathbf{I})$$

and $\qquad$ **X** is nonstochastic with rank k

The first is a combination of assumptions 2, 3, and 6, and the second is a combination of assumptions 4 and 5. We have seen in Eq. (5-31) that

$$\mathbf{b} = \boldsymbol{\beta} + (\mathbf{X}'\mathbf{X})^{-1}\mathbf{X}'\mathbf{u}$$

so **b** is then multivariate normal, and since we have already established the mean vector and the covariance matrix, we have the fundamental result

$$\mathbf{b} \sim N\left(\boldsymbol{\beta}, \sigma^2(\mathbf{X}'\mathbf{X})^{-1}\right) \tag{5-58}$$

From the end of the previous section we also have

$$\mathbf{e}'\mathbf{e} = \mathbf{u}'\mathbf{M}\mathbf{u}$$

From the result in Sec. 5-1 on the distribution of quadratic forms with idempotent matrices it then follows that

$$\frac{1}{\sigma^2}(\mathbf{e}'\mathbf{e}) \sim \chi^2(n-k) \tag{5-59}$$

The degrees of freedom in Eq. (5-59) come from the fact that

$$\rho(\mathbf{M}) = \text{tr}(\mathbf{M})$$

since $\mathbf{M}$ is idempotent, and we have just shown the trace to be $n - k$. Finally, applying condition (5-15) for the independence of a linear and quadratic form to $\mathbf{b}$ and $\mathbf{e}'\mathbf{e}$ gives

$$(\mathbf{X}'\mathbf{X})^{-1}\mathbf{X}'\mathbf{M} = \mathbf{0} \tag{5-60}$$

since $\mathbf{MX} = \mathbf{0}$. Thus

$\mathbf{b}$ *is distributed independently of* s^2.

These results suffice to establish inference procedures for any element of $\mathbf{b}$. Consider, for example, b_i, the estimated coefficient of X_i in the OLS regression. It follows from Eq. (5-58) that

$$b_i \sim N(\beta_i, \sigma^2 a_{ii})$$

where a_{ii} denotes the ith element on the principal diagonal of $(\mathbf{X}'\mathbf{X})^{-1}$. Thus

$$\frac{b_i - \beta_i}{\sigma\sqrt{a_{ii}}} \sim N(0,1)$$

From Eqs. (5-59) and (5-60),

$$\frac{(n-k)s^2}{\sigma^2} \sim \chi^2(n-k)$$

independently of b_i. Thus we can proceed directly to form a t variable, that is,

$$t = \frac{b_i - \beta_i}{\sigma\sqrt{a_{ii}}} \frac{\sigma\sqrt{(n-k)}}{s\sqrt{(n-k)}}$$

or

$$t = \frac{b_i - \beta_i}{s\sqrt{a_{ii}}} \sim t(n-k) \qquad \text{for } i = 1, 2, \ldots, k \tag{5-61}$$

Result (5-61) may be used to test an hypothesis about β_1 or set up a confidence interval for β_i in the usual way. However, we will not pursue the details further at the moment as it is more efficient to develop a general set of inference procedures, of which tests on a single coefficient are just one particular application.

Sets of Linear Hypotheses

Consider the set of linear hypotheses about the elements of $\boldsymbol{\beta}$, embodied in

$$\mathbf{R}\boldsymbol{\beta} = \mathbf{r} \tag{5-62}$$

where $\mathbf{R}$ is a known matrix of order $q \times k$ with $q \leq k$, and $\mathbf{r}$ is a known q-element vector. We also assume $\mathbf{R}$ to have full row rank, that is, that there are no linear dependencies between the hypotheses. It is extremely important to understand the range of various hypotheses represented by Eq. (5-62). We illustrate them with some examples.

1. $\mathbf{R} = [0 \quad \cdots \quad 0 \quad 1 \quad 0 \quad \cdots \quad 0]$ and $\mathbf{r} = 0$
   Here $\mathbf{R}$ contains only a single row ($q = 1$) with a unit in the ith position and zeros everywhere else, and $\mathbf{r}$ is the scalar zero. On substitution in Eq. (5-62) we have

$$\beta_i = 0$$

   Thus this specification of $\mathbf{R}$ and $\mathbf{r}$ sets up the hypothesis that β_i is zero. Choosing a nonzero value for $\mathbf{r}$ would set up the hypothesis that β_i is equal to the specified constant.
2. $\mathbf{R} = [0 \quad 1 \quad -1 \quad \cdots \quad 0]$ and $\mathbf{r} = 0$
   produce the hypothesis

$$\beta_2 - \beta_3 = 0$$

   or

$$\beta_2 = \beta_3$$

3. $\mathbf{R} = [0 \quad 0 \quad 1 \quad 1 \quad 0 \quad \cdots \quad 0]$ and $\mathbf{r} = 1$
   specify the hypothesis

$$\beta_3 + \beta_4 = 1$$

4.

$$\mathbf{R} = \begin{bmatrix} 0 & 1 & 0 & \cdots & 0 \\ 0 & 0 & 1 & \cdots & 0 \\ \cdots & \cdots & \cdots & \cdots & \cdots \\ 0 & 0 & 0 & \cdots & 1 \end{bmatrix}$$

   of order $(k - 1) \times k$ and

$$\mathbf{r} = \begin{bmatrix} 0 \\ 0 \\ \vdots \\ 0 \end{bmatrix}$$

   of order $(k - 1) \times 1$. This is equivalent to the joint hypothesis

$$\begin{bmatrix} \beta_2 \\ \beta_3 \\ \vdots \\ \beta_k \end{bmatrix} = \begin{bmatrix} 0 \\ 0 \\ \vdots \\ 0 \end{bmatrix}$$

   that is, that the set of explanatory variables $X_2, X_3, \ldots, X_k$ *has no influence in the determination of* Y. This is a very important hypothesis. The test of this hypothesis is often referred to as a *test of the overall relation*. Notice that the hypothesis does *not* include $\beta_1 = 0$, since that involves the additional implication that the mean level of Y is zero. Our usual concern is whether the hypothetical explanatory variables help to explain the variation of *Y around its mean value*, but the actual level of the mean is of no particular importance.

5. $\mathbf{R} = [\mathbf{0} \quad \mathbf{I}_s]$ and $\mathbf{r} = \mathbf{0}$
Here $\mathbf{0}$ is a null matrix of order $s \times (k-s)$ and $\mathbf{r}$ is an s-element column vector. This sets up the hypothesis that the last s elements in β are jointly zero,
$$\beta_{k-s+1} = \beta_{k-s+2} = \cdots = \beta_k = 0$$
For example, in an equation explaining the rate of inflation the explanatory variables might be grouped into two subsets—those measuring expectations of inflation and those measuring pressure of demand. The significance of either subset might be tested by using this formulation with the numbering of the variables so arranged that those in the subset to be tested come at the end.

It is thus clear that a procedure for testing the general hypothesis $\mathbf{R}\boldsymbol{\beta} = \mathbf{r}$ will be extremely useful and powerful, since various specifications for $\mathbf{R}$ and $\mathbf{r}$ will cover a range of questions.

To develop such a test procedure, we first of all replace the unknown $\boldsymbol{\beta}$ vector in Eq. (5-62) by the OLS vector $\mathbf{b}$, obtaining the vector $\mathbf{Rb}$. The more this vector departs from $\mathbf{r}$, the greater is the doubt cast on the hypothesis. The problem is to determine the sampling distribution of $\mathbf{Rb}$ and devise a practical test procedure. First of all, we see directly that
$$E(\mathbf{Rb}) = \mathbf{R}\boldsymbol{\beta} \tag{5-63}$$
and
$$\begin{aligned}\operatorname{var}(\mathbf{Rb}) &= E\{\mathbf{R}(\mathbf{b}-\boldsymbol{\beta})(\mathbf{b}-\boldsymbol{\beta})'\mathbf{R}'\} \\ &= \sigma^2\mathbf{R}(\mathbf{X}'\mathbf{X})^{-1}\mathbf{R}' \end{aligned} \tag{5-64}$$
Since $\mathbf{b}$ is multivariate normal,
$$\mathbf{Rb} \sim N\left(\mathbf{R}\boldsymbol{\beta}, \sigma^2\mathbf{R}(\mathbf{X}'\mathbf{X})^{-1}\mathbf{R}'\right)$$
or
$$\mathbf{R}(\mathbf{b}-\boldsymbol{\beta}) \sim N\left(\mathbf{0}, \sigma^2\mathbf{R}(\mathbf{X}'\mathbf{X})^{-1}\mathbf{R}'\right) \tag{5-65}$$
If the hypothesis (5-62) is true, we can replace $\mathbf{R}\boldsymbol{\beta}$ in Eq. (5-65) by $\mathbf{r}$, obtaining
$$(\mathbf{Rb}-\mathbf{r}) \sim N\left(\mathbf{0}, \sigma^2\mathbf{R}(\mathbf{X}'\mathbf{X})^{-1}\mathbf{R}'\right) \tag{5-66}$$
We can now apply Eq. (5-11) directly to Eq. (5-66) and write
$$(\mathbf{Rb}-\mathbf{r})'\left[\sigma^2\mathbf{R}(\mathbf{X}'\mathbf{X})^{-1}\mathbf{R}'\right]^{-1}(\mathbf{Rb}-\mathbf{r}) \sim \chi^2(q) \tag{5-67}$$
where the degrees of freedom q are given by the number of elements in the $\mathbf{Rb}$ vector.†

The only problem hindering practical applications of Eq. (5-67) is the presence of the unknown σ^2, since all other elements are known. However, we

† To show that the inverse of $\mathbf{R}(\mathbf{X}'\mathbf{X})^{-1}\mathbf{R}'$ exists, we show that
$$\mathbf{z}'\mathbf{R}(\mathbf{X}'\mathbf{X})^{-1}\mathbf{R}'\mathbf{z} > 0$$
for $\mathbf{z} \neq \mathbf{0}$, so that the matrix is positive definite and thus nonsingular. Define $\mathbf{v} = \mathbf{R}'\mathbf{z}$. Then $\mathbf{v}$ is a

have already shown that

$$\frac{\mathbf{e'e}}{\sigma^2} \sim \chi^2(n-k)$$

independently of **b**, and hence independently of **Rb**. Thus we can form an F ratio, and the unknown σ^2 will cancel out. The basic result is thus, *if* $\mathbf{R}\boldsymbol{\beta} = \mathbf{r}$ *is true*,

$$\frac{(\mathbf{Rb}-\mathbf{r})'\left[\mathbf{R}(\mathbf{X'X})^{-1}\mathbf{R'}\right]^{-1}(\mathbf{Rb}-\mathbf{r})/q}{\mathbf{e'e}/(n-k)} \sim F(q, n-k) \tag{5-68}$$

The test procedure is then to reject the hypothesis $\mathbf{R}\boldsymbol{\beta} = \mathbf{r}$ if the computed F value exceeds a preselected critical value. Now we must see what this test procedure amounts to in some of the specific applications indicated above.

Testing a Single Coefficient

$$\mathbf{R} = [0 \quad \cdots \quad 0 \quad \underset{\substack{\downarrow \\ i\text{th element}}}{1} \quad 0 \quad \cdots \quad 0] \qquad \text{and} \qquad \mathbf{r} = 0$$

set up the hypothesis

$$H_0\colon \quad \beta_i = 0$$

We then have

$$\mathbf{Rb} - \mathbf{r} = b_i$$

and

$$\mathbf{R}(\mathbf{X'X})^{-1}\mathbf{R'}$$

merely picks out the ith element a_{ii} on the main diagonal of $(\mathbf{X'X})^{-1}$. Thus the test statistic becomes

$$F = \frac{b_i^2}{s^2 a_{ii}} \sim F(1, n-k) \tag{5-69}$$

If instead of testing the hypothesis

$$\beta_i = 0$$

one wishes to test the hypothesis that β_i assumed some specified value,

$$\beta_i = \beta_{i0}$$

---

linear combination of the rows of **R**. Since **R** has full row rank, $\mathbf{v} \neq \mathbf{0}$. Thus

$$\mathbf{z'R}(\mathbf{X'X})^{-1}\mathbf{R'z} = \mathbf{v'}(\mathbf{X'X})^{-1}\mathbf{v}$$

But $(\mathbf{X'X})$ is positive definite by assumption, and so $(\mathbf{X'X})^{-1}$ is positive definite, since its eigenvalues are the reciprocals of the eigenvalues of $(\mathbf{X'X})$. Thus

$$\mathbf{v'}(\mathbf{X'X})^{-1}\mathbf{v} > 0$$

and so $\mathbf{R}(\mathbf{X'X})^{-1}\mathbf{R'}$ is positive definite.

we simply set $r = \beta_{i0}$, and the test statistic becomes

$$F = \frac{(b_i - \beta_{i0})^2}{s^2 a_{ii}}$$

This is, of course, the same result as that already derived by a different route in Eq. (5-61), since $t^2(n-k) = F(1, n-k)$.

Testing the Significance of the Complete Regression

$$\mathbf{R} = \begin{bmatrix} 0 & 1 & 0 & \cdots & 0 \\ 0 & 0 & 1 & \cdots & 0 \\ \cdots & \cdots & \cdots & \cdots & \cdots \\ 0 & 0 & 0 & \cdots & 1 \end{bmatrix}$$

of order $(k-1) \times k$ and $\mathbf{r} = \mathbf{0}$ give the hypothesis

$$\beta_2 = \beta_3 = \cdots = \beta_k = 0$$

The vector $\mathbf{Rb} - \mathbf{r}$ now reduces simply to the $k-1$ vector of OLS regression slopes

$$\mathbf{b}_2 = \begin{bmatrix} b_2 \\ b_3 \\ \vdots \\ b_k \end{bmatrix}$$

$\mathbf{R(X'X)}^{-1}\mathbf{R'}$ picks out the $(k-1) \times (k-1)$ submatrix formed by the last $k-1$ rows and columns in $(\mathbf{X'X})^{-1}$. To see what is implied by this matrix, partition the $\mathbf{X}$ matrix as

$$\mathbf{X} = [\mathbf{i} \quad \mathbf{X}_2]$$

where $\mathbf{i}$ is a column of units and $\mathbf{X}_2$ is the $n \times (k-1)$ matrix of observations on all the explanatory variables. Then

$$\mathbf{X'X} = \begin{bmatrix} n & \mathbf{i'X}_2 \\ \mathbf{X}_2'\mathbf{i} & \mathbf{X}_2'\mathbf{X}_2 \end{bmatrix}$$

By Eq. (4-66) the right lower $k-1$ submatrix in $(\mathbf{X'X})^{-1}$ is

$$\left(\mathbf{X}_2'\mathbf{X}_2 - \mathbf{X}_2'\mathbf{i}\frac{1}{n}\mathbf{i'X}_2\right)^{-1} = (\mathbf{X}_2'\mathbf{AX}_2)^{-1}$$

from Eq. (5-41). Thus the F statistic becomes

$$F = \frac{\mathbf{b}_2'(\mathbf{X}_2'\mathbf{AX}_2)\mathbf{b}_2/(k-1)}{\mathbf{e'e}/(n-k)} \tag{5-70}$$

From the decomposition of the total sum of squares in Eq. (5-49) above this is seen to be

$$F = \frac{\text{ESS}/(k-1)}{\text{RSS}/(n-k)} \tag{5-71}$$

or, in terms of R^2,

$$F = \frac{R^2/(k-1)}{(1-R^2)/(n-k)} \tag{5-72}$$

The *joint significance* of the complete set of explanatory variables is thus tested by computing F from any of these three formulas and seeing whether the computed value exceeds the preselected critical value.

Testing the Significance of a Subset of Coefficients

Specifying

$$\mathbf{R} = [\mathbf{0} \quad \mathbf{I}_s] \qquad \text{and} \qquad \mathbf{r} = \mathbf{0}$$

sets up the hypothesis

$$\beta_{k-s+1} = \beta_{k-s+2} = \cdots = \beta_k = 0$$

We can always renumber the variables, if necessary, so that the subset of interest comes at the end. Let us partition $\mathbf{X}$ and $\mathbf{b}$ conformably so that the complete OLS regression may be written

$$\mathbf{y} = [\mathbf{X}_r \quad \mathbf{X}_s]\begin{bmatrix}\mathbf{b}_r \\ \mathbf{b}_s\end{bmatrix} + \mathbf{e} = \mathbf{X}_r\mathbf{b}_r + \mathbf{X}_s\mathbf{b}_s + \mathbf{e} \tag{5-73}$$

where $\mathbf{X}_r$ is of order $n \times (k-s)$ and denotes the first $k-s$ columns in $\mathbf{X}$, and $\mathbf{X}_s$ denotes the last s columns in $\mathbf{X}$. Now

$$\mathbf{Rb} - \mathbf{r} = \mathbf{b}_s$$

and $\mathbf{R}(\mathbf{X}'\mathbf{X})^{-1}\mathbf{R}'$ picks out the square submatrix of order s in the bottom right-hand corner of $(\mathbf{X}'\mathbf{X})^{-1}$. Let us call that submatrix $\mathbf{C}_{ss}$. From the partitioning of $\mathbf{X}$ above

$$(\mathbf{X}'\mathbf{X}) = \begin{bmatrix}\mathbf{X}_r'\mathbf{X}_r & \mathbf{X}_r'\mathbf{X}_s \\ \mathbf{X}_s'\mathbf{X}_r & \mathbf{X}_s'\mathbf{X}_s\end{bmatrix}$$

and from Eq. (4-66)

$$\begin{aligned}\mathbf{C}_{ss} &= \left(\mathbf{X}_s'\mathbf{X}_s - \mathbf{X}_s'\mathbf{X}_r(\mathbf{X}_r'\mathbf{X}_r)^{-1}\mathbf{X}_r'\mathbf{X}_s\right)^{-1} \\ &= \left\{\mathbf{X}_s'\left[\mathbf{I} - \mathbf{X}_r(\mathbf{X}_r'\mathbf{X}_r)^{-1}\mathbf{X}_r'\right]\mathbf{X}_s\right\}^{-1} \\ &= (\mathbf{X}_s'\mathbf{M}_r\mathbf{X}_s)^{-1}\end{aligned} \tag{5-74}$$

where

$$\mathbf{M}_r = \mathbf{I} - \mathbf{X}_r(\mathbf{X}_r'\mathbf{X}_r)^{-1}\mathbf{X}_r' \tag{5-75}$$

Thus the numerator in the test statistic, Eq. (5-68), becomes†

$$\mathbf{b}_s'(\mathbf{X}_s'\mathbf{M}_r\mathbf{X}_s)\mathbf{b}_s/s$$

†Do not confuse this s, which denotes the number of coefficients under test with the square root of the residual variance defined in Eq. (5-57).

We will now show that this numerator has a very fundamental and important interpretation in terms of sums of squares. Suppose $\mathbf{y}$ is regressed just on the subset of variables in $\mathbf{X}_r$. Let $\mathbf{e}_r$ denote the resultant vector of residuals. From Eq. (5-54) we have

$$\mathbf{e}_r = \mathbf{M}_r\mathbf{y}$$

where $\mathbf{M}_r$ is exactly the matrix just defined in Eq. (5-75).
Thus

$$\begin{aligned}
\mathbf{e}_r'\mathbf{e}_r &= \text{residual sum of squares from regression of } \mathbf{y} \text{ on } \mathbf{X}_r \\
\mathbf{e}'\mathbf{e} &= \text{residual sum of squares from regression of } \mathbf{y} \text{ on } [\mathbf{X}_r \quad \mathbf{X}_s] \\
\mathbf{e}_r'\mathbf{e}_r - \mathbf{e}'\mathbf{e} &= \text{reduction in residual sum of squares due to adding } \mathbf{X}_s \text{ to regression} \\
&= \text{increase in explained sum of squares due to adding } \mathbf{X}_s \text{ to regression}
\end{aligned}$$

Our purpose is to show that

$$\mathbf{b}_s'(\mathbf{X}_s'\mathbf{M}_r\mathbf{X}_s)\mathbf{b}_s = \mathbf{e}_r'\mathbf{e}_r - \mathbf{e}'\mathbf{e}$$

Return to Eq. (5-73) and premultiply by $\mathbf{M}_r$ to get

$$\begin{aligned}
\mathbf{M}_r\mathbf{y} &= \mathbf{M}_r\mathbf{X}_r\mathbf{b}_r + \mathbf{M}_r\mathbf{X}_s\mathbf{b}_s + \mathbf{M}_r\mathbf{e} \\
&= \mathbf{M}_r\mathbf{X}_s\mathbf{b}_s + \mathbf{e}
\end{aligned}$$

for the definition of $\mathbf{M}_r$ in Eq. (5-75) implies $\mathbf{M}_r\mathbf{X}_r = \mathbf{0}$ and $\mathbf{M}_r\mathbf{e} = \mathbf{e}$ since $\mathbf{X}'\mathbf{e} = [\mathbf{X}_r'\mathbf{e} \quad \mathbf{X}_s'\mathbf{e}] = [\mathbf{0} \quad \mathbf{0}]$. Transposing and squaring this equation gives

$$\mathbf{y}'\mathbf{M}_r\mathbf{y} = \mathbf{b}_s'\mathbf{X}_s'\mathbf{M}_r\mathbf{X}_s\mathbf{b}_s + \mathbf{e}'\mathbf{e}$$

but

$$\mathbf{y}'\mathbf{M}_r\mathbf{y} = \mathbf{e}_r'\mathbf{e}_r$$

and the desired result follows. Thus the test statistic, Eq. (5-68), in this case becomes

$$F = \frac{(\mathbf{e}_r'\mathbf{e}_r - \mathbf{e}'\mathbf{e})/s}{(\mathbf{e}'\mathbf{e})/(n-k)} \sim F(s, n-k) \tag{5-76}$$

In words, the test of the joint significance of the subset $\mathbf{X}_s$ is achieved by the following steps:

1. Regress $\mathbf{y}$ on the variables $\mathbf{X}_r$ which are not in the subset, and measure the residual sum of squares $\mathbf{e}_r'\mathbf{e}_r$.
2. Carry out the complete regression and measure the residual sum of squares $\mathbf{e}'\mathbf{e}$. The difference $\mathbf{e}_r'\mathbf{e}_r - \mathbf{e}'\mathbf{e}$ measures the reduction in the residual sum of squares due to adding $\mathbf{X}_s$ to the regression.
3. The mean square $(\mathbf{e}_r'\mathbf{e}_r - \mathbf{e}'\mathbf{e})/s$, associated with the subset, is then contrasted with the overall mean square $\mathbf{e}'\mathbf{e}/(n-k)$. If the resultant F value exceeds a preselected critical value, the hypothesis that the variables in $\mathbf{X}_s$ have zero effect on Y is rejected.

The previous test for the joint significance of *all* the explanatory variables may also be seen to be of the same form as Eq. (5-76). That test was based on

$$F = \frac{\text{ESS}/(k-1)}{\text{RSS}/(n-k)}$$

From Eqs. (5-49) we have

$$\underset{\text{(TSS)}}{\mathbf{y}'\mathbf{A}\mathbf{y}} = \underset{\text{(ESS)}}{\mathbf{b}_2'\mathbf{X}_2'\mathbf{A}\mathbf{X}_2\mathbf{b}_2} + \underset{\text{(RSS)}}{\mathbf{e}'\mathbf{e}}$$

Thus the above F statistic could be written

$$F = \frac{(\mathbf{y}'\mathbf{A}\mathbf{y} - \mathbf{e}'\mathbf{e})/(k-1)}{\mathbf{e}'\mathbf{e}/(n-k)}$$

and $\mathbf{y}'\mathbf{A}\mathbf{y}$, which is the sum of the squared *deviations* of the Y values, can be interpreted as a residual sum of squares when Y is regressed only on a vector of units $\mathbf{i}$, for replacing $\mathbf{X}_r$ in Eq. (5-75) by $\mathbf{i}$ gives

$$\mathbf{M}_r = \mathbf{I} - \frac{1}{n}\mathbf{i}\mathbf{i}'$$

This is the $\mathbf{A}$ matrix of Eq. (5-41), which transforms a variable into deviation form. Thus $\mathbf{e}_r'\mathbf{e}_r$ becomes $\mathbf{y}'\mathbf{A}\mathbf{y}$ in this case.

The test of a single coefficient is merely a special case of the test of a subset. Thus the t or F test for the significance of a single coefficient may also be interpreted in a sums of squares context. The test of

$$H_0\colon\ \beta_i = 0$$

amounts to

1. Regress $\mathbf{y}$ on all X's except X_i.
2. Regress $\mathbf{y}$ on all X's.
3. Compute the reduction in the residual sum of squares from step 1 to step 2 and contrast with $\mathbf{e}'\mathbf{e}/(n-k)$.

Finally, we note another illuminating way of interpreting these various tests. The regression of $\mathbf{y}$ on $\mathbf{X}_r$ leading to the residual vector $\mathbf{e}_r$ may be regarded as a *restricted regression*. The essence of the restriction is that any coefficients which are specified by the hypothesis to be zero *in the population* are actually set at zero in the sample. Thus in testing $\beta_i = 0$, the restricted regression omits X_i, so that in effect $b_i = 0$. Likewise, in testing the overall regression, the restricted regression leaves out all variables except the unit vector, thus setting $b_2 = b_3 = \cdots = b_k = 0$. The complete regression may be regarded as an *unrestricted* regression, since all the variables are included, and the estimated coefficients come out as the sample data determine. Thus

$$\mathbf{e}_r'\mathbf{e}_r = \text{residual sum of squares from restricted regression}$$

$$\mathbf{e}'\mathbf{e} = \text{residual sum of squares from unrestricted regression}$$

and the test of the significance of a restriction, or the set of q restrictions, is

$$F = \frac{(\mathbf{e}_r'\mathbf{e}_r - \mathbf{e}'\mathbf{e})/q}{\mathbf{e}'\mathbf{e}/(n-k)} \tag{5-77}$$

Confidence Intervals

Confidence intervals for a single β coefficient may be readily determined from the result on the t distribution in Eq. (5-61). Joint confidence regions for two or more parameters may also be determined. From Eq. (5-65) we have

$$[\mathbf{R}(\mathbf{b}-\boldsymbol{\beta})]'\left[\sigma^2\mathbf{R}(\mathbf{X}'\mathbf{X})^{-1}\mathbf{R}'\right]^{-1}[\mathbf{R}(\mathbf{b}-\boldsymbol{\beta})] \sim \chi^2(q)$$

and, as usual,

$$\frac{\mathbf{e}'\mathbf{e}}{\sigma^2} \sim \chi^2(n-k)$$

independently of $\mathbf{b}$. Thus

$$F = \frac{[\mathbf{R}(\mathbf{b}-\boldsymbol{\beta})]'\left[\mathbf{R}(\mathbf{X}'\mathbf{X})^{-1}\mathbf{R}'\right]^{-1}[\mathbf{R}(\mathbf{b}-\boldsymbol{\beta})]/q}{\mathbf{e}'\mathbf{e}/(n-k)} \sim F(q, n-k) \qquad (5\text{-}78)$$

Appropriate specifications of $\mathbf{R}$ in Eq. (5-78) will yield confidence regions for various groups of parameters. For example, setting $\mathbf{R} = \mathbf{I}_k$ and equating the expression in Eq. (5-78) to some critical value F_α gives a condition on the unknown $\boldsymbol{\beta}$ vector from which a joint confidence region may be determined.

Example 5-2. Example 5-1 was based on

$$\mathbf{y} = \begin{bmatrix} 3 \\ 1 \\ 8 \\ 3 \\ 5 \end{bmatrix} \qquad \text{and} \qquad \mathbf{X} = \begin{bmatrix} 1 & 3 & 5 \\ 1 & 1 & 4 \\ 1 & 5 & 6 \\ 1 & 2 & 4 \\ 1 & 4 & 6 \end{bmatrix}$$

The estimated regression was

$$\hat{Y} = 4 + 2.5X_2 - 1.5X_3$$

with ESS = 26.5, RSS = 1.5, TSS = 28, and

$$R^2 = 0.9464$$

We also have $n = 5$ and $k = 3$. We will now illustrate tests of various hypotheses with these data. It must be emphasized that the tests are simply meant to illustrate the use of the formulas of this section. The data have been "cooked" to give simple numbers, and the sample size is too small to allow any sharp interpretations.

1. *Testing the joint significance of* X_2 *and* X_3

$$\boxed{H_0\colon\ \beta_2 = \beta_3 = 0}$$

Substitution in Eq. (5-71) gives

$$F = \frac{\text{ESS}/(k-1)}{\text{RSS}/(n-k)} = \frac{26.5/(3-1)}{1.5/(5-3)} = 17.67$$

From the tables of the F distribution, $F_{0.95}(2, 2) = 19.00$, so that the sample F falls short of the 5 percent critical value. Even though the sample R^2 is numerically high, the sample size is so small that it fails to reach significance.

2. *Testing the significance of* $\mathbf{X}_3$

$$\boxed{H_0:\ \beta_3 = 0}$$

Result (5-61) states that

$$t = \frac{b_i - \beta_i}{s\sqrt{a_{ii}}} \sim t(n-k)$$

where a_{ii} is the ith term on the main diagonal of $(\mathbf{X}'\mathbf{X})^{-1}$. We do not need, however, to invert the 3×3 matrix $\mathbf{X}'\mathbf{X}$. In the development of Eq. (5-70) we showed that the right lower $k-1$ submatrix in $(\mathbf{X}'\mathbf{X})^{-1}$ is given by $(\mathbf{X}_2'\mathbf{A}\mathbf{X}_2)^{-1}$, which is simply the inverse of the matrix of sums of squares and products of the variables in deviation form. For this example we have

$$\mathbf{X}_2'\mathbf{A}\mathbf{X}_2 = \begin{bmatrix} 10 & 6 \\ 6 & 4 \end{bmatrix}$$

Thus

$$(\mathbf{X}_2'\mathbf{A}\mathbf{X}_2)^{-1} = \begin{bmatrix} 1 & -1.5 \\ -1.5 & 2.5 \end{bmatrix}$$

giving $a_{33} = 2.5$. Further, $s^2 = \mathbf{e}'\mathbf{e}/(n-k) = 1.5/2 = 0.75$. Finally, substituting -1.5 for b_3 and 0 for β_3 gives the test statistic

$$t = \frac{-1.5}{\sqrt{0.75}\sqrt{2.5}} = \sqrt{1.2} = 1.1$$

which is insignificant.

Alternatively, we may show that the same numerical value for the test statistic comes from the stepwise reduction in the residual sum of squares. It is again simpler to work with the data in deviation form. Regressing Y on X_2 gives an estimated regression coefficient of

$$\frac{\Sigma y x_2}{\Sigma x_2^2} = \frac{16}{10} = 1.6$$

The explained sum of squares due to this regression is then

$$b_2 \Sigma y x_2 = 1.6(16) = 25.6$$

and the residual sum of squares is

$$\Sigma y^2 - b_2 \Sigma y x_2 = 28.0 - 25.6 = 2.4 = \mathbf{e}_r'\mathbf{e}_r$$

When the complete regression X_2 and X_3 is run, we already know the residual sum of squares,

$$\text{RSS} = \mathbf{e}'\mathbf{e} = 1.5$$

Thus substitution in Eq. (5-77) gives

$$F = \frac{(\mathbf{e}_r'\mathbf{e}_r - \mathbf{e}'\mathbf{e})/q}{\mathbf{e}'\mathbf{e}/(n-k)} = \frac{2.4 - 1.5}{1.5/2} = 1.2$$

which is the square of the above t statistic, as it should be.

3. *Coefficients of* X_2 *and* X_3 *equal in magnitude but opposite in sign*

$$\boxed{H_0:\ \beta_2 + \beta_3 = 0}$$

From the general formulation

$$\mathbf{R}\boldsymbol{\beta} = \mathbf{r}$$

this gives

$$\mathbf{R} = [0 \quad 1 \quad 1] \qquad \text{and} \qquad \mathbf{r} = 0$$

with $q = 1$. The appropriate test statistic is given by the general result in Eq. (5-68), namely,

$$F = \frac{(\mathbf{Rb} - \mathbf{r})'\left[\mathbf{R}(\mathbf{X}'\mathbf{X})^{-1}\mathbf{R}'\right]^{-1}(\mathbf{Rb} - \mathbf{r})/q}{\mathbf{e}'\mathbf{e}/(n-k)}$$

We then have

$$\mathbf{Rb} - \mathbf{r} = b_2 + b_3$$

and $\mathbf{R}(\mathbf{X}'\mathbf{X})^{-1}\mathbf{R}$ only involves the elements in the 2×2 submatrix in the lower right-hand corner of $(\mathbf{X}'\mathbf{X})^{-1}$. As we have already seen, this is $(\mathbf{X}_2'\mathbf{A}\mathbf{X}_2)^{-1}$. Thus

$$\mathbf{R}(\mathbf{X}'\mathbf{X})^{-1}\mathbf{R}' = [1 \quad 1]\begin{bmatrix} 1 & -1.5 \\ -1.5 & 2.5 \end{bmatrix}\begin{bmatrix} 1 \\ 1 \end{bmatrix} = 0.5$$

Thus the test statistic becomes

$$F = \frac{(b_2 + b_3)^2}{0.75(0.5)} = 2.66$$

which falls well short of any usual critical value for $F(1, 2)$. Thus the data are not inconsistent with the hypothesis that $\beta_2 + \beta_3 = 0$.

4. *95 percent confidence interval for* β_2

$$b_2 = 2.5$$

$$s^2 = \frac{\mathbf{e}'\mathbf{e}}{2} = 0.75$$

The top diagonal element in $(\mathbf{X}_2'\mathbf{A}\mathbf{X}_2)^{-1} = 1$. Thus

$$\text{var}(b_2) = 0.75$$

$$\text{s.e.}\,(b_2) = 0.866$$

$$t_{0.025}(2) = 4.303$$

Thus the confidence interval is given by

$$2.5 \pm 4.303(0.866) = 2.5 \pm 3.7$$

that is,

$$-1.2 \text{ to } 6.2$$

The fact that the confidence interval includes zero means that b_2 is not statistically significant at the 5 percent level.

5. *Joint confidence region for β_2 and β_3* Returning to Eq. (5-78) we specify

$$\mathbf{R} = \begin{bmatrix} 0 & 1 & 0 \\ 0 & 0 & 1 \end{bmatrix} \qquad \text{and} \qquad q = 2$$

Thus

$$\mathbf{R}(\mathbf{b} - \boldsymbol{\beta}) = \begin{bmatrix} b_2 \\ b_3 \end{bmatrix} - \begin{bmatrix} \beta_2 \\ \beta_3 \end{bmatrix} = \begin{bmatrix} 2.5 - \beta_2 \\ -1.5 - \beta_3 \end{bmatrix}$$

and

$$\left[\mathbf{R}(\mathbf{X}'\mathbf{X})^{-1}\mathbf{R}'\right]^{-1} = \begin{bmatrix} 10 & 6 \\ 6 & 4 \end{bmatrix}$$

Substitution in Eq. (5-78) gives

$$F = \frac{\begin{bmatrix} 2.5 - \beta_2 & -1.5 - \beta_3 \end{bmatrix} \begin{bmatrix} 10 & 6 \\ 6 & 4 \end{bmatrix} \begin{bmatrix} 2.5 - \beta_2 \\ -1.5 - \beta_3 \end{bmatrix}}{1.5}$$

$$= \frac{26.5 - 32\beta_2 - 18\beta_3 + 12\beta_2\beta_3 + 10\beta_2^2 + 4\beta_3^2}{1.5}$$

Choosing, say, the 5 percent critical value of F, we have

$$\Pr\{F < F_{0.95}\} = 0.95$$

Then setting

$$F = F_{0.95}$$

defines a 95 percent confidence ellipse for the unknown β parameters in F. For this problem $F_{0.95}(2, 2) = 19$. Setting $F = F_{0.95}$ then gives

$$\frac{10\beta_2^2 + 12\beta_2\beta_3 + 4\beta_3^2 - 32\beta_2 - 18\beta_3 + 26.5}{1.5} - 19 = 0$$

that is,

$$10\beta_2^2 + 12\beta_2\beta_3 + 4\beta_3^2 - 32\beta_2 - 18\beta_3 - 2 = 0$$

This defines the 95 percent confidence ellipse for β_2 and β_3, which is sketched in Fig. 5-1. The ellipse is centered at the estimated point $b_2 = 2.5$, $b_3 = -1.5$. There is a strong negative covariance between the two estimates and the origin lies just inside the ellipse, in agreement with the result of test 1 above.

6. *Point and interval forecasts* Suppose we wish to forecast the value of Y associated with $X_2 = 10$ and $X_3 = 10$. Plugging these values into the regres-

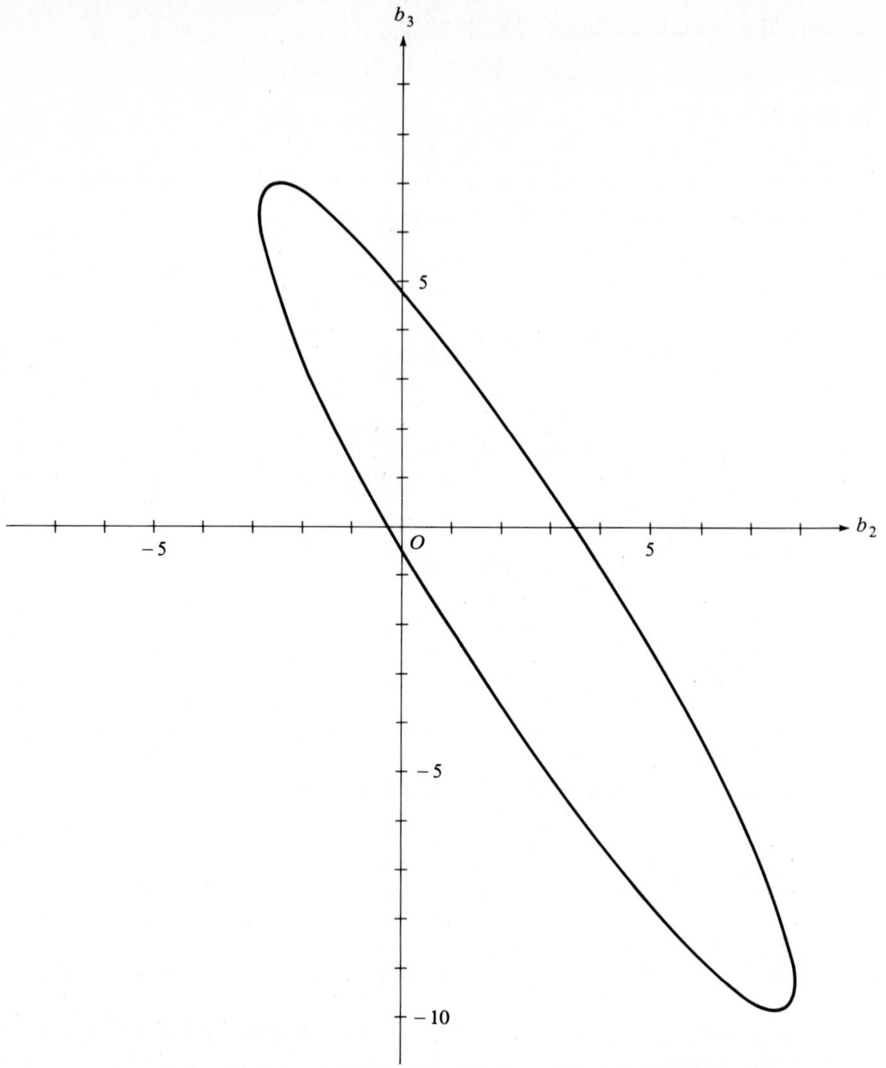

Figure 5-1 95 percent confidence ellipse for b_2, b_3.

sion equation gives the *point* forecast

$$\hat{Y}_f = 4 + 2.5(10) - 1.5(10) = 14$$

A point forecast is of little use unless supplemented by a measure of precision, which enables us to put the forecast in interval form. The forecast may be written

$$\hat{Y}_f = [1 \quad 10 \quad 10]\begin{bmatrix} b_1 \\ b_2 \\ b_3 \end{bmatrix} = \mathbf{Rb}$$

where $$\mathbf{R} = [1 \quad 10 \quad 10]$$

The actual Y value in the forecast period will be

$$Y_f = \mathbf{R}\boldsymbol{\beta} + u_f$$

where u_f denotes the actual value assumed by the disturbance in the forecast period. Let us then define the forecast error e_f as

$$e_f = Y_f - \hat{Y}_f = -\mathbf{R}(\mathbf{b} - \boldsymbol{\beta}) + u_f$$

It follows immediately that

$$E(e_f) = 0$$

since $E(\mathbf{b}) = \boldsymbol{\beta}$ and $E(u_f) = 0$. Also

$$\begin{aligned}\text{var}(e_f) &= E\{[-\mathbf{R}(\mathbf{b} - \boldsymbol{\beta}) + u_f][-\mathbf{R}(\mathbf{b} - \boldsymbol{\beta}) + u_f]'\} \\ &= \sigma^2\mathbf{R}(\mathbf{X}'\mathbf{X})^{-1}\mathbf{R}' + \sigma^2\end{aligned}$$

using Eq. (5-64), and also the fact that u_f will be independent of the sample disturbances and hence independent of $\mathbf{b}$. Thus

$$\frac{Y_f - \hat{Y}_f}{\sigma\sqrt{1 + \mathbf{R}(\mathbf{X}'\mathbf{X})^{-1}\mathbf{R}'}} \sim N(0, 1)$$

Replacing the unknown σ by

$$s = \sqrt{\mathbf{e}'\mathbf{e}/(n - k)}$$

then gives

$$\frac{Y_f - \hat{Y}_f}{s\sqrt{1 + \mathbf{R}(\mathbf{X}'\mathbf{X})^{-1}\mathbf{R}'}} \sim t(n - k)$$

and so a 95 percent confidence interval for Y_f is

$$\hat{Y}_f \pm t_{0.025}s\sqrt{1 + \mathbf{R}(\mathbf{X}'\mathbf{X})^{-1}\mathbf{R}'} \tag{5-79}$$

where $\mathbf{R}$ is a row vector containing the values of X in the forecast period prefaced by unity in the first position. In this example

$$\mathbf{X}'\mathbf{X} = \begin{bmatrix} 5 & 15 & 25 \\ 15 & 55 & 81 \\ 25 & 81 & 129 \end{bmatrix}$$

with

$$(\mathbf{X}'\mathbf{X})^{-1} = \begin{bmatrix} 26.7 & 4.5 & -8.0 \\ 4.5 & 1.0 & -1.5 \\ -8.0 & -1.5 & 2.5 \end{bmatrix}$$

Thus

$$\begin{aligned}\mathbf{R}(\mathbf{X}'\mathbf{X})^{-1}\mathbf{R}' &= [1 \quad 10 \quad 10]\begin{bmatrix} 26.7 & 4.5 & -8.0 \\ 4.5 & 1.0 & -1.5 \\ -8.0 & -1.5 & 2.5 \end{bmatrix}\begin{bmatrix} 1 \\ 10 \\ 10 \end{bmatrix} \\ &= [-8.3 \quad -0.5 \quad 2.0]\begin{bmatrix} 1 \\ 10 \\ 10 \end{bmatrix} = 6.7\end{aligned}$$

We also have

$$s^2 = 0.75$$

and

$$t_{0.025}(2) = 4.303$$

Thus substitution in Eq. (5-79) gives

$$14 \pm 4.303\sqrt{0.75}\sqrt{7.7} = 14 \pm 10.34$$

or

$$\boxed{3.66 \text{ to } 24.34}$$

This is a prediction interval for Y_f, the value of Y in the forecast period. Sometimes an investigator prefers to set up an interval for $E(Y_f)$, that is, the mean or expected value of Y in the forecast period, the reason being that Y_f contains the disturbance u_f, which is essentially unpredictable. We have

$$Y_f = \mathbf{R\beta} + u_f$$

Thus

$$E(Y_f) = \mathbf{R\beta}$$

and the forecast error would now be defined as

$$e_f = E(Y_f) - \hat{Y}_f = -\mathbf{R}(\mathbf{b} - \boldsymbol{\beta})$$

Following through the steps of the previous analysis then gives a 95 percent confidence interval for $E(Y_f)$ as

$$\hat{Y}_f \pm t_{0.025} s \sqrt{\mathbf{R}(\mathbf{X}'\mathbf{X})^{-1}\mathbf{R}'} \tag{5-80}$$

The numerical implementation of Eq. (5-80) gives

$$14 \pm 4.303\sqrt{0.75}\sqrt{6.7}$$

or

$$\boxed{4.36 \text{ to } 23.64}$$

which is a slightly narrower interval than that for Y_f.

There is an alternative way of generating either interval forecast, which is simpler in that it only requires the inversion of a second-order rather than a third-order matrix, and which also provides an illuminating way of looking at the OLS regression. From Eq. (5-48) we can write the OLS regression as

$$Y = \bar{Y} + b_2x_2 + b_3x_3 + \cdots + b_kx_k + e$$

where, as in Chaps. 2 and 3, $x_2 = X_2 - \bar{X}$, and so on. This is equivalent to the regression of $\mathbf{y}$ on $\mathbf{X}$, where $\mathbf{X}$ is now defined as

$$\mathbf{X} = [\mathbf{i} \quad \mathbf{AX}_2]$$

i being a column of units and $\mathbf{AX}_2$ the $n \times (k-1)$ matrix of *deviations*. The OLS estimator is then

$$\mathbf{b} = \begin{bmatrix} n & \mathbf{0} \\ \mathbf{0} & \mathbf{X}_2'\mathbf{AX}_2 \end{bmatrix}^{-1} \begin{bmatrix} \mathbf{i}'\mathbf{y} \\ \mathbf{X}_2'\mathbf{Ay} \end{bmatrix}$$

$$= \begin{bmatrix} \dfrac{1}{n} & \mathbf{0} \\ \mathbf{0} & (\mathbf{X}_2'\mathbf{AX}_2)^{-1} \end{bmatrix} \begin{bmatrix} \mathbf{i}'\mathbf{y} \\ \mathbf{X}_2'\mathbf{Ay} \end{bmatrix}$$

$$= \begin{bmatrix} \bar{Y} \\ (\mathbf{X}_2'\mathbf{AX}_2)^{-1}\mathbf{X}_2'\mathbf{Ay} \end{bmatrix}$$

where we used the result that $\mathbf{i}'\mathbf{AX}_2 = \mathbf{0}$ (the sums of sample deviations being identically zero). The covariance matrix is

$$\text{var}(\mathbf{b}) = \sigma^2 \begin{bmatrix} \dfrac{1}{n} & \mathbf{0} \\ \mathbf{0} & (\mathbf{X}_2'\mathbf{AX}_2)^{-1} \end{bmatrix}$$

The point forecast may be written

$$\hat{Y}_f = \bar{Y} + \mathbf{x}_f\mathbf{b}_2$$

where $\mathbf{x}_f = [x_{2f} \quad \cdots \quad x_{kf}]$ is a row vector of the X deviations in the forecast period and $\mathbf{b}_2$ is a $(k-1)$-element column vector of the OLS regression slopes. Thus

$$E(\hat{Y}_f) = E(\bar{Y}) + \mathbf{x}_f\boldsymbol{\beta}_2$$

and

$$\text{var}(\hat{Y}_f) = \text{var}(\bar{Y}) + \mathbf{x}_f E\{(\mathbf{b}_2 - \boldsymbol{\beta}_2)(\mathbf{b}_2 - \boldsymbol{\beta}_2)'\}\mathbf{x}_f'$$

$$= \sigma^2\left[\frac{1}{n} + \mathbf{x}_f(\mathbf{X}_2'\mathbf{AX}_2)^{-1}\mathbf{x}_f'\right]$$

since the matrix var(**b**) above shows that $\bar{Y}$ and $\mathbf{b}_2$ are distributed independently. For the problem in hand,

$$\bar{Y} = 4 \qquad \bar{X}_2 = 3 \qquad \bar{X}_3 = 5$$

and so

$$\mathbf{x}_f = [7 \quad 5]$$

$$(\mathbf{X}_2'\mathbf{AX}_2)^{-1} = \begin{bmatrix} 1.0 & -1.5 \\ -1.5 & 2.5 \end{bmatrix}$$

and $s^2 = 0.75$. Thus the *estimated* var($\hat{Y}_f$) is

$$0.75(0.2) + 0.75[7 \quad 5]\begin{bmatrix} 1.0 & -1.5 \\ -1.5 & 2.5 \end{bmatrix}\begin{bmatrix} 7 \\ 5 \end{bmatrix} = 0.75(6.7)$$

The point forecast is

$$\hat{Y}_f = 4 + [7 \quad 5]\begin{bmatrix} 2.5 \\ -1.5 \end{bmatrix} = 14$$

and thus the 95 percent confidence interval for $E(Y_f)$ is

$$14 \pm 4.303\sqrt{0.75}\,\sqrt{0.67}$$

or

$$4.36 \text{ to } 23.64$$

as before.

Prediction when the X Variables Are Uncertain

The treatment of interval forecasts given above assumes implicitly that the values of the X variables in the forecast period are known with certainty. In practice, however, it is more realistic to postulate some uncertainty about the X values. Let

$$\mathbf{x}'_f = \begin{bmatrix} 1 & X_{2f} & X_{3f} & \cdots & X_{kf} \end{bmatrix}$$

indicate the true values of the explanatory variables in the forecast period and

$$\hat{\mathbf{x}}'_f = \begin{bmatrix} 1 & \hat{X}_{2f} & \hat{X}_{3f} & \cdots & \hat{X}_{kf} \end{bmatrix}$$

the values that the forecaster thinks will be obtained in the forecast period. The true value Y_f is given by

$$Y_f = \mathbf{x}'_f\boldsymbol{\beta} + u_f$$

and the point prediction will now be

$$\hat{Y}_f = \hat{\mathbf{x}}'_f\mathbf{b}$$

Thus the forecast error is

$$\begin{aligned} e_f &= Y_f - \hat{Y}_f \\ &= u_f + \mathbf{x}'_f\boldsymbol{\beta} - \hat{\mathbf{x}}'_f\mathbf{b} \end{aligned}$$

For simplicity we will drop the f subscript, since there is no ambiguity, and write the forecast error as

$$\begin{aligned} e &= u - \hat{\mathbf{x}}'(\mathbf{b} - \boldsymbol{\beta}) - (\hat{\mathbf{x}} - \mathbf{x})'\boldsymbol{\beta} \\ &= u - \hat{\mathbf{x}}'(\mathbf{b} - \boldsymbol{\beta}) - \boldsymbol{\beta}'(\hat{\mathbf{x}} - \mathbf{x}) \end{aligned} \tag{5-81}$$

If we assume that the forecaster makes unbiased forecasts of the X values, that is,

$$E(\hat{\mathbf{x}}) = \mathbf{x}$$

and, in addition, that there is zero covariance in the population between forecasts of $\mathbf{x}$ and estimate of $\boldsymbol{\beta}$ from the sample data, then

$$E\{\hat{\mathbf{x}}'(\mathbf{b} - \boldsymbol{\beta})\} = 0$$

and so

$$E(e) = 0$$

Hence the variance of the forecast error is found by squaring Eq. (5-81) and taking expectations, to give

$$\sigma_{\hat{y}}^2 = E\{u^2 + \hat{\mathbf{x}}'(\mathbf{b} - \boldsymbol{\beta})(\mathbf{b} - \boldsymbol{\beta})'\hat{\mathbf{x}} + \boldsymbol{\beta}'(\hat{\mathbf{x}} - \mathbf{x})(\hat{\mathbf{x}} - \mathbf{x})'\boldsymbol{\beta} + \text{cross-product terms}\} \tag{5-82}$$

On taking expectations the cross-product terms vanish because of the independence of u, $\hat{\mathbf{x}}$, and $\mathbf{b}$. For the remaining terms

$$\begin{aligned} E\{\boldsymbol{\beta}'(\hat{\mathbf{x}} - \mathbf{x})(\hat{\mathbf{x}} - \mathbf{x})'\boldsymbol{\beta}\} &= \boldsymbol{\beta}'\mathbf{E}\{(\hat{\mathbf{x}} - \mathbf{x})(\hat{\mathbf{x}} - \mathbf{x})'\}\boldsymbol{\beta} \\ &= \boldsymbol{\beta}'\text{var}(\hat{\mathbf{x}})\boldsymbol{\beta} \end{aligned}$$

and

$$\begin{aligned} E\{\hat{\mathbf{x}}'(\mathbf{b} - \boldsymbol{\beta})(\mathbf{b} - \boldsymbol{\beta})'\hat{\mathbf{x}}\} &= E\{\text{tr}[\hat{\mathbf{x}}'(\mathbf{b} - \boldsymbol{\beta})(\mathbf{b} - \boldsymbol{\beta})'\hat{\mathbf{x}}]\} \\ &= E\{\text{tr}[(\mathbf{b} - \boldsymbol{\beta})(\mathbf{b} - \boldsymbol{\beta})'\hat{\mathbf{x}}\hat{\mathbf{x}}']\} \\ &= \text{tr}[E\{(\mathbf{b} - \boldsymbol{\beta})(\mathbf{b} - \boldsymbol{\beta})'\}E\{\hat{\mathbf{x}}\hat{\mathbf{x}}'\}] \end{aligned}$$

Now

$$\begin{aligned} \text{var}(\hat{\mathbf{x}}) &= E\{(\hat{\mathbf{x}} - \mathbf{x})(\hat{\mathbf{x}} - \mathbf{x})'\} \\ &= E(\hat{\mathbf{x}}\hat{\mathbf{x}}') - \mathbf{x}\mathbf{x}' \end{aligned}$$

and so

$$E(\hat{\mathbf{x}}\hat{\mathbf{x}}') = \text{var}(\hat{\mathbf{x}}) + \mathbf{x}\mathbf{x}'$$

Thus

$$E\{\hat{\mathbf{x}}'(\mathbf{b} - \boldsymbol{\beta})(\mathbf{b} - \boldsymbol{\beta})'\hat{\mathbf{x}}\} = \text{tr}[\text{var}(\mathbf{b}) \cdot (\text{var}(\hat{\mathbf{x}}) + \mathbf{x}\mathbf{x}')]$$

and

$$\text{tr}[\text{var}(\mathbf{b})\mathbf{x}\mathbf{x}'] = \text{tr}[\mathbf{x}'\text{var}(\mathbf{b})\mathbf{x}] = \mathbf{x}'\text{var}(\mathbf{b})\mathbf{x}$$

Thus substituting these expressions in Eq. (5-82)

$$\sigma_{\hat{y}}^2 = \sigma_u^2 + \mathbf{x}'\text{var}(\mathbf{b})\mathbf{x} + \boldsymbol{\beta}'\text{var}(\hat{\mathbf{x}})\boldsymbol{\beta} + \text{tr}[\text{var}(\mathbf{b}) \cdot \text{var}(\hat{\mathbf{x}})] \tag{5-83}$$

If there were no uncertainity about the X values in the forecast period, this expression reduces to

$$\sigma_u^2 + \mathbf{x}'\text{var}(\mathbf{b})\mathbf{x}$$

which is the conventional formula for the variance of a forecast. To implement Eq. (5-83) the various unknowns are replaced by estimated values:

- σ_u^2 is replaced by $s^2 = \mathbf{e}'\mathbf{e}/(n - k)$ in the usual fashion.
- $\mathbf{x}$ is replaced by $\hat{\mathbf{x}}$.
- var(**b**) is estimated by the usual OLS program.
- β is replaced by the estimated **b**.

The main practical difficulty is likely to be in the estimation of var($\hat{\mathbf{x}}$), the variance-covariance matrix of the forecast X values. There may be accumulated experience in forecasting from which variances and covariances may be estimated.

Alternatively, the forecaster may have subjective assessments that a forecast value is very likely to be within, say, 5 percent of the true value, which in turn implies a figure for the variance.

The remaining practical difficulty about the use of Eq. (5-83) is that we can no longer determine exact confidence intervals using the t and normal distributions. The reason is that even if normality is assumed for $\hat{\mathbf{x}}$ as well as u, the forecast error in Eq. (5-81) is not normally distributed since it involves $\hat{\mathbf{x}}'(\mathbf{b} - \boldsymbol{\beta})$, which is the sum of products of normal variables. One may follow the suggestion of Feldstein to use the Chebyshev inequality to determine an outer-bound forecast interval.† The practical procedure is as follows. Letting $s_{\hat{y}}$ denote the square root of the estimated value of Eq. (5-83) we can state:

The probability that the observed value of Y *in the forecast period will fall outside the interval* $\hat{Y}_f \pm cs_{\hat{y}}$ *does not exceed* $1/c^2$.

The researcher can set the value of c to make $1/c^2$ equal to 0.05 or whatever is desired. The Chebyshev inequality strictly involves the true $\sigma_{\hat{y}}$, but it is a very conservative statement and unlikely to be seriously affected by the replacement of $\sigma_{\hat{y}}$ by $s_{\hat{y}}$. If the distribution of $\hat{Y}_f$ were sufficiently well behaved to be unimodal and symmetric, the probability of Y_f lying outside the interval $\hat{Y}_f \pm cs_{\hat{y}}$ would not exceed $4/9c^2$.

PROBLEMS

5-1 Test the hypotheses (N.B. plural) $\beta_1 = 1$, $\beta_2 = 1$, $\beta_3 = -2$ in the regression model

$$Y_t = \beta_0 + \beta_1 X_{1t} + \beta_2 X_{2t} + \beta_3 X_{3t} + u_t$$

given the following sums of squares and products of deviations from means for 24 observations:

$$\Sigma y^2 = 60 \qquad \Sigma x_1^2 = 10 \qquad \Sigma x_2^2 = 30 \qquad \Sigma x_3^2 = 20$$

$$\Sigma yx_1 = 7 \qquad \Sigma yx_2 = -7 \qquad \Sigma yx_3 = -26$$

$$\Sigma x_1x_2 = 10 \qquad \Sigma x_1x_3 = 5 \qquad \Sigma x_2x_3 = 15$$

Test also the hypothesis that $\beta_1 + \beta_2 + \beta_3 = 0$. How does this differ from the hypothesis that $[\beta_1 \ \ \beta_2 \ \ \beta_3] = [1 \ \ 1 \ \ -2]$? Test the latter hypothesis.

5-2 The following sums were obtained from 10 sets of observations on Y, X_1, and X_2:

$$\Sigma Y = 20 \qquad \Sigma X_1 = 30 \qquad \Sigma X_2 = 40$$

$$\Sigma Y^2 = 88.2 \qquad \Sigma X_1^2 = 92 \qquad \Sigma X_2^2 = 163$$

$$\Sigma YX_1 = 59 \qquad \Sigma YX_2 = 88 \qquad \Sigma X_1X_2 = 119$$

Estimate the regression of Y on X_1 and X_2, and test the hypothesis that the coefficient of X_2 is zero.

5-3 Let

$\mathbf{y}$ be an $n \times 1$ column vector
$\mathbf{X}$ an $n \times k$ matrix

† M. S. Feldstein, "The Error of Forecast in Econometric Models when the Forecast-Period Exogenous Variables are Stochastic," *Econometrica*, **39**, 1971, pp. 55–60.

$\mathbf{X}[i]$ be $\mathbf{X}$ with the ith column $(\mathbf{x}_i)$ removed
$\mathbf{e}_{yi}$ be the residual vector from the regression of $\mathbf{y}$ on $\mathbf{X}[i]$
$\mathbf{e}_i$ be the residual vector from the regression of $\mathbf{x}_i$ on $\mathbf{X}[i]$

Now consider the two regressions:

1. $\mathbf{e}_{yi}$ on $\mathbf{e}_i$
2. $\mathbf{y}$ on $\mathbf{X}$

Prove that:

(a) The slope $b = \mathbf{e}'_{yi}\mathbf{e}_i/\mathbf{e}'_i\mathbf{e}_i$ from regression 1 and the multiple regression coefficient b_i from regression 2 are identical.

(b) The residuals from the two regressions are identical.

(c) The simple correlation between $\mathbf{e}_{yi}$ and $\mathbf{e}_i$ is the same as the partial correlation between y and $\mathbf{x}_i$ in regression 2.

5-4 The following regression equation is estimated as a production function for Q:

$$\log Q = 1.37 + \underset{(0.257)}{0.632} \log K + \underset{(0.219)}{0.452} \log L$$

$$R^2 = 0.98 \qquad \text{cov}(b_K, b_L) = 0.055$$

and the standard errors are given in parentheses.

Test the following null hypotheses:

(a) The capital K and labor L elasticities of output are identical.

(b) There are constant returns to scale.

(University of Washington, 1980)

Note: The problem does not give the number of sample observations. Does this omission affect your conclusions?

5-5 Consider a multiple regression model for which all classical assumptions hold, but in which there is *no constant term*. Suppose you wish to test the null hypothesis that there is no relationship between y and **X**, that is,

$$H_0: \ \beta_2 = \cdots = \beta_K = 0$$

against the alternative that at least one of the β's is nonzero. Present the appropriate test statistic and state its distribution (including the appropriate number[s] of degrees of freedom).

(University of Michigan, 1978)

5-6 One aspect of the rational expectations hypothesis involves the claim that expectations are unbiased, that is, that the average prediction is equal to the observed realization of the variable under investigation. This claim can be tested by reference to announced predictions and to actual values of the rate of interest on three-month U.S. Treasury Bills published in *The Goldsmith-Nagan Bond and Money Market Letter*. The results of least-squares estimation (based on 30 quarterly observations) of the regression of the actual on the predicted interest rates were as follows:

$$r_t = \underset{(0.86)}{0.24} + \underset{(0.14)}{0.94}\, r_t^* + e_t, \qquad \text{RSS} = 28.56$$

where r_t is the observed interest rate, and r_t^* is the average expectation of r_t held at the end of the preceding quarter. Figures in parentheses are estimated standard errors. The sample data on r^* give

$$\sum_t r_t^*/30 = 10, \qquad \sum_t (r_t^* - \bar{r}^*)^2 = 52$$

Carry out the test, assuming that all basic assumptions of the classical regression model are satisfied.

(University of Michigan, 1981)

5-7 Consider the following regression model in deviation form:

$$y_t = \beta_1 x_{1t} + \beta_2 x_{2t} + u_t$$

with sample data:

$$n = 100, \quad \Sigma y^2 = \frac{493}{3}, \quad \Sigma x_1^2 = 30, \quad \Sigma x_2^2 = 3,$$

$$\Sigma x_1 y = 30 \quad \Sigma x_2 y = 20, \quad \Sigma x_1 x_2 = 0$$

(*a*) Compute the OLS estimates of β_1, β_2, and R^2.
(*b*) Test the hypothesis H_0: $\beta_2 = 7$ against H_1: $\beta_2 \neq 7$.
(*c*) Test the hypothesis H_0: $\beta_1 = \beta_2 = 0$ against H_1: $\beta_1 \neq 0$ or $\beta_2 \neq 0$.
(*d*) Test the hypothesis H_0: $\beta_2 = 7\beta_1$ against H_1: $\beta_2 \neq 7\beta_1$.

(UL, 1981)

5-8 Given the following least-squares estimates:

$$C_t = \text{constant} + 0.92Y_t + e_{1t}$$

$$C_t = \text{constant} + 0.84C_{t-1} + e_{2t}$$

$$C_{t-1} = \text{constant} + 0.78Y_t + e_{3t}$$

$$Y_t = \text{constant} + 0.55C_{t-1} + e_{4t}$$

calculate the least-squares estimates of β_2 and β_3 in

$$C_t = \beta_1 + \beta_2 Y_t + \beta_3 C_{t-1} + u_t$$

(University of Michigan, 1981)

5-9 Prove that R^2 is the square of the simple correlation between $\mathbf{y}$ and $\hat{\mathbf{y}}$, where $\hat{\mathbf{y}} = \mathbf{X}(\mathbf{X}'\mathbf{X})^{-1}\mathbf{X}'\mathbf{y}$.

5-10 Prove that if a regression is fitted *without* a constant term, the residuals will not necessarily sum to zero, and R^2, if calculated as $1 - \mathbf{e}'\mathbf{e}/(\mathbf{y}'\mathbf{y} - n\bar{Y}^2)$, may be negative.

5-11 A researcher wishes to estimate the regression of $\mathbf{y}$ on $\mathbf{X}$ without an intercept term, that is, $\mathbf{X}$ does not contain a column of 1s. Unfortunately, the regression program at hand automatically computes an intercept term. Douglas M. Hawkins suggests that the program can be "tricked" into estimating the correct intercept free regression by entering each data point twice—once in its correct form $(y_i, \mathbf{x}_i)$ and once with the opposite sign $(-\mathbf{y}_i, -\mathbf{x}_i)$.

Prove that:

(*a*) The "trick" regression and the correct regression (with intercept suppressed) yield the same coefficients for $\mathbf{X}$.

(*b*) The residual sum of squares from the "trick" regression is exactly double the value from the correct regression.

Compute the ratio of the standard errors of the two regressions.

(*American Statistician*, **34**, Nov. 1980, p. 233)

5-12 (a) Prove that $\bar{R}^2$ increases with the addition of an extra explanatory variable only if the F $(= t^2)$ statistic for that variable exceeds unity.

(b) Prove that the partial

$$r^2 = \frac{F}{F + \text{df}} = \frac{t^2}{t^2 + \text{df}}$$

where t is the value of the statistic for testing the significance of the coefficient of the X_i to which the partial r is related, and df is the number of degrees of freedom in the regression.

5-13 Let the regression equation be partitioned as

$$\mathbf{y} = \mathbf{X}_1\boldsymbol{\beta}_1 + \mathbf{X}_2\boldsymbol{\beta}_2 + \boldsymbol{\varepsilon}$$

Let $\mathbf{b}_1$ and $\mathbf{b}_2$ be the usual least-squares estimators. Suppose that $E(\boldsymbol{\varepsilon}) = \mathbf{X}_1\boldsymbol{\gamma}$, that is, the mean vector of the disturbances is a linear combination of *some* of the regressors. Prove that $\mathbf{b}_1$ is biased but $\mathbf{b}_2$ is unbiased.

(University of Michigan, 1981)

5-14 Suppose that the $m \times 1$ vector $\mathbf{x}_i$ denotes m observations on the ith individual ($i = 1, \ldots, p$) and $\tilde{\mathbf{x}}_i$ is the corresponding vector of deviations from the ith sample mean. Let the $\mathbf{x}_i$ and $\tilde{\mathbf{x}}_i$ vectors be "stacked" to give $mp \times 1$ vectors

$$\mathbf{x}' = [\mathbf{x}_1' \quad \mathbf{x}_2' \quad \cdots \quad \mathbf{x}_p']$$

and

$$\tilde{\mathbf{x}}' = [\tilde{\mathbf{x}}_1' \quad \tilde{\mathbf{x}}_2' \quad \cdots \quad \tilde{\mathbf{x}}_p']$$

Find a matrix $\mathbf{D}$ such that $\mathbf{D}\mathbf{x} = \tilde{\mathbf{x}}$.

CHAPTER

SIX

FURTHER TOPICS IN THE k-VARIABLE LINEAR MODEL

6-1 ESTIMATION SUBJECT TO LINEAR RESTRICTIONS

In Chap. 5 we have described the procedure for testing the hypothesis that the elements of the population vector $\boldsymbol{\beta}$ obey the set of $\mathbf{q}$ ($\leq k$) linear restrictions embodied in the relations

$$H_0: \quad \mathbf{R}\boldsymbol{\beta} = \mathbf{r}$$

If H_0 is not rejected, one may wish to reestimate the model, incorporating the restrictions in the estimation process. One important reason for such reestimation is that it will improve the efficiency of the estimates. This produces an estimator $\mathbf{b}_*$ which then satisfies

$$\mathbf{R}\mathbf{b}_* = \mathbf{r} \tag{6-1}$$

For example, if the hypothesis of constant returns to scale is not rejected for a production function, the reestimation process would yield a production function with estimated elasticities which sum to unity.

We must first of all show how to derive an estimator $\mathbf{b}_*$ which satisfies Eq. (6-1). Second, we will use this estimator to cast new light on some of the test procedures of Chap. 5, and third, we will look at some important applications of the new estimator.

The assumed model, as before, is

$$\mathbf{y} = \mathbf{X}\boldsymbol{\beta} + \mathbf{u}$$

We define the scalar function

$$\varphi = (\mathbf{y} - \mathbf{X}\mathbf{b}_*)'(\mathbf{y} - \mathbf{X}\mathbf{b}_*) - 2\boldsymbol{\lambda}'(\mathbf{R}\mathbf{b}_* - \mathbf{r}) \tag{6-2}$$

where $\boldsymbol{\lambda}$ denotes a column vector of q Lagrange multipliers. Taking the partial derivatives of φ gives

$$\frac{\partial\varphi}{\partial\mathbf{b}_*} = -2\mathbf{X}'\mathbf{y} + 2\mathbf{X}'\mathbf{X}\mathbf{b}_* - 2\mathbf{R}'\boldsymbol{\lambda}$$

and

$$\frac{\partial\varphi}{\partial\boldsymbol{\lambda}} = -2(\mathbf{R}\mathbf{b}_* - \mathbf{r})$$

Setting these partial derivatives to zero gives the equations to be solved for $\mathbf{b}_*$ and $\boldsymbol{\lambda}$, namely,†

$$\mathbf{X}'\mathbf{X}\mathbf{b}_* - \mathbf{X}'\mathbf{y} - \mathbf{R}'\boldsymbol{\lambda} = \mathbf{0} \tag{6-3}$$

$$\mathbf{R}\mathbf{b}_* - \mathbf{r} = \mathbf{0} \tag{6-4}$$

Premultiplying Eq. (6-3) by $\mathbf{R}(\mathbf{X}'\mathbf{X})^{-1}$ gives

$$\mathbf{R}\mathbf{b}_* - \mathbf{R}(\mathbf{X}'\mathbf{X})^{-1}\mathbf{X}'\mathbf{y} - \mathbf{R}(\mathbf{X}'\mathbf{X})^{-1}\mathbf{R}'\boldsymbol{\lambda} = \mathbf{0}$$

Using Eq. (6-4) and resurrecting the OLS estimator of Chap. 5, that is,

$$\mathbf{b} = (\mathbf{X}'\mathbf{X})^{-1}\mathbf{X}'\mathbf{y}$$

this equation may be solved for $\boldsymbol{\lambda}$ as

$$\boldsymbol{\lambda} = \left[\mathbf{R}(\mathbf{X}'\mathbf{X})^{-1}\mathbf{R}'\right]^{-1}(\mathbf{r} - \mathbf{R}\mathbf{b})$$

Substituting back in Eq. (6-3) gives

$$\mathbf{b}_* = (\mathbf{X}'\mathbf{X})^{-1}\mathbf{X}'\mathbf{y} + (\mathbf{X}'\mathbf{X})^{-1}\mathbf{R}'\left[\mathbf{R}(\mathbf{X}'\mathbf{X})^{-1}\mathbf{R}'\right]^{-1}(\mathbf{r} - \mathbf{R}\mathbf{b})$$

that is,

$$\mathbf{b}_* = \mathbf{b} + (\mathbf{X}'\mathbf{X})^{-1}\mathbf{R}'\left[\mathbf{R}(\mathbf{X}'\mathbf{X})^{-1}\mathbf{R}'\right]^{-1}(\mathbf{r} - \mathbf{R}\mathbf{b}) \tag{6-5}$$

where $\mathbf{b}$ is the *unrestricted* OLS estimator $(\mathbf{X}'\mathbf{X})^{-1}\mathbf{X}'\mathbf{y}$. Formula (6-5) defines the *restricted* least-squares estimator satisfying the set of q restrictions embodied in $\mathbf{R}\mathbf{b}_* = \mathbf{r}$.‡ Corresponding to $\mathbf{b}_*$, we may define the residual vector

$$\mathbf{e}_* = \mathbf{y} - \mathbf{X}\mathbf{b}_*$$

† To keep the notation as simple as possible, we have not distinguished between the vectors $\mathbf{b}_*$ and $\boldsymbol{\lambda}$ which appear in the objective function, Eq. (6-2), and the specific vectors that emerge as the solutions to Eqs. (6-3) and (6-4).

‡ Provided the restrictions $\mathbf{R}\boldsymbol{\beta} = \mathbf{r}$ are true, the variance-covariance matrix of the restricted least-squares estimator may be shown to be

$$\text{var}(\mathbf{b}_*) = \sigma^2\left\{(\mathbf{X}'\mathbf{X})^{-1} - (\mathbf{X}'\mathbf{X})^{-1}\mathbf{R}'\left[\mathbf{R}(\mathbf{X}'\mathbf{X})^{-1}\mathbf{R}'\right]^{-1}\mathbf{R}(\mathbf{X}'\mathbf{X})^{-1}\right\}$$

See Problem 6-6. We should also note that in some problems it may be simpler to obtain $\mathbf{b}_*$ by imposing the restrictions directly on the problem rather than by substituting in Eq. (6-5). For example, suppose the data are already in deviation form and we wish to estimate

$$y = \beta_2 x_2 + \beta_3 x_3 + u$$

which may be written

$$\mathbf{e}_* = \mathbf{y} - \mathbf{Xb} - \mathbf{X}(\mathbf{b}_* - \mathbf{b})$$
$$= \mathbf{e} - \mathbf{X}(\mathbf{b}_* - \mathbf{b})$$

where $\mathbf{e}$ is the OLS residual vector. Transposing and multiplying

$$\mathbf{e}_*'\mathbf{e}_* = \mathbf{e}'\mathbf{e} + (\mathbf{b}_* - \mathbf{b})'\mathbf{X}'\mathbf{X}(\mathbf{b}_* - \mathbf{b})$$

the cross-product term vanishing since $\mathbf{X}'\mathbf{e} = \mathbf{0}$. Thus the difference between the restricted and the unrestricted residual sums of squares may be written

$$\mathbf{e}_*'\mathbf{e}_* - \mathbf{e}'\mathbf{e} = (\mathbf{b}_* - \mathbf{b})'\mathbf{X}'\mathbf{X}(\mathbf{b}_* - \mathbf{b}) \tag{6-6}$$

Substituting for $\mathbf{b}_* - \mathbf{b}$ from Eq. (6-5) and simplifying gives†

$$\mathbf{e}_*'\mathbf{e}_* - \mathbf{e}'\mathbf{e} = (\mathbf{r} - \mathbf{Rb})'\left[\mathbf{R}(\mathbf{X}'\mathbf{X})^{-1}\mathbf{R}'\right]^{-1}(\mathbf{r} - \mathbf{Rb}) \tag{6-7}$$

The right-hand side of Eq. (6-7) is exactly the expression in the numerator of the F statistic for testing H_0: $\mathbf{R}\boldsymbol{\beta} = \mathbf{r}$ derived in Eq. (5-68). Thus an alternative expression of the test statistic for H_0: $\mathbf{R}\boldsymbol{\beta} = \mathbf{r}$ is

$$F = \frac{(\mathbf{e}_*'\mathbf{e}_* - \mathbf{e}'\mathbf{e})/q}{\mathbf{e}'\mathbf{e}/(n-k)} \tag{6-8}$$

where $\mathbf{e}_*'\mathbf{e}_*$ denotes the restricted residual sum of squares derived from the vector $\mathbf{b}_*$, which satisfies the q restrictions $\mathbf{Rb}_* = \mathbf{r}$, and $\mathbf{e}'\mathbf{e}$ denotes the unrestricted residual sum of squares from the usual OLS regression. We have already derived this result for one particular application in Eq. (5-76), but the derivation leading up to Eq. (6-8) is perfectly general and applies to all cases.

To summarize, the test of the hypothesis that the elements of $\boldsymbol{\beta}$ obey a set of q $(\leq k)$ linear restrictions embodied in

$$H_0: \quad \mathbf{R}\boldsymbol{\beta} = \mathbf{r}$$

may be carried out by computing the unrestricted OLS vector $\mathbf{b}$ and the residual vector $\mathbf{e}$ and then calculating the F statistic, Eq. (5-68),

$$F = \frac{(\mathbf{r} - \mathbf{Rb})'\left[\mathbf{R}(\mathbf{X}'\mathbf{X})^{-1}\mathbf{R}'\right]^{-1}(\mathbf{r} - \mathbf{Rb})/q}{\mathbf{e}'\mathbf{e}/(n-k)}$$

rejecting H_0 if F exceeds a preselected critical value taken from the F distribution with $q, n-k$ degrees of freedom. Alternatively one may compute the *restricted* vector $\mathbf{b}_*$ from Eq. (6-5) or otherwise, and the corresponding residual vector

---

subject to the restriction $\beta_2 + \beta_3 = 1$. Substituting the restriction in the equation gives

$$y = \beta_2(x_2 - x_3) + x_3 + u$$

so that the regression of $y - x_3$ on $x_2 - x_3$ yields an estimate b_2, and b_3 is then obtained from $b_3 = 1 - b_2$. For the general version of this approach, see Problem 6-11.

† As shown in the footnote on page 184, $[\mathbf{R}(\mathbf{X}'\mathbf{X})^{-1}\mathbf{R}']^{-1}$ is positive definite. Thus $\mathbf{e}_*'\mathbf{e}_* - \mathbf{e}'\mathbf{e} \geq 0$, with equality only when $\mathbf{Rb} = \mathbf{r}$. Imposing restrictions cannot lower the residual sum of squares.

$\mathbf{e}_* = \mathbf{y} - \mathbf{X}\mathbf{b}_*$. The test statistic is then

$$\mathbf{F} = \frac{(\mathbf{b}_* - \mathbf{b})'\mathbf{X}'\mathbf{X}(\mathbf{b}_* - \mathbf{b})/q}{\mathbf{e}'\mathbf{e}/(n-k)} \tag{6-9}$$

or equivalently

$$F = \frac{(\mathbf{e}_*'\mathbf{e}_* - \mathbf{e}'\mathbf{e})/q}{\mathbf{e}'\mathbf{e}(n-k)}$$

One of the most useful applications of these formulas is in tests of structural change.

6-2 TESTS OF STRUCTURAL CHANGE

Example 6-1 Suppose we have data on two variables,

$$Y = \text{consumption expenditure}$$
$$X = \text{disposable income}$$

The data cover two distinct subperiods, n_1 observations relating to wartime years and n_2 observations relating to peacetime years. Suppose we wish to investigate whether there is any change, or shift, in the consumption function between the wartime and peacetime periods. Such a change is referred to as a *structural* change or structural break. Let us denote the consumption functions by

$$Y = \alpha_1 + \beta_1 X + u \qquad \text{wartime function} \tag{6-10a}$$

$$Y = \alpha_2 + \beta_2 X + u \qquad \text{peacetime function} \tag{6-10b}$$

This is the *unrestricted* form of the model, allowing intercepts and slopes to be different in the two periods. This model would be set up in matrix form as follows:

$$\begin{bmatrix} Y_1 \\ Y_2 \\ \vdots \\ Y_{n_1} \\ \hline Y_{n_1+1} \\ Y_{n_1+2} \\ \vdots \\ Y_{n_1+n_2} \end{bmatrix} = \begin{bmatrix} 1 & X_1 & 0 & 0 \\ 1 & X_2 & 0 & 0 \\ \cdots & \cdots & \cdots & \cdots \\ 1 & X_{n_1} & 0 & 0 \\ \hline 0 & 0 & 1 & X_{n_1+1} \\ 0 & 0 & 1 & X_{n_1+2} \\ \cdots & \cdots & \cdots & \cdots \\ 0 & 0 & 1 & X_{n_1+n_2} \end{bmatrix} \begin{bmatrix} \alpha_1 \\ \beta_1 \\ \alpha_2 \\ \beta_2 \end{bmatrix} + \begin{bmatrix} u_1 \\ u_2 \\ \vdots \\ u_{n_1} \\ \hline u_{n_1+1} \\ u_{n_1+2} \\ \vdots \\ u_{n_1+n_2} \end{bmatrix} \tag{6-11}$$

where the wartime observations have been listed first and the peacetime observations last. More compactly Eq. (6-11) becomes

$$\mathbf{y} = \begin{bmatrix} \mathbf{y}_1 \\ \mathbf{y}_2 \end{bmatrix} = \begin{bmatrix} \mathbf{X}_1 & 0 \\ 0 & \mathbf{X}_2 \end{bmatrix} \begin{bmatrix} \alpha_1 \\ \beta_1 \\ \alpha_2 \\ \beta_2 \end{bmatrix} + \mathbf{u} = \mathbf{X}\boldsymbol{\beta} + \mathbf{u} \tag{6-12}$$

where the data matrix $\mathbf{X}$ is block-diagonal.† Notice that each of the submatrices $\mathbf{X}_1$ and $\mathbf{X}_2$ has a column of units in the first position followed by a column of observations on income, and $\boldsymbol{\beta}$ indicates a column vector of the four structural parameters. Applying OLS to Eq. (6-12) gives

$$\mathbf{b} = \begin{bmatrix} a_1 \\ b_1 \\ \hline a_2 \\ b_2 \end{bmatrix} = (\mathbf{X}'\mathbf{X})^{-1}\mathbf{X}'\mathbf{y}$$

$$= \begin{bmatrix} (\mathbf{X}_1'\mathbf{X}_1)^{-1} & \mathbf{0} \\ \mathbf{0} & (\mathbf{X}_2'\mathbf{X}_2)^{-1} \end{bmatrix} \begin{bmatrix} \mathbf{X}_1'\mathbf{y}_1 \\ \mathbf{X}_2'\mathbf{y}_2 \end{bmatrix}$$

$$= \begin{bmatrix} (\mathbf{X}_1'\mathbf{X}_1)^{-1}\mathbf{X}_1'\mathbf{y}_1 \\ (\mathbf{X}_2'\mathbf{X}_2)^{-1}\mathbf{X}_2'\mathbf{y}_2 \end{bmatrix} \tag{6-13}$$

These estimates are seen to be identical with those obtained by applying OLS separately to Eqs. (6-10a) and (6-10b). One merely sets the data up in the form of Eq. (6-12) and a single regression will produce all four regression parameters. Using Eq. (6-13) one can then obtain the vector $\mathbf{e}$ of $n_1 + n_2$ residuals, and $\mathbf{e}'\mathbf{e}$ gives the unrestricted residual sum of squares.

Now set up the null hypothesis of no structural change. This may be formulated as

$$H_0\colon \quad \begin{bmatrix} \alpha_1 \\ \beta_1 \end{bmatrix} = \begin{bmatrix} \alpha_2 \\ \beta_2 \end{bmatrix} \tag{6-14}$$

or, putting it in the $\mathbf{R}\boldsymbol{\beta} = \mathbf{r}$ framework,

$$H_0\colon \quad \begin{bmatrix} 1 & 0 & -1 & 0 \\ 0 & 1 & 0 & -1 \end{bmatrix} \begin{bmatrix} \alpha_1 \\ \beta_1 \\ \alpha_2 \\ \beta_2 \end{bmatrix} = \begin{bmatrix} 0 \\ 0 \end{bmatrix}$$

so that

$$\mathbf{R} = [\mathbf{I} \; -\mathbf{I}] \qquad \text{and} \qquad \mathbf{r} = \mathbf{0} \tag{6-15}$$

† When using computers the student must take care to understand the properties of the program being used. If the program automatically estimates an intercept, feeding in the block-diagonal $\mathbf{X}$ matrix would produce a linear dependence between the column of units supplied by the computer and the first and third columns of $\mathbf{X}$. Thus one must either feed in $\mathbf{X}$ as it stands and suppress the automatic intercept, or else allow the automatic intercept and modify the $\mathbf{X}$ matrix in a way to be discussed later in this section.

where **I** is a unit matrix of order 2. The *restricted* model may thus be formulated as

$$\begin{bmatrix} \mathbf{y}_1 \\ \mathbf{y}_2 \end{bmatrix} = \begin{bmatrix} \mathbf{X}_1 \\ \mathbf{X}_2 \end{bmatrix} \begin{bmatrix} \alpha \\ \beta \end{bmatrix} + \mathbf{u} \tag{6-16}$$

The contrast with the unrestricted model in Eq. (6-12) is that the $\mathbf{X}_i$ matrices are now stacked vertically, so that only two parameters are required to describe the relation.

We now have two alternative procedures for testing H_0. Using the unrestricted **b** computed from Eq. (6-13) and the **R** matrix and **r** vector defined in Eq. (6-15), we can calculate the F statistic defined in Eq. (5-68). Alternatively, we may compute the $\mathbf{e}_*$ vector that comes from fitting the restricted model (6-16) by OLS and substitute either in Eq. (6-8) or in Eq. (6-9). The second procedure is the simpler, but we will illustrate both with the following data. Again these are artificially simple numbers, designed to keep the arithmetic to the minimum and highlight the methods.

Wartime data

$$\mathbf{y}_1 = \begin{bmatrix} 1 \\ 2 \\ 2 \\ 4 \\ 6 \end{bmatrix} \qquad \mathbf{X}_1 = \begin{bmatrix} 1 & 2 \\ 1 & 4 \\ 1 & 6 \\ 1 & 10 \\ 1 & 13 \end{bmatrix}$$

Peacetime data

$$\mathbf{y}_2 = \begin{bmatrix} 1 \\ 3 \\ 3 \\ 5 \\ 6 \\ 6 \\ 7 \\ 9 \\ 9 \\ 11 \end{bmatrix} \qquad \mathbf{X}_2 = \begin{bmatrix} 1 & 2 \\ 1 & 4 \\ 1 & 6 \\ 1 & 8 \\ 1 & 10 \\ 1 & 12 \\ 1 & 14 \\ 1 & 16 \\ 1 & 18 \\ 1 & 20 \end{bmatrix}$$

The sample sizes are

$$n_1 = 5 \qquad n_2 = 10 \qquad n = 15$$

and we have

$$(\mathbf{X}_1'\mathbf{X}_1) = \begin{bmatrix} 5 & 35 \\ 35 & 325 \end{bmatrix} \qquad (\mathbf{X}_2'\mathbf{X}_2) = \begin{bmatrix} 10 & 110 \\ 110 & 1540 \end{bmatrix}$$

$$(\mathbf{X}_1'\mathbf{X}_1)^{-1} = \frac{1}{400}\begin{bmatrix} 325 & -35 \\ -35 & 5 \end{bmatrix} \qquad (\mathbf{X}_2'\mathbf{X}_2)^{-1} = \frac{1}{330}\begin{bmatrix} 154 & -11 \\ -11 & 1 \end{bmatrix}$$

$$\mathbf{X}_1'\mathbf{y}_1 = \begin{bmatrix} 15 \\ 140 \end{bmatrix} \qquad \mathbf{X}_2'\mathbf{y}_2 = \begin{bmatrix} 60 \\ 828 \end{bmatrix}$$

$$\mathbf{y}_1'\mathbf{y}_1 = 61 \qquad \mathbf{y}_2'\mathbf{y}_2 = 448$$

Substitution in Eq. (6-13) gives the unrestricted OLS estimator

$$\mathbf{b} = \begin{bmatrix} \mathbf{b}_1 \\ \mathbf{b}_2 \end{bmatrix} = \begin{bmatrix} (\mathbf{X}_1'\mathbf{X}_1)^{-1}\mathbf{X}_1'\mathbf{y}_1 \\ (\mathbf{X}_2'\mathbf{X}_2)^{-1}\mathbf{X}_2'\mathbf{y}_2 \end{bmatrix} = \begin{bmatrix} -0.062500 \\ 0.437500 \\ \hdashline 0.400000 \\ 0.509091 \end{bmatrix}$$

Thus the estimated regressions are

$$\hat{Y} = -0.0625 + 0.4375X \qquad \text{wartime}$$

and

$$\hat{Y} = 0.4000 + 0.5091X \qquad \text{peacetime}$$

These point estimates give the wartime function a smaller intercept and lower slope than the peacetime function. The residual sum of squares from the wartime regression is

$$\begin{aligned} \mathbf{e}_1'\mathbf{e}_1 &= \mathbf{y}_1'\mathbf{y}_1 - \mathbf{b}_1'\mathbf{X}_1'\mathbf{y}_1 \\ &= 61 - [-0.0625 \quad 0.4375]\begin{bmatrix} 15 \\ 140 \end{bmatrix} = 61 - 60.3125 \\ &= 0.6875 \end{aligned}$$

Similarly for the peacetime regression

$$\begin{aligned} \mathbf{e}_2'\mathbf{e}_2 &= \mathbf{y}_2'\mathbf{y}_2 - \mathbf{b}_2'\mathbf{X}_2'\mathbf{y}_2 \\ &= 448 - [0.4 \quad 0.509091]\begin{bmatrix} 60 \\ 828 \end{bmatrix} = 448 - 445.5273 \\ &= 2.4727 \end{aligned}$$

Thus the unrestricted residual sum of squares is

$$\begin{aligned} \mathbf{e}'\mathbf{e} &= \mathbf{e}_1'\mathbf{e}_1 + \mathbf{e}_2'\mathbf{e}_2 \\ &= 3.1602 \end{aligned}$$

In fitting the restricted model, Eq. (6-16), the data matrix is now

$$\mathbf{X}_* = \begin{bmatrix} \mathbf{X}_1 \\ \mathbf{X}_2 \end{bmatrix}$$

giving

$$(\mathbf{X}_*'\mathbf{X}_*) = (\mathbf{X}_1'\mathbf{X}_1 + \mathbf{X}_2'\mathbf{X}_2)$$

$$\mathbf{X}_*'\mathbf{y} = \mathbf{X}_1'\mathbf{y}_1 + \mathbf{X}_2'\mathbf{y}_2$$

From the data,

$$(\mathbf{X}_*'\mathbf{X}_*) = \begin{bmatrix} 15 & 145 \\ 145 & 1865 \end{bmatrix} \qquad \text{and} \qquad \mathbf{X}_*'\mathbf{y} = \begin{bmatrix} 75 \\ 968 \end{bmatrix}$$

The restricted coefficient vector is

$$\begin{bmatrix} a \\ b \end{bmatrix} = \frac{1}{6950}\begin{bmatrix} 1865 & -145 \\ -145 & 15 \end{bmatrix}\begin{bmatrix} 75 \\ 968 \end{bmatrix} = \begin{bmatrix} -0.069784 \\ 0.524460 \end{bmatrix}$$

Thus the estimated common regression is

$$\hat{Y} = -0.0698 + 0.5245X$$

and the restricted residual sum of squares is

$$\mathbf{e}_*'\mathbf{e}_* = (61 + 448) - [-0.069784 \quad 0.524460]\begin{bmatrix} 75 \\ 968 \end{bmatrix} = 509 - 502.4435$$

$$= 6.5565$$

Thus substitution in Eq. (6-8) gives

$$F = \frac{(6.5565 - 3.1602)/2}{3.1602/(15 - 4)} = 5.91$$

Notice that the number of degrees of freedom in the numerator is 2, since there are two restrictions embodied in H_0, and in the denominator $n - k = 15 - 4$ since four regression coefficients are estimated in the unrestricted regression. From the tables of the F distribution,

$$F_{0.95}(2, 11) = 3.98 \qquad \text{and} \qquad F_{0.99}(2, 11) = 7.20$$

Thus the hypothesis of no structural change would be rejected at the 5 percent level of significance, but not at the 1 percent level.

The alternative approach is to calculate only the unrestricted $\mathbf{b}$ vector and substitute directly in Eq. (5-68). This requires the evaluation of $\mathbf{R}(\mathbf{X}'\mathbf{X})^{-1}\mathbf{R}'$. From Eqs. (6-12) and (6-15),

$$\mathbf{R}(\mathbf{X}'\mathbf{X})^{-1}\mathbf{R}' = [\mathbf{I} \quad -\mathbf{I}]\begin{bmatrix} (\mathbf{X}_1'\mathbf{X}_1)^{-1} & 0 \\ 0 & (\mathbf{X}_2'\mathbf{X}_2)^{-1} \end{bmatrix}\begin{bmatrix} \mathbf{I} \\ -\mathbf{I} \end{bmatrix}$$

$$= (\mathbf{X}_1'\mathbf{X}_1)^{-1} + (\mathbf{X}_2'\mathbf{X}_2)^{-1}$$

$$= \begin{bmatrix} 1.27916667 & -0.12083333 \\ -0.12083333 & 0.01553030 \end{bmatrix}$$

with

$$\left[\mathbf{R}(\mathbf{X}'\mathbf{X})^{-1}\mathbf{R}'\right]^{-1} = \begin{bmatrix} 2.949641 & 22.965567 \\ 22.965567 & 242.949711 \end{bmatrix}$$

$$\mathbf{Rb} = [\mathbf{I} \quad -\mathbf{I}]\begin{bmatrix} -0.062500 \\ 0.437500 \\ \hline 0.400000 \\ 0.509091 \end{bmatrix} = \begin{bmatrix} -0.462500 \\ -0.071591 \end{bmatrix}$$

and $\mathbf{r} = \mathbf{0}$. Thus

$$(\mathbf{r} - \mathbf{Rb})'\left[\mathbf{R}(\mathbf{X}'\mathbf{X})^{-1}\mathbf{R}'\right]^{-1}(\mathbf{r} - \mathbf{Rb}) = 3.3969$$

and from the previous calculations,

$$\mathbf{e}_*'\mathbf{e}_* - \mathbf{e}'\mathbf{e} = 6.5565 - 3.1602 = 3.3963$$

so that the two numbers agree, subject to rounding errors in the calculation. The F statistic from Eq. (5-68) is

$$F = \frac{3.3969/2}{3.1602/11} = 5.91 \qquad \text{as before}$$

Example 6-2: Tests of change in the regression slope Example 6-1 showed how to test the hypothesis

$$H_0: \quad \begin{bmatrix} \alpha_1 \\ \beta_1 \end{bmatrix} = \begin{bmatrix} \alpha_2 \\ \beta_2 \end{bmatrix}$$

The restricted and unrestricted models are pictured in Fig. 6-1.

Sometimes the investigator is more interested in testing for the homogeneity of the regression slope, the values of the intercept term being of no particular importance. The null hypothesis is now specified as

$$H_0: \quad \beta_1 = \beta_2 \tag{6-17}$$

The α parameter is free to take on different values in the two subperiods. For instance, in simple Keynesian theory the size of the national income multiplier depends only on the marginal propensity to consume β and not at all on the intercept α. Thus the H_0 in Eq. (6-17) is equivalent to asking whether the income multiplier is the same in each subperiod. The restricted and unrestricted models may then be set up as follows:

$$\text{Restricted} \qquad \begin{bmatrix} \mathbf{y}_1 \\ \mathbf{y}_2 \end{bmatrix} = \begin{bmatrix} \mathbf{i}_1 & \mathbf{0} & \mathbf{x}_1 \\ \mathbf{0} & \mathbf{i}_2 & \mathbf{x}_2 \end{bmatrix} \begin{bmatrix} \alpha_1 \\ \alpha_2 \\ \beta \end{bmatrix} + \mathbf{u} \qquad \text{Unrestricted} \qquad \begin{bmatrix} \mathbf{y}_1 \\ \mathbf{y}_2 \end{bmatrix} = \begin{bmatrix} \mathbf{i}_1 & \mathbf{x}_1 & \mathbf{0} & \mathbf{0} \\ \mathbf{0} & \mathbf{0} & \mathbf{i}_2 & \mathbf{x}_2 \end{bmatrix} \begin{bmatrix} \alpha_1 \\ \beta_1 \\ \alpha_2 \\ \beta_2 \end{bmatrix} + \mathbf{u} \tag{6-18}$$

where $\mathbf{i}_1$ denotes a column vector of n_1 units, $\mathbf{i}_2$ a column vector of n_2 units, $\mathbf{x}_1$ a column vector of the n_1 observations on wartime income, and $\mathbf{x}_2$ a column vector of the n_2 observations on peacetime income. OLS may then be applied directly to each model in Eqs. (6-18) and H_0 tested by comparing the

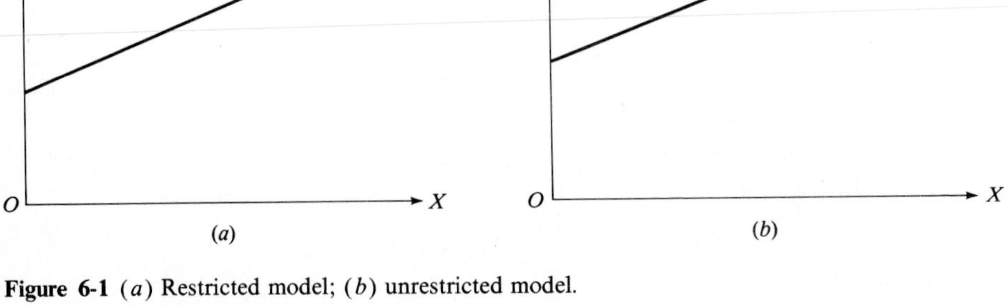

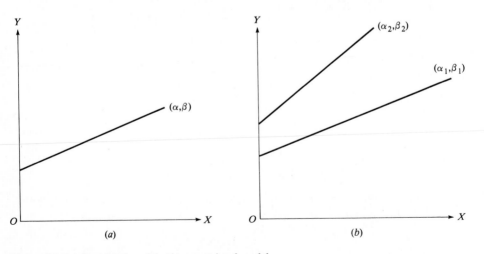

Figure 6-1 (*a*) Restricted model; (*b*) unrestricted model.

residual sums of squares from the restricted and unrestricted models in the usual way. The two models are shown in Fig. 6-2.

The unrestricted model in Eqs. (6-18) is exactly the same as that in Eq. (6-12), so we already have

$$\mathbf{e}'\mathbf{e} = 3.1602$$

For the restricted model,

$$\mathbf{X}_* = \begin{bmatrix} \mathbf{i}_1 & \mathbf{0} & \mathbf{x}_1 \\ \mathbf{0} & \mathbf{i}_2 & \mathbf{x}_2 \end{bmatrix}$$

so

$$\mathbf{X}_*'\mathbf{X}_* = \begin{bmatrix} n_1 & 0 & \mathbf{i}_1'\mathbf{x}_1 \\ 0 & n_2 & \mathbf{i}_2'\mathbf{x}_2 \\ \mathbf{x}_1'\mathbf{i}_1 & \mathbf{x}_2'\mathbf{i}_2 & \mathbf{x}_1'\mathbf{x}_1 + \mathbf{x}_2'\mathbf{x}_2 \end{bmatrix} \qquad \mathbf{X}_*'\mathbf{y} = \begin{bmatrix} \mathbf{i}_1'\mathbf{y}_1 \\ \mathbf{i}_2'\mathbf{y}_2 \\ \mathbf{x}_1'\mathbf{y}_1 + \mathbf{x}_2'\mathbf{y}_2 \end{bmatrix}$$

$$= \begin{bmatrix} 5 & 0 & 35 \\ 0 & 10 & 110 \\ 35 & 110 & 1865 \end{bmatrix} \qquad = \begin{bmatrix} 15 \\ 60 \\ 968 \end{bmatrix}$$

Thus

$$\mathbf{e}_*'\mathbf{e}_* = \mathbf{y}'\mathbf{y} - \mathbf{y}'\mathbf{X}_*(\mathbf{X}_*'\mathbf{X}_*)^{-1}\mathbf{X}_*'\mathbf{y}$$

$$= (61 + 448) - [15 \quad 60 \quad 968]\begin{bmatrix} 5 & 0 & 35 \\ 0 & 10 & 110 \\ 35 & 110 & 1865 \end{bmatrix}^{-1}\begin{bmatrix} 15 \\ 60 \\ 968 \end{bmatrix}$$

$$= 509 - \frac{1}{20{,}500}[15 \quad 60 \quad 968]\begin{bmatrix} 6550 & 3850 & -350 \\ 3850 & 8100 & -550 \\ -350 & -550 & 50 \end{bmatrix}\begin{bmatrix} 15 \\ 60 \\ 968 \end{bmatrix}$$

$$= 509 - 505.5098 = 3.4902$$

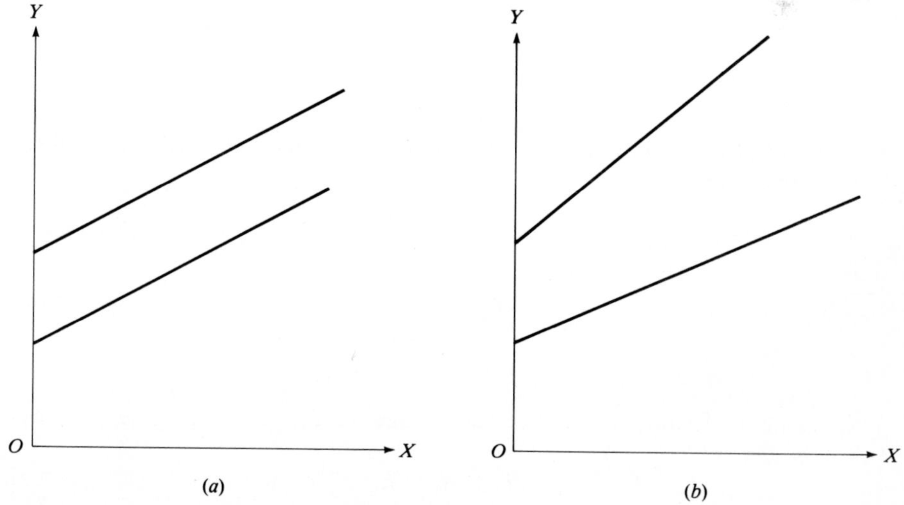

Figure 6-2 (a) Restricted model; (b) unrestricted model.

The test statistic for the null hypothesis that $\beta_1 = \beta_2$ is then

$$F = \frac{3.4902 - 3.1602}{3.1602/11} = 1.15$$

and $F_{0.95}(1, 11) = 4.84$. Thus there is no evidence of a significant difference in the regression slopes in the two periods. Since the F statistic in Example 6-1 was on the borderline of significance, this suggests that any change between the two periods lies in the intercepts rather than the slopes.

Before leaving this example, let us note a much simpler way of calculating $\mathbf{e}'_*\mathbf{e}_*$, based on deviations from the subperiod means. We have earlier introduced in Eq. (5-41) the $\mathbf{A}$ matrix which transforms a vector of n observations into deviation form. Let us define $\mathbf{A}_1$ and $\mathbf{A}_2$ to be such matrices for use with vectors of n_1 and n_2 observations, respectively. Premultiplying the restricted model by the block-diagonal matrix

$$\begin{bmatrix} \mathbf{A}_1 & \mathbf{0} \\ \mathbf{0} & \mathbf{A}_2 \end{bmatrix}$$

then gives

$$\begin{bmatrix} \mathbf{A}_1\mathbf{y}_1 \\ \mathbf{A}_2\mathbf{y}_2 \end{bmatrix} = \begin{bmatrix} \mathbf{0} & \mathbf{0} & \mathbf{A}_1\mathbf{x}_1 \\ \mathbf{0} & \mathbf{0} & \mathbf{A}_2\mathbf{x}_2 \end{bmatrix} \begin{bmatrix} \alpha_1 \\ \alpha_2 \\ \beta \end{bmatrix} + \mathbf{u}$$

since $\mathbf{A}_1\mathbf{i}_1 = \mathbf{0}$ and $\mathbf{A}_2\mathbf{i}_2 = \mathbf{0}$. The β parameter is thus estimated by a simple regression of

$$\begin{bmatrix} \mathbf{A}_1\mathbf{y}_1 \\ \mathbf{A}_2\mathbf{y}_2 \end{bmatrix} \quad \text{on} \quad \begin{bmatrix} \mathbf{A}_1\mathbf{x}_1 \\ \mathbf{A}_2\mathbf{x}_2 \end{bmatrix}$$

Each vector consists of two subvectors, the first being the deviations of the wartime Y (or X) from the wartime sample mean and the second the deviations of the peacetime Y (or X) from the corresponding peacetime sample mean. Denoting the vectors of deviations by $\tilde{\mathbf{y}}$ and $\tilde{\mathbf{x}}$, respectively,

$$\mathbf{b} = \frac{\tilde{\mathbf{y}}'\tilde{\mathbf{x}}}{\tilde{\mathbf{x}}'\mathbf{x}}$$

and

$$\mathbf{e}'_*\mathbf{e}_* = \tilde{\mathbf{y}}'\tilde{\mathbf{y}} - \tilde{\mathbf{y}}'\tilde{\mathbf{x}}(\tilde{\mathbf{x}}'\tilde{\mathbf{x}})^{-1}\tilde{\mathbf{x}}'\tilde{\mathbf{y}}$$

Computing the deviations for the two subperiods and evaluating these expressions gives

$$b = \frac{203}{410} = 0.4951$$

and

$$\mathbf{e}'_*\mathbf{e}_* = 104 - \frac{(203)^2}{410}$$

$$= 3.4902 \qquad \text{as before}$$

Example 6-3: Testing for structural change in the intercept The null hypothesis is now

$$H_0\colon \quad \alpha_1 = \alpha_2 \tag{6-19}$$

We must be very careful in the specification of the restricted and unrestricted models. By analogy with Example 6-2 it might seem reasonable to specify the restricted model as

$$\begin{bmatrix} \mathbf{y}_1 \\ \mathbf{y}_2 \end{bmatrix} = \begin{bmatrix} \mathbf{i}_1 & \mathbf{x}_1 & \mathbf{0} \\ \mathbf{i}_2 & \mathbf{0} & \mathbf{x}_2 \end{bmatrix} \begin{bmatrix} \alpha \\ \beta_1 \\ \beta_2 \end{bmatrix} + u \qquad (6\text{-}20)$$

with the unrestricted model as before. Model (6-20) imposes a common intercept but specifies different slopes. If the functions have different slopes, they must intersect at some X value. There may be cases where it is relevant and important to test that the intersection occurs at $X = 0$, as is implied by specifying Eq. (6-20) as the restricted model. However, this is not usually the case, and the most common practice is to test H_0, *subject to the assumption of a common regression slope*. Thus the restricted and unrestricted models become

$$\underset{\text{Restricted}}{\begin{bmatrix} \mathbf{y}_1 \\ \mathbf{y}_2 \end{bmatrix} = \begin{bmatrix} \mathbf{i}_1 & \mathbf{x}_1 \\ \mathbf{i}_2 & \mathbf{x}_2 \end{bmatrix} \begin{bmatrix} \alpha \\ \beta \end{bmatrix} + \mathbf{u}} \qquad \underset{\text{Unrestricted}}{\begin{bmatrix} \mathbf{y}_1 \\ \mathbf{y}_2 \end{bmatrix} = \begin{bmatrix} \mathbf{i}_1 & \mathbf{0} & \mathbf{x}_1 \\ \mathbf{0} & \mathbf{i}_2 & \mathbf{x}_2 \end{bmatrix} \begin{bmatrix} \alpha_1 \\ \alpha_2 \\ \beta \end{bmatrix} + \mathbf{u}} \qquad (6\text{-}21)$$

Notice that the unrestricted model in this example is the restricted model of Example 6-2 [see Eqs. (6-18)], and the restricted model here is the same as the restricted model in Example 6-1. Thus from our previous calculations the relevant sums of squares are

$$\mathbf{e}'_* \mathbf{e}_* = 6.5565$$

and

$$\mathbf{e}'\mathbf{e} = 3.4902$$

Thus the test statistic for H_0: $\alpha_1 = \alpha_2$, conditional on a common β, is

$$F = \frac{6.5565 - 3.4902}{3.4902/12} = 10.54$$

and $F_{0.99}(1, 12) = 9.33$ so that the difference in the intercepts is significant at the 1 percent level. The models are shown in Fig. 6-3.

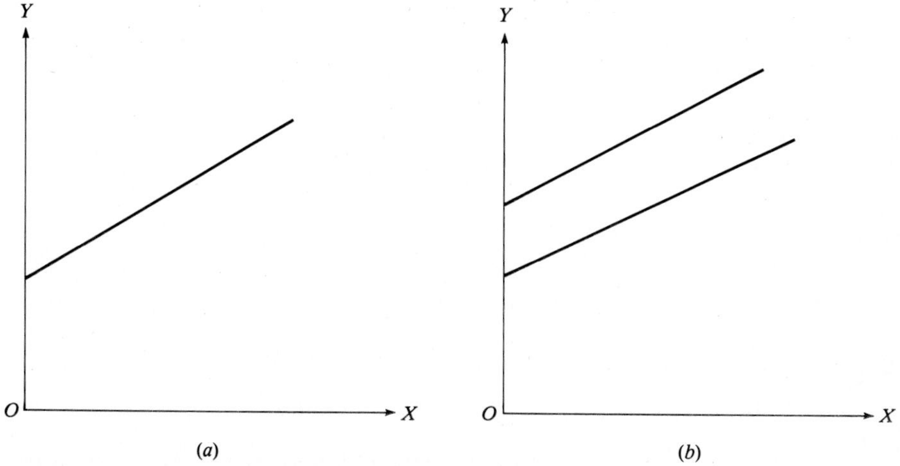

Figure 6-3 (a) Restricted model; (b) unrestricted model.

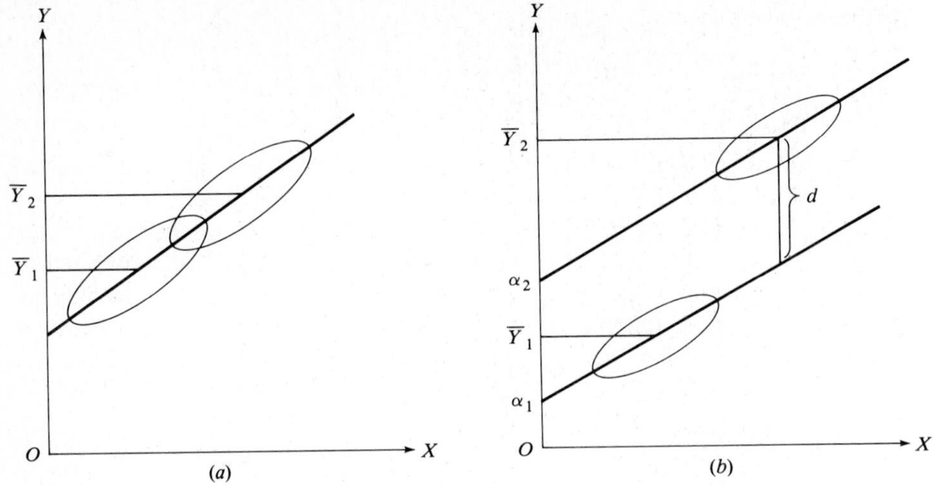

Figure 6-4

This test is a simple example of the *analysis of covariance*, which has widespread applications. Suppose, for instance, that Y denotes the yield of wheat per acre and X indicates hours of sunshine. One set of observations relates to strain 1 of wheat and the other set to strain 2. The crucial question is whether one strain shows a significantly different yield than the other, but suppose that the experimental plots sown with the two strains have not received equal amounts of sunshine. The difference between the sample means would then not only reflect any possible difference between the strains, but also the difference due to the variable hours of sunshine received. In the analysis of covariance, hours of sunshine would be termed an *intervening* variable. The problem is depicted graphically in Fig. 6-4.

In Fig. 6-4*a* the single line denotes the assumed positive relationship between yield and hours of sunshine, and the ellipses denote the samples from each strain. The difference between the sample means is here due solely to a different set of X values for the two varieties. In Fig. 6-4*b* strain 2 is assumed to have a greater yield than strain 1, a difference indicated by the difference between the intercepts,

$$d = \alpha_2 - \alpha_1$$

The observed difference between the sample means is then d plus or minus any differential effect due to sunshine. In testing the hypothesis

$$H_0: \quad \alpha_1 = \alpha_2$$

proper allowance must be made for any possible interference from the intervening variable, but this is precisely what is achieved by the test of the models in Eqs. (6-21), namely, the test of H_0, conditional on the assumption of a common β.

Summary

These three examples are based on a hierarchy of models:

$$\text{I} \qquad \begin{bmatrix} \mathbf{y}_1 \\ \mathbf{y}_2 \end{bmatrix} = \begin{bmatrix} \mathbf{i}_1 & \mathbf{x}_1 \\ \mathbf{i}_2 & \mathbf{x}_2 \end{bmatrix} \begin{bmatrix} \alpha \\ \beta \end{bmatrix} + \mathbf{u} \qquad \text{common regression for both periods}$$

II $\quad \begin{bmatrix} \mathbf{y}_1 \\ \mathbf{y}_2 \end{bmatrix} = \begin{bmatrix} \mathbf{i}_1 & \mathbf{0} & \mathbf{x}_1 \\ \mathbf{0} & \mathbf{i}_2 & \mathbf{x}_2 \end{bmatrix} \begin{bmatrix} \alpha_1 \\ \alpha_2 \\ \beta \end{bmatrix} + \mathbf{u}$ $\quad$ differential intercepts, common slope

III $\quad \begin{bmatrix} \mathbf{y}_1 \\ \mathbf{y}_2 \end{bmatrix} = \begin{bmatrix} \mathbf{i}_1 & \mathbf{x}_1 & \mathbf{0} & \mathbf{0} \\ \mathbf{0} & \mathbf{0} & \mathbf{i}_2 & \mathbf{x}_2 \end{bmatrix} \begin{bmatrix} \alpha_1 \\ \beta_1 \\ \alpha_2 \\ \beta_2 \end{bmatrix} + \mathbf{u}$ $\quad$ differential intercepts, differential slopes

Fitting each model by OLS produces a residual sum of squares. There are three basic tests on the differences between the various residual sums of squares. These are the following:

- Test of differential intercepts—model I contrasted with model II
- Test of differential slope coefficients—model II contrasted with model III
- Test of differential regressions—model I contrasted with model III (slopes and intercepts)

The tests outlined above have implicitly assumed that the disturbance variance σ^2 is the same in each period. Schmidt and Sickles have investigated the effect of departures from this assumption on the significance level of the test.† For equal-sized samples there are modest increases in the true significance level over the nominal level, even for very large departures from the assumption of equal variances. For instance, with $n_1 = n_2 = 25$ the true significance level only rises to 0.059, compared with a nominal value of 0.05, when one variance is 100 times the other. If the X variable is a linear trend, the true significance level rises to 0.063 for a tenfold increase in the variance and to 0.084 for a one-hundredfold increase. When the sample sizes are unequal, the true significance level shows a greater departure from the nominal level, and it may now be less or greater than the nominal level. Full details are given in the reference.

Example 6-4: Tests of structural change (k variables) The previous three examples have only been concerned with a two-variable model for two subperiods. The tests need to be generalized in two directions, namely, extending to k variables and also making comparisons between more than two subperiods. In this example we make the first extension.

The unrestricted model is now

$$\begin{bmatrix} \mathbf{y}_1 \\ \mathbf{y}_2 \end{bmatrix} = \begin{bmatrix} \mathbf{X}_1 & \mathbf{0} \\ \mathbf{0} & \mathbf{X}_2 \end{bmatrix} \begin{bmatrix} \boldsymbol{\beta}_1 \\ \boldsymbol{\beta}_2 \end{bmatrix} + \mathbf{u} \tag{6-22}$$

where $\mathbf{X}_1$ is of order $n_1 \times k$, $\mathbf{X}_2$ is of order $n_2 \times k$, and $\boldsymbol{\beta}_1$ and $\boldsymbol{\beta}_2$ each denotes vectors of k coefficients. This model has exactly the same matrix form as Eq. (6-12), the only difference being in the number of variables in the $\mathbf{X}_1, \mathbf{X}_2$ matrices. Let us partition $\mathbf{X}_1$ and $\mathbf{X}_2$ by the first column of units and the remaining $k - 1$ columns of observations on the explanatory variables as

† P. Schmidt and R. Sickles, "Some Further Evidence on the Use of the Chow Test under Heteroscedasticity," *Econometrica*, **45**, 1977, pp. 1293–1298.

follows:

$$\mathbf{X}_1 = [\mathbf{i}_1 \quad \mathbf{X}_1^*]$$

and

$$\mathbf{X}_2 = [\mathbf{i}_2 \quad \mathbf{X}_2^*]$$

We may then construct the same hierarchy of models as in the two-variable case. This now gives

$$\text{I} \quad \begin{bmatrix} \mathbf{y}_1 \\ \mathbf{y}_2 \end{bmatrix} = \begin{bmatrix} \mathbf{i}_1 & \mathbf{X}_1^* \\ \mathbf{i}_2 & \mathbf{X}_2^* \end{bmatrix} \boldsymbol{\beta} + \mathbf{u} \qquad \text{common regression for both periods}$$

$$\text{II} \quad \begin{bmatrix} \mathbf{y}_1 \\ \mathbf{y}_2 \end{bmatrix} = \begin{bmatrix} \mathbf{i}_1 & \mathbf{0} & \mathbf{X}_1^* \\ \mathbf{0} & \mathbf{i}_2 & \mathbf{X}_2^* \end{bmatrix} \begin{bmatrix} \alpha_1 \\ \alpha_2 \\ \boldsymbol{\beta}^* \end{bmatrix} + \mathbf{u} \qquad \text{differential intercepts, common vector of regression slopes}$$

$$\text{III} \quad \begin{bmatrix} \mathbf{y}_1 \\ \mathbf{y}_2 \end{bmatrix} = \begin{bmatrix} \mathbf{i}_1 & \mathbf{0} & \mathbf{X}_1^* & \mathbf{0} \\ \mathbf{0} & \mathbf{i}_2 & \mathbf{0} & \mathbf{X}_2^* \end{bmatrix} \begin{bmatrix} \alpha_1 \\ \alpha_2 \\ \boldsymbol{\beta}_1^* \\ \boldsymbol{\beta}_2^* \end{bmatrix} + \mathbf{u} \qquad \text{differential intercepts, differential slopes}$$

where we have partitioned the k-element $\boldsymbol{\beta}$ vector as

$$\boldsymbol{\beta} = \begin{bmatrix} \alpha_1 \\ \hline \beta_2 \\ \beta_3 \\ \vdots \\ \beta_k \end{bmatrix} = \begin{bmatrix} \alpha_1 \\ \hline \boldsymbol{\beta}^* \end{bmatrix}$$

Application of OLS to each model will yield a residual sum of squares (RSS) with an associated number of degrees of freedom as indicated by

Model I	RSS_1	$n - k$
Model II	RSS_2	$n - k - 1$
Model III	RSS_3	$n - 2k$

where $n = n_1 + n_2$ indicates the total number of observations in the combined samples. The test statistics for various hypotheses are then as follows:

H_0: $\alpha_1 = \alpha_2$: *Test of differential intercepts*

$$F = \frac{\text{RSS}_1 - \text{RSS}_2}{\text{RSS}_2/(n - k - 1)} \sim F(1, n - k - 1) \qquad (6\text{-}23)$$

H_0: $\boldsymbol{\beta}_1^* = \boldsymbol{\beta}_2^*$: *Test of differential slope vectors*

$$F = \frac{(\text{RSS}_2 - \text{RSS}_3)/(k - 1)}{\text{RSS}_3/(n - 2k)} \sim F(k - 1, n - 2k) \qquad (6\text{-}24)$$

H_0: $\boldsymbol{\beta}_1 = \boldsymbol{\beta}_2$: *Test of differential regressions (intercepts and slopes)*

$$F = \frac{(\text{RSS}_1 - \text{RSS}_3)/k}{\text{RSS}_3/(n-2k)} \sim F(k, n-2k) \tag{6-25}$$

The degrees of freedom in the numerator are simply obtained as the *difference* in the degrees of freedom of the residual sums of squares in the numerator. This is equal to the number of restrictions involved in going from the unrestricted to the restricted model. For example, only one restriction is imposed in going from model II to model I, and $k-1$ restrictions (equality of regression slopes) are imposed in going from model III to model II.

However, a further test is possible in the $k > 1$ case, which did not arise in the two-variable model. We may now test whether a *subset* of coefficients is stable over the two periods. For example, most wage equations take the form

$$\text{Wage change} = f(\text{market pressure, expectations of inflation})$$

One might wish to test whether the reaction to the market pressure variables has changed between two periods, or alternatively, one might hypothesize that the reaction to inflationary expectations is different in "high" inflation and "low" inflation periods. The principle of the test is the same as in all the previous examples, as shown by the following rule.

Fit the restricted model with the subset of coefficients whose stability is being tested, taking the same value in each subperiod, and compute the residual sum of squares $\mathbf{e}_*'\mathbf{e}_*$. All other coefficients are left to vary between the two subperiods. Then fit the completely unrestricted model, where all coefficients are free to vary, with the residual sum of squares $\mathbf{e}'\mathbf{e}$. The test of the stability of the subset is then based on

$$F = \frac{(\mathbf{e}_*'\mathbf{e}_* - \mathbf{e}'\mathbf{e})/q}{\mathbf{e}'\mathbf{e}/(n-k)}$$

where q indicates the number of coefficients in the subset. Formally the restricted model is set up as

$$\begin{bmatrix} \mathbf{y}_1 \\ \mathbf{y}_2 \end{bmatrix} = \begin{bmatrix} \mathbf{X}_{11} & \mathbf{0} & \mathbf{X}_{12} \\ \mathbf{0} & \mathbf{X}_{21} & \mathbf{X}_{22} \end{bmatrix} \begin{bmatrix} \boldsymbol{\beta}_{11} \\ \boldsymbol{\beta}_{21} \\ \boldsymbol{\beta}_2 \end{bmatrix} + \mathbf{u} \tag{6-26}$$

where $\mathbf{X}_{11} = n_1 \times (k-q)$ matrix of observations in period 1 on the variables not being tested

$\mathbf{X}_{21} = n_2 \times (k-q)$ matrix of observations in period 2 on the variables not being tested

$\mathbf{X}_{12} = n_1 \times q$ matrix of observations in period 1 on the variables in the test

$\mathbf{X}_{22} = n_2 \times q$ matrix of observations in period 2 on the variables in the test

$\boldsymbol{\beta}_{11}, \boldsymbol{\beta}_{21}$ = coefficient vectors of $\mathbf{X}_{11}$ and $\mathbf{X}_{21}$, respectively

$\boldsymbol{\beta}_2$ = common coefficient vector for $\mathbf{X}_{12}$ and $\mathbf{X}_{22}$

Example 6-5: Tests of structural change ($n_2 < k$) A special problem arises if one of the subperiods has fewer observations than the number of parameters to be estimated in the model. Let us assume that we have n_1 ($> k$) observations in one subperiod and n_2 ($\leq k$) observations in the other. There is no difficulty about the restricted model in which one set of k parameters is estimated for the n ($= n_1 + n_2$) sample observations, namely,

$$\begin{bmatrix} \mathbf{y}_1 \\ \mathbf{y}_2 \end{bmatrix} = \begin{bmatrix} \mathbf{X}_1 \\ \mathbf{X}_2 \end{bmatrix} \mathbf{b}_* + \mathbf{e}_*$$

and $\mathbf{e}_*'\mathbf{e}_*$ has $n - k$ degrees of freedom. If $n_2 = k$, the unrestricted model can be fitted and will have a residual vector

$$\mathbf{e} = \begin{bmatrix} \mathbf{e}_1 \\ \mathbf{0} \end{bmatrix}$$

where
$$\mathbf{e}_1 = \mathbf{y}_1 - \mathbf{X}_1\mathbf{b}_1$$

denotes the residual vector from the first regression, and $\mathbf{0}$ is a k-element residual vector from the second regression, in which the regression plane fits the k observations exactly. The residual sum of squares $\mathbf{e}'\mathbf{e}$ has

$$n_1 + n_2 - 2k = n_1 - k$$

degrees of freedom. If $n_2 < k$, all k parameters cannot be determined for the second period, but the residual vector is still $\mathbf{0}$ since an infinite number of hyperplanes of dimension k can be passed through a set of less than k observations. Thus the unrestricted residual sum of squares is still

$$\mathbf{e}'\mathbf{e} = \mathbf{e}_1'\mathbf{e}_1 \qquad \text{with } n_1 - k \text{ degrees of freedom}$$

Analogy with the previous tests suggests that the appropriate test of the null hypothesis that the n_2 additional observations belong to the same structure as the first n_1 observations is based on†

$$F = \frac{(\mathbf{e}_*'\mathbf{e}_* - \mathbf{e}_1'\mathbf{e}_1)/n_2}{\mathbf{e}_1'\mathbf{e}_1/(n_1 - k)} \tag{6-27}$$

where n_2 is given by $(n - k) - (n_1 - k)$, the difference between the number of degrees of freedom of the sums of squares in the numerator. Thus the practical procedure is as follows:

- Fit the regression to all $n_1 + n_2$ observations, giving the residual sum of squares $\mathbf{e}_*'\mathbf{e}_*$.
- Fit the regression to the n_1 observations, giving the residual sum of squares $\mathbf{e}_1'\mathbf{e}_1$.
- Compute the F statistic defined in Eq. (6-27) and reject the hypothesis of a common structure if F exceeds a preselected critical value from $F(n_2, n_1 - k)$.

† This is only a heuristic proof. For an exact derivation of Eq. (6-27), see F. M. Fisher, "Tests on Equality between Sets of Coefficients in Two Linear Regressions: An Expository Note," *Econometrica*, **28**, 1970, pp. 361–366. An alternative proof is given in Sec. 10-1.

Example 6-6: Tests of structural change (k variables, p periods) The final extension is going from two periods to more than two periods. For example, we might wish to test whether a Phillips curve has the same structure prior to World War I, between the two world wars, and post–World War II. But the test need not be across periods. We might examine the stability of a relation across countries, industries, social groups, or whatever.

The usual hierarchy of three models may be set up:

$$\text{I} \qquad \begin{bmatrix} \mathbf{y}_1 \\ \mathbf{y}_2 \\ \vdots \\ \mathbf{y}_p \end{bmatrix} = \begin{bmatrix} \mathbf{i}_1 & \mathbf{X}_1^* \\ \mathbf{i}_2 & \mathbf{X}_2^* \\ \cdots & \cdots \\ \mathbf{i}_p & \mathbf{X}_p^* \end{bmatrix} \begin{bmatrix} \alpha \\ \boldsymbol{\beta}^* \end{bmatrix} + \mathbf{u}$$

common intercept, common slope vector in all p classes

$$\text{II} \qquad \begin{bmatrix} \mathbf{y}_1 \\ \mathbf{y}_2 \\ \vdots \\ \mathbf{y}_p \end{bmatrix} = \begin{bmatrix} \mathbf{i}_1 & \mathbf{0} & \cdots & \mathbf{0} & \mathbf{X}_1^* \\ \mathbf{0} & \mathbf{i}_2 & \cdots & \mathbf{0} & \mathbf{X}_2^* \\ \cdots & \cdots & \cdots & \cdots & \cdots \\ \mathbf{0} & \mathbf{0} & \cdots & \mathbf{i}_p & \mathbf{X}_p^* \end{bmatrix} \begin{bmatrix} \alpha_1 \\ \alpha_2 \\ \vdots \\ \alpha_p \\ \boldsymbol{\beta}^* \end{bmatrix} + \mathbf{u}$$

differential intercepts, common slope vector

$$\text{III} \qquad \begin{bmatrix} \mathbf{y}_1 \\ \mathbf{y}_2 \\ \vdots \\ \mathbf{y}_p \end{bmatrix} = \begin{bmatrix} \mathbf{i}_1 & \mathbf{0} & \cdots & \mathbf{0} & \mathbf{X}_1^* & \mathbf{0} & \cdots & \mathbf{0} \\ \mathbf{0} & \mathbf{i}_2 & \cdots & \mathbf{0} & \mathbf{0} & \mathbf{X}_2^* & \cdots & \mathbf{0} \\ \cdots & \cdots & \cdots & \cdots & \cdots & \cdots & \cdots & \cdots \\ \mathbf{0} & \mathbf{0} & \cdots & \mathbf{i}_p & \mathbf{0} & \mathbf{0} & \cdots & \mathbf{X}_p^* \end{bmatrix} \begin{bmatrix} \alpha_1 \\ \alpha_2 \\ \vdots \\ \alpha_p \\ \boldsymbol{\beta}_1^* \\ \boldsymbol{\beta}_2^* \\ \vdots \\ \boldsymbol{\beta}_p^* \end{bmatrix} + \mathbf{u}$$

differential intercepts, differential slope vectors

Here $\mathbf{i}_i$ is the column vector of n_i units $(i = 1, 2, \ldots, p)$ and $\mathbf{X}_i^*$ is the $n_i \times (k-1)$ matrix of observations on the explanatory variables in class i $(i = 1, 2, \ldots, p)$.

The residual sums of squares from the three models have the number of degrees of freedom

$$n - k, \qquad n - p - k + 1, \qquad \text{and} \qquad n - pk$$

where

$$n = n_1 + n_2 + \cdots + n_p$$

Table 6-1

	Class									
	1		2		3		4			
Observation	Y	X	Y	X	Y	X	Y	X		
1	22	29	30	15	12	16	23	5		
2	22	20	32	9	8	31	25	25		
3	20	14	26	1	13	26	28	16		
4	24	21	26	6	25	35	26	10		
5	12	6	37	19	7	12	23	24	Y	X
Sums	100	90	150	50	65	120	125	80	440	340
Means	20	18	30	10	13	24	25	16	22	17

denotes the total number of sample observations. The various hypotheses may then be tested by contrasting residual sums of squares in the usual way.†

Example 6-7 This illustration is based on $p = 4$ classes, but for simplicity of calculation we have kept $k = 2$ (Table 6-1).

Denoting the data matrix in model I by $\mathbf{X}_*$, the residual sum of squares for model I is

$$\text{RSS}_1 = \mathbf{y}'\mathbf{y} - \mathbf{y}'\mathbf{X}_*(\mathbf{X}_*'\mathbf{X}_*)^{-1}\mathbf{X}_*'\mathbf{y}$$

$$= \Sigma Y^2 - [\Sigma Y \quad \Sigma XY]\begin{bmatrix} n & \Sigma X \\ \Sigma X & \Sigma X^2 \end{bmatrix}^{-1}\begin{bmatrix} \Sigma Y \\ \Sigma XY \end{bmatrix}$$

where the summations are over all 20 observations,

$$\text{RSS}_1 = 10{,}876 - [440 \quad 7288]\begin{bmatrix} 20 & 340 \\ 340 & 7462 \end{bmatrix}^{-1}\begin{bmatrix} 440 \\ 7288 \end{bmatrix}$$

$$= 1174.1$$

Using the same approach, the residual sum of squares for model II is given by

$$\text{RSS}_2 = \Sigma Y^2 - [\Sigma_1 Y \quad \Sigma_2 Y \quad \Sigma_3 Y \quad \Sigma_4 Y \quad \Sigma XY]$$

$$\times \begin{bmatrix} n_1 & 0 & 0 & 0 & \Sigma_1 X \\ 0 & n_2 & 0 & 0 & \Sigma_2 X \\ 0 & 0 & n_3 & 0 & \Sigma_3 X \\ 0 & 0 & 0 & n_4 & \Sigma_4 X \\ \Sigma_1 X & \Sigma_2 X & \Sigma_3 X & \Sigma_4 X & \Sigma X^2 \end{bmatrix}^{-1}\begin{bmatrix} \Sigma_1 Y \\ \Sigma_2 Y \\ \Sigma_3 Y \\ \Sigma_4 Y \\ \Sigma XY \end{bmatrix}$$

where Σ_i indicates summation over observations in class i and Σ indicates

† It should be emphasized that the tests for structural change discussed in this section assume that the researcher has strong a priori views about when or where the potential change(s) occurred. Additional complexities arise when the switch point(s) may be unknown. There is also the possibility of a transition phase between regimes. There is some discussion of these topics in Sec. 10-4.

summation over all classes,

$$\text{RSS}_2 = 10{,}876 - [100 \quad 150 \quad 65 \quad 125 \quad 7288]$$

$$\times \begin{bmatrix} 5 & 0 & 0 & 0 & 90 \\ 0 & 5 & 0 & 0 & 50 \\ 0 & 0 & 5 & 0 & 120 \\ 0 & 0 & 0 & 5 & 180 \\ 90 & 50 & 120 & 80 & 7462 \end{bmatrix}^{-1} \begin{bmatrix} 100 \\ 150 \\ 65 \\ 125 \\ 7288 \end{bmatrix}$$

$$= 251.0$$

As shown in Example 6-2, this sum of squares may be more easily calculated by first of all expressing the data in the form of deviations from class means, pooling all the deviations and calculating RSS_2 as the residual sum of squares from the regression of the Y deviations on the X deviations. Table 6-2 shows the data in deviation form. The residual sum of squares from the regression of the Y deviations on the X deviations is then

$$\text{RSS}_2 = \sum_{ij} (Y_{ij} - \bar{Y}_i)^2 - \frac{\left[\Sigma_{ij}(Y_{ij} - \bar{Y}_i)(X_{ij} - \bar{X}_i)\right]^2}{\Sigma_{ij}(X_{ij} - \bar{X}_i)^2}$$

$$= (88 + 94 + 206 + 18) - \frac{(134 + 117 + 177 + 0)^2}{294 + 204 + 382 + 302}$$

$$= 251.0 \qquad \text{as before}$$

Finally, we need to obtain the residual sum of squares from the completely unrestricted model, model III. This is the sum of the residual sums of squares obtained by fitting a linear regression to each class separately. These are most simply obtained from Table 6-2. They are

$$\mathbf{e}_1'\mathbf{e}_1 = 88 - \frac{(134)^2}{294} = 26.925$$

$$\mathbf{e}_2'\mathbf{e}_2 = 94 - \frac{(117)^2}{204} = 26.897$$

$$\mathbf{e}_3'\mathbf{e}_3 = 206 - \frac{(117)^2}{382} = 123.987$$

$$\mathbf{e}_4'\mathbf{e}_4 = 18 - \frac{0}{302} = 18$$

giving

$$\text{RSS}_3 = 195.8$$

The various tests may be set up in an analysis of variance framework as shown in Table 6-3.

The test for a common regression slope is

$$F = \frac{(\text{RSS}_2 - \text{RSS}_3)/3}{\text{RSS}_3/12} = \frac{18.4}{16.3} = 1.1$$

Table 6-2

Observation	Class							
	1		2		3		4	
j	$(Y_{1j} - \bar{Y}_1)$	$(X_{1j} - \bar{X}_1)$	$(Y_{2j} - \bar{Y}_2)$	$(X_{2j} - \bar{X}_2)$	$(Y_{3j} - \bar{Y}_3)$	$(X_{3j} - \bar{X}_3)$	$(Y_{4j} - \bar{Y}_4)$	$(X_{4j} - \bar{X}_4)$
1	2	11	0	5	−1	−8	−2	−11
2	2	2	2	−1	−5	7	0	9
3	0	−4	−4	−9	0	2	3	0
4	4	3	−5	−4	12	11	1	−6
5	−8	−12	7	9	−6	−12	−2	8
$\sum_j (Y_{ij} - \bar{Y}_i)^2$	88		94		206		18	
$\sum_j (X_{ij} - \bar{X}_i)^2$		294		204		382		302
$\sum_j (Y_{ij} - \bar{Y}_i)(X_{ij} - \bar{X}_i)$	134		117		177		0	

Table 6-3

Model	Residual sum of squares	Degrees of freedom	Mean square
I	$RSS_1 = 1174.1$	$n - k = 18$	
II	$RSS_2 = 251.0$	$n - p - k + 1 = 15$	16.7
III	$RSS_3 = 195.8$	$n - pk = 12$	16.3
	$RSS_1 - RSS_2 = 923.1$	3	307.7
	$RSS_2 - RSS_3 = 55.2$	3	18.4
	$RSS_1 - RSS_3 = 978.3$	6	163.0

which is insignificant. Thus we do not reject the assumption of a common X effect in all classes. The test for common intercepts (conditional on a common slope) is

$$F = \frac{(RSS_1 - RSS_2)/3}{RSS_2/15} = \frac{307.7}{16.7} = 18.4$$

and $F_{0.99}(3, 15) = 5.42$. Thus we conclude that a "class effect" is established, that is, that the levels of the regressions do appear to differ between classes. The test for overall homogeneity of regressions across classes is

$$F = \frac{(RSS_1 - RSS_3)/6}{RSS_3/12} = \frac{163.0}{16.3} = 10$$

and $F_{0.99}(6, 12) = 4.82$, so that this too is a highly significant result, but it would appear that the significance is due to variation in the intercepts and not in the slopes.

6-3 DUMMY VARIABLES

Dummy variables have already made their appearance in the previous section, but we have not explicitly labeled them as such. For example, the unrestricted model in Eqs. (6-21) specifies a consumption function which has different intercepts, but a common slope, in wartime and peacetime periods. The specification is repeated here

$$\begin{bmatrix} \mathbf{y}_1 \\ \mathbf{y}_2 \end{bmatrix} = \begin{bmatrix} \mathbf{i}_1 & \mathbf{0} & \mathbf{x}_1 \\ \mathbf{0} & \mathbf{i}_2 & \mathbf{x}_2 \end{bmatrix} \begin{bmatrix} \alpha_1 \\ \alpha_2 \\ \beta \end{bmatrix} + \mathbf{u} \tag{6-28}$$

where the subscript 1 refers to wartime and the subscript 2 to peacetime. This model may be written as

$$Y_t = \alpha_1 D_{1t} + \alpha_2 D_{2t} + \beta X_t + u_t \qquad t = 1, 2, \ldots, n \tag{6-29}$$

D_{1t} and D_{2t} are dummy variables whose sample values are given in the first two columns of the data matrix in Eq. (6-28). That is,

$$D_{1t} = \begin{cases} 1 & \text{if } t \text{ indicates a wartime observation} \\ 0 & \text{if } t \text{ indicates a peacetime observation} \end{cases}$$

and

$$D_{2t} = \begin{cases} 0 & \text{if } t \text{ indicates a wartime observation} \\ 1 & \text{if } t \text{ indicates a peacetime observation} \end{cases}$$

Notice that the model in Eq. (6-29) has no general intercept term. If one runs a regression of Y on D_1, D_2, and X with a computer program that automatically produces an intercept term, the estimation procedure will break down (or possibly give nonsense coefficients, which are merely ratios of rounding errors) since D_1 and D_2 sum to the unit vector. The practical alternatives are

1. Run Eq. (6-29) with the general intercept suppressed.

   or

2. Reformulate Eq. (6-29) as

$$Y_t = \gamma_1 + \gamma_2 D_{2t} + \beta X_t + u_t \tag{6-30}$$

   and run with the standard OLS program.

Comparing intercepts in Eqs. (6-29) and (6-30) gives

	Equation (6-29)	Equation (6-30)
Wartime intercept	α_1	γ_1
Peacetime intercept	α_2	$\gamma_1 + \gamma_2$

Thus the relation between the α's and the γ's is

$$\gamma_1 = \alpha_1 \qquad \text{and} \qquad \gamma_2 = \alpha_2 - \alpha_1$$

The model of Eq. (6-30) may then be put in matrix form as

$$\begin{bmatrix} \mathbf{y}_1 \\ \mathbf{y}_2 \end{bmatrix} = \begin{bmatrix} \mathbf{i}_1 & \mathbf{0} & \mathbf{x}_1 \\ \mathbf{i}_2 & \mathbf{i}_2 & \mathbf{x}_2 \end{bmatrix} \begin{bmatrix} \alpha_1 \\ \alpha_2 - \alpha_1 \\ \beta \end{bmatrix} + \mathbf{u} \tag{6-31}$$

The choice between the two estimation procedures is of no great importance, but it is very important to be clear about precisely what is being tested in either model. For instance, testing the significance of D_2 in Eq. (6-30) is, in effect, testing the hypothesis

$$H_0: \quad \alpha_2 - \alpha_1 = 0$$

which is testing whether the peacetime and the wartime intercepts are significantly different, whereas testing the significance of D_2 in Eq. (6-29) is asking whether the peacetime intercept is significantly different from zero.

The dummy variables may also be allowed to interact with the X variable. Consider

$$Y = \alpha_1 D_1 + \alpha_2 D_2 + \beta_1(D_1 X) + \beta_2(D_2 X) + u \tag{6-32}$$

where the subscript t has been omitted for simplicity. Equation (6-32) implies two separate relations, namely,

$$Y = \alpha_1 + \beta_1 X + u \qquad \text{wartime function}$$

$$Y = \alpha_2 + \beta_2 X + u \qquad \text{peacetime function}$$

Thus performing a single regression of Y on D_1, D_2, D_1X, and D_2X with the general intercept suppressed is equivalent to fitting separate regressions to the two subperiods. An alternative formulation of Eq. (6-32) is

$$Y = \alpha_1 + (\alpha_2 - \alpha_1)D_2 + \beta_1 X + (\beta_2 - \beta_1)D_2 X + u \tag{6-33}$$

This corresponds to a regression of Y on D_2, X, and D_2X with a constant term. One advantage of Eq. (6-33) is that testing the significance of the D_2X variable is a test of the hypothesis

$$H_0\colon \quad \beta_2 - \beta_1 = 0$$

Thus we see that, in the two-variable model, the tests for homogeneity of intercepts and homogeneity of slopes are equivalent to tests of the significance of single coefficients in an appropriately specified regression equation using dummy variables.

Dummy variables may also be usefully applied in more complex models. For the data of the last numerical illustration we may specify

$$\begin{aligned} Y = \alpha_1 &+ (\alpha_2 - \alpha_1)D_2 + (\alpha_3 - \alpha_1)D_3 + (\alpha_4 - \alpha_1)D_4 + \beta_1 X \\ &+ (\beta_2 - \beta_1)D_2 X + (\beta_3 - \beta_1)D_3 X + (\beta_4 - \beta_1)D_4 X + u \end{aligned} \tag{6-34}$$

where

$$D_i = \begin{cases} 1 & \text{for an observation in class } i \qquad i = 2, 3, 4 \\ 0 & \text{otherwise} \end{cases}$$

Equation (6-34) allows intercepts and regression slopes to vary across all four classes. The choice of the class not to be represented by a dummy variable is arbitrary, but once it is made, the coefficients of all the other variables are differences from the coefficients of that class.

Estimating Eq. (6-34) from the data of Table 6-1 gives

$$\begin{aligned} Y = \underset{(2.56)}{11.7959} &+ \underset{(2.19)}{12.4688D_2} - \underset{(-1.41)}{9.9163\,D_3} + \underset{(2.13)}{13.2041D_4} + \underset{(1.19)}{0.4558X} \\ &+ \underset{(0.32)}{0.1177D_2X} + \underset{(0.02)}{0.0076D_3X} - \underset{(-1.38)}{0.4558\,D_4X} \end{aligned}$$

with $R^2 = 0.7468$ and 12 degrees of freedom.† The figures in parentheses are t ratios, and we see that none of the coefficients of the D_iX variables is significantly

† I am indebted to G. Gujarati for discussions of this point and also for the calculations.

different from zero. This, of course, confirms the homogeneity of regression slopes established earlier by the F test. Imposing the assumption of a common regression slope gives the revised regression

$$\underset{(4.79)}{Y = 13.4882} + \underset{(4.68)}{12.8969D_2} - \underset{(-3.42)}{9.1726\, D_3} + \underset{(2.20)}{5.742D_4} + \underset{(3.04)}{0.3621X}$$

with $R^2 = 0.7341$ and 15 degrees of freedom. All three dummies are significantly different from zero at the 5 percent level, thus establishing that the intercepts in the second, third, and fourth classes are different from the intercept in the first class, again in agreement with the earlier F test on intercepts. One advantage of this type of dummy variable setup is that in cases where the tests examine the *joint* significance of a subset of variables the dummy variables can indicate which variables may have made the most important contribution to the overall significance of the group.

The dummy variables specified above play an important role in describing temporal effects (where the classes refer to different time periods), *spatial* effects (where the classes refer to different regions or countries), *industrial* effects (where the classes refer to industries), and so forth. Suppose we have *qualitative* variables such as

- Education (none, grammar, some high school, high school diploma, some college, college degree, advanced degree, foreign education)
- Marital status (unmarried, married 1 year, 2 years, 3 years, 4 years, 5–9 years, 10–20 years, over 20 years)
- Sex (male, female)
- Race (white, black, other)

Only the last two are truly qualitative variables. Education might be treated as a cardinal variable, measured by years of formal education, and likewise, duration of marriage is a cardinal variable. In both cases, however, we may use groupings of a cardinal variable to define a qualitative variable. If a qualitative variable is thought to influence some dependent variable, we may use the categories of that variable to classify the sample observations into various classes, and the preceding method of analysis applies. There are, however, some slight complications if we wish to use two or more qualitative variables in a single equation.

Two or More Sets of Dummy Variables

Suppose we wish to incorporate two qualitative variables in a regression equation, each such variable being represented by a *set* of dummy variables. To be specific, suppose the variables are educational level (3 classes) and sex (2 classes). We then define

$$E_i = \begin{cases} 1 & \text{if observation relates to education level } i, \qquad i = 1, 2, 3 \\ 0 & \text{otherwise} \end{cases}$$

and

$$S_j = \begin{cases} 1 & \text{if observation relates to sex } j, \quad j = 1, 2 \\ 0 & \text{otherwise} \end{cases}$$

Suppose we then wish to examine the relationship between hours spent in reading nonfiction Y and these two qualitative variables. It is instructive to examine first of all what happens if we have only one set of dummy variables in the model. A linear model for the influence of E on Y would be written

$$Y = \alpha_1 E_1 + \alpha_2 E_2 + \alpha_3 E_3 + u \tag{6-35}$$

The data matrix is

$$\mathbf{E} = \begin{bmatrix} \mathbf{i}_1 & \mathbf{0} & \mathbf{0} \\ \mathbf{0} & \mathbf{i}_2 & \mathbf{0} \\ \mathbf{0} & \mathbf{0} & \mathbf{i}_3 \end{bmatrix}$$

so that

$$\mathbf{E}'\mathbf{E} = \begin{bmatrix} n_1 & 0 & 0 \\ 0 & n_2 & 0 \\ 0 & 0 & n_3 \end{bmatrix}$$

and the estimated OLS vector is

$$\begin{bmatrix} a_1 \\ a_2 \\ a_3 \end{bmatrix} = \begin{bmatrix} \bar{Y}_1 \\ \bar{Y}_2 \\ \bar{Y}_3 \end{bmatrix}$$

so that the OLS regression coefficients are simply the mean values of Y in each of the educational classes. If we used the alternative formulation

$$Y = \alpha_1 + \alpha_2^* E_2 + \alpha_3^* E_3 + u \tag{6-36}$$

consistency with Eq. (6-35) requires

$$\alpha_2^* = \alpha_2 - \alpha_1 \quad \text{and} \quad \alpha_3^* = \alpha_3 - \alpha_1$$

The data matrix is now

$$\mathbf{E}^* = \begin{bmatrix} \mathbf{i}_1 & \mathbf{0} & \mathbf{0} \\ \mathbf{i}_2 & \mathbf{i}_2 & \mathbf{0} \\ \mathbf{i}_3 & \mathbf{0} & \mathbf{i}_3 \end{bmatrix}$$

and it is simple to show that the OLS coefficient vector is†

$$\begin{bmatrix} a_1 \\ a_2^* \\ a_3^* \end{bmatrix} = \begin{bmatrix} \bar{Y}_1 \\ \bar{Y}_2 - \bar{Y}_1 \\ \bar{Y}_3 - \bar{Y}_1 \end{bmatrix}$$

† See Problem 6-7.

Table 6-4 $E(Y|E_i, S_j)$

		Educational level		
		E_1	E_2	E_3
Sex	S_1	$\alpha_1 + \beta_1$	$\alpha_2 + \beta_1$	$\alpha_3 + \beta_1$
	S_2	$\alpha_1 + \beta_2$	$\alpha_2 + \beta_2$	$\alpha_3 + \beta_2$

Table 6-5 $E(Y|E_i, S_j)$

		Educational level		
		E_1	E_2	E_3
Sex	S_1	μ	$\mu + \alpha_2$	$\mu + \alpha_3$
	S_2	$\mu + \beta_2$	$\mu + \alpha_2 + \beta_2$	$\mu + \alpha_3 + \beta_2$

If we now specify Y as a function of both education level and sex, we might be tempted to write

$$Y = \alpha_1 E_1 + \alpha_2 E_2 + \alpha_3 E_3 + \beta_1 S_1 + \beta_2 S_2 + u \tag{6-37}$$

Thus there is an expected value of Y for each combination of E and S. These *conditional* expected values are shown in Table 6-4. An immediate difficulty with Eq. (6-37) is that the OLS program (even with the intercept suppressed) will break down, for the column vectors corresponding to E_1, E_2, E_3, S_1, and S_2 form a linearly dependent set. Thus we cannot find unique estimates of the five parameters in Eq. (6-37). As we will see, however, this does *not* imply that we cannot find unique estimates of the *sums* of those parameters appearing in Table 6-4.

One way out of the difficulty is to reformulate Eq. (6-37) as

$$Y = \mu + \alpha_2 E_2 + \alpha_3 E_3 + \beta_2 S_2 + u \tag{6-38}$$

where the dummy variables are the same as before, but the α, β parameters will not have the same meaning (or values) as in Eq. (6-37). The set of conditional means for Eq. (6-38) is shown in Table 6-5.

The parameter μ represents the expected number of hours spent in reading nonfiction for people in the category (E_1, S_1). The α_2, α_3 parameters measure *differential* effects for E_2 and E_3, respectively, compared with E_1. The differential effect for E_3 compared with E_2 is $\alpha_3 - \alpha_2$. Similarly, β_2 represents a differential effect for S_2 compared with S_1.† Notice that the differential sex effect is the same at all educational levels, and similarly the differential educational effects are invariant to sex. The four parameters of Eq. (6-38) may be estimated uniquely by

† We might choose any one of the six cells to be represented by μ. The differential effects would then be measured from that cell, but the numerical estimates of the conditional means will be invariant to the starting position. See Problem 6-8.

Table 6-6 Hours spent in reading nonfiction Y

	E_1	E_2	E_3
S_1	8, 10, 12	12, 14	20
S_2	5, 6	10	20

OLS, and from these we obtain unique estimates of the expected values in Table 6-5.

Example 6-8 Hypothetical data on hours spent in reading nonfiction is shown in Table 6-6 for ten subjects classified by sex and educational level. Taking those data row by row, model (6-38), set out in full, gives

$$
\begin{array}{c}
Y \\
\begin{bmatrix}
8 \\ 10 \\ 12 \\ 12 \\ 14 \\ 20 \\ 5 \\ 6 \\ 10 \\ 20
\end{bmatrix}
\end{array}
=
\begin{array}{cccc}
 & E_2 & E_3 & S_2 \\
\begin{bmatrix}
1 & 0 & 0 & 0 \\
1 & 0 & 0 & 0 \\
1 & 0 & 0 & 0 \\
1 & 1 & 0 & 0 \\
1 & 1 & 0 & 0 \\
1 & 0 & 1 & 0 \\
1 & 0 & 0 & 1 \\
1 & 0 & 0 & 1 \\
1 & 1 & 0 & 1 \\
1 & 0 & 1 & 1
\end{bmatrix}
\end{array}
\begin{bmatrix}
\mu \\ \alpha_2 \\ \alpha_3 \\ \beta_2
\end{bmatrix}
+ \mathbf{u}
\qquad (6\text{-}39)
$$

Letting $\mathbf{X}$ represent the data matrix (often referred to as a *design* matrix in experimental contexts) in Eq. (6-39),

$$
\mathbf{X'X} =
\begin{bmatrix}
10 & 3 & 2 & 4 \\
3 & 3 & 0 & 1 \\
2 & 0 & 2 & 1 \\
4 & 1 & 1 & 4
\end{bmatrix}
\quad \text{and} \quad
\mathbf{X'y} =
\begin{bmatrix}
117 \\ 36 \\ 40 \\ 41
\end{bmatrix}
$$

the estimated equation is

$$
\hat{Y} = 11.14 + 3.31 E_2 + 12.54 E_3 - 7.35 S_2
$$

The corresponding estimates of the expected number of hours are shown in Table 6-7.

Interaction

The main drawback of Eq. (6-38) and the estimates to which it gives rise is the built-in assumption that the differential effect of each factor is constant across the levels of the other factor. Thus Table 6-7 shows that hours for S_2 are 7.35 lower than for S_1, irrespective of the level of education. Conversely, E_2 shows 3.31 more

Table 6-7 Estimated mean hours

	E_1	E_2	E_3
S_1	11.14	14.45	23.68
S_2	3.79	7.10	16.33

hours than E_1, and E_3 shows 12.54 more than E_1, irrespective of whether we are in the S_1 row or the S_2 row. This implies the absence of any interaction between the two factors. If, however, it is to be expected that the differential sex effect varies with the level of education, then an interaction effect exists, and we need to see how to incorporate it into the model and estimate it.

Returning to Eq. (6-38), we would now expand the relation to read

$$Y = \mu + \alpha_2 E_2 + \alpha_3 E_3 + \beta_2 S_2 + \gamma_2 (E_2 S_2) + \gamma_3 (E_3 S_2) + u \qquad (6\text{-}40)$$

There are only two possible interaction variables in this case, and they are found by multiplying each E level by each S level. The conditional expected values are now shown in Table 6-8.

The first row is the same as in Table 6-5, but the second row incorporates the interaction effects. Thus the sex differential is

$$\begin{array}{rl} \beta_2 & \text{for } E_1 \\ \beta_2 + \gamma_2 & \text{for } E_2 \\ \beta_2 + \gamma_3 & \text{for } E_3 \end{array}$$

Likewise, the E_2/E_1 differential is

$$\begin{array}{rl} \alpha_2 & \text{for } S_1 \\ \alpha_2 + \gamma_2 & \text{for } S_2 \end{array}$$

and the E_3/E_1 differential is

$$\begin{array}{rl} \alpha_3 & \text{for } S_1 \\ \alpha_3 + \gamma_3 & \text{for } S_2 \end{array}$$

Table 6-8 $E(Y|E_i, S_j)$

	E_1	E_2	E_3
S_1	μ	$\mu + \alpha_2$	$\mu + \alpha_3$
S_2	$\mu + \beta_2$	$\mu + \alpha_2 + \beta_2 + \gamma_2$	$\mu + \alpha_3 + \beta_2 + \gamma_3$

Table 6-9 Estimated mean hours

	E_1	E_2	E_3
S_1	13.33	13.00	20.00
S_2	0.50	10.00	20.00

Referring back to the data matrix in Eq. (6-39), the data matrix for this problem would now be

$$\begin{array}{cccccc} & E_2 & E_3 & S_2 & E_2S_2 & E_3S_2 \end{array}$$

$$\mathbf{X} = \begin{bmatrix} 1 & & & & & \\ 1 & & & & & \\ 1 & & & & & \\ 1 & 1 & & & & \\ 1 & 1 & & & & \\ 1 & & 1 & & & \\ 1 & & & 1 & & \\ 1 & & & 1 & & \\ 1 & 1 & & 1 & 1 & \\ 1 & & 1 & 1 & & 1 \end{bmatrix}$$

Thus

$$\mathbf{X}'\mathbf{X} = \begin{bmatrix} 10 & 3 & 2 & 4 & 1 & 1 \\ 3 & 3 & 0 & 1 & 1 & 0 \\ 2 & 0 & 2 & 1 & 0 & 1 \\ 4 & 1 & 1 & 4 & 1 & 1 \\ 1 & 1 & 0 & 1 & 1 & 0 \\ 1 & 0 & 1 & 1 & 0 & 1 \end{bmatrix} \quad \text{and} \quad \mathbf{X}'\mathbf{y} = \begin{bmatrix} 117 \\ 36 \\ 40 \\ 41 \\ 10 \\ 20 \end{bmatrix}$$

The OLS equation is now

$$\hat{Y} = 13.33 - 0.33E_2 + 6.67E_3 - 12.83S_2 + 9.83(E_2S_2) + 12.83(E_3S_2)$$

and substitution in Table 6-8 gives the estimated number of mean hours shown in Table 6-9.

Compared with the previous regression, where no interaction effect was incorporated, we now have a large negative sex effect (-12.83) at E_1, which is reduced to -3.00 at E_2 and eliminated completely at E_3. This last result is an automatic consequence of our data, where in the interests of simplicity we had only one observation in each of the E_3 cells and also in the E_2, S_2 cell. The regression values, with interaction, then coincide with these observations. This has also distorted the estimate of the E_2 differential effect to give a small negative number (-0.33) for S_1, but the calculations do illustrate the principles involved.†

† This section has only dealt with dummy variables on the right-hand side of the equation. For a discussion of the application of dummy variables to the left-hand-side variable see Sec. 10-5, Qualitative Dependent Variables.

6-4 SEASONAL ADJUSTMENT

Dummy variables also play an important role in problems of seasonal adjustment. These problems are of two kinds. First there is the conventional and long-standing problem of deseasonalizing a given quarterly or monthly time series, and second there is the problem of estimating an econometric relationship between variables that are available in both unadjusted and deseasonalized forms.

Suppose we have $4n$ quarterly observations on a variable Y, such as unemployment, imports, or food prices. Such variables are likely to display a pronounced seasonal movement, and for purposes of economic intelligence and policy it is important to produce a "deseasonalized" series, from which one can better assess whether unemployment, say, is really increasing or decreasing. There are several methods of deseasonalizing series in practice, but here we are only concerned with applications of dummy variables.

Let us define a $4n \times 4$ matrix $\mathbf{D}$,

$$\mathbf{D} = \begin{bmatrix} 1 & 0 & 0 & 0 \\ 0 & 1 & 0 & 0 \\ 0 & 0 & 1 & 0 \\ 0 & 0 & 0 & 1 \\ 1 & 0 & 0 & 0 \\ 0 & 1 & 0 & 0 \\ \cdots & \cdots & \cdots & \cdots \\ 0 & 0 & 0 & 1 \end{bmatrix}$$

This is the sample matrix for four dummy variables defined by

$$D_{it} = \begin{cases} 1 & \text{if } t \text{ occurs in quarter } i \qquad i = 1, 2, 3, 4 \\ 0 & \text{otherwise} \end{cases}$$

If we regress $\mathbf{y}$ on $\mathbf{D}$, we obtain

$$\mathbf{y} = \mathbf{Db} + \mathbf{y}^{\alpha} \tag{6-41}$$

where $\mathbf{b}$ is the vector of the OLS coefficients and $\mathbf{y}^{\alpha}$ the vector of residuals. From the analysis of Chap. 5,

$$\mathbf{y}^{\alpha} = \mathbf{My} \tag{6-42}$$

where

$$\mathbf{M} = \mathbf{I} - \mathbf{D}(\mathbf{D}'\mathbf{D})^{-1}\mathbf{D}' \tag{6-43}$$

and $\mathbf{M}$ is symmetric idempotent with the property

$$\mathbf{MD} = \mathbf{0} \tag{6-44}$$

The series $\mathbf{y}^{\alpha}$ cannot serve directly as a deseasonalized series for two reasons. First of all, it sums to zero, and it would seem plausible to require a deseasonalized series to have the same sum as the original, unadjusted series. Second, as shown earlier for model (6-35),

$$\mathbf{b} = \begin{bmatrix} \bar{Y}_1 \\ \bar{Y}_2 \\ \bar{Y}_3 \\ \bar{Y}_4 \end{bmatrix}$$

where $\bar{Y}_i$ $(i = 1, \ldots, 4)$ is the mean of all ith-quarter Y values. Thus $\mathbf{y}^{\alpha}$ merely consists of deviations of the Y values from the quarterly means. But if the series contains trend and/or cyclical components, the elements of **b** will be an amalgam of trend, cyclical, and seasonal effects. Thus subtracting **b** year by year from the actual Y values will not yield satisfactory estimates of a deseasonalized series. The remedy is to introduce into the regression a polynomial in time of sufficiently high order to represent the trend and cyclical components, so that the coefficients of **D** will be a more satisfactory estimate of the seasonal component. Thus one computes the regression

$$\mathbf{y} = \mathbf{Pa} + \mathbf{Db} + \mathbf{e} \tag{6-45}$$

where

$$\mathbf{P} = \begin{bmatrix} 1 & 1^2 & \cdots & 1^p \\ 2 & 2^2 & \cdots & 2^p \\ 3 & 3^2 & \cdots & 3^p \\ 4 & 4^2 & \cdots & 4^p \\ \cdots & \cdots & \cdots & \cdots \\ 4n & (4n)^2 & & (4n)^p \end{bmatrix}$$

The deseasonalized series would now be defined as

$$\mathbf{y}^{\alpha} = \mathbf{y} - \mathbf{Db} \tag{6-46}$$

Jorgenson has argued that if the **P** and **D** matrices are properly specified, then **a** and **b** will be best linear unbiased estimates of the systematic and seasonal components, since Eq. (6-45) is then a straightforward example of ordinary least squares.† The estimates of **a** and **b** are given by

$$\begin{bmatrix} \mathbf{a} \\ \mathbf{b} \end{bmatrix} = \begin{bmatrix} \mathbf{P'P} & \mathbf{P'D} \\ \mathbf{D'P} & \mathbf{D'D} \end{bmatrix}^{-1} \begin{bmatrix} \mathbf{P'y} \\ \mathbf{D'y} \end{bmatrix} \tag{6-47}$$

Applying the results for the inverse of a partitioned matrix,

$$\mathbf{b} = (\mathbf{D'ND})^{-1}\mathbf{D'Ny} \tag{6-48}$$

where

$$\mathbf{N} = \mathbf{I} - \mathbf{P}(\mathbf{P'P})^{-1}\mathbf{P'} \tag{6-49}$$

† D. W. Jorgenson, "Minimum Variance, Linear, Unbiased Seasonal Adjustment in Economic Time Series," *Journal of the American Statistical Association*, **59**, 1964, pp. 681–725.

Table 6-10 Quarterly seasonal component of the U.K. Index of Industrial Production, 1948–1957

	Seasonal component			
Method	b_1	b_2	b_3	b_4
Moving average (additive)	3.28	0.77	−7.13	3.08
Regression on **D**	1.85	0.35	−7.15	4.95
Regression on [**P D**] ($p = 4$)	4.87	0.36	−7.17	2.95
Regression on [**P D**] ($p = 6$)	3.35	0.95	−7.54	3.25

Substituting in Eq. (6-46) gives

$$\mathbf{y}^{\alpha} = \mathbf{Ty}$$

where

$$\mathbf{T} = \mathbf{I} - \mathbf{D}(\mathbf{D}'\mathbf{N}\mathbf{D})^{-1}\mathbf{D}'\mathbf{N} \tag{6-50}$$

Thus the deseasonalized series can still be expressed as a linear transformation of **y**. However, in contrast with the **M** matrix defined in Eq. (6-43), the **T** matrix is not symmetric, though it is idempotent and does satisfy the condition $\mathbf{TD} = \mathbf{0}$.

As a numerical illustration of these methods we made several estimates of the quarterly seasonal component in the U.K. Index of Industrial Production for the period 1948–1957. The results are shown in Table 6-10. The centered four-quarter moving average is a flexible method for removing trend and cycle, and we will take the estimates of the seasonal component in the first row of Table 6-10 as a standard by which to judge the various regressions. It is seen that the simple regression on seasonal dummies alone gives misleading estimates of the seasonal component, apart from the pronounced dip in the third quarter which is well picked up by all methods, and it is only when we use a sixth-degree polynomial that the results agree closely with those obtained from the moving average method.

Estimation of Econometric Relationships

Faced with the choice between using raw data or seasonally adjusted data, one should think carefully about the basic decision process underlying any behavioral relation being estimated. For example, in the study of production decisions it is often found that firms attempt to base production rates on "smoothed" sales figures, so that the appropriate regression might be *actual* production on *deseasonalized* sales. A salaried worker may have an income with no seasonal component, but consumption expenditures with a strong seasonal component due to vacation and Christmas spending. The appropriate model would then regress actual consumption on actual income plus a set of seasonal dummies. Income itself may have one seasonal pattern and consumption a different seasonal pattern with deseasonalized consumption a function of deseasonalized income. If one then wished to explain actual consumption, the appropriate regression is

$$\begin{aligned}\text{Actual consumption} &= \text{deseasonalized consumption} + \text{seasonal component} \\ &= f(\text{deseasonalized income}) + \text{seasonal component} \\ &= f(\text{deseasonalized income, dummy variables})\end{aligned}$$

In many cases theory may give no clear guide to the appropriate regression, and as the data are often available in both unadjusted and deseasonalized form, it is sometimes difficult to decide in which form to incorporate variables in the regression. In practice, however, the problem of specification turns out to be less important than might have been expected, because of an important set of results due to Lovell.† To illustrate one of Lovell's basic results, consider the least-squares regression

$$\mathbf{y} = \mathbf{X}\mathbf{c}_1 + \mathbf{D}\mathbf{b}_1 + \mathbf{e}_1 \tag{6-51}$$

This may be interpreted as a regression of unadjusted Y values on unadjusted X values and a set of seasonal dummies. However, it is more instructive to consider a more general specification first of all, and simply regard $\mathbf{X}$ and $\mathbf{D}$ as a partitioning of the set of explanatory variables in the regression model,

$$\mathbf{y} = [\mathbf{X} \quad \mathbf{D}]\begin{bmatrix}\mathbf{c}_1 \\ \mathbf{b}_1\end{bmatrix} + \mathbf{e}_1$$

The OLS coefficients are then given by

$$\begin{bmatrix}\mathbf{c}_1 \\ \mathbf{b}_1\end{bmatrix} = \begin{bmatrix}\mathbf{X}'\mathbf{X} & \mathbf{X}'\mathbf{D} \\ \mathbf{D}'\mathbf{X} & \mathbf{D}'\mathbf{D}\end{bmatrix}^{-1}\begin{bmatrix}\mathbf{X}'\mathbf{y} \\ \mathbf{D}'\mathbf{y}\end{bmatrix} \tag{6-52}$$

Applying Eq. (4-68), the first element in this inverse matrix is

$$\left(\mathbf{X}'\mathbf{X} - \mathbf{X}'\mathbf{D}(\mathbf{D}'\mathbf{D})^{-1}\mathbf{D}'\mathbf{X}\right)^{-1} = (\mathbf{X}'\mathbf{M}\mathbf{X})^{-1}$$

where

$$\mathbf{M} = \mathbf{I} - \mathbf{D}(\mathbf{D}'\mathbf{D})^{-1}\mathbf{D}'$$

This is the $\mathbf{M}$ matrix already defined in Eq. (6-43), which we know to be symmetric and idempotent and to have the property $\mathbf{MD} = \mathbf{0}$. The remaining element in the first row of the inverse matrix is then

$$-(\mathbf{X}'\mathbf{M}\mathbf{X})^{-1}\mathbf{X}'\mathbf{D}(\mathbf{D}'\mathbf{D})^{-1}$$

Equation (6-52) may then be solved for $\mathbf{c}_1$ as

$$\mathbf{c}_1 = (\mathbf{X}'\mathbf{M}\mathbf{X})^{-1}\mathbf{X}'\mathbf{y} - (\mathbf{X}'\mathbf{M}\mathbf{X})^{-1}\mathbf{X}'\mathbf{D}(\mathbf{D}'\mathbf{D})^{-1}\mathbf{D}'\mathbf{y}$$

that is,

$$\mathbf{c}_1 = (\mathbf{X}'\mathbf{M}\mathbf{X})^{-1}\mathbf{X}'\mathbf{M}\mathbf{y} \tag{6-53}$$

† M. C. Lovell, "Seasonal Adjustment of Economic Time Series," *Journal of the American Statistical Association*, **58**, 1963, pp. 93–1010. The basic result goes back to R. Frisch and F. V. Waugh, "Partial Time Regressions as Compared with Individual Trends," *Econometrica*, **1**, 1933, pp. 387–401.

Now consider the transformed variables

$$\mathbf{y}^\alpha = \mathbf{My} \qquad \text{and} \qquad \mathbf{X}^\alpha = \mathbf{MX} \tag{6-54}$$

From Eq. (6-54) it follows that $\mathbf{y}^\alpha$ is the vector of residuals after $\mathbf{y}$ has been regressed on $\mathbf{D}$. Similarly, each column in $\mathbf{X}^\alpha$ is the vector of residuals after the corresponding X variable has been regressed on $\mathbf{D}$. If $\mathbf{y}^\alpha$ is regressed on $\mathbf{X}^\alpha$, the estimated coefficient vector is

$$\begin{aligned}(\mathbf{X'M'MX})^{-1}\mathbf{X'M'My} &= (\mathbf{X'MX})^{-1}\mathbf{X'My} \\ &= \mathbf{c}_1\end{aligned}$$

in view of the symmetry and idempotency of $\mathbf{M}$. Thus we have the important result that if we partition the explanatory variables in a regression into two blocks denoted by

$$[\mathbf{X} \quad \mathbf{D}]$$

the estimated coefficients of the X variables are exactly the same, whether we run the full OLS regression of $\mathbf{y}$ on $\mathbf{X}$ and $\mathbf{D}$ or first "correct" $\mathbf{y}$ and $\mathbf{X}$ for the effect of $\mathbf{D}$ and regress the Y residuals on the X residuals. More formally, if we calculate the two regressions

$$\begin{aligned}\mathbf{y} &= \mathbf{Xc}_1 + \mathbf{Db}_1 + \mathbf{e}_1 \\ \mathbf{y}^\alpha &= \mathbf{X}^\alpha\mathbf{c}_2 + \mathbf{e}_2\end{aligned}$$

the result is

$$\mathbf{c}_1 = \mathbf{c}_2 \tag{6-55}$$

This result is, of course, symmetrical with respect to $\mathbf{X}$ and $\mathbf{D}$, and the $\mathbf{D}$ matrix need not consist of dummy variables; it is merely any subset of explanatory variables. However, Lovell is concerned with seasonal adjustment, and $\mathbf{D}$ is then appropriately an $n \times 4$ matrix of quarterly seasonal dummies.

Two further basic results from Lovell are that the regressions

$$\mathbf{y} = \mathbf{X}^\alpha\mathbf{c}_3 + \mathbf{e}_3$$

and

$$\mathbf{y} = \mathbf{X}^\alpha\mathbf{c}_4 + \mathbf{Db}_4 + \mathbf{e}_4$$

also yield identical vectors of coefficients for the X variables, that is

$$\mathbf{c}_1 = \mathbf{c}_2 = \mathbf{c}_3 = \mathbf{c}_4 \tag{6-56}$$

The proofs are simple. Regressing $\mathbf{y}$ on $\mathbf{X}^\alpha$ gives

$$\begin{aligned}\mathbf{c}_3 &= (\mathbf{X'MX})^{-1}\mathbf{X'My} \\ &= \mathbf{c}_1\end{aligned}$$

and regressing $\mathbf{y}$ on $[\mathbf{X}^\alpha \quad \mathbf{D}]$ gives

$$\begin{aligned}\begin{bmatrix}\mathbf{c}_4 \\ \mathbf{b}_4\end{bmatrix} &= \begin{bmatrix}\mathbf{X'MX} & \mathbf{X'MD} \\ \mathbf{D'MX} & \mathbf{D'D}\end{bmatrix}^{-1}\begin{bmatrix}\mathbf{X'My} \\ \mathbf{D'y}\end{bmatrix} \\ &= \begin{bmatrix}\mathbf{X'MX} & \mathbf{0} \\ \mathbf{0} & \mathbf{D'D}\end{bmatrix}^{-1}\begin{bmatrix}\mathbf{X'My} \\ \mathbf{D'y}\end{bmatrix} \qquad \text{using Eq. (6-44)}\end{aligned}$$

Thus

$$\mathbf{c}_4 = (\mathbf{X'MX})^{-1}\mathbf{X'My}$$
$$= \mathbf{c}_1$$

These results raise some further questions. We have already seen that if $\mathbf{D}$ is merely a matrix of seasonal dummies, then $\mathbf{y}^\alpha$ and $\mathbf{X}^\alpha$, defined in Eqs. (6-54), are not properly deseasonalized series. On the other hand, if properly deseasonalized series are obtained by using the transformation matrix $\mathbf{T}$ defined in Eq. (6-50), this matrix, though idempotent and orthogonal to $\mathbf{D}$, does not have the symmetry property used in the above proofs. Furthermore, many official series are not deseasonalized by least-squares methods at all, but by moving average or other methods. Thus the Lovell results cannot be expected to hold exactly when $\mathbf{y}^\alpha$ and $\mathbf{X}^\alpha$ indicate properly deseasonalized series. Nonetheless some experimental calculations with various equations from the Oxford econometric model of the United Kingdom indicate agreement to several decimal places between estimated coefficients, whether the regression has been run with raw data and dummy variables or with deseasonalized variables produced by moving average methods or by least-squares regressions on $\mathbf{D}$ or on $[\mathbf{P} \quad \mathbf{D}]$.† The years covered by the model showed fairly steady growth and negligible cyclical oscillations. One would not expect such close agreement if the cyclical effects were very strong, and in practical work one should not allow this theorem to be a substitute for careful thought about the proper specification of the relationship.

6-5 MULTICOLLINEARITY

We have seen in Chap. 5 that the OLS estimator is

$$\mathbf{b} = (\mathbf{X'X})^{-1}\mathbf{X'y}$$

and that its variance matrix is

$$\text{var}(\mathbf{b}) = \sigma^2(\mathbf{X'X})^{-1}$$

Thus the sampling variances depend not only on the disturbance variance σ^2, but also on the *sample values* of the explanatory variables. Consider the following hypothetical matrices.

	$\mathbf{X'X}$	$(\mathbf{X'X})^{-1}$	$\lvert\mathbf{X'X}\rvert$
1.	$\begin{bmatrix} 1 & 0 \\ 0 & 1 \end{bmatrix}$	$\begin{bmatrix} 1 & 0 \\ 0 & 1 \end{bmatrix}$	1
2.	$\begin{bmatrix} 1 & 0.9 \\ 0.9 & 1 \end{bmatrix}$	$\begin{bmatrix} 5.26 & -4.74 \\ -4.74 & 5.26 \end{bmatrix}$	0.19
3.	$\begin{bmatrix} 1 & 0.99 \\ 0.99 & 1 \end{bmatrix}$	$\begin{bmatrix} 50 & -49.5 \\ -49.5 & 50 \end{bmatrix}$	0.02

† A. Georgopoulou and J. Johnston, "Seasonal Adjustment of Economic Time Series," University of Manchester, discussion paper.

In case 1 the two explanatory variables are orthogonal and the coefficients of the X's in the multiple regression equation would be the same as those given by the simple regressions of Y on each X in turn.† Orthogonal variables may be set up in experimental designs, but they are the exception, not the rule, in economic data. Cases 2 and 3 display increasing correlation between the two explanatory variables, as evidenced by the increasing numerical value for the off-diagonal (covariation) term. This is also reflected in the dramatic fall in the value of the determinant. This is described as a situation of *collinearity* (or *multicollinearity*) between the explanatory variables. Three important effects are illustrated in the sequence of matrices:

1. The sampling variances of the estimated OLS coefficients increase sharply with increasing collinearity between the explanatory variables. Taking case 1 as the base, they are more than *five* times as great in case 2 and *50* times as great in case 3. Thus in any specific application individual coefficients are likely to differ substantially from their true values.
2. Greater covariances between the explanatory variables produce greater sampling covariances for the OLS coefficients. Comparing the off-diagonal terms in $\mathbf{X'X}$ and $(\mathbf{X'X})^{-1}$ shows that a positive covariance for the X's gives a negative covariance for the b's, and vice versa. Again, in a specific application, if b_2 is below β_2, b_3 is most likely to exceed β_3 and vice versa (provided the X's are positively correlated).
3. Small variations in the data (for instance, dropping or adding a few observations) may produce substantial variations in the OLS coefficients. Suppose the normal equations for case 2 are

$$\begin{aligned} b_2 + 0.9b_3 &= 2.8 \\ 0.9b_2 + b_3 &= 2.9 \end{aligned} \Rightarrow b_2 = 1 \qquad b_3 = 2$$

Now suppose the X_3 variable is somewhat more highly correlated with X_2 and we have normal equations for case 3 as

$$\begin{aligned} b_2 + 0.99b_3 &= 2.8 \\ 0.99b_2 + b_3 &= 3.1 \end{aligned} \Rightarrow b_2 = -13.436 \qquad b_3 = 16.4$$

The only numerical change between the two sets of equations is a 10 percent (or less) increase in two coefficients, yet the solution values change dramati-

† Assuming the variables to be in deviation form

$$\mathbf{b} = \begin{bmatrix} \mathbf{x}_2'\mathbf{x}_2 & 0 \\ 0 & \mathbf{x}_3'\mathbf{x}_3 \end{bmatrix}^{-1} \begin{bmatrix} \mathbf{x}_2'\mathbf{y} \\ \mathbf{x}_3'\mathbf{y} \end{bmatrix} = \begin{bmatrix} \dfrac{\mathbf{x}_2'\mathbf{y}}{\mathbf{x}_2'\mathbf{x}_2} \\ \dfrac{\mathbf{x}_3'\mathbf{y}}{\mathbf{x}_3'\mathbf{x}_3} \end{bmatrix}$$

where each element in the right-hand-side vector is the slope coefficient in a simple two-variable regression.

cally.† Notice, however, that $b_2 + b_3 = 3$ in the first case and $b_2 + b_3 = 2.964$ in the second. Thus the sum of the coefficients appears to be estimated fairly precisely, even though the individual coefficients are subject to large errors of estimation. Even this happy result is dependent on the covariance between the b's being negative (i.e., covariance between the X's being positive) for

$$\text{var}(b_2 + b_3) = \text{var}(b_2) + \text{var}(b_3) + 2\,\text{cov}(b_2, b_3)$$

Thus increasing collinearity increases both $\text{var}(b_2)$ and $\text{var}(b_3)$. However, it also increases the *numerical* value of $\text{cov}(b_2, b_3)$ and, provided this covariance is negative, $\text{var}(b_2 + b_3)$ may not increase at all. For example, case 2 gives

$$\text{var}(b_2 + b_3) = 2(5.26 - 4.74)\sigma^2 = 1.04\sigma^2$$

and case 3 gives

$$\text{var}(b_2 + b_3) = 2(50 - 49.5)\sigma^2 = 1.00\sigma^2$$

For simplicity these three important points have been illustrated for the case of two explanatory variables. It is important to establish that similar results hold for the k-variable case and to discuss how multicollinearity may be detected and what may be done about it. However, before doing that, we will discuss the limiting case of exact, or complete, multicollinearity.

Exact Multicollinearity and Estimable Functions

In the case of two explanatory variables exact collinearity is represented by

$$x_3 = \alpha x_2 \tag{6-57}$$

where we are working with the variables in deviation form. Then

$$\mathbf{X'X} = \Sigma x_2^2 \begin{bmatrix} 1 & \alpha \\ \alpha & \alpha^2 \end{bmatrix}$$

with $|\mathbf{X'X}| = 0$ and $\rho(\mathbf{X'X}) = 1$. This is simply a breakdown of the assumption that $\mathbf{X}$ has full column rank, and so we cannot obtain the unique OLS vector defined by

$$\mathbf{b} = \begin{bmatrix} b_2 \\ b_3 \end{bmatrix} = (\mathbf{X'X})^{-1}\mathbf{X'y}$$

The normal equations

$$(\mathbf{X'X})\mathbf{b} = \mathbf{X'y} \tag{6-58}$$

however, will admit an infinity of solutions for

$$\mathbf{X'y} = \Sigma x_2 y \begin{bmatrix} 1 \\ \alpha \end{bmatrix}$$

† This is only a hypothetical example, but the literature of applied econometrics is full of examples of small changes in the data base producing substantial changes in estimated coefficients. For one example, see J. Johnston, "An Econometric Model of the United Kingdom," *Review of Economic Studies*, **29**, 1961, pp. 29–39.

so that the rows of $\mathbf{X'y}$ exhibit the same linear dependence as the rows of $\mathbf{X'X}$. The set of equations in Eq. (6-58) is thus consistent, and there is an infinity of solution vectors. Taking the first equation in Eq. (6-58), we have

$$\Sigma x_2^2(b_2 + \alpha b_3) = \Sigma x_2 y$$

and the second equation is

$$\alpha\Sigma x_2^2(b_2 + \alpha b_3) = \alpha\Sigma x_2 y$$

Both equations reduce to

$$b_2 + \alpha b_3 = \frac{\Sigma x_2 y}{\Sigma x_2^2} \tag{6-59}$$

Thus no matter which arbitrary solution to Eqs. (6-58) we take, the linear combination $b_2 + \alpha b_3$ will always have the same numerical value. We then define $\beta_2 + \alpha\beta_3$ as an *estimable function*, where we notice that the α in the estimable function is the parameter defining the linear dependence between x_2 and x_3.

The same result may be derived by writing the model in deviation form as

$$y = \beta_2 x_2 + \beta_3 x_3 + (u - \bar{u})$$

and substituting Eq. (6-57) to get

$$y = \beta x_2 + (u - \bar{u}) \tag{6-60}$$

where

$$\beta = \beta_2 + \alpha\beta_3 \tag{6-61}$$

The β parameter may be estimated by applying OLS to Eq. (6-60) to give

$$b = \frac{\Sigma x_2 y}{\Sigma x_2^2} \tag{6-62}$$

which is the same expression as that already obtained in Eq. (6-59). The expected value of y for a given x_2 (and x_3) is

$$\begin{aligned} E(y) &= \beta_2 x_2 + \beta_3 x_3 \\ &= (\beta_2 + \alpha\beta_3)x_2 \\ &= \beta x_2 \end{aligned}$$

Thus $E(y)$ can be estimated uniquely since β can be estimated uniquely by Eq. (6-62).

Example 6-9 Suppose $x_3 = 2x_2$ and the sample data are

$$\mathbf{X'X} = \begin{bmatrix} 10 & 20 \\ 20 & 40 \end{bmatrix} \qquad \mathbf{X'y} = \begin{bmatrix} 5 \\ 10 \end{bmatrix}$$

The normal equations (6-58) are

$$\begin{aligned} 10b_2 + 20b_3 &= 5 \\ 20b_2 + 40b_3 &= 10 \end{aligned}$$

Table 6-11

b_3	b_2	$b_2 + 2b_3$	Estimate of $E(y \mid x_2 = 20)$
0	0.5	0.5	10
1	−1.5	0.5	10
−1	2.5	0.5	10
−10	20.5	0.5	10

with solution

$$b_2 = \frac{5 - 20b_3}{10}$$

Taking some arbitrary values for b_3 gives Table 6-11.

The linear combination $b_2 + 2b_3$ is invariant to the solution chosen for the normal equations, and it is readily seen to be equal to

$$b = \frac{\Sigma x_2 y}{\Sigma x_2^2} = \frac{5}{10} = 0.5$$

Likewise, the regression value for any given x_2 is invariant to the normal solution vector.

To summarize, even though β_2 and β_3 cannot be estimated, a certain linear combination of β_2 and β_3 can be estimated, and $E(y)$ can also be estimated for any given x_2 value.

The nature of the problem may also be illustrated geometrically. In Fig. 6-5a the standard OLS case is shown. The $\mathbf{x}_2, \mathbf{x}_3$ vectors are not perfectly collinear, and they span a two-dimensional subspace in $\mathcal{R}^n$. Dropping a perpendicular from

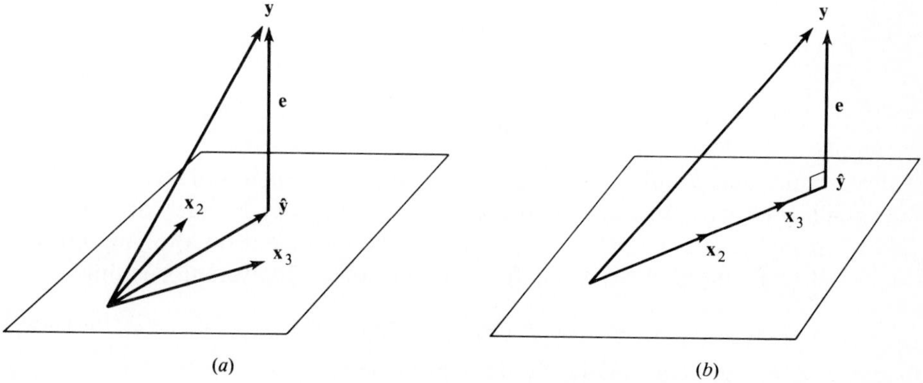

Figure 6-5

y to that subspace splits $\mathbf{y}$ into

$$\mathbf{y} = \hat{\mathbf{y}} + \mathbf{e}$$

where

$$\hat{\mathbf{y}} = \mathbf{Xb} = b_2\mathbf{x}_2 + b_3\mathbf{x}_3$$

The regression vector $\hat{\mathbf{y}}$ is a *unique* linear combination of the column vectors $\mathbf{x}_2, \mathbf{x}_3$. By contrast in Fig. 6-5*b* the $\mathbf{x}_2, \mathbf{x}_3$ vectors only span a one-dimensional subspace (line) in $\mathcal{R}^n$. The $\hat{\mathbf{y}}$ vector is still unambiguously determined by dropping a perpendicular from $\mathbf{y}$ to the line, but $\hat{\mathbf{y}}$ cannot be expressed uniquely in terms of $\mathbf{x}_2$ and $\mathbf{x}_3$.

In the general case perfect multicollinearity exists if $\rho(\mathbf{X}) < k$. Suppose $\rho(\mathbf{X}) = r$. There is then at least one set of r linearly independent columns in $\mathbf{X}$. Let one such set be assembled in the first r columns, so that we partition $\mathbf{X}$ as

$$\mathbf{X} = [\mathbf{X}_r \quad \mathbf{X}_s] \tag{6-63}$$

where $\mathbf{X}_r = n \times r$ matrix of rank r

$\mathbf{X}_s = n \times s$ matrix of the $s = k - r$ remaining columns in $\mathbf{X}$

Each column vector in $\mathbf{X}_s$ may then be expressed as a linear combination of the columns of $\mathbf{X}_r$. Thus we may write

$$\mathbf{X}_s = \mathbf{X}_r\mathbf{W} \tag{6-64}$$

where $\mathbf{W}$ is an $r \times s$ matrix, each column of which gives the coefficients of the linear combination for the corresponding vector in $\mathbf{X}_s$. The numerical values of the elements of $\mathbf{W}$ can, in principle, be determined. Combining Eqs. (6-63) and (6-64) gives

$$\begin{aligned}\mathbf{X} &= \mathbf{X}_r[\mathbf{I}_r \quad \mathbf{W}] \\ &= \mathbf{X}_r\mathbf{Z} \end{aligned} \tag{6-65}$$

where

$$\mathbf{Z} = [\mathbf{I}_r \quad \mathbf{W}] \tag{6-66}$$

The linear model may then be written

$$\begin{aligned}\mathbf{y} &= \mathbf{X}\boldsymbol{\beta} + \mathbf{u} \\ &= \mathbf{X}_r\mathbf{Z}\boldsymbol{\beta} + \mathbf{u} \\ &= \mathbf{X}_r\boldsymbol{\beta}_r + \mathbf{u} \end{aligned} \tag{6-67}$$

where

$$\boldsymbol{\beta}_r = \mathbf{Z}\boldsymbol{\beta} \tag{6-68}$$

Note carefully that $\boldsymbol{\beta}_r$ indicates a *vector of* r *linear combinations* of the original $\boldsymbol{\beta}$'s, the coefficients of those linear combinations being given by the rows of $\mathbf{Z}$, as defined in Eq. (6-66). The elements of $\boldsymbol{\beta}_r$ may be estimated by applying OLS to Eq. (6-67), since the $\mathbf{X}_r$ matrix has full column rank. The estimator is thus

$$\hat{\boldsymbol{\beta}}_r = (\mathbf{X}_r'\mathbf{X}_r)^{-1}\mathbf{X}_r'\mathbf{y} \tag{6-69}$$

Likewise, $E(\mathbf{y})$ can be estimated by the regression vector

$$\hat{\mathbf{y}} = \mathbf{X}_r\hat{\boldsymbol{\beta}}_r \tag{6-70}$$

and the estimates in Eqs. (6-69) and (6-70) will have the usual OLS properties. The operational procedure would be to identify the largest submatrix in $\mathbf{X}$ with full column rank, denote it by $\mathbf{X}_r$, and substitute in Eqs. (6-69) and (6-70). If there is more than one such submatrix, $\hat{\mathbf{y}}$ will be invariant to which is chosen.

As in the case of two explanatory variables, an alternative procedure is to derive *any solution* $\mathbf{b}_0$ to the normal equations

$$(\mathbf{X}'\mathbf{X})\mathbf{b}_0 = \mathbf{X}'\mathbf{y}$$

and compute

$$\hat{\mathbf{y}} = \mathbf{X}\mathbf{b}_0 \tag{6-71}$$

The numerical values for $\hat{\mathbf{y}}$ in Eqs. (6-70) and (6-71) will be identical. One needs to determine the linear dependencies in the $\mathbf{X}$ data (as in the $\mathbf{W}$ and $\mathbf{Z}$ matrices) in order to determine the precise linear combinations of β coefficients that are being estimated in $\boldsymbol{\beta}_r$, but such combinations are not usually of any economic significance. Furthermore, the use of Eq. (6-70) or Eq. (6-71) for forecasting *outside the sample observations* rests on the same linear dependencies holding among the X's in the forecast period.

Near Multicollinearity

The prevalent case in so much econometric work, especially with time series data, is one of high but not exact multicollinearity. This raises three questions:

1. What effects to expect from multicollinearity
2. How to detect the degree of multicollinearity
3. What remedial action to take

Effects

Provided the $\mathbf{X}$ matrix has full column rank, the OLS estimates exist and will still be the best linear unbiased estimates. This property, however, is now cold comfort since the sampling variances of the estimates increase alarmingly with rising collinearity. To prove this in the general case, partition the $\mathbf{X}$ matrix as

$$\mathbf{X} = [\mathbf{x}_i \quad \mathbf{X}_i]$$

where $\mathbf{x}_i$ = column vector of observations on the ith explanatory variable
$\mathbf{X}_i$ = submatrix of observations on the $k-1$ other explanatory variables

Then

$$\mathbf{X}'\mathbf{X} = \begin{bmatrix} \mathbf{x}_i'\mathbf{x}_i & \mathbf{x}_i'\mathbf{X}_i \\ \mathbf{X}_i'\mathbf{x}_i & \mathbf{X}_i'\mathbf{X}_i \end{bmatrix}$$

Applying Eq. (4-68), the leading term in $(\mathbf{X}'\mathbf{X})^{-1}$ is

$$\left[(\mathbf{x}_i'\mathbf{x}_i) - \mathbf{x}_i'\mathbf{X}_i(\mathbf{X}_i'\mathbf{X}_i)^{-1}(\mathbf{X}_i'\mathbf{x}_i)\right]^{-1} = (\mathbf{x}_i'\mathbf{M}_i\mathbf{x}_i)^{-1}$$

where

$$\mathbf{M}_i = \mathbf{I} - \mathbf{X}_i(\mathbf{X}_i'\mathbf{X}_i)^{-1}\mathbf{X}_i'$$

Thus the sampling variance of the OLS estimate of β_i is

$$\text{var}(b_i) = \frac{\sigma^2}{\mathbf{x}_i'\mathbf{M}_i\mathbf{x}_i} \tag{6-72}$$

But from Eq. (5-54) it is seen that

$$\mathbf{x}_i'\mathbf{M}_i\mathbf{x}_i = \begin{array}{l}\text{residual sum of squares from the regression of the } i\text{th explanatory} \\ \text{variable on the other } k-1 \text{ explanatory variables}\end{array}$$

The residual sum of squares decreases with increasing collinearity between the ith explanatory variable and the remaining explanatory variables, and thus the sampling variance of b_i increases. It is clear from Eq. (6-72) that not all coefficients will be affected similarly by collinearity. The denominators in the k sampling variances are the residual sums of squares from the multiple regressions of each explanatory variable in turn on all the other explanatory variables, and these can vary considerably from one to another, as is illustrated in the following numerical examples.

Suppose we have three explanatory variables X_2, X_3, and X_4, all measured in deviation form. We show four illustrative $\mathbf{X'X}$ matrices, and in each case the determinant, the inverse, and the values of the squared multiple correlation coefficients obtained when each explanatory variable in turn is regressed on the remaining explanatory variables.

	$\mathbf{X'X}$	$(\mathbf{X'X})^{-1}$	$R^2_{2.34}$	$R^2_{3.24}$	$R^2_{4.23}$
1.	$\begin{bmatrix} 10 & 0 & 0 \\ 0 & 5 & 0 \\ 0 & 0 & 1 \end{bmatrix}$ det = 50	$\begin{bmatrix} 0.1 & 0 & 0 \\ 0 & 0.2 & 0 \\ 0 & 0 & 1 \end{bmatrix}$	0	0	0
2.	$\begin{bmatrix} 10 & 5 & 2 \\ 5 & 5 & 2 \\ 2 & 2 & 1 \end{bmatrix}$ det = 5	$\begin{bmatrix} 0.2 & -0.2 & 0 \\ -0.2 & 1.2 & -2.0 \\ 0 & -2.0 & 5.0 \end{bmatrix}$	0.5000	0.8333	0.8000
3.	$\begin{bmatrix} 10 & 6 & 3 \\ 6 & 5 & 2 \\ 3 & 2 & 1 \end{bmatrix}$ det = 1	$\begin{bmatrix} 1.0 & 0 & -3.0 \\ 0 & 1.0 & -2.0 \\ -3.0 & -2.0 & 14.0 \end{bmatrix}$	0.9000	0.8000	0.9286
4.	$\begin{bmatrix} 10 & 7 & 1.5 \\ 7 & 5 & 1 \\ 1.5 & 1 & 1 \end{bmatrix}$ det = 0.75	$\begin{bmatrix} 5.3 & -7.3 & -0.7 \\ -7.3 & 10.3 & 0.7 \\ -0.7 & 0.7 & 1.3 \end{bmatrix}$	0.9812	0.9802	0.2500

Case 1 shows perfectly orthogonal variables. The sampling variances are given by σ^2 times the elements in the principal diagonal of $(\mathbf{X}'\mathbf{X})^{-1}$. In the orthogonal case these variances are inversely proportional to the amount of variation in the corresponding explanatory variable. For example, X_2 displays 10 times the variation of X_4, and the sampling variance of its coefficient is one-tenth of that for the coefficient of X_4. To standardize the comparisons, the elements in the principal diagonal of $\mathbf{X}'\mathbf{X}$ have been kept constant throughout, but the cases display increasing collinearity, as reflected in the declining value of the determinant. In case 2 the sampling variances are all larger than in case 1, but they still retain the same order in that

$$\text{var}(b_2) < \text{var}(b_3) < \text{var}(b_4)$$

However, they have been increased by varying factors. We notice that var(b_4) is now 25 times var(b_2), contrasted with 10 times in the orthogonal case. Case 3 shows a large increase in var(b_2), which is now as large as var(b_3). Case 4 is the most interesting of all in that var(b_4) is now the smallest of the three sampling variances, and indeed it is not much larger than in the orthogonal case, whereas var(b_2) and var(b_3) are each more than 50 times as large as in the orthogonal case.

Careful study of the R^2's will show that there is an association between the size of R^2 and the extent to which the corresponding sampling variance is increased over the orthogonal case. The relationship is, in fact, a precise one and may be set out as follows: Let

TSS_i = total sum of squared deviations for X_i

RSS_i = residual sum of squares when X_i is regressed on the other $k - 1$ explanatory variables

R_i^2 = square of multiple correlation coefficient from the same regression

$$= 1 - \frac{\text{RSS}_i}{\text{TSS}_i}$$

Then Eq. (6-72) may be rewritten as

$$\text{var}(b_i) = \frac{\sigma^2}{\text{RSS}_i} = \frac{\sigma^2}{\text{TSS}_i(1 - R_i^2)}$$

Letting b_{io} denote the estimate of β_i in the orthogonal case,

$$\text{var}(b_{io}) = \frac{\sigma^2}{\text{TSS}_i}$$

Thus, if TSS_i is held constant, the magnification of the sampling variance with increasing collinearity is given by

$$\frac{\text{var}(b_i)}{\text{var}(b_{io})} = \frac{1}{1 - R_i^2} \tag{6-73}$$

The orthogonal case is not meant to be a feasible target, but is used as a

Table 6-12 Magnification of sampling variances

R_i^2	0.5	0.8	0.9	0.95	0.96	0.97	0.98	0.99	0.999
$\dfrac{\text{var}(b_i)}{\text{var}(b_{io})}$	2	5	10	20	25	33	50	100	1000

benchmark from which to measure the relative magnification of the sampling variance of different coefficients. Some illustrative calculations from Eq. (6-73) are shown in Table 6-12, and the graph of the function is drawn in Fig. 6-6.

As the table and the figure show, the relationship is highly nonlinear, and the magnification factor increases dramatically as R_i^2 exceeds 0.9. The formula also reveals why different coefficients fare differently in a regression. For example, in case 4 the magnification effect was very serious for b_2 and b_3 and almost negligible for b_4, which is exactly in line with the pattern of R^2's. In that data X_2 and X_3 are highly correlated with one another, but X_4 is not closely correlated with either X_2 or X_3, or with any linear combination of them.

The three main effects already listed for the case of two explanatory variables will thus carry over to the general case, namely

- Very large sampling variances
- Greater covariances
- Great sensitivity of estimated coefficients to small data changes

A common result is to find regressions possibly with a very high overall R^2, but

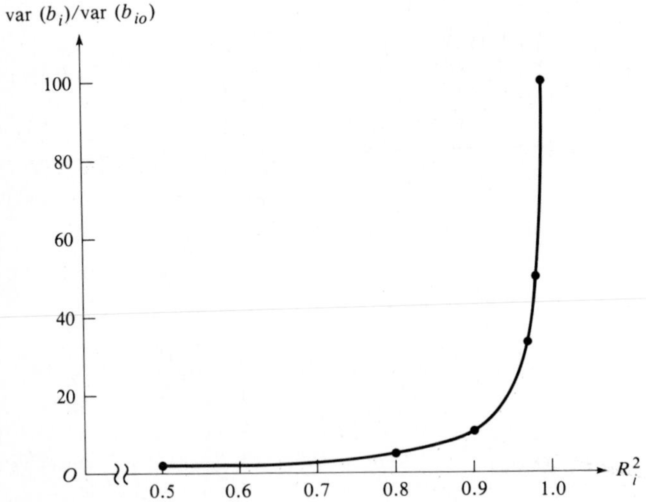

Figure 6-6

with some (or many) individual coefficients apparently insignificant. The high R^2 arises when the $\mathbf{y}$ vector is close to the hyperplane generated by the $\mathbf{x}_i$ vectors and the apparently insignificant coefficients arise because the $\mathbf{x}_i$ vectors are nearly linearly dependent. It is also possible to find a high R^2 and highly significant t values on individual coefficients, even though multicollinearity is serious. This can arise if individual coefficients happen to be numerically well in excess of the true value, so that the effect still shows up in spite of the inflated standard error and/or because the true value itself is so large that even an estimate on the downside still shows up as significant. The multicollinearity would likely show up in varying parameter estimates as some sample observations are dropped or added. For any regression, however, comparison of the R_i^2's shows which coefficients are likely to be most seriously affected by collinearity.

Detection

Computer programs often print out $|\mathbf{X'X}|$. As our numerical examples illustrate, the determinant declines in value with increasing collinearity, tending to zero as collinearity becomes exact. While a useful warning signal, we have no calibration scale for assessing what is serious and what is very serious, and again it gives no guide to the relative effects on individual coefficients. Similar remarks apply to the computation of the eigenvalues of $\mathbf{X'X}$. Since

$$|\mathbf{X'X}| = \lambda_1 \lambda_2 \cdots \lambda_k$$

a small determinant means that some (or many) of the eigenvalues will be small. But again knowledge of the eigenvalues is of little direct help in assessing effects on individual coefficients.†

The most useful single diagnostic guide is the R_i^2's, as shown above. In a sense TSS_i determines the *minimum* sampling variance that might be achieved for b_i in that in the orthogonal case

$$\mathrm{var}(b_{io}) = \frac{\sigma^2}{\mathrm{TSS}_i}$$

Any collinearity in the sample data will *raise all sampling variances*, but the relative magnifications for different coefficients will be indicated by a comparison of the R_i^2's.

Belsley, Kuh, and Welsch suggest the combined use of two diagnostic tools to detect which coefficients are most likely to be affected by the collinearity.‡ The first statistic is the *condition number* of the $\mathbf{X}$ matrix, defined by

$$\kappa(\mathbf{X}) = \frac{\sqrt{\lambda_{\max}}}{\sqrt{\lambda_{\min}}}$$

† The precise relationship between $\mathrm{var}(b_i)$ and the λ's is derived below.

‡ D. A. Belsley, E. Kuh, and R. E. Welsch, *Regression Diagnostics, Identifying Influential Data and Sources of Collinearity*, Wiley, New York, 1980, chap. 3.

where λ_{max} and λ_{min} denote the maximum and minimum eigenvalues of $\mathbf{X'X}$, respectively. If the $\mathbf{X}$ matrix has been standardized so that each column has unit length, then $\kappa(\mathbf{X})$ is unity when the columns of $\mathbf{X}$ are orthogonal and rises above unity with collinearity between the columns. Various applications with experimental and actual data sets suggest that condition numbers in the range of 20 to 30 are probably indicative of serious collinearity problems, and a fortiori for numbers in excess of that range. A *condition index* may be computed for each eigenvalue, starting at unity for $\lambda_i = \lambda_{min}$ and rising to $\kappa(\mathbf{X})$ for $\lambda_i = \lambda_{max}$. Thus a given data matrix may yield one or more condition indexes in excess of a "danger" level. The second and related diagnostic tool is the *regression coefficient variance decomposition*. If $\mathbf{X}$ is $n \times k$ and $\mathbf{V}$ is the $k \times k$ matrix that diagonalized $\mathbf{X'X}$, then

$$(\mathbf{X'X})\mathbf{V} = \mathbf{V\Lambda}$$

where $\mathbf{\Lambda}$ is the diagonal matrix of the eigenvalues of $\mathbf{X'X}$. Thus

$$\text{var}(\mathbf{b}) = \sigma^2(\mathbf{X'X})^{-1} = \sigma^2\mathbf{V\Lambda}^{-1}\mathbf{V}'$$

and

$$\text{var}(b_i) = \sigma^2\left(\frac{v_{i1}^2}{\lambda_1} + \frac{v_{i2}^2}{\lambda_2} + \cdots + \frac{v_{ik}^2}{\lambda_k}\right) \qquad i = 1, \ldots, k$$

where $v_{i1}, v_{i2}, \ldots, v_{ik}$ are the elements of the ith row of $\mathbf{V}$. From this one may compute the *proportions* of $\text{var}(b_i)$ associated with each λ. The two-step procedure recommended by Belsley, Kuh, and Welsch is

1. Compute the λ_i's and identify any λ_i which gives a condition index in excess of the "danger" level (say, 20 to 30).
2. For each of those selected λ_i's inspect the proportions of the sampling variance of each b_j associated with that eigenvalue. Coefficients with proportions in excess of, say, 0.50 are likely to have been adversely affected by the collinearity in the $\mathbf{X}$ matrix. Reference should be made to Belsley, Kuh, and Welsch for detailed examples of the technique.

Remedies

More data is no help in multicollinearity if it is simply "more of the same." What matters is the structure of the $\mathbf{X'X}$ matrix, and this will only be improved by adding data which are less collinear than before. However, there is often no easy way for an econometrician to get better data. The data are produced by the functioning of the economic system, and the collinearities reflect the nature of that system. One hopeful approach in some areas is the joint use of both time-series and cross-section data, which we will take up in Chap. 10. A related approach is to feed in estimates of some parameters which may be available from an independent, relevant study. The classic example is the analysis of demand functions, where an estimate of the income elasticity obtained from cross-section studies is fed into the estimation of the price elasticities from a time-series sample.

This is a *sequential* approach using one set of cross-section data and another set of time-series data, rather than a joint (or simultaneous) set. The latter requires that the observations relate to a common set of decision units.

The general framework for the incorporation of prior estimates of some parameters may be set out as follows. Partition $\mathbf{X}$, $\boldsymbol{\beta}$, and $\mathbf{b}$ as

$$\mathbf{X} = [\mathbf{X}_r \quad \mathbf{X}_s] \qquad \boldsymbol{\beta} = \begin{bmatrix} \boldsymbol{\beta}_r \\ \boldsymbol{\beta}_s \end{bmatrix} \qquad \mathbf{b} = \begin{bmatrix} \mathbf{b}_r \\ \mathbf{b}_s \end{bmatrix}$$

where $\mathbf{X}_r$ is the $n \times r$ submatrix consisting of the first r columns of $\mathbf{X}$, $\mathbf{X}_s$ is the submatrix consisting of the remaining $s = k - r$ columns, and $\boldsymbol{\beta}$ and $\mathbf{b}$ are partitioned conformably. Suppose that a previous study provides the estimated $\mathbf{b}_s$ vector with an estimated variance matrix $\mathbf{V}_s$. We will assume $\mathbf{b}_s$ to be unbiased, that is,

$$E(\mathbf{b}_s) = \boldsymbol{\beta}_s$$

and we will take $\mathbf{V}_s$ to be approximately the true variance matrix

$$E\{(\mathbf{b}_s - \boldsymbol{\beta}_s)(\mathbf{b}_s - \boldsymbol{\beta}_s)'\}$$

The problem now is to estimate the remaining unknown parameters in $\boldsymbol{\beta}_r$. The procedure is to "correct" $\mathbf{y}$ for the $\mathbf{X}_s$ data by forming

$$\mathbf{y}_* = \mathbf{y} - \mathbf{X}_s\mathbf{b}_s \tag{6-74}$$

and then perform an OLS regression of $\mathbf{y}_*$ on $\mathbf{X}_r$. The result is

$$\mathbf{b}_r = (\mathbf{X}_r'\mathbf{X}_r)^{-1}\mathbf{X}_r'\mathbf{y}_* \tag{6-75}$$

Writing

$$\mathbf{y} = \mathbf{X}_r\boldsymbol{\beta}_r + \mathbf{X}_s\boldsymbol{\beta}_s + \mathbf{u}$$

and substituting in Eqs. (6-74) and (6-75) gives

$$\mathbf{b}_r = \boldsymbol{\beta}_r + (\mathbf{X}_r'\mathbf{X}_r)^{-1}\mathbf{X}_r'\mathbf{u} - (\mathbf{X}_r'\mathbf{X}_r)^{-1}\mathbf{X}_r'\mathbf{X}_s(\mathbf{b}_s - \boldsymbol{\beta}_s)$$

Taking expectations

$$E(\mathbf{b}_r) = \boldsymbol{\beta}_r$$

since $E(\mathbf{u}) = \mathbf{0}$ and $E(\mathbf{b}_s) = \boldsymbol{\beta}_s$.† Then

$$\begin{aligned} \text{var}(\mathbf{b}_r) &= E\{(\mathbf{b}_r - \boldsymbol{\beta}_r)(\mathbf{b}_r - \boldsymbol{\beta}_r)'\} \\ &= \sigma^2(\mathbf{X}_r'\mathbf{X}_r)^{-1} + (\mathbf{X}_r'\mathbf{X}_r)^{-1}\mathbf{X}_r'\mathbf{X}_s\mathbf{V}_s\mathbf{X}_s'\mathbf{X}_r(\mathbf{X}_r'\mathbf{X}_r)^{-1} \end{aligned} \tag{6-76}$$

on the assumption that the two sets of data are independent. The first term in Eq. (6-76) is the conventional variance matrix for an OLS regression involving $\mathbf{X}_r$, and the second term shows the elements by which this must be adjusted because of the sampling variation in the $\mathbf{b}_s$ coefficients, used in calculating $\mathbf{y}_*$. The only

† Notice that this operation involves taking expectations over two different sets of data. $E(\mathbf{u})$ refers to expectations over the current sample data and $E(\mathbf{b}_s)$ to expectations over the data underlying the prior estimate $\mathbf{b}_s$.

remaining practical problem is the estimation of σ^2. Defining

$$\mathbf{e} = \mathbf{y}_* - \mathbf{X}_r\mathbf{b}_r = \mathbf{y} - \mathbf{X}_r\mathbf{b}_r - \mathbf{X}_s\mathbf{b}_s$$

the estimate is $\mathbf{e}'\mathbf{e}/(n-k)$, where we divide by $n-k$ rather than by $n-r$ since $\mathbf{e}$ depends on k estimated parameters.

Some authors suggest dealing with multicollinearity in a rather mechanical and purely numerical fashion. For example, a currently fashionable technique is that of *ridge regression*.† The ridge estimate of $\boldsymbol{\beta}$ is defined as

$$\mathbf{b}_R = (\mathbf{X}'\mathbf{X} + c\mathbf{I})^{-1}\mathbf{X}'\mathbf{y} \tag{6-77}$$

where $c > 0$ is an arbitrary constant. The rationale for the estimator may easily be seen by referring back to the $\mathbf{X}'\mathbf{X}$ matrices given in the numerical illustrations. Increasing the diagonal elements and leaving the off-diagonal elements unchanged may be expected to reverse the sequence of effects shown in those examples where the off-diagonal elements have been increased relative to the diagonal elements. It follows directly from Eq. (6-77) that

$$E(\mathbf{b}_R) = (\mathbf{X}'\mathbf{X} + c\mathbf{I})^{-1}\mathbf{X}'\mathbf{X}\boldsymbol{\beta} \tag{6-78}$$

and

$$\text{var}(\mathbf{b}_R) = \sigma^2(\mathbf{X}'\mathbf{X} + c\mathbf{I})^{-1}\mathbf{X}'\mathbf{X}(\mathbf{X}'\mathbf{X} + c\mathbf{I})^{-1} \tag{6-79}$$

The ridge estimator is thus biased, but it may be shown that the variances of the elements of $\mathbf{b}_R$ are less than those of the OLS estimator.‡ This raises the possibility that a ridge estimator may have a smaller mean-square error (MSE) than the OLS estimator.§ The main difficulty centers on the selection of a numerical value for the arbitrary scalar c. In their original article Hoërl and Kennard suggested trying various values of c in an attempt to see if the $\mathbf{b}_R$ vector stabilized. Schmidt, in the source cited, establishes conditions for c to minimize $E(\mathbf{b}_R - \boldsymbol{\beta})'(\mathbf{b}_R - \boldsymbol{\beta})$, the sum of the MSEs of the ridge estimators. These conditions, however, depend on unknown parameters. Using sample estimates of these parameters to determine c would yield an estimator with complicated and as yet unknown sampling properties, so that inferences about $\boldsymbol{\beta}$ could not be made. The ridge technique essentially consists of an arbitrary numerical adjustment to the sample data, and one does not really know how to interpret the resultant estimators.¶

† See A. E. Hoerl and R. W. Kennard, "Ridge Regression: Biased Estimation for Non-Orthogonal Problems," *Technometrics*, 1970, pp. 55–68, for an exposition of the theory; and A. E. Hoerl and R. W. Kennard, "Ridge Regression: Applications to Nonorthogonal Problems," *Technometrics*, 1970, pp. 69–82, for two illustrations.

‡ See P. Schmidt, *Econometrics*, Marcel Dekker, New York, 1976, pp. 48–55, for this result and a very useful discussion of the theory of ridge regression.

§ For a definition of MSE see Chap. 2, pages 27–28.

¶ For further discussion see the series of papers in *Journal of the American Statistical Association*, **75**, 1980, pp. 74–103.

Another approach to improving the MSE involves the suggestion that one or more explanatory variables be dropped in order to improve the MSE of the remaining coefficients. To illustrate the approach consider just a three-variable model,

$$y = \beta_2 x_2 + \beta_3 x_3 + u \tag{6-80}$$

where the variables have been expressed in deviation form.† Let us denote the coefficients resulting from the application of OLS to Eq. (6-80) as

$$b_{12.3} = \text{OLS estimate of } \beta_2$$

$$b_{13.2} = \text{OLS estimate of } \beta_3$$

From the properties of the OLS model we know these estimators are unbiased and their sampling variances are‡

$$\text{var}(b_{12.3}) = \frac{\sigma^2}{\Sigma x_2^2(1 - r_{23}^2)} \tag{6-81}$$

$$\text{var}(b_{13.2}) = \frac{\sigma^2}{\Sigma x_3^2(1 - r_{23}^2)} \tag{6-82}$$

Clearly, as r_{23}^2 gets close to unity, both sampling variances increase dramatically. Now consider the simple regression of y on x_2 and denote the slope coefficient by

$$b_{12} = \frac{\Sigma y x_2}{\Sigma x_2^2}$$

Substituting for y from Eq. (6-80) gives

$$b_{12} = \beta_2 + b_{32}\beta_3 + \frac{\Sigma x_2 u}{\Sigma x_2^2} \tag{6-83}$$

where

$$b_{32} = \frac{\Sigma x_2 x_3}{\Sigma x_2^2}$$

† Strictly speaking, when the relation is written in deviation form, the disturbance term is $u - \bar{u}$, but this slight complication has no effect on any of the derivations in which we are interested and so may be ignored.

‡ These are derived from the general formula

$$\text{var}\begin{bmatrix} b_{12.3} \\ b_{13.2} \end{bmatrix} = \sigma^2(\mathbf{X}'\mathbf{X})^{-1} = \frac{\sigma^2}{\Sigma x_2^2 \Sigma x_3^2 - (\Sigma x_2 x_3)^2}\begin{bmatrix} \Sigma x_3^2 & -\Sigma x_2 x_3 \\ -\Sigma x_2 x_3 & \Sigma x_2^2 \end{bmatrix}$$

which gives

$$\text{var}(b_{12.3}) = \frac{\sigma^2 \Sigma x_3^2}{\Sigma x_2^2 \Sigma x_3^2 - (\Sigma x_2 x_3)^2} = \frac{\sigma^2}{\Sigma x_2^2(1 - r_{23}^2)}$$

where r_{23} is the simple correlation coefficient between x_2 and x_3. A similar derivation yields the result for $\text{var}(b_{13.2})$.

From Eq. (6-83) it follows that

$$E(b_{12}) = \beta_2 + b_{32}\beta_3 \tag{6-84}$$

and†

$$\operatorname{var}(b_{12}) = \frac{\sigma^2}{\Sigma x_2^2} \tag{6-85}$$

Thus b_{12} is a biased estimator of β_2, unless x_2 and x_3 are orthogonal so that $b_{32} = 0$. However, comparison of Eqs. (6-81) and (6-85) shows that b_{12} has a smaller sampling variance than $b_{12.3}$. The possibility then exists of a tradeoff between bias and variance. The crucial question is under what conditions b_{12} may have a smaller MSE than $b_{12.3}$.

As shown in Eq. (2-23),

$$\text{MSE} = \text{sampling variance} + \text{square of bias}$$

Thus

$$\text{MSE}(b_{12}) = \frac{\sigma^2}{\Sigma x_2^2} + b_{32}^2\beta_3^2$$

and

$$\text{MSE}(b_{12.3}) = \frac{\sigma^2}{\Sigma x_2^2(1 - r_{23}^2)}$$

A little algebra then shows‡

$$\frac{\text{MSE}(b_{12})}{\text{MSE}(b_{12.3})} = 1 + r_{23}^2(\tau^2 - 1) \tag{6-86}$$

where

$$\tau^2 = \frac{\beta_3^2}{\sigma^2/\Sigma x_3^2(1 - r_{23}^2)} = \frac{\beta_3^2}{\operatorname{var}(b_{13.2})} \tag{6-87}$$

This τ^2 statistic is the ratio of the square of the *true* (but unknown) β_3 to the *true* (not the estimated) variance of $b_{13.2}$. From Eq. (6-86), if $\tau^2 < 1$,

$$\text{MSE}(b_{12}) < \text{MSE}(b_{12.3})$$

Thus if one were mainly interested in obtaining as accurate an estimate as possible of β_2, and if one felt confident that τ^2 was less than unity, it might seem sensible to drop x_3 from the regression and carry out a simple regression of y on

† Notice that, in this case, $\operatorname{var}(b_{12})$ is the variance about a *biased* expectation. From first principles

$$\operatorname{var}(b_{12}) = E\{[b_{12} - E(b_{12})^2]\} = E\{[b_{12} - \beta_2 - b_{32}\beta_3]^2\}$$

$$= E\left\{\left(\frac{\Sigma x_2 u}{\Sigma x_2^2}\right)^2\right\} = \frac{\sigma^2}{\Sigma x_2^2}$$

‡ See Problem 6-9.

x_2. The snag of course is that τ^2 is unknown, and the consequences of mistakes about its value could be fairly serious. If, for example, β_3 is three times its true standard error and r_{23}^2 is around 0.8, then MSE(b_{12}) will be over seven times as large as MSE($b_{12.3}$).

In view of Eq. (6-86) it might seem plausible to drop x_3 from the regression if the *estimated t* value is numerically less than 1, that is, if

$$F = t^2 = \frac{b_{13.2}^2}{s^2/\Sigma x_3^2\left(1 - r_{23}^2\right)} < 1 \tag{6-88}$$

Thus one may define a *conditional omitted variable* (COV) estimator of β_2 as

$$b_{\text{COV}} = \begin{cases} b_{12} & \text{if } F < 1 \\ b_{12.3} & \text{if } F \geq 1 \end{cases} \tag{6-89}$$

Other COV estimators may be defined using critical F values other than unity. Feldstein has investigated the MSE of b_{COV} relative to MSE($b_{12.3}$) for various values of r_{23}, various values of τ, and also for several critical F values, including unity and the conventional $F_{0.95}$.† When $|\tau| > 1$, sampling fluctuations can still give $F < 1$, and consequently the COV estimators are inferior to OLS. Feldstein's main conclusion is

> *OLS is preferable to any of the COV estimators unless the researcher has a strong prior belief that* $\tau < 1$.‡

Feldstein also investigates the properties of a *weighted* (WTD) estimator which is simply a linear combination of b_{12} and $b_{12.3}$. We define

$$b_{\text{WTD}} = \lambda b_{12.3} + (1 - \lambda) b_{12} \tag{6-90}$$

It may be shown that the value of λ which minimizes MSE (b_{WTD}) is§

$$\lambda^* = \frac{\tau^2}{1 + \tau^2} \tag{6-91}$$

This is the same unknown τ^2 statistic already defined in Eq. (6-87). The WTD estimator could be made operational by computing the t^2 statistic defined in Eq. (6-88), hence computing

$$\lambda = \frac{t^2}{1 + t^2}$$

and substituting this value of λ in Eq. (6-90). Feldstein's simulation experiments show the WTD estimator to be generally superior to the various COV estimators in his study, but to be inferior to OLS when $|\tau| > 1.5$. Thus exhaustive study of

† M. S. Feldstein, "Multicollinearity and the Mean Square Error of Alternative Estimators," *Econometrica*, **41**, 1973, pp. 337–346. See especially Tables I, II, and III.

‡ M. S. Feldstein, op. cit., p. 344.

§ See M. S. Feldstein, op. cit., or work it out directly in Problem 6-10.

the three-variable case suggests that, even in the presence of high correlation between x_2 and x_3, the best procedure is probably the straightforward OLS regression of y on x_2 and x_3. Only if the investigator has really strong prior beliefs that β_3 is less than $\sqrt{\text{var}(b_{13.2})}$, should x_3 be dropped from the regression. Even this nonstartling advice to drop a variable when you are fairly sure its coefficient is "small" is only helpful if the investigator is mainly interested in the other coefficient, β_2.

Even though these results on the three-variable case are not very helpful, considerable work has been done on extensions of the approach to the k-variable case. As we have already seen in Chap. 5, setting a coefficient or group of coefficients at zero is a special case of imposing a set of linear restrictions on the coefficients. Thus the question arises whether the imposition of a set of restrictions will result in estimators which are better in some MSE sense than the unrestricted OLS estimators, even though the restrictions may not, in fact, be true.

The first problem is the generalization of the MSE criterion to a number of estimators. Consider the usual linear model

$$\mathbf{y} = \mathbf{X\beta} + \mathbf{u}$$

with the set of $q\ (\leq k)$ restrictions embodied in

$$\mathbf{R\beta} = \mathbf{r}$$

As seen in Eq. (6-5), the estimator embodying these restrictions is

$$\mathbf{b}_* = \mathbf{b} + (\mathbf{X'X})^{-1}\mathbf{R'}\left[\mathbf{R}(\mathbf{X'X})^{-1}\mathbf{R'}\right]^{-1}(\mathbf{r} - \mathbf{Rb})$$

where

$$\mathbf{b} = (\mathbf{X'X})^{-1}\mathbf{X'y}$$

is the unrestricted OLS estimator. We may define the *MSE matrix* for $\mathbf{b}_*$ as

$$\text{MSE}(\mathbf{b}_*) = E\{(b_* - \boldsymbol{\beta})(\mathbf{b}_* - \boldsymbol{\beta})'\} \tag{6-92}$$

This is a symmetric $k \times k$ matrix with the MSEs of the individual coefficients displayed on the principal diagonal. The typical off-diagonal term is

$$E(b_{*i} - \beta_i)(b_{*j} - \beta_j) \qquad i \neq j$$

which is essentially a covariance defined in terms of the true β_i, β_j values rather than in terms of the expected values of the estimators. One might then say that $\mathbf{b}_*$ is better in MSE than $\mathbf{b}$ if

$$\mathbf{c'}\text{MSE}(\mathbf{b}_*)\mathbf{c} \leq \mathbf{c'}\text{MSE}(\mathbf{b})\mathbf{c} \tag{6-93}$$

for any nonnull k-element vector $\mathbf{c}$.† This is a very strong criterion, requiring that

† Notice that Eq. (6-93) is equivalent to the condition MSE($\mathbf{c'b}_*$) $\leq$ MSE($\mathbf{c'b}$) for

$$\text{MSE}(\mathbf{c'b}_*) = E\{\mathbf{c'}(\mathbf{b}_* - \boldsymbol{\beta})^2\} = E\{\mathbf{c'}(\mathbf{b}_* - \boldsymbol{\beta})(\mathbf{b}_* - \boldsymbol{\beta})'\mathbf{c}\} = \mathbf{c'}\text{MSE}(\mathbf{b}_*)\mathbf{c}$$

and similarly for MSE($\mathbf{c'b}$). Thus Eq. (6-93) requires that the MSE of any linear combination of the elements of $\mathbf{b}_*$ be no greater than the MSE of the same linear combination of the elements of $\mathbf{b}$.

any quadratic form in MSE($\mathbf{b}_*$) be less than or equal to the corresponding quadratic form in MSE($\mathbf{b}$). A much weaker criterion would be

$$\operatorname{tr} \text{MSE}(\mathbf{b}_*) \leq \operatorname{tr} \text{MSE}(\mathbf{b}) \tag{6-94}$$

that is, that the *sum* of the MSEs of the restricted estimators be less than or equal to the *sum* of the MSEs of the unrestricted estimators.

The problem of determining the conditions under which Eq. (6-93) or Eq. (6-94) might hold has been investigated in a number of papers by Wallace, Toro-Vizcarrondo, and Goodnight.† It can be shown that the restricted estimators (even when the restrictions are incorrect) will have smaller variances than the unrestricted OLS estimators. However, taking expectations of Eq. (6-5) shows that

$$E(\mathbf{b}_*) = \boldsymbol{\beta} + (\mathbf{X}'\mathbf{X})^{-1}\mathbf{R}'\left[\mathbf{R}(\mathbf{X}'\mathbf{X})^{-1}\mathbf{R}'\right]^{-1}(\mathbf{r} - \mathbf{R}\boldsymbol{\beta})$$

so that $\mathbf{b}_*$ will be a biased estimator if the restrictions are not correct. This is a generalization of the tradeoff between bias and variance in the previous simple example. Wallace and Toro-Vizcarrondo show that the strong MSE criterion (6-93) will be satisfied if‡

$$\lambda = \frac{(\mathbf{r} - \mathbf{R}\boldsymbol{\beta})'\left[\mathbf{R}(\mathbf{X}'\mathbf{X})^{-1}\mathbf{R}'\right]^{-1}(\mathbf{r} - \mathbf{R}\boldsymbol{\beta})}{2\sigma^2} \leq \frac{1}{2} \tag{6-95}$$

As in the previous simple case, this condition involves the true but unknown $\boldsymbol{\beta}$ vector and the unknown σ^2. If these are replaced by their OLS estimators and the resultant value of the statistic in Eq. (6-95), denoted by $\hat{\lambda}$, it is easy to see that

$$F = \frac{2\hat{\lambda}}{q}$$

† C. Toro-Vizcarrondo and T. D. Wallace, "A Test of the Mean Square Error Criterion for Restrictions in Linear Regression," *Journal of the American Statistical Association*, 1968, pp. 558–572; T. D. Wallace and C. E. Toro-Vizcarrondo, "Tables for the Mean Square Error Test for Exact Linear Restrictions in Regression," *Journal of the American Statistical Association*, 1969, pp. 1649–1663; T. D. Wallace, "Weaker Criteria and Tests for Linear Restrictions in Regression," *Econometrica*, **40**, 1972, pp. 689–698; J. Goodnight and T. D. Wallace, "Operational Techniques and Tables for Making Weak MSE Tests for Restrictions in Regressions," *Econometrica*, **40**, 1972, pp. 699–709.

‡ Notice that dropping x_3 from the model

$$y = \beta_2 x_2 + \beta_3 x_3 + u$$

is equivalent to imposing the restriction

$$[0 \quad 1]\begin{bmatrix}\beta_2 \\ \beta_3\end{bmatrix} = 0$$

and with these specifications of $\mathbf{r}$ and $\mathbf{R}$ condition (6-95) becomes

$$\frac{\beta_3^2}{2\operatorname{var}(b_{13.2})} \leq \frac{1}{2}$$

or $\tau^2 \leq 1$ as derived in Eq. (6-87).

where

$$F = \frac{(\mathbf{e}_*'\mathbf{e}_* - \mathbf{e}'\mathbf{e})/q}{\mathbf{e}'\mathbf{e}/(n-k)}$$

is the sample statistic, defined in Eq. (6-8), for testing the null hypothesis

$$H_0\colon \quad \mathbf{R\beta} = \mathbf{r}$$

When H_0 is true, $\lambda = 0$, and F has the *central F* distribution with q, $n-k$ degrees of freedom. The test of H_0 is made, as we have seen, by comparing the sample F with a preselected critical value from the central F distribution. The basic result of Toro-Vizcarrondo and Wallace (1968) is that when H_0 is *not* true, the F statistic, defined above, follows the *noncentral F* distribution with degrees of freedom q, $n-k$ and noncentrality parameter λ, defined in Eq. (6-95). Thus the test for the improvement in MSE is to compare the sample F statistic with a critical value from the *noncentral* F *distribution with* $\lambda = 0.5$. Critical points of this distribution are tabulated in Wallace and Toro-Vizcarrondo (1969). The practical procedure is as follows:

1. Compute the usual F statistic, based on the difference in the residual sums of squares from the restricted and unrestricted regressions.
2. If $F > F(q, n-k)_{0.95}$, say, in the table by Wallace and Toro-Vizcarrondo, reject the hypothesis that the restricted estimators are better in MSE. If the sample F is less than the critical value, use the restricted estimators.

The above procedure is for the strong MSE criterion, embodied in Eq. (6-93). Wallace (1972) has shown that the weaker MSE criterion (6-94) will be satisfied if

$$\lambda \leq \frac{q}{2}$$

where q is the number of restrictions. The appropriate critical values of F are tabulated in Goodnight and Wallace (1972). As an indication of how these procedures would work, consider the following critical F values, taken from the appropriate tables:

	Noncentrality parameter		
	$\lambda = 0$	$\lambda = 0.5$	$\lambda = q/2$
$F(3, 20)_{0.95}$	3.10	4.06	5.73

If one were testing H_0: $\mathbf{R\beta} = \mathbf{r}$ at the 5 percent level with $q = 3$ and $n - k = 20$, H_0 would be rejected if the sample F exceeded 3.10, and one would conclude that the restrictions were not true. However, a sample F as high as 4.06 in the case of the strong MSE criterion, and as high as 5.73 in the case of the weak MSE criterion, would still lead to the imposition of the restrictions and the use of the restricted estimator on the Wallace criterion.

These procedures, as in the COV estimator of Eq. (6-89), rest on a prior significance test. Their actual performance in repeated applications would need to be evaluated as Feldstein did for the COV estimator in the three-variable case. It is also doubtful whether, in practice, econometricians would wish to impose restrictions, which seem unlikely to be true, in order to improve the estimators in the MSE sense. For example, suppose the estimation of a production function leads to the rejection of the hypothesis of constant returns to scale, but the sample F value does not exceed the critical value for the weak MSE condition. The restricted estimates of capital and labor elasticities may have lower MSEs than the unrestricted estimates, but they will sum to unity and incorrectly indicate constant returns to scale. The investigator must make a value judgment as to whether this kind of tradeoff is desirable.

The upshot of this discussion of multicollinearity is not very comforting. Some data sets contain very little information and do not enable one to disentangle the relative effects of variables with much precision. The multiple correlation coefficients among the explanatory variables will indicate those coefficients which are likely to be most adversely affected by the collinearity, and one should not readily drop these variables from a regression because of low t statistics. Restricted estimators may have greater precision, but at the cost of a bias. Only the accumulation of more and better data sets will yield more precise estimates of complex interrelationships.

6-6 SPECIFICATION ERROR

Strictly speaking the term specification error covers any mistake in the set of assumptions underpinning a model and the associated inference procedures, but it has come to be used particularly for errors in specifying the data matrix **X**.† There are two problems involved in specifying **X**. The first is knowing which variables (such as income, relative prices, etc.) to include, and the second is in what mathematical form each variable is to be included. So far we have blithely assumed such knowledge to be readily available. In practice it is not. Economic theory can normally indicate the set of explanatory variables corresponding to any assumed model (utility maximization, cost minimization, etc.), but theory cannot usually indicate the precise form of the relationship. In less favorable situations where there is no clearly articulated theory there may be no clear guide to relevant explanatory variables. On top of all this one may not be able to obtain measurements on appropriate variables and, hence, have to use proxy variables in their place.

To establish the effects of misspecification of **X**, let us suppose that the true model is

$$\mathbf{y} = \mathbf{X}\boldsymbol{\beta} + \mathbf{u} \tag{6-96}$$

† See H. Theil, "Specification Errors and the Estimation of Economic Relationships," *Review of the International Statistical Institute*, **25**, 1957, pp. 41–51.

 HYE JUNG LEE

with

$$E(\mathbf{u}) = \mathbf{0} \qquad \text{and} \qquad E(\mathbf{uu}') = \sigma^2\mathbf{I}$$

The model specified by the investigator is

$$\mathbf{y} = \mathbf{X}_*\boldsymbol{\beta} + \mathbf{u} \tag{6-97}$$

where, of course, some variables may be common to both $\mathbf{X}$ and $\mathbf{X}_*$. The investigator thus computes the estimated coefficient vector

$$\mathbf{b}_* = (\mathbf{X}_*'\mathbf{X}_*)^{-1}\mathbf{X}_*'\mathbf{y}$$

Substituting for $\mathbf{y}$ from Eq. (6-96) gives

$$\mathbf{b}_* = (\mathbf{X}_*'\mathbf{X}_*)^{-1}\mathbf{X}_*'\mathbf{X}\boldsymbol{\beta} + (\mathbf{X}_*'\mathbf{X}_*)^{-1}\mathbf{X}_*'\mathbf{u}$$

Thus

$$E(\mathbf{b}_*) = (\mathbf{X}_*'\mathbf{X}_*)^{-1}\mathbf{X}_*'\mathbf{X}\boldsymbol{\beta} \tag{6-98}$$

and the expectations of the estimated coefficients are seen to be *not* the true population parameters but rather linear combinations of those parameters. We may distinguish a number of different possibilities.

Case 6-1: Exclusion of relevant variables Suppose that the $\mathbf{X}_*$ and $\mathbf{X}$ matrices are

$$\mathbf{X}_* = [\mathbf{x}_1 \quad \mathbf{x}_2 \quad \cdots \quad \mathbf{x}_r] = \mathbf{X}_1$$

$$\mathbf{X} = \left[\mathbf{x}_1 \quad \mathbf{x}_2 \quad \cdots \quad \mathbf{x}_r \vdots \mathbf{x}_{r+1} \quad \cdots \quad \mathbf{x}_k\right] = [\mathbf{X}_1 \quad \mathbf{X}_2]$$

The investigator has correctly included the first r explanatory variables but mistakenly omitted the remaining $k - r$ variables. It follows directly that

$$\begin{aligned}(\mathbf{X}_*'\mathbf{X}_*)^{-1}\mathbf{X}_*'\mathbf{X} &= (\mathbf{X}_1'\mathbf{X}_1)^{-1}[\mathbf{X}_1'\mathbf{X}_1 \quad \mathbf{X}_1'\mathbf{X}_2] \\ &= \left[\mathbf{I}_r \quad (\mathbf{X}_1'\mathbf{X}_1)^{-1}\mathbf{X}_1'\mathbf{X}_2\right]\end{aligned}$$

Thus

$$E(b_{*i}) = \beta_i + a_{i,r+1}\beta_{r+1} + \cdots + a_{ik}\beta_k \qquad i = 1,\ldots,r$$

where $a_{i,r+1},\ldots,a_{i,k}$ are the elements in the ith row of $(\mathbf{X}_1'\mathbf{X}_1)^{-1}\mathbf{X}_1'\mathbf{X}_2$. The columns of this last matrix are seen to be the OLS coefficients obtained when each excluded variable in turn is regressed on the set of included variables. Thus even though the investigator has managed to include a number of the true explanatory variables, their coefficients will be biased, and the bias is seen to be some linear combination of the true coefficients of the excluded variables. This of course destroys the conventional b.l.u.e. property of OLS estimators. The conventional inference procedures are also undermined, not only because of Eq. (6-98), but also because the disturbance variance cannot be correctly estimated. When $\mathbf{y}$ is regressed on $\mathbf{X}_* = \mathbf{X}_1 = [\mathbf{x}_1 \quad \mathbf{x}_2 \quad \cdots \quad \mathbf{x}_r]$, the residual vector is $\mathbf{M}_1\mathbf{y}$, where

$$\mathbf{M}_1 = \mathbf{I} - \mathbf{X}_1(\mathbf{X}_1'\mathbf{X}_1)^{-1}\mathbf{X}_1'$$

is a symmetric idempotent matrix of rank and trace equal to $n - r$. The residual sum of squares is

$$\text{RSS} = \mathbf{y}'\mathbf{M}_1\mathbf{y}$$

Writing Eq. (6-96) in partitioned form as

$$\mathbf{y} = \mathbf{X}_1\boldsymbol{\beta}_1 + \mathbf{X}_2\boldsymbol{\beta}_2 + \mathbf{u}$$

and substituting in RSS gives

$$\text{RSS} = (\mathbf{X}_2\boldsymbol{\beta}_2 + \mathbf{u})'\mathbf{M}_1(\mathbf{X}_2\boldsymbol{\beta}_2 + \mathbf{u})$$

since $\mathbf{M}_1\mathbf{X}_1 = \mathbf{0}$, and so

$$\text{RSS} = \mathbf{u}'\mathbf{M}_1\mathbf{u} + \boldsymbol{\beta}_2'\mathbf{X}_2'\mathbf{M}_1\mathbf{X}_2\boldsymbol{\beta}_2 + 2\boldsymbol{\beta}_2'\mathbf{X}_2'\mathbf{M}_1\mathbf{u}$$

Thus

$$\begin{aligned} E(\text{RSS}) &= E(\mathbf{u}'\mathbf{M}_1\mathbf{u}) + \boldsymbol{\beta}_2'\mathbf{X}_2'\mathbf{M}_1\mathbf{X}_2\boldsymbol{\beta}_2 \\ &= \sigma^2(n-r) + \boldsymbol{\beta}_2'\mathbf{X}_2'\mathbf{M}_1\mathbf{X}_2\boldsymbol{\beta}_2 \end{aligned}$$

and so

$$E\left(\frac{\text{RSS}}{n-r}\right) = \sigma^2 + \frac{1}{n-r}\boldsymbol{\beta}_2'\mathbf{X}_2'\mathbf{M}_1\mathbf{X}_2\boldsymbol{\beta}_2 \tag{6-99}$$

The matrix of the quadratic form in Eq. (6-99) is the matrix containing the sums of squares and the cross products of the residual vectors obtained when each excluded variable in $\mathbf{X}_2$ is regressed on the set of included variables $\mathbf{X}_1$. Apart from a constant divisor it is a variance-covariance matrix and thus positive semidefinite, so Eq. (6-99) establishes that the residual variance estimated from the specified regression of $\mathbf{y}$ on $\mathbf{X}_1$ will, on average, overestimate the true disturbance variance. As in Eq. (6-98), the bias involves the true but unknown coefficients of the excluded variables. The bias in the regression coefficients would disappear if the included and excluded variables were orthogonal, $\mathbf{X}_1', \mathbf{X}_2 = \mathbf{0}$, but the estimated disturbance variance would have expectation

$$E\left(\frac{\text{RSS}}{n-r}\right) = \sigma^2 + \frac{1}{n-r}\boldsymbol{\beta}_2'\mathbf{X}_2'\mathbf{X}_2\boldsymbol{\beta}_2 > \sigma^2$$

so that faulty inferences would still be made.

Case 6-2: Inclusion of irrelevant variables The $\mathbf{X}_*$ and $\mathbf{X}$ matrices could now be specified as

$$\begin{aligned} \mathbf{X}_* &= [\mathbf{X}_1 \quad \mathbf{X}_2] \\ \mathbf{X} &= [\mathbf{X}_1] \end{aligned}$$

where $\mathbf{X}_1$ is $n \times k$ and $\mathbf{X}_2$ (the matrix of irrelevant variables) is $n \times s$. When each true variable in $\mathbf{X}_1$ is regressed on $[\mathbf{X}_1 \quad \mathbf{X}_2]$, the least-squares fit will force the coefficient of that same variable on the right-hand side to unity and all other coefficients to zero. Thus

$$(\mathbf{X}_*'\mathbf{X}_*)^{-1}\mathbf{X}_*'\mathbf{X} = \begin{bmatrix} \mathbf{I}_k \\ \mathbf{0} \end{bmatrix}$$

where $\mathbf{0}$ is a null matrix of order $s \times k$. Thus the coefficients of the variables in $\mathbf{X}_1$ will be unbiased estimates of the true parameters, and the coefficients of the variables in $\mathbf{X}_2$ will have zero expectations. The residual variance will also be an unbiased estimate of σ^2. The residual sum of squares from the regression of $\mathbf{y}$ on $\mathbf{X}_*$ is

$$\text{RSS} = \mathbf{y}'\mathbf{M}\mathbf{y}$$

where

$$\mathbf{M} = \mathbf{I} - \mathbf{X}_*(\mathbf{X}_*'\mathbf{X}_*)^{-1}\mathbf{X}_*'$$

Since the true model is, by assumption,

$$\begin{aligned} \mathbf{y} &= \mathbf{X}_1\boldsymbol{\beta}_1 + \mathbf{u} \\ \text{RSS} &= (\mathbf{X}_1\boldsymbol{\beta}_1 + \mathbf{u})'\mathbf{M}(\mathbf{X}_1\boldsymbol{\beta}_1 + \mathbf{u}) \\ &= \mathbf{u}'\mathbf{M}\mathbf{u} + 2\boldsymbol{\beta}_1'\mathbf{X}_1'\mathbf{M}\mathbf{u} + \boldsymbol{\beta}_1'\mathbf{X}_1'\mathbf{M}\mathbf{X}_1\boldsymbol{\beta}_1 \\ &= \mathbf{u}'\mathbf{M}\mathbf{u} \end{aligned}$$

since $\mathbf{MX}_1 = \mathbf{0}$ as $\mathbf{MX}_* = \mathbf{M}[\mathbf{X}_1 \quad \mathbf{X}_2] = \mathbf{0}$. Thus

$$\begin{aligned} E(\text{RSS}) &= \sigma^2 \operatorname{tr} \mathbf{M} \\ &= (n - k - s)\sigma^2 \end{aligned}$$

and so

$$E(s^2) = \sigma^2$$

where

$$s^2 = \frac{\text{RSS}}{n - k - s}$$

Notice that although the true model only contains k variables, the correct divisor in s^2 is $n - k - s$, where $k + s$ is the number of variables actually included in the misspecified model.

It would seem from the discussion of these two cases that it is more serious to omit relevant variables than to include irrelevant variables since in the former case the coefficients will be biased, the disturbance variance overestimated, and conventional inference procedures rendered invalid, while in the latter case the coefficients will be unbiased, the disturbance variance properly estimated, and the inference procedures will be valid. This constitutes a fairly strong case for including rather than excluding variables from a regression equation. There is, however, a qualification to this view. Adding extra variables, be they relevant or irrelevant, will lower the precision of estimation of the relevant coefficients. This point has already been illustrated for a simple model in the previous section on multicollinearity. Suppose the true model is

$$y = \beta_2 x_2 + u \tag{6-100}$$

and the assumed model is

$$y = \beta_2 x_2 + \beta_3 x_3 + u \tag{6-101}$$

The sampling variance of the estimate of β_2 obtained by applying OLS to Eq. (6-101) is, as shown in Eq. (6-81),

$$\text{var}(b_2) = \frac{\sigma^2}{\Sigma x_2^2(1 - r_{23}^2)}$$

whereas the correct sampling variance, under Eq. (6-100), is $\sigma^2/\Sigma x_2^2$. More generally if $\mathbf{X}_1$ indicates the set of true explanatory variables, $\mathbf{X}_2$ the set of irrelevant variables, and if $\mathbf{y}$ were regressed just on $\mathbf{X}_1$, the variance matrix for the estimated coefficients would be

$$\sigma^2(\mathbf{X}_1'\mathbf{X}_1)^{-1} \tag{6-102}$$

When $\mathbf{y}$ is regressed on $[\mathbf{X}_1 \quad \mathbf{X}_2]$, the variance matrix for the coefficients of the variables in $\mathbf{X}_1$ is

$$\sigma^2\left(\mathbf{X}_1'\mathbf{X}_1 - \mathbf{X}_1'\mathbf{X}_2(\mathbf{X}_2'\mathbf{X}_2)^{-1}\mathbf{X}_2'\mathbf{X}_1\right)^{-1} \tag{6-103}$$

The diagonal elements in Eq. (6-102) will be smaller than those in Eq. (6-103). In the event of substantial collinearity this drop in precision may be serious, but subject to this qualification, including irrelevant variables would seem a less serious problem than the exclusion of possibly relevant variables. Riddell and Buse derive all the main results for Cases 6-1 and 6-2 in a unified fashion by treating them as special cases of restricted least squares.†

Case 6-3: The general case The general case relates to the mistaken use of the $\mathbf{X}_*$ matrix instead of the $\mathbf{X}$ matrix, as specified in Eqs. (6-96) and (6-97). The residual sum of squares from the regression of $\mathbf{y}$ on $\mathbf{X}_*$ is

$$\mathbf{e}'\mathbf{e} = \mathbf{y}'\mathbf{M}_*\mathbf{y}$$

where

$$\mathbf{M}_* = \mathbf{I} - \mathbf{X}_*(\mathbf{X}_*'\mathbf{X}_*)^{-1}\mathbf{X}_*'$$

Substituting for $\mathbf{y}$ from Eq. (6-96) gives

$$\begin{aligned}\mathbf{e}'\mathbf{e} &= (\mathbf{X}\boldsymbol{\beta} + \mathbf{u})'\mathbf{M}_*(\mathbf{X}\boldsymbol{\beta} + \mathbf{u}) \\ &= \mathbf{u}'\mathbf{M}_*\mathbf{u} + \boldsymbol{\beta}'\mathbf{X}'\mathbf{M}_*\mathbf{X}\boldsymbol{\beta} + 2\boldsymbol{\beta}'\mathbf{X}'\mathbf{M}_*\mathbf{u}\end{aligned}$$

and

$$E\frac{\mathbf{e}'\mathbf{e}}{\text{tr}\,\mathbf{M}_*} = \sigma^2 + \frac{1}{\text{tr}\,\mathbf{M}_*}(\boldsymbol{\beta}'\mathbf{X}'\mathbf{M}_*\mathbf{X}\boldsymbol{\beta}) \tag{6-104}$$

If no specification error were made, the $\mathbf{M}_*$ matrix would become

$$\mathbf{M}_* = \mathbf{I} - \mathbf{X}(\mathbf{X}'\mathbf{X})^{-1}\mathbf{X}'$$

and the quadratic form on the right-hand side of Eq. (6-104) would vanish. For any specification error at all the matrix of the quadratic form, being essentially

† See W. C. Riddell and A. Buse, "An Alternative Approach to Specification Errors," *Australian Economic Papers*, **19**, 1980, pp. 211–214.

the variance-covariance matrix computed from the residual vectors obtained when each variable in $\mathbf{X}$ is regressed on $\mathbf{X}_*$, is positive semidefinite. Thus the expected value of the residual variance computed from the regression of $\mathbf{y}$ on $\mathbf{X}_*$ will exceed σ^2 and would only fall to σ^2 when $\mathbf{X}_* = \mathbf{X}$. This provides a rationalization for the common practice of searching among regressions to find the minimum residual sum of squares (or maximum $\bar{\mathbf{R}}^2$), though, of course, in any specific application sampling fluctuations might yield a lower residual sum of squares for $\mathbf{X}_*$ than for $\mathbf{X}$.

The result obtained in Eq. (6-98) that specification error leads to biased estimates of the population parameters must be interpreted with care. Suppose, for example, that $\mathbf{y}$ indicates observations on the rate of inflation, $\mathbf{X}$ the set of explanatory variables in a "fiscalist" theory of inflation, and $\mathbf{X}_*$ the set of explanatory variables in a "monetarist" theory. A fiscalist will estimate Eq. (6-96) and a monetarist Eq. (6-97). Monetarists will have little interest in the "news" that their monetary coefficients are biased estimates of the coefficients of fiscalist variables, nor would fiscalists be interested in the reverse information. Even if one model really is the "true" model, the substantial correlation existing among economic data may well help the "wrong" theory to put up a reasonably good statistical showing. We are touching on the very difficult problem of the choice between alternative models, which we will discuss in some more detail in Chap. 12.

PROBLEMS

6-1 A data matrix of full column rank is partitioned as

$$\mathbf{X} = [\mathbf{X}_1 \quad \mathbf{X}_2]$$

where $\mathbf{X}_1$ is $n \times k_1$ and $\mathbf{X}_2$ is $n \times k_2$. Show that the upper left-hand block in $(\mathbf{X}'\mathbf{X})^{-1}$ may be expressed as

$$(\mathbf{X}_1'\mathbf{M}_2\mathbf{X}_1)^{-1}$$

where

$$\mathbf{M}_2 = \mathbf{I} - \mathbf{X}_2(\mathbf{X}_2'\mathbf{X}_2)^{-1}\mathbf{X}_2'$$

Give a least-squares interpretation of $\mathbf{M}_2\mathbf{X}_1$ and hence of $\mathbf{X}_1'\mathbf{M}_2\mathbf{X}_1$.

6-2 The following estimated equation was obtained by OLS regression using quarterly data for 1958 to 1976 inclusive:

$$\underset{}{y_t} = \underset{(3.4)}{2.20} + \underset{(0.005)}{0.104}\, x_{t1} - \underset{(2.2)}{3.48} x_{t2} + \underset{(0.15)}{0.34}\, x_{t3}$$

Standard errors are in parentheses, the explained sum of squares was 109.6, and the residual sum of squares 18.48.

(*a*) Test the significance of each of the slope coefficients.

(*b*) Calculate the coefficient of determination R^2.

(*c*) When three seasonal dummy variables were added and the equation was reestimated, the explained sum of squares rose to 114.8. Test for the presence of seasonality.

(*d*) Two further regressions, based on the original specification, were computed for the subperiods 1958, quarter 1, to 1968, quarter 4; and 1969, quarter 1, to 1976, quarter 4, yielding residual sums of squares of 9.32 and 7.46, respectively. Test the following hypotheses:

(i) The error variances are identical in the two subperiods.

(ii) The coefficients are identical in the two superperiods.

(UL, 1981)

6-3 The following regression was estimated from 16 quarterly observations (t ratios in parentheses):

$$\underset{(3.7)}{Y_t = 70.7} \; \underset{(0.27)}{-\,0.90X_t} + \underset{(3.37)}{0.43S_{1t}} + \underset{(3.40)}{6.55S_{2t}} - \underset{(3.37)}{2.83S_{3t}} \qquad R^2 = 0.68$$

where $S_{it} = 1$ in the ith quarter and 0 otherwise. Explain the implied pattern of seasonal variation and interpret the result.

(UL, 1980)

6-4 A production function model is specified as

$$Y_i = \beta_1 + \beta_2 X_{2i} + \beta_3 X_{3i} + u_i$$

where Y_i = log output, X_{2i} = log labor input, and X_{3i} = log capital input. The data refer to a sample of 23 firms, and observations are measured as deviations from the sample means

$$\Sigma x_{2i}^2 = 12 \qquad \Sigma x_{2i}x_{3i} = 8$$

$$\Sigma x_{3i}^2 = 12 \qquad \Sigma y_i x_{2i} = 10$$

$$\Sigma y_i^2 = 10 \qquad \Sigma y_i x_{3i} = 8$$

(a) Estimate β_2, β_3, their standard errors, and R^2.

(b) Test the hypothesis that $\beta_2 + \beta_3 = 1$.

(c) Suppose now that you wish to impose the a priori restriction that $\beta_2 + \beta_3 = 1$. What is the least-squares estimate of β_2 and its standard error? What is the value of R^2 in this case? Compare these results with those obtained in (a) and comment.

(UL, 1979)

6-5 A set of cross-section data on family income y and expenditure c is partitioned into subsets of observations, relating to families headed by:

1. Manual workers
2. Salaried workers
3. Self-employed

A regression of log c on log y is computed for each subsample and for the full sample, yielding:

	$\hat{\beta}$	s^2	T
Manual workers	1.02 (0.06)	0.24	102
Salaried workers	0.91 (0.1)	0.46	104
Self-employed	0.76 (0.08)	0.30	26
All families	0.86 (0.05)	0.39	232

Here $\hat{\beta}$ is the slope coefficient (standard errors in parentheses), s^2 is the residual variance, and T is the sample size.

Test the hypotheses that:

(a) The elasticity of c with respect to y is the same for all occupational classes.

(b) Its value is unity.

Interpret your results and give some possible explanations for the observed differences.

(UL, 1979)

6-6 On the assumption that the elements of $\boldsymbol{\beta}$ obey the restrictions

$$\mathbf{R}\boldsymbol{\beta} = \mathbf{r}$$

show that the variance-covariance matrix of the restricted estimator $\mathbf{b}_*$, defined in Eq. (6-5), is

$$\text{var}(\mathbf{b}_*) = \sigma^2\left\{(\mathbf{X}'\mathbf{X})^{-1} - (\mathbf{X}'\mathbf{X})^{-1}\mathbf{R}'\left[\mathbf{R}(\mathbf{X}'\mathbf{X})^{-1}\mathbf{R}'\right]^{-1}\mathbf{R}(\mathbf{X}'\mathbf{X})^{-1}\right\}$$

6-7 The model

$$Y = \alpha_1 + \alpha_2^* E_2 + \alpha_3^* E_3 + u$$

is estimated by OLS, where E_2 and E_3 are dummy variables indicating membership of the second and third educational classes, respectively. Show that the OLS estimates are

$$\begin{bmatrix} a_1 \\ a_2^* \\ a_3^* \end{bmatrix} \begin{matrix} = \\ = \\ = \end{matrix} \begin{bmatrix} \overline{Y}_1 \\ \overline{Y}_2 - \overline{Y}_1 \\ \overline{Y}_3 - \overline{Y}_1 \end{bmatrix}$$

where $\overline{Y}_i$ denotes the mean value of Y in the ith educational class.

6-8 Rework the estimation problem based on the data in Table 6-6, using any other cell as the starting position and confirm that one obtains the same numerical estimates of the expected number of hours as those given in Table 6-7.

6-9 Prove the result on MSEs stated in Eq. (6-86).

6-10 Derive the result given in Eq. (6-91).

6-11 The set of restrictions $\mathbf{R}\boldsymbol{\beta} = \mathbf{r}$, with appropriate partitions of $\mathbf{R}$ and $\boldsymbol{\beta}$, may be reformulated as

$$\mathbf{R}_1\boldsymbol{\beta}_1 + \mathbf{R}_2\boldsymbol{\beta}_2 = \mathbf{r}$$

where $\mathbf{R}_1$ is $q \times q$ and nonsingular and R_2 is $q \times (k - q)$. Show that the restricted estimator $\mathbf{b}_*$, defined in Eq. (6-5), may be obtained in two stages, namely:

(*a*) Regress the vector $(\mathbf{y} - \mathbf{X}_1\mathbf{R}_1^{-1}\mathbf{r})$ on the matrix $(\mathbf{X}_2 - \mathbf{X}_1\mathbf{R}_1^{-1}\mathbf{R}_2)$ to obtain an estimate $\mathbf{b}_2$ of $\boldsymbol{\beta}_2$.

(*b*) Substitute this estimate in

$$\boldsymbol{\beta}_1 = \mathbf{R}_1^{-1}(\mathbf{r} - \mathbf{R}_2\boldsymbol{\beta}_2)$$

to obtain an estimate of $\boldsymbol{\beta}_1$.

CHAPTER

SEVEN

MAXIMUM LIKELIHOOD ESTIMATORS AND ASYMPTOTIC DISTRIBUTIONS

7-1 REVIEW AND PREVIEW

Chaps. 5 and 6 have set out the main features of the k-variable linear model. It is very important to emphasize that the results obtained so far depend upon the particular set of assumptions made in specifying the model. It will be helpful to review those assumptions and results very briefly as this sets the stage for the remainder of the book, which is concerned with the many problems that arise in econometrics when various assumptions underpinning the simple model that we have considered so far have to be revised and extended.

The k-variable linear model with n sample observations was specified as

$$\underset{(n \times 1)}{\mathbf{y}} = \underset{(n \times k)}{\mathbf{X}} \underset{(k \times 1)}{\boldsymbol{\beta}} + \underset{(n \times 1)}{\mathbf{u}}$$

with two crucial sets of assumptions, namely, assumptions about the $\mathbf{X}$ matrix and assumptions about the disturbance vector $\mathbf{u}$, that is,

1. $\mathbf{X}$ is of full column rank and nonstochastic
2. $\mathbf{u}$ has the properties $E(\mathbf{u}) = \mathbf{0}$ and $\text{var}(\mathbf{u}) = \sigma^2\mathbf{I}$

or

3. $\mathbf{u} \sim N(\mathbf{0}, \sigma^2\mathbf{I})$

The combination of assumptions 1 and 2 yields the result that the OLS estimator $\mathbf{b} = (\mathbf{X}'\mathbf{X})^{-1}\mathbf{X}'\mathbf{y}$ with $\text{var}(\mathbf{b}) = \sigma^2(\mathbf{X}'\mathbf{X})^{-1}$ is a best linear unbiased estimator of $\boldsymbol{\beta}$. The development of inference procedures required an assumption about the *form* of the distribution of the disturbance term, and the combination of assumptions 1 and 3 resulted in a comprehensive set of exact, finite sample inference procedures—tests of coefficients, confidence intervals, analysis of variance procedures, tests of structural change, and so forth.

The above assumptions are very restrictive, and parts of Chap. 6 examined some issues relating to the **X** matrix. Sections 6-3 and 6-4 indicated various applications resulting from the incorporation of dummy variables among the X's. Section 6-5 examined the problems that arise when the X variables are highly correlated, and Sec. 6-6 discussed the problems involved in *specifying* the **X** matrix, that is, in knowing which variables in what functional form should comprise the columns of **X**. None of these issues violates the basic assumption that **X** was nonstochastic. It is, however, very important to relax this assumption. Also important is the relaxation of assumptions about the disturbance term. We will see in Chap. 8 that many real-world situations would preclude var($\mathbf{u}$) from having the extremely simple form set out in assumption 2, and it is important to develop appropriate estimators for these more complicated situations. We also need to ask what are the effects of removing the normality assumption for the disturbance term. Finally we note that when **X** is nonstochastic, there is no question of any statistical dependence between the X's and the u's, but when the nonstochastic assumption is removed, this now becomes a possibility to be investigated, and, in fact, this particular problem has generated some of the major developments in econometric theory.

In tackling this broader range of complex problems, the least-squares principle alone cannot always yield an appropriate estimator. We need, therefore, to introduce the powerful maximum likelihood principle. Furthermore, in many of the new problems it proves excessively laborious and often impossible to derive exact finite sample results, but it is possible to derive results which hold in the limit, or asymptotically, as the sample size becomes infinitely large. Thus we need a simple introduction to asymptotic theory, and this is attempted in Sec. 7-2, followed by an introduction to maximum likelihood estimators in Sec. 7-3.

7-2 SOME REMARKS ON ASYMPTOTIC THEORY

Asymptotic theory is concerned with the behavior of random variables as the sample size tends to infinity. To illustrate, let $\bar{x}_n$ denote the mean of a random sample of n observations drawn from some population of x values. Or let b_n indicate the estimated slope of an OLS regression based on n pairs of sample observations. Both $\bar{x}_n$ and b_n are random variables with probability density functions (pdf) denoted, say, by $f(\bar{x}_n|\mu, \sigma^2)$ and $f(b_n|\alpha, \beta, \sigma_u^2)$. The first pdf assumes that the x distribution involves just two parameters, the mean μ and the variance σ^2. The second pdf involves the three parameters of the two-variable linear model of Chap. 2.

The crucial question in asymptotic theory is how random variables such as $\bar{x}_n$ or b_n and their pdf's behave as $n \to \infty$. For our purposes there are two main aspects of this behavior, the first relating to *convergence in probability* and the second to *convergence in distribution*.

Convergence in Probability

A basic result in elementary statistics states that, if the x's have been drawn at random from some distribution with mean μ and variance σ^2,

$$E(\bar{x}_n) = \mu \qquad \text{and} \qquad \operatorname{var}(\bar{x}_n) = \frac{\sigma^2}{n}$$

Thus $\bar{x}_n$ is an unbiased estimator of μ for any sample size, and the variance tends to zero as n increases indefinitely. It is then intuitively clear that the distribution of $\bar{x}_n$, whatever its precise form, becomes more and more concentrated in the neighborhood of μ as n increases. Formally, if one defines a neighborhood around μ as $\mu \pm \varepsilon$, the expression

$$\Pr\{\mu - \varepsilon < \bar{x}_n < \mu + \varepsilon\} = \Pr\{|\bar{x}_n - \mu| < \varepsilon\}$$

indicates the probability that $\bar{x}_n$ lies in that interval. The interval may be made arbitrarily small by suitable choice of ε. Since $\operatorname{var}(\bar{x}_n)$ declines monotonically with increasing n, there exists a number n^* and a δ ($|\delta| < 1$) such that for all $n > n^*$,

$$\Pr\{|\bar{x}_n - \mu| < \varepsilon\} > 1 - \delta \tag{7-1}$$

The random variable $\bar{x}_n$ is then said to *converge in probability* to the constant μ. As n increases, the probability of $\bar{x}_n$ lying in a specified interval becomes larger, that is, δ becomes smaller. Thus an equivalent statement is

$$\lim_{n \to \infty} \Pr\{|\bar{x}_n - \mu| < \varepsilon\} = 1 \tag{7-2}$$

In words, the probability of $\bar{x}_n$ lying in an arbitrarily small interval about μ can be made as close to unity as we desire by letting n become sufficiently large. A shorthand way of writing Eq. (7-2) is

$$\operatorname{plim} \bar{x}_n = \mu \tag{7-3}$$

where plim is an abbreviation of probability limit. The sample mean is then said to be a *consistent* estimator of the population mean μ. By a similar argument the reader may easily show that, in the two-variable regression, b_n is a consistent estimator of β, since it was shown in Chap. 2 that

$$E(b_n) = \beta \qquad \text{and} \qquad \operatorname{var}(b_n) = \frac{\sigma_u^2}{\Sigma x^2}$$

These two examples are very simple in that the estimators are unbiased for *all* sample sizes. Suppose we have another estimator, m_n, of μ such that

$$E(m_n) = \mu + \frac{c}{n}$$

where c is some constant. This estimator is biased in finite samples, but

$$\lim_{n \to \infty} E(m_n) = \mu$$

and m_n is said to be asymptotically unbiased.† Provided $\text{var}(m_n)$ goes to zero as n increases, it may be shown, by use of Chebysheff's theorem, that m_n is a consistent estimator of μ.

Chebysheff's theorem states that for a random variable X with finite mean and variance, μ and σ^2, and for given $\lambda > 0$,

$$\Pr\{|x - \mu| > \lambda\sigma\} < \frac{1}{\lambda^2}$$

Applying the theorem to this example gives

$$\Pr\left\{\left|m_n - \left(\mu + \frac{c}{n}\right)\right| > \lambda\sqrt{\text{var}(m_n)}\right\} < \frac{1}{\lambda^2}$$

Setting $\varepsilon = \lambda\sqrt{\text{var}(m_n)}$, this becomes

$$\Pr\left\{\left|m_n - \left(\mu + \frac{c}{n}\right)\right| > \varepsilon\right\} < \frac{\text{var}(m_n)}{\varepsilon^2}$$

Taking the limits of each side as n goes to infinity gives

$$\lim_{n \to \infty} \Pr\{|m_n - \mu| > \varepsilon\} = 0 \tag{7-4}$$

Thus m_n is a consistent estimator of μ, since Eq. (7-4) is equivalent to the definition of a consistent estimator in Eq. (7-2). So a sufficient condition for consistency is that an estimator should be asymptotically unbiased and have a variance which converges to zero.‡

One of the great advantages of probability limits is their simplicity of operation, as illustrated by the following examples:

$$\text{plim}(x^2) = (\text{plim}\, x)^2$$

$$\text{plim}(x^{-1}) = (\text{plim}\, x)^{-1}$$

$$\text{plim}\left(\frac{x}{y}\right) = \frac{\text{plim}(x)}{\text{plim}(y)}$$

whether or not x and y are independently distributed. Probability limits may also be extended to vectors and matrices. It simply means taking the probability limit of each element of the vector or matrix, provided of course that such probability limits exist. Operation with these probability limits is again extremely simple. For

† An alternative definition of asymptotic unbiasedness will be given shortly in the discussion of convergence in distribution.

‡ Consistency, however, does not necessarily imply asymptotic unbiasedness. The standard counterexample is given in W. P. Sewell, "Least-Squares, Conditional Predictions and Estimator Properties," *Econometrica*, **37**, 1969, pp. 39–43.

example,

$$\text{plim}(\mathbf{AB}) = \text{plim}\,\mathbf{A} \cdot \text{plim}\,\mathbf{B}$$

$$\text{plim}(\mathbf{A}^{-1}) = (\text{plim}\,\mathbf{A})^{-1}$$

As an illustration, recall the OLS coefficient vector from the basic model in Chap. 5, namely,

$$\begin{aligned} \mathbf{b} &= (\mathbf{X}'\mathbf{X})^{-1}\mathbf{X}'\mathbf{y} \\ &= \boldsymbol{\beta} + (\mathbf{X}'\mathbf{X})^{-1}\mathbf{X}'\mathbf{u} \\ &= \boldsymbol{\beta} + \left(\frac{1}{n}\mathbf{X}'\mathbf{X}\right)^{-1}\left(\frac{1}{n}\mathbf{X}'\mathbf{u}\right) \end{aligned}$$

The matrix

$$\left(\frac{1}{n}\mathbf{X}'\mathbf{X}\right)$$

consists of the mean squares and mean cross products of the explanatory variables. If the $\mathbf{X}$ matrix is constant in repeated samples, then†

$$\lim_{n\to\infty}\left(\frac{1}{n}\mathbf{X}'\mathbf{X}\right) = \left(\frac{1}{n}\mathbf{X}'\mathbf{X}\right)$$

If the explanatory variables are stochastic, it can be shown that the sample moments will converge in probability to the population moments. Thus we write

$$\text{plim}\left(\frac{1}{n}\mathbf{X}'\mathbf{X}\right) = \boldsymbol{\Sigma} \tag{7-5}$$

where $\boldsymbol{\Sigma}$ is a given symmetric, finite, positive definite matrix. It remains to evaluate

$$\text{plim}\left(\frac{1}{n}\mathbf{X}'\mathbf{u}\right) = \begin{bmatrix} \text{plim}\left(\frac{1}{n}\Sigma u_t\right) \\ \text{plim}\left(\frac{1}{n}\Sigma X_{2t}u_t\right) \\ \vdots \\ \text{plim}\left(\frac{1}{n}\Sigma X_{kt}u_t\right) \end{bmatrix}$$

The element inside the first parentheses is $\bar{u}$. Since $E(\bar{u}) = 0$ and $\text{var}(\bar{u}) = \sigma^2/n$, it follows that $\text{plim}(\bar{u}) = 0$. For the ith element

$$E\left(\frac{1}{n}\Sigma X_{it}u_t\right) = 0$$

which holds both for the case where $\mathbf{X}$ is fixed and also for stochastic $\mathbf{X}$ on the assumption of zero covariance with u. Also

$$\text{var}\left(\frac{1}{n}\Sigma X_{it}u_t\right) = \frac{\sigma^2}{n} \cdot \frac{\Sigma_{t=1}^{n} X_{it}^2}{n}$$

† For the proof see H. Theil, *Principles of Econometrics*, Wiley, New York, 1971, pp. 364–365.

In view of Eq. (7-5), the probability limit of $\Sigma X_{it}^2/n$ is a constant. Thus the probability limit of the variance is zero. Repeating the argument for the other terms,

$$\text{plim}\left(\frac{1}{n}\mathbf{X'u}\right) = \mathbf{0}$$

and so

$$\begin{aligned} \text{plim}\,\mathbf{b} &= \boldsymbol{\beta} + \text{plim}\left(\frac{1}{n}\mathbf{X'X}\right)^{-1}\text{plim}\left(\frac{1}{n}\mathbf{X'u}\right) \\ &= \boldsymbol{\beta} + \Sigma^{-1}\cdot\mathbf{0} \\ &= \boldsymbol{\beta} \end{aligned}$$

which proves the consistency of the OLS estimator.

Convergence in Distribution

Return again to the sample mean $\bar{x}_n$. If the population from which the x's are drawn at random may be characterized by

$$x \sim N(\mu, \sigma^2)$$

then $\bar{x}_n$, being a linear combination of normal variables, has a normal pdf. Thus

$$\bar{x}_n \sim N\left(\mu, \frac{\sigma^2}{n}\right)$$

and $f(\bar{x}_n)$ is normal for every n. The *limiting distribution* is found by examining what happens to $f(\bar{x}_n)$ as n goes to infinity. Since var$(\bar{x}_n)$ goes to zero, the whole mass is concentrated on the point μ in the limit and the distribution is said to be *degenerate*. A simple transformation of $\bar{x}_n$, however, can lead to a limiting distribution which does not collapse on a single point. Consider

$$z_n = \sqrt{n}\,(\bar{x}_n - \mu)$$

Clearly, $E(z_n) = 0$ and var$(z_n) = \sigma^2$. Thus

$$f(z_n) \text{ is } N(0, \sigma^2) \qquad \text{for any } n$$

that is, the limiting distribution and all finite sample distributions are identical since the parameters of the distribution do not involve n.

The real application of these ideas comes in situations where finite sample pdf's either cannot be derived at all or are very difficult to derive and manipulate, but a tractable limiting distribution can be obtained. *The limiting distribution may then be taken as an approximation for the unknown or intractable finite sample distribution*. As an illustration, suppose the random variable X has mean μ and variance σ^2, as before, but the distribution of X is no longer normal. A fundamental result, the central limit theorem, states that†

the limiting distribution of $z_n = \sqrt{n}(\bar{x}_n - \mu)$ *is* $N(0, \sigma^2)$.

Thus irrespective of the form of $f(x)$, the limiting distribution of z_n is still normal, though the quality of the approximation to any finite pdf will be influenced by the extent to which $f(x)$ departs from normality. Alternative ways of expressing this result are

$\sqrt{n}(\bar{x}_n - \mu)$ *converges in distribution to* $N(0, \sigma^2)$

or

$$\sqrt{n}(\bar{x}_n - \mu) \xrightarrow{D} N(0, \sigma^2) \tag{7-6}$$

This result is often expressed loosely as "$\bar{x}_n$ is asymptotically normally distributed with mean μ and variance σ^2/n" and σ^2/n is then referred to as the asymptotic variance of $\bar{x}_n$. A shorthand version of this statement is

$$\bar{x}_n \sim \mathrm{AN}\left(\mu, \frac{\sigma^2}{n}\right) \tag{7-7}$$

with

$$\text{asy var}(\bar{x}_n) = \frac{\sigma^2}{n}$$

where AN indicates asymptotically normal and asy var, asymptotic variance. As already emphasized, the limiting (asymptotic) distribution of $\bar{x}_n$ is degenerate. The practical import of Eq. (7-7) is that in cases where $f(\bar{x}_n)$ is intractable we are taking it, for sufficiently large n, to be approximately normal with mean μ and variance σ^2/n. These procedures extend directly to multivariate situations, and we will give an example in Sec. 7-4 with a treatment of the k-variable linear model when the disturbances are nonnormal.

If we consider the class of consistent and asymptotically normal estimators, the one with the minimum asymptotic variance is said to be *asymptotically efficient*. The mean of the asymptotic distribution provides an alternative measure of the asymptotic expectation of an estimator, and hence of asymptotic bias. Previously we implicitly defined the asymptotic expectation (AE) of an estimator $\hat{\theta}$ as

$$\mathrm{AE}(\hat{\theta}) = \lim_{n \to \infty} E(\hat{\theta})$$

The alternative definition is

$$\mathrm{AE}(\hat{\theta}) = \text{mean of the asymptotic distribution of } \hat{\theta}$$

Similar definitions apply to second- and higher-order moments. In many cases the two definitions are equivalent, but there are instances where it is important to

† For a proof see H. Theil, op. cit., pp. 367–369.

distinguish between *limits of sequences of moments* and the corresponding *moments of a limiting distribution*. Sometimes the moments of a finite sampling distribution may not exist or cannot be established, although a limiting distribution with well-defined moments does exist.†

7-3 MAXIMUM LIKELIHOOD ESTIMATORS

We will illustrate the principle of maximum likelihood (ML) estimation in the context of the linear regression model.‡ Let us retain the assumption of a fixed nonstochastic **X** matrix. The model

$$\mathbf{y} = \mathbf{X}\boldsymbol{\beta} + \mathbf{u} \tag{7-8}$$

then defines a transformation from **u** to **y**. The assumption of a multivariate density function for **u** implies a multivariate density function for **y**, which may be written

$$p(\mathbf{y}) = p(\mathbf{u})\left|\frac{\partial \mathbf{u}}{\partial \mathbf{y}}\right|$$

where $|\partial \mathbf{u}/\partial \mathbf{y}|$ indicates the *absolute* value of the determinant formed from the matrix of partial derivatives§

$$\begin{bmatrix} \dfrac{\partial u_1}{\partial y_1} & \dfrac{\partial u_1}{\partial y_2} & \cdots & \dfrac{\partial u_1}{\partial y_n} \\ \dfrac{\partial u_2}{\partial y_1} & \dfrac{\partial u_2}{\partial y_2} & \cdots & \dfrac{\partial u_2}{\partial y_n} \\ \cdots & \cdots & \cdots & \cdots \\ \dfrac{\partial u_n}{\partial y_1} & \dfrac{\partial u_n}{\partial y_2} & \cdots & \dfrac{\partial u_n}{\partial y_n} \end{bmatrix}$$

In the case of Eq. (7-8) this matrix is seen to be the identity matrix whose determinant is unity. Thus

$$p(\mathbf{y}) = p(\mathbf{u})$$

If we further assume, as before, that **u** is multivariate normal with mean vector **0** and variance matrix $\sigma^2\mathbf{I}$, then formula (5-5) gives

$$p(\mathbf{u}) = \frac{1}{(2\pi\sigma^2)^{n/2}}\exp\left(-\frac{1}{2\sigma^2}\mathbf{u}'\mathbf{u}\right)$$

and so

$$p(\mathbf{y}) = \frac{1}{(2\pi\sigma^2)^{n/2}}\exp\left[-\frac{1}{2\sigma^2}(\mathbf{y}-\mathbf{X}\boldsymbol{\beta})'(\mathbf{y}-\mathbf{X}\boldsymbol{\beta})\right] \tag{7-9}$$

† For details see H. Theil, op. cit., pp. 375–378.

‡ For a general account of estimators the reader might consult P. G. Hoel, *Introduction to Mathematical Statistics*, 4th ed., Wiley, New York, 1971, pp. 196–200; L. D. Taylor, *Probability and Mathematical Statistics*, Harper and Row, New York, 1974, pp. 197–230; or M. G. Kendall and A. Stuart, *The Advanced Theory of Statistics*, vol. 2, Griffin, London, 1961, pp. 1–67.

§ See App. A-9, Change of Variables in Density Functions.

Equation (7-9) involves both the observations on $\mathbf{y}$ and the unknown parameters $\boldsymbol{\beta}$ and σ^2. Writing $p(\mathbf{y})$ in the form $L(\mathbf{y}; \boldsymbol{\beta}, \sigma^2)$ emphasizes that it is the probability density for the y's, given the parameters $\boldsymbol{\beta}$ and σ^2. Alternatively, writing it as $L(\boldsymbol{\beta}, \sigma^2; \mathbf{y})$ stresses that for given $\mathbf{y}$ it can be regarded as a function of the parameters. It is termed the *likelihood function* and is conventionally denoted by the symbol L.

The ML principle is to choose as estimators of $\boldsymbol{\beta}$ and σ^2 the values which maximize the likelihood function, given the sample data $\mathbf{y}$. Letting $\boldsymbol{\theta}' = [\boldsymbol{\beta}' \ \sigma^2]$ denote the vector of unknown parameters and $\hat{\boldsymbol{\theta}}$ the ML estimator, $\hat{\boldsymbol{\theta}}$ is obtained as the solution of the equation

$$\frac{\partial L}{\partial \boldsymbol{\theta}} = \mathbf{0} \tag{7-10}$$

In practice the derivation of the ML estimators is often simplified by maximizing the log of the likelihood function, that is, by finding $\hat{\boldsymbol{\theta}}$ as the solution to

$$\frac{\partial (\ln L)}{\partial \boldsymbol{\theta}} = \mathbf{0} \tag{7-11}$$

Since

$$\frac{\partial (\ln L)}{\partial \boldsymbol{\theta}} = \frac{1}{L} \cdot \frac{\partial L}{\partial \boldsymbol{\theta}}$$

the same vector $\hat{\boldsymbol{\theta}}$ is obtained as the solution to Eqs. (7-10) and (7-11) for any $L > 0$.

Taking the natural logarithm of the likelihood in Eq. (7-9) gives

$$\ln L = -\frac{n}{2}\ln(2\pi) - \frac{n}{2}\ln(\sigma^2) - \frac{1}{2\sigma^2}(\mathbf{y} - \mathbf{X}\boldsymbol{\beta})'(\mathbf{y} - \mathbf{X}\boldsymbol{\beta})$$

Differentiating partially with respect to $\boldsymbol{\beta}$ and σ^2 and evaluating these derivatives at the ML estimators gives the specific form of Eq. (7-11) as

$$\begin{aligned} \frac{\partial (\ln L)}{\partial \boldsymbol{\beta}} &= -\frac{1}{2\hat{\sigma}^2}(-2\mathbf{X}'\mathbf{y} + 2\mathbf{X}'\mathbf{X}\hat{\boldsymbol{\beta}}) = \frac{1}{\hat{\sigma}^2}(\mathbf{X}'\mathbf{y} - \mathbf{X}'\mathbf{X}\hat{\boldsymbol{\beta}}) = \mathbf{0} \\ \frac{\partial (\ln L)}{\partial \sigma^2} &= -\frac{1}{2\hat{\sigma}^2} + \frac{1}{2\hat{\sigma}^4}(\mathbf{y} - \mathbf{X}\hat{\boldsymbol{\beta}})'(\mathbf{y} - \mathbf{X}\hat{\boldsymbol{\beta}}) = 0 \end{aligned} \tag{7-12}$$

The simultaneous solution of these $k + 1$ equations gives

$$\hat{\boldsymbol{\beta}} = (\mathbf{X}'\mathbf{X})^{-1}\mathbf{X}'\mathbf{y} \tag{7-13}$$

and

$$\hat{\sigma}^2 = \frac{\mathbf{e}'\mathbf{e}}{n} \tag{7-14}$$

The ML $\hat{\boldsymbol{\beta}}$ is seen, in this case, to be identical with the OLS $\mathbf{b}$. The estimate of σ^2, however, differs from the unbiased s^2 of Eq. (5-57) by the factor $(n - k)/n$, which illustrates the fact that ML estimators are not necessarily unbiased. In this application $\hat{\boldsymbol{\beta}}$ is an unbiased estimator of $\boldsymbol{\beta}$, but $\hat{\sigma}^2$ is a biased estimator of σ^2.

Properties of ML Estimators

ML estimators have a number of desirable properties, some of which hold for finite samples and some of which only hold asymptotically. Of the finite (small sample) results one of the most important is the following:

> *If a minimum variance bound (MVB) estimator exists, it is given by the ML method.*

The minimum variance bound (MVB), developed in the remarkable Cramer-Rao theorem, establishes a minimum for the variance of an unbiased estimator. It is important to note that the theorem relates to the class of unbiased estimators and not just to the subset of *linear* unbiased estimators. Furthermore the theorem establishes a lower bound for the variance, but there may, of course, be situations where the bound cannot be attained, that is, where one can derive a minimum variance unbiased (MVU) estimator, but its variance will exceed the MVB. The bound is derived from the likelihood function.

Consider first of all the case of a single unknown parameter θ, a density function $f(y|\theta)$, and a random sample of n observations from this density. The likelihood function is then

$$L(\theta|\mathbf{y}) = \prod_{i=1}^{n} f(y_i|\theta)$$

Let $\tilde{\theta}$ denote an unbiased estimator θ. Then the Cramer-Rao theorem states

$$\operatorname{var}(\tilde{\theta}) \geq \frac{1}{E\left(\dfrac{\partial \ln L}{\partial \theta}\right)^2} = \frac{-1}{E\left(\dfrac{\partial^2 \ln L}{\partial \theta^2}\right)} \tag{7-15}$$

where either of the expressions on the right-hand side indicates the MVB. For the multiparameter case, let $\tilde{\boldsymbol{\theta}}$ denote an unbiased estimator of the vector $\boldsymbol{\theta}$ of, say, k unknown parameters. Now we have a variance-covariance matrix for the elements of $\tilde{\boldsymbol{\theta}}$, denoted by $\operatorname{var}(\tilde{\boldsymbol{\theta}})$. The multidimensional equivalent of

$$E\left(\frac{\partial^2 \ln L}{\partial \theta^2}\right)$$

in Eq. (7-15) is now the symmetric matrix

$$\mathbf{R}(\boldsymbol{\theta}) = -E\left(\frac{\partial^2 \ln L}{\partial \boldsymbol{\theta}\, \partial \boldsymbol{\theta}'}\right)$$

$$= -E\begin{bmatrix} \dfrac{\partial^2 \ln L}{\partial \theta_1^2} & \dfrac{\partial^2 \ln L}{\partial \theta_1\, \partial \theta_2} & \cdots & \dfrac{\partial^2 \ln L}{\partial \theta_1\, \partial \theta_k} \\ \dfrac{\partial^2 \ln L}{\partial \theta_2\, \partial \theta_1} & \dfrac{\partial^2 \ln L}{\partial \theta_2^2} & \cdots & \dfrac{\partial^2 \ln L}{\partial \theta_2\, \partial \theta_k} \\ \cdots & \cdots & \cdots & \cdots \\ \dfrac{\partial^2 \ln L}{\partial \theta_k\, \partial \theta_1} & \dfrac{\partial^2 \ln L}{\partial \theta_k\, \partial \theta_2} & \cdots & \dfrac{\partial^2 \ln L}{\partial \theta_k^2} \end{bmatrix} \tag{7-16}$$

$\mathbf{R}(\boldsymbol{\theta})$ is often referred to as the information matrix. The multidimensional version of the Cramer-Rao theorem now states

$$\text{var}(\tilde{\boldsymbol{\theta}}) - \mathbf{R}^{-1}(\boldsymbol{\theta}) \text{ *is a positive semidefinite matrix*}$$

Thus the MVB, for any $\tilde{\theta}_i$, is given by the ith element on the principal diagonal of $\mathbf{R}^{-1}(\boldsymbol{\theta})$.†

As an illustration of this result, let us return to the k-variable linear model. The first-order derivatives of the likelihood function were given in Eq. (7-12). Differentiating these again we obtain‡

$$\frac{\partial^2(\ln L)}{\partial\boldsymbol{\beta}\,\partial\boldsymbol{\beta}'} = -\frac{1}{\sigma^2}\mathbf{X}'\mathbf{X}$$

$$\frac{\partial^2(\ln L)}{\partial(\sigma^2)^2} = \frac{n}{2\sigma^4} - \frac{(\mathbf{y}-\mathbf{X}\boldsymbol{\beta})'(\mathbf{y}-\mathbf{X}\boldsymbol{\beta})}{\sigma^6}$$

$$\frac{\partial^2(\ln L)}{\partial\boldsymbol{\beta}\,\partial\sigma^2} = -\frac{1}{2\sigma^4}(\mathbf{X}'\mathbf{y} - \mathbf{X}'\mathbf{X}\boldsymbol{\beta})$$

Taking expectations of these second-order derivatives and reversing signs gives

$$-E\left\{\frac{\partial^2(\ln L)}{\partial\boldsymbol{\beta}\,\partial\boldsymbol{\beta}'}\right\} = \frac{1}{\sigma^2}\mathbf{X}'\mathbf{X}$$

$$-E\left\{\frac{\partial^2(\ln L)}{\partial(\sigma^2)^2}\right\} = -\frac{n}{2\sigma^4} + \frac{n\sigma^2}{\sigma^6} = \frac{n}{2\sigma^4}$$

since

$$E(\mathbf{y}-\mathbf{X}\boldsymbol{\beta})'(\mathbf{y}-\mathbf{X}\boldsymbol{\beta}) = E(\mathbf{u}'\mathbf{u}) = n\sigma^2$$

and

$$-E\left\{\frac{\partial^2(\ln L)}{\partial\boldsymbol{\beta}\,\partial\sigma^2}\right\} = \mathbf{0}$$

since

$$E(\mathbf{X}'\mathbf{y} - \mathbf{X}'\mathbf{X}\boldsymbol{\beta}) = E\{\mathbf{X}'(\mathbf{y}-\mathbf{X}\boldsymbol{\beta})\} = E(\mathbf{X}'\mathbf{u}) = \mathbf{0}$$

Substituting in Eq. (7-16) and inverting the resulting matrix then gives

$$\mathbf{R}^{-1}\begin{pmatrix}\boldsymbol{\beta}\\ \sigma^2\end{pmatrix} = \begin{bmatrix}\sigma^2(\mathbf{X}'\mathbf{X})^{-1} & \mathbf{0}\\ \mathbf{0} & \dfrac{2\sigma^4}{n}\end{bmatrix} \tag{7-17}$$

We see immediately that the ML (OLS) estimator of $\boldsymbol{\beta}$ attains the Cramer-Rao MVB, since $\text{var}(\hat{\boldsymbol{\beta}}) = \text{var}(\mathbf{b}) = \sigma^2(\mathbf{X}'\mathbf{X})^{-1}$, which is identical with the top left-hand

† Derivations of the Cramer-Rao MVB may be found in P. G. Hoel, op. cit., pp. 362–365; L. D. Taylor, op. cit., pp. 209–213, and M. G. Kendall and A. Stuart, op. cit., Chap. 17.

‡ Note that Eq. (7-12) contains $\hat{\boldsymbol{\beta}}$ and $\hat{\sigma}^2$ because the first-order derivatives had been equated to zero. We now ignore the equalities, replace $\hat{\boldsymbol{\beta}}$ by $\boldsymbol{\beta}$, $\hat{\sigma}^2$ by σ^2, and differentiate again.

submatrix in $\mathbf{R}^{-1}$. The same result does not hold for either the OLS or the ML estimator of σ^2. The OLS estimator is

$$s^2 = \frac{\mathbf{e}'\mathbf{e}}{n-k}$$

and it was established in Eq. (5-59) that

$$\frac{1}{\sigma^2}(\mathbf{e}'\mathbf{e}) \sim \chi^2(n-k)$$

Thus

$$s^2 \sim \frac{\sigma^2}{n-k} \cdot \chi^2(n-k)$$

Recalling that the variance of a χ^2 variable is equal to twice its number of degrees of freedom,

$$\text{var}(s^2) = \frac{\sigma^4}{(n-k)^2} 2(n-k) = \frac{2\sigma^4}{n-k}$$

which, for any finite n, is somewhat greater than the variance term given in $\mathbf{R}^{-1}$. There is, in fact, no unbiased estimator of σ^2 which can attain the MVB. The derivation of the variance of the ML estimator, $\hat{\sigma}^2 = \mathbf{e}'\mathbf{e}/n$, is left as an exercise for the reader, but in any case it is a biased estimator of σ^2.

A second important feature of ML estimators is their *invariance* property, which holds for any sample size and may be stated as follows:

The ML estimate of a function $g(\boldsymbol{\theta})$ *is* $g(\hat{\boldsymbol{\theta}})$, *where* $\hat{\boldsymbol{\theta}}$ *is the ML estimate of* $\boldsymbol{\theta}$.

We have seen that the ML estimate of σ^2 in the regression model is $\hat{\sigma}^2 = \mathbf{e}'\mathbf{e}/n$. Thus the ML estimate of σ is simply $\sqrt{\mathbf{e}'\mathbf{e}/n}$.

The most important result about ML estimators relates to their *large sample* or *asymptotic* properties.†

Under certain regularity conditions, ML estimators are consistent, asymptotically normally distributed, and asymptotically efficient.

Specifically, if $\hat{\boldsymbol{\theta}}$ denotes the ML estimate of $\boldsymbol{\theta}$,

$$\text{plim}\,\hat{\boldsymbol{\theta}} = \boldsymbol{\theta} \tag{7-18}$$

$$\hat{\boldsymbol{\theta}} \sim \text{AN}(\boldsymbol{\theta}, \mathbf{R}^{-1}) \tag{7-19}$$

where $\mathbf{R}$ has already been defined in Eq. (7-16) as

$$\mathbf{R} = -E\left(\frac{\partial^2 \ln L}{\partial\boldsymbol{\theta}\,\partial\boldsymbol{\theta}'}\right)$$

† Reference may be made, for example, to Kendall and Stuart, op. cit., for a comprehensive statement of the underpinning assumptions and the derivation of this and other results.

Thus the ML estimators, besides being consistent and asymptotically normal, are efficient in that the asymptotic variance matrix reaches the Cramer-Rao lower bound.

7-4 SOME ASYMPTOTIC RESULTS FOR THE *k*-VARIABLE LINEAR MODEL

In this section we will relax two of the assumptions underpinning the k-variable linear model, namely, the normality of the disturbance term and the nonstochastic nature of the **X** matrix.

Nonnormal Disturbances

Let us retain assumptions 1 and 2 of Sec. 7-1, that is,

1. $\mathbf{X}$ is nonstochastic of full column rank k.
2. $E(\mathbf{u}) = \mathbf{0}$ and $\text{var}(\mathbf{u}) = \sigma^2\mathbf{I}$.

but dispense with the assumption of a normal distribution for the u's. Under assumptions 1 and 2 the OLS $\mathbf{b}$ is still a best linear unbiased estimator of $\boldsymbol{\beta}$ with variance matrix $\sigma^2(\mathbf{X}'\mathbf{X})^{-1}$. Moreover, as already shown, $\mathbf{b}$ is a consistent estimator of $\boldsymbol{\beta}$. Thus even when the disturbances are nonnormal, OLS is still a very acceptable technique for deriving point estimates. The difficulty is that the various exact inference procedures outlined in Chaps. 5 and 6 are no longer strictly valid since their derivation depended on the assumption of normality. However, one may conjecture that the procedures are reasonably robust for moderate departures from normality.† More importantly the tests can be given a large sample justification. This requires the use of two theoretical results.

First, if $\mathbf{X}$ is nonstochastic of full column rank k, $E(\mathbf{u}) = \mathbf{0}$, $\text{var}(\mathbf{u}) = \sigma^2\mathbf{I}$, the elements of $\mathbf{X}$ are uniformly bounded, and $\lim_{n\to\infty}(1/n)\mathbf{X}'\mathbf{X} = \boldsymbol{\Sigma}$, a finite, symmetric, positive definite matrix, then‡

$$\frac{1}{\sqrt{n}}(\mathbf{X}'\mathbf{u}) \sim \text{AN}(0, \sigma^2\boldsymbol{\Sigma}) \tag{7-20}$$

† "... it has been shown that these tests are not very sensitive to departure from normality. If the errors are not normally distributed but have a variance, it is generally true that only trivial errors are made in the powers or the levels of significance if we retain the formulae which are strictly applicable in the case where the errors are normal." E. Malinvaud, *Statistical Methods of Econometrics*, 2nd ed., North-Holland, Amsterdam, 1970, p. 99. See also Malinvaud's discussion on pp. 296–302. Additional references on this topic are P. Schmidt, *Econometrics*, Marcel Dekker, 1976, pp. 55–64; A. C. Harvey, *The Econometric Analysis of Time Series*, Wiley, New York, 1981, pp. 112–117; and G. G. Judge, W. E. Griffiths, R. C. Hill, and T. C. Lee, *The Theory and Practice of Econometrics*, Wiley, New York, 1980, Chap. 7.

‡ For a proof see P. Schmidt, op. cit., pp. 56–60.

Second, let $\{X_n, Y_n\}$ denote a sequence of pairs of random variables, where X_n has a probability limit and Y_n a limiting distribution, that is,

$$\text{plim } X_n = c$$

and

$$Y_n \xrightarrow{D} f(Y)$$

then

$$(X_n Y_n) \xrightarrow{D} f(cY)$$

or, in words, the product $X_n Y_n$ has the limiting distribution $f(cY)$.† If, in particular, Y_n has a normal limiting distribution

$$Y_n \xrightarrow{D} N(\mu, \sigma^2)$$

then

$$X_n Y_n \xrightarrow{D} N(c\mu, c^2\sigma^2)$$

The multidimensional version of the same result is as follows: Let $\mathbf{y}_n$ denote a $k \times 1$ vector with limiting distribution

$$\mathbf{y}_n \xrightarrow{D} N(\boldsymbol{\mu}, \boldsymbol{\Omega})$$

and $\mathbf{z}_n$ an $r \times 1$ vector defined by

$$\mathbf{z}_n = \mathbf{H}_n \mathbf{y}_n \tag{7-21}$$

where $\mathbf{H}_n$ is an $r \times k$ matrix with probability limit

$$\text{plim}\,\mathbf{H}_n = \mathbf{H}$$

then

$$\mathbf{z}_n \xrightarrow{D} N(\mathbf{H}\boldsymbol{\mu}, \mathbf{H}\boldsymbol{\Omega}\mathbf{H}') \tag{7-22}$$

Returning now to the main argument

$$\mathbf{b} - \boldsymbol{\beta} = \left(\frac{1}{n}\mathbf{X}'\mathbf{X}\right)^{-1}\left(\frac{1}{n}\mathbf{X}'\mathbf{u}\right)$$

Thus

$$\sqrt{n}\,(\mathbf{b} - \boldsymbol{\beta}) = \left(\frac{1}{n}\mathbf{X}'\mathbf{X}\right)^{-1}\left(\frac{1}{\sqrt{n}}X'u\right)$$

This is seen to be in the form of Eq. (7-21), and a direct application of Eq. (7-22) gives the result that $\sqrt{n}\,(\mathbf{b} - \boldsymbol{\beta})$ has a limiting normal distribution with zero

† See C. R. Rao, *Linear Statistical Inference and Its Applications*, Wiley, New York, 1965, pp. 101 ff., for this and other important limit theorems.

mean vector and variance matrix given by

$$\sigma^2\Sigma^{-1}\Sigma\Sigma^{-1} = \sigma^2\Sigma^{-1}$$

Thus we may write

$$\sqrt{n}\,(\mathbf{b} - \boldsymbol{\beta}) \xrightarrow{D} N(\mathbf{0}, \sigma^2\Sigma^{-1}) \tag{7-23}$$

or

$$\mathbf{b} \sim \mathrm{AN}\left(\boldsymbol{\beta}, \frac{1}{n}\sigma^2\Sigma^{-1}\right) \tag{7-24}$$

In a practical application Σ is unknown and is replaced by the sample estimate $((1/n)\mathbf{X}'\mathbf{X})$ and σ^2 is estimated by $s^2 = \mathbf{e}'\mathbf{e}/(n-k)$, where $\mathbf{e} = \mathbf{y} - \mathbf{X}\mathbf{b}$. Thus the *estimated* asymptotic variance-covariance matrix for $\mathbf{b}$ is

$$\text{asy var}(\mathbf{b}) = s^2(\mathbf{X}'\mathbf{X})^{-1}$$

which is the finite sample estimator of Chaps. 5 and 6. It can be shown that Eq. (7-24) essentially ensures that all the conventional t and F tests are valid asymptotically.† It is a moot point whether in the test of a single restriction critical values should be taken from $N(0, 1)$ rather than $t(n-k)$, and in the test of a set of q restrictions, whether one should consult the χ^2/q distribution or $F(q, n-k)$. However, it is not a matter of great importance since

$$t(n-k) \xrightarrow{D} N(0, 1)$$

and

$$F(q, n-k) \xrightarrow{D} \frac{\chi^2}{q}$$

and, moreover, under the assumptions made in this section, the procedures are only valid asymptotically so that one should not place undue emphasis on precise levels of significance.

Stochastic X Matrix

The explanatory variables in an econometric relation are not usually subject to control by the economic researcher, the secretary of the U.S. Treasury, or anyone else. Rather they are mostly the outcome of the functioning of some economic/social system. Let us, therefore, characterize the X_{it} $(i = 1, \ldots, k;$ $t = 1, \ldots, n)$ as possessing some multivariate density function $g(\mathbf{X})$. We will make two crucial assumptions about this density function, namely:

1. The parameters of $g(\mathbf{X})$ do not involve the parameters $\boldsymbol{\beta}$ and σ^2 of the regression model.
2. $\mathbf{X}$ and $\mathbf{u}$ are independently distributed. This is the strong assumption of full independence. It implies, for example, that the disturbance u_t is independent of X_{it} for all $i = 1, \ldots, k$ and all $t = 1, \ldots, n$ or, in other words, that u_t is

† For details see P. Schmidt, op. cit., pp. 60–64.

independent of all past values, the current values, and all future values of all explanatory variables. This strong assumption would be violated if a lagged value of Y, such as Y_{t-1}, appeared among the explanatory variables, for u_{t-1} influences Y_{t-1}, so Y_{t-1} is not independent of u_{t-1}. Furthermore u_{t-2} influences Y_{t-2}, which in turn influences Y_{t-1}. Thus Y_{t-1} is dependent on $u_{t-1}, u_{t-2}, \ldots$, but is independent of u_t, u_{t+1}, and all later u's.†

Formally we may express assumption 2 as

$$\begin{aligned} p(\mathbf{u}|\mathbf{X}) &= p(\mathbf{u}) \\ E(\mathbf{u}|\mathbf{X}) &= E(\mathbf{u}) \\ E(\mathbf{y}|\mathbf{X}) &= E(\mathbf{X}\boldsymbol{\beta} + \mathbf{u}|\mathbf{X}) = \mathbf{X}\boldsymbol{\beta} + E(\mathbf{u}) \\ E(\mathbf{uu}'|\mathbf{X}) &= E(\mathbf{uu}') \end{aligned}$$

The likelihood of the sample observations on both Y and X's may be written

$$\begin{aligned} p(\mathbf{y}, \mathbf{X}) &= p(\mathbf{y}|\mathbf{X}) \cdot g(\mathbf{X}) \\ &= p(\mathbf{u}|\mathbf{X}) \cdot g(\mathbf{X}) \\ &= p(\mathbf{u}) \cdot g(\mathbf{X}) \end{aligned}$$

We also retain the assumption:

3. $\mathbf{u} \sim N(\mathbf{0}, \sigma^2\mathbf{I})$

Thus the log likelihood becomes

$$\ln L = -\frac{n}{2}\ln(2\pi) - \frac{n}{2}\ln(\sigma^2) - \frac{1}{2\sigma^2}(\mathbf{y} - \mathbf{Xb})'(\mathbf{y} - \mathbf{Xb}) + \ln g(\mathbf{X})$$

This differs from the likelihood for the fixed **X** model only in the additional term in $\ln g(\mathbf{X})$. Since this term does not involve $\boldsymbol{\beta}$ and σ^2, the ML estimators of these parameters are the same as those already given for the fixed **X** model in Eqs. (7-13) and (7-14). Thus the ML estimator of $\boldsymbol{\beta}$, which still equals the OLS estimator, will at least have desirable asymptotic properties when the X's are stochastic. Furthermore, reworking the development leading up to Eq. (7-17) now gives

$$\mathbf{R}^{-1}\begin{pmatrix} \boldsymbol{\beta} \\ \sigma^2 \end{pmatrix} = \begin{bmatrix} \sigma^2 E(\mathbf{X}'\mathbf{X})^{-1} & \mathbf{0} \\ \mathbf{0} & \dfrac{2\sigma^4}{n} \end{bmatrix} \tag{7-25}$$

so that the asymptotic variance matrix for $\hat{\boldsymbol{\beta}}(= \mathbf{b})$ is $\sigma^2 E(\mathbf{X}'\mathbf{X})^{-1}$, which is the MVB.

Turning to the small sample properties it is easy to show first of all that **b** is an unconditionally unbiased estimator. From Chap. 5,

$$\mathbf{b} = \boldsymbol{\beta} + (\mathbf{X}'\mathbf{X})^{-1}\mathbf{X}'\mathbf{u}$$

† This case is treated in Sec. 9-2.

Thus

$$\begin{aligned} E(\mathbf{b}) &= \boldsymbol{\beta} + E\{(\mathbf{X}'\mathbf{X})^{-1}\mathbf{X}'\mathbf{u}\} \\ &= \boldsymbol{\beta} + E\{(\mathbf{X}'\mathbf{X})^{-1}\mathbf{X}'\} \cdot E(\mathbf{u}) \qquad \text{since } \mathbf{X} \text{ and } \mathbf{u} \text{ are independent} \\ &= \boldsymbol{\beta} \qquad \text{since } E(\mathbf{u}) = \mathbf{0} \end{aligned}$$

For the variance-covariance matrix

$$\begin{aligned} \text{var}(\mathbf{b}) &= E\{(\mathbf{b} - \boldsymbol{\beta})(\mathbf{b} - \boldsymbol{\beta})'\} \\ &= E\{(\mathbf{X}'\mathbf{X})^{-1}\mathbf{X}'\mathbf{u}\mathbf{u}'\mathbf{X}(\mathbf{X}'\mathbf{X})^{-1}\} \\ &= E_{\mathbf{x}}\{E_{\mathbf{u}|\mathbf{x}}(\mathbf{X}'\mathbf{X})^{-1}\mathbf{X}'\mathbf{u}\mathbf{u}'\mathbf{X}(\mathbf{X}'\mathbf{X})^{-1}\} \end{aligned}$$

where $E_{\mathbf{u}|\mathbf{x}}$ indicates the expected value in the *conditional* distribution of **u** given **X**, and $E_{\mathbf{x}}$ indicates the expected value in the *marginal* distribution of **X**.† Thus

$$\begin{aligned} \text{var}(\mathbf{b}) &= E_{\mathbf{x}}\{\sigma^2(\mathbf{X}'\mathbf{X})^{-1}\} \\ &= \sigma^2 E(\mathbf{X}'\mathbf{X})^{-1} \end{aligned} \tag{7-26}$$

This shows that the finite sample variance attains the Cramer-Rao lower bound and differs only from the corresponding formula in the stochastic case in that $(\mathbf{X}'\mathbf{X})^{-1}$ is replaced by $E(\mathbf{X}'\mathbf{X})^{-1}$.

Formula (7-26) may be established in an alternative and instructive fashion. It was shown in Eq. (5-33) that the variance matrix for **b**, given some **X** matrix, was $\sigma^2(\mathbf{X}'\mathbf{X})^{-1}$. Emphasizing the *conditional* nature of this variance we can write

$$\text{var}(\mathbf{b}|\mathbf{X}) = \sigma^2(\mathbf{X}'\mathbf{X})^{-1}$$

or letting $\mathbf{S} = \mathbf{X}'\mathbf{X}$,

$$\text{var}(\mathbf{b}|\mathbf{S}) = \sigma^2\mathbf{S}^{-1}$$

Now suppose that the random X's can, in principle, generate a finite number of **S** matrices $S_1, S_2, \ldots, S_m$ with probabilities $p_1, p_2, \ldots, p_m$. Then the unconditional variance matrix for **b**, determined from the marginal distribution, is

$$\begin{aligned} \text{var}(\mathbf{b}) &= \sum_{i=1}^{m} \text{var}(\mathbf{b}|\mathbf{S}_i) \cdot p_i \\ &= \sigma^2 \sum_{i=1}^{m} \mathbf{S}_i^{-1} p_i \\ &= \sigma^2 \cdot E(\mathbf{S}^{-1}) \\ &= \sigma^2 E(\mathbf{X}'\mathbf{X})^{-1} \qquad \text{as in Eq. (7-26)} \end{aligned}$$

It is clear that the same argument goes through when the X's are continuous.

Unfortunately both elements in Eq. (7-26) are unknown. Intuition suggests replacing

$$\sigma^2 \quad \text{by} \quad s^2 = \frac{\mathbf{e}'\mathbf{e}}{n-k}$$

† See App. A-8, Expectations in Bivariate Distributions.

and $\qquad E(\mathbf{X}'\mathbf{X})^{-1} \quad$ by $\quad (\mathbf{X}'\mathbf{X})^{-1}$

It can be shown that the result is an unbiased estimator of Eq. (7-26) for

$$\begin{aligned} E\{s^2(\mathbf{X}'\mathbf{X})^{-1}\} &= E_{\mathbf{x}}\{E_{s^2|\mathbf{x}}s^2(\mathbf{X}'\mathbf{X})^{-1}\} \\ &= E_{\mathbf{x}}\{\sigma^2(\mathbf{X}'\mathbf{X})^{-1}\} \\ &= \sigma^2 E(\mathbf{X}'\mathbf{X})^{-1} \end{aligned}$$

To summarize the position so far, when the X's are stochastic but independent of the u's, the ML (= OLS) estimators for the fixed **X** case are still ML for the stochastic case, and thus all the conventional test procedures are still justified asymptotically. For finite samples the OLS (ML) $\mathbf{b}(\boldsymbol{\beta})$ is unconditionally unbiased, and var(**b**) attains the Cramer-Rao MVB. Moreover the conventional estimator $s^2(\mathbf{X}'\mathbf{X})^{-1}$ is an unbiased estimator of that MVB.

The only remaining question concerns the finite sample validity of the conventional inference procedures. The basic result is that all confidence interval statements and significance levels derived from the usual formulas are still correct, but the probabilities of type II errors and the widths of confidence intervals will be different. Confidence intervals and hypothesis tests are derived by calculating probabilities from the sampling distribution of some appropriate test statistic under H_0. The test statistic is in general some function of the sample observations and may be denoted by $t(\mathbf{y}, \mathbf{X})$. If, for example, the test statistic is found to follow the t distribution, then we may make the probability statement

$$\Pr\{-t_{\alpha/2} < t(\mathbf{y}, \mathbf{X}) < t_{\alpha/2}\} = 1 - \alpha \tag{7-27}$$

This statement may be used to derive a confidence interval or, equivalently, to determine a critical region for a test of H_0 at the α level of significance.

The statement in Eq. (7-27), however, has been derived under the assumption of a fixed **X** matrix, and so it is a conditional probability statement. We need to find what *unconditional* probability statement can be made about $t(\cdot)$ when the stochastic nature of **X** is allowed for. Let A denote the event

$$A: \quad -t_{\alpha/2} < t(\cdot) < t_{\alpha/2}$$

and let us suppose that the pdf for **X** gives a finite number of **X** matrices,

$$\mathbf{X}_1, \mathbf{X}_2, \ldots, \mathbf{X}_m$$

with associated probabilities

$$p_1, p_2, \ldots, p_m \qquad \text{with } \sum_i^m p_i = 1$$

A restatement of Eq. (7-27) then gives

$$\Pr\{A|\mathbf{X}_i\} = 1 - \alpha \qquad i = 1, \ldots, m$$

and the unconditional probability of A is

$$\Pr(A) = \sum_{i=1}^m \Pr\{A|\mathbf{X}_i\} = (1 - \alpha)\sum_{i=1}^m p_i = 1 - \alpha \tag{7-28}$$

Thus a confidence interval computed in the usual way will have the same confidence coefficient for random **X** as for fixed **X**, and a hypothesis test will have the same significance level in each case. The assumption of a discrete distribution for **X** is only a simplification, and it is clear that the argument carries through for continuous distributions.† Notice that it has not been necessary to derive the sampling distributions of the estimators to establish the above result. These distributions will be more complicated than those already obtained in Chap. 5. As an illustration consider the ML estimator $\hat{\beta}$ of the slope coefficient β in a two-variable model. Letting **x** denote the vector of sample observations on the explanatory variable, we know that the *conditional* distribution of $\hat{\boldsymbol{\beta}}$, given x, is

$$f(\hat{\beta}|\mathbf{x}) = N\left(\beta, \frac{\sigma^2}{\Sigma x^2}\right)$$

When **x** is stochastic, the *marginal* distribution of $\hat{\beta}$ is

$$f(\hat{\beta}) = f(\hat{\beta}|\mathbf{x}) \cdot g(\mathbf{x})$$

where $g(\mathbf{x})$ is the marginal distribution of **x**. Clearly, the marginal distribution depends on the distribution of **x**, but the crux of the matter is that, provided **x** and **u** are fully independent and the parameters of $g(\mathbf{x})$ do not involve $\boldsymbol{\beta}$ or σ^2, the precise form of $g(\mathbf{x})$ does not affect the probability statements underlying confidence coefficients and significance levels.

PROBLEMS

7-1 Derive the mean and the variance of the ML estimator $\hat{\sigma}^2 = \mathbf{e}'\mathbf{e}/n$ of the disturbance variance for the regression model $\mathbf{y} = \mathbf{X}\boldsymbol{\beta} + \mathbf{u}$ with $\mathbf{u} \sim N(\mathbf{0}, \sigma^2\mathbf{I})$. (*Hint*: If $w \sim \chi^2(r)$, then $E(w) = r$ and $\text{var}(w) = 2r$.)

7-2 Prove that the OLS estimator $s^2 = \mathbf{e}'\mathbf{e}/(n - k)$ and the ML estimator of σ^2 in the regression model of Problem 7-1 are both consistent.

7-3 Suppose that we have n independent observations $y_1, y_2, \ldots, y_n$, say, incomes, drawn by simple random sampling from a Pareto distribution which has the following pdf:

$$P(y|\alpha) = \frac{\alpha 10{,}000^{\alpha}}{y^{\alpha+1}} \qquad y \geq 10{,}000;\ \alpha > 0$$

What is the ML estimate for α?

(University of Washington, 1979)

7-4 Consider a regression equation

$$y_i = \alpha + \beta x_i + \varepsilon_i \qquad i = 1, 2, \ldots, n$$

where x_i is nonstochastic and $\varepsilon_1, \varepsilon_2, \ldots, \varepsilon_n$ are independently and identically distributed. The distribution of ε_i is

$$f(\varepsilon_i) = \lambda \varepsilon_i^{-(\lambda+1)} \qquad 1 \leq \varepsilon_i \leq \infty;\ \lambda > 2$$

† A complete derivation of this and other results is given in F. A. Graybill, *Theory and Application of the Linear Model*, Duxburg Press, Mass., 1976, chap. 10.

Suppose λ is not known. Set up the likelihood function for $y_1, y_2, \ldots, y_n$ and describe a way to obtain ML estimates of α, β, and λ.

(University of Michigan, 1977)

7-5 Consider the uniform density

$$f(X) = 1/\alpha \qquad 0 < X < \alpha$$

What is the ML estimator for α? Does it attain the Cramer-Rao lower bound? Compare the asymptotic efficiency of the ML estimator for α with the alternative estimator derived from using the sample mean, and prove the consistency of that estimator for α.

(University of Chicago, 1975)

CHAPTER
EIGHT

GENERALIZED LEAST SQUARES

A basic assumption underpinning the methods outlined in Chaps. 5 and 6 is that

$$E(\mathbf{uu}') = \sigma^2\mathbf{I} \tag{8-1}$$

This is described as the assumption of *spherical disturbances*. It involves the double assumption that the disturbance variance is constant at each observation point and that the disturbance covariances at all possible pairs of observation points are zero. We now seek to do four things, namely:

1. To indicate some of the more important cases in which assumption (8-1) may not be fulfilled
2. To determine the properties of OLS estimators if they are (perhaps inadvertently) applied, even though the underpinning assumption about the disturbances is not valid
3. To develop tests of whether assumption (8-1) has broken down
4. To develop appropriate estimation procedures for cases where assumption (8-1) does not apply

8-1 SOURCES OF NONSPHERICAL DISTURBANCES

If the sample observations relate to households or firms in a cross-section study, the assumption of a common disturbance variance at all observation points is often implausible. For example, if Y refers to family expenditure and X to family income, the variance about the Engel curve is likely to increase with the size of X.

Similarly if Y denotes profits and X is some measure of firm size, the same property is to be expected. The specification of the disturbance variance matrix would then be

$$E(\mathbf{uu}') = \begin{bmatrix} \sigma_1^2 & 0 & \cdots & 0 \\ 0 & \sigma_2^2 & \cdots & 0 \\ \cdots & \cdots & \cdots & \cdots \\ 0 & 0 & \cdots & \sigma_n^2 \end{bmatrix} \tag{8-2}$$

which is the standard case of *heteroscedasticity*. Formulation (8-2) still assumes that the disturbances are pairwise uncorrelated.

Suppose, to take a different example, that an investigator is studying the relationship between wage change and the level of unemployment and that he measures wage movements in terms of four-quarter overlapping changes. That is, the annual rate of wage change in quarter t is specified as

$$\frac{w_t - w_{t-4}}{w_{t-4}}$$

where w_t is the level of the wage index in quarter t. The observed change in the index, $w_t - w_{t-4}$, is the result of some groups securing a wage change in quarter $t - 3$, some others in quarter $t - 2$, and so forth. If one assumes one fourth of the labor force to secure a wage change in each quarter, the dependent variable is an average of these separate changes, and the disturbance term in the macrowage equation is similarly an average of the separate quarterly disturbances and so might be specified as

$$u_t = \tfrac{1}{4}(\varepsilon_t + \varepsilon_{t-1} + \varepsilon_{t-2} + \varepsilon_{t-3}) \tag{8-3}$$

where the ε's indicate the disturbances in the wage change equations for the separate groups. Let us assume

$$E(\boldsymbol{\varepsilon}) = \mathbf{0} \qquad \text{and} \qquad E(\boldsymbol{\varepsilon\varepsilon}') = \sigma_\varepsilon^2\mathbf{I} \tag{8-4}$$

It then follows from Eq. (8-3) that

$$E(u_t^2) = \tfrac{1}{4}\sigma_\varepsilon^2$$

which does not depend on t, so that the $\{u_t\}$ series is homoscedastic. Further

$$E(u_t u_{t-1}) = \tfrac{3}{16}\sigma_\varepsilon^2$$
$$E(u_t u_{t-2}) = \tfrac{2}{16}\sigma_\varepsilon^2$$
$$E(u_t u_{t-3}) = \tfrac{1}{16}\sigma_\varepsilon^2$$

and

$$E(u_t u_{t-s}) = 0 \qquad \text{for } s \geq 4$$

Thus the variance matrix following from Eqs. (8-3) and (8-4) is

$$E(\mathbf{uu}') = \frac{1}{16}\sigma_\varepsilon^2 \begin{bmatrix} 4 & 3 & 2 & 1 & 0 & 0 & 0 & & \cdots & & 0 \\ 3 & 4 & 3 & 2 & 1 & 0 & 0 & & \cdots & & 0 \\ 2 & 3 & 4 & 3 & 2 & 1 & 0 & & \cdots & & 0 \\ 1 & 2 & 3 & 4 & 3 & 2 & 1 & & \cdots & & 0 \\ \cdots & \cdots & \cdots & \cdots & \cdots & \cdots & \cdots & \cdots & \cdots & \cdots & \cdots \\ 0 & & & & & & & 1 & 2 & 3 & 4 \end{bmatrix} \tag{8-5}$$

This again is a departure from Eq. (8-1), but in contrast with Eq. (8-2) there is just one unknown in Eq. (8-5), namely, σ_ε^2. This is an example of *autocorrelated* disturbances. The autocorrelation arose from temporal aggregation over individual disturbances, which were themselves uncorrelated over time.

To continue the wage change model, it was customary in many early studies of the Phillips curve for researchers to employ four-quarter overlapping changes. These, however, have some unfortunate side effects. In consequence it is now more customary to specify a model of the form

$$\frac{w_t - w_{t-1}}{w_{t-1}} = \alpha + \mathbf{x}_t'\boldsymbol{\beta} + u_t \tag{8-6}$$

where the dependent variable is now expressed as a one-quarter change in the wage index, and $\mathbf{x}_t'$ denotes a vector of explanatory variables, such as expected price inflation, the reciprocal of the unemployment rate, and so forth.† With the specification (8-6), however, it becomes less appropriate to specify zero correlations for various disturbances. In particular, neighboring disturbances might be positively correlated. Suppose, for instance, that an "unusually large" settlement was secured by the workers settling in period $t - 1$, where unusually large means "larger than would normally be associated with the vector $\mathbf{x}_{t-1}$." If this leads to a greater than usual "push" by the workers negotiating in period t, then we might specify

$$u_t = \rho u_{t-1} + \varepsilon_t \tag{8-7}$$

where ρ is some parameter, and the $\{\varepsilon_t\}$ series has the usual simple properties specified in Eq. (8-4). Equation (8-7) specifies a first-order autoregressive (Markov) scheme—autoregressive since u is related to lagged values of itself, and first-order because the maximum lag in the autoregression is 1.

Let us introduce the lag operator L such that, when applied to any variable x_t,

$$Lx_t = x_{t-1}$$

$$L^2x_t = L(Lx_t) = Lx_{t-1} = x_{t-2}$$

and, in general,

$$L^s x_t = x_{t-s} \qquad s \geq 1$$

Thus Eq. (8-7) may be rewritten as

$$(1 - \rho L)u_t = \varepsilon_t$$

or‡

$$u_t = \frac{1}{1 - \rho L}\varepsilon_t$$

$$= (1 + \rho L + \rho^2 L^2 + \cdots)\varepsilon_t$$

† Note that we retain our convention of using u to indicate the disturbance term in Eq. (8-6). It does *not* indicate the unemployment rate.

‡ The lag operator may be treated as a scalar for purposes of algebraic manipulation. For any nonzero constant a we have $(1 - a)^{-1} = 1 + a + a^2 + \cdots$. Replacing a by ρL gives the result stated above.

that is,

$$u_t = \varepsilon_t + \rho\varepsilon_{t-1} + \rho^2\varepsilon_{t-2} + \cdots \tag{8-8}$$

Squaring both sides of Eq. (8-8) and taking expectations,

$$\operatorname{var}(u_t) = E(u_t^2) = \frac{\sigma_\varepsilon^2}{1-\rho^2} \qquad |\rho| < 1 \tag{8-9}$$

The right-hand side does not involve t, thus the $\{u_t\}$ series has a constant variance, $\sigma^2 = \sigma_\varepsilon^2/(1-\rho^2)$.

Using the definition of u_t in Eq. (8-8) and the properties of ε_t assumed in Eq. (8-4), it is simple to establish that

$$E(u_t u_{t-1}) = \rho\sigma^2$$

$$E(u_t u_{t-2}) = \rho^2\sigma^2$$

and, in general,

$$E(u_t u_{t-s}) = \rho^s\sigma^2 \tag{8-10}$$

Thus the variance matrix for a disturbance following a first-order autoregressive scheme is

$$E(\mathbf{uu}') = \sigma^2 \begin{bmatrix} 1 & \rho & \rho^2 & \cdots & \rho^{n-1} \\ \rho & 1 & \rho & \cdots & \rho^{n-2} \\ \cdots & \cdots & \cdots & \cdots & \cdots \\ \rho^{n-1} & \rho^{n-2} & \rho^{n-3} & \cdots & 1 \end{bmatrix} \tag{8-11}$$

If ρ were known, this expression, like Eq. (8-5), would involve only one unknown.

There are many other ways, as we shall see later, in which nonspherical disturbances may arise, but these three examples illustrate some important patterns. The general nonspherical disturbance matrix may be specified as

$$E(\mathbf{uu}') = \sigma^2\boldsymbol{\Omega} \tag{8-12a}$$

or

$$E(\mathbf{uu}') = \mathbf{V} \tag{8-12b}$$

The choice of specification depends on whether or not we wish to single out an unknown scalar, which multiplies all the elements in the matrix as in Eqs. (8-5) and (8-11). In either case, since we are dealing with a disturbance matrix, $\boldsymbol{\Omega}$ and $\mathbf{V}$ are assumed to be positive definite matrices.

8-2 PROPERTIES OF OLS ESTIMATORS UNDER NONSPHERICAL DISTURBANCES

Our assumed model is now

$$\mathbf{y} = \mathbf{X}\boldsymbol{\beta} + \mathbf{u}$$

where $\mathbf{X}$ is taken as a nonstochastic matrix with full column rank,

$$E(\mathbf{u}) = \mathbf{0} \qquad \text{and} \qquad E(\mathbf{uu}') = \mathbf{V} \qquad (\text{or } \sigma^2\boldsymbol{\Omega})$$

The OLS estimator of $\boldsymbol{\beta}$ may be expressed as usual as

$$\mathbf{b} = \boldsymbol{\beta} + (\mathbf{X'X})^{-1}\mathbf{X'u}$$

Thus

$$E(\mathbf{b}) = \boldsymbol{\beta}$$

so that OLS is still unbiased. The variance matrix is given by

$$\begin{aligned} \text{var}(\mathbf{b}) &= E\{(\mathbf{b} - \boldsymbol{\beta})(\mathbf{b} - \boldsymbol{\beta})'\} \\ &= E\{(\mathbf{X'X})^{-1}\mathbf{X'uu'X}(\mathbf{X'X})^{-1}\} \\ &= \sigma^2(\mathbf{X'X})^{-1}\mathbf{X'\Omega X}(\mathbf{X'X})^{-1} \end{aligned} \tag{8-13}$$

Thus the conventional formula $\sigma^2(\mathbf{X'X})^{-1}$ no longer measures the sampling variances of the OLS estimators, and any application of it is potentially misleading. More importantly, even if one could use Eq. (8-13) to estimate the sampling variances, the substitution of these numbers in the conventional t formulas and confidence interval formulas is strictly invalid since the assumptions used in deriving those inference procedures no longer apply. For the same reason the optimal minimum variance property of OLS no longer holds. We will illustrate these points for various specific departures from spherical disturbances in later sections and also discuss various specific tests for departures from spherical disturbances. Now it is more important to turn to the development of a more appropriate estimator.

8-3 THE GENERALIZED LEAST-SQUARES ESTIMATOR

Suppose we premultiply the assumed model

$$\mathbf{y} = \mathbf{X}\boldsymbol{\beta} + \mathbf{u}$$

by some $n \times n$ nonsingular transformation matrix $\mathbf{T}$ to obtain

$$\mathbf{Ty} = (\mathbf{TX})\boldsymbol{\beta} + \mathbf{Tu} \tag{8-14}$$

Each element in the vector $\mathbf{Ty}$ is then some linear combination of the elements in $\mathbf{y}$, and so forth. The variance matrix for the disturbance in Eq. (8-14) is

$$E(\mathbf{Tuu'T'}) = \sigma^2\mathbf{T\Omega T'} \tag{8-15}$$

since $E(\mathbf{Tu}) = \mathbf{0}$. If it were possible to specify $\mathbf{T}$ such that

$$\mathbf{T\Omega T'} = \mathbf{I} \tag{8-16}$$

then we could apply OLS to the transformed variables $\mathbf{Ty}$ and $\mathbf{TX}$ in Eq. (8-14), and the resultant estimates would have all the optimal properties of OLS and could be validly subjected to the usual inference procedures.

It is, in fact, possible to find a matrix $\mathbf{T}$ which will satisfy Eq. (8-16), for it was shown in Eq. (4-111) that if $\boldsymbol{\Omega}$ is a symmetric positive definite matrix, a nonsingular matrix $\mathbf{P}$ can be found such that

$$\boldsymbol{\Omega} = \mathbf{PP'}$$

Since $\mathbf{P}$ is nonsingular,

$$\mathbf{P}^{-1}\boldsymbol{\Omega}\mathbf{P}'^{-1} = \mathbf{I} \tag{8-17}$$

Comparison of Eqs. (8-16) and (8-17) shows that the appropriate $\mathbf{T}$ is given by

$$\mathbf{T} = \mathbf{P}^{-1}$$

and it easily follows that

$$\begin{aligned}\boldsymbol{\Omega}^{-1} &= \mathbf{P}'^{-1}\mathbf{P}^{-1} \\ &= (\mathbf{P}^{-1})'\mathbf{P}^{-1} \\ &= \mathbf{T}'\mathbf{T}\end{aligned}$$

Applying OLS to Eq. (8-14) then gives

$$\begin{aligned}\mathbf{b}_* &= (\mathbf{X}'\mathbf{T}'\mathbf{T}\mathbf{X})^{-1}\mathbf{X}'\mathbf{T}'\mathbf{T}\mathbf{y} \\ &= (\mathbf{X}'\boldsymbol{\Omega}^{-1}\mathbf{X})^{-1}\mathbf{X}'\boldsymbol{\Omega}^{-1}\mathbf{y}\end{aligned} \tag{8-18}$$

with the variance-covariance matrix given by

$$\operatorname{var}(\mathbf{b}_*) = \sigma^2(\mathbf{X}'\boldsymbol{\Omega}^{-1}\mathbf{X})^{-1} \tag{8-19}$$

The estimator $\mathbf{b}_*$ is defined to be the generalized least-squares (GLS) or Aitken estimator. Since Eqs. (8-15) and (8-16) imply that Eq. (8-14) satisfies the assumptions required for the application of OLS, it follows that $\mathbf{b}_*$ is a best linear unbiased estimator of $\boldsymbol{\beta}$ in the model $\mathbf{y} = \mathbf{X}\boldsymbol{\beta} + \mathbf{u}$ with $E(\mathbf{u}\mathbf{u}') = \sigma^2\boldsymbol{\Omega}$.

Alternatively Eq. (8-15) may be written

$$E(\mathbf{T}\mathbf{u}\mathbf{u}'\mathbf{T}') = \mathbf{T}\mathbf{V}\mathbf{T}'$$

and setting $\mathbf{T}\mathbf{V}\mathbf{T}' = \mathbf{I}$ gives $\mathbf{T}'\mathbf{T} = \mathbf{V}^{-1}$ so that the GLS estimator may also be written as

$$\mathbf{b}_* = (\mathbf{X}'\mathbf{V}^{-1}\mathbf{X})^{-1}\mathbf{X}'\mathbf{V}^{-1}\mathbf{y} \tag{8-20}$$

with

$$\operatorname{var}(\mathbf{b}_*) = (\mathbf{X}'\mathbf{V}^{-1}\mathbf{X})^{-1} \tag{8-21}$$

Comparing Eqs. (8-18) and (8-20) shows that it makes no difference to $\mathbf{b}_*$ whether var($\mathbf{u}$) is formulated as $\sigma^2\boldsymbol{\Omega}$ or as $\mathbf{V}$, but care has to be taken to select the correct expression for var($\mathbf{b}_*$), as a comparison of Eqs. (8-19) and (8-21) shows.†

If the further assumption of normality for the u's is added, it may be shown that the GLS estimator is also an ML estimator. We specify

$$\mathbf{u} \sim N(\mathbf{0}, \sigma^2\boldsymbol{\Omega})$$

Thus the likelihood function is

$$L = p(\mathbf{y}|\mathbf{X}) = \frac{1}{(2\pi)^{n/2}\sigma^n|\boldsymbol{\Omega}|^{1/2}}\exp\left[-\frac{1}{2\sigma^2}(\mathbf{y} - \mathbf{X}\boldsymbol{\beta})'\boldsymbol{\Omega}^{-1}(\mathbf{y} - \mathbf{X}\boldsymbol{\beta})\right]$$

and the log likelihood is

$$\ln L = -\frac{n}{2}\ln(2\pi) - \frac{n}{2}\ln(\sigma^2) - \frac{1}{2}\ln|\boldsymbol{\Omega}| - \frac{1}{2\sigma^2}(\mathbf{y} - \mathbf{X}\boldsymbol{\beta})'\boldsymbol{\Omega}^{-1}(\mathbf{y} - \mathbf{X}\boldsymbol{\beta})$$

† Note that the transformation matrix $\mathbf{T}$, defined in Eq. (8-16), differs by a scale factor from that defined by $\mathbf{T}\mathbf{V}\mathbf{T}' = \mathbf{I}$.

Maximizing $\ln L$ with respect to $\boldsymbol{\beta}$ implies minimizing the weighted sum of squares

$$(\mathbf{y} - \mathbf{X}\boldsymbol{\beta})'\boldsymbol{\Omega}^{-1}(\mathbf{y} - \mathbf{X}\boldsymbol{\beta}) = \mathbf{y}'\boldsymbol{\Omega}^{-1}\mathbf{y} - 2\boldsymbol{\beta}'\mathbf{X}'\boldsymbol{\Omega}^{-1}\mathbf{y} + \boldsymbol{\beta}'\mathbf{X}'\boldsymbol{\Omega}^{-1}\mathbf{X}\boldsymbol{\beta}$$

Differentiating with respect to $\boldsymbol{\beta}$ and equating to zero gives

$$\mathbf{b}_* = (\mathbf{X}'\boldsymbol{\Omega}^{-1}\mathbf{X})^{-1}\mathbf{X}'\boldsymbol{\Omega}^{-1}\mathbf{y}$$

as in Eq. (8-18).

An unbiased estimator of σ^2 may be derived from the application of OLS to Eq. (8-14). It is

$$\begin{aligned} s^2 &= \frac{(\mathbf{Ty} - \mathbf{TXb}_*)'(\mathbf{Ty} - \mathbf{Txb}_*)}{n-k} \\ &= \frac{(\mathbf{y} - \mathbf{Xb}_*)'\mathbf{T}'\mathbf{T}(\mathbf{y} - \mathbf{Xb}_*)}{n-k} \\ &= \frac{(\mathbf{y} - \mathbf{Xb}_*)'\boldsymbol{\Omega}^{-1}(\mathbf{y} - \mathbf{Xb}_*)}{n-k} \\ &= \frac{\mathbf{y}'\boldsymbol{\Omega}^{-1}\mathbf{y} - \mathbf{b}_*'\mathbf{X}'\boldsymbol{\Omega}^{-1}\mathbf{y}}{n-k} \end{aligned} \tag{8-22}$$

On the assumption of normality for the disturbance term all the inference procedures of Chaps. 5 and 6 carry through for this model. Thus the test of

$$H_0\text{:}\quad \mathbf{R}\boldsymbol{\beta} = \mathbf{r}$$

is based on

$$F = \frac{(\mathbf{r} - \mathbf{Rb}_*)'\left[\mathbf{R}(\mathbf{X}'\boldsymbol{\Omega}^{-1}\mathbf{X})^{-1}\mathbf{R}'\right]^{-1}(\mathbf{r} - \mathbf{Rb}_*)/q}{s^2}$$

having the $F(q, n-k)$ distribution under the null hypothesis, where $\mathbf{b}_*$ is the GLS estimator defined in Eq. (8-18) and s^2 the variance estimator defined in Eq. (8-22).

The above formulas are only operational if the elements of $\boldsymbol{\Omega}$ are known. In some exceptional cases this may be so, but in most practical cases it is not. We must therefore proceed to the development of operational procedures for such cases, but there is, in fact, no single procedure which is generally applicable. One must look for the procedure which is best suited to the features of each specific problem in turn, and that is done in the remaining sections of this chapter.

8-4 HETEROSCEDASTICITY

We have already mentioned in Sec. 8-1 the possibility of heteroscedastic disturbances in *cross-section* studies. Heteroscedasticity may also arise in dealing with grouped data. Suppose the model is

$$Y_t = \alpha + \beta X_t + u_t \qquad t = 1, \ldots, n$$

where the u_t are homoscedastic with zero covariances. However, suppose we only have access to data which have been averaged within m groups, where n_i indicates the number of observations in the ith group. The form of the model appropriate to the data is now

$$\bar{Y}_i = \alpha + \beta \bar{X}_i + \bar{u}_i$$

and clearly

$$\operatorname{var}(\bar{u}_i) = \frac{\sigma^2}{n_i} \qquad i = 1, \ldots, m$$

Thus

$$\sigma^2 \boldsymbol{\Omega} = \sigma^2 \begin{bmatrix} \frac{1}{n_1} & 0 & \cdots & 0 \\ 0 & \frac{1}{n_2} & \cdots & 0 \\ \cdots & \cdots & \cdots & \cdots \\ 0 & 0 & \cdots & \frac{1}{n_m} \end{bmatrix} \tag{8-23}$$

where $\boldsymbol{\Omega}$ is known and the GLS estimator can easily be computed.

Example 8-1 We have taken the same X, Y data as in Example 2-1, only now it is assumed that they relate to group means. The n_i column indicates the number of observations in each group. The overall means are easily computed from

$$\bar{X} = \frac{\Sigma n_i \bar{X}_i}{\Sigma n_i} = \frac{202}{50} = 4.04$$

$$\bar{Y} = \frac{\Sigma n_i \bar{Y}_i}{\Sigma n_i} = \frac{400}{50} = 8.00$$

which are almost identical with the simple means of 4 and 8 in Table 2-1. We assume that Eq. (8-23) is the appropriate assumption about $\operatorname{var}(\bar{\mathbf{u}})$, that is,

$$\operatorname{var}(\bar{\mathbf{u}}) = \sigma^2 \boldsymbol{\Omega} = \sigma^2 \begin{bmatrix} \frac{1}{n_1} & & & \\ & \frac{1}{n_2} & & \\ & & \ddots & \\ & & & \frac{1}{n_5} \end{bmatrix}$$

Thus

$$\Omega^{-1} = \begin{bmatrix} n_1 & & & \\ & n_2 & & \\ & & \ddots & \\ & & & n_5 \end{bmatrix} = \begin{bmatrix} 12 & & & & \\ & 6 & & & \\ & & 11 & & \\ & & & 10 & \\ & & & & 11 \end{bmatrix}$$

It may then be seen that

$$\mathbf{X}'\Omega^{-1}\mathbf{X} = \begin{bmatrix} 1 & 1 & \cdots & 1 \\ \bar{X}_1 & \bar{X}_2 & \cdots & \bar{X}_5 \end{bmatrix} \begin{bmatrix} n_1 & & & \\ & n_2 & & \\ & & \ddots & \\ & & & n_5 \end{bmatrix} \begin{bmatrix} 1 & \bar{X}_1 \\ 1 & \bar{X}_2 \\ \vdots & \vdots \\ 1 & \bar{X}_5 \end{bmatrix}$$

$$= \begin{bmatrix} \Sigma n_i & \Sigma n_i \bar{X}_i \\ \Sigma n_i \bar{X}_i & \Sigma n_i \bar{X}_i^2 \end{bmatrix}$$

and

$$\mathbf{X}'\Omega^{-1}\mathbf{y} = \begin{bmatrix} \Sigma n_i \bar{Y}_i \\ \Sigma n_i \bar{X}_i \bar{Y}_i \end{bmatrix}$$

Formula (8-18) for the GLS estimator now simplifies to

$$\begin{bmatrix} \Sigma n_i & \Sigma n_i \bar{X}_i \\ \Sigma n_i \bar{X}_i & \Sigma n_i \bar{X}_i^2 \end{bmatrix} \mathbf{b}_* = \begin{bmatrix} \Sigma n_i \bar{Y}_i \\ \Sigma n_i \bar{X}_i \bar{Y}_i \end{bmatrix}$$

which is a form of weighted least squares. Applying the data from Table 8-1 gives

$$50b_{1*} + 202b_{2*} = 400$$

$$202b_{1*} + 1254b_{2*} = 2388$$

with solution $b_{1*} = 0.88$ and $b_{2*} = 1.76$. To obtain the sampling variance of these estimates, substitute for Ω^{-1} from Eq. (8-23) in Eq. (8-22) to obtain for

Table 8-1

$\bar{X}_i$	$\bar{Y}_i$	n_i	$n_i\bar{X}_i$	$n_i\bar{Y}_i$	$n_i\bar{X}_i^2$	$n_i\bar{X}_i\bar{Y}_i$	$n_i\bar{Y}_i^2$
2	4	12	24	48	48	96	192
3	7	6	18	42	54	126	294
1	3	11	11	33	11	33	99
5	9	10	50	90	250	450	810
9	17	11	99	187	891	1683	3179
Sums		50	202	400	1254	2388	4574

this example

$$(n-k)s^2 = \Sigma n_i \bar{Y}_i^2 - [b_{1*} \quad b_{2*}]\begin{bmatrix} \Sigma n_i \bar{Y}_i \\ \Sigma n_i \bar{X}_i \bar{Y}_i \end{bmatrix}$$

$$= 4574 - [0.8791 \quad 1.7626]\begin{bmatrix} 400 \\ 2388 \end{bmatrix}$$

$$= 13.2712$$

Thus $$s^2 = \frac{13.2712}{3} = 4.4237$$

Notice that the n which occurs in the denominator of the variance formula, Eq. (8-22), is the number of sample points. It is *not* the total number of observations underlying the sample points. In this example, the latter number is $\Sigma n_i = 50$, but $n = 5$. Finally, substitution in Eq. (8-19) gives

$$\text{var}(\mathbf{b}_*) = s^2(\mathbf{X}'\mathbf{\Omega}^{-1}\mathbf{X})^{-1}$$

$$= 4.4237\begin{bmatrix} 50 & 202 \\ 202 & 1254 \end{bmatrix}^{-1}$$

$$= 4.4237\begin{bmatrix} 0.057271 & -0.009225 \\ -0.009225 & 0.002284 \end{bmatrix}$$

$$= \begin{bmatrix} 0.2533 & -0.0408 \\ -0.0408 & 0.0101 \end{bmatrix}$$

Thus $$\text{var}(b_{1*}) = 0.2533$$

$$\text{var}(b_{2*}) = 0.0101$$

This example might have been treated equivalently by finding the $\mathbf{T}$ matrix satisfying $\mathbf{T}'\mathbf{T} = \mathbf{\Omega}^{-1}$. Given $\mathbf{\Omega}^{-1}$, the $\mathbf{T}$ matrix is simply

$$\mathbf{T} = \begin{bmatrix} \sqrt{n_1} & & & \\ & \sqrt{n_2} & & \\ & & \ddots & \\ & & & \sqrt{n_5} \end{bmatrix}$$

Thus the data of Table 8-1 could have been recorded as

X_i	$2\sqrt{12}$	$3\sqrt{6}$	$1\sqrt{11}$	$5\sqrt{10}$	$9\sqrt{11}$
Y_i	$4\sqrt{12}$	$7\sqrt{6}$	$3\sqrt{11}$	$9\sqrt{10}$	$17\sqrt{11}$

and OLS applied to these five pairs of numbers.

A different variant of a cross-section study is one with *replication* of the Y variable for given values of X. Suppose, for instance, that agronomists are investigating the variation of crop yield in response to varying applications of fertilizer. Let $X_1, \ldots, X_i, \ldots, X_m$ denote the different fertilizer dosages chosen for the experiment. For dosage X_i, n_i plots are chosen, and Y_{ij} $(j = 1,\ldots, n_i)$ denotes the resultant set of n_i yields. A model for the linear effect of fertilizer on yield would then be specified as

$$Y_{ij} = \alpha + \beta X_i + u_{ij} \qquad i = 1,\ldots, m; \quad j = 1,\ldots, n_i \tag{8-24}$$

Denoting the vector of disturbances in the ith application by $\mathbf{u}_i$, we make the conventional assumptions

$$E(\mathbf{u}_i) = \mathbf{0} \qquad \text{and} \qquad E(\mathbf{u}_i\mathbf{u}_i') = \sigma_i^2\mathbf{I}_{n_i} \qquad i = 1,\ldots, m \tag{8-25}$$

Thus Eq. (8-25) allows the disturbance variance to be different in different applications, but assumes homoscedasticity and zero covariances *within* applications. However, an additional assumption is now required to cover the relations between disturbances in different applications. We assume these to be uncorrelated, that is,

$$E(\mathbf{u}_i\mathbf{u}_r') = \mathbf{0} \qquad i, r = 1,\ldots, m; \quad i \neq r \tag{8-26}$$

The complete model may now be written

$$\begin{bmatrix} \mathbf{y}_1 \\ \mathbf{y}_2 \\ \vdots \\ \mathbf{y}_m \end{bmatrix} = \begin{bmatrix} \mathbf{X}_1 \\ \mathbf{X}_2 \\ \vdots \\ \mathbf{X}_m \end{bmatrix} \begin{bmatrix} \alpha \\ \beta \end{bmatrix} + \begin{bmatrix} \mathbf{u}_1 \\ \mathbf{u}_2 \\ \vdots \\ \mathbf{u}_m \end{bmatrix} \tag{8-27}$$

where

$$\mathbf{X}_i = \begin{bmatrix} 1 & X_i \\ 1 & X_i \\ \vdots & \vdots \\ 1 & X_i \end{bmatrix} \qquad i = 1,\ldots, m$$

A more compact form of Eq. (8-27) is

$$\mathbf{y} = \mathbf{X}\boldsymbol{\beta} + \mathbf{u}$$

where $\mathbf{y}' = [\mathbf{y}_1' \quad \mathbf{y}_2' \quad \cdots \quad \mathbf{y}_m']$, and so on. Assumptions (8-25) and (8-26) produce a block-diagonal form for var($\mathbf{u}$), namely,

$$\text{var}(\mathbf{u}) = \begin{bmatrix} \sigma_1^2\mathbf{I}_{n_1} & \mathbf{0} & \cdots & \mathbf{0} \\ \mathbf{0} & \sigma_2^2\mathbf{I}_{n_2} & \cdots & \mathbf{0} \\ \cdots & \cdots & \cdots & \cdots \\ \mathbf{0} & \mathbf{0} & \cdots & \sigma_m^2\mathbf{I}_{n_m} \end{bmatrix} \tag{8-28}$$

Notice that each $\mathbf{X}_i$ submatrix has only unit rank, since the same dosage is applied to all plots within the group, but the $\mathbf{X}$ matrix has full column rank.

Model (8-27) is a special case of a more general model, which may be written

$$\begin{bmatrix} \mathbf{y}_1 \\ \vdots \\ \mathbf{y}_m \end{bmatrix} = \begin{bmatrix} \mathbf{X}_1 \\ \vdots \\ \mathbf{X}_m \end{bmatrix} \boldsymbol{\beta} + \begin{bmatrix} \mathbf{u}_1 \\ \vdots \\ \mathbf{u}_m \end{bmatrix} \tag{8-29}$$

where each $\mathbf{X}_i$ is of order $n_i \times k$, the rows of $\mathbf{X}_i$ are not required to be identical, and the assumption is still made that var(**u**) has the block-diagonal structure given in Eq. (8-28). For example, Y_{ij} might represent investment expenditure by firm i in year j and the X's the variables thought to influence investment expenditures. The study would thus cover m different firms in various years, that is, a pooling of time-series and cross-section data. Model (8-29) assumes a common set of reaction coefficients $\boldsymbol{\beta}$ for all firms, but assumption (8-28) would allow the disturbance variances to differ across firms.†

Testing for Heteroscedasticity

Test for the equality of variances. In the case of replicated data, model (8-27), and $\mathbf{u}_i \sim N(0, \sigma_i^2 \mathbf{I}_{n_i})$, a standard test for the equality of variances is available. The hypothesis of homoscedasticity is

$$H_0: \quad \sigma_1^2 = \sigma_2^2 = \cdots = \sigma_m^2$$

The test is conducted as follows.‡

1. For each class or group, compute the within-group sample variance

$$s_i^2 = \frac{\sum_{j=1}^{n_i}\left(Y_{ij} - \bar{Y}_i\right)^2}{\nu_i} \qquad i = 1, \ldots, m$$

where $\nu_i = n_i - 1$, and

$$\bar{Y}_i = \frac{\sum_{j=1}^{n_i} Y_{ij}}{n_i}$$

2. Then compute the pooled variance

$$s^2 = \frac{\sum_{i=1}^{m} \nu_i s_i^2}{\nu}$$

where

$$\nu = \sum_{i=1}^{m} (n_i - 1)$$

and the quantity

$$Q' = \nu \ln s^2 - \sum_{i=1}^{m} \nu_i \ln s_i^2$$

Under the null hypothesis Q' will be approximately distributed as $\chi^2(m - 1)$. However, the approximation will be improved by dividing Q' by the scaling

† The zero covariances incorporated in Eq. (8-28) may be an oversimplification for this model. See Sec. 8-6, Sets of Equations, and Sec. 10-3, Pooling of Time-Series and Cross-Section Data.

‡ See M. G. Kendall and A. Stuart, *The Advanced Theory of Statistics*, vol. 2, Griffin, London, 1961, pp. 234–236.

constant

$$C = 1 + \frac{1}{3(m-1)}\left(\sum_{i=1}^{m} \frac{1}{\nu_i} - \frac{1}{\nu}\right)$$

to give

$$Q = \frac{Q'}{C}$$

3. If $Q > \chi^2_{0.95}(m-1)$, say, then the null hypothesis would be rejected at the 5 percent level of significance.

Example 8-2 The data of Table 6-1 do not fit this test exactly since the X variable is not constant within each class. However, we will ignore this discrepancy and use the Y data of Tables 6-1 and 6-2 to illustrate this test. We have $\nu_i = 4$ for each i and

$$\nu = \sum_{i=1}^{m} \nu_i = 16 \qquad m = 4$$

Thus

$$C = 1 + \frac{1}{3(3)}\left(1 - \frac{1}{16}\right) = 1.1042$$

$$s_1^2 = \frac{88}{4} = 22 \qquad s_2^2 = 23.5 \qquad s_3^2 = 51.5 \qquad s_4^2 = 4.5$$

$$\ln s_1^2 = 3.0910 \qquad \ln s_2^2 = 3.1570 \qquad \ln s_3^2 = 3.9416 \qquad \ln s_4^2 = 1.5041$$

$$\Sigma \nu_i \ln s_i^2 = 46.4868$$

$$s^2 = \frac{\Sigma \nu_i s_i^2}{\nu} = 25.3750$$

$$\nu \ln s^2 = 51.7402$$

Thus

$$Q = \frac{51.7402 - 25.3750}{1.1042} = 23.88$$

which exceeds

$$\chi^2_{0.95}(3) = 7.81$$

and the hypothesis of homoscedasticity would be rejected on these numbers. Let us repeat, however, that these calculations were for illustrative purposes only since the within-group variability of X violates a basic assumption underlying the test. A more appropriate procedure would be to replace the within-group Y variances by the residual variances around the within-group regressions of Y on X, that is, compute

$$s_i^2 = \frac{(\mathbf{y}_i - \mathbf{X}_i\mathbf{b}_i)'(\mathbf{y}_i - \mathbf{X}_i\mathbf{b}_i)}{n_i - k} \qquad i = 1, \ldots, m$$

where

$$\mathbf{b}_i = (\mathbf{X}_i'\mathbf{X}_i)^{-1}\mathbf{X}_i'\mathbf{y}_i$$

The Breusch-Pagan test.† Situations with replicated observations are rare in practice. The more common situation is one of single observation points. The Breusch-Pagan test for heteroscedasticity is a very general test in that it covers a wide range of heteroscedastic situations, and it is also a very simple test in that it is based on the OLS residuals. The model is

$$\mathbf{y} = \mathbf{X}\boldsymbol{\beta} + \mathbf{u}$$

where the disturbances u_i are assumed to be normally and independently distributed with variance

$$\sigma_i^2 = h(\mathbf{z}_i'\boldsymbol{\alpha}) \tag{8-30}$$

where $h(\cdot)$ denotes some unspecified functional form, $\boldsymbol{\alpha}$ is a $p \times 1$ vector of coefficients unrelated to $\boldsymbol{\beta}$, and $\mathbf{z}_t$ is a $p \times 1$ vector of variables thought to influence the heteroscedasticity. The first element in $\mathbf{z}_i$ is taken to be unity. Thus the null hypothesis

$$H_0\colon \quad \alpha_2 = \alpha_3 = \cdots = \alpha_p = 0$$

specifies homoscedasticity since then $\sigma_i^2 = h(\alpha_1)$, which is constant over all i. The other Z variables may consist partially, or even exclusively, of X variables, that is, the heteroscedasticity may be governed by the explanatory variables in the structural relationship. The test is a large sample or asymptotic test and is conducted as follows.

1. Fit the OLS regression of $\mathbf{y}$ on $\mathbf{X}$ and obtain the vector $\mathbf{e}$ of OLS residuals.
2. From $\mathbf{e}$ compute

$$\hat{\sigma}^2 = \frac{\sum_{t=1}^{n} e_t^2}{n}$$

and the series

$$g_t = \frac{e_t^2}{\hat{\sigma}^2} \qquad t = 1, \ldots, n$$

3. Specify the variables in the vector $\mathbf{z}_t$. Notice that the functional form $h(\cdot)$ in Eq. (8-30) does not have to be specified, merely the variables in the linear combination $\mathbf{z}_t'\boldsymbol{\alpha}$. Then fit the regression of g_t on $\mathbf{z}_t'$ and compute the explained sum of squares (ESS) from the regression.
4. The quantity $Q = \text{ESS}/2$ is, under the null hypothesis, asymptotically distributed as $\chi^2(p-1)$. Thus if $Q > \chi^2_{0.95}(p-1)$ one would reject the hypothesis of homoscedasticity at the 5 percent level.

The Goldfeld-Quandt test. An especially simple and finite sample test, which is applicable if it is thought that *one* of the X variables is the basic explanation of

† T. S. Breusch and A. R. Pagan, "A Simple Test for Heteroscedasticity and Random Coefficient Variation," *Econometrica*, vol. 47, 1979, pp. 1287–1294.

heteroscedasticity, is the Goldfeld-Quandt test.† Suppose it is suspected that σ_t^2 is positively related to one of the X variables, say X_i. The test procedure is then as follows.

1. Reorder the observations by the values of X_i.
2. Omit c central observations.
3. Fit separate regressions by OLS to the first and last $(n - c)/2$ observations, provided, of course, that $(n - c)/2$ exceeds the number of parameters to be estimated.
4. Let RSS_1 and RSS_2 denote the residual sum of squares from the two regressions, with the subscript 1 denoting that from the smaller X_i values and 2 that from the larger X_i values. Then

$$R = \frac{\text{RSS}_2}{\text{RSS}_1}$$

will, on the assumption of homoscedasticity, have the F distribution with $((n - c - 2k)/2, (n - c - 2k)/2)$ degrees of freedom. Under the alternative hypothesis R will tend to be large. Thus if $F > F_{0.95}$, one would reject the assumption of homoscedasticity at the 5 percent level.

The power of the test will depend, among other things, on the number of central observations excluded, and will clearly be small if c is too large (so that RSS_1 and RSS_2 have very few degrees of freedom) or too small (so any possible contrast between RSS_1 and RSS_2 is reduced). A rough guide is to set c at approximately $n/3$.‡

The Glesjer test. None of the previous tests yields any specific estimate of the form of heteroscedasticity which could then be inserted in var(**u**) to help derive the GLS estimator. A test which helps in this direction is that due to Glesjer.§ It is suggested, however, only for the case where a single variable Z is presumed to determine the heteroscedasticity. The Z variable may, of course, be one of the explanatory X variables in the structural relation. The test proceeds as follows.

1. Fit the OLS regression of **y** on **X** and derive the residual vector **e**.
2. Regress the absolute value of the OLS residuals on Z^h, that is,¶

$$|e_t| = \delta_0 + \delta_1 Z_t^h + \text{error} \tag{8-31}$$

† S. M. Goldfeld and R. E. Quandt, "Some Tests for Homoscedasticity," *Journal of the American Statistical Association*, vol. 60, 1965, pp. 539–547; or S. M. Goldfeld and R. E. Quandt, *Nonlinear Methods in Econometrics*, North-Holland, Amsterdam, 1972, Chap. 3, for a more general discussion.

‡ See A. C. Harvey and G. D. A. Phillips, "A Comparison of the Power of Some Tests for Heteroscedasticity in the General Linear Model," *Journal of Econometrics*, vol. 2, 1973, p. 312.

§ H. Glesjer, "A New Test for Heteroscedasticity," *Journal of the American Statistical Association*, vol. 64, 1969, pp. 316–323.

¶ Alternatively one might use e_t^2 as the dependent variable.

As it stands, this relation is nonlinear in δ_0, δ_1, and h. Glesjer suggests trying regressions for a few specific values of h, such as $1, -1, \frac{1}{2}$. The estimated slope coefficient $\hat{\delta}_1$ is then used to test the hypothesis that δ_1 is zero, although the conditions required for the validity of the usual significance test will not, in fact, be satisfied by this regression.† Acceptance of H_0: $\delta_1 = 0$ implies homoscedasticity and its rejection, heteroscedasticity.

Estimation under Heteroscedasticity

1. Example 8-1 has illustrated a simple case of GLS estimation for grouped data, where the $\mathbf{\Omega}$ matrix was known.
2. Another simple case occurs where one of the explanatory variables determines the heteroscedasticity. This may have been determined by a Glesjer type regression or postulated on a priori grounds. Suppose the heteroscedasticity is modeled by

$$\sigma_t^2 = \sigma^2 X_{jt}^2 \qquad t = 1, \ldots, n \tag{8-32}$$

where X_j is the explanatory variable thought to be the source of the heteroscedasticity. The variance matrix of the disturbance term then takes the form

$$\operatorname{var}(\mathbf{u}) = \sigma^2 \begin{bmatrix} X_{j1}^2 & 0 & \cdots & 0 \\ 0 & X_{j2}^2 & \cdots & 0 \\ \cdots & \cdots & \cdots & \cdots \\ 0 & 0 & \cdots & X_{jn}^2 \end{bmatrix}$$

and so the appropriate transformation matrix is

$$\mathbf{T} = \begin{bmatrix} \dfrac{1}{X_{j1}} & 0 & \cdots & 0 \\ 0 & \dfrac{1}{X_{j2}} & \cdots & 0 \\ \cdots & \cdots & \cdots & \cdots \\ 0 & 0 & \cdots & \dfrac{1}{X_{jn}} \end{bmatrix}$$

Thus the original relation

$$Y_t = \beta_1 + \beta_2 X_{2t} + \cdots + \beta_j X_{jt} + \cdots + \beta_k X_{kt} + u_t$$

would be transformed for estimation purposes to

$$\left(\frac{Y_t}{X_{jt}}\right) = \beta_1\left(\frac{1}{X_{jt}}\right) + \beta_2\left(\frac{X_{2t}}{X_{jt}}\right) + \cdots + \beta_j + \cdots + \beta_k\left(\frac{X_{kt}}{X_{jt}}\right) + \left(\frac{u_t}{X_{jt}}\right) \tag{8-33}$$

† See the discussion in S. M. Goldfeld and R. E. Quandt, *Nonlinear Methods in Econometrics*, North-Holland, Amsterdam, 1972, pp. 92–94.

and the inference procedures of Chap. 5 could then be validly applied to the transformed variables in Eq. (8-33). Notice, however, that β_j is estimated by the intercept in the transformed relation, and the original intercept β_1 is estimated by the coefficient of $1/X_j$. Equivalently, the diagonal matrix

$$\mathbf{\Omega}^{-1} = \text{diag}\left\{\frac{1}{X_{j1}^2}, \frac{1}{X_{j2}^2}, \ldots, \frac{1}{X_{jn}^2}\right\}$$

may be inserted along with the original $\mathbf{y}$, $\mathbf{X}$ data in Eqs. (8-18) and (8-19).

3. In cases 1 and 2 we have assumed the elements in the $\mathbf{\Omega}$ matrix to be known exactly. In many realistic cases these elements have to be estimated and the estimates then substituted in the GLS formulas. This is sometimes referred to as a two-stage Aitken estimator (2SAE), or as a *feasible* GLS (Aitken) estimator. For example, in the case of replicated data the within-group, sample Y variances could be estimated and substituted in $\mathbf{\Omega}$. Or if a Glesjer-type assumption postulated

$$\sigma_t^2 = \delta_0 + \delta_1 X_t$$

and these parameters were estimated from

$$e_t^2 = \hat{\delta}_0 + \hat{\delta}_1 X_t + \text{error}$$

the estimated disturbance variance matrix would be

$$\widehat{\text{var}(\mathbf{u})} = \text{diag}\{\hat{\delta}_0 + \hat{\delta}_1 X_1, \hat{\delta}_0 + \hat{\delta}_1 X_2, \ldots, \hat{\delta}_0 + \hat{\delta}_1 X_n\}$$

An unfortunate consequence of replacing unknown disturbance parameters by estimated values is that we no longer have exact finite sample results for the resultant estimators. In general the small sample properties of feasible GLS estimators are unknown. There is, however, some evidence from Monte Carlo studies on the relative performance of feasible GLS estimators compared with OLS.† Furthermore, under fairly general conditions the feasible GLS estimators will have the same asymptotic distribution as the GLS estimators, so that the conventional tests may be given an asymptotic justification.‡

The importance of adjusting for heteroscedasticity depends on the extent of the departure from homoscedasticity. No general pronouncements can be made, but as a very simple illustration consider a two-variable model

$$Y_t = \alpha + \beta X_t + u_t$$

where X_t takes on the values 1, 2, 3, 4, 5. Let b denote the OLS estimator of β and b_* the GLS estimator and let us assume further that the nature of the heteroscedasticity is

$$\sigma_t^2 = \sigma^2 X_t^2$$

† For a summary and detailed references see G. G. Judge, W. E. Griffiths, R. C. Hill, and T. C. Lee, *The Theory and Practice of Econometrics*, Wiley, New York, 1980, Chap. 4.

‡ For the condition under which there is asymptotic equivalence see P. Schmidt, *Econometrics*, Marcel Dekker, New York, 1976, Chap. 2, or H. Theil, *Principles of Econometrics*, Wiley, New York, 1971, Chap. 8. Unfortunately these conditions need to be checked out for each specific application.

A straightforward application of Eqs. (8-13) and (8-19) then gives

$$\frac{\operatorname{var}(b_*)}{\operatorname{var}(b)} = \frac{0.69}{1.24} = 0.56 \tag{8-34a}$$

and if the form of the heteroscedasticity is

$$\sigma_t^2 = \sigma^2 X_t$$

the corresponding result is

$$\frac{\operatorname{var}(b_*)}{\operatorname{var}(b)} = 0.83 \tag{8-34b}$$

Thus in this illustration, the efficiency of the OLS estimator ranges from 56 to 83 percent of the GLS estimator, depending on the postulated range for the heteroscedasticity. Finally, we may note that in the heteroscedastic case, and in other cases where GLS estimation is appropriate, there is no unique measure of goodness of fit. A measure may be based on weighted sums of squares, using $\mathbf{\Omega}^{-1}$ (or $\mathbf{V}^{-1}$) as a weighting matrix, or on sums of squares of the transformed vector **Ty**, although the latter is inappropriate if the transformed relation does not have an intercept term. For details of these and other measures the reader should consult the article by Buse.†

8-5 AUTOCORRELATION

Definitions

The autocorrelation, which is the focus of this section, is that of the $\{u_t\}$ series. There may or may not be autocorrelation in the explanatory variables, but for the moment we are only concerned with possible autocorrelation in the disturbance term. When present, it results in some or all of the off-diagonal terms in the var(**u**) matrix being nonzero. This in turn destroys the optimal properties of OLS and gives rise to another application of GLS.

We assume, as usual, zero mean for the series, that is,

$$E(u_t) = 0 \qquad \text{for all } t$$

The autocovariance at lag s is defined by

$$\gamma_s = E(u_t u_{t-s}) \qquad s = 0, \pm 1, \pm 2, \ldots \tag{8-35}$$

At zero lag we have simply the constant variance of the series

$$\gamma_0 = Eu_t^2 = \sigma_u^2$$

The autocorrelation coefficient at lag s is defined by

$$\rho_s = \frac{\gamma_s}{\gamma_0} \qquad s = \pm 1, \pm 2, \ldots \tag{8-36}$$

† A. Buse, "Goodness of Fit in Generalized Least Squares Estimation," *The American Statistician*, vol. 27, 1973, pp. 106–108.

We note that the γ's and ρ's are symmetrical in s and have been assumed to be independent of the t subscript, that is, these coefficients are constant over time and depend only on the length of lag s. The variance matrix for the disturbance term may then be written as

$$\operatorname{var}(\mathbf{u}) = \begin{bmatrix} \gamma_0 & \gamma_1 & \gamma_2 & \cdots & \gamma_{n-1} \\ \gamma_1 & \gamma_0 & \gamma_1 & \cdots & \gamma_{n-2} \\ \cdots & \cdots & \cdots & \cdots & \cdots \\ \gamma_{n-1} & \gamma_{n-2} & \gamma_{n-3} & \cdots & \gamma_0 \end{bmatrix}$$

$$= \sigma_u^2 \begin{bmatrix} 1 & \rho_1 & \rho_2 & \cdots & \rho_{n-1} \\ \rho_1 & 1 & \rho_1 & \cdots & \rho_{n-2} \\ \cdots & \cdots & \cdots & \cdots & \cdots \\ \rho_{n-1} & \rho_{n-2} & \rho_{n-3} & \cdots & 1 \end{bmatrix} \tag{8-37}$$

The above exposition has implicitly assumed a *temporal*, or time-series, framework, but the same phenomenon may arise with cross-section data, where it is often referred to as *spatial autocorrelation*. Suppose a sample of six observational units is represented by Fig. 8-1. The units might actually be contiguous as in the case of adjoining states, or "nearness" might be defined in terms of some other variable. For instance, if the sample units were households, the first household might have an income close to the incomes of the second and third households but not close to the incomes of the remaining households. If one hypothesized that the disturbance for the ith unit was related to the disturbances of contiguous units, then

$$u_1 = f(u_2, u_3)$$
$$u_2 = f(u_1, u_3, u_4, u_5)$$

and so on, and we would have some nonzero terms in the off-diagonal positions in var(**u**).

Estimation of var(**u**) as in Eq. (8-37) from any finite sample is impossible since the number of unknowns exceeds the number of observations, nor is any relief afforded by increasing the number of observations, as it brings a concomitant increase in the number of unknowns. The practical procedure is to secure a reduction in the number of unknown parameters by postulating some structure

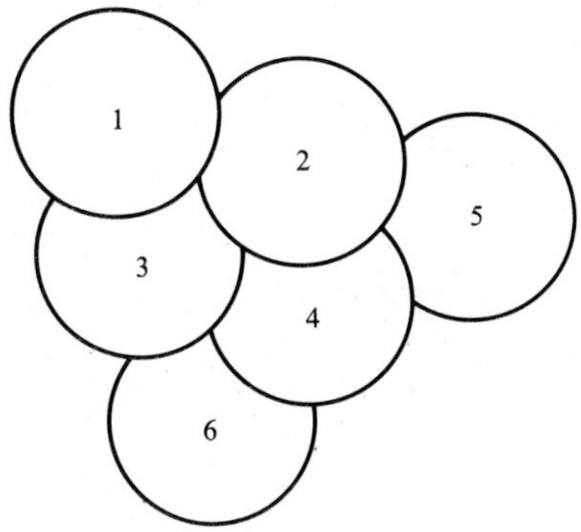

Figure 8-1 A sample of "contiguous" units.

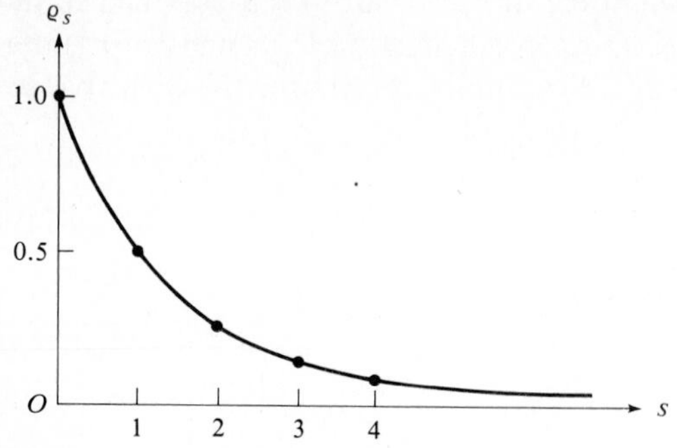

Figure 8-2 Correlogram for AR(1) with $\phi = 0.5$.

for the disturbances. In time-series applications simplified structures are typically *autoregressive* (AR) processes, *moving average* (MA) processes, or joint autoregressive, moving average (ARMA) processes. We have already had an example of an autoregressive process in Eq. (8-7), namely,

$$u_t = \phi u_{t-1} + \varepsilon_t \qquad |\phi| < 1$$

where the coefficient of the lagged term is denoted by ϕ as we now wish to use ρ to denote an autocorrelation coefficient. This is a first-order AR(1) process, and the result already established in Eq. (8-10) gives us the *autocorrelation function* (ACF) of the process as

$$\rho_s = \phi^s \qquad s = 0, 1, 2, \ldots \tag{8-38}$$

Thus the autocorrelations decay exponentially and will oscillate in sign if ϕ is negative. The graph of the autocorrelation function is called the *correlogram*, and a typical correlogram for the AR(1) process, with positive ϕ, is shown in Fig. 8-2.

The AR(2) process is defined as

$$u_t = \phi_1 u_{t-1} + \phi_2 u_{t-2} + \varepsilon_t \tag{8-39}$$

In these and all other applications the $\{\varepsilon_t\}$ series is always assumed to be "well-behaved," that is, $E(\boldsymbol{\varepsilon}) = \mathbf{0}$ and $E(\boldsymbol{\varepsilon}\boldsymbol{\varepsilon}') = \sigma_\varepsilon^2\mathbf{I}$. The condition $|\phi| < 1$ ensured that the AR(1) process had a finite variance. The resultant $\{u_t\}$ series was an example of a *stationary process*.† In the second-order case the conditions for stationarity are‡

$$|\phi_2| < 1 \qquad \phi_2 + \phi_1 < 1 \qquad \phi_2 - \phi_1 < 1$$

To establish the autocorrelation coefficients of the AR(2) process, multiply Eq. (8-39) by u_{t-s} and take expectations, giving

$$\gamma_s = \phi_1\gamma_{s-1} + \phi_2\gamma_{s-2} \qquad s > 0$$

since ε_t has zero covariance with all previous u's. Dividing through by the

† A stationary process has a constant and finite mean and variance and a set of covariances which are independent of time and are functions only of the lag length.

‡ G. E. P. Box and G. M. Jenkins, *Time Series Analysis Forecasting and Control*, revised edition, Holden-Day, San Francisco, 1976, p. 58.

variance γ_0 of the series gives

$$\rho_s = \phi_1 \rho_{s-1} + \phi_2 \rho_{s-2} \qquad s > 0 \tag{8-40}$$

Setting $s = 1$ and using $\rho_0 = 1$ and $\rho_{-1} = \rho_1$, it follows that

$$\rho_1 = \frac{\phi_1}{1 - \phi_2} \tag{8-41}$$

Setting $s = 2$ and using Eq. (8-41) then gives

$$\rho_2 = \phi_2 + \frac{\phi_1^2}{1 - \phi_2} \tag{8-42}$$

These first two autocorrelations, in conjunction with the recurrence relation (8-40), will yield the higher order autocorrelations. The stationarity conditions ensure that the autocorrelation function decays as the lag length increases. To obtain the variance of the u series, square both sides of Eq. (8-39) and take expectations, giving

$$\sigma_u^2 \left[1 - \phi_1^2 - \phi_2^2 - 2\phi_1 \phi_2 \rho_1\right] = \sigma_\varepsilon^2$$

Substituting for ρ_1 from Eq. (8-41) and simplifying gives the result

$$\sigma_u^2 = \frac{(1 - \phi_2) \cdot \sigma_\varepsilon^2}{(1 + \phi_2)\left[(1 - \phi_2)^2 - \phi_1^2\right]} \tag{8-43}$$

The general AR process of order p is defined as

$$u_t = \phi_1 u_{t-1} + \phi_2 u_{t-2} + \cdots + \phi_p u_{t-p} + \varepsilon_t \tag{8-44}$$

where the $\{\varepsilon_t\}$ series is well behaved, and suitable conditions are imposed on the ϕ's to ensure stationarity.

The general MA process of order q is defined as

$$u_t = \varepsilon_t + \theta_1 \varepsilon_{t-1} + \theta_2 \varepsilon_{t-2} + \cdots + \theta_q \varepsilon_{t-q} \tag{8-45}$$

An example of a fourth-order process was given in the context of a wage change model in Eq. (8-3), and the corresponding variance matrix in Eq. (8-5) showed that the autocorrelation coefficients are zero for all lags greater than the order of the MA process. Consider the MA(1) process

$$u_t = \varepsilon_t + \theta \varepsilon_{t-1} \tag{8-46}$$

It follows directly that

$$\gamma_0 = \sigma_u^2 = E\left(u_t^2\right) = \left(1 + \theta^2\right)\sigma_\varepsilon^2$$

and

$$\gamma_1 = E\left(u_t u_{t-1}\right) = \theta \sigma_\varepsilon^2$$

so that

$$\rho_1 = \frac{\gamma_1}{\gamma_0} = \frac{\theta}{1 + \theta^2}$$

and all further autocorrelation coefficients are zero.

A finite-order MA process may be converted into an infinite-order AR process and vice versa. For instance, using the lag operation L, Eq. (8-46) may be rewritten as

$$u_t = (1 + \theta L)\varepsilon_t$$

giving

$$(1 + \theta L)^{-1} u_t = \varepsilon_t$$

or

$$(1 - \theta L + \theta^2 L^2 - \cdots) u_t = \varepsilon_t$$

or

$$u_t = \theta u_{t-1} - \theta^2 u_{t-2} + \theta^3 u_{t-3} - \cdots + \varepsilon_t$$

which is an infinite AR process with the restriction that the coefficients are given by the successive powers of θ with alternating signs. Similarly the AR(1) process may be written

$$(1 - \phi L) u_t = \varepsilon_t$$

or

$$u_t = (1 - \phi L)^{-1} \varepsilon_t = (1 + \phi L + \phi^2 L^2 + \cdots)\varepsilon_t$$

or

$$u_t = \varepsilon_t + \phi \varepsilon_{t-1} + \phi^2 \varepsilon_{t-2} + \cdots$$

which is an infinite MA process with the coefficients given by the successive powers of ϕ. The general ARMA(p, q) process is defined by

$$u_t = \phi_1 u_{t-1} + \cdots + \phi_p u_{t-p} + \varepsilon_t + \theta_1 \varepsilon_{t-1} + \cdots + \theta_q \varepsilon_{t-q} \tag{8-47}$$

This may be written more compactly, using polynomials in the lag operator, as

$$\phi(L) u_t = \theta(L) \varepsilon_t \tag{8-48}$$

where

$$\phi(L) = 1 - \phi_1 L - \phi_2 L^2 - \cdots - \phi_p L^p$$

and

$$\theta(L) = 1 + \theta_1 L + \theta_2 L^2 + \cdots + \theta_q L^q$$

The mixed ARMA formulation enables quite complicated processes to be represented by a suitable choice of *low-order* polynomials.

Returning to the spatial example in Fig. 8-1, a common hypothesis about the structure of the autocorrelation is†

$$u_i = \rho \sum_j w_{ij} u_j + \varepsilon_i \tag{8-49}$$

where

$$w_{ij} = \frac{w_{ij}^*}{\sum_j w_{ij}^*}$$

and

$$w_{ij}^* = \begin{cases} 1 & \text{if units } i, j \text{ are contiguous} \\ 0 & \text{otherwise} \end{cases}$$

In this formulation ρ is a scalar indicating the overall strength of the autocorrelation, and the weights w_{ij} are essentially dummy variables which allow any disturbance to be affected by contiguous disturbances. The matrix formulation of

† See, for example, R. L. Martin, "On Spatial Dependence, Bias and the Use of First Spatial Differences in Regression Analysis," *Area*, vol. 6, 1974, pp. 185–194.

Eq. (8-49) is

$$\mathbf{u} = \rho\mathbf{W}\mathbf{u} + \boldsymbol{\varepsilon} \tag{8-50}$$

and for Fig. 8-1 the **W** matrix would be

$$\mathbf{W} = \begin{bmatrix} 0 & \frac{1}{2} & \frac{1}{2} & 0 & 0 & 0 \\ \frac{1}{4} & 0 & \frac{1}{4} & \frac{1}{4} & \frac{1}{4} & 0 \\ \frac{1}{4} & \frac{1}{4} & 0 & \frac{1}{4} & 0 & \frac{1}{4} \\ 0 & \frac{1}{4} & \frac{1}{4} & 0 & \frac{1}{4} & \frac{1}{4} \\ 0 & \frac{1}{2} & 0 & \frac{1}{2} & 0 & 0 \\ 0 & 0 & \frac{1}{2} & \frac{1}{2} & 0 & 0 \end{bmatrix}$$

From Eq. (8-50) the variance matrix of the disturbance term is

$$\text{var}(\mathbf{u}) = \sigma_\varepsilon^2(\mathbf{I} - \rho\mathbf{W})^{-1}(\mathbf{I} - \rho\mathbf{W})'^{-1} \tag{8-51}$$

In Eq. (8-51) **W** is generally a known matrix, but ρ and σ_ε^2 are unknown scalars. However, we will not consider the resultant estimation problems here.†

Reasons for Autocorrelated Disturbances

Some possible reasons have already been mentioned in Sec. 8-1. A general source of autocorrelated disturbances is the fact that the disturbance represents the *net* influence of omitted explanatory variables. Economic theory cannot prescribe an exhaustive list of explanatory variables to be included in a relation and, in any case, data limitations often curtail the number of variables that can be included. Exclusion of variables would not of itself impart autocorrelation to the disturbance term unless the excluded variables were autocorrelated. Even then autocorrelation in one explanatory variable might offset that in another. However, economic variables tend to be nonrandom over time and also to move roughly in phase so that excluded variables may impart autocorrelation to the disturbance term. A second source of autocorrelation may be a misspecification of the form of the relationship. Suppose the true relationship is represented by line A in Fig. 8-3, and the linear function B is fitted to the data. The sample points will be scattered around A and so the residuals from B will tend to be positive for $X < X_1$, negative for $X_1 < X < X_2$, and positive again for $X > X_2$. Such a case might be spotted simply from an inspection of the scatter diagram, and a transformation to a quadratic or other nonlinear function would yield random disturbances. Even in the case shown in Fig. 8-3 the X variable would need to be reordered in increasing size for the correlation between adjacent residuals to show up. In multiple regression situations misspecifications of the form of the equation cannot usually be detected by graphical means, and some experimentation with different functional forms may be required to judge whether any autocorrelation that shows up may be a reflection of specification error.

† For a discussion of estimation procedures see A. J. Cliff and J. K. Ord, *Spatial Processes, Models and Applications*, Chapman and Hall, London, 1981.

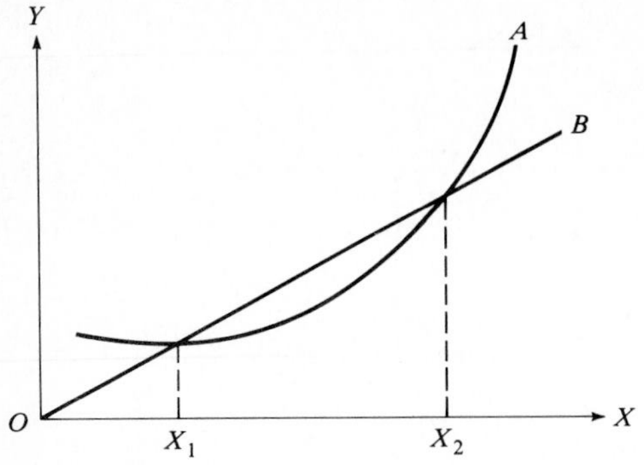

Figure 8-3

A third possible source of autocorrelated disturbances may be measurement error in the dependent variable. Economic statisticians typically have various formalized routines and procedures for estimating (or some say guesstimating) economic magnitudes. The sequential publication of revised estimates is eloquent testimony to the fact that the creators of the series believed their products to contain some error, and indeed a series becomes definitive simply when the statisticians stop revising it, which is not to say that it is then free of error. It is unlikely that the estimating procedures produce errors which are random from period to period and so, letting the $\mathbf{y}$ vector denote the observed Y values and $\mathbf{y}_*$ the true Y values generated by the mechanism $\mathbf{X\beta} + \mathbf{u}$, we have

$$\mathbf{y} = \mathbf{y}_* + \mathbf{v} = \mathbf{X\beta} + (\mathbf{u} + \mathbf{v})$$

where $\mathbf{v}$ is a vector of measurement errors. In the observed relationship the disturbance term is $\mathbf{u} + \mathbf{v}$, which may exhibit autocorrelation through $\mathbf{u}$ or $\mathbf{v}$ or both.

Consequences of Autocorrelation for OLS

The consequences of applying OLS to a relationship with autocorrelated disturbances are qualitatively similar to those already derived for the heteroscedastic case, namely, unbiased but inefficient estimation and invalid inference procedures. It is possible to illustrate some of these factors quantitatively for certain simple cases. Consider the model

$$y_t = \beta x_t + u_t \tag{8-52}$$

with

$$u_t = \rho u_{t-1} + \varepsilon_t$$

where

$$E(\boldsymbol{\varepsilon}) = \mathbf{0} \qquad \text{and} \qquad E(\boldsymbol{\varepsilon\varepsilon}') = \sigma_\varepsilon^2 \mathbf{I}$$

If OLS is applied to Eq. (8-52), we know from Eqs. (8-11) and (8-13) that

$$\text{var}(\text{OLS } b) = \sigma_u^2 (\mathbf{X'X})^{-1}\mathbf{X'\Omega X}(\mathbf{X'X})^{-1} \tag{8-53}$$

where

$$\mathbf{\Omega} = \begin{bmatrix} 1 & \rho & \rho^2 & \cdots & \rho^{n-1} \\ \rho & 1 & \rho & \cdots & \rho^{n-2} \\ \cdots & \cdots & \cdots & \cdots & \cdots \\ \rho^{n-1} & \rho^{n-2} & \rho^{n-3} & \cdots & 1 \end{bmatrix} \tag{8-54}$$

and, as may be verified by multiplying out,

$$\boldsymbol{\Omega}^{-1} = \frac{1}{1-\rho^2}\begin{bmatrix} 1 & -\rho & 0 & \cdots & 0 & 0 & 0 \\ -\rho & 1+\rho^2 & -\rho & \cdots & 0 & 0 & 0 \\ 0 & -\rho & 1+\rho^2 & \cdots & 0 & 0 & 0 \\ \cdots & \cdots & \cdots & \cdots & \cdots & \cdots & \cdots \\ 0 & 0 & 0 & & -\rho & 1+\rho^2 & -\rho \\ 0 & 0 & 0 & & 0 & -\rho & 1 \end{bmatrix} \tag{8-55}$$

Substituting Eq. (8-54) in Eq. (8-53) for the model of Eq. (8-52) gives

$$\operatorname{var}(\text{OLS } b) = \frac{\sigma_u^2}{\sum_{t=1}^n x_t^2}\left(1 + 2\rho\frac{\sum_{t=1}^{n-1} x_t x_{t+1}}{\sum_{t=1}^n x_t^2} + 2\rho^2\frac{\sum_{t=1}^{n-2} x_t x_{t+2}}{\sum_{t=1}^n x_t^2} + \cdots + 2\rho^{n-1}\frac{x_1 x_n}{\sum_{t=1}^n x_t^2}\right) \tag{8-56}$$

If ρ were known and GLS was applied to Eq. (8-52), then substitution of Eq. (8-55) in the general formula

$$\operatorname{var}(\mathbf{b}_*) = \sigma_u^2(\mathbf{X}'\boldsymbol{\Omega}^{-1}\mathbf{X})^{-1}$$

gives

$$\operatorname{var}(\text{GLS } b_*) = \frac{\sigma_u^2}{\sum_{t=1}^n x_t^2}\left(\frac{1-\rho^2}{1+\rho^2 - 2\rho\sum_{t=1}^{n-1} x_t x_{t+1}/\sum_{t=1}^n x_t^2}\right) \tag{8-57}$$

Comparison of Eq. (8-57) with Eq. (8-56) shows that the efficiency of OLS is measured by the ratio of the two terms in parentheses and thus depends not just on ρ but also on the nature of the x variable. Let us suppose that x follows a stable AR(1) scheme with parameter λ. As the sample size n gets very large, the terms involving x are approximated by the autocorrelation coefficients of x, which are simply the successive powers of λ. Thus the asymptotic efficiency of OLS is given by

$$\begin{aligned} \text{asy eff}(\text{OLS } b) &= \frac{1-\rho^2}{(1+\rho^2-2\rho\lambda)(1+2\rho\lambda+2\rho^2\lambda^2+\cdots)} \\ &= \frac{(1-\rho^2)(1-\rho\lambda)}{(1+\rho^2-2\rho\lambda)(1+\rho\lambda)} \end{aligned} \tag{8-58}$$

Table 8-2 shows illustrative values of this asymptotic efficiency for selected values of ρ and λ. Looking first at the right-hand side of the table, where ρ and λ are both positive, it is clear that ρ is the dominant parameter. Efficiency declines from 90 percent to about 10 percent as ρ rises from 0.2 to 0.9, with variations in λ having a relatively minor effect. The diagonal entries are equal to those in the first row since if $\lambda = 0$ or if $\rho = \lambda$, the efficiency measure simplifies to $(1-\rho^2)/(1+\rho^2)$. Looking at the left-hand side of the table, the efficiencies are symmetrical across the first row where the $\{x_t\}$ series is random. The remaining rows show that λ now exerts a much stronger effect and that the combination of a positive λ

Table 8-2 Asymptotic efficiency of OLS b (percent)

λ	ρ							
	−0.9	−0.8	−0.5	−0.2	0.2	0.5	0.8	0.9
0.0	10.5	22.0	60.0	92.3	92.3	60.0	22.0	10.5
0.2	12.6	25.4	63.2	92.9	92.3	58.4	19.8	9.1
0.5	18.5	34.4	71.4	94.6	93.5	60.0	18.4	7.9
0.8	35.9	56.2	85.4	97.5	96.6	71.4	22.0	8.4
0.9	52.8	71.8	92.0	98.7	98.1	81.3	29.3	10.5

and negative ρ can moderate the dramatic declines in efficiency shown in the right-hand side of the table. These calculations are, of course, only illustrative, but they indicate the possibility of a serious loss in efficiency if OLS is applied in the context of autocorrelated disturbances.

A second problem with the application of OLS is that the conventional formula on the computer for var(b) will, in this example, estimate $\sigma_u^2/\Sigma_1^n x_t^2$, whereas Eq. (8-56) shows that this is no longer the true variance. As the sample size gets very large, the ratio of the conventional formula to the true variance is given by

$$\tau = \frac{1 - \rho\lambda}{1 + \rho\lambda}$$

Thus the proportionate bias that the conventional program will impart to the estimation of the true sampling variance of the OLS b is, in the limit,

$$\text{Asymptotic proportionate bias} = \frac{-2\rho\lambda}{1 + \rho\lambda} \tag{8-59}$$

Table 8-3 shows values of this statistic for selected values of ρ and λ. Again it is instructive to consider the table in two halves. A positively autocorrelated disturbance in conjunction with a positively autocorrelated $\{x\}$ series implies underestimation of the sampling variance by the conventional OLS formula. If $\rho = \lambda = 0.9$, the estimated variance will only be about one-tenth of the correct number, which would cause a serious *overestimation* of t statistics and significance levels in conventional inference procedures. On the other hand, different signs for ρ and λ will cause an overestimation of the sampling variance. Casual empiricism

Table 8-3 Percentage bias in estimating var(b)

λ	ρ					
	−0.9	−0.5	−0.2	0.2	0.5	0.9
0	0	0	0	0	0	0
0.2	43.9	22.2	8.3	−7.7	−18.2	−30.5
0.5	163.6	40.0	22.2	−18.2	−40.0	−62.1
0.9	852.6	163.6	43.9	−30.5	−62.1	−89.5

indicates that the predominant situation in applied studies is a conjunction of positive autocorrelation in both disturbance and explanatory variable so that underestimation of var(b) is the more likely situation.

The comparison involved in Table 8-3 has implicitly taken σ_u^2 as known. In practice it must be estimated from the sample data, and here again there is a possibility of bias if the disturbance term is autocorrelated. We saw in Chap. 5 that

$$\mathbf{e}'\mathbf{e} = \mathbf{u}'\mathbf{u} - \mathbf{u}'\mathbf{X}(\mathbf{X}'\mathbf{X})^{-1}\mathbf{X}'\mathbf{u}$$

Thus $$E(\mathbf{e}'\mathbf{e}) = E(\mathbf{u}'\mathbf{u}) - E\{\mathbf{u}'\mathbf{X}(\mathbf{X}'\mathbf{X})^{-1}\mathbf{X}'\mathbf{u}\}$$

Now $$E(\mathbf{u}'\mathbf{u}) = n\sigma_u^2$$

and

$$E\{\mathbf{u}'\mathbf{X}(\mathbf{X}'\mathbf{X})^{-1}\mathbf{X}'\mathbf{u}\} = E\{\mathrm{tr}[\mathbf{u}'\mathbf{X}(\mathbf{X}'\mathbf{X})^{-1}\mathbf{X}'\mathbf{u}]\}$$ since the expression in brackets is a scalar

$$= E\{\mathrm{tr}[\mathbf{X}(\mathbf{X}'\mathbf{X})^{-1}\mathbf{X}'\mathbf{u}\mathbf{u}']\}$$

$$= \sigma_u^2\,\mathrm{tr}\{\mathbf{X}(\mathbf{X}'\mathbf{X})^{-1}\mathbf{X}'\boldsymbol{\Omega}\}$$

$$= \sigma_u^2\,\mathrm{tr}\{(\mathbf{X}'\mathbf{X})^{-1}\mathbf{X}'\boldsymbol{\Omega}\mathbf{X}\} \tag{8-60}$$

For the simple model being analyzed here

$$E(\mathbf{e}'\mathbf{e}) = \sigma_u^2\left\{n - \left(1 + 2\rho\frac{\sum_{t=1}^{n-1}x_t x_{t+1}}{\sum_{t=1}^{n}x_t^2} + 2\rho^2\frac{\sum_{t=1}^{n-2}x_t x_{t+2}}{\sum_{t=1}^{n}x_t^2} + \cdots + 2\rho^{n-1}\frac{x_1 x_n}{\sum_{t=1}^{n}x_t^2}\right)\right\}$$

If $\rho = 0$, then $E(\mathbf{e}'\mathbf{e}) = (n-1)\sigma_u^2$, which confirms the unbiased estimator $s^2 = \mathbf{e}'\mathbf{e}/(n-1)$ of Chap. 5. If we assume the $\{x_t\}$ series to be a stable AR(1) process with parameter λ, then for large n

$$E(\mathbf{e}'\mathbf{e}) \simeq \sigma_u^2\left(n - \frac{1+\rho\lambda}{1-\rho\lambda}\right)$$

If ρ and λ have the same sign, then s^2 will have a downward bias as an estimator of σ_u^2. If, for instance, $\rho = 0.9 = \lambda$ and $n = 101$,

$$E(s^2) \simeq 0.915\sigma_u^2$$

Thus when ρ and λ have the same sign, this bias accentuates the bias analyzed in Table 8-3. It is clear that autocorrelated disturbances are a potentially serious problem, and it is very important to be able to test for their existence.

Tests for Autocorrelation

Suppose that in the model $\mathbf{y} = \mathbf{X}\boldsymbol{\beta} + \mathbf{u}$ one suspects that the disturbance term follows an AR(1) scheme, that is,

$$u_t = \phi u_{t-1} + \varepsilon_t$$

The null hypothesis of zero autocorrelation would then be set up as

$$H_0: \quad \phi = 0$$

and the alternative hypothesis as

$$H_1: \quad \phi \neq 0$$

The null hypothesis is about the u's, which are unobservable. One therefore looks for a test of the null hypothesis using the vector of OLS residuals, $\mathbf{e} = \mathbf{y} - \mathbf{Xb}$. This raises several difficulties. We know from Chap. 5 that

$$\mathbf{e} = \mathbf{Mu}$$

where

$$\mathbf{M} = \mathbf{I} - \mathbf{X}(\mathbf{X'X})^{-1}\mathbf{X'}$$

is symmetric, idempotent of rank $n - k$. Thus the variance-covariance matrix of the e's is

$$E(\mathbf{ee'}) = \sigma_u^2 \mathbf{M}$$

Thus even if the null hypothesis is true, so that $E(\mathbf{uu'}) = \sigma_u^2 \mathbf{I}$, the OLS residuals will display some autocorrelation, for the off-diagonal terms in $\mathbf{M}$ do not vanish. More importantly $\mathbf{M}$ is a function of the sample values of the explanatory variables, so that it is impossible to derive an exact finite sample test on the e's which will be valid for any $\mathbf{X}$ matrix that might ever turn up.

Durbin-Watson test. These problems were treated in a pair of classic and path-breaking articles.† The Durbin-Watson test statistic is computed from the vector of OLS residuals $\mathbf{e} = \mathbf{y} - \mathbf{X}\boldsymbol{\beta}$. It is denoted in the literature variously as d or DW and is defined as

$$d = \frac{\sum_{t=2}^{n}(e_t - e_{t-1})^2}{\sum_{t=1}^{n} e_t^2} \tag{8-61}$$

Figure 8-4 indicates why d might be expected to measure the extent of first-order autocorrelation. The mean residual is zero, so the residuals will be scattered around the horizontal axis. If the e's are positively autocorrelated, successive values will tend to be close to each other, runs above and below the horizontal axis will occur, and the first differences will tend to be numerically smaller than the residuals themselves. Alternatively if the e's have a first-order negative correlation, there is a tendency for successive observations to be on opposite sides of the horizontal axis, so that first differences tend to be numerically larger than the residuals. Thus d will tend to be "small" for positively autocorrelated e's and "large" for negatively autocorrelated e's. If the e's are random, we have an in-between situation with no tendency for runs above and below the axis or for alternate swings across it, and d will take on an intermediate value.

† J. Durbin and G. S. Watson, "Testing for Serial Correlation in Least Squares Regression," *Biometrika*, vol. 37, 1950, pp. 409–428; vol. 38, 1951, pp. 159–178.

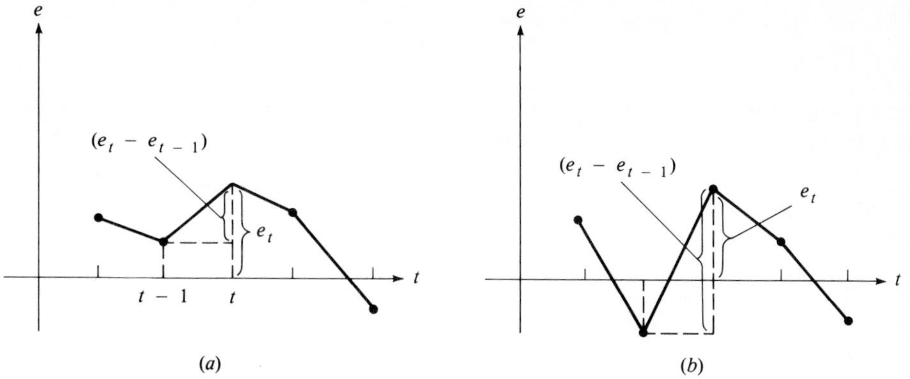

Figure 8-4 (*a*) Positive autocorrelation; (*b*) negative autocorrelation.

The Durbin-Watson statistic is closely related to the sample first-order autocorrelation coefficient of the e's. Expanding Eq. (8-61),

$$d = \frac{\sum_{t=2}^{n} e_t^2 + \sum_{t=2}^{n} e_{t-1}^2 - 2\sum_{t=2}^{n} e_t e_{t-1}}{\sum_{t=1}^{n} e_t^2}$$

For large n the different ranges of summation in numerator and denominator have a diminishing effect and

$$d \simeq 2(1 - r) \tag{8-62}$$

where $r = \Sigma e_t e_{t-1} / \Sigma e_t^2$ is the coefficient in the OLS regression of e_t on e_{t-1}. Formula (8-62) shows heuristically that the range of d is from 0 to 4:

$d < 2$ for positive autocorrelation of the e's
$d > 2$ for negative autocorrelation of the e's
$d \simeq 2$ for zero autocorrelation of the e's

The hypothesis under test is, of course, about the properties of the unobservable u's, which will not be reproduced exactly by the OLS residuals, but the above indicators are nonetheless valid in that d will tend to be less (greater) than 2 for positive (negative) autocorrelation of the u's. For a random u series the expected value of d is

$$E(d) \simeq 2 + \frac{2(k-1)}{n-k} \tag{8-63}$$

where k is the number of variables in the regression.

Because of the dependence of any computed d value on the associated **X** matrix, exact critical values of d cannot be tabulated for all possible cases. Durbin and Watson established upper (d_U) and lower (d_L) bounds for the critical values. The tabulated bounds are to test the hypothesis of zero autocorrelation against the alternative of *positive* first-order autocorrelation. The testing procedure is as follows.

1. If $d < d_L$, reject the hypothesis of nonautocorrelated u in favor of the hypothesis of positive first-order autocorrelation.

2. If $d > d_U$, do not reject the null hypothesis.
3. If $d_L < d < d_U$, the test is inconclusive.

If the sample value of d exceeds 2, we wish to test the null hypothesis against the alternative hypothesis of *negative* first-order autocorrelation. The appropriate procedure is to compute $4 - d$ and compare this statistic with the tabulated values of d_L and d_U as if one were testing for positive autocorrelation. The original DW tables covered sample sizes from 15 to 100, with 5 as the maximum number of regressors. Savin and White have published extended tables for $6 \leq n \leq 200$ and up to 10 regressors.† The 5 percent and 1 percent Savin-White tables are reproduced in App. B-5.

There are two important qualifications to the use of the Durbin-Watson test. First it is necessary to have included a constant term in the regression. Second, it is strictly valid only for a nonstochastic **X**. Thus it is not applicable when a lagged dependent variable appears among the regressors, and indeed it can be shown that the combination of a lagged Y variable and a positively autocorrelated disturbance term will bias the Durbin-Watson statistic upward and thus give misleading indications.‡ Even when the conditions for the validity of the Durbin-Watson test are satisfied, the inconclusive range is an awkward problem, especially as it becomes fairly large at low degrees of freedom. A conservative practical procedure is to use d_U as if it were a conventional critical value and simply reject the null hypothesis if $d < d_U$. The consequences of accepting H_0 when autocorrelation is present are almost certainly more serious than the consequences of incorrectly assuming it to be absent, which is one reason for the procedure.§ Second, it has been shown that when the regressors are slowly changing series, as many economic series are, the true critical value will be close to the Durbin-Watson upper bound.¶

When the regression does not contain an intercept term, d is bounded by

$$d_M \leq d \leq d_U$$

where d_U is the upper bound of the conventional Durbin-Watson tables. Farebrother has provided extensive tabulations of both lower and upper 1 percent and 5 percent significance points for d_M.||

† N. E. Savin and K. J. White, "The Durbin-Watson Test for Serial Correlation with Extreme Sample Sizes or Many Regressors," *Econometrica*, vol. 45, 1977, pp. 1989–1996.

‡ M. Nerlove and K. F. Wallis, "Use of the Durbin-Watson Statistic in Inappropriate Situations," *Econometrica*, vol. 34, 1966, pp. 235–238.

§ A comprehensive Monte Carlo study relevant to this question is J. K. Peck, "The Estimation of a Dynamic Equation Following a Preliminary Test for Autocorrelation," Cowles Foundation Discussion Paper, no. 404, September 9, 1975. After studying the properties of regression estimators following different significance levels for d, the author recommends using a significance level much more likely (than the conventional levels) to reject H_0 when it is true. This is in the same spirit as using d_U as the critical value.

¶ H. Theil and A. L. Nagar, "Testing the Independence of Regression Disturbances," *Journal of the American Statistical Association*, vol. 56, 1961, pp. 793–806; and E. J. Hannan and R. D. Terrell, "Testing for Serial Correlation after Least Squares Regression," *Econometrica*, vol. 36, 1968, pp. 133–150.

|| R. W. Farebrother, "The Durbin-Watson Test for Serial Correlation when There Is No Intercept in the Regression," *Econometrica*, vol. 48, 1980, pp. 1553–1563.

The inconclusive range of the Durbin-Watson statistic can be narrowed if explicit account can be taken of the form of any regressors in addition to the constant term, since that reduces uncertainty about the **X** matrix. King has presented tabulations of d_L and d_U for three classes of linear regression models, namely:

1. Regressions with a full set of quarterly seasonal dummy variables
2. Regressions with an intercept and a linear trend variable
3. Regressions with a full set of quarterly seasonal dummies and a linear trend variable†

The Wallis test for fourth-order autocorrelation.‡ Wallis has pointed out that many applied studies employ quarterly data, and in such cases one might expect to find *fourth-order* autocorrelation in the disturbance term. The appropriate specification is then

$$u_t = \phi_4 u_{t-4} + \varepsilon_t \tag{8-64}$$

and the null hypothesis would be

$$H_0\colon \quad \phi_4 = 0$$

To test the null hypothesis, Wallis proposes a modified Durbin-Watson statistic

$$d_4 = \frac{\sum_{t=5}^{n}(e_t - e_{t-4})^2}{\sum_{t=1}^{n} e_t^2} \tag{8-65}$$

where the e's are the usual OLS residuals. Wallis derives upper and lower bounds for d_4 under the assumption of a nonstochastic **X** matrix. The 5 percent significance points are tabulated in App. B-6. The first table is for use with regressions with an intercept, but without quarterly dummy variables. The second table is for use with regressions incorporating quarterly dummies. As shown in Chap. 6, one may employ a constant term and three quarterly dummies or use four quarterly dummies without a constant term.

Further significance points at 0.5, 1.0, and 2.5 percent levels are provided by Giles and King.§ The same authors also point out that if one is testing H_0 against the alternative hypothesis $H_1\colon \; \phi_4 < 0$, the test statistic $4 - d_4$ may be correctly referred to the critical values $4 - d_{4,U}$ and $4 - d_{4,L}$, where $d_{4,U}$ and $d_{4,L}$ are the 5 percent values tabulated by Wallis, only in the case where seasonal dummies have been included among the regressors. For the case where an intercept but no seasonal dummies have been employed, these critical values are inappropriate and the authors provide a revised set.¶

† M. L. King, "The Durbin-Watson Test for Serial Correlation: Bounds for Regressions with Trend and/or Seasonal Dummy Variables," *Econometrica*, vol. 49, 1981, pp. 1571–1581.

‡ K. F. Wallis, "Testing for Fourth Order Autocorrelation in Quarterly Regression Equations," *Econometrica*, vol. 40, 1972, pp. 617–636.

§ D. E. A. Giles and M. L. King, "Fourth-Order Autocorrelation: Further Significance Points for the Wallis Test," *Journal of Econometrics*, vol. 8, 1978, pp. 255–259.

¶ M. L. King and D. E. A. Giles, "A Note on Wallis' Bounds Test and Negative Autocorrelation," *Econometrica*, vol. 45, 1977, pp. 1023–1026.

Durbin tests for a regression containing lagged values of the dependent variable. As has been pointed out, the Durbin-Watson test procedure was derived under the assumption of a nonstochastic **X** matrix, which is violated by the presence of lagged values of the dependent variable appearing among the explanatory variables. Durbin has derived a large sample (asymptotic) test for the more general case.† Consider the relation

$$Y_t = \beta_1 Y_{t-1} + \cdots + \beta_r Y_{t-r} + \beta_{r+1} X_{1t} + \cdots + \beta_{r+s} X_{st} + u_t \qquad (8\text{-}66)$$

with

$$u_t = \phi u_{t-1} + \varepsilon_t \qquad \text{and} \qquad \varepsilon \sim N(\mathbf{0}, \sigma_\varepsilon^2 \mathbf{I})$$

The basic result is that under the null hypothesis, H_0: $\phi = 0$, the statistic

$$h = r\sqrt{\frac{n}{1 - n\,\mathrm{var}(b_1)}} \sim \mathrm{AN}(0, 1) \qquad (8\text{-}67)$$

where n = sample size

$\mathrm{var}(b_1)$ = estimated sampling variance of the coefficient of Y_{t-1} in the OLS regression of Eq. (8-66)

$r = \sum_{t=2}^{n} e_t e_{t-1} / \sum_{t=2}^{n} e_{t-1}^2$, the estimate of ϕ from the OLS regression of e_t on e_{t-1}, the e's in turn being the residuals from the OLS regression of Eq. (8-66)

Thus the test procedure is as follows.

1. Fit the OLS regression denoted by Eq. (8-66) and note $\mathrm{var}(b_1)$.
2. From the residuals compute r or, alternatively, if the Durbin-Watson statistic has been computed, we may use the approximation $r \simeq 1 - d/2$.
3. Substitute in the formula for h, and if $h > 1.645$, reject the null hypothesis at the 5 percent level of significance in favor of the hypothesis of a positive first-order autocorrelation.
4. A similar one-sided test for negative autocorrelation can be carried out for negative h.

The test breaks down if it should happen that $n \cdot \mathrm{var}(b_1) \geq 1$. Durbin showed that an asymptotically equivalent procedure is the following.

1. Estimate the OLS regression of Eq. (8-66) and obtain the residual e's.
2. Estimate the OLS regression of

$$e_t \qquad \text{on } e_{t-1}, Y_{t-1}, \ldots, Y_{t-r}, X_{1t}, \ldots, X_{st}$$

3. If the coefficient of e_{t-1} in this regression is significantly different from zero by the usual OLS test, reject the null hypothesis H_0: $\phi = 0$.

† J. Durbin, "Testing for Serial Correlation in Least Squares Regression when Some of the Regressors are Lagged Dependent Variables," *Econometrica*, vol. 38, 1970, pp. 410–421.

Breusch-Godfrey test. The procedures considered so far test the significance of a *single* autocorrelation coefficient. One might expect these tests to have reasonable power in the presence of more general forms of autocorrelation. For instance, if

$$u_t = \phi_1 u_{t-1} + \phi_2 u_{t-2} + \cdots + \phi_p u_{t-p} + \varepsilon_t$$

the d test might well show ϕ_1 to be significantly different from zero. But ϕ_1 represents just a part of the autocorrelation now present, and one might find an insignificant value for the first-order statistic. This, however, sheds no light on the significance of $\phi_2, \ldots, \phi_p$. Thus a more general test is clearly desirable. Such a test has been developed, apparently independently, by Breusch and by Godfrey.† They postulate the usual model $\mathbf{y} = \mathbf{X}\boldsymbol{\beta} + \mathbf{u}$, where the $\mathbf{X}$ matrix may include lagged values of the dependent variable. The null hypothesis is

$$H_0: \quad \mathbf{u} \sim N(0, \sigma_u^2 \mathbf{I})$$

Two alternative hypotheses are considered. One is that the $\{u_t\}$ are generated by an AR(p) process,

$$u_t + \alpha_1 u_{t-1} + \cdots + \alpha_p u_{t-p} = \varepsilon_t \tag{8-68}$$

The other hypothesis is that the $\{u_t\}$ are generated by an MA(p) process,

$$u_t = \varepsilon_t + \alpha_1 \varepsilon_{t-1} + \cdots + \alpha_p \varepsilon_{t-p} \tag{8-69}$$

where in each case $\{\varepsilon_t\}$ is well-behaved. The test is based on the OLS residual vector $\mathbf{e}$, and is essentially a test of the joint significance of the first p autocorrelations of these residuals. A remarkable feature of the test is that the same test statistic applies for either alternative hypothesis. The components of the test statistic are

$$\mathbf{e} = \mathbf{y} - \mathbf{X}\mathbf{b}, \text{ the usual } n \times 1 \text{ vector of OLS residuals}$$

$$\hat{\sigma}^2 = \mathbf{e}'\mathbf{e}/n, \text{ the ML estimate of } \sigma_u^2$$

$$\mathbf{E}_p = \begin{bmatrix}\mathbf{e}_1 & \mathbf{e}_2 & \cdots & \mathbf{e}_p\end{bmatrix} = \begin{bmatrix} 0 & 0 & \cdots & 0 \\ e_1 & 0 & \cdots & 0 \\ e_2 & e_1 & \cdots & 0 \\ e_3 & e_2 & \cdots & 0 \\ \cdots & \cdots & \cdots & \cdots \\ & & \cdots & e_1 \\ & & \cdots & e_2 \\ \cdots & \cdots & \cdots & \cdots \\ e_{n-1} & e_{n-2} & \cdots & e_{n-p} \end{bmatrix}$$

The test statistic is

$$l = \mathbf{e}'\mathbf{E}_p\left[\mathbf{E}_p'\mathbf{E}_p - \mathbf{E}_p'\mathbf{X}(\mathbf{X}'\mathbf{X})^{-1}\mathbf{X}'\mathbf{E}_p\right]^{-1}\mathbf{E}_p'\mathbf{e}/\hat{\sigma}^2 \tag{8-70}$$

† L. G. Godfrey, "Testing Against General Autoregressive and Moving Average Error Models when the Regressors Include Lagged Dependent Variables," *Econometrica*, vol. 46, 1978, pp. 1293–1302; and T. S. Breusch, "Testing for Autocorrelation in Dynamic Linear Models," *Australian Economic Papers*, vol. 17, 1978, pp. 334–355.

which, under the null hypothesis, is asymptotically distributed as $\chi^2(p)$. The asymptotic properties of the test would not be affected if $\hat{\sigma}^2$ were replaced by the usual unbiased estimator $s^2 = \mathbf{e}'\mathbf{e}/(n-k)$. Significantly large values of l would lead to the rejection of the null hypothesis, but would not indicate which of the alternative hypotheses, Eq. (8-68) or Eq. (8-69), should be regarded as the more appropriate. Godfrey shows that when the $\mathbf{X}$ matrix contains *only exogenous variables*, the test statistic is asymptotically equivalent to

$$l = n\left(r_1^2 + r_2^2 + \cdots + r_p^2\right)$$

where

$$r_i = \frac{\sum_{t=i+1}^{n} e_t e_{t-i}}{\sum_{t=1}^{n} e_t^2} \qquad i = 1, 2, \ldots$$

is the ith autocorrelation coefficient of the OLS residuals.

The test statistic defined in Eq. (8-70) may seem to imply a burdensome amount of computation, but it can be expressed in a simpler form. Suppose that the OLS regression of $\mathbf{y}$ on $\mathbf{X}$ has been computed. The $\mathbf{X}$ matrix may contain lagged values of the dependent variable. Denoting the residual vector from this regression by $\mathbf{e} = \mathbf{y} - \mathbf{Xb}$, it follows that

$$\{e_t\} \text{ has zero mean}$$

and
$$\mathbf{e}'\mathbf{X} = \mathbf{0}$$

Suppose now that $\mathbf{e}$ is regressed on the matrix $[\mathbf{E}_p \quad \mathbf{X}]$ where $\mathbf{E}_p$ is as defined above. The R^2 from this regression is given by

$$R^2 = \frac{\text{ESS}}{\mathbf{e}'\mathbf{e}}$$

since no correction is required for the mean of the dependent variable. Moreover, from Eq. (5-53),

$$\text{ESS} = \mathbf{e}'\begin{bmatrix}\mathbf{E}_p & \mathbf{X}\end{bmatrix}\begin{bmatrix}\mathbf{E}_p'\mathbf{E}_p & \mathbf{E}_p'\mathbf{X} \\ \mathbf{X}'\mathbf{E}_p & \mathbf{X}'\mathbf{X}\end{bmatrix}^{-1}\begin{bmatrix}\mathbf{E}_p' \\ \mathbf{X}'\end{bmatrix}\mathbf{e}$$

Using $\mathbf{e}'\mathbf{X} = \mathbf{0}$, this simplifies to

$$\text{ESS} = \mathbf{e}'\mathbf{E}_p\left[\mathbf{E}_p'\mathbf{E}_p - \mathbf{E}_p'\mathbf{X}(\mathbf{X}'\mathbf{X})^{-1}\mathbf{X}'\mathbf{E}_p\right]^{-1}\mathbf{E}_p'\mathbf{e}$$

Thus
$$l = \frac{\text{ESS}}{\hat{\sigma}^2}$$

and since $\hat{\sigma}^2 = \mathbf{e}'\mathbf{e}/n$, we have

$$l = nR^2 \tag{8-71}$$

The test procedure is thus as follows.

1. Fit the OLS regression of $\mathbf{y}$ on $\mathbf{X}$ to obtain $\mathbf{e}$.
2. Regress $\mathbf{e}$ on $[\mathbf{E}_p \quad \mathbf{X}]$ and obtain R^2.
3. Refer nR^2 to the $\chi^2(p)$ distribution and reject the null hypothesis if a significantly large value is found.

In practice the second step in the test procedure might be described as

2. Regress e_t on $e_{t-1},\ldots, e_{t-p}$, and $\mathbf{x}_t$ (that is, the tth row of $\mathbf{X}$).

Since there are only n values of e available, this regression might be carried out using only the last $n - p$ observations. The Breusch-Godfrey procedure sets $e_0, e_{-1},\ldots$ at zero. Asymptotically it does not matter which route is taken, and it is a moot point whether it matters in finite samples.

Estimation with Autocorrelated Disturbances

The Durbin test for a regression and the Breusch-Godfrey test for the presence of autocorrelated errors are applicable when lagged values of the dependent variable appear in the $\mathbf{X}$ matrix. In discussing estimation procedures we will restrict consideration in this section to nonstochastic $\mathbf{X}$ matrices. Additional remarks on estimation in the presence of lagged dependent variables will be made in Sec. 9-2.

Consider again the model

$$\mathbf{y} = \mathbf{X}\boldsymbol{\beta} + \mathbf{u}$$

with $$E(\mathbf{u}) = \mathbf{0} \qquad \text{and} \qquad E(\mathbf{uu}') = \sigma^2\boldsymbol{\Omega}$$

From the discussion in Sec. 8-3 it is clear that GLS estimation may be achieved if it is possible to find a transformation matrix $\mathbf{T}$ of known parameters such that $\mathbf{T}'\mathbf{T} = \boldsymbol{\Omega}^{-1}$ and then apply OLS to the transformed variables $\mathbf{Ty}$ and $\mathbf{TX}$. As an illustration, suppose we have just a two-variable regression where the disturbance follows an AR(1) scheme, that is,

$$Y_t = a + bX_t + u_t \qquad t = 1,\ldots, n \tag{8-72}$$

and $$u_t = \rho u_{t-1} + \varepsilon_t$$

with $|\rho| < 1$ and well-behaved ε's. The form of $\boldsymbol{\Omega}$ for this model has already been given in Eq. (8-11) and its inverse in Eq. (8-55) as

$$\boldsymbol{\Omega}^{-1} = \frac{1}{1-\rho^2}\begin{bmatrix} 1 & -\rho & 0 & \cdots & 0 & 0 & 0 \\ -\rho & 1+\rho^2 & -\rho & \cdots & 0 & 0 & 0 \\ \cdots & \cdots & \cdots & \cdots & \cdots & \cdots & \cdots \\ 0 & 0 & 0 & \cdots & -\rho & 1+\rho^2 & -\rho \\ 0 & 0 & 0 & \cdots & 0 & -\rho & 1 \end{bmatrix}$$

Consider first an $(n-1) \times n$ transformation matrix $\mathbf{T}_*$ defined by

$$\mathbf{T}_* = \begin{bmatrix} -\rho & 1 & 0 & \cdots & 0 & 0 \\ 0 & -\rho & 1 & & & \\ \cdots & \cdots & \cdots & \cdots & \cdots & \cdots \\ 0 & 0 & 0 & \cdots & -\rho & 1 \end{bmatrix}$$

Multiplication then shows that $\mathbf{T}_*'\mathbf{T}_*$ gives an $n \times n$ matrix which, apart from a proportionality constant, is identical with $\boldsymbol{\Omega}^{-1}$ except for the first element in the leading diagonal, which is ρ^2 rather than unity. Now consider the $n \times n$ matrix $\mathbf{T}$ obtained from $\mathbf{T}_*$ by adding a new first row with $\sqrt{1-\rho^2}$ in the first position and zeros elsewhere, that is,

$$\mathbf{T} = \begin{bmatrix} \sqrt{1-\rho^2} & 0 & 0 & \cdots & 0 & 0 \\ -\rho & 1 & 0 & \cdots & 0 & 0 \\ 0 & -\rho & 1 & \cdots & 0 & 0 \\ \cdots & \cdots & \cdots & \cdots & \cdots & \cdots \\ 0 & 0 & 0 & \cdots & -\rho & 1 \end{bmatrix}$$

Multiplication shows that $\mathbf{T}'\mathbf{T} = (1 - \rho^2)\mathbf{\Omega}^{-1}$. The difference between $\mathbf{T}_*$ and $\mathbf{T}$ lies only in the treatment of the first sample observation. Applying $\mathbf{T}_*$ to Eq. (8-72) gives the transformed model

$$\begin{bmatrix} Y_2 - \rho Y_1 \\ Y_3 - \rho Y_2 \\ \vdots \\ Y_n - \rho Y_{n-1} \end{bmatrix} = \begin{bmatrix} 1 & X_2 - \rho X_1 \\ 1 & X_3 - \rho X_2 \\ \cdots & \cdots \\ 1 & X_n - \rho X_{n-1} \end{bmatrix} \begin{bmatrix} \alpha(1-\rho) \\ \beta \end{bmatrix} + \begin{bmatrix} \varepsilon_2 \\ \varepsilon_3 \\ \vdots \\ \varepsilon_n \end{bmatrix} \tag{8-73}$$

so that only $n - 1$ transformed observations are used in the OLS estimation. The variables in Eq. (8-73) are sometimes referred to as quasi first differences, and the intercept term being estimated is now $\alpha(1 - \rho)$. The variance matrix of the disturbance term in Eq. (8-73) is an $(n - 1) \times (n - 1)$ matrix,

$$\text{var}(\boldsymbol{\varepsilon}) = (1 - \rho^2)\sigma^2\mathbf{I}$$

Application of $\mathbf{T}$ to Eq. (8-72) gives the transformed model

$$\begin{bmatrix} \sqrt{1-\rho^2}\cdot Y_1 \\ Y_2 - \rho Y_1 \\ \vdots \\ Y_n - \rho Y_{n-1} \end{bmatrix} = \begin{bmatrix} \sqrt{1-\rho^2} & \sqrt{1-\rho^2}\cdot X_1 \\ 1-\rho & X_2 - \rho X_1 \\ \cdots & \cdots \\ 1-\rho & X_n - \rho X_{n-1} \end{bmatrix} \begin{bmatrix} \alpha \\ \beta \end{bmatrix} + \begin{bmatrix} \sqrt{1-\rho^2}\cdot u_1 \\ \varepsilon_2 \\ \vdots \\ \varepsilon_n \end{bmatrix} \tag{8-74}$$

The $\sqrt{1 - \rho^2}$ factor is required to make the transformed disturbances homoscedastic. From Eq. (8-9),

$$\sigma_\varepsilon^2 = \sigma_u^2(1 - \rho^2)$$

for an AR(1) scheme. Thus $\text{var}\left[\sqrt{1-\rho^2}\cdot u_1\right] = \sigma_\varepsilon^2$.

If ρ were known, GLS estimation could be achieved by applying OLS to Eq. (8-74), or the process could be approximated by using Eq. (8-73). The difference between the two procedures can be important when the sample size is small. The extensions to include additional explanatory variables and higher-order AR processes are simple. Additional X's are treated in exactly the same way as the single explanatory variable in the example. If the disturbance term followed an AR(2) scheme,

$$u_t = \phi_1 u_{t-1} + \phi_2 u_{t-2} + \varepsilon_t$$

the transformed variable would take the form

$$Y_t - \phi_1 Y_{t-1} - \phi_2 Y_{t-2} - \cdots \qquad t = 3,\ldots, n$$

Special transformations would also be required for the first two observations.†

The assumption, however, of a known value for ρ is unrealistic. It is a parameter to be estimated along with α, β, and σ_u^2. Lagging Eq. (8-72) one period and subtracting from Eq. (8-72) gives

$$Y_t = \alpha(1 - \rho) + \beta X_t - \beta\rho X_{t-1} + \rho Y_{t-1} + \varepsilon_t \qquad t = 2,\ldots, n \qquad (8\text{-}75)$$

The disturbance in Eq. (8-75) satisfies the assumptions required for OLS. However,

$$\Sigma\varepsilon_t^2 = f(\alpha, \beta, \rho) \qquad (8\text{-}76)$$

which is a function of just *three* unknown parameters, while a straightforward application of OLS to Eq. (8-75) will yield *four* estimated coefficients, namely,

$$b_1 = \widehat{\alpha(1 - \rho)}$$
$$b_2 = \hat{\beta}$$
$$b_3 = -\widehat{\beta\rho}$$
$$b_4 = \hat{\rho}$$

where the circumflex denotes an estimate of the corresponding parameter. These four equations will, in general, be inconsistent in that they do not yield a unique set of estimates of α, β, and ρ. Thus a *nonlinear constraint*, $b_3 = -b_2 b_4$, would have to be imposed on the estimation process. To put the same point another way, minimizing $\Sigma\varepsilon_t^2$ with respect to α, β, and ρ gives equations which are nonlinear in the parameters and thus cannot be solved analytically.

The basis of an *iterative estimation process* can be found by rewriting Eq. (8-75) in two equivalent fashions, namely:

1. $Y_t - \rho Y_{t-1} = \alpha(1 - \rho) + \beta(X_t - \rho X_{t-1}) + \varepsilon_t$

and

2. $(Y_t - \alpha - \beta X_t) = \rho(Y_{t-1} - \alpha - \beta X_{t-1}) + \varepsilon_t$

Starting with any value for ρ, the quasi first differences in the equation of step 1 could be computed, and OLS applied to it would then yield estimates of α and β. These estimates in turn can be used to compute the $Y_t - \alpha - \beta X_t$ series. Regressing this series on itself lagged one period in the equation of step 2 yields a revised estimate of ρ, which can then be fed back into the equation of step 1, and the process continues.

This is known as the Cochrane-Orcutt iterative process, and versions of it are incorporated in almost all social science computer packages.‡ There is a variety of

† For details see F. B. Lempers and T. Kloek, "On a Simple Transformation for Second-Order Autocorrelated Disturbances in Regression Analysis," *Statistica Neerlandica*, vol. 27, 1973, pp. 69–75.

‡ D. Cochrane and G. H. Orcutt, "Application of Least Squares Regressions to Relationships Containing Autocorrelated Error Terms," *Journal of the American Statistical Association*, vol. 44, 1949, pp. 32–61.

starting positions and rules for termination. If the initial value of ρ is set at zero, step 1 is then simply the OLS regression of Y_t on X_t, which yields the OLS residuals $e_t = Y_t - a - bX_t$. In step 2 e_t is regressed on e_{t-1}, without an intercept term, to obtain an estimate r of the first-order autocorrelation coefficient. Alternatively r may be computed from the Durbin-Watson statistic, which is a routine output in an OLS package, as

$$r \simeq 1 - \tfrac{1}{2}d$$

The estimated r is then used to compute the series $\{Y_t - rY_{t-1}\}$ and $\{X_t - rX_{t-1}\}$, which are used in a repeat of step 1. The process may be stopped any time the Durbin-Watson statistic in step 1 indicates random residuals. This frequently occurs after one complete iteration. Alternatively one can stop the process after successive estimates of the parameters differ by less than some prescribed amount.

It is clear that step 1 in the Cochrane-Orcutt process is the use of model (8-73) and the associated transformation matrix $\mathbf{T}_*$. A modification of the process is to use model (8-74), where the first term gets explicit treatment. This is often referred to as the Prais-Winsten method.† The Prais-Winsten modification may be expected to improve the efficiency of the estimation, especially in small sample sizes. Yet another modification is to use a method suggested by Durbin for obtaining the initial estimate of ρ.‡ This is to fit Eq. (8-75) by OLS without worrying about the nonlinear restriction and take r as the coefficient of Y_{t-1}. A Monte Carlo study by Griliches and Rao suggests that a two-step estimator consisting of the Durbin estimate of ρ followed by the Prais-Winsten treatment of the transformed variables performs somewhat better than any of the other variants over a fairly wide range of parameter values.§

The two-step Durbin estimator extends easily to more than one explanatory variable and to higher order autoregressive schemes. For example, suppose the model is

$$Y_t = \beta_1 + \beta_2 X_{2t} + \cdots + \beta_k X_{kt} + u_t$$

with

$$u_t = \phi_1 u_{t-2} + \phi_2 u_{t-2} + \varepsilon_t$$

Combining the two equations gives

$$Y_t = \phi_1 Y_{t-1} + \phi_2 Y_{t-2} + \beta_2 X_{2t} + \cdots + \beta_k X_{kt} - \phi_1 \beta_2 X_{2,t-1} - \cdots$$
$$- \phi_1 \beta_k X_{k,t-1} - \phi_2 \beta_2 X_{2,t-2} - \cdots - \phi_2 \beta_k X_{k,t-2} + (1 - \phi_1 - \phi_2)\beta_1 + \varepsilon_t$$

Let $\hat{\phi}_1$ and $\hat{\phi}_2$ denote the coefficients of Y_{t-1} and Y_{t-2} when this regression is fitted by OLS. The transformed variables are then computed as

$$\left(Y_t - \hat{\phi}_1 Y_{t-1} - \hat{\phi}_2 Y_{t-2}\right), \left(X_{it} - \hat{\phi}_1 X_{i,t-1} - \hat{\phi}_2 X_{i,t-2}\right) \qquad i = 2, \ldots, k;\ t = 3, \ldots, n$$

and OLS is applied to these to obtain estimates of the β's.

† S. J. Prais and C. B. Winsten, "Trend Estimators and Serial Correlation," *Cowles Commission Discussion Paper*, no. 383, Chicago, 1954.

‡ J. Durbin, "Estimation of Parameters in Time Series Regression Models," *Journal of the Royal Statistical Society*, ser. B, vol. 22, 1960, pp. 139–153.

§ Z. Griliches and P. Rao, "Small Sample Properties of Several Two Stage Regression Methods in the Context of Autocorrelated Errors," *Journal of the American Statistical Association*, vol. 64, 1969, pp. 253–272.

The iterative procedures described above will, in general, converge to a solution vector since at each stage one is minimizing a quadratic function in the unknowns. There remains the question of whether one has reached a local or a global minimum of the sum of squares function. This may be investigated by performing a *grid search* over the permissible range of ρ values. For an AR(1) scheme stability requires $|\rho| < 1$. Thus a grid of ρ values might be specified ranging from -1 to $+1$ by increments of 0.1. For each value step 1 of the Cochrane-Orcutt process is applied and the residual sum of squares computed. The ρ value and the associated α and β values with the minimum residual sums of squares are then chosen as the estimates. Or a finer grid may be imposed around this ρ value and a further grid search carried out to achieve greater precision.

When some parameters of the variance matrix have to be estimated, we have a further example of feasible GLS estimation. Thus our conventional test procedures no longer have an exact finite sample justification but are only justified asymptotically. The tests should be based on the final least-squares regression computed in either a two-step or an iterative procedure, as the usual standard error formulas will, in general, yield consistent estimates of the asymptotic errors. The justification for this remark is provided at the end of the next section on ML estimation.

Maximum Likelihood Estimation

A full ML procedure for a regression equation with an AR(1) disturbance has recently been proposed, and the algorithm has been incorporated in some computer packages.† The model considered is

$$\mathbf{Y} = \mathbf{X}\boldsymbol{\beta} + \mathbf{u}$$

with

$$u_t = \rho u_{t-1} + \varepsilon_t \qquad E(\boldsymbol{\varepsilon}) = \mathbf{0} \qquad E(\boldsymbol{\varepsilon}\boldsymbol{\varepsilon}') = \sigma_\varepsilon^2 \mathbf{I}$$

The likelihood function is then

$$L(\boldsymbol{\varepsilon}) = \frac{1}{(2\pi\sigma_\varepsilon^2)^{n/2}} \exp\left[-\frac{1}{2\sigma_\varepsilon^2}(\boldsymbol{\varepsilon}'\boldsymbol{\varepsilon})\right]$$

Using the transformation matrix $\mathbf{T}$ defined above, we have

$$\mathbf{Tu} = \boldsymbol{\varepsilon}$$

where $\mathbf{u}$ and $\boldsymbol{\varepsilon}$ are both $n \times 1$ vectors. Changing variables in the likelihood function gives‡

$$L(\mathbf{u}) = L(\boldsymbol{\varepsilon}) \left| \frac{\partial \boldsymbol{\varepsilon}}{\partial \mathbf{u}} \right|$$

where $|\partial\boldsymbol{\varepsilon}/\partial\mathbf{u}|$ indicates the absolute value of the determinant formed from the matrix of partial derivatives of the ε's with respect to the u's. In this case

$$\left| \frac{\partial \boldsymbol{\varepsilon}}{\partial \mathbf{u}} \right| = |\det \mathbf{T}| = \sqrt{1 - \rho^2}$$

† C. M. Beach and J. G. MacKinnon, "A Maximum Likelihood Procedure for Regression with Autocorrelated Errors," *Econometrica*, vol. 46, 1978, pp. 51–58.

‡ See App. A-9, Change of Variables in Density Functions.

and so

$$\ln L(\mathbf{u}) \propto -\frac{n}{2}\ln \sigma_\varepsilon^2 + \frac{1}{2}\ln(1-\rho^2) - \frac{1}{2\sigma_\varepsilon^2}(\boldsymbol{\varepsilon}'\boldsymbol{\varepsilon}) \tag{8-77}$$

where $\propto$ means *is proportionate to*.

Thus a procedure which minimizes $\boldsymbol{\varepsilon}'\boldsymbol{\varepsilon}$, even one that incorporates the Prais-Winsten treatment of the first observation, is not full ML since it has not taken account of the term in $1-\rho^2$ in the likelihood function. Beach and MacKinnon devised an iterative procedure for maximizing Eq. (8-77), which has now been incorporated in White's SHAZAM program and also in new versions of the time-series processor (TSP).† They also conducted some sampling experiments which suggest that their procedure may yield better estimates than conventional procedures, such as the Cochrane-Orcutt process, and may also be computationally less expensive. Some further experiments conducted by Harvey and McAvinchey compare the full ML procedure not just with the two-step Cochrane-Orcutt process, which was the comparison in the Beach-MacKinnon study, but also with the iterative Cochrane-Orcutt and with the two-step Prais-Winsten procedures.‡ Their study uses the root-mean-square error (RMSE) of estimators as the principle of comparison and confirms the results of the Beach-MacKinnon experiments, but it also brings out a number of important points.

1. The two-step Prais-Winsten method is as efficient as full ML estimation for the parameter values underlying their experiments.
2. The iterative Cochrane-Orcutt process is sometimes inferior to two-step Cochrane-Orcutt, especially when the explanatory variable is basically a time trend.
3. The two-step Cochrane-Orcutt process is in turn inferior to the two-step Prais-Winsten method when the explanatory variable is trending.
4. OLS has RMSEs only about 3 to 4 percent in excess of full ML estimation with trending data, but its relative performance deteriorates when X is a stationary random series.

A more recent study by Park and Mitchell confirms the main findings of Harvey and McAvinchey and adds some additional findings.§

1. Their range of estimators includes an iterative version of Prais-Winsten, with ρ estimated from the least-squares residuals, and they find this to be the best of the feasible estimators.

† K. J. White, "A General Computer Program for Econometric Methods—SHAZAM," *Econometrica*, vol. 46, 1978, pp. 239–240.

‡ A. C. Harvey and I. D. McAvinchey, "The Small Sample Efficiency of Two-Step Estimates in Regression Models with Autoregressive Disturbances," Discussion Paper no. 78-10, University of British Columbia, April 1978. See also, A. C. Harvey, *The Econometric Analysis of Time Series*, Wiley, New York, 1981, pp. 196–199.

§ R. E. Park and B. M. Mitchell, "Estimating the Autocorrelated Error Model with Trended Data," *Journal of Econometrics*, vol. 13, 1980, pp. 185–201.

2. They also investigate how well the various estimators perform in hypothesis testing by looking at the number of type I errors in 1000 trials at the 0.05 significance level. The results are only reported for positively autocorrelated disturbances, but the message is very clear. All estimators seriously underestimate standard errors, making estimated coefficients appear to be much more significant than they actually are. This is, of course, to be expected for OLS, but it is also fairly substantial for two-stage Prais-Winsten (2SPW), iterative Prais-Winsten (ITERPW), and Beach-MacKinnon ML (BM). For a sample size of 20, $\rho = 0.8$, and GNP as the trending explanatory variable, the number of type I errors reported are OLS (449), 2SPW (251), ITERPW (246), and BM (258). These numbers should be contrasted with an expected range of 37 to 63. Thus it would be advisable to apply more stringent significance levels than usual in testing coefficients in models with autocorrelated disturbances.

Beach and MacKinnon have extended their ML approach to accommodate an AR(2) process.† The treatment of relationships where the disturbance term follows an MA or ARMA process is less well developed than the AR case.‡

As an illustration of the derivation of the asymptotic errors for ML estimation of a relationship with an AR(1) disturbance, consider the simple model

$$Y_t = \alpha + \beta X_t + u_t \qquad t = 1, \ldots, n$$

with

$$u_t = \rho u_{t-1} + \varepsilon_t \qquad |\rho| < 1$$

and

$$\varepsilon \sim N(\mathbf{0}, \sigma_\varepsilon^2 \mathbf{I})$$

We need to evaluate the information matrix. We are only concerned with asymptotic results, and so the treatment of the first sample observation does not matter since its effect becomes negligible as the sample size increases. Thus we may write the model as

$$\varepsilon_t = u_t - \rho u_{t-1} = (Y_t - \alpha - \beta X_t) - \rho(Y_{t-1} - \alpha - \beta X_{t-1}) \qquad t = 2, \ldots, n$$

The log likelihood function is then

$$\ln(L) = -\frac{n-1}{2}\ln(2\pi) - \frac{n-1}{2}\ln \sigma_\varepsilon^2 - \frac{1}{2\sigma_\varepsilon^2}\sum_{t=2}^{n} \varepsilon_t^2$$

The first-order partial derivatives with respect to the unknown parameters α, β, ρ,

† C. M. Beach and J. G. MacKinnon, "Full Maximum Likelihood Estimation of Second-Order Autoregressive Error Models," *Journal of Econometrics*, vol. 7, 1978, pp. 187–198.

‡ For an account of recent developments see A. C. Harvey, *The Econometric Analysis of Time Series*, Wiley, New York, 1981, Chap. 6. See also A. C. Harvey and I. D. McAvinchey, "On the Relative Efficiency of Various Estimators of Regression Models with Moving Average Disturbances," in E. G. Charatsis, Ed., *Proceedings of the Econometric Society European Meeting, Athens, 1979*, North-Holland, Amsterdam, 1981, pp. 105–118.

and σ_ε^2 are

$$\frac{\partial \ln L}{\partial \alpha} = \frac{1-\rho}{\sigma_\varepsilon^2}\Sigma\varepsilon_t$$

$$\frac{\partial \ln L}{\partial \beta} = \frac{1}{\sigma_\varepsilon^2}\Sigma(X_t - \rho X_{t-1})\varepsilon_t$$

$$\frac{\partial \ln L}{\partial \rho} = \frac{1}{\sigma_\varepsilon^2}\Sigma u_{t-1}\varepsilon_t$$

$$\frac{\partial \ln L}{\partial \sigma_\varepsilon^2} = -\frac{n-1}{2\sigma_\varepsilon^2} + \frac{1}{2\sigma_\varepsilon^4}\Sigma\varepsilon_t^2$$

where all summations are over $t = 2, \ldots, n$. Setting these derivatives to zero and solving for the parameters gives *conditional* ML estimators (conditional, that is, on X, which is taken as fixed). We may note in passing that the first three equations give

$$\Sigma(Y_t - \hat{\rho}Y_{t-1}) = (n-1)\hat{\alpha} + \hat{\beta}\Sigma(X_t - \hat{\rho}X_{t-1})$$

$$\Sigma(Y_t - \hat{\rho}Y_{t-1})(X_t - \hat{\rho}X_{t-1}) = \hat{\alpha}\Sigma(X_t - \hat{\rho}X_{t-1}) + \hat{\beta}\Sigma(X_t - \hat{\rho}X_{t-1})^2$$

$$\hat{\rho} = \frac{\Sigma(Y_t - \hat{\alpha} - \hat{\beta}X_t)(Y_{t-1} - \hat{\alpha} - \hat{\beta}X_{t-1})}{\Sigma(Y_{t-1} - \hat{\alpha} - \hat{\beta}X_{t-1})^2}$$

which are the equations of the iterative Cochrane-Orcutt process, the first two being the least-squares equations on the quasi first differences and the third the first-order autoregressive coefficient of the estimated residuals.

Turning to the second-order partial derivatives

$$\frac{\partial^2 \ln L}{\partial \alpha^2} = -\frac{(n-1)(1-\rho)^2}{\sigma_\varepsilon^2}$$

$$\frac{\partial^2 \ln L}{\partial \beta^2} = -\frac{1}{\sigma_\varepsilon^2}\Sigma(X_t - \rho X_{t-1})^2$$

$$\frac{\partial^2 \ln L}{\partial \rho^2} = -\frac{1}{\sigma_\varepsilon^2}\Sigma u_{t-1}^2$$

$$\frac{\partial^2 \ln L}{\partial (\sigma_\varepsilon^2)^2} = \frac{n-1}{2\sigma_\varepsilon^4} - \frac{1}{\sigma_\varepsilon^6}\Sigma\varepsilon_t^2$$

The cross partial derivatives are

$$\frac{\partial^2 \ln L}{\partial \alpha\, \partial \beta} = -\frac{1-\rho}{\sigma_\varepsilon^2}\Sigma(X_t - \rho X_{t-1})$$

$$\frac{\partial^2 \ln L}{\partial \alpha\, \partial \rho} = -\frac{1}{\sigma_\varepsilon^2}\{\Sigma\varepsilon_t + (1-\rho)\Sigma u_{t-1}\}$$

$$\frac{\partial^2 \ln L}{\partial \alpha\, \partial \sigma_\varepsilon^2} = -\frac{1-\rho}{\sigma_\varepsilon^2}\Sigma\varepsilon_t$$

$$\frac{\partial^2 \ln L}{\partial \beta\, \partial \rho} = -\frac{1}{\sigma_\varepsilon^2}\{\Sigma\varepsilon_t X_{t-1} - \Sigma\varepsilon_{t-1}(X_t - \rho X_{t-1})\}$$

$$\frac{\partial^2 \ln L}{\partial \beta\, \partial \sigma_\varepsilon^2} = -\frac{1}{\sigma_\varepsilon^4}\Sigma\varepsilon_t(X_t - \rho X_{t-1})$$

$$\frac{\partial^2 \ln L}{\partial \rho\, \partial \sigma_\varepsilon^2} = -\frac{1}{\sigma_\varepsilon^4}\Sigma\varepsilon_t u_{t-1}$$

Taking the negative of the expectations gives the information matrix

$$\mathbf{R} = \frac{1}{\sigma_\varepsilon^2}\begin{bmatrix} (n-1)(1-\rho)^2 & (1-\rho)\Sigma(X_t - \rho X_{t-1}) & 0 & 0 \\ (1-\rho)\Sigma(X_t - \rho X_{t-1}) & \Sigma(X_t - \rho X_{t-1})^2 & 0 & 0 \\ 0 & 0 & (n-1)\sigma_u^2 & 0 \\ 0 & 0 & 0 & \dfrac{n-1}{2\sigma_\varepsilon^2} \end{bmatrix}$$

The crucial feature of this information matrix is its block-diagonal nature. Asymptotically the estimates of the regression parameters α and β are distributed independently of the estimate of the autocorrelation parameter ρ and of the estimate of σ_ε^2. Referring back to Eq. (8-73), the data matrix for this regression is given by the $(n-1) \times 2$ matrix $\mathbf{X}_*$, where

$$\mathbf{X}'_* = \begin{bmatrix} 1-\rho & 1-\rho & \cdots & 1-\rho \\ X_2 - \rho X_1 & X_3 - \rho X_2 & \cdots & X_n - \rho X_{n-1} \end{bmatrix}$$

with unknown parameters α and β. The 2×2 submatrix in $\mathbf{R}$ is easily seen to be $\mathbf{X}'_*\mathbf{X}_*$. Since the asymptotic variance matrix is given by $\mathbf{R}^{-1}$ and since this has the same diagonal form as $\mathbf{R}$, we have

$$\text{asy var}\begin{pmatrix} \hat{\alpha} \\ \hat{\beta} \end{pmatrix} = \sigma_\varepsilon^2(\mathbf{X}'_*\mathbf{X}_*)^{-1}$$

which is consistently estimated by the usual least-squares procedures, justifying the remark at the end of the previous section. We also see from $\mathbf{R}^{-1}$ that

$$\text{asy var}(\hat{\rho}) = \frac{1-\rho^2}{n-1}$$

remembering that $\sigma_u^2 = \sigma_\varepsilon^2/(1-\rho^2)$.

Prediction in the Presence of Autocorrelated Disturbances

If the model

$$Y_t = \alpha + \beta X_t + u_t \qquad u_t = \rho u_{t-1} + \varepsilon_t$$

has been estimated from n sample observations, the best prediction of Y in period $n+1$ is no longer

$$\hat{Y}_{n+1} = a + bX_{n+1}$$

where a and b are estimates obtained by any of the above methods, since this prediction sets the disturbance term at zero, and the AR(1) process implies

$E(u_{n+1}) = \rho u_n$. Both elements in ρu_n are unknown, but might be estimated by

$$r\hat{u}_n = r(Y_n - a - bX_n)$$

The suggested predictor is then

$$\hat{Y}_{n+1} = a + bX_{n+1} + r\hat{u}_n$$

This, in fact, would be a best linear unbiased predictor if ρ were known and r set equal to ρ since it is the predictor that would emerge from the relation

$$Y_t - \rho Y_{t-1} = \alpha(1 - \rho) + \beta(X_t - \rho X_{t-1}) + \varepsilon_t$$

which may be rewritten as

$$Y_t = \alpha + \beta X_t + \rho(Y_{t-1} - \alpha - \beta X_{t-1}) + \varepsilon_t$$

giving the predictor.†

$$\hat{Y}_{n+1} = a + bX_{n+1} + \rho\hat{u}_n$$

8-6 SETS OF EQUATIONS

Sets of equations occur in various branches of economic theory. In the theory of consumer behavior the decision maker faces a given money income M and a set of prices $P_1, \ldots, P_r$. The assumption of utility maximization leads to a set of demand equations

$$Q_i = f_i(P_1, P_2, \ldots, P_r, M) \qquad i = 1, \ldots, r$$

where Q_i indicates the optimal rate of consumption of the ith commodity. Theory imposes various conditions on these demand equations. The assumption of a specific form of utility function will impose yet further conditions. For example, if one postulates an indirect addilog utility function

$$u^* = \sum_i a_i \left(\frac{M}{P_i}\right)^{b_i}$$

the ith demand equation is‡

$$Q_i = \frac{a_i b_i M^{b_i} P_i^{-b_i - 1} e^{\varepsilon_i}}{\sum_j a_j b_j M^{b_j - 1} P_j^{-b_j}} \qquad i = 1, \ldots, r \tag{8-78}$$

where we have inserted a multiplicative disturbance term e^{ε_i} to prepare the way for empirical estimation.§ Expenditure $Z_i = P_i Q_i$ on the ith commodity is then given by

$$Z_i = \frac{a_i b_i M^{b_i} P_i^{-b_i} e^{\varepsilon_i}}{\sum_j a_j b_j M^{b_j - 1} P_j^{-b_j}} \qquad i = 1, \ldots, r \tag{8-79}$$

† For a detailed treatment of this topic see A. S. Goldberger, "Best Linear Unbiased Prediction in the Generalized Linear Regression Model," *Journal of the American Statistical Association*, vol. 57, 1962, pp. 369–375.

‡ For this result and indeed for an elegant and lucid presentation of the theory and measurement of demand systems see L. Phlips, *Applied Consumption Analysis*, North-Holland, Amsterdam, 1974.

§ The e in the disturbance term indicates the mathematical constant $e = 2.71828$, and should not be confused with the use of the same symbol for OLS residuals.

The expenditure equation (8-79) is nonlinear in the a's and b's. However, if the logarithm of the ratio Z_i/Z_j is taken,

$$\ln Z_i - \ln Z_j = A_{ij} + b_i \ln\left(\frac{M}{P_i}\right) - b_j \ln\left(\frac{M}{P_j}\right) + u_{ij} \tag{8-80}$$

where
$$A_{ij} = \ln\left(\frac{a_i b_i}{a_j b_j}\right)$$

and
$$u_{ij} = \varepsilon_i - \varepsilon_j$$

This is clearly an estimable equation. Given r commodities, there are $r(r-1)/2$ such equations, but most are redundant. As an illustration, for commodities i and k we have

$$\ln Z_i - \ln Z_k = A_{ik} + b_i \ln\left(\frac{M}{P_i}\right) - b_k \ln\left(\frac{M}{P_k}\right) + u_{ik} \tag{8-81}$$

Subtracting Eq. (8-80) from Eq. (8-81) gives

$$\ln Z_j - \ln Z_k = A_{jk} + b_j \ln\left(\frac{M}{P_j}\right) - b_k \ln\left(\frac{M}{P_k}\right) + u_{jk}$$

where
$$A_{jk} = \ln\left(\frac{a_j b_j}{a_k b_k}\right)$$

and
$$u_{jk} = \varepsilon_j - \varepsilon_k$$

Thus of the three possible equations for commodities i, j, and k only two are independent. Given any pair of equations, the third follows by subtraction. For r commodities there are just $r - 1$ independent equations, and for estimation purposes one may select any set of $r - 1$ independent equations. Thus one might write the system

$$\begin{aligned}
\ln Z_{1t} - \ln Z_{2t} &= A_{12} + b_1 \ln\left(\frac{M_t}{P_{1t}}\right) - b_2 \ln\left(\frac{M_t}{P_{2t}}\right) + u_{12t} \\
\ln Z_{1t} - \ln Z_{3t} &= A_{13} + b_1 \ln\left(\frac{M_t}{P_{1t}}\right) - b_3 \ln\left(\frac{M_t}{P_{3t}}\right) + u_{13t} \qquad t = 1, \ldots, n \\
&\cdots\cdots\cdots\cdots\cdots\cdots\cdots\cdots\cdots\cdots \\
\ln Z_{1t} - \ln Z_{rt} &= A_{1r} + b_1 \ln\left(\frac{M_t}{P_{1t}}\right) - b_r \ln\left(\frac{M_t}{P_{rt}}\right) + u_{1rt}
\end{aligned} \tag{8-82}$$

Define $Y_{1t} = \ln Z_{1t} - \ln Z_{2t}$ and $\mathbf{y}_1 = [Y_{11} \quad Y_{12} \quad \cdots \quad Y_{1n}]'$.

The sample observations on the first equation in Eqs. (8-82) may then be written as

$$\mathbf{y}_1 = \mathbf{X}_1 \boldsymbol{\beta}_1 + \mathbf{u}_1$$

where

$$\mathbf{X}_1 = \begin{bmatrix} | & | & | \\ \mathbf{i} & \ln\left(\frac{M}{P_1}\right) & -\ln\left(\frac{M}{P_2}\right) \\ | & | & | \end{bmatrix} \qquad \boldsymbol{\beta}_1 = \begin{bmatrix} A_{12} \\ b_1 \\ b_2 \end{bmatrix} \qquad \mathbf{u}_1 = \begin{bmatrix} \varepsilon_{11} - \varepsilon_{21} \\ \varepsilon_{12} - \varepsilon_{22} \\ \vdots \\ \varepsilon_{1n} - \varepsilon_{2n} \end{bmatrix}$$

Likewise, defining $Y_{2t} = \ln Z_{1t} - \ln Z_{3t}$, the sample observations on the second equation in Eqs. (8-82) may be written as

$$\mathbf{y}_2 = \mathbf{X}_2\boldsymbol{\beta}_2 + \mathbf{u}_2$$

where

$$\mathbf{X}_2 = \begin{bmatrix} | & | & | \\ \mathbf{i} & \ln\left(\frac{M}{P_1}\right) & -\ln\left(\frac{M}{P_3}\right) \\ | & | & | \end{bmatrix} \qquad \boldsymbol{\beta}_2 = \begin{bmatrix} A_{13} \\ b_1 \\ b_3 \end{bmatrix} \qquad \mathbf{u}_2 = \begin{bmatrix} \varepsilon_{11} - \varepsilon_{31} \\ \varepsilon_{12} - \varepsilon_{32} \\ \vdots \\ \varepsilon_{1n} - \varepsilon_{3n} \end{bmatrix}$$

The complete model implied by Eqs. (8-82) is then

$$\begin{aligned} \mathbf{y}_1 &= \mathbf{X}_1\boldsymbol{\beta}_1 + \mathbf{u}_1 \\ \mathbf{y}_2 &= \mathbf{X}_2\boldsymbol{\beta}_2 + \mathbf{u}_2 \\ &\cdots\cdots\cdots \\ \mathbf{y}_m &= \mathbf{X}_m\boldsymbol{\beta}_m + \mathbf{u}_m \end{aligned} \tag{8-83}$$

where $m = r - 1$. This set of equations may be written equivalently

$$\begin{bmatrix} \mathbf{y}_1 \\ \mathbf{y}_2 \\ \vdots \\ \mathbf{y}_m \end{bmatrix} = \begin{bmatrix} \mathbf{X}_1 & & & \\ & \mathbf{X}_2 & & \\ & & \ddots & \\ & & & \mathbf{X}_m \end{bmatrix} \begin{bmatrix} \boldsymbol{\beta}_1 \\ \boldsymbol{\beta}_2 \\ \vdots \\ \boldsymbol{\beta}_m \end{bmatrix} + \begin{bmatrix} \mathbf{u}_1 \\ \mathbf{u}_2 \\ \vdots \\ \mathbf{u}_m \end{bmatrix} \tag{8-84}$$

or as

$$\mathbf{y} = \mathbf{X}\boldsymbol{\beta} + \mathbf{u} \tag{8-85}$$

Because of the block-diagonal form of **X** the application of OLS to Eq. (8-85), treated as a simple regression, would be exactly equivalent to the application of OLS to each of the m equations in Eqs. (8-83) separately. However, the application of OLS to Eq. (8-85) would not be optimal for two reasons. First of all the **u** vector is not homoscedastic. From the structure of the u's

$$u_i = \varepsilon_1 - \varepsilon_{i+1} \qquad i = 1, \ldots, r - 1$$

Thus
$$\operatorname{var}(u_i) = \operatorname{var}(\varepsilon_1) + \operatorname{var}(\varepsilon_{i+1}) - 2\operatorname{cov}(\varepsilon_1, \varepsilon_{i+1})$$

Even if the original ε's are contemporaneously uncorrelated,

$$\operatorname{var}(u_i) = \operatorname{var}(\varepsilon_1) + \operatorname{var}(\varepsilon_{i+1})$$

and
$$\operatorname{var}(u_j) = \operatorname{var}(\varepsilon_1) + \operatorname{var}(\varepsilon_{j+1})$$

Thus the u's would only be homoscedastic if the ε's were homoscedastic, but there is no a priori reason for the disturbance variances in the various expenditure equations to be equal.

A second reason for the nonoptimality of OLS is that the off-diagonal terms in var(**u**) will not be zero.

$$\begin{aligned} E(u_i u_j) &= E(\varepsilon_1 - \varepsilon_{i+1})(\varepsilon_1 - \varepsilon_{j+1}) \\ &= E(\varepsilon_1^2) - E(\varepsilon_1\varepsilon_{i+1}) - E(\varepsilon_1\varepsilon_{j+1}) + E(\varepsilon_{i+1}\varepsilon_{j+1}) \end{aligned}$$

Even if the covariances of the ε's vanish, $E(u_i u_j)$ does not vanish. Thus var(**u**) is not spherical, and GLS is the appropriate estimation procedure.

These conditions on the disturbances may be embodied in the set of assumptions

$$E(\mathbf{u}_i\mathbf{u}_i') = \sigma_{ii}\mathbf{I} \qquad i = 1,\ldots, m$$

and

$$E(\mathbf{u}_i\mathbf{u}_j') = \sigma_{ij}\mathbf{I} \qquad i \neq j;\ i,\ j = 1,\ldots, m$$

The first condition allows the disturbance variance to be different in the various equations, but within each equation the assumptions of homoscedasticity and zero covariances are still imposed. The second condition allows for nonzero covariances between the disturbances in different equations and assumes that, for any pair, the covariance is the same at each sample point; all lagged covariances, however, are assumed to be zero. Collecting these variances and covariances in the symmetric positive definite matrix

$$\boldsymbol{\Sigma} = \begin{bmatrix} \sigma_{11} & \sigma_{12} & \cdots & \sigma_{1m} \\ \sigma_{21} & \sigma_{22} & \cdots & \sigma_{2m} \\ \cdots & \cdots & \cdots & \cdots \\ \sigma_{m1} & \sigma_{m2} & \cdots & \sigma_{mm} \end{bmatrix}$$

the variance matrix for the **u** vector in Eq. (8-85) may be written†

$$\text{var}(\mathbf{u}) = \mathbf{V} = \boldsymbol{\Sigma} \otimes \mathbf{I} \tag{8-86}$$

Thus a set of demand equations should almost certainly be considered as a group and estimated by GLS because of the nature of the variance matrix of the disturbance term. In addition, theoretical considerations will impose restrictions across equations. For example, in the addilog demand system above the second parameter, b_1 in each $\boldsymbol{\beta}_i$ vector is constrained to be equal across all m equations. This constraint has not been imposed in the specification (8-84). Implementation of that system would allow a different estimate of the coefficient b_1 to be made for each commodity. One may wish to test for constancy of b_1 across commodities and to reestimate the system with constancy imposed.‡

A second illustration of sets of equations with cross-equation restrictions and connections between the various disturbances is found in sets of "share" equations approximated by transcendental logarithmic functions, which has recently become the dominant methodology in the estimation of various substitution elasticities, especially in the field of energy economics.§ Consider a production function

$$Q = f(X_1, X_2, \ldots, X_r)$$

where Q denotes the rate of output and X_i $(i = 1,\ldots, r)$ the rate of input of the ith productive factor. If one assumes the firm to face a given set of factor prices

† See Eqs. (4-76) and (4-77) for the definition of a Kronecker product and its inverse.

‡ For an illustration of the estimation and testing of three different demand systems see R. W. Parks, "Systems of Demand Equations: An Empirical Comparison of Alternative Functional Forms," *Econometrica*, vol. 37, 1969, pp. 629–650.

§ See, for instance, E. A. Hudson and D. W. Jorgenson, "U.S. Energy Policy and Economic Growth," *Bell Journal of Economics*, vol. 5, 1974, pp. 461–514; E. R. Berndt and D. O. Wood, "Technology, Prices and the Derived Demand for Energy," *Review of Economics and Statistics*, vol. 57, 1975, pp. 259–268; and J. M. Griffin and P. R. Gregory, "An Intercountry Translog Model of Energy Substitution Responses," *American Economic Review*, vol. 66, 1976, pp. 845–857.

$P_1, \ldots, P_r$, one formulation of the firm's decision problem is to choose the input mix to minimize the cost of producing a given output $\bar{Q}$. This gives rise to a set of factor demand functions

$$X_i = f_i(P_1, \ldots, P_r, \bar{Q}) \qquad i = 1, \ldots, r$$

Denoting the optimal inputs by X_i^*, the optimal (minimal) cost level is

$$C^* = \sum_i P_i X_i^* = f(P_1, \ldots, P_r, \bar{Q})$$

Differentiating C^* with respect to the factor prices gives†

$$\frac{\partial C^*}{\partial P_i} = X_i^*$$

† This result is an application of Shephard's lemma. (R. W. Shephard, *Theory of Cost and Production Functions*, Princeton University Press, Princeton, NJ, 1970, p. 170.) The lemma may be illustrated for a two-factor production function $Q = f(X_1, X_2)$. Suppose the firm is required to produce some stated output Q at minimum cost, given factor prices P_1 and P_2. If we define

$$\phi = (P_1 X_1 + P_2 X_2) - \lambda[f(X_1, X_2) - Q]$$

where λ is a Lagrange multiplier, we then seek the minimum of ϕ. The first-order conditions are

$$\frac{\partial \phi}{\partial X_1} = P_1 - \lambda f_1 = 0$$

$$\frac{\partial \phi}{\partial X_2} = P_2 - \lambda f_2 = 0 \qquad (1)$$

$$\frac{\partial \phi}{\partial \lambda} = f(X_1, X_2) - Q = 0$$

The solution of these equations gives the cost-minimizing factor demands X_1^* and X_2^*, expressed as functions of P_1, P_2, and Q. The minimum achievable cost is then given by

$$C^* = P_1 X_1^* + P_2 X_2^* \qquad (2)$$

Differentiating Eq. (2) partially with respect to P_1 gives

$$\frac{\partial C^*}{\partial P_1} = X_1^* + P_1 \frac{\partial X_1^*}{\partial P_1} + P_2 \frac{\partial X_1^*}{\partial P_1}$$

Thus Shephard's lemma requires that

$$P_1 \frac{\partial X_1^*}{\partial P_1} + P_2 \frac{\partial X_2^*}{\partial P_1} = 0$$

and, similarly, that

$$P_1 \frac{\partial X_1^*}{\partial P_2} + P_2 \frac{\partial X_2^*}{\partial P_2} = 0$$

Differentiate the system (1) totally, setting $dP_2 = dQ = 0$. This gives

$$\lambda f_{11}\, dX_1 + \lambda f_{12}\, dX_2 + f_1\, d\lambda = dP_1$$

$$\lambda f_{21}\, dX_1 + \lambda f_{22}\, dX_2 + f_2\, d\lambda = 0 \qquad (3)$$

$$f_1\, dX_1 + f_2\, dX_2 = 0$$

Further

$$\frac{\partial C^*}{\partial P_i} \cdot \frac{P_i}{C^*} = \frac{P_i X_i^*}{C^*}$$

or

$$\frac{\partial \ln C^*}{\partial \ln P_i} = \frac{P_i X_i^*}{C^*} = S_i$$

where S_i denotes the cost share of the ith factor, that is, the proportion of total cost absorbed by the ith factor. Since C^* depends on the factor prices and output, the cost shares will be functions of the same variables, that is,

$$S_i = g_i(P_1, \ldots, P_r, \bar{Q}) \qquad i = 1, \ldots, r$$

By estimating the parameters of the share equations one may be able to estimate the parameters of the cost function. All depends on the functional form postulated for the cost function.

A currently favored specification is the transcendental logarithmic (or translog) function.† This is a very flexible form, capable of approximating a wide variety of functional forms. As an illustration, the production function for the industrial sector of an economy is often specified as

$$Q = f(K, L, E, M)$$

where the inputs distinguished are capital K, labor L, energy E, and materials M. Assuming constant returns to scale plus exogenous factor prices P_K, P_L, P_E, and P_M, and imposing symmetry on the second-order partial derivatives, gives the translog cost function

$$\begin{aligned}\ln C = {} & \alpha_0 + \ln Q + \alpha_K \ln P_K + \alpha_L \ln P_L + \alpha_E \ln P_E + \alpha_M \ln P_M \\ & + \tfrac{1}{2}\beta_{KK}(\ln P_K)^2 + \beta_{KL}(\ln P_K)(\ln P_L) + \beta_{KE}(\ln P_K)(\ln P_E) \\ & + \beta_{KM}(\ln P_K)(\ln P_M) + \tfrac{1}{2}\beta_{LL}(\ln P_L)^2 + \beta_{LE}(\ln P_L)(\ln P_E) \\ & + \beta_{LM}(\ln P_L)(\ln P_M) + \tfrac{1}{2}\beta_{EE}(\ln P_E)^2 + \beta_{EM}(\ln P_E)(\ln P_M) \\ & + \tfrac{1}{2}\beta_{MM}(\ln P_M)^2.\end{aligned}$$

---

with the solution

$$dX_1 = -\frac{1}{\Delta} f_2^2 \, dP_1$$

$$dX_2 = \frac{1}{\Delta} f_1 f_2 \, dP_1$$

where Δ is the determinant of the 3×3 matrix of coefficients on the left-hand side of Eq. (3). Thus

$$\begin{aligned} P_1 \frac{\partial X_1^*}{\partial P_1} + P_2 \frac{\partial X_2^*}{\partial P_1} &= \frac{1}{\Delta}\left(P_2 f_1 f_2 - P_1 f_2^2\right) \\ &= 0 \qquad \text{from the first two equations in Eqs. (1).}\end{aligned}$$

† See, for example, L. R. Christensen, D. W. Jorgenson, and L. J. Lau, "Transcendental Logarithmic Production Frontiers," *Review of Economics and Statistics*, vol. 55, 1973, pp. 28–45.

Differentiating $\ln C$ with respect to the logs of the prices gives the cost share equations

$$\begin{aligned}
S_K &= \alpha_K + \beta_{KK}\ln P_K + \beta_{KL}\ln P_L + \beta_{KE}\ln P_E + \beta_{KM}\ln P_M \\
S_L &= \alpha_L + \beta_{KL}\ln P_K + \beta_{LL}\ln P_L + \beta_{LE}\ln P_E + \beta_{LM}\ln P_M \\
S_E &= \alpha_E + \beta_{KE}\ln P_K + \beta_{LE}\ln P_L + \beta_{EE}\ln P_E + \beta_{EM}\ln P_M \\
S_M &= \alpha_M + \beta_{KM}\ln P_K + \beta_{LM}\ln P_L + \beta_{EM}\ln P_E + \beta_{MM}\ln P_M
\end{aligned}$$

Since the shares must sum to unity,

$$\alpha_K + \alpha_L + \alpha_E + \alpha_M = 1$$

and the β's sum to zero in each column (and row). Imposing the rowwise β constraints on the first three share equations gives the system

$$\begin{aligned}
S_K &= \alpha_K + \beta_{KK}\ln\left(\frac{P_K}{P_M}\right) + \beta_{KL}\ln\left(\frac{P_L}{P_M}\right) + \beta_{KE}\ln\left(\frac{P_E}{P_M}\right) \\
S_L &= \alpha_L + \beta_{KL}\ln\left(\frac{P_K}{P_M}\right) + \beta_{LL}\ln\left(\frac{P_L}{P_M}\right) + \beta_{LE}\ln\left(\frac{P_E}{P_M}\right) \qquad (8\text{-}87) \\
S_E &= \alpha_E + \beta_{KE}\ln\left(\frac{P_K}{P_M}\right) + \beta_{LE}\ln\left(\frac{P_L}{P_M}\right) + \beta_{EE}\ln\left(\frac{P_E}{P_M}\right)
\end{aligned}$$

Because of the symmetry in the β's there are just nine independent parameters in this system. Estimation of these, in conjunction with the summation conditions on the α's and β's, will yield estimates of all the coefficients of the cost function except α_0.

For the translog cost function the Allen partial elasticities of substitution are given by

$$\delta_{ij} = \frac{\beta_{ij} + S_i S_j}{S_i S_j} \qquad i \neq j$$

and

$$\delta_{ii} = \frac{\beta_{ii} + S_i^2 - S_i}{S_i^2}$$

and the factor price elasticities by

$$\eta_{ij} = \delta_{ij} S_j$$

Since the four shares sum identically to unity, one must expect nonzero contemporaneous covariances between disturbances in different equations, and there is also no a priori reason to expect the same disturbance variance in different share equations. However, this system differs in one major aspect from the addilog demand functions in Eqs. (8-82). In Eqs. (8-87) the same set of explanatory variables appears in each share equation, but that is not true in Eqs. (8-82), and we will return to the significance of this point below. At the next level of disaggregation a production function could be specified for the energy sector with various specific fuels as inputs and the parameters estimated from a set of energy cost share equations. There have been many applications of this cost share approach in recent years. However, a word of caution is required. As the derivation made clear, a basic assumption underlying the derivation of the share equations is that in each observation period in the sample there has been a full and complete adjustment of the input mix to the factor prices ruling in that period so that the minimum cost level C^* is achieved. This is an implausible assumption for many production processes, and actual cost shares probably represent various *lagged* adjustments to changing factor prices. The assumption of instantaneous adjustment is likely to produce seriously biased estimates of the various elasticities.

Feasible GLS Estimation

Returning now to the general set of equations set out in Eqs. (8-83) to (8-86), the GLS estimator of $\boldsymbol{\beta}$ is

$$\mathbf{b}_* = (\mathbf{X}'\mathbf{V}^{-1}\mathbf{X})^{-1}\mathbf{X}'\mathbf{V}^{-1}\mathbf{y}$$

From Eqs. (8-86)

$$\mathbf{V}^{-1} = \boldsymbol{\Sigma}^{-1} \otimes \mathbf{I} = \begin{bmatrix} \sigma^{11}\mathbf{I} & \cdots & \sigma^{1m}\mathbf{I} \\ \cdots & \cdots & \cdots \\ \sigma^{m1}\mathbf{I} & \cdots & \sigma^{mm}\mathbf{I} \end{bmatrix}$$

where σ^{ij} denotes the i, jth element in $\boldsymbol{\Sigma}^{-1}$. Substituting for $\mathbf{V}^{-1}$ in the formula for $\mathbf{b}_*$ gives

$$\mathbf{b}_* = \begin{bmatrix} \sigma^{11}\mathbf{X}_1'\mathbf{X}_1 & \sigma^{12}\mathbf{X}_1'\mathbf{X}_2 & \cdots & \sigma^{1m}\mathbf{X}_1'\mathbf{X}_m \\ \cdots & \cdots & \cdots & \cdots \\ \sigma^{m1}\mathbf{X}_m'\mathbf{X}_1 & \sigma^{m2}\mathbf{X}_m'\mathbf{X}_2 & \cdots & \sigma^{mm}\mathbf{X}_m'\mathbf{X}_m \end{bmatrix}^{-1} \begin{bmatrix} \sum_{j=1}^{m} \sigma^{1j}\mathbf{X}_1'\mathbf{y}_j \\ \vdots \\ \sum_{j=1}^{m} \sigma^{mj}\mathbf{X}_m'\mathbf{y}_j \end{bmatrix} \tag{8-88}$$

and the associated variance matrix is

$$\operatorname{var}(\mathbf{b}_*) = (\mathbf{X}'\mathbf{V}^{-1}\mathbf{X})^{-1} \tag{8-89}$$

The obvious operational difficulty with Eq. (8-88) is that $\boldsymbol{\Sigma}$ is unknown. Zellner has proposed the construction of a feasible estimator as follows.†

1. Apply OLS separately to each equation in Eqs. (8-83), obtaining the vectors of sample residuals $\mathbf{e}_1, \mathbf{e}_2, \ldots, \mathbf{e}_m$ where

$$\mathbf{e}_i = \left[\mathbf{I} - \mathbf{X}_i(\mathbf{X}_i'\mathbf{X}_i)^{-1}\mathbf{X}_i'\right]\mathbf{y}_i \qquad i = 1, \ldots, m$$

2. The diagonal elements σ_{ii} of $\boldsymbol{\Sigma}$ are estimated by

$$s_{ii} = \frac{e_i'e_i}{n - k_i}$$

† A. Zellner, "An Efficient Method of Estimating Seemingly Unrelated Regressions and Tests for Aggregation Bias," *Journal of the American Statistical Association*, vol. 57, 1962, pp. 348–368.

and the off-diagonal elements s_{ij} by

$$s_{ij} = \frac{\mathbf{e}_i'\mathbf{e}_j}{(n-k_i)^{1/2}(n-k_j)^{1/2}}$$

where k_i denotes the number of columns in $\mathbf{X}_i$.† The denominator in these estimates may alternatively be taken simply as n since the usual test procedures will now only be valid asymptotically. Thus an estimated $\hat{\Sigma}$ matrix is computed and substituted in Eq. (8-88) to give a feasible estimator. The usual significance tests based on an estimated version of var($\mathbf{b}_*$) now have an asymptotic justification rather than small sample validity.

This estimator is often referred to as SURE (seemingly unrelated regression equations) estimator after the title of Zellner's original paper. This title is something of a misnomer, since the most natural application of the technique is to sets of equations which are indeed theoretically related, as in the two examples. The gain in efficiency yielded by the Zellner estimator over OLS increases directly with the correlation between disturbances from the different equations and decreases as the correlation between the different sets of explanatory variables increases. Indeed the GLS estimator reduces to OLS if either (1) the σ_{ij} are all zero or (2) the $\mathbf{X}_i$ are identical.‡ Even if the true correlation between equation disturbances is zero, the sample OLS residuals may yield nonnegligible covariances, and one might mistakenly compute GLS estimates. The result will be estimates with somewhat greater standard errors than those of the OLS coefficients. This will even be true for very small disturbance correlations, but as these correlations increase, the efficiency of the GLS over the OLS estimates rises substantially.§

Tests of Linear Restrictions

In order to see how to test a set of linear restrictions in the SURE model we must extend the test developed in Chap. 5 under the OLS assumptions to fit the new GLS assumptions. As we have seen in Sec. 8-3, the GLS estimator may be obtained by applying OLS to the transformed equation

$$\mathbf{Ty} = (\mathbf{TX})\boldsymbol{\beta} + \mathbf{Tu}$$

where

$$\mathbf{T'T} = \mathbf{V}^{-1}$$

Making the appropriate substitution of **Ty** for **y** and **TX** for **X** in the OLS test

† In the two illustrative examples the $\mathbf{X}_i$ matrices had an equal number of columns, but there is no need to impose such a condition generally. The exposition also assumes an equal sample size in each regression, but this is merely a simplification and need not be imposed generally.

‡ See Problem 8-2.

§ J. Kmenta and R. F. Gilbert, "Small Sample Properties of Alternative Estimators of Seemingly Unrelated Regressions," *Journal of the American Statistical Association*, vol. 63, 1968, pp. 1180–1200.

statistic for H_0: $\mathbf{R\beta} = \mathbf{r}$, now gives the statistic

$$\frac{(\mathbf{r} - \mathbf{Rb}_*)'\left[\mathbf{R}(\mathbf{X}'\mathbf{V}^{-1}\mathbf{X})^{-1}\mathbf{R}'\right]^{-1}(\mathbf{r} - \mathbf{Rb}_*)/q}{\mathbf{e}'\mathbf{V}^{-1}\mathbf{e}/(n-k)} \tag{8-90}$$

where $\mathbf{b}_*$ is the GLS estimator, q is the number of restrictions embodied in the null hypothesis, and $\mathbf{e} = \mathbf{y} - \mathbf{Xb}_*$. Under the null hypothesis this statistic follows the $F(q, n-k)$ distribution.

The SURE model specified in Eqs. (8-84) to (8-86) gives a special case of this statistic. There are m separate equations with n observations on each, giving $N = mn$ observations in all. There are k_i variables in $\mathbf{X}_i$, and the estimation of the *unrestricted* model, Eq. (8-84), will thus yield estimates of $K = \Sigma_{i=1}^{m} k_i$ parameters. Finally the $\mathbf{V}$ matrix has the special form shown in Eq. (8-86). Thus the test statistic becomes

$$\frac{(\mathbf{r} - \mathbf{Rb}_*)'\left\{\mathbf{R}\left[\mathbf{X}'(\mathbf{\Sigma}^{-1} \otimes \mathbf{I})\mathbf{X}\right]^{-1}\mathbf{R}'\right\}^{-1}(\mathbf{r} - \mathbf{Rb}_*)/q}{\mathbf{e}'(\mathbf{\Sigma}^{-1} \otimes \mathbf{I})\mathbf{e}/(N-K)} \tag{8-91}$$

Finally the unknown $\mathbf{\Sigma}$ in Eq. (8-91) has to be replaced by $\hat{\mathbf{\Sigma}}$, containing the s_{ij} defined above, and the test now has only an asymptotic justification.

As an illustration of the construction of the $\mathbf{R}$ matrix consider an addilog system, Eqs. (8-82), with just four commodity groups and hence three estimated equations. Application of the SURE technique to Eq. (8-84) will give the GLS vector $\mathbf{b}_*$, containing nine estimated parameters, namely,

$$\mathbf{b}_* = \begin{bmatrix} \hat{A}_{12} & \hat{b}_1^{(1)} & \hat{b}_2 & \hat{A}_{13} & \hat{b}_1^{(2)} & \hat{b}_3 & \hat{A}_{14} & \hat{b}_1^{(3)} & \hat{b}_4 \end{bmatrix}'$$

Thus each of the equations gives an estimate of the b_1 parameter, as indicated by the superscript. The null hypothesis is that the true value of this parameter is the same in all three equations. This translates into a two-element constraint, namely,

$$b_1^{(1)} - b_1^{(2)} = 0$$

$$b_1^{(1)} - b_1^{(3)} = 0$$

Thus $$\mathbf{R} = \begin{bmatrix} 0 & 1 & 0 & 0 & -1 & 0 & 0 & 0 & 0 \\ 0 & 1 & 0 & 0 & 0 & 0 & 0 & -1 & 0 \end{bmatrix}$$

and

$$\mathbf{r} = \begin{bmatrix} 0 \\ 0 \end{bmatrix}$$

If the null hypothesis is not rejected and one wishes to reestimate the system with the constraint imposed, one may take the formula for the restricted OLS estimator, given in Eq. (6-5), and replace $\mathbf{X}$ by $\mathbf{TX}$ to obtain

$$\mathbf{b}_{**} = \mathbf{b}_* + (\mathbf{X}'\mathbf{V}^{-1}\mathbf{X})^{-1}\mathbf{R}'\left[\mathbf{R}(\mathbf{X}'\mathbf{V}^{-1}\mathbf{X})^{-1}\mathbf{R}'\right]^{-1}(\mathbf{r} - \mathbf{Rb}_*) \tag{8-92}$$

Equivalently one may arrange the columns of the data matrix in such a way that a direct application of GLS gives an estimator obeying the constraints. For a three-equation version of Eqs. (8-82) the arrangement would be

$$\begin{bmatrix} \mathbf{y}_1 \\ \mathbf{y}_2 \\ \mathbf{y}_3 \end{bmatrix} = \begin{bmatrix} \mathbf{i} & \mathbf{0} & \mathbf{0} & \mathbf{x}_1 & -\mathbf{x}_2 & \mathbf{0} & \mathbf{0} \\ \mathbf{0} & \mathbf{i} & \mathbf{0} & \mathbf{x}_1 & \mathbf{0} & -\mathbf{x}_3 & \mathbf{0} \\ \mathbf{0} & \mathbf{0} & \mathbf{i} & \mathbf{x}_1 & \mathbf{0} & \mathbf{0} & -\mathbf{x}_4 \end{bmatrix} \begin{bmatrix} A_{12} \\ A_{13} \\ A_{14} \\ b_1 \\ b_2 \\ b_3 \\ b_4 \end{bmatrix} + \begin{bmatrix} \mathbf{u}_1 \\ \mathbf{u}_2 \\ \mathbf{u}_3 \end{bmatrix} \tag{8-93}$$

where $\mathbf{i}$ denotes a column vector of n units and $\mathbf{x}_1$ the n observations on $\ln(M/P_1)$, and so on. Repeating the $\mathbf{x}_1$ vector in a single column of the data matrix ensures just a single estimate of its coefficient. The efficient estimation procedure for Eq. (8-93) is still the Zellner SURE technique since the disturbance variance matrix has the form of Eq. (8-86). There is a moot point whether the estimates of the elements of $\mathbf{\Sigma}$ in the first stage of the technique should be obtained from the application of OLS to each equation separately, as previously described, or from the application of OLS to Eq. (8-93), which incorporates the restrictions implied by the null hypothesis. The two procedures are equivalent asymptotically.

Looking now at the cost share equations (8-87), *unrestricted* estimation of the equations would be achieved by OLS, even with a nonspherical disturbance matrix, since the matrix of explanatory variables is identical in each equation. However, the test of the symmetry restrictions still requires the computation of the test statistic (8-91): the GLS $\mathbf{b}_*$ in that formula is now replaced by the OLS $\mathbf{b}$, but the elements of the $\mathbf{\Sigma}$ matrix must be estimated from the OLS residuals as before. The specification of the appropriate $\mathbf{R}$ matrix and $\mathbf{r}$ vector for the test of the symmetry conditions is left as an exercise for the reader.† Equations (8-87) already embody summation restrictions on both α's and β's. One may wish to test these restrictions before looking at Eqs. (8-87), or one may wish to test the complete set of summation and symmetry conditions.‡ Finally if one wishes to estimate Eqs. (8-87) with the symmetric restrictions imposed, the Zellner SURE technique is again required, as in the addilog example. The details are left as an exercise.

The choice of which of the four share equations to drop in obtaining the set of three equations (8-87) is an arbitrary one. The SURE estimates are not invariant to the choice of equation to drop. However, iteration of the SURE technique will produce parameter estimates that converge to the ML parameter estimates, which are unique and independent of the equation omitted.§

† See Problem 8-3.

‡ See Problem 8-4.

§ See the very useful discussion and references to other relevant papers in E. R. Berndt and L. R. Christensen, "The Translog Function and the Substitution of Equipment, Structures and Labor in U.S. Manufacturing, 1929–68," *Journal of Econometrics*, vol. 1, 1973, pp. 81–113.

The iterative process goes as follows.

1. Compute the s_{ij} from the OLS residuals, as described above, and hence obtain $\boldsymbol{\Sigma}$.
2. Compute the elements of $\boldsymbol{\Sigma}^{-1}$ and substitute in Eq. (8-88) to compute $\mathbf{b}_*$.
3. Using $\mathbf{b}_*$ compute a new set of residuals $\mathbf{e}_* = \mathbf{y} - \mathbf{X}\mathbf{b}_*$.
4. Partition $\mathbf{e}_*$ into the subvectors corresponding to each equation and use these subvectors to compute new s_{ij}, thus starting the process over again.

The SURE process may be further complicated to allow for autocorrelation in the disturbance terms, but we will not pursue that topic here.†

PROBLEMS

8-1 Derive the results on the efficiency of the OLS estimator under the two forms of heteroscedasticity, given in Eqs. (8-34*a*) and (8-34*b*).

8-2 Prove that the SURE estimator in Eqs. (8-88) reduces to the application of OLS to each equation separately if

(*a*) $\sigma_{ij} = 0$ for all $i \neq j$

or

(*b*) $\mathbf{X}_1 = \mathbf{X}_2 = \cdots = \mathbf{X}_m$

8-3 Specify the **R** matrix and **r** vector for testing the symmetry conditions in the set of equations (8-87).

8-4 Consider the four cost share equations prior to Eqs. (8-87) and explain how to test the full set of summation restrictions (on α's and β's) and symmetry conditions. Which, if any, of these restrictions might be satisfied exactly by the estimated coefficients?

8-5 Consider a heteroscedastic model (for which all other classical assumptions hold)

$$Y_{ij} = \alpha + \beta X_i + u_{ij} \qquad i = 1, 2, \ldots, m \qquad (m > 1)$$
$$j = 1, 2, \ldots, n_i \qquad (n_i > 2)$$

Suppose $\operatorname{var}(u_i) = \sigma_i^2$. A sample estimator of σ_i^2 is

$$s_i^2 = \frac{\sum_{j=1}^{n_i} \left(Y_{ij} - \bar{Y}_i\right)^2}{n_i - 1}$$

where

$$\bar{Y}_i = \frac{\sum_{j=1}^{n_i} Y_{ij}}{n_i}$$

Determine $E(s_i^2)$.

(University of Michigan, 1981)

† See R. W. Parks, "Efficient Estimation of a System of Regression Equations when Disturbances Are Both Serially and Contemporaneously Correlated," *Journal of the American Statistical Association*, vol. 62, 1967, pp. 500–509, for a treatment of first-order serial correlation; and see G. G. Judge, W. E. Griffiths, R. C. Hill, and T. C. Lee, *The Theory and Practice of Econometrics*, Wiley, New York, 1980, Chap. 6, for more general cases.

8-6 In the model

$$y_{1t} = \alpha x_{1t} + u_{1t}$$

$$y_{2t} = \beta x_{2t} + u_{2t}$$

the x_{it} are nonrandom exogenous variables and the u_{it} are serially independent random disturbances that are normally distributed with zero means and second moments

$$E(u_{1t}^2) = 1 \qquad E(u_{2t}^2) = 2 \qquad E(u_{1t}u_{2t}) = 1$$

for all values of t. The sample second moment matrix below was calculated from 20 sample observations:

$$\begin{array}{c} \\ y_1 \\ y_2 \\ x_1 \\ x_2 \end{array} \begin{array}{c} \begin{array}{cccc} y_1 & y_2 & x_1 & x_2 \end{array} \\ \begin{bmatrix} 10 & -1 & 1 & -1 \\ -1 & 15 & 5 & 1 \\ 1 & 5 & 11 & 1 \\ -1 & 1 & 1 & 1 \end{bmatrix} \end{array}$$

(*a*) Find the best linear unbiased estimates of the parameters α and β.
(*b*) Test the null hypothesis

$$H_0: \quad \alpha = \beta$$

against the alternative H_1: $\alpha \neq \beta$.

(University of Michigan, 1980)

CHAPTER

NINE

LAGGED VARIABLES

We will use the term "lagged variables" to cover the inclusion on the right-hand side of the regression equation of lagged-values of the explanatory variables, the X's, and/or lagged values of the dependent variable Y.

9-1 SOURCES OF LAGGED VARIABLES

Realistic formulations of economic relations often require the insertion of lagged values of the explanatory variables. For instance, a rise in "permanent" income is likely to have an effect on consumption, which is distributed over a number of time periods, or a change in investment allowances may be expected to result in changed investment allocations, which, in turn, will have an effect on actual investment spending spread over a number of time periods because of production and other lags.

In general let us suppose that a causal variable X_t exerts a distributed lag effect on Y as follows:

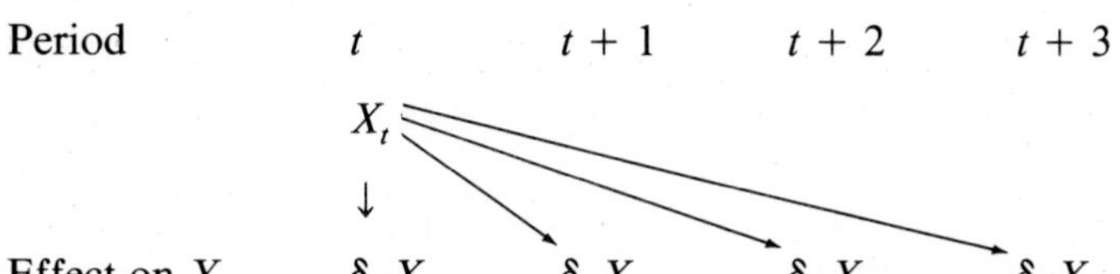

Period
t
t + 1
t + 2
t + 3
X_t
Effect on Y
δ_0 X_t
δ_1 X_t
δ_2 X_t
δ_3 X_t

Assuming the lag pattern to persist through time, any Y_t is seen to be built up as the sum of effects from current and previous values of X. Thus the lagged effect assumed above would generate the relation

$$Y_t = \mu + \delta_0 X_t + \delta_1 X_{t-1} + \delta_2 X_{t-2} + \delta_3 X_{t-3} + u_t$$

where we have also allowed for an intercept and a disturbance term. In practice one does not usually have any strong a priori information about the maximum length of lag, and one formulates the general relation

$$Y_t = \mu + D(L) X_t + u_t \tag{9-1}$$

where $D(L)$ is a polynomial of some degree s in the lag operator, that is,

$$D(L) = \delta_0 + \delta_1 L + \cdots + \delta_s L^s \tag{9-2}$$

If X has remained constant at some level $\bar{X}$ for s periods, then, apart from disturbances, Y will have reached an equilibrium value

$$\bar{Y} = \mu + D(1)\bar{X}$$

where $D(1)$ indicates the value of the polynomial when L is replaced by unity, and is simply the sum of the δ_i coefficients, namely,

$$D(1) = \sum_{i=0}^{s} \delta_i$$

If $\bar{X}$ changes in period t by an amount ΔX_t and is then held constant at the new level, Y will gradually adjust from $\bar{Y}$ to a new equilibrium. The changes are

Period	t	$t+1$	$t+2$	$\cdots$
Change in Y	$\delta_0 \Delta X_t$	$\delta_1 \Delta X_t$	$\delta_2 \Delta X_t$	$\cdots$

The coefficient δ_0 $(= \Delta Y_t / \Delta X_t)$ thus represents the impact multiplier for X. Partial sums of the δ's indicate intermediate multipliers. The δ's may also be standardized by dividing by their sum $D(1)$. Partial sums of the standardized δ's then indicate the *proportion* of the total effect achieved by a certain period. For example, knowledge of the δ's enables one to estimate how many periods must elapse before, say, 90 percent of the total effect is achieved. An important concept is that of the *median lag*, which is the number of periods required for 50 percent of the total effect to be achieved. When all the δ's are positive, another useful statistic is the *mean lag* defined as

$$\frac{\sum_{i=0}^{s} i\delta_i}{\sum_{i=0}^{s} \delta_i} = \frac{\delta_1 + 2\delta_2 + \cdots + s\delta_s}{\delta_0 + \delta_1 + \delta_2 + \cdots + \delta_s}$$

From Eq. (9-2) it is seen that differentiating $D(L)$ with respect to L gives

$$D'(L) = \delta_1 + 2\delta_2 L + \cdots + s\delta_s L^{s-1}$$

Thus
$$\text{Mean lag} = \frac{D'(1)}{D(1)}$$

As an illustration suppose an estimated version of Eq. (9-1) yields

$$D(L) = 0.10 + 0.25L + 0.35L^2 + 0.15L^3 + 0.05L^4$$

Then
$$D(1) = 0.90$$
so that the final or total effect of a unit change in X is a change of 0.9 in Y. Also
$$D'(1) = 0.25 + 0.70 + 0.45 + 0.20 = 1.60$$
and the mean lag is computed as $1.6/0.9 = 1.78$ periods. The standardized coefficients and their cumulated values are as follows:

Period	0	1	2	3	4
Standardized coefficients	0.11	0.28	0.39	0.17	0.05
Cumulated values	0.11	0.39	0.78	0.95	1.00

The median lag would be computed by interpolation as
$$1 + \frac{0.50 - 0.39}{0.78 - 0.39} = 1.28 \text{ periods}$$

In practice the maximum lag s may have to be fairly large to provide an adequate representation of the relationship between Y and X. It is frequently possible to achieve a more parsimonious representation (that is, using a smaller number of parameters) by postulating a distributed lag on both Y_t and X_t as in
$$A(L)(Y_t - \mu) = B(L)X_t + v_t \tag{9-3}$$
where
$$A(L) = 1 - \alpha_1 L - \cdots - \alpha_p L^p \tag{9-4a}$$
$$B(L) = \beta_0 + \beta_1 L + \cdots + \beta_q L^q \tag{9-4b}$$
and it is expected that $p + q$ will be less than s. The stability of Eq. (9-3) imposes conditions on the α's, which may be expressed in the form that the roots of $A(L)$ lie outside the unit circle.† Relation (9-3) may be rewritten as
$$Y_t = \mu + \frac{B(L)}{A(L)} X_t + u_t \tag{9-5}$$
where we are assuming the disturbances to be related by $v_t = A(L)u_t$. Comparison of Eqs. (9-1) and (9-5) gives
$$\frac{B(L)}{A(L)} = D(L) \tag{9-6}$$
As an example, suppose that
$$A(L) = 1 - \alpha_1 L \tag{9-7a}$$
and
$$B(L) = \beta_0 + \beta_1 L \tag{9-7b}$$
Then‡
$$\frac{B(L)}{A(L)} = \beta_0 + (\alpha_1\beta_0 + \beta_1)L + \alpha_1(\alpha_1\beta_0 + \beta_1)L^2 + \alpha_1^2(\alpha_1\beta_0 + \beta_1)L^3 + \cdots$$

† See C. E. P. Box and G. M. Jenkins, *Time Series Analysis: Forecasting and Control*, revised edition, Holden-Day, San Francisco, 1976, pp. 53–54.

‡ Note that $(1 - \alpha_1 L)^{-1} = 1 + \alpha_1 L + \alpha_1^2 L^2 + \cdots$.

and the correspondence between the α's, β's, and δ's is

$$\begin{aligned} \delta_0 &= \beta_0 \\ \delta_1 &= \alpha_1\beta_0 + \beta_1 \\ \delta_2 &= \alpha_1\delta_1 \\ \delta_3 &= \alpha_1\delta_2 \end{aligned} \tag{9-8}$$

and so on. Two first-order polynomials $A(L)$ and $B(L)$ thus generate an infinite polynomial for $D(L)$, but there are, of course, implied restrictions on the δ's. As shown by Eq. (9-8), the first two δ's are "free" and subsequent δ's decline exponentially. They decline since the stability requirement that the root of

$$A(L) = 1 - \alpha_1 L = 0$$

lie *outside* the unit circle ensures that α_1 $(= 1/L)$ has modulus *less* than unity. The same condition ensures that the infinite sum of the δ's converges. From Eq. (9-8) this sum is seen to be

$$\begin{aligned} D(1) &= \beta_0 + \frac{\alpha_1\beta_0 + \beta_1}{1 - \alpha_1} \\ &= \frac{\beta_0 + \beta_1}{1 - \alpha_1} \\ &= \frac{B(1)}{A(1)} \end{aligned}$$

Clearly, extending the power of the $B(L)$ polynomial would extend the number of "free" δ coefficients before the exponential decline sets in. The mean lag may also be derived from the $A(L)$, $B(L)$ polynomials. Since $D(L) = B(L)/A(L)$,

$$\frac{D'(L)}{D(L)} = \frac{B'(L)}{B(L)} - \frac{A'(L)}{A(L)}$$

and so

$$\text{Mean lag} = \frac{B'(1)}{B(1)} - \frac{A'(1)}{A(1)} \tag{9-9}$$

This expression is often easier to compute than the equivalent expression in terms of the δ's. For the above example

$$\text{Mean lag} = \frac{\beta_1}{\beta_0 + \beta_1} - \frac{-\alpha_1}{1 - \alpha_1} = \frac{\alpha_1\beta_0 + \beta_1}{(1 - \alpha_1)(\beta_0 + \beta_1)}$$

The Koyck Scheme

We have seen that, starting with an equation like Eq. (9-1), which involves only lagged X values on the right-hand side, one may be led by considerations of parsimonious parameterization to reformulate it as in Eq. (9-3), which introduces lagged values of the dependent variable Y among the regressors. When the $A(L)$ polynomial is just of the first degree, as in Eq. (9-7*a*), we have an example of a

Koyck scheme of declining exponential weights.† The simple Koyck scheme has the coefficients on the X's declining exponentially from the start, that is,

$$\delta_i = \alpha_1 \delta_{i-1} \qquad i = 1, 2, \ldots$$

This corresponds to the specification

$$A(L) = 1 - \alpha_1 L \qquad \text{and} \qquad B(L) = \beta_0$$

and the relationship may be formulated as

$$Y_t = \mu + \delta_0 X_t + \alpha_1 \delta_0 X_{t-1} + \alpha_1^2 \delta_0 X_{t-2} + \cdots + u_t \tag{9-10}$$

or, equivalently, as

$$(1 - \alpha_1 L)(Y_t - \mu) = \beta_0 X_t + v_t$$

which may be written

$$Y_t = \mu(1 - \alpha_1) + \alpha_1 Y_{t-1} + \beta_0 X_t + v_t \tag{9-11}$$

Equivalence between Eqs. (9-10) and (9-11) requires

$$\beta_0 = \delta_0$$

and

$$v_t = (1 - \alpha_1 L) u_t = u_t - \alpha_1 u_{t-1} \tag{9-12}$$

Thus if the original disturbances $\{u_t\}$ in Eq. (9-10) are serially independent, the transformed disturbances $\{v_t\}$ in Eq. (9-11) are *serially dependent*, which has implications for the estimation procedures to be considered in Sec. 9-2. Since $A(1) = 1 - \alpha_1$, $A'(1) = -\alpha_1$, $B(1) = \beta_0$, and $B'(1) = 0$, the mean lag for the simple Koyck process is $\alpha_1/(1 - \alpha_1)$. As has already been indicated, raising the degree of the $B(L)$ polynomial, while retaining $A(L) = 1 - \alpha_1 L$, increases the number of "free" coefficients before the Koyck exponential decline comes into play.

So far we have considered the distributed lag effect of just a single explanatory variable. Suppose there are two explanatory variables, each with a Koyck lag. There may be no a priori reason to expect an identical decay parameter in each lag. Thus the relation might be formulated as

$$\begin{aligned} Y_t = \mu + \beta X_t + \alpha_1 \beta X_{t-1} + \alpha_1^2 \beta X_{t-2} + \cdots + \gamma Z_t \\ + \alpha_2 \gamma Z_{t-1} + \alpha_2^2 \gamma Z_{t-2} + \cdots + u_t \end{aligned} \tag{9-13}$$

or

$$Y_t = \mu + \frac{\beta}{1 - \alpha_1 L} X_t + \frac{\gamma}{1 - \alpha_2 L} Z_t + u_t$$

which gives

$$Y_t = \mu^* + (\alpha_1 + \alpha_2) Y_{t-1} - \alpha_1 \alpha_2 Y_{t-2} + \beta X_t - \alpha_2 \beta X_{t-1} + \gamma Z_t - \alpha_1 \gamma Z_{t-1} + v_t \tag{9-14}$$

where

$$\mu^* = \mu(1 - \alpha_1)(1 - \alpha_2)$$

and

$$v_t = u_t - (\alpha_1 + \alpha_2) u_{t-1} + \alpha_1 \alpha_2 u_{t-2}$$

† L. M. Koyck, *Distributed Lags and Investment Analysis*, North-Holland, Amsterdam, 1954.

so that, compared with the single-variable Koyck scheme in Eq. (9-11), we have two lagged values of Y and lagged values of each explanatory variable. For estimation purposes the essential point to notice about Koyck schemes is that they may be formulated either with only lagged values of explanatory variables on the right-hand side, as in Eqs. (9-10) and (9-13), or with lagged Y's appearing on the right-hand side, as in Eqs. (9-11) and (9-14). The former have nonlinear restrictions on the parameters combined with presumably "well-behaved" disturbance terms, while the latter have a dramatic reduction in the number of right-hand side variables, but "complicated" disturbance terms and sometimes restrictions on the coefficients [as in Eq. (9-14) but not in Eq. (9-11)].

Adaptive Expectations

Lagged dependent variables may also appear among the regressors in various expectational models. A firm may base its production rate Y_t not on the current sales rate X_t, but on the expected, permanent, or trend sales rate X_t^*. Thus one may specify

$$Y_t = \alpha + \beta X_t^* + u_t \qquad (9\text{-}15)$$

where a disturbance u_t has been included to allow accidental over- or under-achievement of the production target. Equation (9-15) is not usually statistically operational since there is a dearth of published information on expected or forecast sales rates and similar variables. It is therefore customary to add an auxiliary hypothesis about the formation of expectations, and one of the most widely used (if not, indeed, abused) schemes is that of *adaptive expectations*, which is that expectations get updated each period on the basis of the latest information about the actual value of the variable. The formal specification is

$$X_t^* - X_{t-1}^* = (1-\lambda)(X_t - X_{t-1}^*) \qquad 0 \le \lambda \le 1 \qquad (9\text{-}16)$$

In this formulation X_t^* indicates the expectation formed at the end of period t, when the information about the current level X_t has become available. If expectations were formed at the beginning of the period, X_t in Eq. (9-16) should be replaced by X_{t-1}. If $\lambda = 0$ in Eq. (9-16), the expected value adjusts period by period to the current observation and all previous history is irrelevant. If $\lambda = 1$, an expectation, once formed, continues unchanged, irrespective of current or earlier observations. The intermediate and more realistic case of λ being a positive fraction means that expectations get adjusted each period by some proportion of the discrepancy between the latest observation and the expectation for that period. Low values of λ imply substantial adjustments in expectations, and large values imply slowly changing expectations.

Equation (9-16) may be reformulated as

$$(1-\lambda L)X_t^* = (1-\lambda)X_t$$

or

$$X_t^* = \frac{1-\lambda}{1-\lambda L}X_t \qquad (9\text{-}17)$$

This in turn may be written

$$X_t^* = (1-\lambda)X_t + \lambda(1-\lambda)X_{t-1} + \lambda^2(1-\lambda)X_{t-2} + \cdots$$

so that the adaptive expectations hypothesis gives the current expectation as a Koyck-weighted combination of the current and all previously observed values of the variable in question. Substitution of Eq. (9-17) in Eq. (9-15) then gives

$$Y_t = \alpha + \frac{\beta(1-\lambda)}{1-\lambda L}X_t + u_t$$

or

$$Y_t = \alpha(1-\lambda) + \lambda Y_{t-1} + \beta(1-\lambda)X_t + (u_t - \lambda u_{t-1}) \qquad (9\text{-}18)$$

This equation is formally identical to the simple Koyck scheme in Eq. (9-11) in terms of the variables included, the MA(1) disturbance process, and the fact that the parameter of the MA(1) process is also the coefficient of the lagged dependent variable.

Partial Adjustment

Another process which can generate lagged dependent variables among the regressors is that of partial adjustment. Consider the adjustment of gasoline consumption to a substantial price rise such as that engineered by OPEC in 1973/1974. Initially the scope for economies in consumption, even in the face of very substantial price rises, was limited by such factors as

1. The existing geographical distribution of residences and work places
2. The existing stock of vehicles
3. The existing supply of alternative transport systems

In the short run, economies could be made in shopping and vacation trips, car pooling on work trips, and so forth. In the longer run, one expects adjustments in the more fundamental factors, such as the fuel efficiency of the vehicle fleet. Such adjustment has its own costs and, in any case, must take time to be achieved. Thus one may postulate Y_t^*, the optimal consumption rate appropriate to a gasoline price of X_t, with income and other factors being held constant, as

$$Y_t^* = \alpha + \beta X_t \qquad (9\text{-}19)$$

For reasons such as those suggested one would not expect actual consumption Y_t to adjust completely to X_t in period t. Instead, a partial adjustment process is frequently specified as

$$Y_t - Y_{t-1} = (1-\lambda)(Y_t^* - Y_{t-1}) + u_t \qquad 0 \le \lambda \le 1 \qquad (9\text{-}20)$$

Notice that no disturbance term has been inserted in the calculation of the optimal Y_t^*, but it would seem essential to include one in the specification of the actual Y_t in Eq. (9-20). An alternative form of Eq. (9-20) is

$$(1-\lambda L)Y_t = (1-\lambda)Y_t^* + u_t \qquad (9\text{-}21)$$

which, in turn, gives

$$Y_t = (1-\lambda)Y_t^* + \lambda(1-\lambda)Y_{t-1}^* + \lambda^2(1-\lambda)Y_{t-2}^* + \cdots + (u_t - \lambda u_{t-1})$$

so that the current consumption rate is a Koyck-weighted combination of current and all previously desired rates. Substitution of Eq. (9-21) into Eq. (9-19) gives

$$(1-\lambda L)Y_t = \alpha(1-\lambda) + \beta(1-\lambda)X_t + u_t$$

or

$$Y_t = \alpha(1-\lambda) + \lambda Y_{t-1} + \beta(1-\lambda)X_t + u_t \tag{9-22}$$

Again notice the formal equivalence of Eq. (9-22) to the adaptive expectations equation (9-18) and the Koyck-weighted lag scheme in Eq. (9-11). The only difference is that in Eq. (9-22) the disturbance term may have simpler properties than in the other two cases.

Demand functions are frequently specified in constant elasticity form. Thus Eq. (9-19) could be respecified as

$$Y_t^* = AX_t^{\beta} \tag{9-23}$$

The partial adjustment process would then have to be specified conformably as

$$\left(\frac{Y_t}{Y_{t-1}}\right) = \left(\frac{Y_t^*}{Y_{t-1}}\right)^{1-\lambda} e^{u_t} \tag{9-24}$$

Combining the two relations produces

$$Y_t = A^{1-\lambda} Y_{t-1}^{\lambda} X_t^{\beta(1-\lambda)} e^{u_t}$$

which, using lowercase letters to denote natural logarithms, gives

$$y_t = \alpha(1-\lambda) + \lambda y_{t-1} + \beta(1-\lambda)x_t + u_t \tag{9-25}$$

Since Eq. (9-25) is double logarithmic, the coefficients represent elasticities. Thus the short-run (or impact) elasticity of Y with respect to X is $\beta(1-\lambda)$, while the long-run (or full adjustment) elasticity is seen from Eq. (9-23) to be β. If the estimated form of Eq. (9-25) is denoted by

$$\hat{y}_t = c_0 + c_1 y_{t-1} + c_2 x_t$$

then

$$\text{Estimated short-run elasticity} = c_2$$

$$\text{Estimated adjustment parameter} = c_1$$

$$\text{Estimated long-run elasticity} = \frac{c_2}{1-c_1}$$

The partial adjustment process specified in Eq. (9-20) has been widely used in applied work because of the simplicity of the resultant estimating equation, such as Eq. (9-25). Nonetheless it implies a pattern of adjustment that may sometimes be implausible. Suppose X had been constant at $\bar{X}$ sufficiently long for Y to have settled at the desired level, $\bar{Y} = \alpha + \beta\bar{X}$. In period t we assume X to become $\bar{X} + \Delta X$ and then to remain at the new level indefinitely. The new desired Y is given by $\bar{\bar{Y}} = \alpha + \beta(\bar{X} + \Delta X)$, and the adjustment to that level implied by Eq. (9-20) for a λ value of, say, 0.5 and a negative β is shown in Fig. 9-1.

In the first period one-half of the total desired adjustment is achieved; in the second period one-half of the remaining adjustment is accomplished, and so

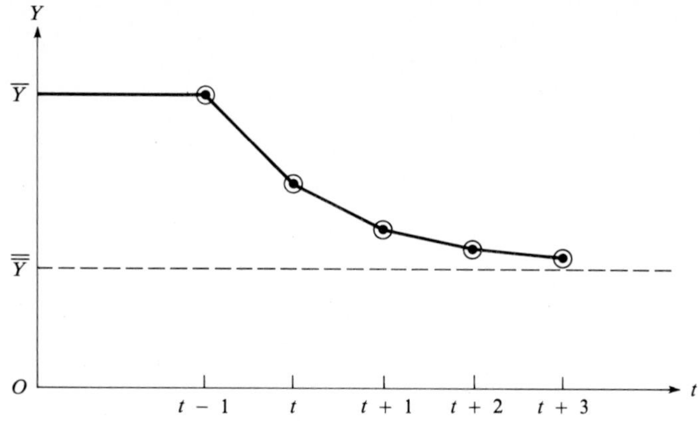

Figure 9-1

forth. Thus the maximum adjustment is achieved in the first period, and each successive adjustment is a fraction λ of the previous adjustment. This might be a plausible reaction pattern for, say, the consumption of broiler chickens in response to a significant price change, but it is less plausible for the consumption of gasoline since that consumption is mediated through durable equipment.

A further difficulty with the simple partial adjustment process arises when Y^* is a function of more than one explanatory variable. Suppose, for example, the optimal level of energy consumption depends on both the relative price of energy and the level of output in the economy. Applying the partial adjustment process to actual energy demand imposes the *same* adjustment parameter on each explanatory variable. Even if the *form* of the adjustment process is similar for each variable, the *speed* of the process may well be different. Thus at given prices, one might expect energy consumption to move more or less in step with output, but to react much more slowly to price changes.

Combination of Adaptive Expectations and Partial Adjustment

Suppose X^* represents "permanent" or long-run income, and Y^* the corresponding level of "permanent" or long-run consumption.† One might then write

$$Y_t^* = \alpha + \beta X_t^* \tag{9-26}$$

This is not an operational equation since there are no direct observations on the variables. However, the adaptive expectations hypothesis may be used to explain X^* and partial adjustment to explain the adjustment of Y to Y^*. Thus combining Eqs. (9-17) and (9-21) with Eq. (9-26) and allowing the λ parameter to be different

† See M. Friedman, *A Theory of the Consumption Function*, Princeton University Press, Princeton, NJ, 1957.

in the two processes gives

$$
\begin{aligned}
(1-\lambda_1 L)Y_t &= (1-\lambda_1)Y_t^* + u_t \\
&= \alpha(1-\lambda_1) + \beta(1-\lambda_1)X_t^* + u_t \\
&= \alpha(1-\lambda_1) + \frac{\beta(1-\lambda_1)(1-\lambda_2)}{1-\lambda_2 L}X_t + u_t
\end{aligned}
\tag{9-27}
$$

or

$$
\begin{aligned}
Y_t = \alpha(1-\lambda_1)(1-\lambda_2) + (\lambda_1+\lambda_2)Y_{t-1} - \lambda_1\lambda_2 Y_{t-2} \\
+\beta(1-\lambda_1)(1-\lambda_2)X_t + (u_t - \lambda_2 u_{t-1})
\end{aligned}
$$

The parameters λ_1 and λ_2 appear symmetrically in the systematic part of Eq. (9-27). Thus if one ignores the structure of the disturbance term and runs a regression of Y_t on Y_{t-1}, Y_{t-2}, and X_t, the resultant coefficients would not yield estimates of the separate lag parameters λ_1 and λ_2. The sum $\lambda_1 + \lambda_2$ and the product $\lambda_1\lambda_2$ can be estimated directly, and hence the term $(1-\lambda_1)(1-\lambda_2)$ is estimable and so are α and β. However, taking account of the structure of the disturbance term can lead to estimates of the λ's, as will be shown in Sec. 9-2.

9-2 ESTIMATION METHODS

Let us begin with the estimation of the distributed lag function (9-1), that is,

$$
Y_t = \mu + \delta_0 X_t + \delta_1 X_{t-1} + \cdots + \delta_s X_{t-s} + u_t \tag{9-28}
$$

where, for simplicity, we restrict consideration to the lagged values of a single explanatory variable. We usually cannot expect theory to indicate the maximum length of lag, but one would ordinarily expect significance tests on the δ's to give some indication both of the maximum lag length and of any delay in the initial transmission of an effect from X to Y. The validity of such significance tests depends on the properties of the disturbance process $\{u_t\}$ and the associated estimation methods. If $E(\mathbf{u}) = \mathbf{0}$ and $\text{var}(\mathbf{u}) = \sigma^2\mathbf{I}$, then, in principle, OLS would be an appropriate estimation technique. In practice, however, its application is likely to be plagued by collinearity between the regressors, leading to great imprecision in the estimates of the δ's.

Almon Lags

A general strategy for dealing with this collinearity and the associated imprecision is to reduce the number of parameters to be estimated by the assumption of some pattern for the δ's. The Koyck scheme of Sec. 9-1 is perhaps an extreme example of such a pattern. The Almon lag scheme provides a more flexible method for reduced parameterization.† Under the Almon scheme one rules out the direct

† S. Almon, "The Distributed Lag between Capital Appropriations and Expenditures," *Econometrica*, vol. 30, 1962, pp. 407–423.

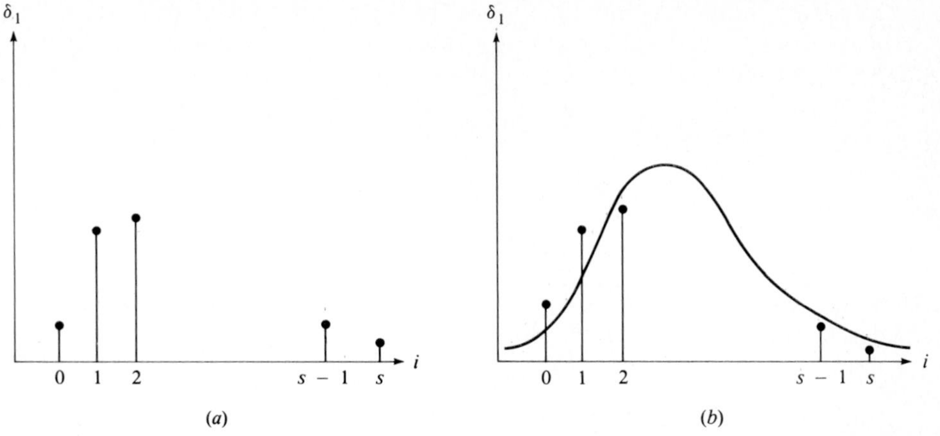

Figure 9-2

approach of attempting to estimate all $(s+1)$ δ's and assumes instead that the δ's can be approximated by some function $\delta_i \simeq f(i)$, as in Fig. 9-2*b*. The basis of the approximation is Weierstrass's theorem, which states that a function continuous in a closed interval may be approximated over the whole interval by a *polynomial* of suitable degree, which differs from the function by less than any given positive quantity at every point of the interval.†

As an illustration suppose we postulate a third-degree polynomial, that is,

$$f(i) = \alpha_0 + \alpha_1 i + \alpha_2 i^2 + \alpha_3 i^3$$

Then approximately

$$\begin{aligned}
\delta_0 &= f(0) = \alpha_0 \\
\delta_1 &= f(1) = \alpha_0 + \alpha_1 + \alpha_2 + \alpha_3 \\
\delta_2 &= f(2) = \alpha_0 + 2\alpha_1 + 4\alpha_2 + 8\alpha_3 \\
\delta_3 &= f(3) = \alpha_0 + 3\alpha_1 + 9\alpha_2 + 27\alpha_3 \\
&\cdots\cdots\cdots\cdots\cdots\cdots\cdots\cdots \\
\delta_s &= f(s) = \alpha_0 + s\alpha_1 + s^2\alpha_2 + s^3\alpha_3
\end{aligned} \tag{9-29}$$

Substituting Eq. (9-29) in Eq. (9-28) and rearranging gives

$$\begin{aligned}
Y_t = \mu &+ \alpha_0(X_t + X_{t-1} + X_{t-2} + X_{t-3} + \cdots + X_{t-s}) \\
&+ \alpha_1(X_{t-1} + 2X_{t-2} + 3X_{t-3} + \cdots + sX_{t-s}) \\
&+ \alpha_2(X_{t-1} + 4X_{t-2} + 9X_{t-3} + \cdots + s^2X_{t-s}) \\
&+ \alpha_3(X_{t-1} + 8X_{t-2} + 27X_{t-3} + \cdots + s^3X_{t-s}) + u_t
\end{aligned} \tag{9-30}$$

Thus four new regressors are formed as linear combinations of the lagged X's. The regression of Y on these variables yields estimates of the α's, which in turn

† R. Courant, *Differential and Integral Calculus*, vol. 1, 2d edition, Blackie & Son, Glasgow, United Kingdom, 1937, p. 423.

yield estimates of the δ's from Eq. (9-29). The sampling variances and covariances of the $\hat{\delta}$'s can be computed from those of the $\hat{\alpha}$'s and significance tests carried out on the δ's. Defining $\mathbf{W}_3$ as the matrix of coefficients in Eq. (9-29),

$$\mathbf{W}_3 = \begin{bmatrix} 1 & 0 & 0 & 0 \\ 1 & 1 & 1 & 1 \\ 1 & 2 & 4 & 8 \\ 1 & 3 & 9 & 27 \\ \cdots & \cdots & \cdots & \cdots \\ 1 & s & s^2 & s^3 \end{bmatrix}$$

where the subscript 3 indicates the use of a third-degree approximating polynomial. Equation (9-29) then becomes

$$\boldsymbol{\delta} = \mathbf{W}_3 \boldsymbol{\alpha} \tag{9-31}$$

and, given $\hat{\boldsymbol{\alpha}}$,

$$\hat{\boldsymbol{\delta}} = \mathbf{W}_3 \hat{\boldsymbol{\alpha}} \tag{9-32}$$

The matrix form of the original equation (9-28) is

$$\mathbf{y} = \mathbf{i}\mu + \mathbf{X}\boldsymbol{\delta} + \mathbf{u}$$

Using Eq. (9-31),

$$\mathbf{y} = \mathbf{i}\mu + \mathbf{X}\mathbf{W}_3\boldsymbol{\alpha} + \mathbf{u}$$

An OLS regression of $\mathbf{y}$ on $[\mathbf{i} \quad \mathbf{XW}_3]$, where $\mathbf{XW}_3$ is the matrix of observations on the "new" regressors shown explicitly in Eq. (9-30), gives the estimated coefficients

$$\begin{bmatrix} \hat{\mu} \\ \hat{\boldsymbol{\alpha}} \end{bmatrix} = \begin{bmatrix} \mathbf{i}'\mathbf{i} & \mathbf{i}'\mathbf{XW}_3 \\ \mathbf{W}_3'\mathbf{X}'\mathbf{i} & \mathbf{W}_3'\mathbf{X}'\mathbf{XW}_3 \end{bmatrix}^{-1} \begin{bmatrix} \mathbf{i}'\mathbf{y} \\ \mathbf{W}_3'\mathbf{X}'\mathbf{y} \end{bmatrix}$$

with

$$\operatorname{var}(\hat{\boldsymbol{\alpha}}) = \sigma_u^2 \left[\mathbf{W}_3'\mathbf{X}'\mathbf{XW}_3 - \frac{1}{n}\mathbf{W}_3'\mathbf{X}'\mathbf{ii}'\mathbf{XW}_3 \right]^{-1} \tag{9-33}$$

From Eqs. (9-31) and (9-32)

$$E(\hat{\boldsymbol{\delta}}) = \mathbf{W}_3 E(\hat{\boldsymbol{\alpha}}) = \boldsymbol{\delta}$$

and

$$\operatorname{var}(\hat{\boldsymbol{\delta}}) = \mathbf{W}_3 \cdot \operatorname{var}(\hat{\boldsymbol{\alpha}}) \cdot \mathbf{W}_3' \tag{9-34}$$

Substitution of Eq. (9-33) in Eq. (9-34) then gives the matrix of sampling variances and covariances for the $\hat{\delta}$'s.

The above would be very useful if, in fact, one knew the appropriate degree for the approximating polynomial. In practice the determination of that degree is an important problem, even given an assumption about the maximum lag length. The problem may be approached in two ways. From Eq. (9-30) it is seen that the coefficient of the last "new" regressor α_3 is the coefficient of the highest power in the approximating polynomial. Testing the significance of α_3 is, in effect, asking whether we need a third-degree polynomial. However, finding α_3 insignificant does not necessarily imply that higher-order α's would also be found insignificant.

The recommended procedure would be to start with a fairly high degree of polynomial, say, fourth or fifth, test the last coefficient for significance, and keep reducing the degree of the polynomial until the last coefficient is found significant. The disadvantage of this procedure is that, in order to carry out the tests, various "new" regressors have to be computed which may not in fact be required in the final regression.

The second approach avoids this computational difficulty. Tests of the degree of the approximating polynomial can be based on the unrestricted OLS estimates of Eq. (9-28) for some assumed value of s, and once the degree has been determined, the Almon estimators can be found by an application of restricted OLS estimation. Consider again a third-degree approximation given by

$$\delta_i = \alpha_0 + \alpha_1 i + \alpha_2 i^2 + \alpha_3 i^3$$

Taking the first difference of this function gives a polynomial of the second degree, and so on, for each successive difference until†

$$\Delta^4 \delta_i = 0$$

But

$$\begin{aligned} \Delta\delta_i &= \delta_i - \delta_{i-1} \\ \Delta^2\delta_i &= (\delta_i - \delta_{i-1}) - (\delta_{i-1} - \delta_{i-2}) \\ &= \delta_i - 2\delta_{i-1} + \delta_{i-2} \\ \Delta^3\delta_i &= \delta_i - 3\delta_{i-1} + 3\delta_{i-2} - \delta_{i-3} \\ \Delta^4\delta_i &= \delta_i - 4\delta_{i-1} + 6\delta_{i-2} - 4\delta_{i-3} + \delta_{i-4} \end{aligned}$$

Thus the assumption of a third-degree polynomial places a set of linear restrictions on the δ's. The full set of restrictions is

$$\begin{aligned} \delta_4 - 4\delta_3 + 6\delta_2 - 4\delta_1 + \delta_0 &= 0 \\ \delta_5 - 4\delta_4 + 6\delta_3 - 4\delta_2 + \delta_1 &= 0 \\ \cdots\cdots\cdots\cdots\cdots\cdots\cdots\cdots \\ \delta_s - 4\delta_{s-1} + 6\delta_{s-2} - 4\delta_{s-3} + \delta_{s-4} &= 0 \end{aligned} \tag{9-35}$$

†

$$\begin{aligned} \Delta\delta_i &= \delta_i - \delta_{i-1} \\ &= \alpha_0 + \alpha_1 i + \alpha_2 i^2 + \alpha_3 i^3 \\ &\quad -\alpha_0 - \alpha_1(i-1) - \alpha_2(i-1)^2 - \alpha_3(i-1)^3 \\ &= (\alpha_1 - \alpha_2 + \alpha_3) + (2\alpha_2 - 3\alpha_3)i + 3\alpha_3 i^2 \end{aligned}$$

The second difference of δ_i is found by repeating the first difference operation. Thus

$$\begin{aligned} \Delta^2\delta_i &= (2\alpha_2 - 3\alpha_3)i + 3\alpha_3 i^2 - (2\alpha_2 - 3\alpha_3)(i-1) - 3\alpha_3(i-1)^2 \\ &= (2\alpha_2 - 6\alpha_3) + 6\alpha_3 i \end{aligned}$$

The degree of the polynomial in i decreases by 1 with each differencing. The third and fourth differences are then

$$\Delta^3\delta_i = 6\alpha_3$$

and

$$\Delta^4\delta_i = 0$$

No restriction involves the intercept term μ. Thus the restrictions (9-35) may be expressed as

$$\mathbf{R}_3\begin{bmatrix}\mu \\ \boldsymbol{\delta}\end{bmatrix} = \mathbf{0} \tag{9-36}$$

where $\mathbf{R}_3$ is the $(s-3) \times (s+2)$ matrix

$$\mathbf{R}_3 = \begin{bmatrix} 0 & 1 & -4 & 6 & -4 & 1 & 0 & \cdots & 0 \\ 0 & 0 & 1 & -4 & 6 & -4 & 1 & \cdots & 0 \\ & & \ddots & \ddots & \ddots & \ddots & \ddots & & \\ 0 & & & & & & & & \end{bmatrix}$$

A second-degree approximating polynomial would imply the set of $s-2$ linear restrictions given by

$$\mathbf{R}_2\begin{bmatrix}\mu \\ \boldsymbol{\delta}\end{bmatrix} = \mathbf{0}$$

where $\mathbf{R}_2$ is the $(s-2) \times (s+2)$ matrix

$$\mathbf{R}_2 = \begin{bmatrix} 0 & -1 & 3 & -3 & 1 & 0 & \cdots & 0 \\ 0 & 0 & -1 & 3 & -3 & 1 & \cdots & 0 \\ & & \ddots & \ddots & \ddots & \ddots & & \\ 0 & & & & & & & \end{bmatrix} \tag{9-37}$$

Notice that the nonzero elements in the rows of the **R** matrices are given by the appropriate set of binomial coefficients with alternating signs.† If r denotes the degree of the approximating polynomial, the nonzero elements in $\mathbf{R}_r$ are the coefficients of L in the polynomial $(1-L)^{r+1}$, but in *reverse* order. However, since the restriction sets linear combinations of the δ's equal to zero, we can multiply the rows of $\mathbf{R}_2$ by -1 and get the coefficients in natural order.

For a given maximum lag s the sequential procedure for finding a suitable degree of the approximating polynomial would be as follows.

1. Start with a polynomial of fairly high degree, say, the fourth or fifth.
2. Set out the corresponding **R** matrix and test the null hypothesis

$$H_0\colon\ \mathbf{R}\begin{bmatrix}\mu \\ \boldsymbol{\delta}\end{bmatrix} = \mathbf{0}$$

by substituting in Eq. (5-68) the results of the unrestricted OLS estimation of

$$Y_t = \mu + \delta_0 X_t + \delta_1 X_{t-1} + \cdots + \delta_s X_{t-s} + u_t$$

† The binomial coefficients may be simply obtained from Pascal's triangle

				1					Almon-polynomial
			1		1				
		1		2		1			
	1		3		3		1		second degree
1		4		6		4		1	third degree

where an internal element in any row is the sum of the pair of elements immediately above.

Under the null hypothesis the resultant test statistic has the $F(s - r, n - s - 2)$ distribution, where r is the degree of the approximating polynomial.

3. If the null hypothesis is rejected, the initial polynomial has not been of sufficiently high degree.
4. If the null hypothesis is accepted, proceed to the next lower degree and test the new set of linear restrictions, proceeding in this way until the null hypothesis is rejected.

If the null hypothesis is accepted, say, for $\mathbf{R}_3$ but rejected for $\mathbf{R}_2$, the appropriate procedure is to find a third-degree approximating polynomial. This may be done by computing the four "new" regressors specified in Eq. (9-30), estimating the α's by OLS and then using Eq. (9-32) to estimate the δ's. Alternatively one may use the formula for the *restricted* estimator given in Eq. (6-5), and inferences may be made by using the variance matrix given in the footnote to Eq. (6-5).

The above procedure is conditional on some assumed value for the maximum lag s. It may be repeated for various values of s and a judgment made by looking at the overall fit and the significance of the higher-order δ's.

An implication of the Almon procedure, which does not seem to have attracted much attention, is that it is likely to yield biased and, indeed, inconsistent estimates. Write the original model, Eq. (9-28), for simplicity as

$$\mathbf{y} = \mathbf{X}\boldsymbol{\delta} + \mathbf{u} \tag{9-38}$$

If the δ's do not lie *exactly* on the approximating polynomial, then a formula such as Eq. (9-31) has to be amended to

$$\boldsymbol{\delta} = \mathbf{W}\boldsymbol{\alpha} + \mathbf{v} \tag{9-39}$$

where $\mathbf{v}$ is an $r \times 1$ vector of errors involved in the use of an rth-degree approximating polynomial. Notice that $\mathbf{v}$ is independent of time and is a vector of unknown constants, which does not vanish with increasing sample size. Substituting Eq. (9-39) in Eq. (9-38) gives

$$\mathbf{y} = \mathbf{XW}\boldsymbol{\alpha} + (\mathbf{Xv} + \mathbf{u}) \tag{9-40}$$

In Eq. (9-40) there is obviously some correlation between the explanatory variables $\mathbf{XW}$ and the expanded disturbance term $\mathbf{Xv} + \mathbf{u}$, which would lead one to expect inconsistency in the estimation of α and hence of δ. Looking directly at the estimator of δ,

$$\begin{aligned}\hat{\boldsymbol{\delta}} &= \mathbf{W}\hat{\boldsymbol{\alpha}} \\ &= \mathbf{W}(\mathbf{W}'\mathbf{X}'\mathbf{X}\mathbf{W})^{-1}\mathbf{W}'\mathbf{X}'\mathbf{y} \\ &= \mathbf{W}\left[\mathbf{W}'\left(\frac{1}{n}\mathbf{X}'\mathbf{X}\right)\mathbf{W}\right]^{-1}\mathbf{W}'\left\{\left(\frac{1}{n}\mathbf{X}'\mathbf{X}\right)\boldsymbol{\delta} + \frac{1}{n}\mathbf{X}'\mathbf{u}\right\}\end{aligned}$$

Assuming

$$\operatorname{plim}\frac{1}{n}(\mathbf{X}'\mathbf{X}) = \boldsymbol{\Sigma}_{xx}$$

and

$$\text{plim}\left(\frac{1}{n}\mathbf{X}'\mathbf{u}\right) = \mathbf{0}$$

we have

$$\text{plim}\,\hat{\boldsymbol{\delta}} = \mathbf{W}[\mathbf{W}'\boldsymbol{\Sigma}_{xx}\mathbf{W}]^{-1}\mathbf{W}'\boldsymbol{\Sigma}_{xx}\boldsymbol{\delta} \tag{9-41}$$

Substitution of Eq. (9-39) in Eq. (9-41) gives

$$\text{plim}\,\hat{\boldsymbol{\delta}} = \boldsymbol{\delta} + \mathbf{W}[\mathbf{W}'\boldsymbol{\Sigma}_{xx}\mathbf{W}]^{-1}\mathbf{W}'\boldsymbol{\Sigma}_{xx}\mathbf{v} \tag{9-42}$$

so that the Almon estimator is inconsistent unless the unknown δ's lie *exactly* on the chosen polynomial, in which case $\mathbf{v} = \mathbf{0}$. The finite sample bias of the Almon estimator can be serious if one fits a polynomial of too low degree. This bias, combined with the smaller sampling variation (as compared with unrestricted OLS), can sometimes give sampling distributions for the Almon estimators which fail to contain the true δ parameter altogether or else have it located near an extremity of the distribution.

Computer packages with Almon lag estimators usually offer the facility of including *end-point* restrictions such as $\delta_{-1} = 0$ and/or $\delta_{s+1} = 0$. Since δ_{-1} is the notional coefficient of X_{t+1} and that variable has no effect on Y_t, it might seem sensible to incorporate that end-point constraint. As Dhrymes and Schmidt and Waud have pointed out, that is a fallacious argument.† Setting $\delta_{-1} = 0$ implies a restriction on the α's and hence on the δ's, which in turn is a restriction on how $X_t, X_{t-1}, \ldots, X_{t-s}$ affect Y_t. For a second-order polynomial the implied restriction is

$$\alpha_0 - \alpha_1 + \alpha_2 = 0$$

Such a restriction could, of course, be tested by estimating the α's and using the variance matrix in Eq. (9-33). The purpose of the Almon polynomial is to give a good approximation to the unknown δ's over the interval 0 to s. Its behavior if extrapolated outside that interval is irrelevant. The second end-point restriction, $\beta_{s+1} = 0$, may not produce much distortion in the approximation if the coefficients are decaying with increasing lags but, again, it implies a restriction on the α's and δ's, and there seems little valid reason for imposing it.

Direct Estimation of a Koyck Lag

If one assumes Eq. (9-28) to obey a simple Koyck lag, the relation becomes

$$Y_t = \mu + \delta X_t + \alpha\delta X_{t-1} + \alpha^2\delta X_{t-2} + \cdots + u_t \qquad |\alpha| < 1 \tag{9-43}$$

with four parameters to be estimated, namely μ, δ, α, and σ_u^2. The lag is now infinite, but the coefficients decay exponentially. The relation (9-43) may be

† P. J. Dhrymes, *Distributed Lags: Problems of Estimation and Formulation*, Holden-Day, San Francisco, 1971, pp. 232–234; P. Schmidt and R. N. Waud, "Almon Lag Technique and the Monetary versus Fiscal Policy Debate," *Journal of the American Statistical Association*, vol. 68, 1973, pp. 11–19.

rewritten as

$$Y_t = \mu + \delta(X_t + \alpha X_{t-1} + \cdots + \alpha^{t-1}X_1) + \alpha^t\delta(X_0 + \alpha X_{-1} + \cdots) + u_t$$

or

$$Y_t = \mu + \delta X_t^* + \alpha^t\gamma + u_t \tag{9-44}$$

where

$$X_t^* = X_t + \alpha X_{t-1} + \cdots + \alpha^{t-1}X_1$$

and

$$\gamma = \delta \sum_{i=0}^{\infty} \alpha^i X_{-i} = E(Y_0 - \mu)$$

The γ parameter may be regarded as the expected difference between Y and μ in the period preceding the first sample observation. If $\mathbf{u} \sim N(\mathbf{0}, \sigma_u^2\mathbf{I})$, the application of OLS to Eq. (9-44) would yield ML estimates. The matrix formulation of Eq. (9-44) would be

$$\mathbf{y} = \begin{bmatrix} 1 & X_1^* & \alpha \\ 1 & X_2^* & \alpha^2 \\ \cdots & \cdots & \cdots \\ 1 & X_n^* & \alpha^n \end{bmatrix} \begin{bmatrix} \mu \\ \delta \\ \gamma \end{bmatrix} + \mathbf{u} \tag{9-45}$$

where the X^*'s may be built up recursively as

$$X_1^* = X_1$$

$$X_2^* = X_2 + \alpha X_1 = X_2 + \alpha X_1^*$$

$$X_3^* = X_3 + \alpha X_2 + \alpha^2 X_1 = X_3 + \alpha X_2^*$$

Since two columns of the data matrix depend on the unknown α, one can proceed with a grid search over the interval $0 \le \alpha < 1$. For each specified value of α the data matrix in Eq. (9-45) is computed and OLS applied, the final choice of regression being based on the minimum residual sum of squares. The standard errors for $\hat{\mu}$ and $\hat{\delta}$ from the OLS program would only be correct if α were known exactly, which is not the case. The asymptotic standard errors can be obtained from the information matrix, which is†

$$\mathbf{R}\begin{pmatrix} \mu \\ \delta \\ \gamma \\ \alpha \end{pmatrix} = \frac{1}{\sigma_u^2} \begin{bmatrix} n & \Sigma X_t^* & \Sigma \alpha^t & \Sigma\left(\delta \dfrac{\partial X_t^*}{\partial \alpha} + t\alpha^{t-1}\gamma\right) \\ & \Sigma X_t^{*2} & \Sigma \alpha^t X_t^* & \Sigma\left(\delta \dfrac{\partial X_t^*}{\partial \alpha} + t\alpha^{t-1}\gamma\right) X_t^* \\ & & \Sigma \alpha^{2t} & \Sigma\left(\delta \dfrac{\partial X_t^*}{\partial \alpha} + t\alpha^{t-1}\gamma\right)\alpha^t \\ & & & \Sigma\left(\delta \dfrac{\partial X_t^*}{\partial \alpha} + t\alpha^{t-1}\gamma\right)^2 \end{bmatrix} \tag{9-46}$$

This matrix is symmetric and so only the upper triangular portion has been shown. The unknown parameters in Eq. (9-46) would be replaced by their

† See Problem 9-4.

estimated values, and the inverse would give the estimated variance matrix for the parameters.

Estimation with a Lagged Dependent Variable

Instead of estimating the simple Koyck scheme directly, as above, one might use the derived relation

$$Y_t = \mu(1 - \alpha_1) + \alpha_1 Y_{t-1} + \beta_0 X_t + (u_t - \alpha_1 u_{t-1})$$

already established in Eq. (9-11). The adaptive expectations scheme is formally identical, as shown in Eq. (9-18). The partial adjustment model, derived in Eq. (9-22), gives

$$Y_t = \alpha(1 - \lambda) + \lambda Y_{t-1} + \beta(1 - \lambda) X_t + u_t$$

Both relations incorporate a lagged Y among the regressors and differ only with respect to the properties of the disturbance term. We must now examine the estimation problems occasioned by the lagged Y value, and we shall do so under various assumptions about the disturbance term.

Lagged Dependent Variable and Well-Behaved Disturbances

Consider the relation

$$Y_t = \beta_1 + \beta_2 X_t + \beta_3 Y_{t-1} + u_t \tag{9-47}$$

where we assume the u's to be independently and identically distributed with zero mean and variance σ_u^2. The relation (9-47) may be rewritten to show the dependence of Y_t on the stream of current and previous values of X and u, that is,

$$(1 - \beta_3 L) Y_t = \beta_1 + \beta_2 X_t + u_t$$

giving

$$Y_t = \alpha + \beta_2 (X_t + \beta_3 X_{t-1} + \beta_3^2 X_{t-2} + \cdots) + v_t \tag{9-48}$$

where
$$\alpha = \frac{\beta_1}{1 - \beta_3}$$

and
$$v_t = (1 - \beta_3 L)^{-1} u_t$$

If X were held constant at some level $\bar{X}$ and $\bar{Y}$ denotes the corresponding level of Y, then

$$E(\bar{Y}) = \frac{\beta_1}{1 - \beta_3} + \frac{\beta_2}{1 - \beta_3} \bar{X}$$

provided $|\beta_3| < 1$. If $|\beta_3| \geq 1$, $E(\bar{Y})$ would explode. In practice a $\{Y_t\}$ series may have explosive tendencies, which are held in check by various "floors" and/or "ceilings." A model of such a process would be highly nonlinear, and the statistical treatment of such models is still in its infancy. We therefore impose the constraint

$$|\beta_3| < 1 \tag{9-49}$$

It is also clear from Eq. (9-48) that expressions such as $(\Sigma Y_t^2/n)$ and $(\Sigma X_t Y_{t-1}/n)$ will involve linear combinations of quantities such as

$$\frac{1}{n}\Sigma X_t^2,\ \frac{1}{n}\Sigma X_{t-1}^2, \ldots$$

and
$$\frac{1}{n}\Sigma X_t X_{t-1},\ \frac{1}{n}\Sigma X_t X_{t-2}, \ldots$$

The additional assumption is then made that the X_t are bounded and that the above quantities have finite limits as n tends to infinity.

The model of Eq. (9-47) may be written in matrix form as

$$\mathbf{y} = \mathbf{Z}\boldsymbol{\beta} + \mathbf{u} \tag{9-50}$$

where

$$\mathbf{Z} = \begin{bmatrix} 1 & X_1 & Y_0 \\ 1 & X_2 & Y_1 \\ \cdots & \cdots & \cdots \\ 1 & X_n & Y_{n-1} \end{bmatrix}$$

To make Eq. (9-50) operational Y_0 has to be known.† The **Z** matrix is stochastic since the **Y**'s are stochastic, even though the **X**'s may be assumed to be exogenous and nonstochastic. However, the case is not an exact parallel of the stochastic data matrix considered in Sec. 7-3. There the strong assumption of full independence between the disturbance and the explanatory variables was valid. In this model it is clear from Eq. (9-47) that, while u_t is independent of X_s for all t and all s and also independent of Y_{t-s} for *positive* s, it is *not* independent of Y_t, and since Y_t in turn influences Y_{t+1}, u_t is not independent of $Y_{t+1}, Y_{t+2}, \ldots$. This apparently small difference has an important effect on the estimates of Eq. (9-50).

The underpinning assumptions for Eq. (9-50) may now be stated:

1. $E(\mathbf{u}) = \mathbf{0}$ and $E(\mathbf{uu}') = \sigma_u^2\mathbf{I}$
2. $E(X_t u_t) = E(Y_{t-1}u_t) = 0$ for all t
3. $$\text{plim}\left(\frac{1}{n}\mathbf{Z}'\mathbf{Z}\right) = \boldsymbol{\Sigma}_{zz}$$

   a symmetric positive definite matrix

Assumption 3 follows from the stability assumption on β_3 and the assumption about limiting values for the second-order moments of X.‡ The Mann-Wald

† If it is not, the effective sample size is $n - 1$, and the statistical inference procedures are conditional on Y_1 with $n - 1$ observations, rather than conditional on Y_0 with n observations. Asymptotically, of course, it makes no difference.

‡ For a complete derivation see E. Malinvaud, *Statistical Methods of Econometrics*, 2d edition, North Holland, Amsterdam, 1970, pp. 540 ff.

theorem can then be applied to give the results.†

$$\operatorname{plim}\left(\frac{1}{n}\mathbf{Z}'\mathbf{u}\right) = \mathbf{0} \tag{9-51}$$

and

$$\left(\frac{1}{\sqrt{n}}\mathbf{Z}'\mathbf{u}\right) \xrightarrow{D} N\left(0, \sigma_u^2 \boldsymbol{\Sigma}_{zz}\right) \tag{9-52}$$

The OLS estimator of $\boldsymbol{\beta}$ in Eq. (9-50) is

$$\begin{aligned} \hat{\boldsymbol{\beta}} &= (\mathbf{Z}'\mathbf{Z})^{-1}\mathbf{Z}'\mathbf{y} \\ &= \boldsymbol{\beta} + (\mathbf{Z}'\mathbf{Z})^{-1}\mathbf{Z}'\mathbf{u} \end{aligned}$$

Thus

$$\sqrt{n}\,(\hat{\boldsymbol{\beta}} - \boldsymbol{\beta}) = \left(\frac{1}{n}\mathbf{Z}'\mathbf{Z}\right)^{-1} \frac{1}{\sqrt{n}}\mathbf{Z}'\mathbf{u} \tag{9-53}$$

Using Eqs. (9-51), (9-52), and (7-24) gives

$$\sqrt{n}\,(\hat{\boldsymbol{\beta}} - \boldsymbol{\beta}) \sim \text{AN}\left(\mathbf{0}, \sigma_u^2 \boldsymbol{\Sigma}_{zz}^{-1}\right)$$

or

$$\hat{\boldsymbol{\beta}} \sim \text{AN}\left(\boldsymbol{\beta}, \sigma_u^2 \frac{1}{n} \boldsymbol{\Sigma}_{zz}^{-1}\right) \tag{9-54}$$

Thus even without the assumption of normality for the u's the OLS estimators will be consistent and asymptotically normally distributed. The unknown variance matrix in Eq. (9-54) can be consistently estimated by the usual formula $s^2(\mathbf{Z}'\mathbf{Z})^{-1}$. If, in addition, the u's are normally distributed, the estimators are also ML and efficient. These results extend simply to the general case of various lagged Y values and several X's. Thus there is substantial justification for the continued use of OLS in relationships containing lagged dependent variables, provided the disturbance term is serially independent. The estimators will, however, be subject to finite sample bias, and one should also recall the problems of testing for autocorrelated disturbances in this case.‡

Lagged Dependent Variable and Autocorrelated Disturbances

Suppose now that we repeat the relation (9-47)

$$Y_t = \beta_1 + \beta_2 X_t + \beta_3 Y_{t-1} + u_t \qquad t = 1, \ldots, n$$

as before, but the u's are now assumed to follow an AR(1) scheme§

$$u_t = \rho u_{t-1} + \varepsilon_t \qquad |\rho| < 1 \tag{9-55}$$

where $\qquad E(\boldsymbol{\varepsilon}) = \mathbf{0} \qquad \text{and} \qquad E(\boldsymbol{\varepsilon}\boldsymbol{\varepsilon}') = \sigma_\varepsilon^2 \mathbf{I}$

† H. B. Mann and A. Wald, "On the Statistical Treatment of Linear Stochastic Difference Equations," *Econometrica*, vol. 11, 1943, pp. 173–220, especially pp. 185–190.

‡ See Sec. 8-5.

§ Note that this is different from the error structure in Eq. (9-11) associated with the Koyck lag; the latter [an MA(1) error] is considered below.

This new assumption has an important effect. From Eq. (9-55) it is seen that u_{t-1} influences u_t, but from Eq. (9-47), in period $t-1$, u_{t-1} influences Y_{t-1}. This sets up a dependence between u_t and Y_{t-1} in Eq. (9-47), that is,

$$E(Y_{t-1}u_t) \neq 0$$

From Eqs. (9-47) and (9-55) it follows that†

$$\text{plim}\left(\frac{1}{n}\Sigma Y_{t-1}u_t\right) = \frac{\rho\sigma_u^2}{1-\beta_3\rho} \tag{9-56}$$

The consequence is that the application of OLS to Eq. (9-47) will yield inconsistent estimates of all parameters. This is so because

$$\text{plim}(\hat{\boldsymbol{\beta}}) = \boldsymbol{\beta} + \boldsymbol{\Sigma}_{zz}^{-1} \cdot \text{plim}\left(\frac{1}{n}\mathbf{Z}'\mathbf{u}\right)$$

and

$$\text{plim}\left(\frac{1}{n}\mathbf{Z}'\mathbf{u}\right) = \begin{bmatrix} \text{plim}\left(\frac{1}{n}\Sigma u_t\right) \\ \text{plim}\left(\frac{1}{n}\Sigma X_t u_t\right) \\ \text{plim}\left(\frac{1}{n}\Sigma Y_{t-1}u_t\right) \end{bmatrix} = \begin{bmatrix} 0 \\ 0 \\ \dfrac{\rho\sigma_u^2}{1-\beta_3\rho} \end{bmatrix}$$

It only takes one nonzero element in $\text{plim}((1/n)\mathbf{Z}'\mathbf{u})$ in general to render all elements in $\hat{\boldsymbol{\beta}}$ inconsistent. There are two main methods of obtaining consistent estimators in this model, namely, instrumental variables and ML.

Instrumental Variables

Consider

$$\mathbf{y} = \mathbf{Z}\boldsymbol{\beta} + \mathbf{u}$$

Premultiply by $\mathbf{Z}'$ to give

$$\mathbf{Z}'\mathbf{y} = \mathbf{Z}'\mathbf{Z}\boldsymbol{\beta} + \mathbf{Z}'\mathbf{u} \tag{9-57}$$

The OLS estimator $\mathbf{b}$ of Chap. 5 may be obtained from this equation simply by setting $\mathbf{Z}'\mathbf{u} = \mathbf{0}$, giving

$$\mathbf{Z}'\mathbf{y} = \mathbf{Z}'\mathbf{Z}\mathbf{b} \tag{9-58}$$

On the assumption that

$$\text{plim}\left(\frac{1}{n}\mathbf{Z}'\mathbf{Z}\right) = \boldsymbol{\Sigma}_{zz} \qquad \text{and} \qquad \text{plim}\left(\frac{1}{n}\mathbf{Z}'\mathbf{u}\right) = \mathbf{0}$$

we can divide Eqs. (9-57) and (9-58) by n, take probability limits, and equate the right-hand sides to find

$$\boldsymbol{\Sigma}_{zz}\text{plim}(\mathbf{b}) = \boldsymbol{\Sigma}_{zz}\boldsymbol{\beta}$$

so that

$$\text{plim}(\mathbf{b}) = \boldsymbol{\beta}$$

which is the standard result on the consistency of the OLS estimator.

† See Problem 9-5.

In the present model the assumption that $\text{plim}((1/n)\mathbf{Z}'\mathbf{u})$ is the zero vector cannot be sustained. Suppose, however, that one can find an $n \times k$ matrix $\mathbf{W}$ containing variables which are thought to be contemporaneously uncorrelated with the disturbance term. That is, we assume

$$E(W_{it}u_t) = 0 \qquad i = 1, \ldots, k;\ t = 1, \ldots, n \tag{9-59}$$

Premultiplying the model by $\mathbf{W}'$ and setting $\mathbf{W}'\mathbf{u}$ to the zero vector, by analogy with the OLS procedure, gives the instrumental variable (IV) estimator $\mathbf{b}_{\text{IV}}$,

$$\mathbf{W}'\mathbf{y} = (\mathbf{W}'\mathbf{Z})\mathbf{b}_{\text{IV}}$$

which, on the assumption that $\mathbf{W}'\mathbf{Z}$ is nonsingular, may be written

$$\mathbf{b}_{\text{IV}} = (\mathbf{W}'\mathbf{Z})^{-1}\mathbf{W}'\mathbf{y} \tag{9-60}$$

On the further assumptions that

$$\text{plim}\left(\frac{1}{n}\mathbf{W}'\mathbf{Z}\right) = \mathbf{\Sigma}_{wz} \qquad \text{a nonsingular matrix} \tag{9-61}$$

and

$$\text{plim}\left(\frac{1}{n}\mathbf{W}'\mathbf{u}\right) = \mathbf{0} \tag{9-62}$$

it is easy to see that

$$\begin{aligned} \text{plim}(\mathbf{b}_{\text{IV}}) &= \boldsymbol{\beta} + \text{plim}\left(\frac{1}{n}\mathbf{W}'\mathbf{Z}\right)^{-1}\text{plim}\left(\frac{1}{n}\mathbf{W}'\mathbf{u}\right) \\ &= \boldsymbol{\beta} + \mathbf{\Sigma}_{wz}^{-1} \cdot \mathbf{0} \\ &= \boldsymbol{\beta} \end{aligned}$$

so that the IV estimator would be consistent.

The variables in $\mathbf{W}$ are referred to as instruments. Some of them may simply be variables from the original $\mathbf{Z}$ matrix. In the present model there is no need to replace X_t since it is already assumed to be independent of the disturbance term. In addition to being uncorrelated with the disturbance term, the instruments should not be totally uncorrelated with the explanatory variables since $\mathbf{W}'\mathbf{Z}$ would then be a null matrix and the estimating technique would break down. If, in fact, $\mathbf{W}'\mathbf{Z}$ is "nearly" null, the IV technique will give very poor results.

In Eq. (9-47) we need just one instrument, and it is customary to select X_{t-1} as the instrument for Y_{t-1}. The appropriate matrices are then

$$\mathbf{W} = \begin{bmatrix} 1 & X_1 & X_0 \\ 1 & X_2 & X_1 \\ \cdots & \cdots & \cdots \\ 1 & X_n & X_{n-1} \end{bmatrix} \qquad \mathbf{Z} = \begin{bmatrix} 1 & X_1 & Y_0 \\ 1 & X_2 & Y_1 \\ \cdots & \cdots & \cdots \\ 1 & X_n & Y_{n-1} \end{bmatrix}$$

and the IV estimator is

$$\mathbf{b}_{\mathrm{IV}} = \begin{bmatrix} n & \Sigma X_t & \Sigma Y_{t-1} \\ \Sigma X_t & \Sigma X_t^2 & \Sigma X_t Y_{t-1} \\ \Sigma X_{t-1} & \Sigma X_t X_{t-1} & \Sigma X_{t-1} Y_{t-1} \end{bmatrix}^{-1} \begin{bmatrix} \Sigma Y_t \\ \Sigma X_t Y_t \\ \Sigma X_{t-1} Y_t \end{bmatrix}$$

where all summations run from $t = 1$ to $t = n$.†

IV estimators are, in general, biased in finite samples and their variances difficult to establish.‡ It is, however, possible to derive a fairly simple and important asymptotic result. The result requires three assumptions. The first is Eq. (9-59),

$$E(W_{it}u_t) = 0 \qquad \text{for all } i, t$$

that is, that the instruments are contemporaneously uncorrelated with the disturbances. The second is that the instruments possess finite probability limits for all second-order moments, that is,

$$\operatorname{plim}\left(\frac{1}{n}\mathbf{W}'\mathbf{W}\right) = \mathbf{\Sigma}_{ww}$$

a symmetric positive definite matrix. The third is that

$$E(\mathbf{u}) = \mathbf{0} \qquad \text{and} \qquad E(\mathbf{uu}') = \sigma_u^2\mathbf{I}$$

Because of Eq. (9-55) this last assumption is *not* true for model (9-47). However, we will ignore this complication for the moment. Under the above three assumptions the Mann-Wald theorem applies so that

$$\operatorname{plim}\left(\frac{1}{n}\mathbf{W}'\mathbf{u}\right) = \mathbf{0}$$

and

$$\left(\frac{1}{\sqrt{n}}\mathbf{W}'\mathbf{u}\right) \xrightarrow{D} N\left(\mathbf{0}, \sigma_u^2\mathbf{\Sigma}_{ww}\right)$$

The IV estimator of Eq. (9-60) is

$$\mathbf{b}_{\mathrm{IV}} = \boldsymbol{\beta} + (\mathbf{W}'\mathbf{Z})^{-1}\mathbf{W}'\mathbf{u}$$

Thus

$$\sqrt{n}\,(\mathbf{b}_{\mathrm{IV}} - \boldsymbol{\beta}) = \left(\frac{1}{n}\mathbf{W}'\mathbf{Z}\right)^{-1}\left(\frac{1}{\sqrt{n}}\mathbf{W}'\mathbf{u}\right)$$

† Should the values X_0 and Y_0 not be available, the first row is dropped from $\mathbf{W}$ and $\mathbf{X}$, the summations run from $t = 2$ to $t = n$, and n is replaced by $n - 1$ in the formula for $\mathbf{b}_{\mathrm{IV}}$.

‡ Contrast the assertion by P. J. Dhrymes, *Econometrics—Statistical Foundations and Applications*, Harper and Row, New York, 1970, p. 297: "All IV estimators, no matter what the choice of instruments, are unbiased and consistent." This statement comes after a passage in which the only explicit assumptions relate to probability limits. The IV estimators are consistent. A possible explanation of the incorrect assertion about unbiasedness is given in App. A-8, Expectations in Bivariate Distributions, where the matter is discussed in detail. The same type of error can also affect the derivation of results about finite sample variance matrices, as in formula (6-4-12) of Dhrymes.

Recalling assumption (9-61) that

$$\text{plim}\left(\frac{1}{n}\mathbf{W}'\mathbf{z}\right) = \boldsymbol{\Sigma}_{wz}$$

a nonsingular matrix, an application of Eq. (7-24) gives

$$\sqrt{n}\,(\mathbf{b}_{\text{IV}} - \boldsymbol{\beta}) \sim \text{AN}\left(\mathbf{0}, \sigma_u^2\boldsymbol{\Sigma}_{wz}^{-1}\boldsymbol{\Sigma}_{ww}\boldsymbol{\Sigma}_{wz}'^{-1}\right)$$

or

$$\mathbf{b}_{\text{IV}} \sim \text{AN}\left(\boldsymbol{\beta}, \sigma_u^2\frac{1}{n}\boldsymbol{\Sigma}_{wz}^{-1}\boldsymbol{\Sigma}_{ww}\boldsymbol{\Sigma}_{wz}'^{-1}\right) \tag{9-63}$$

Under the full assumptions the IV estimator would be a consistent and asymptotically normal estimator of $\boldsymbol{\beta}$. The variance matrix would be estimated by the formula

$$\text{est var}(\mathbf{b}_{\text{IV}}) = s^2(\mathbf{W}'\mathbf{Z})^{-1}(\mathbf{W}'\mathbf{W})(\mathbf{Z}'\mathbf{W})^{-1} \tag{9-64}$$

where

$$s^2 = \frac{(\mathbf{y} - \mathbf{X}\mathbf{b}_{\text{IV}})'(\mathbf{y} - \mathbf{X}\mathbf{b}_{\text{IV}})}{n - k}$$

The statement in Eq. (9-63) is not strictly valid for the model (9-47) since the u's are not independently distributed in consequence of Eq. (9-55). It also follows that Eq. (9-64) would not be the appropriate formula for estimating the sampling variances of the IV estimators, though it is often applied for want of anything better. Results (9-63) and (9-64) hold for the IV estimator under the full set of three assumptions outlined above, and we shall have need of them subsequently. The main use of the IV estimator in this model is to provide a consistent estimator as a starting point in an iterative ML technique.

Maximum-Likelihood Estimator

Combining Eq. (9-47) with the AR(1) disturbance process in Eq. (9-55) gives

$$Y_t = \beta_1 - \beta_1\rho + \beta_2 X_t - \beta_2\rho X_{t-1} + (\beta_3 + \rho)Y_{t-1} - \beta_3\rho Y_{t-2} + \varepsilon_t \tag{9-65}$$

If one assumes

$$\boldsymbol{\varepsilon} \sim N\left(\mathbf{0}, \sigma_\varepsilon^2\mathbf{I}\right)$$

then ML estimators of the β's and ρ would be given by the values minimizing $\Sigma\varepsilon_t^2$. However, the first-order conditions would not yield linear equations in the estimators, since there are five variables in Eq. (9-65) but only four parameters to be estimated. An iterative Cochrane-Orcutt procedure may be used, based on two alternative ways of rewriting Eq. (9-65), namely,

$$(Y_t - \rho Y_{t-1}) = \beta_1(1 - \rho) + \beta_2(X_2 - \rho X_{t-1}) + \beta_3(Y_{t-1} - \rho Y_{t-2}) + \varepsilon_t \tag{9-66a}$$

$$(Y_t - \beta_1 - \beta_2 X_t - \beta_3 Y_{t-1}) = \rho(Y_{t-1} - \beta_1 - \beta_2 X_{t-1} - \beta_3 Y_{t-2}) + \varepsilon_t \tag{9-66b}$$

Given a starting value for ρ, the transformed variables in Eq. (9-66a) could be computed and OLS applied to yield estimates of the β's. These estimates in turn could be used to compute the transformed variables in Eq. (9-66b) and OLS applied to produce a revised estimate of ρ with the iterations continuing till convergence.

Setting up the log likelihood for Eq. (9-65) and differentiating gives the information matrix†

$$\mathbf{R}\begin{pmatrix}\beta_1\\ \beta_2\\ \beta_3\\ \rho\\ \sigma_\varepsilon^2\end{pmatrix} = \frac{1}{\sigma_\varepsilon^2}\begin{bmatrix} n(1-\rho)^2 & (1-\rho)\Sigma X_t^* & (1-\rho)E\{\Sigma Y_{t-1}^*\} & 0 & 0 \\ & \Sigma X_t^{*2} & E\{\Sigma X_t^* Y_{t-1}^*\} & 0 & 0 \\ & & \Sigma Y_{t-1}^{*2} & \dfrac{n\sigma_\varepsilon^2}{1-\beta_3\rho} & 0 \\ & & & \dfrac{n\sigma_\varepsilon^2}{1-\rho^2} & 0 \\ & & & & \dfrac{n}{2\sigma_\varepsilon^2} \end{bmatrix} \tag{9-67}$$

where

$$X_t^* = X_t - \rho X_{t-1} \qquad \text{and} \qquad Y_{t-1}^* = Y_{t-1} - \rho Y_{t-2}$$

This matrix is symmetric, and we have just shown the upper triangular portion. As usual it involves the unknown parameters, but it would be calculated using the estimated parameters.

It has recently been shown that the iterative Cochrane-Orcutt process may lead to inconsistent estimates.‡ The basic point is that, while for a finite sample the Cochrane-Orcutt estimators will always converge to some fixed point, that point may correspond to a local minimum of the sum of squares rather than the global minimum, and the probability limit of the fixed point will not be the true parameter vector. To ensure consistency of the iterative process, one must start with a consistent estimator. Thus starting the process by setting ρ to zero in Eq. (9-66a) would be inappropriate since that corresponds to estimating the β's by applying OLS directly to Eq. (9-47), which is an inconsistent procedure. On the other hand, the process could be started consistently by computing, say, the IV estimators of the β's as described earlier.

An alternative approach to minimizing $\Sigma\varepsilon_t^2$ in Eq. (9-65) is to use a grid search over the permissible range of ρ values. Thus a set of ρ values is specified in the interval $(-1, 1)$. Each value is used to compute the quasi first differences in Eq. (9-66a), and OLS is then applied to minimize $\Sigma\varepsilon_t^2$. A fine enough grid should distinguish the global minimum from any local minima. If necessary a finer grid

† See Problem 9-6.

‡ R. Betancourt and H. Kelejan, "Lagged Endogenous Variables and the Cochrane-Orcutt Procedure," *Econometrica*, vol. 49, 1981, pp. 1073–1078.

may be imposed around the ρ value chosen in the first grid search and a second grid search applied to obtain a finer estimate of the minimizing ρ value. This value and the corresponding β's obtained from Eq. (9-66a) constitute the point estimates, and the asymptotic standard errors can be obtained from Eq. (9-67).

MA(1) Disturbance

Instead of the AR(1) disturbance process assumed in Eq. (9-55), let us now consider an MA(1) process. As has been shown, this is likely to occur in a simple Koyck scheme or in an adaptive expectations model. In each of these cases there is the further significant feature that the parameter of the MA(1) process is also the coefficient of the lagged dependent variable. The model to be considered is thus

$$Y_t = \alpha + \lambda Y_{t-1} + \beta X_t + (u_t - \lambda u_{t-1}) \qquad |\lambda| < 1 \tag{9-68}$$

where it is assumed that

$$\mathbf{u} \sim N(\mathbf{0}, \sigma_u^2 \mathbf{I})$$

Utilizing the existence of the common parameter, this relation may be rewritten as

$$Z_t = \alpha + \lambda Z_{t-1} + \beta X_t \tag{9-69}$$

where

$$Z_t = Y_t - u_t$$

Successive substitution for the Z variable in Eq. (9-69) gives

$$Z_t = \alpha(1 + \lambda + \lambda^2 + \cdots + \lambda^{t-1})$$
$$+\beta(X_t + \lambda X_{t-1} + \lambda^2 X_{t-2} + \cdots + \lambda^{t-1} X_1) + Z_0 \lambda^t$$

or

$$Y_t = \alpha(1 + \lambda + \cdots + \lambda^{t-1}) + \beta X_t^* + Z_0 \lambda^t + u_t \tag{9-70}$$

where now

$$X_t^* = X_t + \lambda X_{t-1} + \lambda^2 X_{t-2} + \cdots + \lambda^{t-1} X_1$$

which may be computed recursively, for any given λ, as

$$X_t^* = X_t + \lambda X_{t-1}^* \qquad \text{with } X_1^* = X_1$$

Relation (9-70) has a well-behaved disturbance term suitable for ML (or equivalently OLS) estimation, with Z_0 treated as a nuisance parameter. The data matrix for OLS estimation would be

$$\mathbf{X}(\lambda) = \begin{bmatrix} 1 & X_1^* & \lambda \\ 1 + \lambda & X_2^* & \lambda^2 \\ 1 + \lambda + \lambda^2 & & \\ \cdots & \cdots & \cdots \\ 1 + \lambda + \cdots + \lambda^{n-1} & X_n^* & \lambda^n \end{bmatrix}$$

The appropriate procedure is then a grid search over the interval $0 < \lambda \leq 1$. For each value of λ, $\mathbf{X}(\lambda)$ is computed, OLS applied to Eq. (9-70), and the set of parameters is chosen which minimizes the residual sum of squares.

The asymptotic standard errors may be obtained from the information matrix in the usual way. The log likelihood for Eq. (9-70) may be written

$$\ln L = -\frac{n}{2}\ln(2\pi) - \frac{n}{2}\ln\sigma_u^2 - \frac{1}{2\sigma_u^2}\Sigma u_t^2 \tag{9-71}$$

where

$$u_t = Y_t - \alpha W_t - \beta X_t^* - Z_0\lambda^t$$

and

$$W_t = 1 + \lambda + \cdots + \lambda^{t-1}$$

The unknown parameters in Eq. (9-71) are α, β, λ, Z_0, and σ_u^2. It may be shown that the expected values of the cross second-order partial derivatives involving σ_u^2 are all zero. Thus inferences about σ_u^2 may be made independently of the other parameters. The ML estimator is

$$\hat{\sigma}_u^2 = \frac{\Sigma \hat{u}_t^2}{n}$$

with asymptotic variance $2\sigma_u^4/n$. The information matrix for the remaining four parameters is†

$$\mathbf{R}\begin{pmatrix}\alpha\\ \beta\\ \lambda\\ Z_0\end{pmatrix} = \frac{1}{\sigma_u^2}\begin{bmatrix}\Sigma W_t^2 & \Sigma W_t X_t^* & \Sigma W_t V_t & \Sigma W_t \lambda^t\\ & \Sigma X_t^{*2} & \Sigma X_t^* V_t & \Sigma X_t^* \lambda^t\\ & & \Sigma V_t^2 & \Sigma V_t \lambda^t\\ & & & \Sigma \lambda^{2t}\end{bmatrix} \tag{9-72}$$

where W_t and X_t^* have already been defined and

$$\begin{aligned} V_t &= -\frac{\partial u_t}{\partial \lambda}\\ &= \alpha\left[1 + 2\lambda + \cdots + (t-1)\lambda^{t-2}\right] + \beta\left[X_{t-1} + 2\lambda X_{t-1} + \cdots\right.\\ &\quad \left. + (t-1)\lambda^{t-2}X_1\right] + tZ_0\lambda^{t-1}\end{aligned}$$

For a penultimate problem we return to Eq. (9-27), which represents a combination of adaptive expectations and partial adjustment. The equation is

$$\begin{aligned} Y_t = {} & \alpha(1-\lambda_1)(1-\lambda_2) + (\lambda_1+\lambda_2)Y_{t-1} - \lambda_1\lambda_2 Y_{t-2}\\ & + \beta(1-\lambda_1)(1-\lambda_2)X_t + (u_t - \lambda_2 u_{t-1})\end{aligned}$$

Defining $Z_t = Y_t - u_t$, this may be rewritten as

$$Z_t = \alpha_0 + \lambda_1 Y_{t-1}^* + \beta_0 X_t + \lambda_2 Z_{t-1} \tag{9-73}$$

where

$$\alpha_0 = \alpha(1-\lambda_1)(1-\lambda_2)$$

$$\beta_0 = \beta(1-\lambda_1)(1-\lambda_2)$$

$$Y_{t-1}^* = Y_{t-1} - \lambda_2 Y_{t-2}$$

† See Problem 9-7.

Successive substitution for Z and transformation back to Y gives

$$\begin{aligned} Y_t = \alpha_0\left[1 + \lambda_2 + \cdots + \lambda_2^{t-1}\right] \\ +\lambda_1\left[Y_{t-1}^* + \lambda_2 Y_{t-2}^* + \cdots + \lambda_2^{t-1} Y_0^*\right] \\ +\beta_0\left[X_t + \lambda_2 X_{t-1} + \cdots + \lambda_2^{t-1} X_1\right] + \lambda_2^t Z_0 + u_t \end{aligned} \tag{9-74}$$

The disturbance term in Eq. (9-74) is well-behaved. The "variables" in square brackets are all dependent on λ_2. Thus a grid search over $0 < \lambda_2 \le 1$ and the choice of the error minimizing version of Eq. (9-74) will yield point estimates of all the parameters.

Finally we take a look at the estimation problems of Eq. (9-14) where it was assumed that Y_t responded to two separate Koyck lags with different parameters. The equation was

$$Y_t = \mu^* + (\alpha_1 + \alpha_2)Y_{t-1} - \alpha_1\alpha_2 Y_{t-2} + \beta X_t - \alpha_2\beta X_{t-1} + \gamma Z_t - \alpha_1\gamma Z_{t-1} + v_t$$

with

$$v_t = u_t - (\alpha_1 + \alpha_2)u_{t-1} + \alpha_1\alpha_2 u_{t-2}$$

The disturbance series $\{v_t\}$ follows an MA(2) process. Ignoring this complication for the moment and assuming the v's to be independently and identically distributed normal variables, the application of unrestricted OLS to Eq. (9-14) would not yield the ML estimators since the seven coefficients are functions of only five parameters. However, the relation may be rewritten as

$$Y_t^* = \mu^* + \beta X_t^* + \gamma Z_t^* + v_t \tag{9-75}$$

where

$$\begin{aligned} Y_t^* &= Y_t - (\alpha_1 + \alpha_2)Y_{t-1} + \alpha_1\alpha_2 Y_{t-2} \\ X_t^* &= X_t - \alpha_2 X_{t-1} \\ Z_t^* &= Z_t - \alpha_1 Z_{t-1} \end{aligned}$$

The transformed variables in Eq. (9-75) depend on the α_1, α_2 parameters. Given any pair of α_1, α_2 values and assuming the v's to be independently distributed, OLS could then be applied to Eq. (9-75) to yield estimates of μ^*, β, γ, and the residual sum of squares. The indicated estimation procedure would be a *two-dimensional grid* search over α_1, α_2 pairs, each parameter being constrained to the (0, 1) interval.

Alternatively, if one makes the explicit assumption that the v_t follow an MA(2) process and if $\mathbf{u} \sim N(\mathbf{0}, \sigma_u^2\mathbf{I})$, the variance matrix for the v's is given by

$$E(\mathbf{vv}') = \sigma_u^2 \begin{bmatrix} \delta_0 & \delta_1 & \delta_2 & 0 & 0 & \cdots & & & 0 \\ \delta_1 & \delta_0 & \delta_1 & \delta_2 & 0 & \cdots & & & 0 \\ \delta_2 & \delta_1 & \delta_0 & \delta_1 & \delta_2 & \cdots & & & 0 \\ & \ddots & & \ddots & & \ddots & & & \\ & & & & & & & & \\ 0 & 0 & 0 & 0 & 0 & \cdots & \delta_2 & \delta_1 & \delta_0 \end{bmatrix} \tag{9-76}$$

Table 9-1 Lagged variable models

Model	Assumption	Estimators
1. $Y_t = \mu + D(L)X_t + u_t$	$D(L)$ a polynomial in the lag operator: $\{u_t\}$ white noise†	OLS (ML) possibly plagued with imprecision due to collinearity
2. $Y_t = \mu + D(L)X_t + u_t$	Almon approximation to $D(L)$	OLS (ML)
3. $Y_t = \mu + D(L)X_t + u_t$	Koyck approximation to $D(L)$	ML (grid search)
4. $Y_t = \beta_1 + \beta_2 X_t + \beta_3 Y_{t-1} + u_t$	$\{u_t\}$ white noise	OLS asymptotically normal and efficient
5. $Y_t = \beta_1 + \beta_2 X_t + \beta_3 Y_{t-1} + u_t$	$\{u_t\}$ follows AR(1) process	OLS now inconsistent; consistent estimators via IV or ML
6. $Y_t = \alpha + \lambda Y_{t-1} + \beta X_t + (u_t - \lambda u_{t-1})$	$\{u_t\}$ white noise	ML (grid search)
7. $Y_t = \alpha(1-\lambda_1)(1-\lambda_2) + (\lambda_1 + \lambda_2)Y_{t-1}$ $-\lambda_1\lambda_2 Y_{t-2} + \beta(1-\lambda_1)(1-\lambda_2)X_t$ $+(u_t - \lambda_2 u_{t-1})$	Combination of adaptive expectations and partial adjustment	ML (grid search)
8. $Y_t = \mu^* + (\alpha_1 + \alpha_2)Y_{t-1} - \alpha_1\alpha_2 Y_{t-2}$ $+\beta X_t - \alpha_2\beta X_{t-1} + \gamma Z_t$ $-\alpha_1 \gamma Z_{t-1} + v_t$	Two explanatory variables with separate Koyck lags	ML (grid search) or GLS depending on treatment of $\{v_t\}$

†If the u_t are independently and identically distributed as $N(0, \sigma_u^2)$, then $\{u_t\}$ is said to be a white noise series.

where

$$\delta_0 = 1 + (\alpha_1 + \alpha_2)^2 + \alpha_1^2\alpha_2^2$$
$$\delta_1 = -(\alpha_1 + \alpha_2)(1 + \alpha_1\alpha_2)$$
$$\delta_2 = \alpha_1\alpha_2$$

The appropriate estimation procedure for Eq. (9-75) is then a combination of GLS and a two-dimensional grid search over α_1, α_2. For each α_1, α_2 pair the variance matrix in Eq. (9-76) is computed and then GLS applied to Eq. (9-75). One chooses the set of parameters that minimizes the weighted sum of squares $\mathbf{e}'\mathbf{\Omega}^{-1}\mathbf{e}$, where $\mathbf{e}$ is the vector of residuals computed from Eq. (9-75) by using the GLS estimates and $\mathbf{\Omega}$ is the matrix in Eq. (9-76).

Various models have been considered in this section, and it may be helpful to summarize them briefly in Table 9-1.

9-3 TIME-SERIES METHODS

The models summarized in Table 9-1 incorporated various theoretical specifications. The first model embodied the least a priori specification, but direct estimation was liable to be somewhat imprecise, which led to the development of

Almon approximations. The Koyck hypothesis in model 3 is a very strong assumption. Models 4 to 6 are versions of adaptive expectations and partial adjustment depending on the treatment of the disturbance term. Model 7 is a combination of adaptive expectations and partial adjustment, while model 8 incorporates two explanatory variables with separate Koyck lags.

In recent years time-series methods of estimating a lagged relationship such as Eq. (9-1)

$$Y_t = \mu + D(L)X_t + u_t$$

have come to be more extensively employed. As seen in Sec. 9-1, this relation may be formulated equivalently as Eq. (9-5),

$$Y_t = \mu + \frac{B(L)}{A(L)}X_t + u_t$$

where $D(L)$, $B(L)$, and $A(L)$ are all polynomials in the lag operator, but the orders of $B(L)$ and $A(L)$ are expected to be small relative to the order of $D(L)$. The relation (9-5) is known as a *transfer function* in the time-series literature.† There are four main characteristics which distinguish time-series estimation methods from the various estimation procedures described in Sec. 9-2.

1. Before estimating the transfer function, the "input" series $\{X_t\}$ and the "output" series $\{Y_t\}$ are subjected to sufficient differencing to render both resultant series *stationary*.
2. The orders of the $A(L)$, $B(L)$ polynomials are determined *empirically* from the data by an *identification* process and without imposing any a priori theoretical specifications, such as a set of declining exponential coefficients.
3. The disturbance term in the transfer function is estimated as a general ARMA process, as described in Sec. 8-5, rather than as a low-order AR or MA process as in some of the models in Sec. 9-2.
4. The transfer function approach has been most extensively developed for the *single-input* case (that is, one explanatory variable with various lagged values), and there is no firm agreement yet on the appropriate extension to cope with two or more inputs, each with a set of lags.

To get a grasp of the methodology we need to discuss each of these four points in greater detail.

Stationarity

The simplest example of a stationary process is the white noise series $\{\varepsilon_t\}$, where the ε's are independently and identically distributed as $N(0, \sigma_\varepsilon^2)$. It follows from

† The basic reference is G. E. P. Box and G. M. Jenkins, *Time Series Analysis: Forecasting and Control*, revised edition, Holden-Day, San Francisco, 1976, especially Chaps. 10 and 11.

the definition that

$$E(\varepsilon_t) = 0 \qquad \text{for all } t$$

$$\text{var}(\varepsilon_t) = E(\varepsilon_t^2) = \sigma_\varepsilon^2 \qquad \text{for all } t$$

$$\gamma_s = \text{cov}(\varepsilon_t, \varepsilon_{t-s}) = E(\varepsilon_t \varepsilon_{t-s}) = 0 \qquad \text{for all } t \text{ and } s \neq 0$$

$$\rho_s = \gamma_s/\gamma_0 = \begin{cases} 1 & \text{for } s = 0 \\ 0 & \text{for } s \neq 0 \end{cases}$$

Thus the mean and the variance of the series are constant, finite, and independent of the time subscript, as are the covariances and the autocorrelations. These conditions constitute a definition of *second-order*, or *weak*, stationarity. A series is said to be *strictly* stationary if the joint probability distribution of $X_{t_1}, \ldots, X_{t_n}$ is the same as the joint distribution of $X_{t_1+\tau}, \ldots, X_{t_n+\tau}$ for all $t_1, \ldots, t_n, \tau$. Since a multivariate normal distribution is completely specified by the first- and second-order moments, the $\{\varepsilon_t\}$ series is also strictly stationary.

Now consider

$$X_t = \phi X_{t-1} + \varepsilon_t \tag{9-77}$$

where $\{\varepsilon_t\}$ is white noise. This process may also be expressed as

$$\varphi(L) X_t = (1 - \phi L) X_t = \varepsilon_t$$

giving

$$X_t = \varepsilon_t + \phi \varepsilon_{t-1} + \phi^2 \varepsilon_{t-2} + \cdots$$

Thus

$$E(X_t) = 0 \qquad \text{for all } t$$

and

$$\text{var}(X_t) = E(X_t^2) = \sigma_\varepsilon^2 (1 + \phi^2 + \phi^4 + \cdots)$$

This last expression only converges if $|\phi| < 1$. We have already seen in Sec. 8-5 that if $|\phi| < 1$,

$$\sigma_x^2 = \frac{\sigma_\varepsilon^2}{1 - \phi^2}$$

and the autocorrelation function is given by

$$\rho_s = \phi^s$$

Thus Eq. (9-77) is a stationary process if $|\phi| < 1$. This condition is also stated equivalently as the root of $\varphi(L)$, or the zero of the polynomial $\varphi(L)$, lying *outside the unit circle*. This root is obtained by setting

$$\varphi(L) = 1 - \phi L = 0$$

and solving for L to find $L = 1/\phi$. Clearly, the condition $|\phi| < 1$ implies $|L| > 1$.

If $|\phi| > 1$, the root of $\varphi(L)$ lies inside the unit circle and Eq. (9-77) is an explosive series.† Now consider the in-between case where $\phi = 1$. Relation (9-77)

† See Problem 9-8.

then defines the random walk

$$X_t = X_{t-1} + \varepsilon_t$$

Clearly, var(X_t) still explodes and X_t is not a stationary series. However, $\Delta X_t = (1 - L)X_t$ is a stationary series since it is equal to ε_t. Thus *first differencing* the random walk series produces a stationary series, but no finite number of differences of Eq. (9-77) can produce a stationary series if $|\phi| > 1$.

Extending the model to a second-order scheme gives

$$X_t = \phi_1 X_{t-1} + \phi_2 X_{t-2} + \varepsilon_t \tag{9-78}$$

or

$$\varphi(L) X_t = \varepsilon_t \tag{9-79}$$

where

$$\varphi(L) = 1 - \phi_1 L - \phi_2 L^2$$

By analogy with the first-order case we seek conditions on the roots of $\varphi(L)$ which might distinguish between the stationary case, the explosive case, and the intermediate case, where differencing might produce a stationary series. The polynomial may be factorized as

$$\varphi(L) = (1 - c_1 L)(1 - c_2 L)$$

and so the roots of the polynomial are c_1^{-1} and c_2^{-1}. From Eq. (9-79)

$$X_t = \varphi^{-1}(L)\varepsilon_t$$

$$= \frac{1}{(1 - c_1 L)(1 - c_2 L)} \varepsilon_t$$

The term $1/(1 - c_1 L)(1 - c_2 L)$ may be expanded in partial fractions as

$$\frac{1}{(1 - c_1 L)(1 - c_2 L)} = \frac{d}{(1 - c_1 L)} + \frac{1 - d}{(1 - c_2 L)}$$

where $d = c_1/(c_1 - c_2)$, as may be verified by multiplying out. Thus

$$X_t = \frac{d}{1 - c_1 L}\varepsilon_t + \frac{1 - d}{1 - c_2 L}\varepsilon_t$$

$$= d\left(\varepsilon_t + c_1\varepsilon_{t-1} + c_1^2\varepsilon_{t-2} + \cdots\right)$$

$$+ (1 - d)\left(\varepsilon_t + c_2\varepsilon_{t-1} + c_2^2\varepsilon_{t-2} + \cdots\right)$$

and the variance of X_t will only be finite and constant if $|c_1|$ and $|c_2|$ are both less than unity, that is, if the *roots of* φ(L) *lie outside the unit circle*. The condition on the roots may be stated equivalently in terms of the ϕ_1, ϕ_2 parameters of Eq. (9-78) as†

$$|\phi_2| < 1$$

$$\phi_2 + \phi_1 < 1$$

$$\phi_2 - \phi_1 < 1$$

† G. E. P. Box and G. M. Jenkins, *Time Series Analysis: Forecasting and Control*, revised edition, Holden-Day, San Francisco, 1976, p. 58.

If the polynomial factorizes as

$$\varphi(L) = (1 - c_1 L)(1 - L)$$

Eq. (9-79) becomes

$$(1 - c_1 L)(1 - L)X_t = (1 - c_1 L)\,\Delta X_t = \varepsilon_t \tag{9-80}$$

Even if $|c_1| < 1$, the X_t series is nonstationary since the other root lies on the unit circle. However, it is clear from Eq. (9-80) that the ΔX_t series is stationary as long as $|c_1| < 1$. If a third-degree polynomial factorizes as

$$\varphi(L) = (1 - c_1 L)(1 - L)^2$$

then second differencing the X_t series will yield a stationary series as long as $|c_1| < 1$.

So far we have just considered AR processes of the form $\varphi(L)X_t = \varepsilon_t$, where ε_t is white noise, and have seen that the condition for stationarity can be expressed in terms of the roots of $\varphi(L)$. The same conditions hold when the disturbance of the right-hand side follows an MA scheme, for if we write

$$\varphi(L)X_t = \theta(L)\varepsilon_t \tag{9-81}$$

where $\theta(L)$ is a finite MA operator,

$$\theta(L) = 1 - \theta_1 L - \theta_2 L^2 - \cdots - \theta_q L^q$$

then $\theta(L)\varepsilon_t$ is a stationary series. It has zero mean, a constant variance, and an autocorrelation function which is nonzero for the first q lags and zero thereafter. Thus the stationarity of the X_t series still depends on the roots of $\varphi(L)$. The general form of Eq. (9-81) is

$$\left(1 - \phi_1 L - \phi_2 L^2 - \cdots - \phi_p L^p\right)(1 - L)^d X_t$$

$$= \left(1 - \theta_1 L - \theta_2 L^2 - \cdots - \theta_q L^q\right)\varepsilon_t \tag{9-82}$$

This is an autoregressive, integrated, moving average, ARIMA(p, d, q) scheme, where p is the order of the AR polynomial, d is the degree of differencing required to yield a stationary series (or equivalently, the number of unit roots in $\varphi(L)$), and q is the order of the MA polynomial. The term integrated refers to the reverse of the differencing operation since the differenced series have to be *summed* (or integrated) to retrieve the original series. It did not arise in Sec. 8-5 where ARMA processes were introduced to model a disturbance series which was already stationary.

The general ARIMA model of Eq. (9-82) has been found to be a very flexible tool for the univariate modeling and forecasting of a wide variety of *homogeneous nonstationary* series—series that are not explosive, but which may display drift or apparent short-run trends as well as various irregular oscillations. The univariate modeling procedure consists of first determining the amount of differencing required to produce approximate stationarity. Typically it appears that, if differencing is required, first or at most second differences suffice. Defining

$$x_t = (1 - L)^d X_t$$

the second stage is making a judgment about the orders p and q in

$$\left(1 - \phi_1 L - \phi_2 L^2 - \cdots - \phi_p L^p\right) x_t = \left(1 - \theta_1 L - \theta_2 L^2 - \cdots - \theta_q L^q\right) \varepsilon_t$$

This is done by comparing the pattern of the estimated autocorrelation coefficients of the $\{x_t\}$ series with the theoretical patterns corresponding to various small values of p and q. An initial estimate of the ϕ, θ parameters is then derived, which serves as the first round in a nonlinear iterative estimation process. Finally various diagnostic checks are applied to the fitted model.

Econometricians are naturally more interested in the estimation of transfer functions than in univariate time-series modeling. However, the latter turns out to be an essential component of the former. Returning to the transfer function (9-5), we may write it explicitly as

$$\left(1 - \alpha_1 L - \alpha_2 L^2 - \cdots - \alpha_r L^r\right) y_t = \left(\beta_0 + \beta_1 L + \cdots + \beta_s L^s\right) x_{t-b} + u_t$$

or

$$A(L) y_t = B(L) x_{t-b} + u_t$$

which is a transfer function of order (r, s, b), where $b \geq 0$ represents any delay in the transmission of an effect from X to Y. The X and Y series are appropriately differenced to achieve (near) stationarity and are also expressed as deviations from the sample means, if necessary.† The problem now is the determination of the values of r, s, and b and the estimation of the consequent α and β parameters. The Box-Jenkins starting point is the calculation of the covariances (current and lagged) between x and y and the autocovariances of the x series. The solution of a set of simultaneous equations yields estimates of the δ coefficients.‡ From the resultant δ coefficients rough guesses are made of the values of r, s, and b on the basis of a comparison between the pattern of the δ coefficients and the theoretical patterns for various values of r, s, and b. From the δ's initial estimates of the α's and β's can be derived and an iterative estimation process carried out, with interaction between the estimation of the transfer function weights and the fitting of an ARIMA scheme to the disturbance term. If the original disturbance was a white noise series, any differencing will have produced an MA process in the transformed disturbances, and if the original disturbance was complicated, the transformed disturbance will normally be more complicated.

Box and Jenkins also suggest that the efficiency of the above process could be improved if an ARIMA model was first fitted to the x_t series. Denote such a

† It is assumed that the same degree of differencing has been applied to each series. However, Box and Jenkins state, "the procedures outlined can equally well be used when different degrees of differencing are employed for input and output" (op. cit., ftn., p. 378). Consider

$$Y_t = \alpha + \beta X_t + u_t$$

First differencing both Y and X gives

$$\Delta Y_t = \beta \Delta X_t + \Delta u_t$$

so that the original β coefficient is retained while the intercept disappears. If different degrees of differencing are applied to each variable, one would no longer be estimating the original β coefficient.

‡ These are the coefficients of the various lagged values of X, defined earlier in Eq. (9-1).

model by

$$\phi_x(L)x_t = \theta_x(L)\eta_t$$

where η_t is approximately a white noise series. Now multiply through the model

$$y_t = D(L)x_t + u_t$$

by $\theta_x^{-1}(L)\phi_x(L)$. The result is

$$y_t^* = D(L)\eta_t + v_t \tag{9-83}$$

where

$$y_t^* = \theta_x^{-1}(L)\phi_x(L)y_t \quad \text{and} \quad v_t = \theta_x^{-1}(L)\phi_x(L)u_t$$

Equation (9-83) still preserves the δ coefficients of the original equation, but the η_t variable is approximately white noise and so its lagged covariances will be approximately zero. This leads to a considerable simplification in obtaining the original δ estimates, since a series of single equations is solved rather than a set of simultaneous equations. The process leading to Eq. (9-83) is termed *prewhitening* the input series. The expression $\theta_x^{-1}(L)\phi_x(L)$ is termed a *filter*, and the same filter is applied to both the input and the output series.

There is an analogy between these procedures and the transformation conventionally applied in econometrics. The model (9-1) with various lagged values of just a single input may be written in the usual matrix form as

$$\mathbf{y} = \mathbf{X}\boldsymbol{\delta} + \mathbf{u} \tag{9-84}$$

As seen in Chap. 8, a nonspherical variance matrix for the disturbance term leads to GLS estimation procedures. The GLS procedure is equivalent to premultiplying Eq. (9-84) by a transformation matrix **T** and applying OLS to the transformed data **Ty** and **TX**. The matrix **T** is chosen according to the assumed properties of the disturbance term so as to make **Tu** a white noise series. The time-series approach concentrates first of all on the properties of **y** and **X** in Eq. (9-84) and not on the nature of **u**. A common differencing procedure is applied to Y_t and X_t, followed by a common filter derived from the ARIMA model fitted to X_t. The $D(L)$ polynomial containing the "long" series of δ coefficients is finally represented by the ratio of two low-order polynomials which are estimated along with an ARIMA model for the disturbance term.

It is impossible to give here a detailed operational description of the time-series procedures.† However, it is clear that a considerable amount of "judgment" is required at various stages in choosing between different ARIMA and different transfer function models. Time-series analysts also stress that long runs of observations, preferably in excess of 100, are desirable, which requires the

† Reference should be made to G. E. P. Box and G. M. Jenkins, *Time Series Analysis: Forecasting and Control*, revised edition, Holden-Day, San Francisco, 1976, or to G. W. J. Granger and P. Newbold, *Forecasting Economic Time Series*, Academic Press, New York, 1977. A lucid introduction to a wide range of time series topics is provided by C. Chatfield, *The Analysis of Time Series: Theory and Practice*, Chapman and Hall, London, 1975.

assumption that the underlying economic structure has been stable for that length of time. The estimation of even the single-input case is fairly complicated. The model is perhaps most appropriate to a "black-box" situation where interest centers on a single input variable which can be controlled in any desired manner but the researcher has no clearly articulated theory of the relation between the input and the output.

The approach described above cannot be simply extended to multiple-input models, since the covariances between the output and any input are contaminated by the effects of the other inputs, unless the inputs are orthogonal. Spectral methods are a possibility, but are not yet well developed for this case. A somewhat different approach for dealing with two or more inputs has recently been suggested by Liu and Hanssens.† Their approach is a modification of the corner method for ARMA identification proposed by Beguin, Gourieroux, and Monfort.‡ Much work is proceeding in this field, and it is too soon to assess the likely practical significance of the methods currently under development.

A final time-series approach that may be noted for the two-variable case is the *prewhitening of both series*. Letting y_t and x_t denote appropriately differenced series as usual, a separate ARMA model is fitted to each series, denoted by

$$\hat{\phi}_y(L)y_t = \hat{\theta}_y(L)\hat{u}_{yt}$$

and

$$\hat{\phi}_x(L)x_t = \hat{\theta}_x(L)\hat{u}_{xt} \tag{9-85}$$

where $\hat{u}_{yt}$ and $\hat{u}_{xt}$ denote estimated residuals which are approximately white noise series. Thus y_t is prewhitened by the filter $\hat{\theta}_y^{-1}(L)\hat{\phi}_y(L)$ to yield $\hat{u}_{yt}$, and x_t is prewhitened by its filter to yield $\hat{u}_{xt}$. It is argued that this approach is useful in cases where there is doubt about the direction of causation. Does x cause y so that one expects nonzero correlations between y and earlier values of x, or is it the other way around, or is there joint causation and feedback? The suggested procedure is to compute the cross correlations at various lags, positive and negative, between $\hat{u}_{yt}$ and $\hat{u}_{xt}$. Inspection of these correlations should lead to a decision about causation. For example, if causation is thought to run from x to y, a transfer function model is estimated for $\hat{u}_{yt}$ on $\hat{u}_{xt}$, say,

$$\hat{u}_{yt} = \hat{\Gamma}(L)\hat{u}_{xt} + \text{noise} \tag{9-86}$$

where the parameters of this transfer function are indicated by

$$\Gamma(L) = \gamma_0 + \gamma_1 L + \gamma_2 L^2 + \cdots$$

to emphasize that they are *not* the original structural coefficients $D(L)$ connecting

† L. M. Liu and D. M. Hanssens, "Identification of Multiple-Input Transfer Function Models," *Communications in Statistics*, 1982.

‡ J. M. Beguin, C. Gourieroux, and A. Monfort, "Identification of a Mixed Autoregressive-Moving Average Process: The Corner Method," in O. D. Anderson, Ed., *Time Series Analysis*, North-Holland, Amsterdam, 1980.

y and x. Finally substituting for $\hat{u}_{yt}$ and $\hat{u}_{xt}$ from Eq. (9-85) gives

$$\hat{\theta}_y^{-1}(L)\hat{\phi}_y(L)y_t = \hat{\Gamma}(L)\hat{\theta}_x^{-1}(L)\hat{\phi}_x(L)x_t + \text{noise} \tag{9-87}$$

which is a relation connecting y and x. The resultant estimates of the structural coefficients are obtained by equating coefficients of the powers of L in

$$\hat{D}(L) = \hat{\theta}_y(L)\hat{\phi}_y^{-1}(L)\hat{\Gamma}(L)\hat{\theta}_x^{-1}(L)\hat{\phi}_x(L) \tag{9-88}$$

This is a rather different procedure than just prewhitening the input, applying the same filter to the output, and then estimating $D(L)$ directly as in Eq. (9-83). In principle the $D(L)$ polynomial is recoverable and capable of being estimated by either method. For example, suppose y_t and x_t simply follow different AR(1) processes,

$$(1 - \alpha_1 L)y_t = u_{yt} \qquad \text{and} \qquad (1 - \alpha_2 L)x_t = u_{xt}$$

Substituting for y_t and x_t in $y = D(L)x_t$ gives

$$u_{yt} = (1 - \alpha_1 L)D(L)(1 - \alpha_2 L)^{-1}u_{xt}$$

which is the implied transfer function between the separate white noise processes. Substituting now for u_{yt} and u_{xt} gives

$$(1 - \alpha_1 L)y_t = (1 - \alpha_1 L)D(L)(1 - \alpha_2 L)^{-1}(1 - \alpha_2 L)x_t$$

which gets us back to

$$y_t = D(L)x_t$$

However, the above is in terms of the true coefficients and has also ignored the noise terms. In practice the bivariate prewhitening approach requires the estimation of more parameters and greater manipulations of those estimated parameters than does the univariate prewhitening method. It would be interesting to see comparative case studies of the results yielded by the two approaches, but there do not yet appear to be any. An extensive application of the bivariate prewhitening approach to various time series of money and interest rates yielded "a surprising, probably disconcerting, lack of relationship among several variables."† Pierce's main conclusion was, "Extensions of time series modeling procedures of Box and Jenkins reveal that numerous economic variables which are generally regarded as being strongly interrelated may with equal validity, based on recent empirical evidence, be regarded as independent or only weakly related." A further study by Haugh and Box illustrated the same approach to the study of the connection between the GNP X and the unemployment rate Y in the United Kingdom.‡ Each series was first differenced to yield $x_t = X_t - X_{t-1}$ and $y_t =$

† D. A. Pierce, "Relationships—and the Lack Thereof—Between Economic Time Series, with Special Reference to Money and Interest Rates," *Journal of the American Statistical Association*, vol. 72, 1977, pp. 11–22.

‡ L. D. Haugh and G. E. P. Box, "Identification of Dynamic Regression (Distributed Lag) Models Connecting Two Time Series," *Journal of the American Statistical Association*, vol. 72, 1977, pp. 121–130.

Table 9-2 Cross correlations $r_{\hat{u}_x\hat{u}_y}(k)$†

Lag (k)	−15	−14	−13	−12	−11	−10	−9	−8	−7	−6	−5	−4	−3	−2	−1	
$r_{\hat{u}_x\hat{u}_y}$	−0.19	0.06	−0.16	0.27	0.04	−0.05	0.01	0.26	0.14	0.10	0.03	0.08	−0.02	−0.16	−0.19	
Lag (k)	0	1	2	3	4	5	6	7	8	9	10	11	12	13	14	15
$r_{\hat{u}_x\hat{u}_y}$	−0.39	−0.24	−0.26	0.03	−0.03	0.09	−0.16	0.18	0.24	0.08	0.09	0.01	0.29	0.18	0.05	−0.22

†L. D. Haugh and G. E. P. Box, "Identification of Dynamic Regression (Distributed Lag) Models Connecting Two Time Series," *Journal of the American Statistical Association*, vol. 72, 1977, p. 127.

Table 9-3 Summary statistics for $r_{\hat{u}_x \hat{u}_y}$

	Number of coefficients exceeding		Mean absolute
	Two standard errors	One standard error	coefficient
Negative lags	2	7	0.13
Positive lags	2	8	0.14

$Y_t - Y_{t-1}$. The separate ARMA models were estimated from 56 deseasonalized quarterly observations as

$$(1 - 0.63L)y_t = \hat{u}_{yt}$$

and

$$x_t = 0.66 + \hat{u}_{xt}$$

The first concern was the direction of causation. Table 9-2 shows the various lagged cross correlations. A positive lag is here defined as the y series lagging behind the x series. The asymptotic standard error for r is 0.13. Table 9-3 presents three summary statistics computed by the author from the data in Table 9-2. The data in these two tables hardly seem to give any clear indication of the direction of causation. However the authors of the paper state, "It is concluded that any feedback effect is of secondary importance, as evidenced by the small cross correlations at negative lags.... This direction of causation from x to y agrees with that considered by Bray."† Another time series analyst might well interpret these cross correlations differently and fit a different transfer function to the residuals.

There is as yet no clear consensus on the relative roles of time-series techniques and the more orthodox econometric methods. Some mistakenly view them as competitive rather than complementary. Each is still an "art," as distinct from a "science," in that time-series practitioners have to make various subjective judgments in the course of their analyses just as econometricians conventionally "choose" between different regressions and specifications. Investigators with strong prior beliefs can usually see "patterns" in the data that may be invisible to more sceptical colleagues.‡

PROBLEMS

9-1 Deduce the δ coefficients implied for $D(L) = B(L)/A(L)$ where

$$A(L) = 1 - \alpha_1 L - \alpha_2 L^2$$

$$B(L) = \beta_0 + \beta_1 L$$

Derive an expression for the mean lag in this process.

† Haugh and G. E. P. Box, op. cit., p. 127.

‡ Years ago in Ireland "reading the tea cups" was a favorite social pastime before the advent of the ubiquitous tea bag. On draining the tea cup the haphazard pattern of the remaining leaves could be interpreted by the skilled "reader" as full of meaning and significance. Nowadays a different class of professionals apply similar "skills" to the interpretation of computer printouts.

9-2 A model is specified as

$$Y_t = \delta Y_{t-1} + u_t \qquad |\delta| < 1$$
$$u_t = \varepsilon_t + \alpha\varepsilon_{t-1}$$

with

$$\boldsymbol{\varepsilon} \sim N(\mathbf{0}, \sigma_\varepsilon^2\mathbf{I})$$

The δ parameter is estimated by $\hat{\delta} = \Sigma Y_t Y_{t-1}/\Sigma Y_{t-1}^2$. Show:

(*a*) $\text{plim}\,\hat{\delta} = \delta + \dfrac{\phi(1-\delta^2)}{1+2\delta\phi}$ where $\phi = \dfrac{\alpha}{1+\alpha^2}$

(*b*) $\text{plim}\left(\dfrac{1}{n}\Sigma\hat{u}_t^2\right) = \sigma_\varepsilon^2[1 + \alpha(\alpha - \alpha^*)]$

where

$$\alpha^* = \frac{\phi(1-\delta^2)}{1+2\delta\phi} \qquad \text{and} \qquad \hat{u}_t = Y_t - \hat{\delta}Y_{t-1}$$

9-3 Show that a second-degree approximation for the Almon lag implies the restrictions

$$\delta_3 - 3\delta_2 + 3\delta_1 - \delta_0 = 0$$
$$\delta_4 - 3\delta_3 + 3\delta_2 - \delta_1 = 0$$
$$\cdots\cdots\cdots\cdots\cdots\cdots\cdots\cdots$$
$$\delta_s - 3\delta_{s-1} + 3\delta_{s-2} - \delta_{s-3} = 0$$

and hence verify the $\mathbf{R}_2$ matrix shown in Eq. (9-37).

9-4 Verify that the information matrix for the model of Eq. (9-44) is given by Eq. (9-46).

9-5 Prove Eq. (9-56). [*Hint*: Use the lag operator to express Eq. (9-47) as

$$Y_t = \text{constant} + \beta_2(X_t + \beta_3 X_{t-1} + \beta_3^2 X_{t-2} + \cdots) + (u_t + \beta_3 u_{t-1} + \beta_3^2 u_{t-2} + \cdots)]$$

9-6 Derive the information matrix (9-67). [*Hint*: Write ε_t in the alternative forms

$$\varepsilon_t = Y_t^* - \beta_1(1-\rho) - \beta_2 X_t^* - \beta_3 Y_{t-1}^*$$

and

$$\varepsilon_t = u_t - \rho u_{t-1}$$

where

$$Y_t^* = Y_t - \rho Y_{t-1} \qquad X_t^* = X_t - \rho X_{t-1} \qquad u_t = Y_t - \beta_1 - \beta_2 X_t - \beta_3 Y_{t-1}$$

and then find all the second-order partial derivatives of

$$\ln L = -\frac{n}{2}\ln(2\pi) - \frac{n}{2}\ln\sigma_\varepsilon^2 - \frac{1}{2\sigma^2}\Sigma\varepsilon_t^2$$

9-7 Derive the information matrix (9-72) and show also that in this model the estimator of σ_u^2 is asymptotically independent of the remaining estimators.

9-8 Consider $X_t = 2X_{t-1} + \varepsilon_t$ where $\{\varepsilon_t\}$ is a white noise series. Draw some sets of ε's from a table of random normal deviates and compute the corresponding sample realizations of the process for $t = 1, \ldots, 10$, starting each realization off by setting $X_0 = 0$. Satisfy yourself that X_t can become "very large" in both positive and negative directions.

9-9 If $u_t = (1 - \theta_1 L - \theta_2 L^2 - \cdots - \theta_q L^q)\varepsilon_t$ and $\{\varepsilon_t\}$ is white noise, derive the autocorrelation function of the $\{u_t\}$ series.

9-10 In the rational lag equation

$$y_t = \frac{3L}{1 - 0.9L + 0.2L^2}x_t + u_t$$

determine:

(*a*) The total multiplier
(*b*) The mean lag
(*c*) The coefficients of x_{t-j} for $j = 0, 1, 2, 3$.

(UL, 1980)

9-11 The model generating the $\{y_t\}$ series is presumed to be

$$y_t = \alpha y_{t-1} + u_t \qquad |\alpha| < 1$$

with

$$u_t = \rho u_{t-1} + \varepsilon_t \qquad |\rho| < 1$$

and the ε's independently and identically distributed with zero mean and constant variance σ^2. Show that

$$\hat{\rho} = \frac{\sum_{t=2}^{n} \hat{u}_t \hat{u}_{t-1}}{\sum_{t=2}^{n} \hat{u}_{t-1}^2}$$

where $\hat{u}_t = y_t - \hat{\alpha} y_{t-1}$ and $\hat{\alpha}$ is the OLS estimator of α, is not a consistent estimator of ρ.

(UL, 1973)

9-12 A simple stochastic version of the permanent income model is

$$z_t = x_t + u_t$$

where z_t is observed income, x_t is permanent income which is unobserved, and u_t is a serially random transitory element. Let x_t evolve according to $x_t = x_{t-1} + v_t$. Assume u and v are independent.

(*a*) What constraints does this model place on the autocorrelation function of $(z_t - z_{t-1})$?

(*b*) Discuss how you would estimate σ_u^2 and σ_v^2 from data on z.

(*c*) What would positive sample autocorrelation at lag 1 in $z_t - z_{t-1}$ suggest about the plausibility of the model?

Suppose now that u and v are not assumed to be independent but have covariance σ_{uv}:

(*d*) Are the parameters σ_u^2, σ_v^2, and σ_{uv} identified?

(*e*) What would positive autocorrelation in $z_t - z_{t-1}$ imply about the sign of σ_{uv}? About the magnitude of σ_v^2 relative to σ_u^2?

(University of Washington, 1980)

CHAPTER

TEN

A SMORGASBORD OF FURTHER TOPICS

Chaps. 5 to 9 have presented the "standard fare" of the single-equation linear model. This chapter outlines a number of additional topics, some of which are "golden oldies" that have been around for some time, while others have come into prominence more recently. Some enthusiasts may wish to study all the topics; other readers may be interested in some topics but not in others. To a large degree the sections stand alone and can be read independently.

10-1 RECURSIVE RESIDUALS

As shown in Chap. 5, the vector of OLS residuals is given by

$$\mathbf{e} = \mathbf{Mu}$$

where

$$\mathbf{M} = \mathbf{I} - \mathbf{X}(\mathbf{X}'\mathbf{X})^{-1}\mathbf{X}'$$

which is a symmetric idempotent matrix of rank $n - k$. If the u's are independently and identically distributed, it then follows that

$$E(\mathbf{ee}') = \sigma_u^2\mathbf{M}$$

Thus the calculated residuals will, in general, display heteroscedasticity and nonzero covariances, even when homoscedasticity and zero covariances hold for the true disturbances. This leads to the difficulties in testing for heteroscedasticity and autocorrelation already discussed in Secs. 8-4 and 8-5.

Recursive residuals are a set of residuals which, if the disturbances are independently and identically distributed, will themselves be independently and identically distributed, thus greatly facilitating tests of the null hypothesis.† We postulate the usual linear model

$$\mathbf{y} = \mathbf{X}\mathbf{b} + \mathbf{u} \qquad \text{with} \qquad \mathbf{u} \sim N(\mathbf{0}, \sigma^2\mathbf{I}) \tag{10-1}$$

and $\mathbf{X}$ a nonstochastic matrix of order $n \times k$. Let $\mathbf{x}_j$ denote the $k \times 1$ vector of observations on the k explanatory variables at sample point j.‡ Thus

$$\mathbf{X} = \begin{bmatrix} - & \mathbf{x}_1' & - \\ - & \mathbf{x}_2' & - \\ & \vdots & \\ - & \mathbf{x}_n' & - \end{bmatrix}$$

Let $\mathbf{X}_{r-1}$ denote the $(r-1) \times k$ matrix consisting of the first $r-1$ rows of $\mathbf{X}$. Provided $r - 1 \geq k$, this matrix may be used to estimate $\boldsymbol{\beta}$. Denote the resultant estimator by $\mathbf{b}_{r-1}$, that is,

$$\mathbf{b}_{r-1} = (\mathbf{X}_{r-1}'\mathbf{X}_{r-1})^{-1}\mathbf{X}_{r-1}'\mathbf{y}_{r-1}$$

where $\mathbf{y}_{r-1}$ denotes the subvector consisting of the first $r-1$ elements of $\mathbf{y}$. Using $\mathbf{b}_{r-1}$ one may "forecast" y_r at sample point r, corresponding to the vector $\mathbf{x}_r$ of explanatory variables at that point. The forecast error is

$$y_r - \mathbf{x}_r'\mathbf{b}_{r-1}$$

and, as shown in Sec. 5-4, the variance of this forecast error is

$$\sigma^2\left(1 + \mathbf{x}_r'(\mathbf{X}_{r-1}'\mathbf{X}_{r-1})^{-1}\mathbf{x}_r\right)$$

Define the recursive residual w_r as

$$w_r = \frac{y_r - \mathbf{x}_r'\mathbf{b}_{r-1}}{\sqrt{\{1 + \mathbf{x}_r'(\mathbf{X}_{r-1}'\mathbf{X}_{r-1})^{-1}\mathbf{x}_r\}}} \tag{10-2}$$

Clearly, under assumption (10-1)

$$w_r \sim N(0, \sigma^2)$$

since it is a linear function of normal variables and the OLS forecast is unbiased. A *sequence* of recursive residuals may be generated as follows.

1. Choose a base of k observations. For the moment let this be the first k observations in the sample, whether it be composed of time-series or cross-

† Recursive residuals are a member of the general class of LUS residuals (linear unbiased with a scalar variance matrix). Another important set is the BLUS residuals due to Theil. See H. Theil, *Principles of Econometrics*, Wiley, New York, 1971, Chap. 5.

‡ As is customary, the first element in each $\mathbf{x}$ vector will be unity to accommodate the intercept term.

section data. Compute the vector $\mathbf{b}_k$ and the recursive residual

$$w_{k+1} = \frac{y_{k+1} - \mathbf{x}'_{k+1}\mathbf{b}_k}{\sqrt{\{1 + \mathbf{x}'_{k+1}(\mathbf{X}'_k\mathbf{X}_k)^{-1}\mathbf{x}_{k+1}\}}}$$

2. Update, or extend, the base to include the first $k + 1$ observations; compute $\mathbf{b}_{k+1}$ and hence w_{k+2}.
3. Repeat step 2, adding one new observation point at a time.

There is thus a sequence of $n - k$ recursive residuals as defined in Eq. (10-2) for $r = k + 1, \ldots, n$. The practical importance of recursive residuals is due to the fact that, under assumption (10-1), the vector of residuals defined by Eq. (10-2) is multivariate normal with zero mean vector and scalar variance matrix, that is,

$$\mathbf{w} \sim N(\mathbf{0}, \sigma^2\mathbf{I}_{n-k}) \tag{10-3}$$

Since we have already seen that each w_r is normal with zero mean and variance σ^2, the proof of Eq. (10-3) just requires the establishment of zero covariances. The numerator in Eq. (10-2) may be written

$$y_r - \mathbf{x}'_r\mathbf{b}_{r-1} = u_r - \mathbf{x}'_r(\mathbf{X}'_{r-1}\mathbf{X}_{r-1})^{-1}\mathbf{X}'_{r-1}\mathbf{u}_{r-1}$$

Thus

$$E\{(y_r - \mathbf{x}'_r\mathbf{b}_{r-1})(y_s - \mathbf{x}'_s\mathbf{b}_{s-1})\}$$
$$= E\{[u_r - \mathbf{x}'_r(\mathbf{X}'_{r-1}\mathbf{X}_{r-1})^{-1}\mathbf{X}'_{r-1}\mathbf{u}_{r-1}][u_s - \mathbf{x}'_s(\mathbf{X}'_{s-1}\mathbf{X}_{s-1})^{-1}\mathbf{X}'_{s-1}\mathbf{u}_{s-1}]\} \tag{10-4}$$

We may assume that $r < s$ without any loss of generality. Thus

$$E(u_r u_s) = 0$$

$$E(\mathbf{u}_{r-1}u_s) = \begin{bmatrix} E(u_1u_s) \\ E(u_2u_s) \\ \vdots \\ E(u_{r-1}u_s) \end{bmatrix} = \mathbf{0}$$

$$E(u_r\mathbf{u}'_{s-1}) = [0 \quad \cdots \quad 0 \quad \underset{\substack{\downarrow \\ r\text{th position}}}{\sigma^2} \quad 0 \quad \cdots \quad 0]$$

$$E(\mathbf{u}_{r-1}\mathbf{u}'_{s-1}) = E\left\{\begin{bmatrix} u_1 \\ u_2 \\ \vdots \\ u_{r-1} \end{bmatrix}[u_1 \quad u_2 \quad \cdots \quad u_{r-1}u_r \quad \cdots \quad u_{s-1}]\right\}$$

$$= \sigma^2(\mathbf{I}_{r-1} \ \mathbf{0}_{(r-1)\times(s-r)})$$

Multiplying out the right-hand side of Eq. (10-4), remembering that the expectation of a scalar can also be written as the expectation of the transpose of the scalar, and using the above results, easily establishes

$$E(w_r w_s) = 0 \qquad \text{for all } r, s;\ r \neq s$$

and so Eq. (10-3) is proved.

The computation of the recursive residuals might be achieved by using the conventional OLS formula repeatedly to compute each $\mathbf{b}$ vector in the sequence $\mathbf{b}_k, \mathbf{b}_{k+1}, \ldots, \mathbf{b}_n$. However, the calculations are simplified by using the following recursion formulas:†

$$(\mathbf{X}_r'\mathbf{X}_r)^{-1} = (\mathbf{X}_{r-1}'\mathbf{X}_{r-1})^{-1} - \frac{(\mathbf{X}_{r-1}'\mathbf{X}_{r-1})^{-1}\mathbf{x}_r\mathbf{x}_r'(\mathbf{X}_{r-1}'\mathbf{X}_{r-1})^{-1}}{1 + \mathbf{x}_r'(\mathbf{X}_{r-1}'\mathbf{X}_{r-1})^{-1}\mathbf{x}_r} \tag{10-5}$$

and

$$\mathbf{b}_r = \mathbf{b}_{r-1} + (\mathbf{X}_r'\mathbf{X}_r)^{-1}\mathbf{x}_r(y_r - \mathbf{x}_r'\mathbf{b}_{r-1}) \tag{10-6}$$

Since

$$\mathbf{X}_r = \begin{bmatrix} \mathbf{X}_{r-1} \\ \mathbf{x}_r' \end{bmatrix}$$

it follows that

$$\mathbf{X}_r'\mathbf{X}_r = \mathbf{X}_{r-1}'\mathbf{X}_{r-1} + \mathbf{x}_r\mathbf{x}_r'$$

Eq. (10-5) may then be checked by multiplying the left-hand side by $\mathbf{X}_r'\mathbf{X}_r$, the right-hand side by $\mathbf{X}_{r-1}'\mathbf{X}_{r-1} + \mathbf{x}_r\mathbf{x}_r'$, and seeing that both reduce to the identity matrix.‡ Relation (10-6) may be simply derived since

$$\begin{aligned}
(\mathbf{X}_r'\mathbf{X}_r)\mathbf{b}_r &= \mathbf{X}_r'\mathbf{y} \\
&= \mathbf{X}_{r-1}'\mathbf{y}_{r-1} + \mathbf{x}_r y_r \\
&= (\mathbf{X}_{r-1}'\mathbf{X}_{r-1})\mathbf{b}_{r-1} + \mathbf{x}_r y_r \\
&= (\mathbf{X}_r'\mathbf{X}_r)\mathbf{b}_{r-1} + \mathbf{x}_r(y_r - \mathbf{x}_r'\mathbf{b}_{r-1})
\end{aligned}$$

Finally, relations (10-5) and (10-6) may be used to derive the following: §

$$\text{RSS}_r = \text{RSS}_{r-1} + w_r^2 \qquad r = k+1, \ldots, n \tag{10-7}$$

where

$$\text{RSS}_r = (\mathbf{y}_r - \mathbf{X}_r\mathbf{b}_r)'(\mathbf{y}_r - \mathbf{X}_r\mathbf{b}_r)$$

These theoretical results on recursive residuals have a number of important practical applications. First of all they provide an alternative derivation of the test

† See R. L. Brown, J. Durbin, and J. M. Evans, "Techniques for Testing the Constancy of Regression Relationships over Time," *Journal of the Royal Statistical Society*, ser. B, vol. 37, 1975, pp. 149–192, for a statement of these formulas and some notes on their history. A useful survey of recursion formulas for various models is to be found in W. C. Riddell, "Recursive Estimation Algorithms for Economic Research," *Annals of Economic and Social Measurement*, vol. 4, 1975, pp. 397–406.

‡ See Problems 10-1 and 10-2.

§ See Problem 10-3.

for structural change in the case where the second sample contains fewer than k observations.† Based only on a heuristic proof, it was asserted in Eq. (6-27) that under the hypothesis of no structural change

$$F = \frac{(\mathbf{e}_*'\mathbf{e}_* - \mathbf{e}_1'\mathbf{e}_1)/n_2}{\mathbf{e}_1'\mathbf{e}_1/(n_1 - k)} \sim F(n_2, n_1 - k)$$

where $\mathbf{e}_*'\mathbf{e}_*$ denotes the residual sum of squares from a regression fitted to all $n_1 + n_2$ observations and $\mathbf{e}_1'\mathbf{e}_1$ is the residual sum of squares from a regression fitted to the first n_1 observations. From Eq. (10-7) it follows that for a regression with n observations,

$$\text{RSS}_n = \sum_{r=k+1}^{n} w_r^2$$

since $\text{RSS}_k = 0$, as a regression with k parameters fitted to k observation points will have zero residuals. Thus

$$\mathbf{e}_1'\mathbf{e}_1 = \sum_{r=k+1}^{n_1} w_r^2$$

$$\mathbf{e}_*'\mathbf{e}_* = \sum_{r=k+1}^{n_1+n_2} w_r^2$$

and so the F statistic defined above becomes

$$F = \frac{\sum_{r=n_1+1}^{n_1+n_2} w_r^2/n_2}{\sum_{r=k+1}^{n_1} w_r^2/(n_1 - k)}$$

Since under the null hypothesis the w_r are independently and identically distributed normal variables, the F statistic is seen to be the ratio of two independent χ^2 variables, each divided by the appropriate number of degrees of freedom, and so it has the $F(n_2, n_1 - k)$ distribution.

A second useful application of recursive residuals lies in testing for heteroscedasticity.‡ If the alternative hypothesis to homoscedasticity is that σ_t^2 varies with X_{jt}, the procedure would be as follows.

1. Order the data according to the values of X_j and choose a base of at least k points from among the central observations.
2. From that base compute a vector $\mathbf{w}_1$ of recursive residuals corresponding to the first m observations, and another vector $\mathbf{w}_2$ of recursive residuals corresponding to the last m observations.§ Since the smallest feasible base is of size k, the maximum value of m is $(n - k)/2$.

† See A. C. Harvey, "An Alternative Proof and Generalization of a Test for Structural Change," *The American Statistician*, vol. 30, 1976, pp. 122–123.

‡ A. C. Harvey and G. D. A. Phillips, "A Comparison of the Power of Some Tests for Heteroscedasticity in the General Linear Model," *Journal of Econometrics*, vol. 2, 1974, pp. 307–316.

§ Notice that there is no problem in computing recursive residuals backward or forward in a sample from any suitably chosen base, or indeed in adding "new" observations in any order.

3. Under the null hypothesis it follows directly from the properties of recursive residuals that the test statistic

$$F = \frac{\mathbf{w}_2'\mathbf{w}_2}{\mathbf{w}_1'\mathbf{w}_1} \sim F(m, m) \tag{10-8}$$

Some sampling experiments by Harvey and Phillips indicate that the power of the test in Eq. (10-8) compares favorably with that of the Goldfeld-Quandt test described in Sec. 8-4. They recommend setting m at approximately $n/3$. An advantage of the recursive residuals test over that of Goldfeld and Quandt is the greater flexibility of the former. If, for example, one now wished to test whether σ^2 varies with some other variable X_i, one could simply regroup the existing recursive residuals according to low and high values of X_i and compute Eq. (10-8) afresh, whereas the Goldfeld-Quandt test would require the computation of two new regressions.

A third application of recursive residuals is in testing for autocorrelation.† In a time-series application one may take the first k observations as the base. From the resultant $n - k$ recursive residuals the conventional von Neumann ratio is‡

$$\frac{\delta^2}{s^2} = \frac{\sum_{t=k+2}^{n}(w_t - w_{t-1})^2/(n-k-1)}{\sum_{t=k+1}^{n}(w_t - \bar{w})^2/(n-k)}$$

where $\bar{w} = \sum_{t=k+1}^{n} w_t/(n-k)$. This is the ratio of the mean-square successive difference to the variance. An exact test against serial correlation would be provided by referring the calculated value of δ^2/s^2 to the significance points of the von Neumann ratio.§ These critical values, however, were derived for the general case where the expected value of the series being tested is some unknown constant. In this application the w's are known to have zero mean. Incorporating this information, Press and Brooks have computed significance points for a *modified* von Neumann ratio¶

$$\left(\frac{\delta^2}{s^2}\right)^* = \frac{\sum_{t=k+2}^{n}(w_t - w_{t-1})^2/(n-k-1)}{\sum_{t=k+1}^{n} w_t^2/(n-k)} \tag{10-9}$$

These points are tabulated in App. B-7. The von Neumann ratio is *arithmetically* closely related to the Durbin-Watson statistic, which could, of course, be computed from the recursive residuals. The crucial point, however, is that the multivariate normal distribution for $\mathbf{w}$ specified in Eq. (10-3) satisfies the assumptions underlying the derivation of the von Neumann (Press and Brooks) signifi-

† G. D. A. Phillips and A. C. Harvey, "A Simple Test for Serial Correlation in Regression Analysis," *Journal of the American Statistical Association*, vol. 69, 1974, pp. 935–939.

‡ J. von Neumann, "Distribution of the Ratio of the Mean Square Successive Difference to the Variance," *Annals of Mathematical Statistics*, vol. 12, 1941, pp. 367–395.

§ B. I. Hart, "Significance Levels for the Ratio of the Mean Square Successive Difference to the Variance," *Annals of Mathematical Statistics*, vol. 13, 1942, pp. 445–447.

¶ S. J. Press and R. B. Brooks, "Testing for Serial Correlation in Regression," Report no. 6911, Center for Mathematical Studies in Business and Economics, University of Chicago, Chicago, 1969.

cance points so that an exact test is available, thus avoiding the inconclusive zone associated with the Durbin-Watson statistic calculated from the OLS residuals. Some sampling experiments by Phillips and Harvey suggest that the power of this test may be increased by forming the initial base from a mixture of the first and last observations.

Fourth, recursive residuals provide a test of some possible forms of misspecification.† Since, under the null hypothesis, the recursive residuals are independently and identically distributed normal variables with zero expectation, the mean of the residuals divided by its estimated standard error will follow a t distribution. Formally

$$t = \frac{\bar{w}}{s/\sqrt{n-k}} \sim t(n-k-1) \tag{10-10}$$

where

$$\bar{w} = \frac{\sum_{j=k+1}^{n} w_j}{n-k}$$

and

$$s^2 = \frac{\sum_{j=k+1}^{n} (w_j - \bar{w})^2}{n-k-1}$$

As an illustration of the use of this test in specification analysis suppose the postulated model is a linear relation between Y and X. If the true relation is convex (concave) and the data are ordered by the size of X, the recursive residuals would be expected to be mainly positive (negative) and the computed t statistic will tend to be large in absolute value. In a multivariate situation this specification test could still be carried out for any *single* explanatory variable, if it were thought that the other explanatory variables were correctly specified, but this type of a priori knowledge is seldom available. Several specification errors might have a self-canceling effect on the recursive residuals, so this test is not likely to be very effective in multivariate situations.

Finally Brown, Durbin, and Evans describe‡ an important application of recursive residuals in testing for structural change over time. The null hypothesis of no structural change for the model $\mathbf{y} = \mathbf{X}\boldsymbol{\beta} + \mathbf{u}$ is specified as

$$H_0: \quad \boldsymbol{\beta}_1 = \boldsymbol{\beta}_2 = \cdots = \boldsymbol{\beta}_n = \boldsymbol{\beta}$$

$$\sigma_1^2 = \sigma_2^2 = \cdots = \sigma_n^2 = \sigma^2$$

where $\boldsymbol{\beta}_t$ denotes the vector of coefficients ruling in period t and σ_t^2 the disturbance variance in that period. It is clear that the null hypothesis would be violated if the $\boldsymbol{\beta}$ vectors remained constant but σ^2 varies. This would be the classic

† A. C. Harvey and P. Collier, "Testing for Functional Misspecification in Regression Analysis," *Journal of Econometrics*, vol. 6, 1977, pp. 103–119.

‡ R. L. Brown, J. Durbin, and J. M. Evans, "Techniques for Testing the Constancy of Regression Relationships over Time," *Journal of the Royal Statistical Society*, ser. B, vol. 37, 1975, pp. 149–192.

case of heteroscedasticity, which might be tested by some of the procedures already outlined. The main concern in problems of structural change, however, is variation in the $\boldsymbol{\beta}$'s.

The authors suggest a pair of tests, namely, the cusum test and the cusum of squares test. The first test statistic is the cusum quantity

$$W_r = \sum_{k+1}^{r} w_j/\hat{\sigma} \qquad r = k+1, \ldots, n \tag{10-11}$$

where

$$\hat{\sigma}^2 = \frac{\text{RSS}_n}{n-k}$$

W_r is seen to be a *cumulative* sum, and it should be plotted against r. As long as the $\boldsymbol{\beta}$ vectors are constant, $E(W_r) = 0$, but if the $\boldsymbol{\beta}$'s change W_r, will tend to diverge from the zero mean value line. For a forward recursion the significance of the departure of W_r from the zero line may be assessed by reference to a pair of straight lines which pass through the points

$$\{k, \pm a\sqrt{n-k}\} \qquad \text{and} \qquad \{n, \pm 3a\sqrt{n-k}\}$$

where a is a parameter depending on the significance level α chosen for the test. The correspondence for some conventional significance levels is

$$\begin{array}{ll} \alpha = 0.01 & a = 1.143 \\ \alpha = 0.05 & a = 0.948 \\ \alpha = 0.10 & a = 0.850 \end{array}$$

The lines are shown in Fig. 10-1.

The equation of the upper line in Fig. 10-1 may be determined from

$$\frac{W_t - a\sqrt{n-k}}{t-k} = \frac{2a\sqrt{n-k}}{n-k}$$

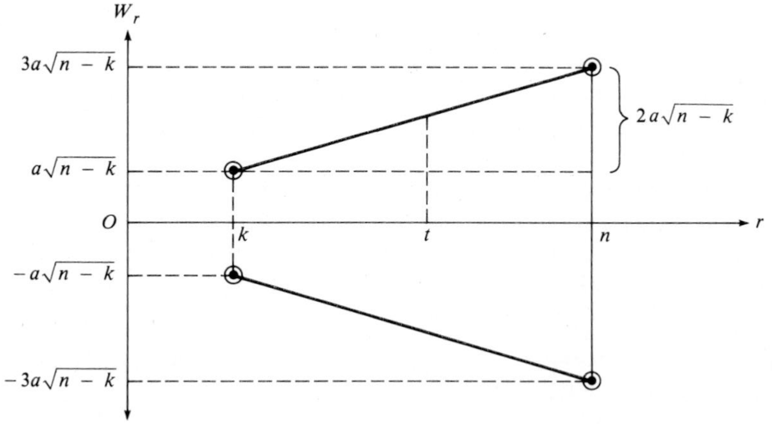

Figure 10-1 Cusum plot.

or

$$W_t = a\sqrt{n-k} + \frac{2a(t-k)}{\sqrt{n-k}}$$

and the equation of the lower line is given by its negative.

The second test statistic is based on cumulative sums of the squared residuals, namely,

$$s_r = \frac{\sum_{k+1}^{r} w_j^2}{\sum_{k+1}^{n} w_j^2} \qquad r = k+1, \ldots, n \tag{10-12}$$

The mean value line giving the expected value of the test statistic under the null hypothesis is

$$E(s_r) = \frac{r-k}{n-k}$$

which goes from zero at $r = k$ to unity at $r = n$. The significance of the departure of s_r from its expected value may be assessed by reference to a pair of lines drawn parallel to the $E(s_r)$ line at a distance c_0 above and below. Values of c_0 for various sample sizes and levels of significance are tabulated in App. B-8. Reference should be made to the Brown, Durbin, and Evans article for practical illustrations of the technique and for interpretations of various plots. The basic idea is that instability of the parameters would be indicated if the plot of W_r or s_r crossed the significance lines described above. There is some evidence that the cusum test is less powerful than the cusum of squares test. Some Monte Carlo experiments by Garbade also suggest that the latter may not be very powerful in comparison with tests based on variable parameter models.† However, the explanatory variable in his experiments was random over time, and it would be interesting to see if the same result was obtained with an autoregressive explanatory variable.

10-2 SPLINE FUNCTIONS

In an interesting study Poirier and Garber examined the determinants of profit rates in the aerospace industry over the period 1951–1971.‡ They were particularly interested in the behavior of profit rates, ceteris paribus, in three distinct periods, 1951–1954 (Korean war), 1954–1965 (peace), and 1965–1971 (Vietnam war). To cover the ceteris paribus proviso, they included eleven explanatory variables, apart from time, in their equation. They treated time by means of spline functions, and to illustrate the basic idea we will assume that the profit rate has been adjusted for the effects of the eleven variables and look at the behavior of the net, or adjusted, profit rate over time. Assuming a linear time trend, the

† K. Garbade, "Two Methods for Examining the Stability of Regression Coefficients," *Journal of the American Statistical Association*, vol. 72, 1977, pp. 54–63.

‡ See D. J. Poirier and S. G. Garber, "The Determinants of Aerospace Profit Rates, 1951–1971," *Southern Economic Journal*, vol. 41, 1974, pp. 228–238; or D. J. Poirier, *The Econometrics of Structural Change*, North-Holland, Amsterdam, 1974, Chap. 2.

postulated model would be

$$\begin{array}{llll} \text{Period 1} & y_t = \alpha_1 + \beta_1 t + u_t & t \le a & \\ \text{Period 2} & y_t = \alpha_2 + \beta_2 t + u_t & a < t \le b & (10\text{-}13) \\ \text{Period 3} & y_t = \alpha_3 + \beta_3 t + u_t & b < t & \end{array}$$

In this example we might take the origin of time to be 1950. Measuring in years then gives $a = 4$ (i.e., 1954) and $b = 15$ (1965). The data might be split into three distinct subsets and three separate time trends estimated. The result, in general, would look like Fig. 10-2*a*. There is nothing in the unrestricted estimation process to ensure that the functions meet at the join points $t = a$ and $t = b$. Fig. 10-2*b* illustrates a *linear spline*, or piecewise linear, function, which eliminates instantaneous jumps or discontinuities in the function at the join points or knots.

The linear spline function may be fitted in two alternative fashions. One is to define the following variables:

$$w_{1t} = t$$

$$w_{2t} = \begin{cases} 0 & \text{if } t \le a \\ t - a & \text{if } a < t \end{cases}$$

$$w_{3t} = \begin{cases} 0 & \text{if } t \le b \\ t - b & \text{if } b < t \end{cases}$$

and reparameterize the function as

$$y_t = \alpha_1 + \delta_1 w_{1t} + \delta_2 w_{2t} + \delta_3 w_{3t} + u_t \qquad (10\text{-}14)$$

Comparing Eqs. (10-13) and (10-14) it is easy to see that

$$\begin{array}{lll} \beta_1 = \delta_1 & & \\ \beta_2 = \delta_1 + \delta_2 & \alpha_2 = \alpha_1 - \delta_2 a & (10\text{-}15) \\ \beta_3 = \delta_1 + \delta_2 + \delta_3 & \alpha_3 = \alpha_2 - \delta_3 b & \end{array}$$

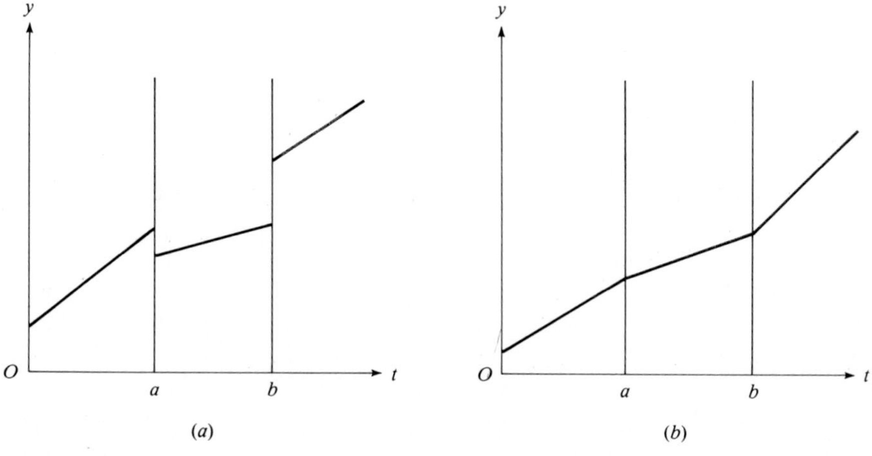

Figure 10-2

Fitting Eq. (10-14) directly by OLS will yield estimated functions which meet at the knots, and the estimated α and β parameters of those functions can be determined from Eqs. (10-15). Tests on α's and β's imply equivalent tests on the δ's. Thus testing the significance of $\delta_1(=\beta_1)$ is asking whether there is a positive (or negative) trend in the first period. Testing the significance of δ_2 is asking whether the trend slope in the second period differs significantly from that in the first, and similarly, testing the significance of δ_3 amounts to asking whether the trend slope in the third period differs from that in the second. Setting up the null hypothesis

$$H_0: \quad \begin{bmatrix} \delta_2 \\ \delta_3 \end{bmatrix} = \begin{bmatrix} 0 \\ 0 \end{bmatrix}$$

is equivalent to postulating that the β's *and* the α's are the same in all three periods, that is, that the data may be adequately described by a single linear trend. This test may be carried out most simply by fitting

$$y_t = \alpha + \delta w_{1t} + u_t$$

as the *restricted* model, the full spline function (10-14) as the *unrestricted* model, and calculating the test statistic defined in Eq. (6-8).

An alternative estimation procedure is restricted least squares. Returning to Eqs. (10-13), the restrictions implied by the join points are

$$\alpha_1 + \beta_1 a = \alpha_2 + \beta_2 a$$
$$\alpha_2 + \beta_2 b = \alpha_3 + \beta_3 b$$

which may be set up in the conventional framework as

$$\overset{\mathbf{R}}{\begin{bmatrix} 1 & a & -1 & -a & 0 & 0 \\ 0 & 0 & 1 & b & -1 & -b \end{bmatrix}} \overset{\boldsymbol{\beta}}{\begin{bmatrix} \alpha_1 \\ \beta_1 \\ \alpha_2 \\ \beta_2 \\ \alpha_3 \\ \beta_3 \end{bmatrix}} = \overset{\mathbf{r}}{\begin{bmatrix} 0 \\ 0 \end{bmatrix}} \tag{10-16}$$

Thus the model

$$\begin{bmatrix} \mathbf{y}_1 \\ \hline \mathbf{y}_2 \\ \hline \mathbf{y}_3 \end{bmatrix} = \left[\begin{array}{cc|cc|cc} 1 & 1 & & & & \\ 1 & 2 & & & & \\ \cdots & \cdots & & & & \\ 1 & a & & & & \\ \hline & & 1 & a+1 & & \\ & & 1 & a+2 & & \\ & & \cdots & \cdots & & \\ & & 1 & b & & \\ \hline & & & & 1 & b+1 \\ & & & & 1 & b+2 \\ & & & & \cdots & \cdots \\ & & & & 1 & n \end{array}\right] \begin{bmatrix} \alpha_1 \\ \beta_1 \\ \alpha_2 \\ \beta_2 \\ \alpha_3 \\ \beta_3 \end{bmatrix} + \mathbf{u} \tag{10-17}$$

where the empty cells in the data matrix are all zero, is fitted subject to the restrictions in Eq. (10-16). The appropriate formula is given in Eq. (6-5). The estimates of the α and β parameters will be identical to those derived from the estimated coefficients of the spline function in Eq. (10-14).†

This simplified example used time as an explanatory variable. The procedure works equally well for any explanatory variable x with *known* join points, or knots, at x_a, x_b, and so on. A possible disadvantage of the linear spline is that while the function itself is continuous at the knots, there is a discontinuity or jump in the first derivative. This may be overcome by the introduction of quadratic or cubic splines. To illustrate a cubic spline function, suppose we have a two-variable relation with known knots at x_a and x_b. Within each subset y is expressed as a third-degree polynomial in x, namely,

$$y = \alpha_{i1} + \beta_{i1}x + \beta_{i2}x^2 + \beta_{i3}x^3 + u \qquad i = 1, 2, 3 \tag{10-18}$$

where the subsets are defined by

$$i = 1 \qquad x \leq x_a$$

$$i = 2 \qquad x_a < x \leq x_b$$

$$i = 3 \qquad x_b < x$$

The restrictions implied by continuity at the knots are then

$$\alpha_{11} + \beta_{11}x_a + \beta_{12}x_a^2 + \beta_{13}x_a^3 = \alpha_{21} + \beta_{21}x_a + \beta_{22}x_a^2 + \beta_{23}x_a^3$$

$$\alpha_{21} + \beta_{21}x_b + \beta_{22}x_b^2 + \beta_{23}x_b^3 = \alpha_{31} + \beta_{31}x_b + \beta_{32}x_b^2 + \beta_{33}x_b^3$$

We further impose continuity of the *first* derivatives of the cubic spline function, which implies

$$\beta_{11} + 2\beta_{12}x_a + 3\beta_{13}x_a^2 = \beta_{21} + 2\beta_{22}x_a + 3\beta_{23}x_a^2$$

$$\beta_{21} + 2\beta_{22}x_b + 3\beta_{23}x_b^2 = \beta_{31} + 2\beta_{32}x_b + 3\beta_{33}x_b^2$$

In addition, continuity of the *second* derivatives implies

$$2\beta_{12} + 6\beta_{13}x_a = 2\beta_{22} + 6\beta_{23}x_a$$

$$2\beta_{22} + 6\beta_{23}x_b = 2\beta_{32} + 6\beta_{33}x_b$$

The cubic spline merely allows discontinuities in the third derivatives at the join points. Thus the cubic spline may be estimated by fitting Eq. (10-18) and estimating the twelve parameters subject to the six restrictions set out above.‡

† See Problem 10-4.

‡ See A. Buse and L. Lim, "Cubic Splines as a Special Case of Restricted Least Squares," *Journal of the American Statistical Association*, vol. 72, 1977, pp. 64–72, which develops the restricted least squares approach; and D. J. Poirier, op. cit., Chap. 3, for an alternative estimation procedure.

Both previous examples have been in terms of spline functions on a single explanatory variable. There are now several examples of applications of *bilinear* splines, where linear splines are specified for two variables with main effects and interaction effects at a two-dimensional grid of specified knots.†

10-3 POOLING OF TIME-SERIES AND CROSS-SECTION DATA

In many problems the investigator may have access to observations on the behavior of a "panel" of decision units at a number of different (and usually successive) time periods. We will assume there are p distinct decision units or groups indexed by $i = 1, \ldots, p$ and m successive time periods indexed by $t = 1, \ldots, m$, giving a total of $n = pm$ sample points. The variables are denoted by

Y_{it} = value of the dependent variable for unit i in period t

$$i = 1, \ldots, p; \; t = 1, \ldots, m$$

X_{jit} = value of jth explanatory variable for unit i in period t $\qquad j = 2, \ldots, k$

The linear hypothesis would then be

$$Y_{it} = \alpha + \beta_2 X_{2it} + \beta_3 X_{3it} + \cdots + \beta_k X_{kit} + u_{it} \tag{10-19}$$

where, for the moment, we assume a common set of parameters for all units in all time periods. To illustrate some of the many possible applications of the model consider some examples.

1. The panel consists of, say, 1000 households whose savings behavior Y_{it} is monitored along with various explanatory variables X_{jit}, such as income, family size, and composition over a number of time periods.
2. The panel consists of a set of firms, and the object of study is the size and timing of their investment expenditures Y_{it} as a function of the group of explanatory variables thought to influence investment.
3. The panel might consist of the 50 states of the United States, and the focus of investigation are the determinants of the unemployment rate Y_{it} across states and over time.
4. The panel consists of the OECD countries, and Y_{it} indicates the per capita consumption of gasoline in country i in year t. The relevant question is whether the usual economic variables such as income and relative prices can adequately explain the variation in Y_{it}.

The most common way of organizing the data in Eq. (10-19) is by decision units. Thus let

$$\mathbf{y}_i = \begin{bmatrix} Y_{i1} \\ \vdots \\ Y_{im} \end{bmatrix} \qquad \mathbf{X}_i = \begin{bmatrix} X_{2i1} & X_{3i1} & \cdots & X_{ki1} \\ \cdots & \cdots & \cdots & \cdots \\ X_{2im} & X_{3im} & \cdots & X_{kim} \end{bmatrix} \qquad \mathbf{u}_i = \begin{bmatrix} u_{i1} \\ \vdots \\ u_{im} \end{bmatrix}$$

† See D. J. Poirier, *The Econometrics of Structural Change*, North-Holland, Amsterdam, 1974, Chap. 4.

denote the data and the disturbances relevant to the ith unit. The data may be "stacked" to form

$$\mathbf{y} = \begin{bmatrix} \mathbf{y}_1 \\ \vdots \\ \mathbf{y}_p \end{bmatrix} \qquad \mathbf{X} = \begin{bmatrix} \mathbf{X}_1 \\ \vdots \\ \mathbf{X}_p \end{bmatrix} \qquad \mathbf{u} = \begin{bmatrix} \mathbf{u}_1 \\ \vdots \\ \mathbf{u}_p \end{bmatrix} \tag{10-20}$$

where $\mathbf{y}$ is $n \times 1$, $\mathbf{X}$ is $n \times (k-1)$, and $\mathbf{u}$ is $n \times 1$. The model in Eq. (10-19) may be expressed as

$$\mathbf{y} = [\mathbf{i} \quad \mathbf{X}]\begin{bmatrix} \alpha \\ \boldsymbol{\beta} \end{bmatrix} + \mathbf{u} \tag{10-21}$$

where $\mathbf{i}$ is an $n \times 1$ vector of units, α is a scalar, and $\boldsymbol{\beta} = (\beta_2 \quad \beta_3 \quad \cdots \quad \beta_k)'$.

A variety of models has been proposed for time-series and cross-section data, and most have been fitted to some data set or another. These models may all be derived from Eq. (10-21) by varying the assumptions made about the systematic part of the equation and/or the assumptions made about the disturbance vector. A possible taxonomy of models is indicated in Table 10-1. The meaning of various terms in the table may not be clear at first sight but will become so as the models are explained.

Model I(a) is perfectly straightforward. The systematic part of Eq. (10-21) postulates a common intercept and a common set of slope coefficients for all units at all time periods. The disturbance assumption is

$$u_{it} \sim \text{iid}(0, \sigma_u^2) \qquad \text{for all } i, t$$

where iid means independently and identically distributed. Thus there is no serial correlation in the disturbances for any individual unit, there is no dependence between the disturbances for different units, either contemporaneous or lagged, and the disturbance has a constant variance at all points. The appropriate estimation method is OLS applied to the stacked data of Eqs. (10-20). If, in addition, the u_{it} are assumed to be normally distributed, all the finite sample inference procedures of Chaps. 5 and 6 are valid.

Model I(b) allows a richer specification for the disturbance term. There are, in fact, several versions of model I(b) depending upon the precise assumptions

Table 10-1 Taxonomy of time-series, cross-section models

	Assumptions about		
Model	Intercept α	Vector of slope coefficients $\boldsymbol{\beta}$	Disturbance term u_{it}
I(a)	Common for all i, t	Common for all i, t	$E(\mathbf{uu}') = \sigma_u^2\mathbf{I}_n$
I(b)	Common for all i, t	Common for all i, t	$E(\mathbf{uu}') = \mathbf{V}$
II(a)	Varying over i	Common for all i, t	Fixed effects model
II(b)	Varying over i	Common for all i, t	Random effects model
III(a)	Varying over i, t	Common for all i, t	Fixed effects model
III(b)	Varying over i, t	Common for all i, t	Random effects model
IV	Varying over i	Varying over i	$E(\mathbf{uu}') = \sigma_u^2\mathbf{I}$ or $E(\mathbf{uu}') = \mathbf{V}$

made about var(**u**). Suppose, for instance, one postulates

$$E(u_{it}^2) = \sigma_{ii} \qquad \text{for all } t;\ i = 1, \ldots, p$$
$$E(u_{it}u_{jt}) = \sigma_{ij} \qquad \text{for all } t \text{ and } i \neq j$$
$$E(u_{it}u_{js}) = 0 \qquad \text{for all } i,\ j, \text{ and } t \neq s$$

These assumptions allow for heteroscedasticity of the disturbance term across units and for nonzero contemporaneous covariances between the disturbances in different units but rule out lagged correlations within and between disturbances. The resultant variance matrix is

$$E(\mathbf{uu}') = \mathbf{V} = \begin{bmatrix} \sigma_{11}\mathbf{I}_m & \sigma_{12}\mathbf{I}_m & \cdots & \sigma_{1p}\mathbf{I}_m \\ \sigma_{12}\mathbf{I}_m & \sigma_{22}\mathbf{I}_m & \cdots & \sigma_{2p}\mathbf{I}_m \\ \cdots & \cdots & \cdots & \cdots \\ \sigma_{1p}\mathbf{I}_m & \sigma_{2p}\mathbf{I}_m & \cdots & \sigma_{pp}\mathbf{I}_m \end{bmatrix} \tag{10-22}$$

The application of GLS to Eq. (10-21) using Eq. (10-22) would now yield the b.l.u.e. of $\boldsymbol{\beta}$,

$$\mathbf{b}_* = (\mathbf{X}'\mathbf{V}^{-1}\mathbf{X})^{-1}\mathbf{X}'\mathbf{V}^{-1}\mathbf{y}$$

The σ_{ij}, however, are unknown. They may be estimated by the following procedure.

Fit Eq. (10-21) by OLS and partition the residual vector into the subvectors $\mathbf{e}_i$ $(i = 1, \ldots, p)$ relating to decision units. Then calculate

$$s_{ij} = \frac{\mathbf{e}_i'\mathbf{e}_j}{m - k}$$

Substitution of the s_{ij} in Eq. (10-22) gives a $\hat{\mathbf{V}}$ matrix which may be used to compute the feasible GLS estimator. The usual inference procedures now apply asymptotically. Another version of model I(b) could be produced by adding an assumption of autocorrelated disturbances within each decision unit.†

Model II relaxes the assumption of a common intercept but retains the assumption of a common vector of slope coefficients for all decision units. The matrix formulation of this model is then

$$\begin{bmatrix} \mathbf{y}_1 \\ \mathbf{y}_2 \\ \vdots \\ \mathbf{y}_p \end{bmatrix} = \begin{bmatrix} \mathbf{i}_m & \mathbf{0} & \cdots & \mathbf{0} & \mathbf{X}_1 \\ \mathbf{0} & \mathbf{i}_m & \cdots & \mathbf{0} & \mathbf{X}_2 \\ \cdots & \cdots & \cdots & \cdots & \cdots \\ \mathbf{0} & \mathbf{0} & \cdots & \mathbf{i}_m & \mathbf{X}_p \end{bmatrix} \begin{bmatrix} \alpha_1 \\ \alpha_2 \\ \vdots \\ \alpha_p \\ \boldsymbol{\beta} \end{bmatrix} + \mathbf{u} \tag{10-23}$$

or

$$\mathbf{y} = \mathbf{Z}\boldsymbol{\alpha} + \mathbf{X}\boldsymbol{\beta} + \mathbf{u} \tag{10-24}$$

† See Problem 10-5 and also J. Kmenta, *Elements of Econometrics*, Macmillan, New York, 1971, pp. 512–514, for a discussion of this case.

where the definition of $\mathbf{Z}$ is obvious from the comparison of Eqs. (10-23) and (10-24). Define the matrix $\mathbf{B}$ as

$$\mathbf{B} = \mathbf{Z}(\mathbf{Z}'\mathbf{Z})^{-1}\mathbf{Z}'$$

It is easily seen that $\mathbf{B}$ is an $n \times n$ matrix given by

$$\mathbf{B} = \frac{1}{m}\begin{bmatrix} \mathbf{J}_m & \mathbf{0} & \cdots & \mathbf{0} \\ \mathbf{0} & \mathbf{J}_m & \cdots & \mathbf{0} \\ \cdots & \cdots & \cdots & \cdots \\ \mathbf{0} & \mathbf{0} & \cdots & \mathbf{J}_m \end{bmatrix}$$

where

$$\mathbf{J}_m = \mathbf{i}_m \mathbf{i}'_m$$

is an $m \times m$ matrix consisting entirely of ones. From the definition of $\mathbf{J}_m$

$$\frac{1}{m}\mathbf{J}_m \mathbf{y}_i = \begin{bmatrix} \bar{Y}_i \\ \bar{Y}_i \\ \vdots \\ \bar{Y}_i \end{bmatrix}$$

where

$$\bar{Y}_i = \frac{1}{m}\sum_{j=1}^{m} Y_{ij}$$

Thus premultiplication of any $n \times 1$ vector by $\mathbf{B}$ will replace each observation for any decision unit by the sample mean of that variable for the decision unit. If we then define

$$\mathbf{P} = \mathbf{I}_n - \mathbf{B}$$

premultiplication by $\mathbf{P}$ will replace the original observations by the *deviations from their unit sample means*. It is also clear that $\mathbf{P}$ is a symmetric idempotent matrix, which is orthogonal to $\mathbf{Z}$, that is,

$$\mathbf{PZ} = \mathbf{0}$$

Premultiplication of Eq. (10-24) by $\mathbf{P}$ then gives

$$\mathbf{Py} = (\mathbf{PX})\boldsymbol{\beta} + \mathbf{Pu} \tag{10-25}$$

Thus estimation of the $\boldsymbol{\beta}$ vector may be achieved by applying OLS to the data expressed in terms of deviations from group (unit) means. The resultant estimator is

$$\mathbf{b} = (\mathbf{X}'\mathbf{PX})^{-1}\mathbf{X}'\mathbf{Py} \tag{10-26}$$

This is, of course, exactly the same vector as results from the application of OLS to Eq. (10-24). The normal equations are

$$\mathbf{Z}'\mathbf{Za} + \mathbf{Z}'\mathbf{Xb} = \mathbf{Z}'\mathbf{y}$$

$$\mathbf{X}'\mathbf{Za} + \mathbf{X}'\mathbf{Xb} = \mathbf{X}'\mathbf{y}$$

Solving the first equation for **a**,

$$\mathbf{a} = (\mathbf{Z}'\mathbf{Z})^{-1}(\mathbf{Z}'\mathbf{y} - \mathbf{Z}'\mathbf{X}\mathbf{b}) \tag{10-27}$$

Substituting in the second normal equation and solving for **b** gives, after some manipulation,

$$\mathbf{b} = (\mathbf{X}'\mathbf{P}\mathbf{X})^{-1}\mathbf{X}'\mathbf{P}\mathbf{y}$$

as before. From the definition of **Z** it may be seen that $(\mathbf{Z}'\mathbf{Z})^{-1}$ is a $p \times p$ diagonal matrix, namely,

$$(\mathbf{Z}'\mathbf{Z})^{-1} = \text{diag}\{m^{-1} \quad m^{-1} \quad \cdots \quad m^{-1}\}$$

and premultiplying an $n \times 1$ vector by $\mathbf{Z}'$ serves to sum elements within each group. Thus Eq. (10-27) implies

$$a_i = \bar{Y}_i - b_2\bar{X}_{2i} - \cdots - b_k\bar{X}_{ki} \qquad i = 1, \ldots, p \tag{10-28}$$

This model, which is designated as model II(a), is usually known as the *fixed effects* model. The fixed effects are the intercepts α_i, one for each group. It is usually assumed that the **u** vector in Eq. (10-24) is homoscedastic and nonautocorrelated so that OLS provides b.l.u.e.'s, though GLS estimators could be constructed on the lines of model I(b). The **b** vector of Eq. (10-26) is also sometimes referred to as the "within" estimator, since it is based on the within-group deviations $(Y_{it} - \bar{Y}_i)$ and $(X_{jit} - \bar{X}_{ji})$. Equations (10-21) and (10-24) have already appeared in Sec. 6-2 on Tests of Structural Change. The exposition in that section was solely in terms of a time-series application where the "groups" referred to p different subperiods, not necessarily all of the same length. Equation (10-21) is a restricted version of Eq. (10-24), and tests of the restrictions may be made in the context of OLS estimates as in Sec. 6-2, or in the context of GLS estimates as in Sec. 8-6.

Model II(b) is the *random effects*, or *error component*, model. Instead of assuming a set of given (unknown) constants $\alpha_1, \ldots, \alpha_p$ for the p groups, a single intercept α is postulated, and the differential intercepts are merged with the disturbance term. The model is now formulated as in Eq. (10-21), namely,

$$\mathbf{y} = [\mathbf{i} \quad \mathbf{X}]\begin{bmatrix} \alpha \\ \boldsymbol{\beta} \end{bmatrix} + \mathbf{u}$$

but the assumptions about **u** are

$$u_{it} = \alpha_i + \varepsilon_{it}$$

where the α_i are drawn at random from $N(0, \sigma_\alpha^2)$ and the ε_{it} are drawn at random from $N(0, \sigma_\varepsilon^2)$. The α_i are now increments (positive or negative) to the common intercept α. To derive the variance matrix of **u** we note that for the ith group we may write

$$\mathbf{u}_i = \alpha_i\mathbf{i}_m + \boldsymbol{\varepsilon}_i$$

It then follows directly that

$$E(\mathbf{u}_i\mathbf{u}_i') = \sigma_\alpha^2\mathbf{J}_m + \sigma_\varepsilon^2\mathbf{I}_m \qquad i = 1,\ldots,p$$

$$= \begin{bmatrix} \sigma_\alpha^2 + \sigma_\varepsilon^2 & \sigma_\alpha^2 & \cdots & \sigma_\alpha^2 \\ \sigma_\alpha^2 & \sigma_\alpha^2 + \sigma_\varepsilon^2 & \cdots & \sigma_\alpha^2 \\ \cdots & \cdots & \cdots & \cdots \\ \sigma_\alpha^2 & \sigma_\alpha^2 & \cdots & \sigma_\alpha^2 + \sigma_\varepsilon^2 \end{bmatrix}$$

$$= \sigma_u^2 \begin{bmatrix} 1 & \rho & \cdots & \rho \\ \rho & 1 & \cdots & \rho \\ \cdots & \cdots & \cdots & \cdots \\ \rho & \rho & \cdots & 1 \end{bmatrix} = \sigma_u^2\mathbf{A}$$

where

$$\sigma_u^2 = \sigma_\alpha^2 + \sigma_\varepsilon^2 \qquad \text{and} \qquad \rho = \frac{\sigma_\alpha^2}{\sigma_u^2}$$

Since $E(\mathbf{u}_i\mathbf{u}_j') = \mathbf{0}$,

$$\mathbf{V} = E(\mathbf{u}\mathbf{u}') = \sigma_u^2 \begin{bmatrix} \mathbf{A} & \mathbf{0} & \cdots & \mathbf{0} \\ \mathbf{0} & \mathbf{A} & \cdots & \mathbf{0} \\ \cdots & \cdots & \cdots & \cdots \\ \mathbf{0} & \mathbf{0} & \cdots & \mathbf{A} \end{bmatrix}$$

$$= \sigma_u^2\mathbf{I}_p \otimes \mathbf{A}$$

The matrix $\mathbf{A}$ may also be expressed as

$$\mathbf{A} = (1 - \rho)\mathbf{I}_m + \rho\mathbf{J}_m$$

This facilitates finding the inverse. Let

$$\mathbf{A}^{-1} = \lambda_1\mathbf{J}_m + \lambda_2\mathbf{I}_m \tag{10-29}$$

where λ_1 and λ_2 are constants to be determined. Multiplying out and noting that $\mathbf{J}_m^2 = m\mathbf{J}_m$,

$$\mathbf{A}\mathbf{A}^{-1} = (1 - \rho)\lambda_2\mathbf{I}_m + [(1 - \rho)\lambda_1 + m\rho\lambda_1 + \rho\lambda_2]\mathbf{J}_m$$

Equating the right-hand side to $\mathbf{I}_m$ gives

$$\lambda_1 = \frac{-\rho}{(1 - \rho)(1 - \rho + m\rho)} \qquad \lambda_2 = \frac{1}{1 - \rho} \tag{10-30}$$

which, on substitution in Eq. (10-29), gives $\mathbf{A}^{-1}$. The GLS estimator of model II(a) might then be obtained from Eq. (10-21) using

$$\mathbf{V}^{-1} = \frac{1}{\sigma_u^2} \begin{bmatrix} \mathbf{A}^{-1} & \mathbf{0} & \cdots & \mathbf{0} \\ \mathbf{0} & \mathbf{A}^{-1} & \cdots & \mathbf{0} \\ \cdots & \cdots & \cdots & \cdots \\ \mathbf{0} & \mathbf{0} & \cdots & \mathbf{A}^{-1} \end{bmatrix} \tag{10-31}$$

The difficulty, however, is that $\mathbf{V}^{-1}$ involves the unknown σ_u^2 and σ_α^2. Before dealing with this problem it may be shown that the GLS estimates can also be achieved by applying OLS to suitably transformed variables. From Eq. (10-29) we may write

$$\mathbf{A}^{-1} = \begin{bmatrix} \lambda_1 + \lambda_2 & \lambda_1 & \cdots & \lambda_1 \\ \lambda_1 & \lambda_1 + \lambda_2 & \cdots & \lambda_1 \\ \cdots & \cdots & \cdots & \cdots \\ \lambda_1 & \lambda_1 & \cdots & \lambda_1 + \lambda_2 \end{bmatrix}$$

Let $\mathbf{z} = [z_1 \quad z_2 \quad \cdots \quad z_m]'$ denote a column vector of m observations on some variable.† It then follows that

$$\begin{aligned} \mathbf{z}'\mathbf{A}^{-1}\mathbf{z} &= \lambda_1(\Sigma z)^2 + \lambda_2 \Sigma z^2 \\ &= \lambda_2\left[\Sigma z^2 - \frac{\rho}{1 - \rho + m\rho}(\Sigma z)^2\right] \qquad \text{using Eq. (10-30)} \\ &= \lambda_2\left[\Sigma z^2 - \frac{m^2\rho}{1 - \rho + m\rho}\bar{z}^2\right] \end{aligned}$$

The form of this expression suggests defining a quasi deviation as

$$\tilde{z} = z - c\bar{z}$$

and asking whether a constant c can be found such that

$$\Sigma \tilde{z}^2 = \Sigma z^2 - \frac{m^2\rho}{1 - \rho + m\rho}\bar{z}^2$$

Now

$$\Sigma \tilde{z}^2 = \Sigma z^2 - (2cm - c^2 m)\bar{z}^2$$

Solving for c gives

$$\begin{aligned} c &= 1 \pm \sqrt{\frac{1 - \rho}{1 - \rho + m\rho}} \\ &= 1 \pm \sqrt{\frac{\sigma_\varepsilon^2}{\sigma_\varepsilon^2 + m\sigma_\alpha^2}} \end{aligned} \qquad (10\text{-}32)$$

recalling that $\rho = \sigma_\alpha^2/(\sigma_\alpha^2 + \sigma_\varepsilon^2)$. It is customary to take the negative sign in Eq. (10-32), and thus we have

$$\mathbf{z}'\mathbf{A}^{-1}\mathbf{z} = \sum_{t=1}^{m} (z_t - c\bar{z})^2 \qquad (10\text{-}33)$$

where‡

$$c = 1 - \sqrt{\frac{\sigma_\varepsilon^2}{\sigma_\varepsilon^2 + m\sigma_\alpha^2}} \qquad (10\text{-}34)$$

† **z** can thus represent the sample observations on the dependent or an independent variable for any given unit.

‡ This result is stated without proof in J. A. Hausman, "Specification Tests in Econometrics," *Econometrica*, vol. 46, 1978, p. 1262.

The estimation of Eq. (10-21) by GLS using the $\mathbf{V}^{-1}$ defined in Eq. (10-31) then gives

$$\begin{bmatrix} a_* \\ \mathbf{b}_* \end{bmatrix} = [[\mathbf{i}_n \quad \mathbf{X}]'\mathbf{V}^{-1}[\mathbf{i}_n \quad \mathbf{X}]]^{-1}[\mathbf{i}_n \quad \mathbf{X}]'\mathbf{V}^{-1}\mathbf{y} \tag{10-35}$$

From the definition of $\mathbf{V}^{-1}$ in Eq. (10-31) the elements in the matrix and vector on the right-hand side of Eq. (10-35) are of the form

$$\mathbf{z}_i\mathbf{A}^{-1}\mathbf{z}_j$$

where $\mathbf{z}_i$ and $\mathbf{z}_j$ represent $m \times 1$ vectors. Thus the GLS estimator defined in Eq. (10-35) is equivalent to applying OLS to the quasi deviations

$$\begin{aligned} y_{it} &= Y_{it} - c\bar{Y}_i \\ x_{jit} &= X_{jit} - c\bar{X}_{ji} \qquad i = 1, \ldots, p;\ t = 1, \ldots, m;\ j = 2, \ldots, k \end{aligned}$$

Either procedure requires an estimate of the variances appearing in $\mathbf{V}^{-1}$ or in c. These may be developed as follows. The disturbance in this model is

$$u_{it} = \alpha_i + \varepsilon_{it}$$

Averaging over t for unit i gives

$$\bar{u}_i = \alpha_i + \bar{\varepsilon}_i$$

Averaging then over i gives

$$\bar{\bar{u}} = \bar{\alpha} + \bar{\bar{\varepsilon}}$$

and the usual decomposition of sums of squares gives

$$\sum_{i,t}(u_{it} - \bar{\bar{u}})^2 = \sum_{i,t}(u_{it} - \bar{u}_i)^2 + \sum_{i,t}(\bar{u}_i - \bar{\bar{u}})^2$$

The resulting analysis of variance is shown in Table 10-2.

Looking first of all at the within-group mean square,

$$\sum_{i,t}(u_{it} - \bar{u}_i)^2 = \sum_{i,t}(\varepsilon_{it} - \bar{\varepsilon}_i)^2$$

Recall that if $x_1, x_2, \ldots, x_m$ are drawn at random from $x \sim N(0, \sigma_x^2)$,†

$$E\left\{\frac{\Sigma(x_i - \bar{x})^2}{m - 1}\right\} = \sigma_x^2$$

Thus
$$E\left\{\sum_{t=1}^{m}(\varepsilon_{it} - \bar{\varepsilon}_i)^2\right\} = (m - 1)\sigma_\varepsilon^2$$

and
$$E\left\{\sum_{i=1}^{p}\sum_{t=1}^{m}(\varepsilon_{it} - \bar{\varepsilon}_i)^2\right\} = p(m - 1)\sigma_\varepsilon^2$$

† The assumption of normality is not required for this result, only that $x \sim \text{iid}(0, \sigma_x^2)$.

Table 10-2 ANOVA of the disturbance term

Source	Sum of squares	Degrees of freedom	Mean square	Expected mean square
Between groups	$\sum_{i,t}(\bar{u}_i - \bar{\bar{u}})^2$	$p - 1$	$\frac{1}{p-1}\sum_{i,t}(\bar{u}_i - \bar{\bar{u}})^2$	$\sigma_\varepsilon^2 + m\sigma_\alpha^2$
Within groups	$\sum_{i,t}(u_{it} - \bar{u}_i)^2$	$p(m - 1)$	$\frac{1}{p(m-1)}\sum_{i,t}(u_{it} - \bar{u}_i)^2$	σ_ε^2
Total	$\sum_{i,t}(u_{it} - \bar{\bar{u}})^2$	$pm - 1$		

giving σ_ε^2 as the expected, within-group mean square. Similarly,

$$\sum_{i,t}(\bar{u}_i - \bar{\bar{u}})^2 = \sum_{i,t}(\alpha_i - \bar{\alpha})^2 + \sum_{i,t}(\bar{\varepsilon}_i - \bar{\bar{\varepsilon}})^2 + 2\sum_{i,t}(\alpha_i - \bar{\alpha})(\bar{\varepsilon}_i - \bar{\bar{\varepsilon}})$$

But
$$E\left\{\sum_{i=1}^{p}(\alpha_i - \bar{\alpha})^2\right\} = (p-1)\sigma_\alpha^2$$

and
$$E\left\{\sum_{i=1}^{p}(\bar{\varepsilon}_i - \bar{\bar{\varepsilon}})^2\right\} = (p-1)\frac{\sigma_\varepsilon^2}{m}$$

since the $\bar{\varepsilon}_i$ are drawn at random from $N(0, \sigma_\varepsilon^2/m)$. Thus

$$E\left\{\sum_{i,t}(\bar{u}_i - \bar{\bar{u}})^2\right\} = m(p-1)\sigma_\alpha^2 + (p-1)\sigma_\varepsilon^2$$

and the expected between-group mean square is $m\sigma_\alpha^2 + \sigma_\varepsilon^2$. The u_{it} in Table 10-2 are, of course, unobserved, but we can estimate the relevant disturbance variances by substituting estimated u's in these formulas.

The estimation procedures may be summarized as follows.

OLS on transformed data

1. Fit the basic model, Eq. (10-21), by OLS and obtain the $n \times 1$ vector $\hat{\mathbf{u}}$ of OLS residuals. Compute also the mean residual $\bar{\hat{u}}_i$ for each unit, and note that
$\bar{\bar{\hat{u}}} = 0$.
2. Compute

$$c = 1 - \sqrt{\frac{\sum_{i=1}^{p}\sum_{t=1}^{m}(\hat{u}_{it} - \bar{\hat{u}}_i)^2/p(m-1)}{m\sum_{i=1}^{p}(\bar{\hat{u}}_i - \bar{\bar{\hat{u}}})^2/(p-1)}}$$

3. Compute the quasi deviations $y_{it} = Y_{it} - c\bar{Y}_i$, and so on, and apply OLS.

The direct application of the GLS formula requires estimates of $\rho = \sigma_\alpha^2/\sigma_u^2$ and of σ_u^2. These are also obtained from the OLS residuals. The steps are as follows.

1. As in OLS procedure.
2. Compute

$$s_\varepsilon^2 = \frac{1}{p(m-1)} \sum_{i=1}^{p} \sum_{t=1}^{s} \left(\hat{u}_{it} - \bar{\hat{u}}_i\right)^2$$

$$s_\alpha^2 = \frac{1}{m}\left\{\frac{m}{p-1} \sum_{i=1}^{p} \left(\bar{\hat{u}}_i - \bar{\bar{\hat{u}}}\right)^2 - s_\varepsilon^2\right\}$$

$$s_u^2 = s_\alpha^2 + s_\varepsilon^2$$

$$\hat{\rho} = \frac{s_\alpha^2}{s_u^2}$$

3. Using $\hat{\rho}$ and s_u^2, compute **V** and the GLS estimator defined in Eq. (10-35).

The estimation of the variance component from the OLS residuals is *not* to be recommended when lagged values of Y appear in the **X** matrix. Since $\rho = \sigma_\alpha^2/(\sigma_\alpha^2 + \sigma_\varepsilon^2)$ is constrained to be in the (0, 1) interval, a grid search over this interval for the ML estimator is a feasible procedure.†

The final question with respect to model II is the choice between fitting either the fixed effects or the random effects model. The choice basically has to be made by the researcher based on the institutional realities relevant to the problem being studied. Returning to the examples given at the beginning of this section, suppose certain monetary/fiscal policies are set in place in an attempt to reduce unemployment rates across the country, and after some time an analysis is made of the experience of the various states. As a result of historical developments, the states have variable mixtures of industrial, commercial, private, and public structures. One would thus expect differential effects across states, which would be modeled appropriately by the fixed effects assumption. On the other hand, if we look at the per capita consumption of gasoline in the OECD countries, we will certainly observe very different levels of the dependent variable in different countries. However, it is also true that for tax and other reasons the real price of gasoline has historically been very different in different countries. For sound economic reasons this may be expected to have *long-run effects* on the size of automobiles and on per capita gasoline consumption. Inserting dummy variables to allow different intercepts across countries removes this variation from the data, and the "effects" of the explanatory variables are estimated solely from the within

† See P. Balestra and M. Nerlove, "Pooling Cross-Section and Time Series Data in the Estimation of a Dynamic Model: The Demand for Natural Gas," *Econometrica*, vol. 34, 1966, pp. 585–612; and G. S. Maddala, "The Use of Variance Components Models in Pooling Cross-Section and Time-Series Data," *Econometrica*, vol. 39, 1971, pp. 341–358.

estimator, Eq. (10-26), which is based on the within-country variation and is not influenced by the between-country variation. Thus a fixed effects model would be liable to underestimate the price elasticity. The random effects model would be equally inappropriate since it would attribute significant variations in consumption to unidentified stochastic factors rather than to price. In this case a more sensible estimator of long-run price and income effects would be obtained by computing the between estimator based on country (group) means. Averaging Eq. (10-19) over groups gives

$$\bar{Y}_i = \alpha + \beta_2 \bar{X}_{2i} + \cdots + \beta_k \bar{X}_{ki} + \bar{u}_i \qquad i = 1, \ldots, p$$

This is the same as transforming the original data by premultiplication by the **B** matrix defined earlier and computing the OLS estimator†

$$\begin{bmatrix} a \\ \mathbf{b} \end{bmatrix} = [[\mathbf{i}_n \quad \mathbf{X}]'\mathbf{B}[\mathbf{i}_n \quad \mathbf{X}]]^{-1}[\mathbf{i}_n \quad \mathbf{X}]'\mathbf{B}\mathbf{y} \tag{10-36}$$

The random effects model would seem appropriate when the decision units (say, households or firms) have been drawn from some population of such units. Conditional on the explanatory variables, there will be an average level of response in the population, and individual levels will vary around that average as a consequence of unidentified stochastic factors.

Looking at the statistic defined in Eq. (10-34), which produces the quasi deviations underlying the GLS (random effects) model, we see

1. As $m \to \infty$, $c \to 1$, and the GLS (random effects) estimator of $\boldsymbol{\beta}$ tends to the fixed effects estimator of $\boldsymbol{\beta}$.
2. As σ_α^2 becomes very large relative to σ_ε^2, $c \to 1$, and again the random effects and fixed effects estimators of $\boldsymbol{\beta}$ will tend to coincide.
3. As $\sigma_\alpha^2 \to 0$, $c \to 0$, and the random effects estimator would tend to the OLS estimator $(\mathbf{X}'\mathbf{X})^{-1}\mathbf{X}'\mathbf{y}$.

Returning to the taxonomy in Table 10-1, model III allows the intercept to vary over units *and* time periods, while retaining the assumption of a common $\boldsymbol{\beta}$ vector for all i, t. This again may be estimated by a fixed effects or random effects approach. The former extends Eq. (10-24) to include dummy variables for the time periods, taking care to use only $m - 1$ such dummies in order to avoid a singular data matrix. The random effects model postulates the disturbance to be

$$u_{it} = \alpha_i + \gamma_t + \varepsilon_{it}$$

where the γ's are assigned at random to the time periods from some postulated distribution. Just as α_i is assumed common to the ith unit for all time periods, so

† For a lucid and practical discussion of these issues see J. M. Griffin, *Energy Conservation in the OECD: 1980 to 2000*. Ballinger, Mass., 1979, Chap. 2.

is γ_t assumed common to all units in the tth time period. The extensions from model II are relatively straightforward, and we will not go into them here.†

Model IV allows both the intercept and the $\boldsymbol{\beta}$ vector, or some components of it, to vary across units. This model has already been studied in Sec. 6-2 under the simplest possible assumptions about the disturbance term and in Sec. 8-6 in the context of the SURE model. The random effects version of model IV might also be extended to allow for time-specific as well as unit-specific error components. In testing for the stability of the $\boldsymbol{\beta}$ vector (whether across unit or over time) it is then especially important to use the procedures of Sec. 8-6 with an appropriately specified variance matrix for the disturbance.‡

10-4 VARIABLE-PARAMETER MODELS

This topic has already appeared in several places. Sec. 6-2 on structural change investigated variations in some or all of the parameters of a relation, but it was known a priori at which point possible structural breaks might have occurred (peacetime, wartime, and so on). Section 10-2 on spline functions showed how different functions might be fitted so as to meet at the known join points. Section 10-3 on time-series and cross-section data considered many possible variations in parameters, but again, as in Sec. 6-2, there were obvious points at which such changes might be expected. Only in Sec. 10-1 on recursive residuals was there some discussion of the case where the $\boldsymbol{\beta}$ vector might change at unknown points.

We must now consider cases where there is no a priori information on the observational points at which structural changes might have taken place, and in this brief section we will consider just two possible approaches. The approach of switching regressions is based on the assumption that there is a known (small) number of different regimes, but the switching points are unknown. The other approach is based on the assumption of continuous parameter variation.

Switching Regimes

The simplest case of switching regimes is based on the assumption of just two different regimes. The switch may depend on time or on a "threshold" value for some variable, or it may be triggered stochastically. For instance, wage and price decisions may be different in periods of low inflation and in periods of high inflation. The pioneering treatment of switching regimes is due to Quandt.§ To

† Reference may be made to the articles by Maddala and by Balestra and Nerlove already cited, and also to T. D. Wallace and A. Hussain, "The Use of Error Component Models in Combining Cross-Section with Time-Series Data," *Econometrica*, vol. 37, 1969, pp. 55–72; and Y. Mundlak, "On the Pooling of Time-Series and Cross-Section Data," *Econometrica*, vol. 46, 1978, pp. 69–86.

‡ See Problem 10-7 and B. H. Baltagi, "An Experimental Study of Alternative Testing and Estimation Procedures in a Two-Way Error Component Model," *Journal of Econometrics*, vol. 17, 1981, pp. 21–49.

§ See S. M. Goldfeld and R. Quandt, *Studies in Nonlinear Estimation*, Ballinger, Mass., 1976, Chap. 1, and references therein.

illustrate the approach suppose we have $t = 1, \ldots, n$ sample observations and the hypothesis is that

$$\text{Regime 1:}\quad y_t = \alpha_1 + \beta_1 x_t + u_{1t} \text{ holds for } t \le t^*$$

$$\text{Regime 2:}\quad y_t = \alpha_2 + \beta_2 x_t + u_{2t} \text{ holds for } t > t^*$$

where t^* is unknown. Assuming the u's to be normally and independently distributed with zero means and variances σ_1^2 and σ_2^2, the log likelihood is

$$\ln L = -\frac{n}{2}\ln 2\pi - \frac{t^*}{2}\ln\sigma_1^2 - \frac{n-t^*}{2}\ln\sigma_2^2$$

$$-\frac{1}{2\sigma_1^2}\sum_{t=1}^{t^*}(y_t - \alpha_1 - \beta_1 x_t)^2 - \frac{1}{2\sigma_2^2}\sum_{t=t^*+1}^{n}(y_t - \alpha_2 - \beta_2 x_t)^2 \tag{10-37}$$

ML estimates of α_i, β_i, and σ_i^2 $(i = 1, 2)$ would be given by two separate OLS regressions for any assumed value of t^*. On replacing these parameters by their ML estimates the last two terms in Eq. (10-37) become

$$-\frac{t^*\hat{\sigma}_1^2}{2\hat{\sigma}_1^2} - \frac{(n-t^*)\hat{\sigma}_2^2}{2\hat{\sigma}_2^2} = -\frac{n}{2}$$

and so

$$\ln L = -\frac{n}{2}\ln 2\pi - \frac{n}{2} - \frac{t^*}{2}\ln\hat{\sigma}_1^2 - \frac{n-t^*}{2}\ln\hat{\sigma}_2^2 \tag{10-38}$$

An estimate of the switch point t^* could then be made by evaluating Eq. (10-38) for all possible values of t^* and choosing the one that maximizes the likelihood. With n sample observations and two variables the possible range for t^* is from $t^* = 3$ to $t^* = n - 3$, implying the calculation of $n - 5$ pairs of regressions. Riddell, however, has recently pointed out that the computational burden is considerably reduced by making use of recursive residuals.† Consider the set of *forward* recursive residuals $w_3, w_4, \ldots$. From Eq. (10-7) we have

$$\text{RSS}_t = \text{RSS}_{t-1} + w_t^2$$

Thus

$$\text{RSS}_{t^*} = \sum_{t=3}^{t^*} w_t^2$$

and

$$\hat{\sigma}_1^2(t^*) = \frac{\text{RSS}_{t^*}}{t^*}$$

In a similar fashion $\hat{\sigma}_2^2(t^*)$ can be constructed from the set of *backward* recursive residuals. Thus just two passes of a recursive residuals program will generate all the data required to find the maximum of Eq. (10-38).

† W. C. Riddell, "Estimating Switching Regressions: A Computational Note," *Journal of Statistical Computation and Simulation*, vol. 10, 1980, pp. 95–101.

The null hypothesis that no switch occurred may be examined by means of the likelihood ratio statistic.† Let

$$\lambda = \frac{L(\hat{\omega})}{L(\hat{\Omega})}$$

where $L(\hat{\Omega})$ is the unrestricted maximum of the likelihood function over the entire parameter space. In this example it is the antilogarithm of the maximum of Eq. (10-38) since it is assumed to be known that there is at most one switch point and the restriction of a single regression (no switch point) has not been imposed. $L(\hat{\omega})$ is the maximum of the likelihood function over the subspace $\omega \subset \Omega$ to which one is restricted by the hypothesis. In this problem it is the maximum value of the likelihood for a single regression. Under the hypothesis of no switch

$$\ln L(\hat{\omega}) = -\frac{n}{2}\ln 2\pi - \frac{n}{2} - \frac{n}{2}\ln \hat{\sigma}^2$$

where

$$\hat{\sigma}^2 = \sum_{t=1}^{n} \left(y_t - \hat{\alpha} - \hat{\beta}x_t\right)^2$$

$\hat{\alpha}$ and $\hat{\beta}$ being the OLS coefficients. Thus

$$\lambda = \frac{\left(\hat{\sigma}_1^2\right)^{t^*/2}\left(\hat{\sigma}_2^2\right)^{(n-t^*)/2}}{\left(\hat{\sigma}^2\right)^{n/2}}$$

The conditions required for $-2\ln\lambda$ to follow an approximate χ^2 distribution are not fulfilled since the likelihood function is only defined for integral values of t^*. However, the graph of λ (or $\ln\lambda$) against t can be instructive, as shown in Brown, Durbin, and Evans, especially when considered in conjunction with other tests.‡ For a discussion of procedures when the switch is triggered in various other deterministic or stochastic fashions the reader should consult Goldfeld and Quandt.§ A special case of switching regimes arises in the context of disequilibrium models where in some periods we have observations on the demand function and in others on the supply function.¶

† For a brief account of likelihood ratio tests see P. G. Hoel, *Introduction to Mathematical Statistics*, 4th edition, Wiley, New York, 1971, pp. 211–217.

‡ R. L. Brown, J. Durbin, and J. M. Evans, "Techniques for Testing the Constancy of Regression Relationships over Time," *Journal of the Royal Statistical Society*, ser. B, vol. 37, 1975, pp. 149–192, especially p. 161.

§ S. M. Goldfeld and R. Quandt, *Studies in Nonlinear Estimation*, Ballinger, Mass., 1976.

¶ A treatment of disequilibrium models is beyond the scope of this book. Some important references are R. C. Fair and D. M. Jaffee, "Methods of Estimation for Markets in Disequilibrium," *Econometrica*, vol. 40, 1972, pp. 497–514; R. C. Fair and H. H. Kelejian, "Methods of Estimation for Markets in Disequilibrium: A Further Study," *Econometrica*, vol. 42, 1974, pp. 177–190; T. Amemiya, "A Note on a Fair and Jaffee Model," *Econometrica*, vol. 42, 1974, pp. 759–762; G. S. Maddala and F. D. Nelson, "Maximum Likelihood Methods for Models of Markets in Disequilibrium," *Econometrica*, vol. 42, 1974, pp. 1013–1030; S. M. Goldfeld and R. E. Quandt, "Estimation in a Disequilibrium Model and the Value of Information," *Journal of Econometrics*, vol. 3, 1975, pp. 325–348.

Continuous Parameter Variation

The capacity of econometric theorists to "invent" new varieties of models with continuous parameter variation tends to exceed the willingness and sometimes even the computational ability of researchers to apply them to real-world situations. We will illustrate two main approaches, namely, random coefficient models and adaptive regression models, and in each case emphasize one or two major publications without attempting to give a comprehensive coverage of all recent theoretical developments.

Random coefficient models. The traditional single-equation model $\mathbf{y} = \mathbf{X}\boldsymbol{\beta} + \mathbf{u}$ puts the ignorance or uncertainty into the disturbance vector $\mathbf{u}$, while the $\boldsymbol{\beta}$ vector is assumed to be fixed at all sample points. An alternative assumption is to make the $\boldsymbol{\beta}$ vector stochastic and write the model as

$$Y_j = (\beta_1 + v_{1j}) + (\beta_2 + v_{2j})X_{2j} + \cdots + (\beta_k + v_{kj})X_{kj} \qquad j = 1, \ldots, n \tag{10-39}$$

The β's in Eq. (10-39) are unknown constants common to all sample points. The v_{ij} are stochastic variables which determine the coefficient vector for the jth sample point. The n sample points might, for example, be a cross section of households where important explanatory variables may be unobserved, and their influence affects slope coefficients as well as the disturbance term. The reaction of mortgage debt to, say, the measured rate of interest may well depend on the unobserved age of the head of household. There is no need to insert the usual equation disturbance term in Eq. (10-39) since it will merge with v_{1j}. Equation (10-39) may be rewritten as

$$Y_j = \mathbf{x}_j'\boldsymbol{\beta} + u_j \qquad j = 1, \ldots, n \tag{10-40}$$

where

$$u_j = \mathbf{x}_j'\mathbf{v}_j$$

$$\mathbf{x}_j' = \begin{bmatrix} 1 & X_{2j} & \cdots & X_{kj} \end{bmatrix}$$

$$\mathbf{v}_j' = \begin{bmatrix} v_{1j} & v_{2j} & \cdots & v_{kj} \end{bmatrix}$$

Assumptions about the $\mathbf{v}_j$ are required to make the model operational. A simple set of assumptions is

$$\begin{aligned} E(\mathbf{v}_j) &= \mathbf{0} && j = 1, \ldots, n \\ E(\mathbf{v}_j\mathbf{v}_j') &= \begin{bmatrix} \alpha_1 & 0 & \cdots & 0 \\ 0 & \alpha_2 & \cdots & 0 \\ \cdots & \cdots & \cdots & \cdots \\ 0 & 0 & \cdots & \alpha_k \end{bmatrix} = \mathbf{A} && j = 1, \ldots, n \\ E(\mathbf{v}_j\mathbf{v}_i') &= \mathbf{0} && i, j = 1, \ldots, n;\ i \neq j \end{aligned} \tag{10-41}$$

The stochastic elements in the coefficients are thus assumed to have zero means and to be uncorrelated between sample points and also between different coefficients for any given sample point. The last assumption is possibly the least plausible. If, for example, age has an effect on the reaction of mortgage debt to the rate of interest, it may have a related effect on the response to income. These, however, are the assumptions of the original Hildreth-Houck random coefficient model.†

From Eqs. (10-41) the disturbances in Eq. (10-40) have the following properties:

$$\begin{aligned} E(u_j) &= 0 & j &= 1,\ldots,n \\ E(u_j^2) &= E(\mathbf{x}_j'\mathbf{v}_j\mathbf{v}_j'\mathbf{x}_j) & j &= 1,\ldots,n \\ &= \mathbf{x}_j'\mathbf{A}\mathbf{x}_j \\ E(u_ju_i) &= 0 & i, j &= 1,\ldots,n;\ i \neq j \end{aligned}$$

Since $\mathbf{A}$ is diagonal, $\text{var}(u_j)$ simplifies to

$$\begin{aligned} \sigma_j^2 = E\left(u_j^2\right) &= \sum_{i=1}^{k} X_{ij}^2\alpha_i \\ &= \dot{\mathbf{x}}_j'\boldsymbol{\alpha} \end{aligned} \tag{10-42}$$

where $\dot{x}_j' = \begin{bmatrix}1 & X_{2j}^2 & \cdots & X_{kj}^2\end{bmatrix}$

and $\boldsymbol{\alpha}' = \begin{bmatrix}\alpha_1 & \alpha_2 & \cdots & \alpha_k\end{bmatrix}$

Thus Eq. (10-40) constitutes a model with a heteroscedastic disturbance term, the variance at each sample point being the same linear combination of the *squares* of the explanatory variables at that point. Collecting the n variances in Eq. (10-42) gives

$$\boldsymbol{\sigma}^2 = \begin{bmatrix}\sigma_1^2 \\ \vdots \\ \sigma_n^2\end{bmatrix} = \dot{\mathbf{X}}\boldsymbol{\alpha}$$

where $\dot{\mathbf{X}}$ denotes the matrix obtained from $\mathbf{X}$ by squaring each element. The form of this relation suggests that if estimates of the left-hand vector could be obtained, a regression on $\dot{\mathbf{X}}$ could yield an estimate of $\boldsymbol{\alpha}$. Looking at the residuals obtained from the OLS fit to Eq. (10-40), $\mathbf{e} = \mathbf{y} - \mathbf{Xb}$, we know from Chap. 5 that

$$E(\mathbf{ee}') = \mathbf{M}E(\mathbf{uu}')\mathbf{M} \tag{10-43}$$

where $\mathbf{M} = \mathbf{I} - \mathbf{X}(\mathbf{X}'\mathbf{X})^{-1}\mathbf{X}'$

† C. Hildreth and J. P. Houck, "Some Estimates for a Linear Model with Random Coefficients," *Journal of the American Statistical Association*, vol. 63, 1968, pp. 584–595.

It follows from Eq. (10-43) that

$$E(\dot{\mathbf{e}}) = \begin{bmatrix} Ee_1^2 \\ \vdots \\ Ee_n^2 \end{bmatrix} = \dot{\mathbf{M}}\boldsymbol{\sigma}^2$$

Thus

$$E(\dot{e}) = \dot{\mathbf{M}}\dot{\mathbf{X}}\boldsymbol{\alpha} \tag{10-44}$$

Equation (10-44) leads to the following procedure for constructing a feasible GLS estimator.

1. Fit OLS to Eq. (10-40) and square each residual to obtain the vector $\dot{\mathbf{e}}$.
2. Regress $\dot{\mathbf{e}}$ on $\dot{\mathbf{M}}\dot{\mathbf{X}}$, which can be constructed from the original data matrix $\mathbf{X}$, to obtain an estimated vector $\hat{\boldsymbol{\alpha}}$.
3. Substitute $\hat{\boldsymbol{\alpha}}$ in Eq. (10-42) to obtain estimates s_j^2 of the variances of the u's.
4. Using the s_j^2 obtain the GLS estimate of $\boldsymbol{\beta}$ in Eq. (10-40).

As Hildreth and Houck pointed out, there is no constraint on step 2 of this process that ensures that the $\hat{\alpha}$'s are all nonnegative. They suggest setting any negative $\hat{\alpha}$'s to zero. They also suggest a number of other methods of obtaining consistent estimators of $\boldsymbol{\beta}$, but it is difficult to know how to choose between them, and their small sample properties are unknown. A small sample test of the significance of the $\boldsymbol{\alpha}$ vector (that is, whether the v's have nonzero variances) might be based on the OLS regression of $\dot{\mathbf{e}}$ on $\dot{\mathbf{M}}\dot{\mathbf{X}}$, but the precise significance levels are unknown.

The Hildreth-Houck model is applicable to a sample where there is just one observation per unit. The Swamy model is designed for cross-section time-series data.† The data for the ith unit or group are modeled by

$$\mathbf{y}_i = \mathbf{X}_i(\boldsymbol{\beta} + \mathbf{v}_i) + \mathbf{u}_i \qquad i = 1,\ldots,p \tag{10-45}$$

There are p separate units with m sample observations on each. The $\mathbf{X}_i$ are all of order $m \times k$ and rank k. The $\boldsymbol{\beta}$ vector of k coefficients is common to all units. The $\mathbf{v}_i$ vectors model the stochastic variation of the coefficient vector across units. For all i, $j = 1,\ldots,p$ it is assumed that

$$\begin{aligned}
&1.\ E\mathbf{u}_i = \mathbf{0} \qquad E(\mathbf{u}_i\mathbf{u}_j') = \begin{cases} \sigma_{ii}\mathbf{I}_m & \text{if } i = j \\ \mathbf{0} & \text{if } i \neq j \end{cases} \\
&2.\ E\mathbf{v}_i = \mathbf{0} \\
&3.\ E(\mathbf{v}_i\mathbf{v}_j') = \begin{cases} \boldsymbol{\Delta} & \text{if } i = j \\ \mathbf{0} & \text{if } i \neq j \end{cases} \\
&4.\ \mathbf{v}_i \text{ and } \mathbf{u}_j \text{ are independent}
\end{aligned} \tag{10-46}$$

† P. A. V. B. Swamy, "Efficient Inference in a Random Coefficient Regression Model," *Econometrica*, vol. 38, 1970, pp. 311–323.

The model would be written in full as

$$\begin{bmatrix} \mathbf{y}_1 \\ \mathbf{y}_2 \\ \vdots \\ \mathbf{y}_p \end{bmatrix} = \begin{bmatrix} \mathbf{X}_1 \\ \mathbf{X}_2 \\ \vdots \\ \mathbf{X}_p \end{bmatrix} \boldsymbol{\beta} + \begin{bmatrix} \mathbf{X}_1 & \mathbf{0} & \cdots & \mathbf{0} \\ \mathbf{0} & \mathbf{X}_2 & \cdots & \mathbf{0} \\ \cdots & \cdots & \cdots & \cdots \\ \mathbf{0} & \mathbf{0} & \cdots & \mathbf{X}_p \end{bmatrix} \begin{bmatrix} \mathbf{v}_1 \\ \mathbf{v}_2 \\ \vdots \\ \mathbf{v}_p \end{bmatrix} + \begin{bmatrix} \mathbf{u}_1 \\ \mathbf{u}_2 \\ \vdots \\ \mathbf{u}_p \end{bmatrix} \tag{10-47}$$

The disturbance vector is the sum of the last two terms in this expression. Using the assumptions in Eqs. (10-46), the variance matrix for the composite disturbance term is

$$\mathbf{V} = \begin{bmatrix} \mathbf{X}_1 \Delta \mathbf{X}_1' + \sigma_{11}\mathbf{I}_m & \mathbf{0} & \cdots & \mathbf{0} \\ \mathbf{0} & \mathbf{X}_2 \Delta \mathbf{X}_2' + \sigma_{22}\mathbf{I}_m & \cdots & \mathbf{0} \\ \cdots & \cdots & \cdots & \cdots \\ \mathbf{0} & \mathbf{0} & \cdots & \mathbf{X}_p \Delta \mathbf{X}_p' + \sigma_{pp}\mathbf{I}_m \end{bmatrix} \tag{10-48}$$

A feasible GLS estimator of $\boldsymbol{\beta}$ could be constructed by first obtaining estimates of Δ and the σ_{ii} in $\mathbf{V}$. These estimates are obtained as follows.

1. Compute the OLS vectors for each unit separately, that is,

$$\mathbf{b}_i = (\mathbf{X}_i'\mathbf{X}_i)^{-1}\mathbf{X}_i'\mathbf{y}_i$$

and the vectors of OLS residuals $\mathbf{e}_i = \mathbf{y}_i - \mathbf{X}_i\mathbf{b}_i$.

2. An unbiased estimator of σ_{ii} is given by

$$s_{ii} = \frac{\mathbf{e}_i'\mathbf{e}_i}{m-k}$$

3. An unbiased estimator of Δ is given by

$$\hat{\Delta} = \frac{S_b}{p-1} - \frac{1}{p}\sum_{i=1}^{p} s_{ii}(\mathbf{X}_i'\mathbf{X}_i)^{-1}$$

where

$$S_b = \sum_{i=1}^{p} \mathbf{b}_i\mathbf{b}_i' - \frac{1}{p}\sum_{i=1}^{p}\mathbf{b}_i \sum_{i=1}^{p}\mathbf{b}_i'$$

4. Substitution in Eq. (10-48) gives $\hat{V}$ which may then be used to derive the feasible GLS estimator of $\boldsymbol{\beta}$ in Eq. (10-47) as

$$\mathbf{b}_* = (\mathbf{X}'\hat{\mathbf{V}}^{-1}\mathbf{X})^{-1}\mathbf{X}'\hat{\mathbf{V}}^{-1}\mathbf{y}$$

where $\mathbf{y}$ and $\mathbf{X}$ denote the stacked vector and matrix in Eq. (10-47). The estimated variance matrix is

$$\text{est var}(\mathbf{b}_*) = (\mathbf{X}'\hat{\mathbf{V}}^{-1}\mathbf{X})^{-1}$$

and the conventional tests on $\mathbf{b}_*$ would be valid asymptotically.

Before fitting Eq. (10-47) by the above procedure it is desirable to test whether the coefficient vectors are truly different across units. Letting $\boldsymbol{\beta}_i = \boldsymbol{\beta} + \mathbf{v}_i$

denote the $k \times 1$ vector of coefficients for the ith unit, we set up the null hypothesis

$$H_0: \quad \boldsymbol{\beta}_1 = \boldsymbol{\beta}_2 = \cdots = \boldsymbol{\beta}_p = \boldsymbol{\beta}$$

This hypothesis may be tested by computing the test statistic defined in Eq. (8-91) for the SURE model, where the $\boldsymbol{\Sigma}$ in that formula is the variance matrix of the u's defined in Eq. (10-46), line 1. The **R** matrix would be set up by reformulating the null hypothesis as

$$\begin{aligned} \boldsymbol{\beta}_1 &= \boldsymbol{\beta}_2 \\ \boldsymbol{\beta}_1 &= \boldsymbol{\beta}_3 \\ &\cdots \\ \boldsymbol{\beta}_1 &= \boldsymbol{\beta}_p \end{aligned}$$

However, as shown in Sec. 6-1, the same test statistic can be derived from the residual sums of squares from the restricted and unrestricted versions of the model. Under the null hypothesis the restricted model is

$$\begin{bmatrix} \mathbf{y}_1 \\ \vdots \\ \mathbf{y}_p \end{bmatrix} = \begin{bmatrix} \mathbf{X}_1 \\ \vdots \\ \mathbf{X}_p \end{bmatrix} \boldsymbol{\beta} + \begin{bmatrix} \mathbf{u}_1 \\ \vdots \\ \mathbf{u}_p \end{bmatrix}$$

and the unrestricted model is

$$\begin{bmatrix} \mathbf{y}_1 \\ \vdots \\ \mathbf{y}_p \end{bmatrix} = \begin{bmatrix} \mathbf{X}_1 & & \\ & \ddots & \\ & & \mathbf{X}_p \end{bmatrix} \begin{bmatrix} \boldsymbol{\beta}_1 \\ \vdots \\ \boldsymbol{\beta}_p \end{bmatrix} + \begin{bmatrix} \mathbf{u}_1 \\ \vdots \\ \mathbf{u}_p \end{bmatrix}$$

The assumptions about the $\mathbf{u}_i$ in Eq. (10-46), line 1, give

$$E(\mathbf{u}\mathbf{u}') = \begin{bmatrix} \sigma_{11} & & \\ & \ddots & \\ & & \sigma_{pp} \end{bmatrix} \otimes \mathbf{I}_m$$

Thus GLS estimates of each model are achieved by applying OLS to *transformed* variables, where the transformation is to divide the observations for the ith unit by $\sqrt{\sigma_{ii}}$ $(i = 1, \ldots, p)$. The residual sum of squares from the restricted model is then

$$\mathbf{e}_*'\mathbf{e}_* = \Sigma \frac{1}{\sigma_{ii}} \mathbf{y}_i'\mathbf{y}_i - \Sigma \frac{1}{\sigma_{ii}} \mathbf{y}_i'\mathbf{X}_i\mathbf{b}$$

where $$\mathbf{b} = \left(\Sigma \frac{1}{\sigma_{ii}} \mathbf{X}_i'\mathbf{X}_i \right)^{-1} \Sigma \frac{1}{\sigma_{ii}} \mathbf{X}_i'\mathbf{y}_i \tag{10-49}$$

and all summations are over $i = 1, \ldots, p$. The residual sum of squares from the unrestricted model is

$$\mathbf{e}'\mathbf{e} = \Sigma \frac{1}{\sigma_{ii}} \mathbf{y}_i'\mathbf{y}_i - \Sigma \frac{1}{\sigma_{ii}} \mathbf{y}_i'\mathbf{X}_i\mathbf{b}_i \tag{10-50}$$

where

$$\mathbf{b}_i = (\mathbf{X}_i'\mathbf{X}_i)^{-1}\mathbf{X}'_i\mathbf{y}_i \tag{10-51}$$

Thus

$$\begin{aligned}\mathbf{e}_*'\mathbf{e}_* - \mathbf{e}'\mathbf{e} &= \Sigma \frac{1}{\sigma_{ii}} \mathbf{y}_i'\mathbf{X}_i\mathbf{b}_i - \Sigma \frac{1}{\sigma_{ii}} \mathbf{y}_i'\mathbf{X}_i\mathbf{b} \\ &= \Sigma \frac{1}{\sigma_{ii}} (\mathbf{b}_i - \mathbf{b})'\mathbf{X}_i'\mathbf{y}_i \\ &= \Sigma \frac{1}{\sigma_{ii}} (\mathbf{b}_i - \mathbf{b})'\mathbf{X}_i'\mathbf{X}_i\mathbf{b}_i\end{aligned}$$

Finally it may be shown that†

$$\mathbf{e}_*'\mathbf{e}_* - \mathbf{e}'\mathbf{e} = \sum_{i=1}^{p} \frac{1}{\sigma_{ii}} (\mathbf{b}_i - \mathbf{b})'\mathbf{X}_i'\mathbf{X}_i(\mathbf{b}_i - \mathbf{b}) \tag{10-52}$$

where $\mathbf{b}$ and $\mathbf{b}_i$ are defined in Eqs. (10-49) and (10-51). If, in addition to the assumptions already made, the u's are normally distributed, then under the null hypothesis,

$$F = \frac{(\mathbf{e}_*'\mathbf{e}_* - \mathbf{e}'\mathbf{e})/k(p-1)}{\mathbf{e}'\mathbf{e}/p(m-k)} \sim F[k(p-1), p(m-k)]$$

This development has, however, used the unknown σ_{ii}. Replacing them by the estimated values s_{ii}, the same test statistic can be computed, but it will now just have asymptotic validity. This model has been extended to include lagged variables and more complicated assumptions about the $\mathbf{v}_i$ vectors.‡

Adaptive regression models. A different form of modeling variable-parameter schemes is the adaptive regression model associated mainly with the names of Cooley and Prescott.§ The model is designed for application to time-series data. We will illustrate the basic idea first of all with reference to the intercept term.

† See Problem 10-9.

‡ See P. A. V. B. Swamy, *Statistical Inference in Random Coefficient Regression Models*, Springer-Verlag, New York, 1971; P. A. V. B. Swamy, "Criteria, Constraints and Multicollinearity in Random Coefficient Regression Models," *Annals of Economic and Social Measurement*, vol. 2, 1973, pp. 429–450; and P. A. V. B. Swamy, "Linear Models with Random Coefficients," in P. Zarembka, Ed., *Frontiers in Econometrics*, Academic Press, New York, 1974.

§ T. F. Cooley and E. C. Prescott, "An Adaptive Regression Model," *International Economic Review*, vol. 14, 1973, pp. 364–371; T. F. Cooley and E. C. Prescott, "Tests of an Adaptive Regression Model," *Review of Economics and Statistics*, vol. 55, 1973, pp. 248–256; and T. F. Cooley and E. C. Prescott, "Systematic (Non-Random) Variation Models: Varying Parameter Regression: A Theory and Some Applications," *Annals of Economic and Social Measurement*, vol. 2, 1973, pp. 463–474.

Consider the relation

$$y_t = \alpha_t + \beta x_t + u_t \tag{10-53}$$

The additive disturbance u_t shifts the function up or down period by period. Cooley and Prescott make the additional assumption that the intercept term is subject to change according to

$$\alpha_t = \alpha_{t-1} + v_{t-1} \tag{10-54}$$

Assume the u's and v's to be independently distributed with zero means and variances σ_u^2 and σ_v^2 and assume also that u_t and v_s are independent for all t, s. The model is similar to the conventional regression with fixed parameters and an autoregressive disturbance process. The difference is that autoregressive shocks are subject to exponential decay while the effects of the v's persist. An AR(1) disturbance process would give

$$y_t = \alpha + \beta x_t + \left(\varepsilon_t + \rho\varepsilon_{t-1} + \rho^2\varepsilon_{t-2} + \cdots + \rho^{t-1}\varepsilon_1 + \rho^t u_0\right)$$

while the adaptive model gives

$$y_t = \alpha_0 + \beta x_t + \left(v_{t-1} + v_{t-2} + \cdots + v_0\right) + u_t$$

where α_0 is the intercept in the immediate presample period. One might estimate the adaptive model in the form just given, in which case the parameters would be α_0, β, σ_u^2, and σ_v^2. Cooley and Prescott, with an emphasis on forecasting, express the model in terms of α_{n+1}, the intercept in the first postsample period. From Eq. (10-54)

$$\alpha_{n+1} = \alpha_t + \sum_{s=t}^{n} v_s$$

Thus Eq. (10-53) may be written

$$y_t = \alpha_{n+1} + \beta x_t + w_t \tag{10-55}$$

where $$w_t = u_t - \sum_{s=t}^{n} v_s$$

Estimation of Eq. (10-55) is simplified by reparameterizing the disturbance variances as

$$\sigma_u^2 = (1-\gamma)\sigma^2 \qquad \sigma_v^2 = \gamma\sigma^2 \qquad 0 \le \gamma \le 1 \tag{10-56}$$

The larger γ, the greater is the importance of the "permanent" component v in the shift of the function relative to that of the transient component u. Using Eqs. (10-56) and the assumptions previously made about u and v gives the variance matrix of w as

$$E(\mathbf{ww}') = \sigma^2\boldsymbol{\Omega}$$

where

$$\boldsymbol{\Omega} = (1-\gamma)\begin{bmatrix} 1 & 0 & \cdots & 0 \\ 0 & 1 & \cdots & 0 \\ \cdots & \cdots & \cdots & \cdots \\ 0 & 0 & \cdots & 1 \end{bmatrix} + \gamma\begin{bmatrix} n & n-1 & \cdots & 3 & 2 & 1 \\ n-1 & n-1 & \cdots & 3 & 2 & 1 \\ \cdots & \cdots & \cdots & \cdots & \cdots & \cdots \\ 3 & 3 & \cdots & 3 & 2 & 1 \\ 2 & 2 & \cdots & 2 & 2 & 1 \\ 1 & 1 & \cdots & 1 & 1 & 1 \end{bmatrix} \tag{10-57}$$

If the u's and v's are normally distributed, the log likelihood is

$$\ln L = -\frac{n}{2}\ln 2\pi - \frac{n}{2}\ln\sigma^2 - \frac{1}{2}\ln|\mathbf{\Omega}| - \frac{1}{2\sigma^2}(\mathbf{y} - \mathbf{X\beta})'\mathbf{\Omega}^{-1}(\mathbf{y} - \mathbf{X\beta})$$

where $\mathbf{X\beta}$ represents the systematic part, $\alpha_{n+1} + \beta X_t$, of Eq. (10-55). If γ, and hence $\mathbf{\Omega}$, were known, the ML estimates of $\mathbf{\beta}$ and σ^2 could be computed from

$$\hat{\mathbf{\beta}} = (\mathbf{X}'\mathbf{\Omega}^{-1}\mathbf{X})^{-1}\mathbf{X}'\mathbf{\Omega}^{-1}\mathbf{y}$$

and

$$\hat{\sigma}^2 = (\mathbf{y} - \mathbf{X}\hat{\mathbf{\beta}})'\mathbf{\Omega}^{-1}(\mathbf{y} - \mathbf{X}\hat{\mathbf{\beta}})$$

However, γ is unknown, but it is confined to the interval (0, 1), which suggests a grid search. Substituting $\hat{\mathbf{\beta}}$ and $\hat{\sigma}^2$ for $\mathbf{\beta}$ and σ^2 in the log likelihood gives the concentrated function

$$\ln L = \text{constant} - \frac{n}{2}\ln s^2 - \frac{1}{2}\ln|\mathbf{\Omega}| \tag{10-58}$$

Maximizing Eq. (10-58) over γ yields $\hat{\gamma}$, which then gives $\hat{\mathbf{\Omega}}$. The feasible GLS estimators are then

$$\mathbf{b}_* = (\mathbf{X}'\hat{\mathbf{\Omega}}^{-1}\mathbf{X})^{-1}\mathbf{X}'\hat{\mathbf{\Omega}}^{-1}\mathbf{y}$$

and

$$s^2 = (\mathbf{y} - \mathbf{X}\mathbf{b}_*)'\hat{\mathbf{\Omega}}^{-1}(\mathbf{y} - \mathbf{X}\mathbf{b}_*)$$

The asymptotic distribution of $\mathbf{b}_*$ is normal with mean $\mathbf{\beta}$ and variance matrix $\sigma^2(\mathbf{X}'\mathbf{\Omega}^{-1}\mathbf{X})^{-1}$. The asymptotic variance matrix for (γ, σ^2) is more complicated and is given in the first of the Cooley-Prescott papers.

The idea of adaptive coefficients can obviously be extended to slopes as well as intercepts. This is done in the third of the Cooley-Prescott papers. To illustrate the treatment consider the three-variable model

$$Y_t = \begin{bmatrix} 1 & X_{2t} & X_{3t} \end{bmatrix} \begin{bmatrix} \beta_{1t} \\ \beta_{2t} \\ \beta_{3t} \end{bmatrix}$$

The assumptions now are

$$\begin{aligned} \beta_{it} &= \beta_{it}^p + u_{it} \\ \beta_{it}^p &= \beta_{i,t-1}^p + v_{it} \end{aligned} \qquad i = 1, 2, 3 \tag{10-59}$$

where the superscript p denotes the permanent part of a coefficient. The Cooley-Prescott assumptions about u_{it} and v_{it} are

$$\begin{aligned} \mathbf{u}_t &\sim N(\mathbf{0}, (1 - \gamma)\sigma^2\mathbf{\Sigma}_u) \\ \mathbf{v}_t &\sim N(\mathbf{0}, \gamma\sigma^2\mathbf{\Sigma}_v) \end{aligned} \qquad t = 1, \ldots, n \tag{10-60}$$

where $\mathbf{u}_t$ and $\mathbf{v}_t$ are 3×1 vectors. In addition the $\mathbf{u}_t$ and the $\mathbf{v}_t$ are serially independent, and $\mathbf{u}_t$ and $\mathbf{v}_s$ are independent for all s, t. The new feature is the appearance of the 3×3 variance matrices $\mathbf{\Sigma}_u$ and $\mathbf{\Sigma}_v$. *For the estimation method to work, these matrices have to be known up to scale factors.* Thus they can be normalized by setting, say, the element in the top left-hand position to unity. Writing $\boldsymbol{\Sigma}_u$ as

$$\boldsymbol{\Sigma}_u = \begin{bmatrix} 1 & 0 & 0 \\ 0 & \sigma_{22}^u & \sigma_{23}^u \\ 0 & \sigma_{23}^u & \sigma_{33}^u \end{bmatrix}$$

implies that u_{1t} is independent of u_{2t} and u_{3t} for all t, that the random components in β_2 and β_3 have variances proportional to σ_{22}^u and σ_{33}^u, respectively, and that these same random components have a covariance proportional to σ_{23}^u. If one has no reason to expect a nonzero covariance, σ_{23}^u is set at zero and $\boldsymbol{\Sigma}_u$ becomes diagonal with only two elements to specify. If one assumes that the intercept is the only coefficient subject to transitory changes and that the permanent changes are independent, the matrices become

$$\boldsymbol{\Sigma}_u = \begin{bmatrix} 1 & 0 & 0 \\ 0 & 0 & 0 \\ 0 & 0 & 0 \end{bmatrix} \qquad \boldsymbol{\Sigma}_v = \begin{bmatrix} 1 & 0 & 0 \\ 0 & \sigma_{22}^v & 0 \\ 0 & 0 & \sigma_{33}^v \end{bmatrix}$$

Finally if one assumes the slope coefficients to be constant, the matrices reduce to

$$\boldsymbol{\Sigma}_u = \boldsymbol{\Sigma}_v = \begin{bmatrix} 1 & 0 & 0 \\ 0 & 0 & 0 \\ 0 & 0 & 0 \end{bmatrix}$$

and

$$\beta_{1t} = \beta_{1t}^p + u_{1t}$$

$$\beta_{1t}^p = \beta_{1,t-1}^p + v_{1t}$$

which is simply another way of writing the adaptive intercept case already studied. The intercept is then β_{it}^p $(= \alpha_t)$, the equation disturbance is u_{1t}, and $\alpha_t = \alpha_{t-1} + v_{1t}$.

For the general case of variability in all coefficients Cooley and Prescott suggest that unless there is special a priori knowledge, one assumes the matrices $\boldsymbol{\Sigma}_u$ and $\boldsymbol{\Sigma}_v$ to be equal. In one practical application the diagonal elements in this common matrix were set equal to the estimated sampling variances of the parameters computed under the assumption of parameter constancy. The authors, however, report that losses in efficiency are surprisingly small, even for sizable errors, in specifying $\boldsymbol{\Sigma}_u$ and $\boldsymbol{\Sigma}_v$.

The general model may now be sketched briefly:

$$Y_t = \mathbf{x}_t'\boldsymbol{\beta}_t \qquad t = 1, \ldots, n$$

where $\mathbf{x}_t$ is the $k \times 1$ vector of explanatory variables at time t, including unity in the first position to take care of the intercept. The variable-parameter assumptions are

$$\boldsymbol{\beta}_t = \boldsymbol{\beta}_t^p + \mathbf{u}_t \qquad \boldsymbol{\beta}_t^p = \boldsymbol{\beta}_{t-1}^p + \mathbf{v}_t \qquad t = 1, \ldots, n$$

It then follows that

$$\boldsymbol{\beta}_{n+1}^p = \boldsymbol{\beta}_t^p + \sum_{s=t+1}^{n+1} \mathbf{v}_s$$

and so

$$Y_t = \mathbf{x}'_t \boldsymbol{\beta}^p_{n+1} + w_t \tag{10-61}$$

where

$$w_t = \mathbf{x}'_t \mathbf{u}_t - \mathbf{x}'_t \sum_{s=t+1}^{n+1} \mathbf{v}_s$$

and emphasis is placed on estimating the permanent coefficients for the first postsample period. The variance matrix for the disturbance term in Eq. (10-61) is

$$E(\mathbf{ww}') = \sigma^2[(1-\gamma)\mathbf{R} + \gamma\mathbf{Q}] = \sigma^2\boldsymbol{\Omega} \tag{10-62}$$

where **R** is a diagonal matrix with

$$r_{ii} = \mathbf{x}'_i \boldsymbol{\Sigma}_u \mathbf{x}_i$$

and **Q** is defined by

$$q_{ij} = \min(n-i+1, n-j+1)\mathbf{x}'_i \boldsymbol{\Sigma}_v \mathbf{x}_j$$

Given $\boldsymbol{\Sigma}_u$ and $\boldsymbol{\Sigma}_v$, **Q** depends only on γ. Thus a grid search over the (0, 1) interval will yield a $\hat{\gamma}$ which in turn gives $\hat{\boldsymbol{\Omega}}$ and the estimators

$$\mathbf{b}^p_{n+1} = (\mathbf{X}'\hat{\boldsymbol{\Omega}}^{-1}\mathbf{X})^{-1}\mathbf{X}'\hat{\boldsymbol{\Omega}}^{-1}\mathbf{y}$$

and

$$s^2 = \frac{(\mathbf{y} - \mathbf{X}\mathbf{b}^p_{n+1})'\hat{\boldsymbol{\Omega}}^{-1}(\mathbf{y} - \mathbf{X}\mathbf{b}^p_{n+1})}{n}$$

The grid search for $\hat{\gamma}$ is in terms of the concentrated likelihood function Eq. (10-58), with $\boldsymbol{\Omega}$ now defined in Eq. (10-62).

10-5 QUALITATIVE DEPENDENT VARIABLES

We saw in Sec. 6-3 on dummy variables that there was no essential difficulty in the incorporation of qualitative variables in the **X** matrix. It is, however, quite a different matter when the dependent variable is qualitative or categorical in nature. We may distinguish three main cases.

1. *Dichotomous, binary, or quantal responses*. These can be characterized by a variable Y which takes on the value one or zero according to which of two possible results occurs. For example, $Y_i = 1$ or 0 if individual i dies (lives); if person i goes to college (does not go to college); if family i goes abroad on vacation (does not go abroad); and so on.
2. *Polytomous responses*. This case refers to more than two possible responses. Thus a family may have
   - no vacation
   - a vacation in the United States
   - a vacation in Europe
   - a vacation elsewhere
3. *Limited dependent variable*. This includes both cases 1 and 2 as special cases, but is also more general. One may have a *quantitative* dependent variable

which is subject to some limit, whether upper or lower, or both. This is also referred to as the case of *censored*, or *truncated*, variables.

Space forbids a treatment of all three cases. We will concentrate on the basic ideas underlying the binary case, which are also the foundation for any treatment of the more complicated cases.

A Single Dichotomous Variable

Suppose the members of a union who have been on strike in a wage dispute are now being asked to vote on a specific wage increase w_0. Let us assume that each worker has a reservation wage increase and there is some distribution $f(w)$ of this figure over the population of workers. The response of an individual worker is denoted by the dichotomous variable

$$Y = \begin{cases} 1 & \text{if the worker accepts the offer} \\ 0 & \text{if the worker rejects the offer} \end{cases}$$

A worker accepts the offer if it exceeds his or her reservation figure. Thus the proportion of the population accepting the specific offer w_0 is given by

$$\pi_0 = \int_0^{w_0} f(w)\,dw \tag{10-63}$$

Management would clearly like to know as much as possible about the distribution $f(w)$. What value of w_0, for example, would be required in Eq. (10-63) to yield a probability in excess of, say, 0.5? If the distribution $f(w)$ remained constant over a sequence of contracts and various wage increases were subjected to ballots, estimation of the parameters of $f(w)$ would be a possibility. Alternatively, at a given period in time, one might imagine a government mediator sampling various groups of workers with a variety of hypothetical wage increases in an attempt to chart the $f(w)$ distribution.

The main use of this type of analysis has not been in economics but in bioassay.† Applications in economics are, however, increasing with the ever expanding supply of micropanel data. In bioassay a specific *dosage* z_0 of, say, a poison is administered to each member of a population (insect, animal, human). The *responses* of the individual members are presumed independent of each other. For a great variety of reasons the *tolerance* to the poison varies from individual to individual and may be described by some distribution $f(z)$. If the tolerance is less than the dosage, the individual succumbs to the poison. Thus the proportion of the population dying at dosage z_0 is

$$\pi_0 = \int_0^{z_0} f(z)\,dz$$

Finney suggests that the distribution of tolerances is often skew and approxi-

† Two basic references are D. J. Finney, *Probit Analysis*, 3d edition, Cambridge University Press, New York, 1971; and D. R. Cox, *The Analysis of Binary Data*, Methuen, London, 1970.

mately log normal. Thus a transformation of tolerances (and dosage) by

$$x = \ln z$$

will render $f(x)$ approximately normal. The dosage-response curve would then be represented by the cumulative normal distribution as shown in Fig. 10-3, where $x \sim N(\mu, \sigma^2)$. At dosage x_1 the proportion dying is read off from the curve as π_1, at x_2 the proportion is π_2, and so forth. The practical problem is now the estimation of μ and σ^2. Suppose, to this end, an experimenter selects a set of dosages $x_1, x_2, \ldots, x_k$. The ith dose is administered to n_i individuals and the proportion p_i dying is measured. On the assumption of a normal distribution for the tolerances the sample proportions will be scattered around the cumulative curve in Fig. 10-3. The use of p_i to estimate μ and σ^2 is difficult since p is a nonlinear function of x. The *probit* transformation linearizes the relationship and makes the estimation of μ and σ^2 relatively straightforward. First define

$$y = \frac{x - \mu}{\sigma}$$

Thus $$y \sim N(0, 1)$$

and any dosage x_i can also be expressed in terms of y. The probability of death with dosage x_0 is now given by

$$\pi_0 = F(y_0) \tag{10-64}$$

where $F(\cdot)$ is the cumulative standard normal distribution and $y_0 = (x_0 - \mu)/\sigma$. This is shown in Fig. 10-4, which is simply a repeat of Fig. 10-3 with the horizontal axis translated to y. Inverting Eq. (10-64) gives

$$F^{-1}(\pi_0) = y_0 = \frac{x_0 - \mu}{\sigma} \tag{10-65}$$

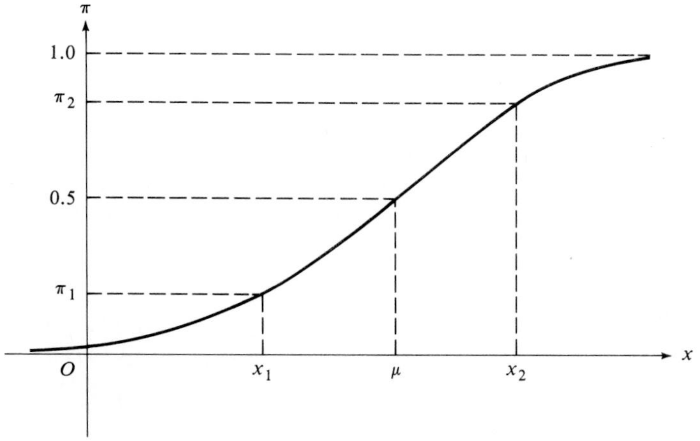

Figure 10-3

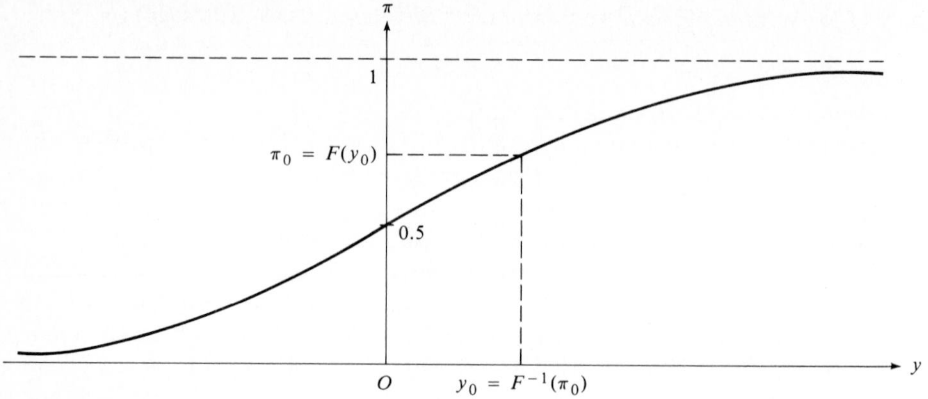

Figure 10-4

Given a value of y, one can read off the corresponding π. Conversely, given π, one can read off the corresponding value of y. The y variable is defined as the *normal equivalent deviate* (n.e.d.) or by the somewhat unattractive term "normit." A probit is defined as

$$\text{Probit} = y + 5$$

From Eq. (10-65) there is an exact linear relationship between the n.e.d. and dosage or, equivalently, between probit and dosage. The n.e.d. will be negative whenever $\pi < 0.5$, whereas the probit will almost never be negative.† Fisher and Yates give a table transforming percentages to probits.‡

In a typical experiment dosages $x_1, x_2, \ldots, x_g$ are administered to $n_1, n_2, \ldots, n_g$ subjects, respectively. The resultant proportions $p_1, p_2, \ldots, p_g$ are measured. The estimation procedure then follows directly from Eq. (10-65).

1. Convert the sample proportions $p_1, p_2, \ldots, p_g$ into n.e.d.'s and plot against dosage x.
2. If the scatter in step 1 is approximately linear, then fit the regression

$$\widehat{\text{NED}} = a + bx \tag{10-66}$$

where§

$$a = \text{estimate of } \frac{-\mu}{\sigma}$$

$$b = \text{estimate of } \frac{1}{\sigma}$$

† The number 5 was chosen to eliminate negative probits, since negative standard normal deviates with absolute values approaching 5 will almost never be found. As Finney explains, "At a time when most biologists lacked even simple calculating machines, and many had little skill in statistical arithmetic, avoidance of negative quantities was an appreciable practical advantage." D. J. Finney, op. cit., p. 23.

‡ R. A. Fisher and F. Yates, *Statistical Tables for Biological, Agricultural and Medical Research*, 6th edition, Oliver and Boyd, Edinburgh, 1963, Table IX.

§ If probits are used instead of n.e.d.'s, a is an estimate of $5 - \mu/\sigma$.

A simple OLS regression would be unbiased but inefficient since it ignores the properties of the error structure. A GLS estimator may be obtained by taking account of the likely nature of the errors. Write the sample proportions as

$$p_i = \pi_i + \varepsilon_i \qquad i = 1,\ldots, g$$

Thus†

$$p_i \sim \text{binomial}\left(\pi_i, \frac{\pi_i(1-\pi_i)}{n_i}\right)$$

The exact relationship is

$$F^{-1}(\pi_i) = -\frac{\mu}{\sigma} + \frac{1}{\sigma}x_i \qquad i = 1,\ldots, g$$

The computed n.e.d.'s are given by

$$F^{-1}(p_i) = F^{-1}(\pi_i + \varepsilon_i)$$

Applying a first-order Taylor expansion

$$F^{-1}(p_i) = F^{-1}(\pi_i) + \varepsilon_i \left.\frac{dF^{-1}}{dp_i}\right|_{p_i=\pi_i}$$

Thus

$$F^{-1}(p_i) = -\frac{\mu}{\sigma} + \frac{1}{\sigma}x_i + u_i \tag{10-67}$$

where

$$u_i = \varepsilon_i \left.\frac{dF^{-1}}{dp_i}\right|_{p_i=\pi_i}$$

Returning to

$$p_i = F(y_i) = \int_{-\infty}^{y_i} \frac{1}{2\pi} e^{-y^2/2}\, dy$$

$$\frac{dF}{dy_i} = \frac{1}{2\pi} e^{-y_i^2/2} = Z_i \qquad \text{ordinate of the standard normal curve at } y_i$$

Thus‡

$$\frac{dF^{-1}}{dp_i} = \frac{1}{Z_i}$$

† The binomial distribution applies since each individual in the ith group is subjected to dosage x_i and hence to a probability π_i of death or whatever. Moreover, individual responses are assumed to be independent of one another.

‡ $p = F(y)$ is a monotonic function, and so is its inverse. We have

$$dp = \frac{dF}{dy}dy \qquad \text{and} \qquad dy = \frac{dF^{-1}}{dp}dp$$

Thus

$$\frac{dF^{-1}}{dp} = \frac{dy}{dp} = \frac{1}{dF/dy}$$

and
$$\operatorname{var}(u_i) = \frac{\pi_i(1 - \pi_i)}{n_i Z_i^2} \tag{10-68}$$

The regression equation (10-67) thus has a heteroscedastic disturbance given by Eq. (10-68). Feasible GLS estimators would be achieved by computing a *weighted* regression of the empirical n.e.d.'s on dosage x using $n_i Z_i^2 / p_i(1 - p_i)$ as weights.

The next extension to consider is where the stimulus or dosage is not a single variable but some linear combination of variables. Thus the ith level of the stimulus might be denoted by†

$$s_i = \mathbf{x}_i'\boldsymbol{\beta}$$

where $\mathbf{x}_i$ is a column vector of k variables and $\boldsymbol{\beta}$ is a $k \times 1$ vector of coefficients presumed constant over all individuals. For example, in the question of whether or not to purchase a new car in a given year the $\mathbf{x}$ vector would include such variables as income, the relative prices of cars and gasoline, the age of the present car, and so forth. We still assume that each individual has a threshold level for car purchase, and we postulate a distribution $f(s)$ over the population, where s indicates the threshold or minimum stimulus required to trigger a new car purchase. Thus the probability of a car purchase at stimulus level s_i is

$$\pi_i = \int_{-\infty}^{s_i} f(s)\, ds$$

If the $f(s)$ distribution were normal with mean μ and variance σ^2, then

$$\pi_i = F\left(\frac{s_i - \mu}{\sigma}\right)$$

where $F(\cdot)$ again indicates the cumulative standard normal distribution. The observed sample proportions p_i are transformed into n.e.d.'s, and the appropriate regression is

$$y_i = F^{-1}(p_i) = F^{-1}(\pi_i) + u_i$$

or
$$y_i = \frac{s_i - \mu}{\sigma} + u_i = \frac{\mathbf{x}_i'\boldsymbol{\beta} - \mu}{\sigma} + u_i$$

The relationship actually estimated is then

$$y_i = \mathbf{x}_i'\boldsymbol{\beta}^* + u_i \qquad i = 1, \ldots, g \tag{10-69}$$

where
$$\boldsymbol{\beta}^* = \frac{1}{\sigma}\left[(\beta_1 - \mu) \quad \beta_2 \quad \cdots \quad \beta_k\right]'$$

Since p_i is still a binomial variable with mean π_i and variance $\pi_i(1 - \pi_i)/n_i$, the disturbance term u_i will have the same properties as above. Thus GLS may be applied to Eq. (10-69) with the correction for heteroscedasticity implied by Eq. (10-68).

† We are now using s (rather than x) to indicate stimulus or dosage, since we wish to use $\mathbf{x}_i$ to indicate a vector of explanatory variables, in conformity with the notation in regression analysis.

An obvious problem with the application of this model in economics is the difficulty of ensuring that n_i individuals are subjected to a given stimulus $\mathbf{x}'_i\boldsymbol{\beta}$. The $\boldsymbol{\beta}$ vector, of course, is unknown, but an appropriate method available with large data sets is to classify units into subsets with given values of explanatory variables such as income, age of car, and so on. A second problem is that we may have little justification for the normality assumption underlying the n.e.d. or probit approach. This may be explored by making different assumptions about the relationship between the probabilities π_i and the stimulus level $s_i = \mathbf{x}'_i\boldsymbol{\beta}$.

The simplest alternative assumption is that of a *linear* relationship, namely,

$$\pi_i = \mathbf{x}'_i\boldsymbol{\beta}$$

or

$$p_i = \mathbf{x}'_i\boldsymbol{\beta} + u_i$$

If this is estimated by OLS, or by GLS taking account of the heteroscedasticity in u, it may give a reasonable fit to "middle-range" data, but it is doomed to run into difficulty for extreme values of $\mathbf{x}'_i\boldsymbol{\beta}$ since there is nothing in either procedure to prevent *estimated* probabilities turning out to be negative or in excess of unity.

The more common and more sensible procedure is to model the probabilities π_i by some distribution function other than the cumulative normal. Perhaps the most frequently used is the *logistic*.† This may be formulated as

$$\pi_i = \frac{e^{\mathbf{x}'_i\boldsymbol{\beta}}}{1 + e^{\mathbf{x}'_i\boldsymbol{\beta}}} = \frac{1}{1 + e^{-\mathbf{x}'_i\boldsymbol{\beta}}} \tag{10-70}$$

Clearly, π is constrained to the (0, 1) interval. It increases monotonically with the stimulus $\mathbf{x}'\boldsymbol{\beta}$, it equals 0.5 when $\mathbf{x}'\boldsymbol{\beta} = 0$, and it has a shape similar to that of the cumulative normal.‡ It is, however, simpler to work with than the cumulative normal.

It follows directly from Eq. (10-70) that

$$\ln\left(\frac{\pi_i}{1 - \pi_i}\right) = \mathbf{x}'_i\boldsymbol{\beta} \tag{10-71}$$

that is, the logarithm of the odds ratio or *logit* is an exact linear function of the x's. As before, the observed sample proportions $p_i = \pi_i + \varepsilon_i$ follow the binomial distribution

$$p_i \sim \text{binomial}\left(\pi_i, \frac{\pi_i(1 - \pi_i)}{n_i}\right)$$

We seek a relationship between the observed logits and the true logits. Letting

$$f(p_i) = \ln\left(\frac{p_i}{1 - p_i}\right)$$

† The classic reference is D. McFadden, "Conditional Logit Analysis of Qualitative Choice Behavior," in P. Zarembka, Ed., *Frontiers in Econometrics*, Academic Press, New York, 1974, Chap. 4.

‡ See D. R. Cox, *The Analysis of Binary Data*, Methuen, London, 1970, p. 28, Table 2.1.

a first-order Taylor expansion around π_i gives

$$f(p_i) \simeq f(\pi_i) + \varepsilon_i \left.\frac{\partial f}{\partial p_i}\right|_{p_i=\pi_i}$$

and
$$\left.\frac{\partial f}{\partial p_i}\right|_{p_i=\pi_i} = \frac{1}{\pi_i(1-\pi_i)}$$

Thus

$$\ln\left(\frac{p_i}{1-p_i}\right) = \mathbf{x}_i'\boldsymbol{\beta} + u_i \tag{10-72}$$

where
$$u_i = \frac{\varepsilon_i}{\pi_i(1-\pi_i)}$$

so that

$$E(u_i) = 0 \qquad \text{and} \qquad \text{var}(u_i) = \frac{1}{n_i\pi_i(1-\pi_i)} \tag{10-73}$$

The appropriate estimation procedure is then as follows.

1. Compute the observed logits $\ln[p_i/(1-p_i)]$ from the sample proportions.
2. Carry out a GLS regression of Eq. (10-72) using the disturbance variances obtained from Eq. (10-73) by replacing the unknown π_i by p_i.

So far in both the probit and the logit approaches we have assumed that there were several observations at each level of the stimulus so that sample proportions could be computed. In some cases this may be infeasible and we just have a single observation, $y = 1$ or $y = 0$, at each $\mathbf{x}_i'\boldsymbol{\beta}$. The scatter would then look like Fig. 10-5.

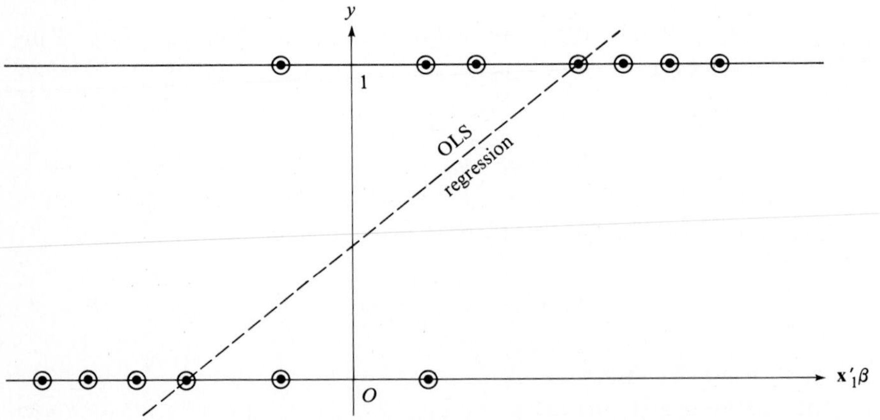

Figure 10-5

Fitting a linear regression of y on $\mathbf{x}'\boldsymbol{\beta}$ is unlikely to approximate the true probabilities over the middle range and gives nonsense results at the extremities. The logistic assumption, however, allows the derivation of a fairly simple ML estimator, which does not violate the constraints on the probability number.

For each of n individuals in the sample we now observe a $k \times 1$ vector $\mathbf{x}_i$ of stimulus variables and a response variable y_i $(i = 1, \ldots, n)$. The scalar stimulus experienced by an individual is given by $s_i = \mathbf{x}_i'\boldsymbol{\beta}$, and y_i is a dummy variable, taking the value unity when a response is observed and the value zero when there is no response. The probability of a response is assumed to be logistic, that is,

$$\pi_i = \Pr(y_i = 1) = \frac{e^{s_i}}{1 + e^{s_i}}$$

and

$$1 - \pi_i = \Pr(y_i = 0) = \frac{1}{1 + e^{s_i}} \tag{10-74}$$

Suppose that r responses and $n - r$ nonresponses occur in a sample. Let us reorder the sample observations so that the responses come first and the nonresponses last. The log likelihood is then

$$\ln L = \sum_{i=1}^{r} \ln \pi_i + \sum_{i=r+1}^{n} \ln(1 - \pi_i)$$

From Eqs. (10-74)

$$\frac{\partial \ln \pi_i}{\partial \boldsymbol{\beta}} = \left(1 - \frac{e^{s_i}}{1 + e^{s_i}}\right)\mathbf{x}_i = (1 - \pi_i)\mathbf{x}_i$$

and

$$\frac{\partial \ln(1 - \pi_i)}{\partial \boldsymbol{\beta}} = -\frac{e^{s_i}}{1 + e^{s_i}}\mathbf{x}_i = -\pi_i \mathbf{x}_i$$

Thus

$$\frac{\partial \ln L}{\partial \boldsymbol{\beta}} = \sum_{i=1}^{r} (1 - \pi_i)\mathbf{x}_i - \sum_{i=r+1}^{n} \pi_i \mathbf{x}_i$$

$$= \sum_{i=1}^{r} \mathbf{x}_i - \sum_{i=1}^{n} \pi_i \mathbf{x}_i$$

The ML estimates of $\boldsymbol{\beta}$ must then satisfy the equation

$$\sum_{i=1}^{r} \mathbf{x}_i = \sum_{i=1}^{n} \pi_i \mathbf{x}_i \tag{10-75}$$

The left-hand side is the sum of the $\mathbf{x}$ vectors just for the individuals displaying a response. The right-hand side is nonlinear in $\boldsymbol{\beta}$, and an iterative nonlinear program is required for the estimation of $\boldsymbol{\beta}$. The asymptotic standard errors may be obtained as follows. From Eqs. (10-74)

$$\frac{\partial \pi_i}{\partial s_i} = \frac{e^{s_i}}{(1 + e^{s_i})^2} = \pi_i(1 - \pi_i)$$

Thus

$$\frac{\partial \pi_i}{\partial \boldsymbol{\beta}} = \frac{\partial \pi_i}{\partial s_i} \cdot \frac{\partial s_i}{\partial \boldsymbol{\beta}} = \pi_i(1 - \pi_i)\mathbf{x}_i$$

and

$$\frac{\partial^2 \ln L}{\partial \boldsymbol{\beta}\, \partial \boldsymbol{\beta}'} = -\sum_{i=1}^{n} \mathbf{x}_i \frac{\partial \pi_i}{\partial \boldsymbol{\beta}} = -\sum_{i=1}^{n} \pi_i(1 - \pi_i)\mathbf{x}_i\mathbf{x}_i'$$

If the x's are treated as nonstochastic, the information matrix is

$$\mathbf{R}(\boldsymbol{\beta}) = \sum_{i=1}^{n} \pi_i(1 - \pi_i)\mathbf{x}_i\mathbf{x}_i'$$

and the asymptotic variance matrix is $R^{-1}(\boldsymbol{\beta})$.†

10-6 ERRORS IN VARIABLES

So far we have implicitly assumed that the X variables have been measured without error and that the only form of error in the equation has been in the disturbance term u. The latter has generally been thought of as representing the influence of various explanatory variables that have not actually been included in the relation. It could, of course, also have a component representing measurement error in the dependent variable Y, and the previous results would still be valid. We now pose the question of what happens if the X variables are subject to measurement error. We assume that the $\boldsymbol{\beta}$ vector represents the coefficients of the correctly measured X variables. Thus the model is assumed to be

$$\mathbf{y} = \tilde{\mathbf{X}}\boldsymbol{\beta} + \mathbf{u} \tag{10-76}$$

where $\tilde{\mathbf{X}}$ is the $n \times k$ matrix of the true (but *unobserved*) values of the explanatory variables. The matrix of *observed* values is

$$\mathbf{X} = \tilde{\mathbf{X}} + \mathbf{V} \tag{10-77}$$

where $\mathbf{V}$ is the $n \times k$ matrix of measurement errors. If some variables are measured without error, the appropriate columns of $\mathbf{V}$ are zero vectors. Combining Eqs. (10-76) and (10-77) gives the following relation between the observed variables:

$$\mathbf{y} = \mathbf{X}\boldsymbol{\beta} + (\mathbf{u} - \mathbf{V}\boldsymbol{\beta}) \tag{10-78}$$

The OLS estimator of $\boldsymbol{\beta}$ in Eq. (10-78) is then

$$\mathbf{b} = \boldsymbol{\beta} + (\mathbf{X}'\mathbf{X})^{-1}\mathbf{X}'(\mathbf{u} - \mathbf{V}\boldsymbol{\beta})$$

Conventional assumptions about the error terms are as follows.

† For extensions of the material in this section the reader should refer to the works of Cox and Finney already cited; also to M. Nerlove and S. J. Press, *Univariate and Multivariate Log-Linear and Logistic Models*, Rand Corporation, R-1306-EDA/NIH, 1973; G. G. Judge et al., *The Theory and Practice of Econometrics*, Wiley, New York, 1980, Chap. 14; and T. Amemya, "Qualitative Response Models: A Survey," *Journal of Economic Literature*, vol. 19, 1981, pp. 1483–1536.

1. The measurement errors in $\mathbf{X}$ are uncorrelated in the limit with the true values $\tilde{\mathbf{X}}$. Thus

$$\operatorname{plim}\left(\frac{1}{n}\tilde{\mathbf{X}}'\mathbf{V}\right) = \mathbf{0}$$

and so

$$\operatorname{plim}\left(\frac{1}{n}\mathbf{X}'\mathbf{X}\right) = \operatorname{plim}\left(\frac{1}{n}\tilde{\mathbf{X}}'\tilde{\mathbf{X}}\right) + \operatorname{plim}\left(\frac{1}{n}\mathbf{V}'\mathbf{V}\right)$$
$$= \boldsymbol{\Sigma} + \boldsymbol{\Omega}$$

2. The equation disturbance (plus any measurement error in Y) is uncorrelated in the limit both with $\tilde{\mathbf{X}}$ and $\mathbf{V}$, that is,

$$\operatorname{plim}\left(\frac{1}{n}\mathbf{V}'\mathbf{u}\right) = \mathbf{0} \qquad \text{and} \qquad \operatorname{plim}\left(\frac{1}{n}\tilde{\mathbf{X}}'\mathbf{u}\right) = \mathbf{0}$$

With these assumptions

$$\operatorname{plim}\mathbf{b} = \boldsymbol{\beta} - (\boldsymbol{\Sigma} + \boldsymbol{\Omega})^{-1}\boldsymbol{\Omega}\boldsymbol{\beta} \tag{10-79}$$

and so OLS estimates are inconsistent. The inconsistency is due to the correlation between the data matrix $\mathbf{X}$ and the composite disturbance term $(\mathbf{u} - \mathbf{V}\boldsymbol{\beta})$ in Eq. (10-78).

As an illustration of the result consider the two-variable model

$$Y_t = \alpha + \beta\tilde{X}_t + u_t$$

where

$$X_t = \tilde{X}_t + v_t$$

Then

$$\boldsymbol{\Sigma} = \operatorname{plim}\left(\frac{1}{n}\tilde{\mathbf{X}}'\tilde{\mathbf{X}}\right) = \operatorname{plim}\begin{bmatrix} 1 & \frac{1}{n}\Sigma\tilde{X}_t \\ \frac{1}{n}\Sigma\tilde{X}_t & \frac{1}{n}\Sigma\tilde{X}_t^2 \end{bmatrix}$$
$$= \begin{bmatrix} 1 & \mu \\ \mu & \mu^2 + \sigma^2 \end{bmatrix}$$

where μ and σ^2 denote, respectively, the mean and the variance of $\tilde{X}$. Further

$$\boldsymbol{\Omega} = \operatorname{plim}\left(\frac{1}{n}\mathbf{V}'\mathbf{V}\right) = \operatorname{plim}\begin{bmatrix} 0 & 0 \\ 0 & \frac{1}{n}\Sigma v_t^2 \end{bmatrix}$$
$$= \begin{bmatrix} 0 & 0 \\ 0 & \sigma_v^2 \end{bmatrix}$$

since there is no error in the dummy variable for the intercept term. Substitution in Eq. (10-79) gives

$$\operatorname{plim}\begin{bmatrix} a \\ b \end{bmatrix} = \begin{bmatrix} \alpha \\ \beta \end{bmatrix} - \frac{1}{\sigma^2 + \sigma_v^2}\begin{bmatrix} -\mu\sigma_v^2\beta \\ \sigma_v^2\beta \end{bmatrix}$$

from which

$$\text{plim}(b) = \beta - \frac{\sigma_v^2 \beta}{\sigma^2 + \sigma_v^2} = \frac{\beta}{1 + \sigma_v^2/\sigma^2}$$

Errors of measurement in X thus bias the estimate of β downward. The percentage bias is approximately given by the error variance as a percentage of the variance of the X values. The estimate of the intercept is also inconsistent, and this result extends to the multivariate case: even if some explanatory variables are measured correctly, all coefficients will in general be inconsistent.

The measurement error in the X variables thus poses a possibly serious estimation problem, and alternative estimators are required. There are two main types of estimator described in the literature. One is based on instrumental variables of various kinds and the other on ML methods, buttressed with fairly strong assumptions about the covariance matrix of the measurement errors. Before describing the estimators it is worth emphasizing the possibility that in certain circumstances economic agents may react to the measured values rather than the true values of economic variables. Firms may base investment decisions on some extrapolation of national income trends and in so doing will use the latest national income statistics complete with such errors as they contain. If decision makers respond to measured data, then the measurement error is irrelevant and our previous techniques will be valid.

Instrumental Variable Estimators

The IV method requires a matrix $\mathbf{Z}$ of variables which are correlated with the true $\tilde{\mathbf{X}}$ but uncorrelated in the limit with the measurement errors $\mathbf{V}$. The IV estimator is

$$\mathbf{b}_{\text{IV}} = (\mathbf{Z}'\mathbf{X})^{-1}\mathbf{Z}'\mathbf{y} \tag{10-80}$$

which will then be consistent and have asymptotic variance matrix

$$\text{asy var}(\mathbf{b})_{\text{IV}} = \sigma_u^2 (\mathbf{Z}'\mathbf{X})^{-1}\mathbf{Z}'\mathbf{Z}(\mathbf{X}'\mathbf{Z})^{-1}$$

To illustrate some of the instrumental variables that have been suggested, consider first the two-variable model, which may be written

$$Y_t = \alpha + \beta X_t + (u_t - \beta v_t)$$

Suppose there is an even number of sample observations. Define $\mathbf{Z}$ as

$$\mathbf{Z}' = \begin{bmatrix} 1 & 1 & 1 & \cdots & 1 \\ -1 & 1 & 1 & \cdots & -1 \end{bmatrix}$$

where the elements in the second row are plus or minus 1 according to whether the corresponding value of X is above or below the median X value. Application of Eq. (10-80) then gives

$$\begin{bmatrix} a_{\text{IV}} \\ b_{\text{IV}} \end{bmatrix} = \begin{bmatrix} n & n\bar{X} \\ 0 & \frac{n}{2}(\bar{X}_2 - \bar{X}_1) \end{bmatrix}^{-1} \begin{bmatrix} n\bar{Y} \\ \frac{n}{2}(\bar{Y}_2 - \bar{Y}_1) \end{bmatrix}$$

where $\bar{X}_2$ and $\bar{X}_1$ denote the means of the values above and below the median and $\bar{Y}_2$ and $\bar{Y}_1$ the means of the corresponding Y values. The estimator of the slope is

$$b_{\mathrm{IV}} = \frac{\bar{Y}_2 - \bar{Y}_1}{\bar{X}_2 - \bar{X}_1}$$

and the intercept is estimated by

$$a_{\mathrm{IV}} = \bar{Y} - b\bar{X}$$

This procedure amounts to partitioning the data into two subsets by the median X value and passing a straight line through the mean points $(\bar{X}_1, \bar{Y}_1)$ and $(\bar{X}_2, \bar{Y}_2)$. If n is odd, one should omit the central observation before beginning the computations. This estimator was first proposed by Wald.† Under fairly general conditions the Wald estimator is consistent but likely to have a large sampling variance. Bartlett has shown that the efficiency may be increased by dividing the X values into approximately three equally sized groups, the first containing the $n/3$ smallest X values and the third the $n/3$ greatest X values.‡ Omitting the central $n/3$ observation, the slope is estimated by

$$b_{\mathrm{IV}} = \frac{\bar{Y}_3 - \bar{Y}_1}{\bar{X}_3 - \bar{X}_1}$$

and the intercept as usual by $a_{\mathrm{IV}} = \bar{Y} - b\bar{X}$.

Extension of the grouping methods of Wald and Bartlett to more than one explanatory variable is cumbersome and tedious. A somewhat different IV estimator suggested by Durbin does not have this drawback.§ The suggestion is to rank the X values in ascending order and then define the **Z** matrix as

$$\mathbf{Z}' = \begin{bmatrix} 1 & 1 & 1 & \cdots & 1 \\ 1 & 2 & 3 & \cdots & n \end{bmatrix}$$

where the second row indicates the rank values of the X's.¶ Substitution in Eq. (10-80) then gives the estimate of the slope as

$$b_{\mathrm{IV}} = \frac{\sum_{i=1}^{n} i y_i}{\sum_{i=1}^{n} i x_i} \tag{10-81}$$

where $y_i = Y_i - \bar{Y}$ and $x_i = X_i - \bar{X}$. The estimate of the intercept turns out to be

$$a_{\mathrm{IV}} = \frac{\bar{Y}\Sigma i X_i - \bar{X}\Sigma i Y_i}{\Sigma i x_i} \tag{10-82}$$

† A. Wald, "The Fitting of Straight Lines if Both Variables Are Subject to Error," *Annals of Mathematical Statistics*, vol. 11, 1940, pp. 284–300.

‡ M. S. Bartlett, "Fitting a Straight Line when Both Variables Are Subject to Error," *Biometrics*, vol. 5, 1949, pp. 207–212. It is easily seen that this is equivalent to making the second row in **Z**′ consist of equal numbers of zeros and plus and minus ones according to the ranks of the X values.

§ J. M. Durbin, "Errors in Variables," *Review of the International Statistical Institute*, vol. 22, 1954, pp. 23–32.

¶ With this formulation plim$((1/n)\mathbf{Z}'\mathbf{Z})$ would not exist as required for the consistency of the IV estimator. However, if the second row is replaced by $1/n, 2/n, \ldots, 1$, the condition will be satisfied and the same estimates as in Eqs. (10-81) and (10-82) will result.

This procedure can easily be extended to replace additional explanatory variables by their ranks. Asymptotic standard errors may be estimated by the usual IV formula. It is likely that the instrumental variables for these grouping schemes will not be highly correlated with the X variables. Thus the IV estimators will probably have fairly large standard errors compared with those of OLS, which is the price that has to be paid for consistency.

To illustrate ML methods, which depend on some specific prior knowledge of the disturbance variances, consider again the two-variable model

$$\begin{aligned} Y_t &= \alpha + \beta \tilde{X}_t + u_t \\ \text{with} \qquad X_t &= \tilde{X}_t + v_t \end{aligned} \qquad t = 1, \cdots, n \tag{10-83}$$

where X denotes the observed value and $\tilde{X}$ the true unobserved value. The u term is an amalgam of the conventional disturbance term and any measurement error in Y. Thus the model might be written equivalently as an *exact* relation between two variables, both subject to error, that is,

$$\begin{aligned} \tilde{Y}_t &= \alpha + \beta \tilde{X}_t \\ \text{with} \qquad Y_t &= \tilde{Y}_t + u_t \qquad \text{and} \qquad \tilde{X}_t = X_t + v_t \end{aligned} \tag{10-84}$$

The errors u_t and v_t are assumed to follow normal distributions with the following properties:

$$\begin{aligned} E(u_t) = E(v_t) = 0 \qquad E(u_t^2) &= \sigma_u^2 \qquad E(v_t^2) = \sigma_v^2 \qquad \text{for all } t \\ E(u_t u_s) = E(v_t v_s) &= 0 \qquad s \neq t \\ E(u_t v_s) &= 0 \qquad \text{for all } s, t \end{aligned} \tag{10-85}$$

Thus the errors are taken to be serially and mutually independent. The relation between the errors and the true $\tilde{X}$, $\tilde{Y}$ values depends on the nature of these latter variables. We will distinguish two cases.

Case 10-1. $\tilde{X}_1, \tilde{X}_2, \ldots, \tilde{X}_n$ are a set of given numbers. This case has two possible interpretations. One is that the set of $\tilde{X}$'s can be held fixed in repeated sampling. This situation would be of little interest, even in the experimental sciences, for if the $\tilde{X}$'s are truly unobservable, how can the experimenter know that they have been held constant in repeated trials. The more useful interpretation, especially in the social sciences, is the one treating the $\tilde{X}$'s as fixed amounts to making inferences *conditional* on the set of $\tilde{X}$'s underlying the sample observations.

Case 10-2. The $\tilde{X}$'s are random drawings from a normal distribution with mean μ and variance σ^2. This is hardly a plausible description of the generating mechanism of most economic variables, but this case leads to the simplest estimating equations and there are interesting parallels between the estimators in the two cases.

If the $\tilde{X}$'s are fixed, then so are the $\tilde{Y}$'s, and the assumptions already made in Eq. (10-85) would ensure zero covariances between errors and true values.

Specifically

$$E(\tilde{X}_t u_t) = E(\tilde{X}_t v_t) = E(\tilde{Y}_t u_t) = E(\tilde{Y}_t v_t) = 0 \qquad \text{for all } t \qquad (10\text{-}86)$$

If, however, the assumptions of Case 10-2 apply and the $\tilde{X}$'s and hence the $\tilde{Y}$'s are random variables, the conditions in Eq. (10-86) would constitute an additional set of assumptions.

Estimation of Case 10-2. Given the assumptions listed above, the observed X, Y values would come from a bivariate normal distribution which is fully determined by the following five parameters:

$$\begin{aligned} E(X) &= E(\tilde{X}) = \mu \\ E(Y) &= E(\tilde{Y}) = \alpha + \beta\mu \\ \text{var}(X) &= \sigma^2 + \sigma_v^2 \\ \text{var}(Y) &= \sigma_{\tilde{y}}^2 + \sigma_u^2 = \beta^2\sigma^2 + \sigma_u^2 \\ \text{cov}(X, Y) &= \text{cov}(\tilde{X}, \tilde{Y}) = \beta\sigma^2 \end{aligned} \qquad (10\text{-}87)$$

The ML estimates of the parameters on the left-hand side of Eqs. (10-87) are given by the corresponding sample statistics, and we then hope to solve the resultant equations for estimates of the parameters of the model. The estimating equations for $\alpha, \beta, \ldots$ are

$$\begin{aligned} \bar{X} &= \hat{\mu} \\ \bar{Y} &= \hat{\alpha} + \hat{\beta}\hat{\mu} \\ m_{xx} &= \hat{\sigma}^2 + \hat{\sigma}_v^2 \\ m_{yy} &= \hat{\beta}^2\hat{\sigma}^2 + \hat{\sigma}_u^2 \\ m_{xy} &= \hat{\beta}\hat{\sigma}^2 \end{aligned} \qquad (10\text{-}88)$$

where the m's indicate second-order moments of the sample data, that is,

$$m_{xy} = \frac{1}{n}\sum_{t=1}^{n}(X_t - \bar{X})(Y_t - \bar{Y})$$

and so on. The dilemma with Eqs. (10-88) is that there are six unknowns but only five equations. Only μ is identifiable and estimable. There is no hope of estimating the other parameters unless additional information can be brought to bear. Three possible sources of additional information are conventionally considered.

1. *Knowledge of* σ_v^2. It is becoming more common for economic statisticians to indicate the approximate degree of error in major statistical series. Thus in some circumstances it may be possible to gauge the probable error in the explanatory variable and to replace σ_v^2 by an estimate s_v^2. The third and fifth equations in Eq. (10-88) then give

$$\hat{\beta} = \frac{m_{xy}}{m_{xx} - s_v^2} \qquad (10\text{-}89)$$

Thus the sample variance in X is reduced by the estimated error variance before dividing into the covariance term. If there were zero measurement error in X, Eq. (10-89) reduces to the slope of the OLS regression of Y on X. The first and second equations in Eqs. (10-88) give

$$\hat{\alpha} = \bar{Y} - \hat{\beta}\bar{X} \tag{10-90}$$

2. *Knowledge of* σ_u^2. This is perhaps a less likely situation than prior knowledge of σ_v^2 since σ_u^2 incorporates both the measurement error in Y and also the conventional equation error. If, however, we have a prior estimate s_u^2, the fourth and fifth equations in Eq. (10-88) yield

$$\hat{\beta} = \frac{m_{yy} - s_u^2}{m_{xy}} \tag{10-91}$$

If s_u^2 were zero, this estimate becomes the reciprocal of the slope in the OLS regression of X on Y.

3. *Knowledge of the ratio* $\lambda = \sigma_u^2/\sigma_v^2$. After some manipulation the last three equations of Eq. (10-88) now give

$$m_{xy}\hat{\beta}^2 - (m_{yy} - \lambda m_{xx})\hat{\beta} - \lambda m_{xy} = 0 \tag{10-92}$$

with roots

$$\hat{\beta} = \frac{(m_{yy} - \lambda m_{xx}) \pm \sqrt{(m_{yy} - \lambda m_{xx})^2 + 4\lambda m_{xy}^2}}{2m_{xy}} \tag{10-93}$$

The sign of $\hat{\beta}$ must be the same as that of m_{xy}. This will be so only if the numerator of Eq. (10-93) is positive, and that in turn will be so only if the positive sign before the square root is taken. Thus the estimator is

$$\hat{\beta} = \frac{(m_{yy} - \lambda m_{xx}) + \sqrt{(m_{yy} - \lambda m_{xx})^2 + 4\lambda m_{xy}^2}}{2m_{xy}} \tag{10-94}$$

Estimation of Case 10-1. We now assume that there is a set of unknown values $\tilde{X}_1, \tilde{X}_2, \ldots, \tilde{X}_n$ underlying the sample data, and we wish to make inferences conditional on this set. We still retain assumptions (10-84) and (10-85). The log likelihood function is

$$\ln L = \text{constant} - \frac{n}{2}\ln\sigma_u^2 - \frac{n}{2}\ln\sigma_v^2 - \frac{1}{2\sigma_v^2}\sum_{i=1}^{n}(X_i - \tilde{X}_i)^2 - \frac{1}{2\sigma_u^2}\sum_{i=1}^{n}(Y_i - \alpha - \beta\tilde{X}_i)^2 \tag{10-95}$$

The major difficulty is that the likelihood function now contains $n + 4$ parameters, namely, α, β, σ_u^2, σ_v^2, and the n values of $\tilde{X}$. Straightforward maximization of

Eq. (10-95) leads to unacceptable results.† The situation cannot be rescued by increasing the sample size since this automatically increases the number of unknown $\tilde{X}$'s. It can, however, be improved by the use of prior knowledge, typically that $\lambda = \sigma_u^2/\sigma_v^2$ is known. Making this substitution in the log likelihood and carrying through the maximization process gives exactly the same quadratic in $\hat{\beta}$ as already derived in Eq. (10-92) for Case 10-2.‡ Thus the $\hat{\beta}$ defined in Eq. (10-94) is the ML estimator for Case 10-1.

The range of λ is zero to infinity. The extremes correspond to the two simple regressions in Case 10-2, information 1 and 2. The estimator defined in Eq. (10-94), which is based on a known λ, will lie between the two OLS regression lines. This estimator is a consistent estimator of β. Kendall and Stuart show that a consistent estimator of σ_u^2 is provided by

$$\hat{\sigma}_u^2 = \frac{2n}{n-2} \cdot \frac{\lambda}{2(\lambda + \hat{\beta}^2)} \left(m_{yy} - 2\hat{\beta} m_{xy} + \hat{\beta}^2 m_{xx} \right) \tag{10-96}$$

The hypothesis H_0: $\beta = 0$ may be tested by computing the sample correlation coefficient

$$r = \frac{m_{xy}}{\sqrt{m_{xx} m_{yy}}}$$

and using the result that, under the null hypothesis,

$$\frac{r\sqrt{n-2}}{\sqrt{1-r^2}} \sim t(n-2)$$

The computation of a confidence interval for β is somewhat more complicated.§ Define the angle $\hat{\theta}$ by $\hat{\beta} = \tan \hat{\theta}$, or $\hat{\theta} = \arctan \hat{\beta}$. The 95 percent confidence interval for θ is given by

$$\hat{\theta} \pm \frac{1}{2} \arcsin \left\{ 2t_{0.025} \left[\frac{m_{xx} m_{yy} - m_{xy}^2}{(n-2)\left[(m_{xx} - m_{yy})^2 + 4m_{xy}^2 \right]} \right]^{1/2} \right\} \tag{10-97}$$

The corresponding limits for β are the tangents of these angles. The assumptions required for the development of Eq. (10-97) render this essentially a large sample method, and, of course, all the above rests on exact knowledge of λ, which is not often likely to be forthcoming. The technique may be extended to a multivariate regression if the investigator has knowledge of the ratios of all the error variances. Details are given in the Kendall and Stuart treatise.

† See M. G. Kendall and A. Stuart, *The Advanced Theory of Statistics*, vol. 2, Griffin, London, 1961, pp. 383 ff.

‡ M. G. Kendall and A. Stuart, op. cit., pp. 385–386.

§ M. G. Kendall and A. Stuart, op. cit., pp. 388–391.

PROBLEMS

10-1 Prove Eq. (10-5) by the method suggested in the text. [*Hint*: Remember that expressions such as $\mathbf{x}'_r(\mathbf{X}'_{r-1}\mathbf{X}_{r-1})^{-1}\mathbf{x}_r$ are scalars and may be moved back and forth in matrix formulas, that is, $c\mathbf{AB} = \mathbf{A}c\mathbf{B} = \mathbf{AB}c$, where c is a scalar and $\mathbf{A}$ and $\mathbf{B}$ are matrices.]

10-2 Relation (10-5) is a special case of a general result given by Plackett.† His problem and method of proof may be stated as follows:

First sample data	$\mathbf{y}_1, \mathbf{X}_1(n \times k)$
Additional data	$\mathbf{y}_2, \mathbf{X}_2(m \times k)$
Complete sample	$\mathbf{y} = \begin{bmatrix} \mathbf{y}_1 \\ \mathbf{y}_2 \end{bmatrix} \quad \mathbf{X} = \begin{bmatrix} \mathbf{X}_1 \\ \mathbf{X}_2 \end{bmatrix}$

The problem is to find the simplest computational way of updating least-squares statistics from the first sample to the complete sample.

Method: Define

$$\mathbf{R}_1 = \mathbf{X}_2(\mathbf{X}'_1\mathbf{X}_1)^{-1}\mathbf{X}'_2$$

and

$$\mathbf{R} = \mathbf{X}_2(\mathbf{X}'\mathbf{X})^{-1}\mathbf{X}'_2$$

Prove that

$$\mathbf{R}_1\mathbf{R} = \mathbf{R}_1 - \mathbf{R}$$

and hence that

$$(\mathbf{I}_m + \mathbf{R}_1)(\mathbf{I}_m - \mathbf{R}) = \mathbf{I}_m$$

Then show that

$$(\mathbf{I}_m + \mathbf{R}_1)^{-1}\mathbf{X}_2(\mathbf{X}'_1\mathbf{X}_1)^{-1} = \mathbf{X}_2(\mathbf{X}'\mathbf{X})^{-1}$$

and thus that

$$(\mathbf{X}'\mathbf{X})^{-1} = (\mathbf{X}'_1\mathbf{X}_1)^{-1} - (\mathbf{X}'_1\mathbf{X}_1)^{-1}\mathbf{X}'_2[\mathbf{I}_m + \mathbf{R}_1]^{-1}\mathbf{X}_2(\mathbf{X}'_1\mathbf{X}_1)^{-1}$$

Finally show that this result yields Eq. (10-5) when $\mathbf{X}_2$ is just a row vector of observations on one additional sample point.

10-3 For the recursive residuals defined in Sec. 10-1, prove

$$\text{RSS}_r = \text{RSS}_{r-1} + w_r^2$$

[*Hint*: Express $\mathbf{y}_r - \mathbf{X}_r\mathbf{b}_r$ as $\mathbf{y}_r - \mathbf{X}_r\mathbf{b}_{r-1} - \mathbf{X}_r(\mathbf{b}_r - \mathbf{b}_{r-1})$. Partition

$$\mathbf{y}_r = \begin{bmatrix} \mathbf{y}_{r-1} \\ y_r \end{bmatrix} \quad \text{and} \quad \mathbf{X}_r = \begin{bmatrix} \mathbf{X}_{r-1} \\ \mathbf{x}'_r \end{bmatrix}$$

and using Eq. (10-6) show that

$$\text{RSS}_r = (\mathbf{y}_r - \mathbf{X}_r\mathbf{b}_{r-1})'(\mathbf{y}_r - \mathbf{X}_r\mathbf{b}_{r-1}) - \mathbf{x}'_r(\mathbf{X}'_r\mathbf{X}_r)^{-1}\mathbf{x}_r(y_r - \mathbf{x}'_r\mathbf{b}_{r-1})^2$$

Applying the partitioning again and using Eq. (10-5) gives the desired result.]

10-4 Take a simple time series and verify that the restricted estimation of Eq. (10-17) yields the same point estimates of the α and β parameters as those derived from the estimated coefficients of the spline function (10-14).

† R. L. Plackett, "Some Theorems in Least Squares," *Biometrika*, vol. 37, 1950, pp. 149–157.

10-5 For the disturbance term in Eq. (10-21) make the following assumptions:

$$E(u_{it}^2) = \sigma_{ii}$$

$$E(u_{it}u_{jt}) = \sigma_{ij}$$

$$u_{it} = \rho_i u_{i,t-1} + \varepsilon_{it} \qquad |\rho_i| < 1$$

$$\varepsilon_{it} = \text{iid}(0, \sigma_\varepsilon^2)$$

Derive var(**u**) and discuss how a feasible GLS estimator of the parameters of Eq. (10-21) might be constructed.

10-6 Show that in Table 10-2

$$E\left\{\frac{1}{p(m-1)}\sum_{i=1}^{p}\sum_{t=1}^{n}\left(u_{it}-\bar{\bar{u}}\right)^2\right\} = \sigma_\varepsilon^2 + \frac{m(p-1)}{pm-1}\sigma_\alpha^2$$

and hence show that it is a biased estimator of $\sigma_u^2 = \sigma_\varepsilon^2 + \sigma_\alpha^2$.

10-7 For a two-way error component model assume

$$u_{it} = \mu_i + \lambda_t + \varepsilon_{it} \qquad i = 1, \ldots, p;\ t = 1, \ldots, m$$

where μ_i is a unit-specific time-invariant effect, λ_t is a period-specific unit-invariant effect, and, ε_{it} is a random disturbance at observation i, t.

The μ_i, λ_t, and ε_{it} are random variables having zero means, independent among themselves and with each other, with variances σ_μ^2, σ_λ^2, and σ_ε^2, respectively. Show that

$$\mathbf{V} = E(\mathbf{uu}') = \sigma^2\left[\rho\mathbf{A} + w\mathbf{B} + (1-\rho-w)\mathbf{I}_{pm}\right]$$

where

$$\mathbf{A} = \mathbf{I}_p \otimes \mathbf{J}_m$$

$$\mathbf{B} = \mathbf{J}_p \otimes \mathbf{I}_m$$

$$\sigma^2 = \sigma_\mu^2 + \sigma_\lambda^2 + \sigma_\varepsilon^2 \qquad \rho = \frac{\sigma_\mu^2}{\sigma^2} \qquad w = \frac{\sigma_\lambda^2}{\sigma^2}$$

and $\mathbf{J}_m$ is an $m \times m$ matrix of ones.

10-8 For the disturbance u_{it} defined in Problem 10-7 develop the ANOVA table similar to Table 10-2. Hence indicate possible estimators of σ_μ^2, σ_λ^2, and σ_ε^2.

10-9 Establish the result stated in Eq. (10-52).

10-10 Prove Eq. (10-57).

10-11 Derive formulas (10-81) and (10-82).

10-12 Consider the following regression model for a sample of panel data:

$$Y_{ij} = \alpha_0 + \alpha_1 X_{1ij} + \alpha_2 X_{2ij} + \alpha_3 X_{3ij} + \varepsilon_{ij}$$

$i = 1, 2, \ldots, n$ (panel members), $j = 1, 2, \ldots, t$ (time periods), and the X's are exogenous variables. The ε_{ij} are assumed to be normally and independently distributed with zero mean and constant variance for all i, j.

(a) If X_{3ij} is not observed and an investigator regresses Y_{ij} on just X_{1ij} and X_{2ij} with a constant term in the regression, what is the bias in the least-squares estimate of α_2? If the algebraic sign of the simple correlation coefficient for X_{3ij} and X_{2ij} were known, is this sufficient information to determine the algebraic sign of the bias? If not, explain what information is required to determine the algebraic sign of the bias.

(b) If the unobserved independent variable X_{3ij} is assumed to satisfy $X_{3ij} = X_{3i}$ for all j and is assumed to be nonstochastic, explain how to obtain estimates of α_1 and α_2 and their associated standard errors.

(University of Chicago, 1977)

10-13 Consider the following errors in variables model:

$$y_{it}^* = a + bx_{it}^* \qquad i = 1, \ldots, N;\ t = 1, 2$$

$$x_{it} = x_{it}^* + \varepsilon_{it} \qquad y_{it} = y_{it}^* + e_{it}$$

$$E\varepsilon_{it} = Ee_{it} = E(x_{it}^* \varepsilon_{is}) = E(x_{it}^* e_{is}) = E(y_{it}^* \varepsilon_{is}) = 0$$

$$E(y_{it}^* e_{is}) = E(\varepsilon_{it} e_{is}) = 0$$

$$E(\varepsilon_{it}^2) = \sigma_\varepsilon^2 \qquad E(e_{it}^2) = \sigma_e^2 \qquad E(\varepsilon_{i1}\varepsilon_{i2}) = \rho_\varepsilon \sigma_\varepsilon^2 \qquad E(e_{i1} e_{i2}) = \rho_e \sigma_e^2$$

$$E(x_{it}^{*2}) = \sigma_x^2 \qquad E(x_{i1}^* x_{i2}^*) = \rho_x \sigma_x^2 \qquad \text{for all } i;\ t = 1, 2;\ s = 1, 2$$

x_{it}, y_{it} are observed for $i = 1, \ldots, N$; $t = 1, 2$. Let $\hat{b}$ be the IV estimate of b from a cross-section regression using data from the second time period and x_{i1} as the instrument. Let $\hat{\hat{b}}$ be the IV estimate of b using the same cross section but with y_{i1} as the instrument. Show that if ρ_e, ρ_ε, and ρ_x are all positive, then $\text{plim}(\hat{b}) \le b \le \text{plim}(\hat{\hat{b}})$.

(UL, 1981)

CHAPTER

ELEVEN

SIMULTANEOUS EQUATION SYSTEMS

So far our interest has centered mainly on the inference problems associated with a single equation, although there was some discussion of groups of equations in Chap. 8. Economists, of course, often focus on a single equation, such as an aggregate consumption function, a demand function for gasoline, a wage-change equation, and so forth. However, economic theory teaches that such equations are embedded in a system or subset of related equations. Thus one must examine whether the presence of these related equations has any implications for the estimation of the focus equation. More importantly, the estimation of a *complete* system of equations is often an important practical problem, whether the objective is to test economic theories about the nature of the system or to use the complete system to make joint predictions of a set of related variables.

11-1 SOME ILLUSTRATIVE SIMULTANEOUS SYSTEMS

In this section we will consider a few very simplified systems in order to illustrate the main problems that arise, and then in subsequent sections we will give a more general and formal treatment.

Consider first an even simpler income determination model than the one outlined in Chap. 1. This one consists solely of a consumption function and the national income identity, namely,

$$C_t = \alpha + \beta Y_t + u_t \qquad (11\text{-}1)$$

$$Y_t \equiv C_t + Z_t \qquad (11\text{-}2)$$

where C = aggregate consumption expenditure
Y = national income
Z = nonconsumption expenditure
u = a stochastic disturbance term

We regard the model as explaining the values taken by C_t and Y_t conditional on Z_t. Thus C and Y are classified as endogenous variables and Z as an exogenous variable. We will make two assumptions, namely:

1. $\mathbf{u} \sim N(\mathbf{0}, \sigma_u^2\mathbf{I})$
2. Z and u are independent, which will be satisfied if either Z is a set of fixed numbers or Z is a random variable distributed independently of u. Z could be taken as representing autonomous investment and government spending controlled by some central authority. The model does not discuss the determinants of Z.

The reduced form of the model is†

$$C_t = \frac{\alpha}{1-\beta} + \frac{\beta}{1-\beta}Z_t + v_t \tag{11-3}$$

$$Y_t = \frac{\alpha}{1-\beta} + \frac{1}{1-\beta}Z_t + v_t \tag{11-4}$$

where $v_t = u_t/(1-\beta)$, so that

$$\mathbf{v} \sim N\left(\mathbf{0}, \frac{\sigma_u^2}{(1-\beta)^2}\mathbf{I}\right)$$

It is immediately obvious from Eq. (11-4) that v_t, and hence u_t, influences Y_t. In fact,

$$\text{plim}\left(\frac{1}{n}\Sigma Y_t v_t\right) = \text{plim}\left(\frac{1}{n}\Sigma v_t^2\right) = \frac{\sigma_u^2}{(1-\beta)^2}$$

Thus the application of OLS to the consumption function (11-1) would yield inconsistent estimates.‡ The nature of the inconsistency is illustrated diagrammatically in Fig. 11-1. The line $\alpha + \beta Y$ shows the relation between C and Y if the disturbance u were zero. The line $Y - Z'$ illustrates the identity (11-2) for a specified Z'. The equilibrium of the system would then be indicated by the point P_0. Imagine now that Z is held constant at Z' and that the disturbance takes on various positive and negative values in some finite range.§ The economy would

† As shown in Chap. 1, the reduced form is obtained by solving the model so as to express each current endogenous variable solely in terms of exogenous variables and lagged endogenous variables.

‡ If necessary, review the discussion of consistency in Sec. 7-2 and illustrations of inconsistency in the presence of lagged variables in Sec. 9-2 and in the presence of errors of measurement in Sec. 10-6.

§ The range is, of course, infinite for a normally distributed disturbance, but the finite range is a convenient assumption to keep the diagram simple.

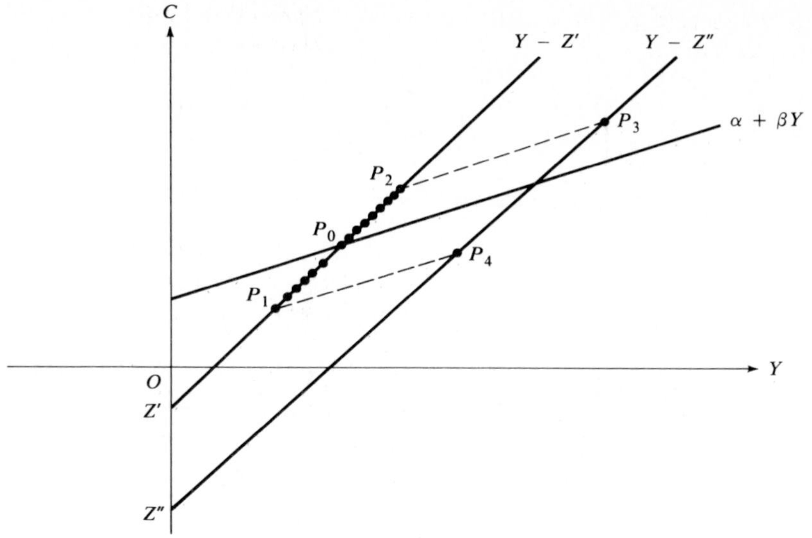

Figure 11-1

then trace out points in successive periods in the range P_1 to P_2 along the $Y - Z'$ line. If Z never changed from Z', these would be the only points ever observed for this economy, no matter how many observations were taken. The estimated regression of C on Y would coincide with the line $Y - Z'$, and *the estimated marginal propensity to consume would be unity, no matter what the true* β *happened to be*. Now suppose that over a large number of time periods Z ranges between Z' and Z''. Observations on C and Y would then fill in the parallelogram $P_1P_2P_3P_4$. The least-squares regression of C on Y minimizes the sum of squares of the residuals measured in the *vertical* (that is, C) direction. Thus in the limit the OLS line will tend to pass through the points P_1, P_3. The estimated slope will now be less than unity but will still be greater than the true β, so that the asymptotic bias is positive.†

Instrumental Variable Estimation

We saw in Sec. 9-2 that the use of suitable instrumental variables can produce consistent estimators. The obvious instrument in the present model is the Z variable which, by assumption, is independent of u, and by Eq. (11-4) will be correlated with Y. Applying the IV estimator defined in Eq. (9-60) to this model gives

$$a_{\text{IV}} = \bar{C} - b_{\text{IV}}\bar{Y} \tag{11-5}$$

and

$$b_{\text{IV}} = \frac{\Sigma cz}{\Sigma yz} \tag{11-6}$$

† See Problem 11-1.

where c, y, and z denote deviations from the sample means. From Eqs. (11-3) and (11-4) we may derive

$$\Sigma cz = \frac{\beta}{1-\beta}\Sigma z^2 + \Sigma zv$$

$$\Sigma yz = \frac{1}{1-\beta}\Sigma z^2 + \Sigma zv$$

Thus, provided

$$\operatorname{plim}\left(\frac{1}{n}\Sigma zv\right) = 0 \qquad \text{and} \qquad \operatorname{plim}\left(\frac{1}{n}\Sigma z^2\right) = \bar{m}_{zz}$$

a finite number,

$$\operatorname{plim}(b_{\text{IV}}) = \beta$$

and hence

$$\operatorname{plim}(a_{\text{IV}}) = \alpha$$

Indirect Least-Squares Estimation

The above development already contains a clue to a second estimation principle, that of indirect least squares (ILS). Looking at the reduced-form equations it is clear that they satisfy the assumptions under which OLS estimators are consistent (and indeed best linear unbiased) so that

$$\frac{\Sigma cz}{\Sigma z^2} \quad \text{is a consistent estimator of} \quad \frac{\beta}{1-\beta}$$

and

$$\frac{\Sigma yz}{\Sigma z^2} \quad \text{is a consistent estimator of} \quad \frac{1}{1-\beta}$$

which suggests taking the ratio

$$b_{\text{ILS}} = \frac{\Sigma cz}{\Sigma z^2} \div \frac{\Sigma yz}{\Sigma z^2} \qquad \text{as an estimate of } \beta$$

The principle of ILS is to estimate reduced-form coefficients by OLS and then to compute structural coefficients by an appropriate transformation of the estimated reduced-form coefficients. We see immediately that in this case

$$b_{\text{ILS}} = \frac{\Sigma cz}{\Sigma yz} = b_{\text{IV}}$$

Two-Stage Least-Squares Estimation

A third estimation principle is that of two-stage least squares (2SLS). It starts from the problem of Y_t and u_t in Eq. (11-1) being correlated. The first stage is to regress Y on the exogenous variables in the model, which in this case are Z, and a dummy variable that is always unity to allow for the intercept term. This reduced-form regression yields an estimated $\hat{Y}$ series, which it is hoped will display less correlation with the u series than does the original Y series. We may write Eq. (11-4) in deviation form as

$$y_t = \delta z_t + v_t$$

where $\delta = 1/(1-\beta)$, and we have also omitted $\bar{v}$ as it does not affect the subsequent derivation. The regression values are then given by

$$\hat{y}_t = \hat{\delta} z_t = \left(\frac{\Sigma yz}{\Sigma z^2} \right) z_t$$

$$= \left(\delta + \frac{\Sigma zv}{\Sigma z^2} \right) z_t$$

Thus
$$\Sigma \hat{y} u = \delta \Sigma zu + \frac{\Sigma zv}{\Sigma z^2} \cdot \Sigma zu$$

On the assumptions made earlier,

$$\text{plim}\left(\frac{1}{n} \Sigma zv \right) = \text{plim}\left(\frac{1}{n} \Sigma zu \right) = 0$$

so that in the limit $\hat{Y}$ is uncorrelated with u. In the second stage C is regressed on $\hat{Y}$ to estimate α and β, that is, Eq. (11-1) is reformulated as

$$C_t = \alpha + \beta \hat{Y}_t + \left[u_t + \beta \left(Y_t - \hat{Y}_t \right) \right]$$

with C_t as the dependent variable and $\hat{Y}_t$ as the explanatory variable. The disturbance term is shown in square brackets. From the OLS regression of Y on Z it follows that $\hat{Y}_t$ will have zero correlation in the sample with the residual $Y_t - \hat{Y}_t$, and we have just shown that $\hat{Y}_t$ is uncorrelated in the limit with u_t. Thus $\hat{Y}_t$ is uncorrelated in the limit with the combined disturbance term $[u_t + \beta(Y_t - \hat{Y}_t)]$, and the 2SLS estimators will be consistent. The 2SLS estimate of the slope β is

$$b_{2SLS} = \frac{\Sigma c \hat{y}}{\Sigma \hat{y}^2} = \frac{\hat{\delta} \Sigma cz}{\hat{\delta}^2 \Sigma z^2} = \frac{\Sigma cz}{\Sigma z^2} \cdot \frac{\Sigma z^2}{\Sigma yz} = \frac{\Sigma cz}{\Sigma yz}$$

Thus we see that in this case all three principles of estimation, IV, ILS, and 2SLS, would yield identical consistent estimates.

The two-equation model of Eqs. (11-1) and (11-2) is the simplest possible simultaneous equation model, consisting of just one stochastic behavioral equation and an identity, but that is enough to generate a dependence between the explanatory variable and the disturbance in the structural relation, rendering OLS inconsistent. More complicated models may be expected to generate further problems in addition to those already encountered.

Consider next a two-equation model in which both equations are stochastic behavioral relations. With a slight change of notation we write

$$\begin{aligned} y_{1t} + \beta_{12} y_{2t} + \gamma_{11} &= u_{1t} \\ \beta_{21} y_{1t} + y_{2t} + \gamma_{21} &= u_{2t} \end{aligned} \qquad t = 1, \ldots, n \qquad (11\text{-}7)$$

In this and subsequent models lowercase letters denote the actual values of the variables and not deviations from sample means. We will reserve the letter y for endogenous variables so that y_{it} denotes the tth observation on the ith endogenous variable. Likewise x_{jt} will denote the tth observation on the jth exogenous variable. The structural parameters β and γ also have two subscripts, the first indicating the equation and the second the variable to which it is attached.

Model (11-7) would be a conventional demand-and-supply model if y_1 denotes price, y_2 denotes quantity, and we impose the restrictions

$$\beta_{12} > 0 \qquad \beta_{21} < 0$$

so that the first equation represents a downward sloping demand curve and the second an upward sloping supply curve. We would also want to impose an additional restriction $\gamma_{11} < 0$ to ensure a positive intercept for the demand function. If the disturbances in period t were both zero ($u_{1t} = 0 = u_{2t}$), the model would be represented by the D, S lines in Fig. 11-2, and we would observe the equilibrium price and quantity indicated by y_1^*, y_2^*. Nonzero disturbances shift the D, S curves up or down from the position shown in Fig. 11-2. Thus a set of random disturbances would generate a two-dimensional scatter of observations clustered around the y_1^*, y_2^* point.

A fundamentally new problem now arises. Given this two-dimensional scatter in price-quantity space, demand analysts might fit a regression and think they were estimating a demand function. Supply analysts might fit a regression to the same data and presume they were estimating a supply function. "General equilibrium" economists, wishing to estimate both functions, would presumably be halted on their way to the computer by the thought, "How can we estimate two separate functions from one two-dimensional scatter?" The new problem is labeled the *identification problem*. It is concerned with the question of whether any specific equation in a model can in fact be estimated. It is not a question of the *method* of estimation nor of sample size, but of whether meaningful estimates of structural coefficients can be obtained. On the assumptions made so far neither equation in Eqs. (11-7) is identified. A regression fitted to the scatter in y_1, y_2 space is not an estimate of either the demand or the supply function.

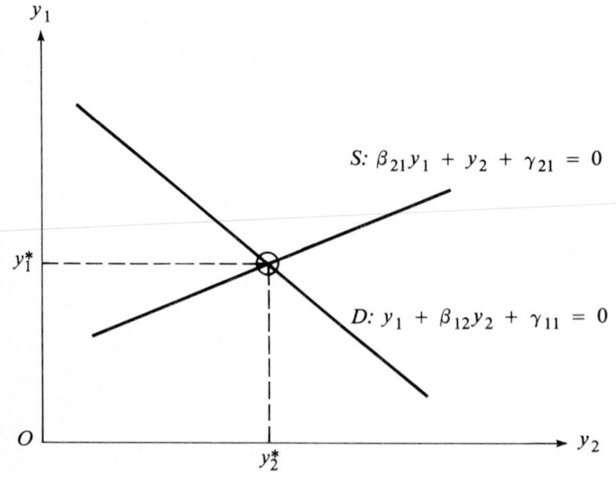

Figure 11-2

The identification problem may be investigated by looking at the relation between the structural and the reduced forms of the model. The reduced-form equations corresponding to Eq. (11-7) are†

$$\begin{aligned} y_{1t} &= \frac{1}{\Delta}\left[(-\gamma_{11} + \beta_{12}\gamma_{21}) + (u_{1t} - \beta_{12}u_{2t})\right] \\ y_{2t} &= \frac{1}{\Delta}\left[(\beta_{21}\gamma_{11} - \gamma_{21}) + (-\beta_{21}u_{1t} + u_{2t})\right] \end{aligned} \qquad (11\text{-}8)$$

where $\Delta = 1 - \beta_{12}\beta_{21}$. The first term on the right-hand side of each equation is a constant. Thus we may write the reduced form more simply as

$$\begin{aligned} y_{1t} &= \mu_1 + v_{1t} \\ y_{2t} &= \mu_2 + v_{2t} \end{aligned} \qquad (11\text{-}9)$$

where

$$\begin{aligned} \mu_1 &= \frac{-\gamma_{11} + \beta_{12}\gamma_{21}}{\Delta} \\ \mu_2 &= \frac{\beta_{21}\gamma_{11} - \gamma_{21}}{\Delta} \\ v_{1t} &= \frac{u_{1t} - \beta_{12}u_{2t}}{\Delta} \\ v_{2t} &= \frac{-\beta_{21}u_{1t} + u_{2t}}{\Delta} \end{aligned} \qquad (11\text{-}10)$$

If we postulate that

$$E(\mathbf{u}_t) = \begin{bmatrix} E(u_{1t}) \\ E(u_{2t}) \end{bmatrix} = \mathbf{0}$$

and

$$E(\mathbf{u}_t\mathbf{u}_t') = \mathbf{\Sigma} = \begin{bmatrix} \sigma_{11} & \sigma_{12} \\ \sigma_{12} & \sigma_{22} \end{bmatrix}$$

then

$$E(\mathbf{v}_t) = \mathbf{0}$$

$$\operatorname{var}(v_1) = E(v_{1t}^2) = \frac{\sigma_{11} + \beta_{12}^2\sigma_{22} - 2\beta_{12}\sigma_{12}}{\Delta^2}$$

$$\operatorname{var}(v_2) = E(v_{2t}^2) = \frac{\beta_{21}^2\sigma_{11} + \sigma_{22} - 2\beta_{21}\sigma_{12}}{\Delta^2}$$

and

$$\operatorname{cov}(v_1, v_2) = E(v_{1t}v_{2t}) = \frac{-\beta_{21}\sigma_{11} - \beta_{12}\sigma_{22} + (1 + \beta_{12}\beta_{21})\sigma_{12}}{\Delta^2}$$

† Here there are no lagged endogenous variables and the only exogenous variable is the dummy variable $x_{1t} = 1$ for all t, which is required to take care of the intercept term in the structural equations.

It also follows from Eqs. (11-9) that

$$\begin{aligned} E(y_1) &= \mu_1 \\ E(y_2) &= \mu_2 \\ \mathrm{var}(y_1) &= \mathrm{var}(v_1) \\ \mathrm{var}(y_2) &= \mathrm{var}(v_2) \\ \mathrm{cov}(y_1, y_2) &= \mathrm{cov}(v_1, v_2) \end{aligned} \tag{11-11}$$

Sample data on y_1, y_2 can only yield estimates of the *five* parameters in Eqs. (11-11). These in turn are functions of the *seven* parameters of the structural model, namely, β_{12}, β_{21}, γ_{11}, γ_{21}, σ_{11}, σ_{22}, and σ_{12}. On the assumptions made so far the structural parameters are unidentifiable.

As a numerical illustration of this situation suppose the true structure corresponding to Eqs. (11-7) is

$$\begin{aligned} y_1 + 2y_2 - 10 &= u_1 \\ -3y_1 + y_2 + 2 &= u_2 \\ \sigma_{11} = \sigma_{22} = 1 \qquad \sigma_{12} &= 0.5 \end{aligned} \tag{11-12}$$

Equations (11-7) define a *model*, and a *structure* like Eqs. (11-12) is obtained from a model by assigning specific numerical values to the β and γ parameters and also to the variances and the covariance of the u's. Solving this structure for Eqs. (11-9) gives

$$y_1 = 2 + v_1$$

$$y_2 = 4 + v_2$$

where

$$v_1 = \frac{u_1 - 2u_2}{7}$$

$$v_2 = \frac{3u_1 + u_2}{7}$$

Thus

$$\begin{aligned} E(y_1) &= \mu_1 = 2 \\ E(y_2) &= \mu_2 = 4 \\ \mathrm{var}(y_1) &= \mathrm{var}(v_1) = \frac{3}{49} \\ \mathrm{var}(y_2) &= \mathrm{var}(v_2) = \frac{13}{49} \\ \mathrm{cov}(y_1, y_2) &= \mathrm{cov}(v_1, v_2) = \frac{-1.5}{49} \end{aligned} \tag{11-13}$$

The true structure (11-12) is, of course, known only to the "deity" who sets the economic system in motion. Now suppose that one of the deity's vice-presidents tinkers with the institutions in an attempt to confuse the econometricians of the world and concocts a new structure by the following rule, where (1) and (2) indicate the first and second equations in Eqs. (11-12),

$$\text{New first equation} = 4(1) + 1(2)$$

$$\text{New second equation} = -(1) + 3(2)$$

This yields the structure

$$\begin{aligned} y_1 + 9y_2 - 38 &= u_1^* \\ -10y_1 + y_2 + 16 &= u_2^* \end{aligned} \tag{11-14}$$

where

$$u_1^* = 4u_1 + u_2$$

$$u_2^* = -u_1 + 3u_2$$

The new structure obeys the same a priori constraints on signs as Eqs. (11-12). Solving this structure for Eqs. (11-9) gives

$$y_1 = 2 + v_1^*$$

$$y_2 = 4 + v_2^*$$

where

$$v_1^* = \frac{u_1^* - 9u_2^*}{91} = \frac{u_1 - 2u_2}{7} = v_1$$

$$v_2^* = \frac{10u_1^* + u_2^*}{91} = \frac{3u_1 + u_2}{7} = v_2$$

Thus the five parameters of the reduced form $E(y_1)$, $E(y_2)$, $\text{var}(y_1)$, $\text{var}(y_2)$, and $\text{cov}(y_1, y_2)$ are identical for the two different structures and indeed for all structures derived by taking linear combinations of the original structural equations.

It is instructive to see what type of further information might help identify one or both equations of this model. There are three basic possibilities, namely, (1) restrictions on the β and γ parameters, (2) restrictions on the Σ matrix, and (3) respecifications of the model to incorporate additional variables. To illustrate the first category, suppose the supply function is presumed to go through the origin. The a priori restriction is thus

$$\gamma_{21} = 0$$

This reduces the number of structural parameters to six, but the number of reduced-form parameters is five, as before, so that it is still not clear that any structural parameters can be identified. However, making the substitution $\gamma_{21} = 0$ in Eqs. (11-10) gives

$$\mu_1 = \frac{-\gamma_{11}}{\Delta}$$

$$\mu_2 = \frac{\beta_{21}\gamma_{11}}{\Delta}$$

so that

$$\beta_{21} = \frac{-\mu_2}{\mu_1}$$

showing that β_{21} can be determined from a knowledge of the reduced-form parameters and also suggesting a possible estimator as $\hat{\beta}_{21} = -\bar{y}_2/\bar{y}_1$. This restriction would enable the supply function to be identified, but the demand equation remains unidentified. Linear combinations of the demand and supply equations would be statistically indistinguishable from the original demand equation. However, any linear combination that assigns a nonzero weight to the demand function will fail, with probability 1, to have a zero intercept and thus will not look like the new supply function.

Now suppose we return to Eqs. (11-7) and impose the restriction

$$\text{var}(u_1) = \sigma_{11} = 0$$

This also implies that $\sigma_{12} = 0$. Looking at Eqs. (11-11) we now find

$$\text{var}(y_1) = \frac{\beta_{12}^2\sigma_{22}}{\Delta^2}$$

$$\text{var}(y_2) = \frac{\sigma_{22}}{\Delta^2}$$

$$\text{cov}(y_1, y_2) = \frac{-\beta_{12}\sigma_{22}}{\Delta^2}$$

so that

$$\beta_{12} = \sqrt{\frac{\text{var}(y_1)}{\text{var}(y_2)}} = \frac{-\text{cov}(y_1, y_2)}{\text{var}(y_2)}$$

$$= \frac{-\text{var}(y_1)}{\text{cov}(y_1, y_2)}$$

and thus the slope of the demand function is identified. Taking expectations of the demand function in Eqs. (11-7) gives

$$\gamma_{11} = -\mu_1 - \beta_{12}\mu_2$$

and substitution for μ_1 and μ_2 from Eqs. (11-10) verifies that this relation holds. Thus γ_{11} and β_{12} can both be expressed in terms of the parameters in Eqs. (11-11), and the demand equation is identified. This case is pictured in Fig.11-3. The combination of $\sigma_{11} = 0$ and $\sigma_{22} \neq 0$ generates a set of observations on the demand function.

A less extreme version of this case would occur if σ_{11} were "small" as compared with σ_{22}. The scatter of observations would then tend to be concentrated around the demand function rather than lying exactly on it. However, knowledge about the relative sizes of disturbance variances is not likely to be generally available, though a possible reason for a large σ_{22} might be the omission of important explanatory variables from the supply function in Eqs. (11-7). The appropriate remedy is the respecification of the supply function to include such variables. In practice the demand function should also be looked at since the simple two-variable model of Eqs. (11-7) is hardly a realistic specification with which to commence empirical work.

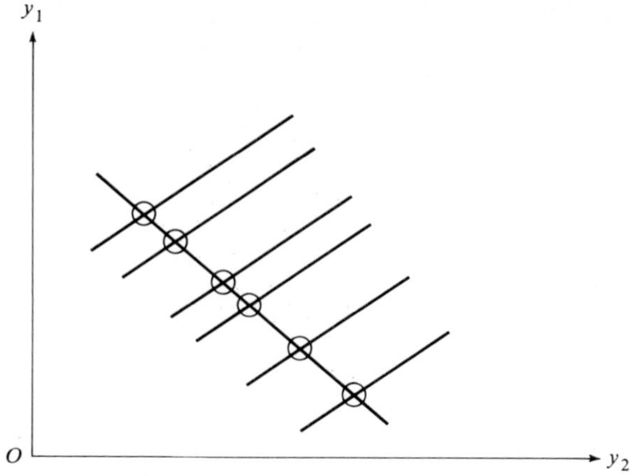

Figure 11-3

Consider now a respecification of Eqs. (11-7) which is, say,

$$\begin{aligned} y_1 + \beta_{12} y_2 + \gamma_{11} x_1 + \gamma_{12} x_2 \qquad\qquad\qquad\quad &= u_1 \\ \beta_{21} y_1 + \quad y_2 + \gamma_{21} x_1 \qquad\qquad + \gamma_{23} x_3 + \gamma_{24} x_4 &= u_2 \end{aligned} \tag{11-15}$$

where we still retain the restrictions $\beta_{12} > 0$ and $\beta_{21} < 0$ to conform with the demand-and-supply analogy. The variable x_1 could be taken as a dummy with a value of unity in all periods to cater for the intercept term, x_2 might represent income, which is expected to influence demand, and x_3 and x_4 would represent variables influencing supply. The reduced form of this model is

$$\begin{bmatrix} y_1 \\ y_2 \end{bmatrix} = \frac{1}{\Delta} \begin{bmatrix} (-\gamma_{11} + \beta_{12}\gamma_{21}) & -\gamma_{12} & \beta_{12}\gamma_{23} & \beta_{12}\gamma_{24} \\ (\beta_{21}\gamma_{11} - \gamma_{21}) & \beta_{21}\gamma_{12} & -\gamma_{23} & -\gamma_{24} \end{bmatrix} \begin{bmatrix} x_1 \\ x_2 \\ x_3 \\ x_4 \end{bmatrix} + \begin{bmatrix} v_1 \\ v_2 \end{bmatrix}$$

where $\Delta = 1 - \beta_{12}\beta_{21}$ and the v's are given in Eqs. (11-10). Let us denote the reduced-form coefficients by π_{ij} $(i = 1, 2;\ j = 1, \ldots, 4)$. It is clear that the structural coefficients can be obtained from the reduced-form coefficients. For example,

$$\beta_{21} = \frac{-\pi_{22}}{\pi_{12}}$$

$$\beta_{12} = \frac{-\pi_{13}}{\pi_{23}} = \frac{-\pi_{14}}{\pi_{24}}$$

and having found the β's, the γ's can be obtained from π_{11} and π_{21}. Leaving the disturbance parameters aside, there are eight reduced-form coefficients and just seven structural coefficients. The imbalance is reflected in the existence of two alternative (but equivalent) expressions for β_{12}. This indicates, however, that we may expect the ILS technique to run into trouble here since the *estimated* reduced-form coefficients will in general not satisfy the equality $\pi_{13}/\pi_{23} = \pi_{14}/\pi_{24}$ that holds for the *true* coefficients.

Further investigation of identification and estimation problems by way of specific models of increasing size and complexity would be inefficient. We now move to a more general and more formal treatment, which can then be specialized to deal with particular cases.

11-2 THE IDENTIFICATION PROBLEM

Let us assume a linear model containing G structural relations. The ith relation at time t may be written

$$\beta_{i1}y_{1t} + \cdots + \beta_{iG}y_{Gt} + \gamma_{i1}x_{1t} + \cdots + \gamma_{iK}x_{Kt} = u_{it} \qquad (11\text{-}16)$$
$$i = 1, \ldots, G;\ t = 1, \ldots, n$$

where the y_{it} denote endogenous variables at time t, and the x_{it} indicate exogenous variables (current or lagged) and may also include lagged endogenous variables.† The latter two groups constitute the class of *predetermined* variables. The model may then be regarded as a theory explaining the determination of the G jointly dependent variables y_{it} $(i = 1, \ldots, G;\ t = 1, \ldots, n)$ in terms of the predetermined variables x_{it} $(i = 1, \ldots, K;\ t = 1, \ldots, n)$ and the disturbances u_{it} $(i = 1, \ldots, G;$ $t = 1, \ldots, n)$. The underlying theory will in general specify that some of the β, γ coefficients are zero. If it did not, all the equations in the model would look alike statistically, as in Eqs. (11-7), and no equation could be identified. As mentioned earlier, the lowercase letters denote actual values of the variables and not deviations from arithmetic means, and setting one of the x variables at unity caters for a constant term in any equation that requires it.

The model may be written in matrix form as

$$\mathbf{B}\mathbf{y}_t + \mathbf{\Gamma}\mathbf{x}_t = \mathbf{u}_t \qquad t = 1, \ldots, n \qquad (11\text{-}17)$$

where $\mathbf{B}$ is a $G \times G$ matrix of coefficients of current endogenous variables, $\mathbf{\Gamma}$ is a $G \times K$ matrix of coefficients of predetermined variables, and $\mathbf{y}_t$, $\mathbf{x}_t$, and $\mathbf{u}_t$ are column vectors of G, K, and G elements, respectively,

$$\mathbf{B} = \begin{bmatrix} \beta_{11} & \beta_{12} & \cdots & \beta_{1G} \\ \beta_{21} & \beta_{22} & \cdots & \beta_{2G} \\ \cdots & \cdots & \cdots & \cdots \\ \beta_{G1} & \beta_{G2} & \cdots & \beta_{GG} \end{bmatrix} \qquad \mathbf{\Gamma} = \begin{bmatrix} \gamma_{11} & \gamma_{12} & \cdots & \gamma_{1K} \\ \gamma_{21} & \gamma_{22} & \cdots & \gamma_{2K} \\ \cdots & \cdots & \cdots & \cdots \\ \gamma_{G1} & \gamma_{G2} & \cdots & \gamma_{GK} \end{bmatrix}$$

$$\mathbf{y}_t = \begin{bmatrix} y_{1t} \\ y_{2t} \\ \vdots \\ y_{Gt} \end{bmatrix} \qquad \mathbf{x}_t = \begin{bmatrix} x_{1t} \\ x_{2t} \\ \vdots \\ x_{Kt} \end{bmatrix} \qquad \mathbf{u}_t = \begin{bmatrix} u_{1t} \\ u_{2t} \\ \vdots \\ u_{Gt} \end{bmatrix}$$

It is plausible to assume that the $\mathbf{B}$ matrix is nonsingular since, if it were not, one

† Notice that for the moment we have not normalized the structural equations by setting any of the β coefficients at unity.

or more of the structural relations would merely be a linear combination of other structural relations, thus being redundant, or, if the rows of the $\boldsymbol{\Gamma}$ matrix did not obey the same linear restrictions as the rows of $\mathbf{B}$, the G structural equations would be inconsistent. Assuming, therefore, that $\mathbf{B}^{-1}$ exists, the reduced form of the model is

$$\mathbf{y}_t = \boldsymbol{\Pi}\mathbf{x}_t + \mathbf{v}_t \qquad t = 1,\ldots, n \tag{11-18}$$

where

$$\boldsymbol{\Pi} = -\mathbf{B}^{-1}\boldsymbol{\Gamma} \qquad \text{and} \qquad \mathbf{v}_t = \mathbf{B}^{-1}\mathbf{u}_t \tag{11-19}$$

The $\boldsymbol{\Pi}$ matrix is of order $G \times K$ and thus contains GK elements. The $\mathbf{B}$ and $\boldsymbol{\Gamma}$ matrices contain at most $G^2 + GK$ elements. There is thus an infinity of $\mathbf{B}$ and $\boldsymbol{\Gamma}$ structures corresponding to any given $\boldsymbol{\Pi}$ matrix.

The identification problem arises because the most that can be determined from observational data on $\mathbf{y}_t$ and $\mathbf{x}_t$ $(t = 1,\ldots, n)$ is a knowledge of the elements of $\boldsymbol{\Pi}$ and the elements of the variance-covariance matrix of the v's. This may be seen in a number of ways. The reduced form Eqs. (11-18) show explicitly that the model provides an explanation of $\mathbf{y}_t$ *conditional on* $\mathbf{x}_t$ and on the disturbance vector $\mathbf{v}_t$. From Eqs. (11-19) it is clear that the stochastic properties of $\mathbf{v}_t$ depend on the assumed stochastic properties of the structural disturbance vector $\mathbf{u}_t$. Assuming $E(\mathbf{u}_t) = \mathbf{0}$ for all t then gives†

$$E(\mathbf{y}_t|\mathbf{x}_t) = \boldsymbol{\Pi}\mathbf{x}_t$$

Thus the mean of the conditional distribution of $\mathbf{y}_t$, given $\mathbf{x}_t$, depends solely on the $\boldsymbol{\Pi}$ matrix. A finite sample of observations $(\mathbf{y}_t, \mathbf{x}_t;\ t = 1,\ldots, n)$ will yield some estimate $\hat{\boldsymbol{\Pi}}$, which will deviate from the true $\boldsymbol{\Pi}$ due to the fluctuations of random sampling. Suppose, however, that we dispense with sampling problems by assuming that an infinitely large sample of observations can be made available. In general the true $\boldsymbol{\Pi}$ may then be determined with any desired degree of precision. This is all that can be afforded by the sample data. Thus knowledge of $\mathbf{B}$ and $\boldsymbol{\Gamma}$ can only come from knowledge of $\boldsymbol{\Pi}$.

To see the same point in a likelihood context, let us assume

$$\mathbf{u}_t \sim N(\mathbf{0}, \boldsymbol{\Sigma})$$

and also that the $\mathbf{u}_t$ vectors are serially independent. It then follows from Eqs. (11-19) that

$$\mathbf{v}_t \sim N(\mathbf{0}, \boldsymbol{\Omega})$$

where

$$\boldsymbol{\Omega} = \mathbf{B}^{-1}\boldsymbol{\Sigma}\mathbf{B}^{-1\prime} \tag{11-20}$$

and the $\mathbf{v}_t$ are serially independent. From the reduced-form equation (11-18)

$$p(\mathbf{y}_t|\mathbf{x}_t) = p(\mathbf{v}_t) = (2\pi)^{-G/2}|\boldsymbol{\Omega}|^{-1/2}\exp\left(-\tfrac{1}{2}\mathbf{v}_t'\boldsymbol{\Omega}^{-1}\mathbf{v}_t\right)$$

† When $\mathbf{x}_t$ contains lagged y values, this expectation has to be read as conditional on these lagged endogenous values.

Thus the likelihood of the sample y's conditional on the x's is

$$L = p(\mathbf{y}_1, \mathbf{y}_2, \ldots, \mathbf{y}_n | \mathbf{X}) = 2\pi^{-nG/2} |\boldsymbol{\Omega}|^{-n/2} \exp\left(-\frac{1}{2} \sum_{t=1}^{n} \mathbf{v}_t' \boldsymbol{\Omega}^{-1} \mathbf{v}_t \right)$$

$$= (2\pi)^{-nG/2} |\boldsymbol{\Omega}|^{-n/2} \exp\left[-\frac{1}{2} \sum_{t=1}^{n} (\mathbf{y}_t - \boldsymbol{\Pi}\mathbf{x}_t)' \boldsymbol{\Omega}^{-1} (\mathbf{y}_t - \boldsymbol{\Pi}\mathbf{x}_t) \right] \quad (11\text{-}21)$$

Alternatively one might set up the likelihood in terms of the structural equations (11-17). This gives

$$p(\mathbf{y}_t | \mathbf{x}_t) = p(\mathbf{u}_t) \left| \frac{\partial \mathbf{u}_t}{\partial \mathbf{y}_t} \right|$$

$$= p(\mathbf{u}_t) \cdot \|\mathbf{B}\|$$

where $\|\mathbf{B}\|$ denotes the absolute value of the determinant of $\mathbf{B}$. The likelihood of the sample y's conditions on the x's is then

$$L = (2\pi)^{-nG/2} \|\mathbf{B}\|^n |\boldsymbol{\Sigma}|^{-n/2} \exp\left(-\frac{1}{2} \sum_{t=1}^{n} \mathbf{u}_t' \boldsymbol{\Sigma}^{-1} \mathbf{u}_t \right)$$

$$= (2\pi)^{-nG/2} \|\mathbf{B}\|^n |\boldsymbol{\Sigma}|^{-n/2} \exp\left[-\frac{1}{2} \sum_{t=1}^{n} (\mathbf{B}\mathbf{y}_t + \boldsymbol{\Gamma}\mathbf{x}_t)' \boldsymbol{\Sigma}^{-1} (\mathbf{B}\mathbf{y}_t + \boldsymbol{\Gamma}\mathbf{x}_t) \right] \quad (11\text{-}22)$$

Comparing Eqs. (11-21) and (11-22) it is easily seen, using Eq. (11-20), that

$$(\mathbf{y}_t - \boldsymbol{\Pi}\mathbf{x}_t)' \boldsymbol{\Omega}^{-1} (\mathbf{y}_t - \boldsymbol{\Pi}\mathbf{x}_t) = (\mathbf{B}\mathbf{y}_t + \boldsymbol{\Gamma}\mathbf{x}_t)' \boldsymbol{\Sigma}^{-1} (\mathbf{B}\mathbf{y}_t + \boldsymbol{\Gamma}\mathbf{x}_t)$$

and $$|\boldsymbol{\Omega}|^{-n/2} = \|\mathbf{B}\|^n |\boldsymbol{\Sigma}|^{-n/2}$$

so that Eqs. (11-21) and (11-22) are equivalent. Leaving aside the variance matrices $\boldsymbol{\Sigma}$ and $\boldsymbol{\Omega}$, each of which contains $G(G+1)/2$ parameters, there are $G^2 + GK$ parameters in Eq. (11-22) and just GK in Eq. (11-21). The likelihood function is thus completely specified by the GK parameters in $\boldsymbol{\Pi}$. Identification of structural parameters in $\mathbf{B}$ and $\boldsymbol{\Gamma}$ thus depends on the addition of further information to the model specified in Eq. (11-16). Such information usually takes the form of restrictions on various elements of $\mathbf{B}$ and $\boldsymbol{\Gamma}$ and, less frequently, on the elements of $\boldsymbol{\Sigma}$.

Restrictions on the Structural Coefficients

We will consider the identification of the *first* equation in the system. The methods derived can then be applied to any structural equation. Let us rewrite the structural form of the model (11-17) as

$$\mathbf{A}\mathbf{z}_t = [\mathbf{B} \quad \boldsymbol{\Gamma}] \begin{bmatrix} \mathbf{y}_t \\ \mathbf{x}_t \end{bmatrix} = \mathbf{u}_t \quad (11\text{-}23)$$

where $\mathbf{A} = [\mathbf{B} \quad \boldsymbol{\Gamma}]$ is the $G \times (G+K)$ matrix of all structural coefficients and $\mathbf{z}_t$ is a $(G+K) \times 1$ vector of observations on all variables at time t. The first structural equation may then be written as

$$\boldsymbol{\alpha}_1 \mathbf{z}_t = u_{1t}$$

where $\boldsymbol{\alpha}_1$ denotes the first row of $\mathbf{A}$.

Economic theory typically places restrictions on the elements of $\boldsymbol{\alpha}_1$. The most common restrictions are *exclusion* restrictions, which specify that certain variables do *not* appear in certain equations. Suppose, for example, that y_3 does not appear in the first equation. The appropriate restriction is then

$$\beta_{13} = 0$$

which may be expressed as a linear restriction on the elements of $\boldsymbol{\alpha}_1$, namely,

$$[\beta_{11} \quad \beta_{12} \quad \beta_{13} \quad \cdots \quad \gamma_{11} \quad \cdots \quad \gamma_{1K}] \begin{bmatrix} 0 \\ 0 \\ 1 \\ 0 \\ \vdots \\ 0 \end{bmatrix} = 0$$

There may also be linear homogeneous restrictions involving two or more elements of α_1. The specification that, say, the coefficients of y_1 and y_2 are equal would be expressed as

$$[\beta_{11} \quad \beta_{12} \quad \cdots \quad \gamma_{11} \quad \cdots \quad \gamma_{1K}] \begin{bmatrix} 1 \\ -1 \\ 0 \\ \vdots \\ 0 \end{bmatrix} = 0$$

If these were the only a priori restrictions on $\boldsymbol{\alpha}_1$, they may be expressed in the form

$$\boldsymbol{\alpha}_1 \boldsymbol{\Phi} = \mathbf{0} \tag{11-24}$$

where

$$\boldsymbol{\Phi} = \begin{bmatrix} 0 & 1 \\ 0 & -1 \\ 1 & 0 \\ 0 & 0 \\ \vdots & \vdots \\ 0 & 0 \end{bmatrix}$$

The $\boldsymbol{\Phi}$ matrix has $G + K$ rows and a column for each a priori restriction on the first equation.

In addition to the restrictions embodied in Eq. (11-24) there will also be restrictions on $\boldsymbol{\alpha}_1$ arising from the relations between structural and reduced-form coefficients. From Eqs. (11-19) we may write

$$\mathbf{B\Pi} + \mathbf{\Gamma} = \mathbf{0}$$

or

$$\mathbf{AW} = \mathbf{0}$$

where
$$\mathbf{W} = \begin{bmatrix} \mathbf{\Pi} \\ \mathbf{I}_k \end{bmatrix}$$

The restrictions on the coefficients of the first structural equation are thus

$$\boldsymbol{\alpha}_1 \mathbf{W} = \mathbf{0} \tag{11-25}$$

Combining Eqs. (11-24) and (11-25) gives

$$\boldsymbol{\alpha}_1 [\mathbf{W} \quad \mathbf{\Phi}] = \mathbf{0} \tag{11-26}$$

There are $G + K$ unknowns in $\boldsymbol{\alpha}_1$. The matrix $[\mathbf{W} \quad \mathbf{\Phi}]$ is of order $(G + K) \times (K + R)$, where R is the number of columns in $\mathbf{\Phi}$. On the assumption that Π is known all the elements in $[\mathbf{W} \quad \mathbf{\Phi}]$ are known. Thus Eq. (11-26) constitutes a set of $K + R$ equations in $G + K$ unknowns. Identification of the first equation requires that the rank of $[\mathbf{W} \quad \mathbf{\Phi}]$ be $G + K - 1$, for then all solutions to Eq. (11-26) would lie on a single ray through the origin. This suffices to determine the coefficients of the first equation uniquely, for in specifying the general model in Eq. (11-17) a β or γ coefficient was attached to each variable in every equation. Normalizing the first equation by setting one coefficient at unity (say, $\beta_{11} = 1$) will now give a single point on the solution ray, and this determines $\boldsymbol{\alpha}_1$ uniquely.

$$\rho[\mathbf{W} \quad \mathbf{\Phi}] = G + K - 1 \tag{11-27}$$

is clearly a necessary and sufficient condition for the identifiability of the first equation. The condition for the identification of the ith structural equation is

$$\rho[\mathbf{W} \quad \mathbf{\Phi}_i] = G + K - 1$$

where $\mathbf{\Phi}_i$ is the matrix embodying the a priori restrictions on the ith equation. The basic difficulty with the rank condition, as stated in Eq. (11-27), is that it is not a convenient one to apply since it requires the construction of the Π matrix, which is complicated even in small models. We will give below an equivalent condition in terms of structural parameters which is easier to apply. However, condition (11-27) does yield *necessary* conditions for identification which are very simple to apply. Since $[\mathbf{W} \quad \mathbf{\Phi}]$ has $K + R$ columns, a necessary condition for Eq. (11-27) to hold is that

$$K + R \geq G + K - 1$$

or
$$R \geq G - 1 \tag{11-28}$$

that is,

> *The number of a priori restrictions should not be less than the number of equations in the model less* 1.

When the restrictions are solely exclusion restrictions, the necessary condition is restated as:

> *The number of variables excluded from the equation must be at least as great as the number of equations in the model less* 1.

Finally, an alternative form of this last condition may be derived by letting

g = number of current endogenous variables included in equation

k = number of predetermined variables included in equation

Then

$$R = (G - g) + (K - k)$$

and the necessary condition becomes

$$(G - g) + (K - k) \geq G - 1$$

or

$$K - k \geq g - 1$$

that is,

The number of predetermined variables excluded from the equation must be at least as great as the number of endogenous variables included less 1.

The necessary condition is referred to as the *order* condition for identifiability. In large models this is often the only condition that can be applied since application of the rank condition becomes difficult, if not impossible.

The rank condition (11-27) may be restated as†

$$\rho[\mathbf{W} \quad \mathbf{\Phi}] = G + K - 1 \qquad \text{if and only if } \rho(\mathbf{A\Phi}) = G - 1 \qquad (11\text{-}29)$$

Note carefully that $[\mathbf{W} \quad \mathbf{\Phi}]$ is a matrix consisting of the two indicated submatrices, while $\mathbf{A\Phi}$ is the *product* of two matrices. The second form of this condition only involves the structural coefficients and thus affords an easier application. When the restrictions are all exclusion restrictions, the first row of $\mathbf{A\Phi}$ is a zero vector and the remaining $G - 1$ rows consist of the coefficients in the other structural equations of the variables which do not appear in the first equation.

If equality holds in Eq. (11-28), that is, $R = G - 1$, so that the number of restrictions on the first equation is just equal to the number of structural equations less 1, the matrix $\mathbf{A\Phi}$ is then of order $G \times (G - 1)$. However, the first row of this matrix is zero by virtue of $\boldsymbol{\alpha}_1\mathbf{\Phi} = \mathbf{0}$. This leaves a square matrix of order $G - 1$ which, apart from some freakish conjunction of coefficients, will be nonsingular. The first equation is then said to be *exactly identified* or *just identified*. Suppose instead that $R > G - 1$. Then $\mathbf{A\Phi}$ has G or more columns. There are now more restrictions than strictly required for identification, and in general there will be more than one square submatrix of order $G - 1$ to satisfy the rank condition. The equation is then said to be *overidentified*.

A direct proof of the rank condition in terms of the $\mathbf{A\Phi}$ matrix may be obtained from an alternative approach to the identification problem. We saw in one of the examples how taking linear combinations of the equations in a given

† See F. M. Fisher, *The Identification Problem in Econometrics*, McGraw-Hill, New York, 1966, Chap. 2; or for a shorter proof, R. W. Farebrother, "A Short Proof of the Basic Lemma of the Linear Identification Problem," *International Economic Review*, vol. 12, 1971, pp. 515–516.

structure could yield a new structure which satisfied the same a priori constraints as the original structure and had identical reduced-form coefficients. Let

$$\mathbf{A} = [\mathbf{B} \quad \mathbf{\Gamma}]$$

denote an original set of structural coefficients (that is, with specific numerical values), and let **FA** denote a new structure obtained from **A** by premultiplication with an arbitrary $G \times G$ nonsingular transformation matrix **F**. The new structure is said to be *admissible*, or equivalently **F** is said to be an admissible transformation matrix, if **FA** satisfies all a priori restrictions on **A**.† Identifiability of the first equation then requires that the first equation of every admissible structure be some scalar multiple of the true first equation. The first row of **A** may be expressed as

$$\boldsymbol{\alpha}_1 = \mathbf{e}_1\mathbf{A}$$

where $\mathbf{e}_1$ is a $1 \times G$ row vector with unity in the first position and zero elsewhere. Thus the a priori restrictions on the first equation may be written

$$\mathbf{e}_1(\mathbf{A\Phi}) = \mathbf{0}$$

The first row of coefficients in the transformed structure may be written as $\mathbf{f}_1\mathbf{A}$, where $\mathbf{f}_1$ denotes the first row of **F**. For an admissible structure this must obey the same restrictions as $\boldsymbol{\alpha}_1$, and so we must have

$$\mathbf{f}_1(\mathbf{A\Phi}) = \mathbf{0}$$

Identifiability requires that $\mathbf{f}_1\mathbf{A}$ be a scalar multiple of $\mathbf{e}_1\mathbf{A}$, that is, that $\mathbf{f}_1$ be a scalar multiple of $\mathbf{e}_1$, which gives the condition that $\rho(\mathbf{A\Phi}) = G - 1$. If all the equations of a model are identified, the only admissible transformation matrices are diagonal matrices.

Examples. To illustrate the application of the conditions for identifiability we shall work with the two-equation system

$$\beta_{11}y_{1t} + \beta_{12}y_{2t} + \gamma_{11}x_{1t} + \gamma_{12}x_{2t} = u_{1t}$$
$$\beta_{21}y_{1t} + \beta_{22}y_{2t} + \gamma_{21}x_{1t} + \gamma_{22}x_{2t} = u_{2t}$$

As it stands, both equations are unidentifiable since no a priori restrictions have yet been imposed. Each example will postulate a different set of restrictions.

Example 11-1 Suppose the a priori restrictions are

$$\gamma_{12} = 0 \qquad \gamma_{21} = 0$$

For the first equation $\mathbf{\Phi}$ is then a four-element column vector

$$\mathbf{\Phi} = \begin{bmatrix} 0 \\ 0 \\ 0 \\ 1 \end{bmatrix}$$

† The general definition of admissibility also requires that the variance matrix of the transformed disturbances satisfy all the a priori restrictions on the original variance matrix, but we are restricting consideration here to the structural coefficients.

and
$$\mathbf{A\Phi} = \begin{bmatrix} \gamma_{12} \\ \gamma_{22} \end{bmatrix} = \begin{bmatrix} 0 \\ \gamma_{22} \end{bmatrix}$$

Thus $\rho(\mathbf{A\Phi}) = 1 = G - 1$, and the first equation is identified, provided, of course, that $\gamma_{22} \neq 0$. If γ_{22} were zero, the variable x_2 would not appear in either equation, and so the fact that it was absent from the first would be of no help in identifying that equation. In a similar fashion, the restriction on the second equation gives

$$\mathbf{\Phi} = \begin{bmatrix} 0 \\ 0 \\ 1 \\ 0 \end{bmatrix}$$

$$\mathbf{A\Phi} = \begin{bmatrix} \gamma_{11} \\ 0 \end{bmatrix}$$

and
$$\rho(\mathbf{A\Phi}) = 1 = G - 1$$

Alternatively the equations

$$\boldsymbol{\alpha}_1[\mathbf{W} \quad \mathbf{\Phi}] = \mathbf{0}$$

in the parameters of the first equation give

$$[\beta_{11} \quad \beta_{12} \quad \gamma_{11} \quad \gamma_{12}] \begin{bmatrix} \pi_{11} & \pi_{12} & 0 \\ \pi_{21} & \pi_{22} & 0 \\ 1 & 0 & 0 \\ 0 & 1 & 1 \end{bmatrix} = [0 \quad 0 \quad 0]$$

that is,

$$\beta_{11}\pi_{11} + \beta_{12}\pi_{21} + \gamma_{11} = 0$$
$$\beta_{11}\pi_{12} + \beta_{12}\pi_{22} + \gamma_{12} = 0$$
$$\gamma_{12} = 0$$

If we normalize by setting, say, $\beta_{11} = 1$, these give

$$\beta_{12} = \frac{-\pi_{12}}{\pi_{22}}$$

and
$$\gamma_{11} = \frac{\pi_{12}\pi_{21} - \pi_{11}\pi_{22}}{\pi_{22}}$$

which shows explicitly how the parameters of the first equation may be derived uniquely from those of the reduced form. The parameters of the second equation may be obtained in a similar fashion.

Example 11-2 The restrictions are

$$\gamma_{12} = 0 \qquad \gamma_{22} = 0$$

For the first equation

$$\mathbf{\Phi} = \begin{bmatrix} 0 \\ 0 \\ 0 \\ 1 \end{bmatrix}$$

and $$\mathbf{A\Phi} = \begin{bmatrix} 0 \\ 0 \end{bmatrix}$$

which has zero rank. Thus the first equation is not identifiable; nor is the second, for this is the case we alluded to in Example 11-1, where x_2 appears in neither equation.

Example 11-3 The restrictions are

$$\gamma_{11} = 0 \qquad \gamma_{12} = 0 \qquad \gamma_{22} = 0$$

This example might be treated in two ways. In one approach we note that the restrictions $\gamma_{12} = 0 = \gamma_{22}$ mean that x_2 does not appear in the model at all. Thus the model could be reduced to one with just a single exogenous variable, in which case the only restriction is $\gamma_{11} = 0$, and that suffices to identify the first equation, but leaves the second unidentified. Alternatively, retaining the dimensions of the original model, the restrictions on the first equation give

$$\mathbf{\Phi} = \begin{bmatrix} 0 & 0 \\ 0 & 0 \\ 1 & 0 \\ 0 & 1 \end{bmatrix} \qquad \text{with } \mathbf{A\Phi} = \begin{bmatrix} 0 & 0 \\ \gamma_{21} & 0 \end{bmatrix}$$

Thus $\rho(\mathbf{A\Phi}) = 1 = G - 1$, and so the first equation is identified. For the second equation

$$\mathbf{\Phi} = \begin{bmatrix} 0 \\ 0 \\ 0 \\ 1 \end{bmatrix} \qquad \text{with } \mathbf{A\Phi} = \begin{bmatrix} 0 \\ 0 \end{bmatrix}$$

so that this equation is not identified. Alternatively, for the second equation

$$\boldsymbol{\alpha}_2[\mathbf{W} \quad \mathbf{\Phi}] = \mathbf{0}$$

gives

$$[\beta_{21} \quad \beta_{22} \quad \gamma_{21} \quad \gamma_{22}] \begin{bmatrix} \pi_{11} & \pi_{12} & 0 \\ \pi_{21} & \pi_{22} & 0 \\ 1 & 0 & 0 \\ 0 & 1 & 1 \end{bmatrix} = [0 \quad 0 \quad 0]$$

This appears to give three equations in four unknowns. Setting $\beta_{22} = 1$ would then determine the remaining parameters of the second equation. However, the restrictions $\gamma_{12} = 0 = \gamma_{22}$ imply $\pi_{12} = 0 = \pi_{22}$. Thus the second and third columns in $[\mathbf{W} \quad \mathbf{\Phi}]$ are identical, and so we only have two equations plus a normalization rule, which are insufficient to identify the second equation.

Example 11-4 The restrictions are

$$\gamma_{11} = 0 \qquad \gamma_{12} = 0$$

For the first equation

$$\mathbf{\Phi} = \begin{bmatrix} 0 & 0 \\ 0 & 0 \\ 1 & 0 \\ 0 & 1 \end{bmatrix}$$

and

$$\mathbf{A\Phi} = \begin{bmatrix} 0 & 0 \\ \gamma_{21} & \gamma_{22} \end{bmatrix}$$

so $\rho(\mathbf{A\Phi}) = 1$ and the first equation is identified, while the second is not.

$$\boldsymbol{\alpha}_1[\mathbf{W} \quad \mathbf{\Phi}] = \mathbf{0}$$

gives

$$\beta_{11}\pi_{11} + \beta_{12}\pi_{21} + \gamma_{11} = 0$$
$$\beta_{11}\pi_{12} + \beta_{12}\pi_{22} + \gamma_{12} = 0$$
$$\gamma_{11} = 0$$
$$\gamma_{12} = 0$$

which, on setting $\beta_{11} = 1$, gives

$$\beta_{12} = -\frac{\pi_{11}}{\pi_{21}} = -\frac{\pi_{12}}{\pi_{22}}$$

This does not imply a contradiction, for both expressions for β_{12} will yield an identical value. The prior specifications and the normalization rule in this example give the model

$$y_{1t} + \beta_{12}y_{2t} = u_{1t}$$
$$\beta_{21}y_{1t} + y_{2t} + \gamma_{21}x_{1t} + \gamma_{22}x_{2t} = u_{2t}$$

The matrix of reduced-form coefficients is

$$\Pi = \begin{bmatrix} \pi_{11} & \pi_{12} \\ \pi_{21} & \pi_{22} \end{bmatrix} = \frac{1}{\Delta}\begin{bmatrix} \beta_{12}\gamma_{21} & \beta_{12}\gamma_{22} \\ -\gamma_{21} & -\gamma_{22} \end{bmatrix}$$

where $\Delta = 1 - \beta_{12}\beta_{21}$. Although Π is a 2×2 matrix, its rank is only 1. This is an example of *overidentification*. Only one prior restriction is needed to identify the first equation, but we have two. The consequence is a restriction on the reduced-form coefficients. Notice also that even in the overidentified case $\rho(\mathbf{A\Phi})$ cannot exceed $G - 1$. $\mathbf{A\Phi}$ has G rows, but the first row is always zero for homogeneous restrictions, so $\rho(\mathbf{A\Phi}) \leq G - 1$ even in cases of overidentification where $\mathbf{A\Phi}$ has G or more columns. If Π is replaced in an actual two-equation problem by $\hat{\Pi}$, the matrix of *estimated* reduced-form coefficients, then $\rho(\hat{\Pi})$ will almost certainly be 2 and not 1, so that estimating β_{12} by $-\hat{\pi}_{11}/\hat{\pi}_{21}$ or by $-\hat{\pi}_{12}/\hat{\pi}_{22}$ would yield two different values. ILS is thus not a suitable estimation method for overidentified equations, since it fails to yield unique estimates.

Example 11-5 The restrictions are

$$\gamma_{11} = 0 \qquad \gamma_{12} = 0 \qquad \beta_{21} + \gamma_{21} = 0 \qquad \gamma_{22} = 0$$

This is Example 11-3 with the additional specification $\beta_{21} + \gamma_{21} = 0$. In Example 11-3 the first equation was identifiable and the second not. Leaving x_2 out of the model, we now have for the second equation

$$\mathbf{\Phi} = \begin{bmatrix} 1 \\ 0 \\ 1 \end{bmatrix}$$

and
$$\mathbf{A\Phi} = \begin{bmatrix} \beta_{11} \\ 0 \end{bmatrix}$$

so $\rho(\mathbf{A\Phi}) = 1$ and the second equation is now identified.

In all the above examples readers should check for themselves that the necessary condition (or *order* condition, as it is often called) would correctly indicate the presence or absence of identification. This need not always be the case. For example, if β_{11} in Example 11-5 were zero, the rank condition would fail even though there is one restriction on the second equation.

Treatment of Identities

Identities themselves do not raise any identification problems since in general the coefficients are known and indeed are usually unity. The general model

$$\mathbf{By}_t + \mathbf{\Gamma x}_t = \mathbf{u}_t$$

may, however, be formulated in two alternative fashions. In one version all identities appear explicitly in the model. In the alternative version the identities may be substituted in other structural equations, thus effectively reducing the size of the model. The identification rules may be applied to either version. Solving out the identities will not change any conclusions about the identifiability of any behavioral or other structural equation whether in its original or revised form.

As an illustration consider the simple supply-and-demand model

$$q^D = \alpha_0 + \alpha_1 p + u_1$$

$$q^S = \beta_0 + \beta_1 p + \beta_2 w + u_2$$

$$q^D \equiv q^S$$

where
q^D = quantity demanded

q^S = quantity supplied

p = price

w = an index of weather conditions

This is a model containing three endogenous variables q^D, q^S, and p ($G = 3$) and two exogenous variables w and z (a dummy variable) set at unity to take care of the intercept term in the first two equations. Rearranging the model in more suitable form we have

$$\begin{bmatrix} 1 & 0 & -\alpha_1 & 0 & -\alpha_0 \\ 0 & 1 & -\beta_1 & -\beta_2 & -\beta_0 \\ 1 & -1 & 0 & 0 & 0 \end{bmatrix} \begin{bmatrix} q^D \\ q^S \\ p \\ w \\ z \end{bmatrix} = \begin{bmatrix} u_1 \\ u_2 \\ 0 \end{bmatrix}$$

For the first equation

$$\mathbf{A\Phi} = \begin{bmatrix} 0 & 0 \\ 1 & -\beta_2 \\ -1 & 0 \end{bmatrix}$$

and $\rho(\mathbf{A\Phi}) = 2 = G - 1$ so that the equation is identified. Notice that when we have exclusion restrictions, the $\mathbf{A\Phi}$ matrix can be written down directly by taking the columns of the $\mathbf{A}$ matrix which contain zeros in the row corresponding to the equation under study. For the second equation

$$\mathbf{A\Phi} = \begin{bmatrix} 1 \\ 0 \\ 1 \end{bmatrix}$$

which only has rank unity, and so the second equation is not identified.

If we rewrite the model without the identity, it becomes a two-equation model in two endogenous variables q and p,

$$q = \alpha_0 + \alpha_1 p + u_1$$

$$q = \beta_0 + \beta_1 p + \beta_2 w + u_2$$

where now $G = 2$, and the first equation is again just identified because it has one restriction on its coefficients while the second equation is not identified because there are no restrictions on its coefficients.

Inhomogeneous Linear Restrictions

The linear restrictions embodied in Eq. (11-24) are all *homogeneous*, that is, specified coefficients or linear combinations of coefficients are set equal to zero. Many restrictions indicated by economic theory occur naturally in a nonhomogeneous form, an illustration being the specification, say, that the elasticities in a production function sum to unity. Such restrictions, however, have no meaning until a normalization rule has been imposed. Thus if we have the restriction

$$\beta_{12} + \gamma_{11} = 1$$

it can be written as

$$\beta_{12} + \gamma_{11} - \beta_{11} = 0$$

plus the normalization rule $\beta_{11} = 1$. Thus inhomogeneous restrictions can be recast in homogeneous form before normalization and the previous procedures still apply.

Restrictions across Equations

So far we have only considered linear restrictions within a structural equation. There are cases, however, where theory suggests restrictions across equations, some examples of which have already been encountered in Sec. 8-6. These can also serve to ensure identifiability, as is shown in the following simplified examples.

Example 11-6 Consider the model

$$y_1 + \beta_{12}y_2 + \gamma_{11}x_1 = u_1$$
$$\beta_{21}y_1 + y_2 + \gamma_{21}x_1 = u_2$$

Without further restrictions neither equation is identified. The imposition of cross-equation restrictions requires that each equation be normalized, otherwise the restriction is ambiguous. Suppose there is a theoretical basis for postulating

$$\gamma_{11} + \gamma_{21} = 0$$

Identifiability in the presence of the restriction may be examined either by looking at the relationship between structural and reduced-form parameters or by investigating the set of admissible transformed structures that satisfy the restriction. The reduced-form equations are

$$y_1 = \frac{-\gamma_{11}}{\Delta}(1 + \beta_{12})x_1 + v_1$$

$$y_2 = \frac{\gamma_{11}}{\Delta}(1 + \beta_{21})x_1 + v_2$$

where

$$\Delta = 1 - \beta_{12}\beta_{21}$$

The reduced form yields only two parameters and, even with the restriction, there are still three structural parameters. It is clear that neither equation is identified.†

Example 11-7 Consider

$$y_1 + \gamma_{11}x_1 = u_1$$
$$\beta_{21}y_1 + y_2 + \gamma_{21}x_1 = u_2$$

† The argument to the contrary in G. S. Maddala, *Econometrics*, McGraw-Hill, New York, 1977, p. 230, is incorrect. Maddala investigates identifiability via transformation matrices. However, he essentially postulates a transformation matrix

$$\mathbf{F} = \begin{bmatrix} 1 & \lambda \\ 0 & 1 \end{bmatrix}$$

and then finds that the restriction implies $\lambda = 0$, which leads him to conclude that both equations are identified. But $\mathbf{F}$ has already assumed that the second equation is identified, which is an invalid assumption. The identifiability of *both* equations has to be considered *jointly*.

Postulating the transformation matrix

$$\mathbf{F} = \begin{bmatrix} f_{11} & f_{12} \\ f_{21} & f_{22} \end{bmatrix}$$

the transformed structure is

$$(f_{11} + f_{12}\beta_{21})y_1 + f_{12}y_2 + (f_{11}\gamma_{11} + f_{12}\gamma_{21})x_1 = u_1^*$$
$$(f_{21} + f_{22}\beta_{21})y_1 + f_{22}y_2 + (f_{21}\gamma_{11} + f_{22}\gamma_{21})x_1 = u_2^*$$

The requirement that the transformed structure satisfies the same a priori constraints as the original structure, namely, that y_2 does not appear in the first equation, gives

$$f_{12} = 0$$

The *normalized* transformed structure is then

$$y_1 + \gamma_{11}x_1 = u_1^{**}$$
$$\left(\frac{f_{21} + f_{22}\beta_{21}}{f_{22}}\right)y_1 + y_2 + \left(\frac{f_{21}\gamma_{11} + f_{22}\gamma_{21}}{f_{22}}\right)x_1 = u_2^{**}$$

If we now impose the cross-equation constraint $\gamma_{11} + \gamma_{21} = 0$ on the original structure, the same condition on the transformed structure gives

$$\gamma_{11} + \frac{f_{21}\gamma_{11} + f_{22}\gamma_{21}}{f_{22}} = 0$$

or

$$f_{21}\gamma_{11} = 0$$

giving

$$f_{21} = 0$$

so that all admissible transformation matrices are diagonal and both equations are identified.

Alternatively the reduced form of the model is

$$y_1 = -\gamma_{11}x_1 + v_1$$
$$y_2 = (\beta_{21}\gamma_{11} - \gamma_{21})x_1 + v_2 = \gamma_{11}(\beta_{21} + 1)x_1 + v_2$$

The parameter γ_{11} can be obtained from the first reduced-form coefficient and β_{21} can be derived from the second reduced-form coefficient, so that both equations are identified.

Restrictions on the Variance Matrix

So far the only explicit assumption about the disturbances has been that of serial independence, but we have made no explicit assumptions about contemporaneous correlations between disturbances in different structural equations. Let

$$\boldsymbol{\Sigma} = E(\mathbf{u}_t\mathbf{u}_t')$$

$\boldsymbol{\Sigma}$ is then a $G \times G$ matrix, the terms on the principal diagonal indicating the variances (assumed constant) of the disturbances in the G structural equations and the off-diagonal terms indicating the covariances between pairs of disturbances. If specific restrictions can be placed on some of these elements, they constitute an additional source of identifying power.

Let us examine first of all restrictions on covariances. Consider the model

$$y_1 + \gamma_{11}x_1 = u_1$$
$$\beta_{21}y_1 + y_2 + \gamma_{21}x_1 = u_2$$

As is easily seen, the first equation of this model is identifiable and the second is not. We shall, however, examine the identifiability of the model again by considering admissible transformation matrices, as this approach facilitates the study of restrictions on variances and covariances.

Using

$$\mathbf{F} = \begin{bmatrix} f_{11} & f_{12} \\ f_{21} & f_{22} \end{bmatrix}$$

the transformed first equation becomes

$$(f_{11} + f_{12}\beta_{21})y_1 + f_{12}y_2 + (f_{11}\gamma_{11} + f_{12}\gamma_{21})x_1 = f_{11}u_1 + f_{12}u_2$$

If the coefficients of the transformed equation are to obey the same restrictions as those of the original equation, we must have

$$f_{11} + f_{12}\beta_{21} = 1$$
$$f_{12} = 0$$

giving $f_{11} = 1$ and $f_{12} = 0$. The only restriction on the second equation is the normalization condition, which is held in abeyance. Thus admissible transformation matrices are given by

$$\mathbf{F} = \begin{bmatrix} 1 & 0 \\ f_{21} & f_{22} \end{bmatrix}$$

showing that the first equation is identified and the second not.

Suppose we can now postulate

$$\mathbf{\Sigma} = \begin{bmatrix} \sigma_{11} & 0 \\ 0 & \sigma_{22} \end{bmatrix}$$

The vector of disturbances in the transformed structure is $\mathbf{Fu}_t$, and so the variance-covariance matrix for the disturbances of the transformed structure is

$$\mathbf{\Psi} = E(\mathbf{Fu}_t\mathbf{u}_t'\mathbf{F}')$$
$$= \mathbf{F\Sigma F}'$$

This must obey the restriction that the covariance between the two transformed disturbances is zero, that is,

$$\mathbf{f}_1\mathbf{\Sigma f}_2' = 0$$

or

$$\begin{bmatrix} 1 & 0 \end{bmatrix}\begin{bmatrix} \sigma_{11} & 0 \\ 0 & \sigma_{22} \end{bmatrix}\begin{bmatrix} f_{21} \\ f_{22} \end{bmatrix} = 0$$

that is,

$$f_{21}\sigma_{11} = 0$$

which gives

$$f_{21} = 0$$

The value of f_{22} is then settled by the normalization condition that the coefficient of y_2 in the second equation must be unity. The coefficients of the transformed structure are given by

$$\mathbf{FA} = \begin{bmatrix} 1 & 0 \\ f_{21} & f_{22} \end{bmatrix} \begin{bmatrix} 1 & 0 & \gamma_{11} \\ \beta_{21} & 1 & \gamma_{21} \end{bmatrix}$$

giving the coefficient of y_2 in the second equation as f_{22}. Thus $f_{22} = 1$, and the only admissible transformation matrix is

$$\mathbf{F} = \begin{bmatrix} 1 & 0 \\ 0 & 1 \end{bmatrix}$$

so that both equations are identified.†

As a further illustration consider the model

$$\begin{aligned} y_1 + \gamma_{11}x_1 &= u_1 \\ \beta_{21}y_1 + y_2 + \gamma_{21}x_1 &= u_2 \\ \beta_{31}y_1 + \beta_{32}y_2 + y_3 + \gamma_{31}x_1 &= u_3 \end{aligned}$$

Without further restrictions only the first equation is identifiable. If, however, we assume

$$\boldsymbol{\Sigma} = \begin{bmatrix} \sigma_{11} & 0 & 0 \\ 0 & \sigma_{22} & 0 \\ 0 & 0 & \sigma_{33} \end{bmatrix}$$

the second and third equations become identifiable. Consider

$$\mathbf{FA} = \begin{bmatrix} 1 & 0 & 0 \\ f_{21} & f_{22} & f_{23} \\ f_{31} & f_{32} & f_{33} \end{bmatrix} \begin{bmatrix} 1 & 0 & 0 & \gamma_{11} \\ \beta_{21} & 1 & 0 & \gamma_{21} \\ \beta_{31} & \beta_{32} & 1 & \gamma_{31} \end{bmatrix}$$

The normalization condition on y_2 in the second equation and on y_3 in the third give

$$\begin{aligned} f_{22} + f_{23}\beta_{32} &= 1 \\ f_{33} &= 1 \end{aligned}$$

† It is convenient algebraically, but not necessary, to impose the normalization condition on the coefficients of y_1 and y_2 in the first and second equations, respectively, of the transformed structure. The absence of y_2 from the first equation gives $f_{12} = 0$. The zero covariance term then gives $f_{21} = 0$ and so the class of admissible transformation matrices is

$$\mathbf{F} = \begin{bmatrix} f_{11} & 0 \\ 0 & f_{22} \end{bmatrix}$$

which secures the identification of both equations.

and the exclusion of y_3 from the second equation gives

$$f_{23} = 0$$

which also implies

$$f_{22} = 1$$

Thus **F** is now

$$\mathbf{F} = \begin{bmatrix} 1 & 0 & 0 \\ f_{21} & 1 & 0 \\ f_{31} & f_{32} & 1 \end{bmatrix}$$

We have not yet considered the effect of the zero covariance restrictions $\sigma_{12} = \sigma_{13} = \sigma_{23} = 0$. These must be satisfied by the transformed structure. Hence

$$\mathbf{f}_1 \boldsymbol{\Sigma} \mathbf{f}'_2 = 0$$
$$\mathbf{f}_1 \boldsymbol{\Sigma} \mathbf{f}'_3 = 0$$
$$\mathbf{f}_2 \boldsymbol{\Sigma} \mathbf{f}'_3 = 0$$

The first of these gives

$$[1 \quad 0 \quad 0] \begin{bmatrix} \sigma_{11} & 0 & 0 \\ 0 & \sigma_{22} & 0 \\ 0 & 0 & \sigma_{33} \end{bmatrix} \begin{bmatrix} f_{21} \\ 1 \\ 0 \end{bmatrix} = f_{21}\sigma_{11} = 0$$

so that

$$f_{21} = 0$$

and in a similar fashion the second and third conditions gives $f_{31} = 0$ and $f_{32} = 0$. Thus the only admissible transformation matrix is

$$\mathbf{F} = \begin{bmatrix} 1 & 0 & 0 \\ 0 & 1 & 0 \\ 0 & 0 & 1 \end{bmatrix}$$

and all three equations are identified.

The above model has two special features, namely, a triangular **B** matrix and a diagonal $\boldsymbol{\Sigma}$ matrix. The presence of these two features defines a *recursive* system. All the equations of the recursive system are identified and, as we shall see below, simple estimation procedures are available for this model.

Zero covariances can aid identification and not necessarily just in recursive systems. For example, in

$$y_1 + \beta_{12} y_2 = u_1$$
$$\beta_{21} y_1 + y_2 + \gamma_{21} x_1 = u_2$$

the first equation is identified and the second is not. However, the additional specification $\sigma_{12} = 0$ would serve to identify the second equation as readers can easily prove for themselves. There is no simple necessary and sufficient condition for the zero covariance case as there was for restrictions on the β and γ parameters, so each case must be examined from first principles.

The discussion has dealt only with models which are linear in variables and parameters. Many realistic models, however, may be nonlinear in variables and/or a priori restrictions. Identification theory for such models is difficult and has only been partially developed. Owing to the unsatisfactory state of the theory it will not be summarized here. Interested readers should consult Fisher.†

11-3 ESTIMATION OF SIMULTANEOUS EQUATION MODELS

Whether we wish to estimate an equation which is one of a set of equations constituting a complete model or whether we wish to estimate all the equations of a model we are in a situation where OLS and the variants of OLS that we have considered so far in the context of a single-equation model are, in general, unsatisfactory estimating techniques. If OLS is applied to an equation in a model, there will usually be more than one current endogenous variable in the relation, and whichever variable one selects as the "dependent" variable, the remaining endogenous variable(s) will generally be correlated with the disturbance term in the equation so that OLS estimates will be biased and inconsistent. Only in the case of *recursive* models will OLS be an optimal estimating technique.

In the more general simultaneous case, where the special assumptions of a recursive system are not fulfilled, the main estimating techniques are indirect least squares (ILS), two-stage least squares (2SLS), both of which may be interpreted as IV estimators, limited-information maximum likelihood (LIML), three-stage least squares (3SLS), and full-information maximum likelihood (FIML). ILS, 2SLS, and LIML are essentially single-equation methods, in which attention is focused on one equation at a time without using all the information contained in the detailed specification of the rest of the model. 3SLS and FIML are system methods, where all the equations of the fully specified structural model are estimated simultaneously.

Recursive Systems

As we have seen already, the two crucial features of a recursive system are a triangular **B** matrix and a diagonal **Σ** matrix. As an illustration consider the model

$$y_{1t} + \gamma_{11}x_t = u_{1t}$$
$$\beta_{21}y_{1t} + y_{2t} + \gamma_{21}x_t = u_{2t}$$

with the specification

$$E(\mathbf{uu}') = \boldsymbol{\Sigma} = \begin{bmatrix} \sigma_{11} & 0 \\ 0 & \sigma_{22} \end{bmatrix}$$

† F. M. Fisher, *The Identification Problem in Econometrics*, McGraw-Hill, New York, 1966, Chap. 5.

To explore the connection between the y's and the u's we look at the reduced-form equations which are

$$y_{1t} = -\gamma_{11}x_t + u_{1t}$$
$$y_{2t} = (\beta_{21}\gamma_{11} - \gamma_{21})x_t + (u_{2t} - \beta_{21}u_{1t})$$

The first equation is the same in each case. Since the exogenous variable x is by assumption uncorrelated with the u's, the first equation may be estimated consistently by OLS. The second reduced-form equation shows y_{2t} to be a function of both u_{1t} and u_{2t}. Thus it would be inappropriate to estimate the second structural equation by an OLS regression of y_1 on y_2 and x. However, y_{1t} is uncorrelated with u_{2t} since it is a function only of u_{1t}, which has zero correlation with u_{2t}. Thus an OLS regression of y_2 on y_1 and x will yield consistent estimates of the second structural equation.

More generally, the disturbance vector in the reduced form of a model is

$$\mathbf{v}_t = \begin{bmatrix} v_{1t} \\ v_{2t} \\ \vdots \\ v_{Gt} \end{bmatrix} = \mathbf{B}^{-1}\mathbf{u}_t \tag{11-30}$$

When $\mathbf{B}$ is lower triangular, then so is $\mathbf{B}^{-1}$. Thus Eq. (11-30) gives

$$y_{1t} = f(u_{1t})$$
$$y_{2t} = f(u_{1t}, u_{2t})$$
$$y_{3t} = f(u_{1t}, u_{2t}, u_{3t})$$
$$0$$
$$y_{Gt} = f(u_{1t}, u_{2t}, \ldots, u_{Gt})$$

The assumption of a diagonal $\boldsymbol{\Sigma}$ matrix then ensures that y_{1t} is uncorrelated with u_{2t}, that y_{2t} is uncorrelated with u_{3t}, and so forth. Thus the second structural equation may be estimated consistently by an OLS regression with y_2 as the dependent variable, the third with y_3 as the dependent variable, and so on.

It is also easy to show that if the u's are normally distributed, OLS yields ML estimates. As was shown in the previous section, the likelihood of the sample y's, conditional on the x's, for the model

$$\mathbf{B}\mathbf{y}_t + \boldsymbol{\Gamma}\mathbf{x}_t = \mathbf{u}_t$$

is given by

$$L = (2\pi)^{-nG/2}\|\mathbf{B}\|^n \cdot |\boldsymbol{\Sigma}|^{-n/2}\exp\left(-\frac{1}{2}\sum_{t=1}^{n}\mathbf{u}_t'\boldsymbol{\Sigma}^{-1}\mathbf{u}_t\right)$$

For recursive systems $|\mathbf{B}|$ is unity and $\boldsymbol{\Sigma}$ and $\boldsymbol{\Sigma}^{-1}$ are both diagonal. Thus finding the $\hat{\mathbf{B}}$ and $\hat{\boldsymbol{\Gamma}}$ to minimize L is equivalent to finding the $\hat{\mathbf{B}}$ and $\hat{\boldsymbol{\Gamma}}$ to minimize

$$\sum_{t=1}^{n}\mathbf{u}_t'\boldsymbol{\Sigma}^{-1}\mathbf{u}_t$$

For a three-equation system this sum of squares is

$$S = \sum_{t=1}^{n} [u_{1t} \quad u_{2t} \quad u_{3t}] \begin{bmatrix} \frac{1}{\sigma_{11}} & 0 & 0 \\ 0 & \frac{1}{\sigma_{22}} & 0 \\ 0 & 0 & \frac{1}{\sigma_{33}} \end{bmatrix} \begin{bmatrix} u_{1t} \\ u_{2t} \\ u_{3t} \end{bmatrix}$$

$$= \sum_{t=1}^{n} \left(\frac{u_{1t}^2}{\sigma_{11}} + \frac{u_{2t}^2}{\sigma_{22}} + \frac{u_{3t}^2}{\sigma_{33}} \right)$$

Thus the partial derivatives of $\ln L$ with respect to the coefficients of the ith structural equation are simply the partial derivatives of

$$\sum_{t=1}^{n} \frac{u_{it}^2}{\sigma_{ii}}$$

Setting these partial derivatives to zero gives the OLS equations for the ith structural equation. Thus under the special assumptions of the recursive model the OLS estimators of the structural equations will have the desirable properties of consistency, asymptotic normality, and efficiency. They will also have the usual small sample properties.†

Indirect Least Squares

As indicated in Sec. 11-1, ILS is a feasible estimation technique for an equation which is just identified. The first step consists of estimating the matrix of reduced-form coefficients by the application of OLS to each of the reduced-form equations. The estimates of the structural coefficients are then obtained from the algebraic relations existing between structural and reduced-form coefficients.

The structural model at time period t has been written as

$$\mathbf{B}\mathbf{y}_t + \mathbf{\Gamma}\mathbf{x}_t = \mathbf{u}_t \tag{11-31}$$

where

$$\mathbf{y}_t = \begin{bmatrix} y_{1t} \\ y_{2t} \\ \vdots \\ y_{Gt} \end{bmatrix} \quad \text{and} \quad \mathbf{x}_t = \begin{bmatrix} x_{1t} \\ x_{2t} \\ \vdots \\ x_{Kt} \end{bmatrix}$$

are, respectively, the $G \times 1$ vector of observations on the jointly dependent endogenous variables at time t and the $K \times 1$ vector of observations on the

† For a proof that the usual small sample inference procedures apply see E. Malinvaud, *Statistical Methods of Econometrics*, 2nd edition, North-Holland, Amsterdam, 1970, pp. 679–681.

predetermined variables at time t. Let us define $\mathbf{Y}$ and $\mathbf{X}$ as

$$\mathbf{Y} = \begin{bmatrix} - & \mathbf{y}_1' & - \\ - & \mathbf{y}_2' & - \\ - & \vdots & - \\ - & \mathbf{y}_n' & - \end{bmatrix} \qquad \mathbf{X} = \begin{bmatrix} - & \mathbf{x}_1' & - \\ - & \mathbf{x}_2' & - \\ - & \vdots & - \\ - & \mathbf{x}_n' & - \end{bmatrix}$$

so that $\mathbf{Y}$ is the $n \times G$ matrix of the sample observations on the endogenous variables and $\mathbf{X}$ is the $n \times K$ matrix of sample observations on the predetermined variables. From Eq. (11-31) we then have

$$\mathbf{YB}' + \mathbf{X\Gamma}' = \mathbf{U} \tag{11-32}$$

where $\mathbf{U}$ is the $n \times G$ matrix of all the sample disturbances. The reduced form may then be written

$$\mathbf{Y} = \mathbf{X\Pi}' + \mathbf{V} \tag{11-33}$$

where

$$\mathbf{\Pi}' = -\mathbf{\Gamma}'(\mathbf{B}')^{-1} \tag{11-34}$$

and

$$\mathbf{V} = \mathbf{U}(\mathbf{B}')^{-1}$$

The matrix of reduced-form coefficients defined in Eq. (11-34) is simply the transpose of the matrix previously defined in Eqs. (11-19). The estimation of $\mathbf{\Pi}'$ is accomplished by applying OLS to Eq. (11-33) giving

$$\mathbf{P}' = (\mathbf{X}'\mathbf{X})^{-1}\mathbf{X}'\mathbf{Y} \tag{11-35}$$

This yields the set of estimated reduced-form coefficients for the first stage of ILS.

Let us denote the equation we are interested in estimating by

$$\mathbf{y} = \mathbf{Y}_1\boldsymbol{\beta} + \mathbf{X}_1\boldsymbol{\gamma} + \mathbf{u} \tag{11-36}$$

where $\mathbf{y} = n \times 1$ vector of observations on the dependent (endogenous) variable in the equation

$\mathbf{Y}_1 = n \times (g-1)$ matrix of observations on the other $g-1$ current endogenous variables in the equation

$\mathbf{X}_1 = n \times k$ matrix of observations on the k predetermined variables in the equation

$\mathbf{u} = n \times 1$ vector of disturbances in the equation.

Rewriting Eq. (11-36) gives

$$[\mathbf{y} \quad \mathbf{Y}_1 \quad \mathbf{X}_1] \begin{bmatrix} 1 \\ -\boldsymbol{\beta} \\ -\boldsymbol{\gamma} \end{bmatrix} = \mathbf{u}$$

or, more fully,

$$[\mathbf{y} \quad \mathbf{Y}_1 \quad \mathbf{Y}_2 \quad \mathbf{X}_1 \quad \mathbf{X}_2] \begin{bmatrix} 1 \\ -\boldsymbol{\beta} \\ \mathbf{0} \\ -\boldsymbol{\gamma} \\ 0 \end{bmatrix} = \mathbf{u}$$

where $\mathbf{Y}_2$ and $\mathbf{X}_2$ are matrices of observations on $G - g$ endogenous and $K - k$ predetermined variables which are excluded from the equation.

The relations between structural and reduced-form equations are given in Eq. (11-34), which may be rewritten as

$$\mathbf{\Pi}'\mathbf{B}' = -\mathbf{\Gamma}'$$

The relations holding for the coefficients of the structural equation (11-36) are then

$$\underset{K \times G}{\mathbf{\Pi}'} \underset{G \times 1}{\begin{bmatrix} 1 \\ -\boldsymbol{\beta} \\ \mathbf{0} \end{bmatrix}} = \underset{K \times 1}{\begin{bmatrix} \boldsymbol{\gamma} \\ \mathbf{0} \end{bmatrix}} \tag{11-37}$$

Substituting in this from Eq. (11-35) gives the ILS coefficients as the vectors **b** and **c** obtained by solving

$$(\mathbf{X}'\mathbf{X})^{-1}\mathbf{X}'\mathbf{Y}\begin{bmatrix} 1 \\ -\mathbf{b} \\ \mathbf{0} \end{bmatrix} = \begin{bmatrix} \mathbf{c} \\ \mathbf{0} \end{bmatrix} \tag{11-38}$$

The crucial question is whether there are unique solution vectors **b** and **c**. Rewriting Eq. (11-38) as

$$(\mathbf{X}'\mathbf{X})^{-1}\mathbf{X}'[\mathbf{y} \quad \mathbf{Y}_1 \quad \mathbf{Y}_2]\begin{bmatrix} 1 \\ -\mathbf{b} \\ \mathbf{0} \end{bmatrix} = \begin{bmatrix} \mathbf{c} \\ \mathbf{0} \end{bmatrix}$$

gives

$$(\mathbf{X}'\mathbf{X})^{-1}\mathbf{X}'\mathbf{y} - (\mathbf{X}'\mathbf{X})^{-1}\mathbf{X}'\mathbf{Y}_1\mathbf{b} = \begin{bmatrix} \mathbf{c} \\ \mathbf{0} \end{bmatrix} \tag{11-39}$$

Premultiplying by $(\mathbf{X}'\mathbf{X})$, partitioning $\mathbf{X}$ as $[\mathbf{X}_1 \quad \mathbf{X}_2]$, and rearranging gives the pair of equations

$$(\mathbf{X}_1'\mathbf{Y}_1)\mathbf{b} + (\mathbf{X}_1'\mathbf{X}_1)\mathbf{c} = \mathbf{X}_1'\mathbf{y} \tag{11-40}$$

$$(\mathbf{X}_2'\mathbf{Y}_1)\mathbf{b} + (\mathbf{X}_2'\mathbf{X}_1)\mathbf{c} = \mathbf{X}_2'\mathbf{y} \tag{11-41}$$

Together these constitute K equations in $(g - 1) + k$ unknowns. Since the necessary condition for exact identification is

$$K - k = g - 1$$

we have the same number of equations as unknowns so that, in general, Eqs. (11-40) and (11-41) solve uniquely for the ILS estimates **b** and **c**.

These equations also indicate how the ILS estimates may be interpreted as IV estimates. Returning to the structural equation

$$\mathbf{y} = \mathbf{Y}_1\boldsymbol{\beta} + \mathbf{X}_1\boldsymbol{\gamma} + \mathbf{u}$$

the inconsistency of OLS arises from the correlations between $\mathbf{Y}_1$ and **u**. The x variables, however, are uncorrelated with **u**, and in the exactly identified case $\mathbf{X}_2$

will have the same number of columns as $\mathbf{Y}_1$. This suggests using

$$[\mathbf{X}_2 \quad \mathbf{X}_1]$$

as the set of instruments for $[\mathbf{Y}_1 \quad \mathbf{X}_1]$. The resultant IV estimates are given by

$$\begin{bmatrix} \mathbf{X}_2'\mathbf{Y}_1 & \mathbf{X}_2'\mathbf{X}_1 \\ \mathbf{X}_1'\mathbf{Y}_1 & \mathbf{X}_1'\mathbf{X}_1 \end{bmatrix} \begin{bmatrix} \mathbf{b}_{\text{IV}} \\ \mathbf{c}_{\text{IV}} \end{bmatrix} = \begin{bmatrix} \mathbf{X}_2'\mathbf{y} \\ \mathbf{X}_1'\mathbf{y} \end{bmatrix}$$

which are identical with Eqs. (11-40) and (11-41). Notice that the ordering of the instrumental variables is unimportant. We can just as well take

$$\mathbf{X} = [\mathbf{X}_1 \quad \mathbf{X}_2]$$

as the matrix of instrumental variables. Rewriting Eq. (11-36) as

$$\mathbf{y} = \mathbf{Z}_1\boldsymbol{\delta} + \mathbf{u}$$

where

$$\mathbf{Z}_1 = [\mathbf{Y}_1 \quad \mathbf{X}_1] \qquad \text{and} \qquad \boldsymbol{\delta} = \begin{bmatrix} \boldsymbol{\beta} \\ \boldsymbol{\gamma} \end{bmatrix}$$

the IV estimator of $\boldsymbol{\delta}$ is

$$\mathbf{d}_{\text{IV}} = \begin{bmatrix} \mathbf{b}_{\text{IV}} \\ \mathbf{c}_{\text{IV}} \end{bmatrix} = (\mathbf{X}'\mathbf{Z}_1)^{-1}\mathbf{X}'\mathbf{y} \tag{11-42}$$

which is easily seen to be identical to the ILS estimator defined in Eqs. (11-40) and (11-41).

Two-Stage Least Squares

In practice ILS is not a widely used technique since it is rare for an equation to be exactly identified. 2SLS is perhaps the most important and widely used procedure. It is applicable to equations which are overidentified or exactly identified. Moreover, it turns out that in the case of an exactly identified equation the 2SLS estimates are identical with the ILS estimates given by Eqs. (11-40) and (11-41).

Consider again the estimation of the equation

$$\mathbf{y} = \mathbf{Y}_1\boldsymbol{\beta} + \mathbf{X}_1\boldsymbol{\gamma} + \mathbf{u}$$

where the necessary condition for identification requires that

$$K - k \geq g - 1$$

As we have seen, the trouble about applying OLS directly to this equation is that the embedding of the equation in a simultaneous equation model makes the variables in $\mathbf{Y}_1$ correlated with $\mathbf{u}$. The 2SLS technique consists of replacing $\mathbf{Y}_1$ by a computed matrix $\hat{\mathbf{Y}}_1$, which hopefully is purged of the stochastic element, and then performing an OLS regression of $\mathbf{y}$ on $\hat{\mathbf{Y}}_1$ and $\mathbf{X}_1$.

The matrix $\hat{\mathbf{Y}}_1$ is computed in the first stage by regressing each variable in $\mathbf{Y}_1$ on all the predetermined variables in the complete model and replacing the actual observations on the y variables by the corresponding regression values. Thus

$$\hat{\mathbf{Y}}_1 = \mathbf{X}(\mathbf{X}'\mathbf{X})^{-1}\mathbf{X}'\mathbf{Y}_1 \tag{11-43}$$

In the second stage the regression of $\mathbf{y}$ on $\hat{\mathbf{Y}}_1$ and $\mathbf{X}_1$ yields the estimating equations

$$\begin{bmatrix} \hat{\mathbf{Y}}_1'\hat{\mathbf{Y}}_1 & \hat{\mathbf{Y}}_1'\mathbf{X}_1 \\ \mathbf{X}_1'\hat{\mathbf{Y}}_1 & \mathbf{X}_1'\mathbf{X}_1 \end{bmatrix} \begin{bmatrix} \mathbf{b} \\ \mathbf{c} \end{bmatrix} = \begin{bmatrix} \hat{\mathbf{Y}}_1'\mathbf{y} \\ \mathbf{X}_1'\mathbf{y} \end{bmatrix} \tag{11-44}$$

where $\begin{bmatrix} \mathbf{b} \\ \mathbf{c} \end{bmatrix}$ now denotes the 2SLS estimator of $\begin{bmatrix} \boldsymbol{\beta} \\ \boldsymbol{\gamma} \end{bmatrix}$. For the actual estimation there is no need to compute the regression values in $\hat{\mathbf{Y}}_1$ explicitly. An alternative form of Eq. (11-44) can be derived which involves only the matrices of actual observations. The matrix $\mathbf{Y}_1$ can be written as

$$\mathbf{Y}_1 = \hat{\mathbf{Y}}_1 + \mathbf{V}_1$$

where $\hat{\mathbf{Y}}_1$ is given by Eq. (11-43) and $\mathbf{V}_1$ is the $n \times (g - 1)$ matrix of OLS residuals. The usual properties of OLS residuals give

$$\hat{\mathbf{Y}}_1'\mathbf{V}_1 = 0$$

and

$$\mathbf{X}'\mathbf{V}_1 = \mathbf{0}$$

Thus

$$\begin{aligned} \hat{\mathbf{Y}}_1'\hat{\mathbf{Y}}_1 &= \hat{\mathbf{Y}}_1'(\mathbf{Y}_1 - \mathbf{V}_1) \\ &= \hat{\mathbf{Y}}_1'\mathbf{Y}_1 \\ &= \mathbf{Y}_1'\mathbf{X}(\mathbf{X}'\mathbf{X})^{-1}\mathbf{X}'\mathbf{Y}_1 \end{aligned}$$

and

$$\begin{aligned} \hat{\mathbf{Y}}_1'\mathbf{X}_1 &= (\mathbf{Y}_1 - \mathbf{V}_1)'\mathbf{X}_1 \\ &= \mathbf{Y}_1'\mathbf{X}_1 \end{aligned}$$

Thus the equations for the 2SLS estimator can now be written

$$\begin{bmatrix} \mathbf{Y}_1'\mathbf{X}(\mathbf{X}'\mathbf{X})^{-1}\mathbf{X}'\mathbf{Y}_1 & \mathbf{Y}_1'\mathbf{X}_1 \\ \mathbf{X}_1'\mathbf{Y}_1 & \mathbf{X}_1'\mathbf{X}_1 \end{bmatrix} \begin{bmatrix} \mathbf{b} \\ \mathbf{c} \end{bmatrix} = \begin{bmatrix} \mathbf{Y}_1'\mathbf{X}(\mathbf{X}'\mathbf{X})^{-1}\mathbf{X}'\mathbf{y} \\ \mathbf{X}_1'\mathbf{y} \end{bmatrix} \tag{11-45}$$

Yet another form of the 2SLS equations, which is useful for further theoretical developments, is

$$\begin{bmatrix} \mathbf{Y}_1'\mathbf{Y}_1 - \mathbf{V}_1'\mathbf{V}_1 & \mathbf{Y}_1'\mathbf{X}_1 \\ \mathbf{X}_1'\mathbf{Y}_1 & \mathbf{X}_1'\mathbf{X}_1 \end{bmatrix} \begin{bmatrix} \mathbf{b} \\ \mathbf{c} \end{bmatrix} = \begin{bmatrix} (\mathbf{Y}_1 - \mathbf{V}_1)'\mathbf{y} \\ \mathbf{X}_1'\mathbf{y} \end{bmatrix} \tag{11-46}$$

The equivalence between Eqs. (11-45) and (11-46) may be proved by the reader as an exercise.

Example 11-8 The first structural equation in a three-equation model is

$$y_{1t} = \beta_{12}y_{2t} + \gamma_{11}x_{1t} + \gamma_{12}x_{2t} + u_t$$

There are four predetermined variables in the complete model, and the $\mathbf{X}'\mathbf{X}$

matrix is

$$\mathbf{X'X} = \begin{bmatrix} 10 & 0 & 0 & 0 \\ 0 & 5 & 0 & 0 \\ 0 & 0 & 4 & 0 \\ 0 & 0 & 0 & 2 \end{bmatrix}$$

In addition we are given

$$\begin{bmatrix} | & | \\ \mathbf{y}_1 & \mathbf{y}_2 \\ | & | \end{bmatrix}' \mathbf{X} = \begin{bmatrix} 2 & 3 & 4 & 1 \\ 1 & 0 & 2 & 1 \end{bmatrix}$$

The necessary condition for identification is satisfied since $K - k = 2$ and $g - 1 = 1$ so that the equation is overidentified. To estimate the parameters by 2SLS we need to establish a correspondence between the data in this problem and the vectors and matrices in Eq. (11-44). Thus

$$\mathbf{y} = \begin{bmatrix} | \\ \mathbf{y}_1 \\ | \end{bmatrix} \qquad \mathbf{Y}_1 = \begin{bmatrix} | \\ \mathbf{y}_2 \\ | \end{bmatrix} \qquad \mathbf{X}_1 = \begin{bmatrix} | & | \\ \mathbf{x}_1 & \mathbf{x}_2 \\ | & | \end{bmatrix} \qquad \mathbf{X}_2 = \begin{bmatrix} | & | \\ \mathbf{x}_3 & \mathbf{x}_4 \\ | & | \end{bmatrix}$$

$$\mathbf{Y}_1'\mathbf{X} = [1 \quad 0 \quad 2 \quad 1] \qquad \mathbf{Y}_1'\mathbf{X}_1 = [1 \quad 0]$$

$$\mathbf{X}_1'\mathbf{X}_1 = \begin{bmatrix} 10 & 0 \\ 0 & 5 \end{bmatrix} \qquad \mathbf{X'y} = \begin{bmatrix} 2 \\ 3 \\ 4 \\ 1 \end{bmatrix} \qquad \mathbf{X}_1'\mathbf{y} = \begin{bmatrix} 2 \\ 3 \end{bmatrix}$$

and so

$$\mathbf{Y}_1'\mathbf{X}(\mathbf{X'X})^{-1}\mathbf{X'Y}_1 = [1 \quad 0 \quad 2 \quad 1] \begin{bmatrix} 0.1 & 0 & 0 & 0 \\ 0 & 0.2 & 0 & 0 \\ 0 & 0 & 0.25 & 0 \\ 0 & 0 & 0 & 0.5 \end{bmatrix} \begin{bmatrix} 1 \\ 0 \\ 2 \\ 1 \end{bmatrix} = 1.6$$

$$\mathbf{Y}_1'\mathbf{X}(\mathbf{X'X})^{-1}\mathbf{X'y} = [0.1 \quad 0 \quad 0.5 \quad 0.5] \begin{bmatrix} 2 \\ 3 \\ 4 \\ 1 \end{bmatrix} = 2.7$$

The 2SLS equations are then

$$\begin{bmatrix} 1.6 & 1 & 0 \\ 1 & 10 & 0 \\ 0 & 0 & 5 \end{bmatrix} \begin{bmatrix} b_{12} \\ c_{11} \\ c_{12} \end{bmatrix} = \begin{bmatrix} 2.7 \\ 2 \\ 3 \end{bmatrix}$$

with solution

$$\begin{bmatrix} b_{12} \\ c_{11} \\ c_{12} \end{bmatrix} = \begin{bmatrix} 1.6667 \\ 0.0333 \\ 0.6000 \end{bmatrix}$$

Example 11-9 For a model

$$y_{1t} = \beta_{12} y_{2t} + \gamma_{11} x_{1t} + u_{1t}$$
$$y_{2t} = \beta_{21} y_{1t} + \gamma_{22} x_{2t} + \gamma_{23} x_{3t} + u_{2t}$$

The sample matrices are†

$$\mathbf{X'X} = \begin{bmatrix} 1 & 0 & 0 \\ 0 & 20 & 0 \\ 0 & 0 & 10 \end{bmatrix} \qquad \mathbf{X'Y} = \begin{bmatrix} 5 & 10 \\ 40 & 20 \\ 20 & 30 \end{bmatrix}$$

We will illustrate the application of 2SLS and ILS, as appropriate, to this model and also look at the estimation of the reduced-form coefficients.

The first equation is overidentified and is estimated by 2SLS. The correspondence between the variables in the equation and the matrix expressions in Eq. (11-44) is given by

$$\mathbf{y} = \begin{bmatrix} | \\ \mathbf{y}_1 \\ | \end{bmatrix} \qquad \mathbf{Y}_1 = \begin{bmatrix} | \\ \mathbf{y}_2 \\ | \end{bmatrix} \qquad \mathbf{X}_1 = \begin{bmatrix} | \\ \mathbf{x}_1 \\ | \end{bmatrix} \qquad \mathbf{X}_2 = \begin{bmatrix} | & | \\ \mathbf{x}_2 & \mathbf{x}_3 \\ | & | \end{bmatrix}$$

Thus

$$\mathbf{X'Y}_1 = \begin{bmatrix} 10 \\ 20 \\ 30 \end{bmatrix} \qquad \mathbf{X}_1'\mathbf{Y}_1 = 10 \qquad \mathbf{X'y} = \begin{bmatrix} 5 \\ 40 \\ 20 \end{bmatrix} \qquad \mathbf{X}_1'\mathbf{y} = 5 \qquad \mathbf{X}_1'\mathbf{X}_1 = 1$$

$$\mathbf{Y}_1'\mathbf{X}(\mathbf{X'X})^{-1}\mathbf{X'Y}_1 = [10 \quad 20 \quad 30] \begin{bmatrix} 1 & 0 & 0 \\ 0 & 0.05 & 0 \\ 0 & 0 & 0.1 \end{bmatrix} \begin{bmatrix} 10 \\ 20 \\ 30 \end{bmatrix}$$

$$= [10 \quad 1 \quad 3] \begin{bmatrix} 10 \\ 20 \\ 30 \end{bmatrix} = 210$$

$$\mathbf{Y}_1'\mathbf{X}(\mathbf{X'X})^{-1}\mathbf{X'y} = [10 \quad 1 \quad 3] \begin{bmatrix} 5 \\ 40 \\ 20 \end{bmatrix} = 150$$

The 2SLS equations are thus

$$\begin{bmatrix} 210 & 10 \\ 10 & 1 \end{bmatrix} \begin{bmatrix} b_{12} \\ c_{11} \end{bmatrix} = \begin{bmatrix} 150 \\ 5 \end{bmatrix}$$

with solution

$$\begin{bmatrix} b_{12} \\ c_{11} \end{bmatrix} = \begin{bmatrix} \frac{10}{11} \\ -4\frac{1}{11} \end{bmatrix}$$

The second equation is just identified and thus may be estimated by 2SLS or ILS. For the 2SLS approach

$$\mathbf{y} = \begin{bmatrix} | \\ \mathbf{y}_2 \\ | \end{bmatrix} \qquad \mathbf{Y}_1 = \begin{bmatrix} | \\ \mathbf{y}_1 \\ | \end{bmatrix} \qquad \mathbf{X}_1 = \begin{bmatrix} | & | \\ \mathbf{x}_2 & \mathbf{x}_3 \\ | & | \end{bmatrix} \qquad \mathbf{X}_2 = \begin{bmatrix} | \\ \mathbf{x}_1 \\ | \end{bmatrix}$$

† In this and the previous example the **X′X** matrices are assumed to be diagonal to keep the arithmetic simple. In realistic situations orthogonal variables are, of course, very rare.

Thus

$$\mathbf{X'Y}_1 = \begin{bmatrix} 5 \\ 40 \\ 20 \end{bmatrix} \qquad \mathbf{X}_1'\mathbf{Y}_1 = \begin{bmatrix} 40 \\ 20 \end{bmatrix} \qquad \mathbf{X'y} = \begin{bmatrix} 10 \\ 20 \\ 30 \end{bmatrix}$$

$$\mathbf{X}_1'\mathbf{y} = \begin{bmatrix} 20 \\ 30 \end{bmatrix} \qquad \mathbf{X}_1'\mathbf{X}_1 = \begin{bmatrix} 20 & 0 \\ 0 & 10 \end{bmatrix}$$

$$\mathbf{Y}_1'\mathbf{X}(\mathbf{X'X})^{-1}\mathbf{X'Y}_1 = [5 \quad 40 \quad 20] \begin{bmatrix} 1 & 0 & 0 \\ 0 & 0.05 & 0 \\ 0 & 0 & 0.1 \end{bmatrix} \begin{bmatrix} 5 \\ 40 \\ 20 \end{bmatrix}$$

$$= [5 \quad 2 \quad 2] \begin{bmatrix} 5 \\ 40 \\ 20 \end{bmatrix} = 145$$

$$\mathbf{Y}_1'\mathbf{X}(\mathbf{X'X})^{-1}\mathbf{X'y} = [5 \quad 2 \quad 2] \begin{bmatrix} 10 \\ 20 \\ 30 \end{bmatrix} = 150$$

The 2SLS equations are thus

$$\begin{bmatrix} 145 & 40 & 20 \\ 40 & 20 & 0 \\ 20 & 0 & 10 \end{bmatrix} \begin{bmatrix} b_{21} \\ c_{22} \\ c_{23} \end{bmatrix} = \begin{bmatrix} 150 \\ 20 \\ 30 \end{bmatrix}$$

with solution

$$\begin{bmatrix} b_{21} \\ c_{22} \\ c_{23} \end{bmatrix} = \begin{bmatrix} 2 \\ -3 \\ -1 \end{bmatrix}$$

To obtain the ILS estimates of the second equation we need to specify the additional matrices appearing in Eq. (11-42). These are

$$\mathbf{X}_2'\mathbf{Y}_1 = 5 \qquad \mathbf{X}_2'\mathbf{X}_1 = [0 \quad 0] \qquad \mathbf{X}_2'\mathbf{y} = 10$$

The ILS equations are then

$$\begin{bmatrix} 5 & 0 & 0 \\ 40 & 20 & 0 \\ 20 & 0 & 10 \end{bmatrix} \begin{bmatrix} b_{21} \\ c_{22} \\ c_{23} \end{bmatrix} = \begin{bmatrix} 10 \\ 20 \\ 30 \end{bmatrix}$$

with the same solution vector as 2SLS. This is an illustration of a general result that 2SLS and ILS estimates, where the latter exist, are identical. The general result will be proved below, but in the meantime we continue with the numerical example.

The reduced-form coefficients, estimated by OLS, are

$$\mathbf{P}' = (\mathbf{X'X})^{-1}\mathbf{X'Y}$$

$$= \begin{bmatrix} 1 & 0 & 0 \\ 0 & 0.05 & 0 \\ 0 & 0 & 0.1 \end{bmatrix} \begin{bmatrix} 5 & 10 \\ 40 & 20 \\ 20 & 30 \end{bmatrix}$$

$$= \begin{bmatrix} 5 & 10 \\ 2 & 1 \\ 2 & 3 \end{bmatrix}$$

giving

$$y_{1t} = 5x_{1t} + 2x_{2t} + 2x_{3t} + v_{1t}$$

and

$$y_{2t} = 10x_{1t} + x_{2t} + 3x_{3t} + v_{2t}$$

The reduced-form matrix may also be estimated by substituting the estimated structural coefficients $\hat{\mathbf{B}}$ and $\hat{\mathbf{\Gamma}}$ in Eq. (11-19),

$$\hat{\Pi} = -\hat{\mathbf{B}}^{-1}\hat{\mathbf{\Gamma}}$$

However, care must be taken in making this substitution since Eq. (11-19) was derived from the structural equations specified as $\mathbf{By}_t + \mathbf{\Gamma x}_t = \mathbf{u}_t$, whereas the equations of this model have been specified with just a single endogenous variable on the left-hand side of each equation. The 2SLS estimates of the structure are

$$y_{1t} = \tfrac{10}{11}y_{2t} - 4\tfrac{1}{11}x_{1t} + u_{1t}$$

$$y_{2t} = 2y_{1t} - 3x_{2t} - x_{3t} + u_{2t}$$

Rearranging with all variables on the left-hand side gives

$$\begin{bmatrix} 1 & -\frac{10}{11} \\ -2 & 1 \end{bmatrix}\begin{bmatrix} y_{1t} \\ y_{2t} \end{bmatrix} + \begin{bmatrix} 4\frac{1}{11} & 0 & 0 \\ 0 & 3 & 1 \end{bmatrix}\begin{bmatrix} x_{1t} \\ x_{2t} \\ x_{3t} \end{bmatrix} = \begin{bmatrix} u_{1t} \\ u_{2t} \end{bmatrix}$$

Thus

$$\hat{\Pi} = -\begin{bmatrix} 1 & -\frac{10}{11} \\ -2 & 1 \end{bmatrix}^{-1}\begin{bmatrix} 4\frac{1}{11} & 0 & 0 \\ 0 & 3 & 1 \end{bmatrix}$$

$$= \begin{bmatrix} 5 & 3\frac{1}{3} & 1\frac{1}{9} \\ 10 & 3\frac{2}{3} & 1\frac{2}{9} \end{bmatrix}$$

These are somewhat different than the OLS estimates. The reason is that the OLS estimates are unrestricted and thus fail to satisfy the restrictions placed on the reduced-form parameters by the overidentification in the system. With two endogenous and three predetermined variables there are six reduced-form coefficients, which are functions of just five structural coefficients. The true reduced-form matrix is

$$\Pi = \frac{1}{(1 - \beta_{12}\beta_{21})}\begin{bmatrix} \gamma_{11} & \beta_{12}\gamma_{22} & \beta_{12}\gamma_{23} \\ \beta_{21}\gamma_{11} & \gamma_{22} & \gamma_{23} \end{bmatrix}$$

in which the second and third columns are linearly dependent.

Interpretation of Two-Stage Least Squares as an Instrumental Variable Estimator

The structural equation to be estimated may be written as

$$\mathbf{y} = \mathbf{Y}_1\boldsymbol{\beta} + \mathbf{X}_1\boldsymbol{\gamma} + \mathbf{u} = \mathbf{Z}_1\boldsymbol{\delta} + \mathbf{u} \tag{11-47}$$

where

$$\mathbf{Z}_1 = [\mathbf{Y}_1 \quad \mathbf{X}_1] \qquad \text{and} \qquad \boldsymbol{\delta} = \begin{bmatrix} \boldsymbol{\beta} \\ \boldsymbol{\gamma} \end{bmatrix}$$

Let us recapitulate the discussion of IV estimates in Chap. 9, with the vector of unknown parameters now indicated by $\boldsymbol{\delta}$ rather than $\boldsymbol{\beta}$ and with the matrix of explanatory variables simply indicated by $\mathbf{Z}$. The equation to be estimated is $\mathbf{y} = \mathbf{Z}\boldsymbol{\delta} + \mathbf{u}$, the problem being that

$$\operatorname{plim}\left(\frac{1}{n}\mathbf{Z}'\mathbf{u}\right) \neq \mathbf{0}$$

which is the difficulty with $\mathbf{Z}_1$ in Eq. (11-47). Provided a matrix $\mathbf{W}$ can be found such that

1. $\operatorname{plim}\left(\frac{1}{n}\mathbf{W}'\mathbf{W}\right) = \boldsymbol{\Sigma}_{ww}$ a finite symmetric positive definite matrix
2. $\operatorname{plim}\left(\frac{1}{n}\mathbf{W}'\mathbf{Z}\right) = \boldsymbol{\Sigma}_{wz}$ a finite nonsingular matrix
3. $\operatorname{plim}\left(\frac{1}{n}\mathbf{W}'\mathbf{u}\right) = \mathbf{0}$

the IV estimator

$$\mathbf{d}_{\mathrm{IV}} = (\mathbf{W}'\mathbf{Z})^{-1}\mathbf{W}'\mathbf{y} \tag{11-48}$$

will be consistent and will have an asymptotic variance matrix estimated by

$$\operatorname{asy\,var}(\mathbf{d}_{\mathrm{IV}}) = s^2(\mathbf{W}'\mathbf{Z})^{-1}(\mathbf{W}'\mathbf{W})(\mathbf{Z}'\mathbf{W})^{-1} \tag{11-49}$$

where $$s^2 = \frac{(\mathbf{y} - \mathbf{Z}\mathbf{d}_{\mathrm{IV}})'(\mathbf{y} - \mathbf{Z}\mathbf{d}_{\mathrm{IV}})}{n}$$

In the present case let us set

$$\mathbf{Z} = \mathbf{Z}_1 = [\mathbf{Y}_1 \quad \mathbf{X}_1]$$

and $$\mathbf{W} = [\hat{\mathbf{Y}}_1 \quad \mathbf{X}_1]$$

so that $\hat{\mathbf{Y}}_1$ is the set of instruments for $\mathbf{Y}_1$. The IV estimator defined in Eq. (11-48) is then

$$\begin{bmatrix} \hat{\mathbf{Y}}_1'\mathbf{Y}_1 & \hat{\mathbf{Y}}_1'\mathbf{X}_1 \\ \mathbf{X}_1'\mathbf{Y}_1 & \mathbf{X}_1'\mathbf{X}_1 \end{bmatrix} \begin{bmatrix} \mathbf{b}_{\mathrm{IV}} \\ \mathbf{c}_{\mathrm{IV}} \end{bmatrix} = \begin{bmatrix} \hat{\mathbf{Y}}_1'\mathbf{y} \\ \mathbf{X}_1'\mathbf{y} \end{bmatrix} \tag{11-50}$$

but we have already seen that $\hat{\mathbf{Y}}_1'\mathbf{Y}_1 = \hat{\mathbf{Y}}_1'\hat{\mathbf{Y}}_1$ and $\hat{\mathbf{Y}}_1'\mathbf{X}_1 = \mathbf{Y}_1'\mathbf{X}_1$. Thus Eqs. (11-50) and (11-44) are identical, so that 2SLS is in fact an IV estimator with $\hat{\mathbf{Y}}_1$ as the instruments for $\mathbf{Y}_1$.

The consistency of the 2SLS (IV) estimator requires the three conditions on $\mathbf{W}$, stated above, to be fulfilled. We will assume that

$$\operatorname{plim}\left(\frac{1}{n}\mathbf{W}'\mathbf{W}\right) \quad \text{and} \quad \operatorname{plim}\left(\frac{1}{n}\mathbf{W}'\mathbf{Z}\right)$$

are both finite.† The third condition is

$$\operatorname{plim}\left(\frac{1}{n}\mathbf{W}'\mathbf{u}\right) = \begin{bmatrix} \operatorname{plim}\left(\frac{1}{n}\hat{\mathbf{Y}}_1'\mathbf{u}\right) \\ \operatorname{plim}\left(\frac{1}{n}\mathbf{X}_1'\mathbf{u}\right) \end{bmatrix} = \mathbf{0}$$

Insofar as $\mathbf{X}_1$ contains exogenous variables, whether current or lagged, these are, by assumption, uncorrelated in the limit with the equation disturbance. The same result will also hold for any lagged endogenous variables in $\mathbf{X}_1$ provided the disturbance term is serially uncorrelated. The remaining term is

$$\begin{aligned} \operatorname{plim}\left(\frac{1}{n}\hat{\mathbf{Y}}_1'\mathbf{u}\right) &= \operatorname{plim}\left(\frac{1}{n}\mathbf{Y}_1'\mathbf{X}(\mathbf{X}'\mathbf{X})^{-1}\mathbf{X}'\mathbf{u}\right) \\ &= \operatorname{plim}\left(\frac{1}{n}\mathbf{Y}_1'\mathbf{X}\right)\cdot \operatorname{plim}\left(\frac{1}{n}\mathbf{X}'\mathbf{X}\right)^{-1}\cdot \operatorname{plim}\left(\frac{1}{n}\mathbf{X}'\mathbf{u}\right) \\ &= \mathbf{0} \end{aligned}$$

since the first two terms are finite and the last is the zero vector.

It was also shown in Sec. 9-2 that the IV estimators are asymptotically normally distributed with an asymptotic variance matrix estimated by Eq. (11-49). Substituting for $\mathbf{W}$ and $\mathbf{Z}$ and using the fact that $\hat{\mathbf{Y}}_1'\hat{\mathbf{Y}}_1 = \hat{\mathbf{Y}}_1'\mathbf{Y}_1$ and $\hat{\mathbf{Y}}_1'\mathbf{X}_1 = \mathbf{Y}_1'\mathbf{X}_1$ gives

$$\begin{aligned} \text{asy var}\begin{pmatrix} \mathbf{b} \\ \mathbf{c} \end{pmatrix} &= s^2\begin{bmatrix} \hat{\mathbf{Y}}_1'\hat{\mathbf{Y}}_1 & \hat{\mathbf{Y}}_1'\mathbf{X}_1 \\ \mathbf{X}_1'\hat{\mathbf{Y}}_1 & \mathbf{X}_1'\mathbf{X}_1 \end{bmatrix}^{-1} \\ &= s^2\begin{bmatrix} \mathbf{Y}_1'\mathbf{X}(\mathbf{X}'\mathbf{X})^{-1}\mathbf{X}'\mathbf{Y}_1 & \mathbf{Y}_1'\mathbf{X}_1 \\ \mathbf{X}_1'\mathbf{Y}_1 & \mathbf{X}_1'\mathbf{X}_1 \end{bmatrix}^{-1} \end{aligned} \tag{11-51}$$

where

$$s^2 = \frac{(\mathbf{y} - \mathbf{Y}_1\mathbf{b} - \mathbf{X}_1\mathbf{c})'(\mathbf{y} - \mathbf{Y}_1\mathbf{b} - \mathbf{X}_1\mathbf{c})}{n} \tag{11-52}$$

which is a consistent estimator of σ_u^2. Some authors prefer to use the number of degrees of freedom $n - g - k + 1$ as the divisor in s^2 rather than n. This is also a consistent estimator of σ_u^2. The 2SLS estimators are thus consistent and asymptotically normally distributed with estimated variance matrix given in Eq. (11-51).

A problem sometimes arises in the application of 2SLS to equations in medium-size or large-size econometric models. The difficulty is that the number of predetermined variables in such a model may become large in relation to the number of observation points. Suppose, to consider a special case, that the number of predetermined variables becomes as great as the number of observations, $K = n$. The $\mathbf{X}$ matrix is then square and, in the absence of any exact linear

† The detailed conditions for this to be true are set out in H. Theil, *Principles of Econometrics*, Wiley, New York, 1971, pp. 484–488.

relations between the predetermined variables, nonsingular. Formula (11-43) thus reduces to

$$\begin{aligned}\hat{\mathbf{Y}}_1 &= \mathbf{X}(\mathbf{X}'\mathbf{X})^{-1}\mathbf{X}'\mathbf{Y}_1 \\ &= \mathbf{X}\mathbf{X}^{-1}(\mathbf{X}')^{-1}\mathbf{X}'\mathbf{Y}_1 \\ &= \mathbf{Y}_1\end{aligned}$$

and 2SLS is equivalent to OLS. The 2SLS estimates would, of course, no longer be consistent, since the matrix of instrumental variables is now $\mathbf{W} = [\mathbf{Y}_1 \quad \mathbf{X}_1]$ and

$$\operatorname{plim}\left(\frac{1}{n}\mathbf{Y}_1'\mathbf{u}\right) \neq \mathbf{0} \qquad \text{so that } \operatorname{plim}\left(\frac{1}{n}\mathbf{W}'\mathbf{u}\right) \neq \mathbf{0}$$

as was required for consistency.

When $K > n$, the $\mathbf{X}'\mathbf{X}$ matrix is of order $K \times K$ and of rank n. Thus it is singular, and the inverse $(\mathbf{X}'\mathbf{X})^{-1}$ does not exist. This has often led to the conclusion that the 2SLS estimator will not exist, since Eq. (11-45), for example, involves $(\mathbf{X}'\mathbf{X})^{-1}$. Fisher and Wadycki have pointed out that this is not necessarily the case.† They argue that the $\hat{\mathbf{Y}}_1$ matrix will be unique in spite of the multiplicity of solutions for the reduced-form coefficients. Consider, for instance, the first variable in $\mathbf{Y}_1$ and denote the $n \times 1$ vector of observations on that variable by $\mathbf{y}_1$. Letting $\mathbf{p}$ denote the $K \times 1$ vector of OLS reduced-form coefficients for that variable, the usual formula gives

$$(\mathbf{X}'\mathbf{X})\mathbf{p} = \mathbf{X}'\mathbf{y}_1 \tag{11-53}$$

Since $\mathbf{X}'\mathbf{X}$ is of order $K \times K$ with rank $n < K$, Eq. (11-53) has an infinity of solutions. Letting $\mathbf{p}_1$ and $\mathbf{p}_2$ be any two solution vectors, we have

$$(\mathbf{X}'\mathbf{X})\mathbf{p}_1 = \mathbf{X}'\mathbf{y}_1$$

$$(\mathbf{X}'\mathbf{X})\mathbf{p}_2 = \mathbf{X}'\mathbf{y}_1$$

Thus

$$(\mathbf{X}'\mathbf{X})(\mathbf{p}_1 - \mathbf{p}_2) = \mathbf{0}$$

Premultiplying by $(\mathbf{p}_1 - \mathbf{p}_2)'$ gives

$$(\mathbf{p}_1 - \mathbf{p}_2)'(\mathbf{X}'\mathbf{X})(\mathbf{p}_1 - \mathbf{p}_2) = 0$$

Thus

$$\mathbf{X}(\mathbf{p}_1 - \mathbf{p}_2) = \mathbf{0}$$

so that

$$\hat{\mathbf{y}}_1 = \mathbf{X}\mathbf{p}_1 = \mathbf{X}\mathbf{p}_2$$

Moreover Eq. (11-53) may be rewritten as

$$\underset{K \times n}{\mathbf{X}'}\underset{n \times 1}{(\mathbf{X}\mathbf{p} - \mathbf{y}_1)} = \mathbf{0}$$

Since $\mathbf{X}'$ has rank n $(< K)$, the only solution vector is $\mathbf{X}\mathbf{p} - \mathbf{y}_1 = \mathbf{0}$ so that

† W. D. Fisher and W. J. Wadycki, "Estimating a Structural Equation in a Large System," *Econometrica*, vol. 39, 1971, pp. 461–465.

$\hat{\mathbf{y}}_1 = \mathbf{y}_1$. The same result will hold for each variable in $\mathbf{Y}_1$ so that once again $\hat{\mathbf{Y}}_1 = \mathbf{Y}_1$, and 2SLS would be equivalent to OLS.

Various suggestions have been made for dealing with the problem of an excess of predetermined variables. Kloek and Mennes suggested replacing $\mathbf{X}_2$ in the first-stage regressions by a smaller number of principal components.† Let $\mathbf{F}$ denote the $n \times l$ matrix of the l chosen principal components and then define

$$\mathbf{Z} = [\mathbf{X}_1 \quad \mathbf{F}]$$

This $\mathbf{Z}$ matrix takes the place of the $\mathbf{X}$ matrix in Eq. (11-45), and the 2SLS estimates based on the principal components approach would then be given by

$$\begin{bmatrix} \mathbf{Y}_1'\mathbf{Z}(\mathbf{Z}'\mathbf{Z})^{-1}\mathbf{Z}'\mathbf{Y}_1 & \mathbf{Y}_1'\mathbf{X}_1 \\ \mathbf{X}_1'\mathbf{Y}_1 & \mathbf{X}_1'\mathbf{X}_1 \end{bmatrix} \begin{bmatrix} \mathbf{b}_{\text{PC}} \\ \mathbf{c}_{\text{PC}} \end{bmatrix} = \begin{bmatrix} \mathbf{Y}_1'\mathbf{Z}(\mathbf{Z}'\mathbf{Z})^{-1}\mathbf{Z}'\mathbf{y} \\ \mathbf{X}_1'\mathbf{y} \end{bmatrix} \tag{11-54}$$

Various problems arise with this approach. The first concerns the number l of principal components to be used. Kloek and Mennes state that identification requires

$$l \geq g - 1$$

but it is difficult to see the reason for this condition since the problem is to find a suitable matrix $\mathbf{Z}$ for the first-stage regressions in which $\mathbf{Y}_1$ is replaced by an estimated matrix $\hat{\mathbf{Y}}_1$. It is, of course, true that identification of the structural equation requires that the number of columns in $\mathbf{X}_2$, namely, $K - k$, should be at least equal to $g - 1$, but there is no reason to carry this condition over to the choice of variables used in computing $\hat{\mathbf{Y}}_1$.

A second problem concerns the criterion to be used in selecting principal components. One possibility is to choose the components with the greatest eigenvalues, that is, the components which account for the greatest variance of the variables in $\mathbf{X}_2$. Some of these components, however, may be highly correlated with variables in $\mathbf{X}_1$, thus providing little additional assistance in explaining $\mathbf{Y}_1$ and possibly also causing $\mathbf{Z}'\mathbf{Z}$ to be nearly singular, so that numerical difficulties arise in computing the inverse. Kloek and Mennes have suggested components which have the *least* correlation with the $\mathbf{X}_1$ matrix. Both approaches involve substantial computation and also imply different sets of principal components for different structural equations.

The last difficulty is avoided by calculating, once and for all, principal components of the *complete* set of predetermined variables and using a subset of these in the first-stage regressions for each structural equation. In a very interesting study Klein estimated a revised version of the Klein-Goldberger model of the U. S. economy by using just the principal components corresponding (1) to the four largest and (2) to the eight largest eigenvalues of $\mathbf{X}'\mathbf{X}$ in the first stage of the 2SLS procedure. Comparing the predictions of GNP in the sample period

† T. Kloek and L. B. M. Mennes, "Simultaneous Equation Estimation Based on Principal Components of Predetermined Variables," *Econometrica*, vol. 28, 1960, pp. 45–61. For a review of principal components see App. A-10.

from these two estimators with OLS and FIML, Klein found 2SLS based on just four principal components to give the smallest absolute percentage error followed by the other 2SLS estimator, OLS, and FIML in that order.†

An alternative approach based on instrumental variables has been suggested by Brundy and Jorgenson to bypass the substantial computation involved in calculating the reduced-form coefficients required for $\hat{\mathbf{Y}}_1$.‡ Let

$$E(\mathbf{Y}_1) = \mathbf{X}\mathbf{\Pi}_1$$

where $\mathbf{\Pi}_1$ is the $K \times (g - 1)$ submatrix of reduced-form coefficients relevant to the variables in $\mathbf{Y}_1$. The Brundy-Jorgenson suggestion is as follows.

1. Define a matrix of instrumental variables as

$$\mathbf{W}_1 = \left[\mathbf{X}\hat{\mathbf{\Pi}}_1 \quad \mathbf{X}_1\right] \tag{11-55}$$

where $\hat{\mathbf{\Pi}}_1$ is any consistent estimator of $\mathbf{\Pi}_1$.

2. Then compute the structural coefficient estimator from the IV formula as

$$\mathbf{d} = \begin{bmatrix} \mathbf{b} \\ \mathbf{c} \end{bmatrix} = (\mathbf{W}_1'\mathbf{Z}_1)^{-1}\mathbf{W}_1'\mathbf{y} \tag{11-56}$$

where $$\mathbf{Z}_1 = [\mathbf{Y}_1 \quad \mathbf{X}_1]$$

The regular 2SLS estimator satisfies these conditions, for $\hat{\mathbf{\Pi}}_1 = (\mathbf{X}'\mathbf{X})^{-1}\mathbf{X}'\mathbf{Y}_1$ is a consistent estimator of $\mathbf{\Pi}_1$ and $\mathbf{W}_1$ then becomes $[\hat{\mathbf{Y}}_1 \quad \mathbf{X}_1]$. The novelty of the Brundy-Jorgenson approach is to avoid computing reduced-form coefficients and to derive an appropriate $\hat{\mathbf{\Pi}}_1$ by first obtaining $\hat{\mathbf{B}}$ and $\hat{\mathbf{\Gamma}}$ as consistent estimators of $\mathbf{B}$ and $\mathbf{\Gamma}$ and then using

$$\hat{\mathbf{\Pi}} = -\hat{\mathbf{B}}^{-1}\hat{\mathbf{\Gamma}}$$

from which the relevant submatrix $\hat{\mathbf{\Pi}}_1$ can be extracted and $\mathbf{X}\hat{\mathbf{\Pi}}_1$ computed for insertion in Eq. (11-55). Thus even if one is interested in just a single structural equation, this approach requires the initial computation of consistent estimators of *all* structural coefficients. On the other hand, if one is estimating all the equations of a model, the single $\hat{\mathbf{\Pi}}$ matrix is used to provide all relevant $\hat{\mathbf{\Pi}}_i$ submatrices.

Several suggestions are offered for initial consistent estimation of the $\mathbf{B}$ and $\mathbf{\Gamma}$ matrices, all of them essentially IV estimators. Considering Eq. (11-47) again, the matrix of right-hand side variables is

$$\mathbf{Z}_1 = [\mathbf{Y}_1 \quad \mathbf{X}_1]$$

where $\mathbf{Y}_1$ is $n \times (g - 1)$ and $\mathbf{X}_1$ is $n \times k$. Define

$$\mathbf{W}_1^* = [\mathbf{X}_1^* \quad \mathbf{X}_1]$$

† L. R. Klein, "Estimation of Interdependent Systems in Macroeconometrics," *Econometrica*, vol. 37, 1969, pp. 171–192.

‡ J. M. Brundy and D. W. Jorgenson, "Efficient Estimation of Simultaneous Equations by Instrumental Variables," *Review of Economics and Statistics*, vol. 53, 1971, pp. 207–224.

where $\mathbf{X}_1^*$ is the matrix of any $g - 1$ predetermined variables which do *not* appear in the first structural equation. These variables could be chosen from the predetermined variables appearing in the structural equations for $\mathbf{Y}_1$, as suggested by Fisher.† The resultant IV estimator of $\boldsymbol{\delta}$ is $(\mathbf{W}_1^{*\prime}\mathbf{Z}_1)^{-1}\mathbf{W}_1^{*\prime}\mathbf{y}$. Repeating this procedure for each structural equation yields the preliminary consistent estimators $\hat{\mathbf{B}}$ and $\hat{\boldsymbol{\Gamma}}$ for insertion in $\hat{\boldsymbol{\Pi}} = -\hat{\mathbf{B}}^{-1}\hat{\boldsymbol{\Gamma}}$, and the computations outlined in Eqs. (11-55) and (11-56) would then yield the final estimator. Another possibility is to define

$$\mathbf{W}_1^* = [\mathbf{F}_1 \quad \mathbf{X}_1]$$

where $\mathbf{F}_1$ is a subset of $g - 1$ principal components of $\mathbf{X}$. This differs, of course, from the Kloek and Mennes procedure, where the principal components were used in quasireduced-form estimation to compute $\hat{\mathbf{Y}}_1$. Here the principal components are used as instrumental variables in a first-round estimation of structural coefficients. The Brundy-Jorgenson estimator is known as the limited-information instrumental variables efficient (LIVE) estimator. The asymptotic variance-covariance matrix for $\mathbf{d}$ is estimated by

$$\text{asy var}(\mathbf{d}) = s^2(\mathbf{W}_1'\mathbf{W}_1)^{-1} \tag{11-57}$$

where $\mathbf{W}_1$ is defined in Eq. (11-55) and

$$s^2 = \frac{(\mathbf{y} - \mathbf{Zd})'(\mathbf{y} - \mathbf{Zd})}{n}$$

The LIVE estimates can thus be computed even where the 2SLS estimates cannot, but the actual point estimates will, of course, vary with the variables chosen as instruments.

Limited-Information Maximum Likelihood (Least Variance Ratio) Estimators

This alternative approach to the estimation of a structural equation preceded the development of 2SLS, which has largely replaced it on grounds of greater simplicity. Consider again the structural equation

$$\mathbf{y} = \mathbf{Y}_1\boldsymbol{\beta} + \mathbf{X}_1\boldsymbol{\gamma} + \mathbf{u}$$

and rewrite it as

$$\mathbf{Y}_\Delta\boldsymbol{\beta}_\Delta - \mathbf{X}_1\boldsymbol{\gamma} = \mathbf{u} \tag{11-58}$$

where

$$\mathbf{Y}_\Delta = [\mathbf{y} \quad \mathbf{Y}_1] \qquad \text{and} \qquad \boldsymbol{\beta}_\Delta = \begin{bmatrix} 1 \\ -\boldsymbol{\beta} \end{bmatrix} \tag{11-59}$$

† F. M. Fisher, "Dynamic Structure and Estimation in Economy-Wide Econometric Models," in J. Duesenberry, G. Fromm, L. R. Klein, and E. Kuh, Eds., *The Brookings Quarterly Econometric Model of the United States*, Rand-McNally, Skokie, IL, 1965, pp. 589–636.

Let us suppose that the endogenous variables have been so numbered that $\mathbf{Y}_\Delta$ constitutes the first g such variables and likewise that $\mathbf{X}_1$ refers to the first k predetermined variables. The likelihood function for the endogenous variables in $\mathbf{Y}_\Delta$ will involve the parameters in the first g rows of the reduced-form matrix $\boldsymbol{\Pi}$. Let these rows be partitioned into the two submatrices $[\boldsymbol{\Pi}_{\Delta 1} \quad \boldsymbol{\Pi}_{\Delta 2}]$ which are of order $g \times k$ and $g \times (K - k)$, respectively. We know that

$$\mathbf{B}\boldsymbol{\Pi} = -\boldsymbol{\Gamma}$$

The first row of each side of this equation may be written

$$[\boldsymbol{\beta}_\Delta' \quad \mathbf{0}_1]\boldsymbol{\Pi} = [-\boldsymbol{\gamma}' \quad \mathbf{0}_2]$$

where $\mathbf{0}_1$ indicates a row vector of $G - g$ zeros and $\mathbf{0}_2$ a row vector of $K - k$ zeros. Using the partitioning of $\boldsymbol{\Pi}$ then gives

$$\boldsymbol{\beta}_\Delta'\boldsymbol{\Pi}_{\Delta 1} = -\boldsymbol{\gamma}' \tag{11-60}$$

$$\boldsymbol{\beta}_\Delta'\boldsymbol{\Pi}_{\Delta 2} = \mathbf{0}_2 \tag{11-61}$$

Eq. (11-61) constitutes $K - k$ homogeneous equations in the g elements of $\boldsymbol{\beta}_\Delta$. However, one of the β's has been set at unity so that we merely need to determine the ratios of the elements in $\boldsymbol{\beta}_\Delta$. This can be done uniquely if the rank of $\boldsymbol{\Pi}_{\Delta 2}$ is $g - 1$. Even in the overidentified case where $K - k > g - 1$ and $\boldsymbol{\Pi}_{\Delta 2}$ thus has g rows and at least g columns, the rank of $\boldsymbol{\Pi}_{\Delta 2}$ cannot exceed $g - 1$.† This is obvious intuitively since Eq. (11-61) is just a subset of equations from $\mathbf{B}\boldsymbol{\Pi} = -\boldsymbol{\Gamma}$, which gives the relations between the *true* structural coefficients and the *true* reduced-form coefficients. However, the true $\boldsymbol{\Pi}_{\Delta 2}$ is unknown, and when it is replaced in Eq. (11-61) by, say, the ML estimate $\hat{\boldsymbol{\Pi}}_{\Delta 2}$, this matrix in the overidentified case will almost certainly have rank g so that one cannot solve for nonzero $\hat{\boldsymbol{\beta}}_\Delta$, except by arbitrarily dropping one of the equations.

The limited-information maximum likelihood (LIML) approach is to maximize the likelihood function for the g endogenous variables in $\mathbf{Y}_\Delta$ subject to the restriction that $\rho(\hat{\boldsymbol{\Pi}}_{\Delta 2}) = g - 1$. This approach was developed by Anderson and Rubin.‡ The application of the method requires one to know, in addition to the specification of the equation being estimated, merely the predetermined variables appearing in the other equations of the model, as in 2SLS. The mathematical development of the LIML estimator is complicated and lengthy, but it may be shown that it reduces to the choice of the elements of $\boldsymbol{\beta}_\Delta$ to minimize

$$l = \frac{\boldsymbol{\beta}'_\Delta \mathbf{W}^*_{\Delta\Delta} \boldsymbol{\beta}_\Delta}{\boldsymbol{\beta}_\Delta' \mathbf{W}_{\Delta\Delta} \boldsymbol{\beta}_\Delta} \tag{11-62}$$

† See W. C. Hood and T. C. Koopmans, *Studies in Econometric Method*, Wiley, New York, 1953, pp. 185–186.

‡ T. W. Anderson and H. Rubin, "Estimation of the Parameters of a Single Equation in a Complete System of Stochastic Equations," *Annals of Mathematical Statistics*, vol. 20, pp. 46–63, 1949.

where $\mathbf{W}^*_{\Delta\Delta}$ and $\mathbf{W}_{\Delta\Delta}$ are certain matrices of residuals.† The explanation of these residuals is given in the following account of least variance ratio (LVR) estimators.

Rewrite Eq. (11-58) as

$$\mathbf{z} = \mathbf{X}_1\boldsymbol{\gamma} + \mathbf{u}$$

where
$$\mathbf{z} = \mathbf{Y}_\Delta\boldsymbol{\beta}_\Delta$$

so that the $\mathbf{z}$ vector is a linear combination of the endogenous variables appearing in the equation, the coefficients of the combination being the unknown $\boldsymbol{\beta}$ parameters. If $\mathbf{z}$ is regressed on $\mathbf{X}_1$, the residual sum of squares is

$$\mathbf{z}'\mathbf{z} - \mathbf{z}'\mathbf{X}_1(\mathbf{X}_1'\mathbf{X}_1)^{-1}\mathbf{X}_1'\mathbf{z} = \boldsymbol{\beta}_\Delta'\mathbf{Y}_\Delta'\mathbf{Y}_\Delta\boldsymbol{\beta}_\Delta - \boldsymbol{\beta}_\Delta'\mathbf{Y}_\Delta'\mathbf{X}_1(\mathbf{X}_1'\mathbf{X}_1)^{-1}\mathbf{X}_1'\mathbf{Y}_\Delta\boldsymbol{\beta}_\Delta = \boldsymbol{\beta}_\Delta'\mathbf{W}^*_{\Delta\Delta}\boldsymbol{\beta}_\Delta$$

where
$$\mathbf{W}^*_{\Delta\Delta} = \mathbf{Y}_\Delta'\mathbf{Y}_\Delta - \mathbf{Y}_\Delta'\mathbf{X}_1(\mathbf{X}_1'\mathbf{X}_1)^{-1}\mathbf{X}_1'\mathbf{Y}_\Delta \tag{11-63}$$

Similarly, if $\mathbf{z}$ is regressed on all the predetermined variables, $\mathbf{X} = [\mathbf{X}_1 \quad \mathbf{X}_2]$, the residual sum of squares is

$$\boldsymbol{\beta}_\Delta'\mathbf{W}_{\Delta\Delta}\boldsymbol{\beta}$$

where
$$\mathbf{W}_{\Delta\Delta} = \mathbf{Y}_\Delta'\mathbf{Y}_\Delta - \mathbf{Y}_\Delta'\mathbf{X}(\mathbf{X}'\mathbf{X})^{-1}\mathbf{X}'\mathbf{Y}_\Delta \tag{11-64}$$

The second residual sum of squares will be no greater than the first since the second regression includes all the explanatory variables in the first regression $\mathbf{X}_1$ plus the set $\mathbf{X}_2$. However, the specification of the structural equation asserts that $\mathbf{z}$ depends on $\mathbf{X}_1$ but not on $\mathbf{X}_2$. Thus the LVR principle suggests that the estimate of $\boldsymbol{\beta}_\Delta$ should be chosen to keep this reduction in the residual sum of squares as small as possible, that is, to minimize the ratio

$$l = \frac{\boldsymbol{\beta}_\Delta'\mathbf{W}^*_{\Delta\Delta}\boldsymbol{\beta}_\Delta}{\boldsymbol{\beta}_\Delta'\mathbf{W}_{\Delta\Delta}\boldsymbol{\beta}_\Delta}$$

which is the same criterion as that for the LIML estimator. Differentiating l with respect to $\boldsymbol{\beta}_\Delta$ and setting the result equal to the zero vector gives

$$(\mathbf{W}^*_{\Delta\Delta} - l\mathbf{W}_{\Delta\Delta})\boldsymbol{\beta}_\Delta = \mathbf{0} \tag{11-65}$$

This set of equations will only have a nontrivial solution if the determinantal equation

$$|\mathbf{W}^*_{\Delta\Delta} - l\mathbf{W}_{\Delta\Delta}| = 0$$

is satisfied. This gives a polynomial in l, which must be solved for the smallest root $\hat{l}$. This root is substituted back on Eq. (11-65) and the estimator $\hat{\boldsymbol{\beta}}_\Delta$ obtained

† T. W. Anderson and H. Rubin, op. cit.; see also W. C. Hood and T. C. Koopmans, op. cit., Chap. 6. Hood and Koopmans arrive at Eq. (11-62) by a different method from the original approach of Anderson and Rubin, who maximized the likelihood function subject to appropriate constraints by using Lagrange multipliers. Hood and Koopmans start with the likelihood function for the complete model of G equations for all G endogenous variables and then, by a series of stepwise maximizations, eliminate from the likelihood function all parameters other than those of the equation to be estimated. Finally, even $\boldsymbol{\gamma}$ is eliminated and the concentrated likelihood function expressed in term of $\boldsymbol{\beta}_\Delta$.

from

$$(\mathbf{W}^*_{\Delta\Delta} - \hat{l}\mathbf{W}_{\Delta\Delta})\hat{\boldsymbol{\beta}}_\Delta = \mathbf{0} \tag{11-66}$$

by setting the first element of $\hat{\boldsymbol{\beta}}_\Delta$ equal to unity. Defining

$$\hat{\mathbf{z}} = \mathbf{Y}_\Delta\hat{\boldsymbol{\beta}}_\Delta$$

and regressing $\hat{\mathbf{z}}$ on $\mathbf{X}_1$ gives

$$\hat{\boldsymbol{\gamma}} = (\mathbf{X}_1'\mathbf{X}_1)^{-1}\mathbf{X}_1'\mathbf{Y}_\Delta\hat{\boldsymbol{\beta}}_\Delta \tag{11-67}$$

Equations (11-66) and (11-67) define the LIML estimates of the structural equation. The LIML estimators have the same asymptotic variance-covariance matrix as 2SLS. The estimates of the asymptotic variances, however, will differ since s^2 is computed from the estimated structural coefficients, which will be different in the two cases.

Three-Stage Least Squares and Full-Information Maximum Likelihood

The estimators considered so far, namely ILS, 2SLS, LIVE, and LIML, are all essentially limited-information estimators in that in the estimation of any structural equation complete information on all the other structural equations in the model is not taken into account.† In principle information on the complete structure, if correct, will yield estimators with greater asymptotic efficiency than that attainable by limited-information methods. There are two main full-information methods, namely, three-stage least squares, (3SLS) and full-information maximum likelihood (FIML).

The initial development of 3SLS is due to Zellner and Theil.‡ Consider again the general linear model containing G jointly dependent endogenous variables and K predetermined variables. The ith equation may be written

$$\mathbf{y}_i = \mathbf{Y}_i\boldsymbol{\beta}_i + \mathbf{X}_i\boldsymbol{\gamma}_i + \mathbf{u}_i \tag{11-68}$$

where $\mathbf{y}_i$ is an $n \times 1$ vector of sample observations on the dependent variable in the ith equation, $\mathbf{Y}_i$ is an $n \times g_i$ matrix of observations on the other endogenous variables in the equation, $\mathbf{X}_i$ is an $n \times k_i$ matrix of observations on the predetermined variables in the equation, $\boldsymbol{\beta}_i$ and $\boldsymbol{\gamma}_i$ are vectors of structural parameters, and $\mathbf{u}_i$ is a vector of disturbances. Rewrite Eq. (11-68) as

$$\mathbf{y}_i = \mathbf{Z}_i\boldsymbol{\delta}_i + \mathbf{u}_i \tag{11-69}$$

where

$$\mathbf{Z}_i = [\mathbf{Y}_i \quad \mathbf{X}_i] \qquad \text{and} \qquad \boldsymbol{\delta}_i = \begin{bmatrix} \boldsymbol{\beta}_i \\ \boldsymbol{\gamma}_i \end{bmatrix}$$

If Eq. (11-69) is premultiplied by $\mathbf{X}$, the $n \times K$ matrix of all the predetermined variables in the model, then

$$\mathbf{X}'\mathbf{y}_i = \mathbf{X}'\mathbf{Z}_i\boldsymbol{\delta}_i + \mathbf{X}'\mathbf{u}_i \qquad i = 1,\ldots, G \tag{11-70}$$

† An exception is the LIVE estimator where initial estimates of the $\mathbf{B}$ and $\boldsymbol{\Gamma}$ matrices are made to derive an estimate of $\boldsymbol{\Pi}$.

‡ A. Zellner and H. Theil, "Three Stage Least Squares: Simultaneous Estimation of Simultaneous Equations," *Econometrica*, vol. 30, 1962, pp. 54–78.

The variance-covariance matrix of the disturbance term in Eq. (11-70) is

$$E(\mathbf{X}'\mathbf{u}_i\mathbf{u}_i'\mathbf{X}) = \sigma_{ii}\mathbf{X}'\mathbf{X} \tag{11-71}$$

on the assumption that $E(\mathbf{u}_i\mathbf{u}_i') = \sigma_{ii}\mathbf{I}$. Considering Eq. (11-70) as a relationship between a dependent variable $\mathbf{X}'\mathbf{y}_i$ and explanatory variables $\mathbf{X}'\mathbf{Z}_i$, the nonspherical disturbance matrix in Eq. (11-71) suggests using generalized least squares. The GLS estimator of $\boldsymbol{\delta}_i$ is then

$$\mathbf{d}_i = \left[\mathbf{Z}_i'\mathbf{X}(\mathbf{X}'\mathbf{X})^{-1}\mathbf{X}'\mathbf{Z}_i\right]^{-1}\mathbf{Z}_i'\mathbf{X}(\mathbf{X}'\mathbf{X})^{-1}\mathbf{X}'\mathbf{y}_i \tag{11-72}$$

Equation (11-72) is simply another way of writing the 2SLS estimator of Eq. (11-69), as may be verified by substituting for $\mathbf{Z}_i$, multiplying out, and comparing with the original expression for the 2SLS estimator in Eq. (11-45).

We may note in passing that Eq. (11-72) affords a simple demonstration of the equivalence of 2SLS and ILS in the case of a just identified equation. The order condition for exact identification of the ith structural equation is

$$K - k_i = g_i - 1 \qquad \text{or} \qquad k_i + g_i - 1 = K$$

Thus $\mathbf{Z}_i$ is of order $n \times K$ so that $\mathbf{X}'\mathbf{Z}_i$ is of order $K \times K$ and may be assumed to be nonsingular. In this special case Eq. (11-72) gives

$$\mathbf{d}_i = (\mathbf{X}'\mathbf{Z}_i)^{-1}(\mathbf{X}'\mathbf{X})(\mathbf{Z}_i'\mathbf{X})^{-1}(\mathbf{Z}_i'\mathbf{X})(\mathbf{X}'\mathbf{X})^{-1}\mathbf{X}'\mathbf{y}_i = (\mathbf{X}'\mathbf{Z}_i)^{-1}\mathbf{X}'\mathbf{y}_i$$

which, from Eq. (11-42), is seen to be the ILS estimator for the ith structural equation.

We also know from the discussion of GLS estimators in Chap. 8 that it is possible to interpret the GLS estimator as equivalent to the estimator given by the application of OLS to suitably transformed data. The present case may be so interpreted, and this leads to a considerable simplification in the presentation of the 3SLS estimator. Consider again Eq. (11-70) whose disturbance has a variance matrix given by $\sigma_{ii}\mathbf{X}'\mathbf{X}$. Since $\mathbf{X}'\mathbf{X}$ is positive definite, we know from Chap. 4 that its inverse is also positive definite and that a nonsingular matrix $\mathbf{P}$ exists such that

$$(\mathbf{X}'\mathbf{X})^{-1} = \mathbf{P}\mathbf{P}' \tag{11-73}$$

from which it follows that

$$\mathbf{P}'\mathbf{X}'\mathbf{X}\mathbf{P} = \mathbf{I} \tag{11-74}$$

Premultiplying Eq. (11-70) by $\mathbf{P}'$ gives

$$\mathbf{P}'\mathbf{X}'\mathbf{y}_i = \mathbf{P}'\mathbf{X}'\mathbf{Z}_i\boldsymbol{\delta}_i + \mathbf{P}'\mathbf{X}'\mathbf{u}_i$$

or

$$\mathbf{w}_i = \mathbf{W}_i\boldsymbol{\delta}_i + \mathbf{v}_i \tag{11-75}$$

where

$$\mathbf{w}_i = \mathbf{P}'\mathbf{X}'\mathbf{y}_i$$
$$\mathbf{W}_i = \mathbf{P}'\mathbf{X}'\mathbf{Z}_i$$
$$\mathbf{v}_i = \mathbf{P}'\mathbf{X}'\mathbf{u}_i$$

The variance matrix for the disturbance term in Eq. (11-75) is

$$\begin{aligned} E(\mathbf{v}_i\mathbf{v}_i') &= E(\mathbf{P}'\mathbf{X}'\mathbf{u}_i\mathbf{u}_i'\mathbf{X}\mathbf{P}) \\ &= \sigma_{ii}\mathbf{P}'\mathbf{X}'\mathbf{X}\mathbf{P} \\ &= \sigma_{ii}\mathbf{I} \end{aligned} \tag{11-76}$$

The application of OLS to Eq. (11-75) then gives

$$\mathbf{d}_i = (\mathbf{W}_i'\mathbf{W}_i)^{-1}\mathbf{W}_i'\mathbf{w}_i \tag{11-77}$$

which is easily seen to reduce to the 2SLS estimator in Eq. (11-72).

Collecting all G structural equations gives

$$\begin{bmatrix} \mathbf{w}_1 \\ \mathbf{w}_2 \\ \vdots \\ \mathbf{w}_G \end{bmatrix} = \begin{bmatrix} \mathbf{W}_1 & \mathbf{0} & \cdots & \mathbf{0} \\ \mathbf{0} & \mathbf{W}_2 & \cdots & \mathbf{0} \\ \cdots & \cdots & \cdots & \cdots \\ \mathbf{0} & \mathbf{0} & \cdots & \mathbf{W}_G \end{bmatrix} \begin{bmatrix} \boldsymbol{\delta}_1 \\ \boldsymbol{\delta}_2 \\ \vdots \\ \boldsymbol{\delta}_G \end{bmatrix} + \begin{bmatrix} \mathbf{v}_1 \\ \mathbf{v}_2 \\ \vdots \\ \mathbf{v}_G \end{bmatrix} \tag{11-78}$$

or, more compactly,

$$\mathbf{w} = \mathbf{W}\boldsymbol{\delta} + \mathbf{v} \tag{11-79}$$

where the definition of the symbols in Eq. (11-79) is obvious from the comparison with Eq. (11-78). The variance matrix for the $\mathbf{v}$ vector is

$$\mathbf{V} = E(\mathbf{v}\mathbf{v}') = \begin{bmatrix} \sigma_{11}\mathbf{I} & \sigma_{12}\mathbf{I} & \cdots & \sigma_{1G}\mathbf{I} \\ \sigma_{21}\mathbf{I} & \sigma_{22}\mathbf{I} & \cdots & \sigma_{2G}\mathbf{I} \\ \cdots & \cdots & \cdots & \cdots \\ \sigma_{G1}\mathbf{I} & \sigma_{G2}\mathbf{I} & \cdots & \sigma_{GG}\mathbf{I} \end{bmatrix} = \boldsymbol{\Sigma} \otimes \mathbf{I} \tag{11-80}$$

The variance terms in Eq. (11-80) follow directly from Eq. (11-76). The typical covariance term is

$$E(\mathbf{v}_i\mathbf{v}_j') = E(\mathbf{P}'\mathbf{X}'\mathbf{u}_i\mathbf{u}_j'\mathbf{X}\mathbf{P}) = \sigma_{ij}\mathbf{I}$$

Thus the basic assumption is that each structural equation has a homoscedastic nonautocorrelated error term and that the disturbances in different structural equations may be contemporaneously correlated. Provided that at least some σ_{ij} are nonzero, the arguments underlying the Zellner SURE estimator, already considered in Chap. 8, would suggest that any of the G equations defined by Eq. (11-75) would be more efficiently estimated as a member of the complete set defined in Eqs. (11-78) and (11-79). 3SLS is, in fact, simply the SURE estimator of $\boldsymbol{\delta}$ in Eq. (11-79). The only difficulty is that the $\boldsymbol{\Sigma}$ matrix in Eq. (11-80) is unknown. The Zellner-Theil suggestion is to estimate first each structural equation by 2SLS, giving the residual vectors

$$\hat{\mathbf{u}}_i = \mathbf{y}_i - \mathbf{Z}_i\mathbf{d}_i \qquad i = 1, \ldots, G$$

where $\mathbf{d}_i$ is the 2SLS estimator of δ_i. The elements of $\boldsymbol{\Sigma}$ are then estimated by

$$s_{ij} = \frac{\hat{\mathbf{u}}_i'\hat{\mathbf{u}}_j}{n} \qquad \text{for all } i, j$$

giving

$$\hat{\mathbf{V}} = \hat{\boldsymbol{\Sigma}} \otimes \mathbf{I}$$

The 3SLS estimator of $\boldsymbol{\delta}$ is then

$$\mathbf{d}_{3\text{SLS}} = (\mathbf{W}'\hat{\mathbf{V}}^{-1}\mathbf{W})^{-1}\mathbf{W}'\hat{\mathbf{V}}^{-1}\mathbf{w} \tag{11-81}$$

with asymptotic variance matrix estimated by

$$\text{asy var}(\mathbf{d}_{3SLS}) = (\mathbf{W}'\hat{\mathbf{V}}^{-1}\mathbf{W})^{-1}$$

Substituting in Eq. (11-81) for the elements of $\mathbf{w}$ and $\mathbf{W}$, the 3SLS estimator may be expressed in terms of the original data as

$$\mathbf{d}_{3SLS} = \begin{bmatrix} s^{11}\mathbf{Z}_1'\mathbf{X}(\mathbf{X}'\mathbf{X})^{-1}\mathbf{X}'\mathbf{Z}_1 & s^{12}\mathbf{Z}_1'\mathbf{X}(\mathbf{X}'\mathbf{X})^{-1}\mathbf{X}'\mathbf{Z}_2 & \cdots & s^{1G}\mathbf{Z}_1'\mathbf{X}(\mathbf{X}'\mathbf{X})^{-1}\mathbf{X}'\mathbf{Z}_G \\ s^{21}\mathbf{Z}_2'\mathbf{X}(\mathbf{X}'\mathbf{X})^{-1}\mathbf{X}'\mathbf{Z}_1 & s^{22}\mathbf{Z}_2'\mathbf{X}(\mathbf{X}'\mathbf{X})^{-1}\mathbf{X}'\mathbf{Z}_2 & \cdots & s^{2G}\mathbf{Z}_2'\mathbf{X}(\mathbf{X}'\mathbf{X})^{-1}\mathbf{X}'\mathbf{Z}_G \\ \cdots & \cdots & \cdots & \cdots \\ s^{G1}\mathbf{Z}_G'\mathbf{X}(\mathbf{X}'\mathbf{X})^{-1}\mathbf{X}'\mathbf{Z}_1 & s^{G2}\mathbf{Z}_G'\mathbf{X}(\mathbf{X}'\mathbf{X})^{-1}\mathbf{X}'\mathbf{Z}_2 & \cdots & s^{GG}\mathbf{Z}_G'\mathbf{X}(\mathbf{X}'\mathbf{X})^{-1}\mathbf{X}'\mathbf{Z}_G \end{bmatrix}$$

$$\times \begin{bmatrix} \sum_{j=1}^{G} s^{1j}\mathbf{Z}_1'\mathbf{X}(\mathbf{X}'\mathbf{X})^{-1}\mathbf{X}'\mathbf{y}_j \\ \sum_{j=1}^{G} s^{2j}\mathbf{Z}_2'\mathbf{X}(\mathbf{X}'\mathbf{X})^{-1}\mathbf{X}'\mathbf{y}_j \\ \cdots \\ \sum_{j=1}^{G} s^{Gj}\mathbf{Z}_G'\mathbf{X}(\mathbf{X}'\mathbf{X})^{-1}\mathbf{X}'\mathbf{y}_j \end{bmatrix} \qquad (11\text{-}82)$$

where the s^{ij} denote the elements in $\hat{\boldsymbol{\Sigma}}^{-1}$.

A crucial question concerns the conditions under which 3SLS will be asymptotically more efficient than 2SLS. A necessary condition for the superior efficiency of a full-information, or complete-system, method of estimation over a limited-information method is that the specification of the complete model should be correct. In many systems this is a formidable requirement, and the larger and more detailed the system, the more difficult does it become. Even granted a correct full-system specification, there are two conditions under which 2SLS and 3SLS will give identical point estimates with identical asymptotic sampling variances. The first is

$$\sigma_{ij} = 0 \qquad \text{for all } i \neq j$$

that is, the contemporaneous correlations between the disturbances in different structural equations are all zero. The equivalence follows directly from the result for the SURE model that a diagonal $\boldsymbol{\Sigma}$ matrix gives equality between the SURE and OLS coefficients.† It may also be seen directly by substituting $s^{ij} = 0$ in Eq. (11-82).‡ The other condition under which one would find equivalence of 2SLS and 3SLS estimators is all equations being exactly identified. We have already seen that the order condition for exact identification of the ith equation leads to the result that $\mathbf{X}'\mathbf{Z}_i$ is of order $K \times K$ and may be assumed to be nonsingular. The

† See Problem 8-2.

‡ Notice that Eq. (11-82) refers to the *feasible* 3SLS estimator where $\boldsymbol{\Sigma}^{-1}$ has been replaced by $\hat{\boldsymbol{\Sigma}}^{-1}$. If $\boldsymbol{\Sigma}$ is diagonal, then so is $\boldsymbol{\Sigma}^{-1}$ and $s^{ij} = 0$ for all $i \neq j$. However, even if this condition is satisfied, the s_{ij} (and hence the s^{ij}) estimated from 2SLS residuals will in general not vanish.

P matrix defined in Eq. (11-73) is also square of order K and nonsingular. Thus

$$\mathbf{W}_i = \mathbf{P}'\mathbf{X}'\mathbf{Z}_i$$

is $K \times K$ and nonsingular. This result holds for all $i = 1, \ldots, G$. Thus the block-diagonal **W** matrix defined in Eqs. (11-78) and (11-79) is nonsingular and each component submatrix is nonsingular. The 3SLS estimator defined in Eq. (11-81) may then be written

$$\begin{aligned}\mathbf{d}_{3\text{SLS}} &= \mathbf{W}^{-1}\hat{\mathbf{V}}(\mathbf{W}')^{-1}\mathbf{W}'\hat{\mathbf{V}}^{-1}\mathbf{w} \\ &= \mathbf{W}^{-1}\mathbf{w}\end{aligned}$$

Under the same assumption the 2SLS estimator for the ith equation defined in Eq. (11-77) reduces to

$$\mathbf{d}_i = \mathbf{W}_i^{-1}\mathbf{w}_i$$

Thus the collection of 2SLS estimators for the complete system may be written

$$\mathbf{d}_{2\text{SLS}} = \begin{bmatrix} \mathbf{d}_1 \\ \mathbf{d}_2 \\ \vdots \\ \mathbf{d}_G \end{bmatrix} = \begin{bmatrix} \mathbf{W}_1^{-1} & \mathbf{0} & \cdots & \mathbf{0} \\ \mathbf{0} & \mathbf{W}_2^{-1} & \cdots & \mathbf{0} \\ \cdots & \cdots & \cdots & \cdots \\ \mathbf{0} & \mathbf{0} & \cdots & \mathbf{W}_G^{-1} \end{bmatrix} \begin{bmatrix} \mathbf{w}_1 \\ \mathbf{w}_2 \\ \vdots \\ \mathbf{w}_G \end{bmatrix} = \mathbf{W}^{-1}\mathbf{w}$$

which is identical with $\mathbf{d}_{3\text{SLS}}$.

So far we have assumed that all the structural equations in the model are identified. Before attempting to apply 3SLS in practice one must omit all unidentified equations and also all identities, since the latter have zero disturbances which would render the $\boldsymbol{\Sigma}$ matrix singular. Suppose that there remain G identified equations of which G_* are exactly identified and G_{**} overidentified. Zellner and Theil have shown that the 3SLS estimator of the G_{**} equations, treated as a complete group, is the same as that obtained from the application of 3SLS to the complete system of G equations. Thus it is computationally efficient to obtain the 3SLS estimates in two steps. First compute the 3SLS estimates of the overidentified equations. The 3SLS estimates of the just identified equations are then obtained by adding to the relevant 2SLS estimates a linear combination of the 3SLS estimates of the overidentified equations.†

Full-Information Maximum Likelihood

As with 3SLS this is a complete system method of estimation. It is computationally more expensive than 3SLS as it involves the solution of nonlinear equations. We will merely sketch the outlines of the approach. Consider again the linear simultaneous equation model in G current endogenous variables

$$\mathbf{B}\mathbf{y}_t + \boldsymbol{\Gamma}\mathbf{x}_t = \mathbf{u}_t \qquad t = 1, \ldots, n$$

† The precise formula is given in A. Zellner and H. Theil, "Three Stage Least Squares: Simultaneous Estimation of Simultaneous Equations," *Econometrica*, vol. 30, 1962, p. 67.

with
$$E(\mathbf{u}_t) = \mathbf{0} \qquad t = 1, \ldots, n$$
$$E(\mathbf{u}_t\mathbf{u}_t') = \mathbf{\Sigma}$$

If it is assumed that the G disturbances follow a multivariate normal distribution, we may write

$$f(\mathbf{u}_t) = \frac{1}{(2\pi)^{G/2}(\det \mathbf{\Sigma})^{1/2}} \exp\left(-\frac{1}{2}\mathbf{u}_t'\mathbf{\Sigma}^{-1}\mathbf{u}_t \right)$$

Assuming, in addition, that the $\mathbf{u}$ vectors are serially uncorrelated, the likelihood for the n vectors $\mathbf{u}_1, \mathbf{u}_2, \ldots, \mathbf{u}_n$ is then

$$p(\mathbf{u}_1, \mathbf{u}_2, \ldots, \mathbf{u}_n) = \prod_{t=1}^{n} f(\mathbf{u}_t)$$
$$= (2\pi)^{-nG/2}(\det \mathbf{\Sigma})^{-n/2} \exp\left(-\frac{1}{2} \sum_{t=1}^{n} \mathbf{u}_t'\mathbf{\Sigma}^{-1}\mathbf{u}_t \right)$$

The likelihood for $\mathbf{y}_1, \mathbf{y}_2, \ldots, \mathbf{y}_n$ is

$$p(\mathbf{y}_1, \mathbf{y}_2, \ldots, \mathbf{y}_n) = (2\pi)^{-nG/2} |\det \mathbf{B}|^n (\det \mathbf{\Sigma})^{-n/2}$$
$$\times \exp\left[-\frac{1}{2} \sum_{t=1}^{n} (\mathbf{B}\mathbf{y}_t + \mathbf{\Gamma}\mathbf{x}_t)'\mathbf{\Sigma}^{-1}(\mathbf{B}\mathbf{y}_t + \mathbf{\Gamma}\mathbf{x}_t) \right] \qquad (11\text{-}83)$$

If we write

$$\mathbf{B}\mathbf{y}_t + \mathbf{\Gamma}\mathbf{x}_t = [\mathbf{B} \quad \mathbf{\Gamma}] \begin{bmatrix} \mathbf{y}_t \\ \mathbf{x}_t \end{bmatrix} = \mathbf{A}\mathbf{z}_t$$

the exponent in the likelihood in Eq. (11-83) can be written

$$-\frac{1}{2} \sum_{t=1}^{n} \mathbf{z}_t'\mathbf{A}'\mathbf{\Sigma}^{-1}\mathbf{A}\mathbf{z}_t = -\frac{1}{2} \operatorname{tr}(\mathbf{Z}\mathbf{A}'\mathbf{\Sigma}^{-1}\mathbf{A}\mathbf{Z}')$$
$$= -\frac{1}{2} \operatorname{tr}(\mathbf{\Sigma}^{-1}\mathbf{A}\mathbf{Z}'\mathbf{Z}\mathbf{A}')$$

where

$$\mathbf{Z} = [\mathbf{Y} \quad \mathbf{X}] = \begin{bmatrix} \mathbf{y}_1' & \mathbf{x}_1' \\ \mathbf{y}_2' & \mathbf{x}_2' \\ \cdots & \cdots \\ \mathbf{y}_n' & \mathbf{x}_n' \end{bmatrix}$$

is the $n \times (G + K)$ matrix of observations on all the endogenous and predetermined variables. Defining

$$\mathbf{M} = \frac{1}{n}\mathbf{Z}'\mathbf{Z}$$

$$\operatorname{tr}(\mathbf{\Sigma}^{-1}\mathbf{A}\mathbf{Z}'\mathbf{Z}\mathbf{A}') = n \operatorname{tr}(\mathbf{\Sigma}^{-1}\mathbf{A}\mathbf{M}\mathbf{A}')$$

Table 11-1 Estimation methods in the models of Project Link

Country	Data†	Total number of equations	Number of stochastic equations	Estimation method
Australia	*Q*	82	42	OLS
Austria	*A*	128	54	OLS
Belgium	*Q*	25	19	OLS
Canada	*A*	183	44	OLS
Finland	*Q*	144	60	OLS
France	*A*	32	19	OLS
West Germany	*A*	137	51	FIML
Italy	*Q*	104	53	OLS
Japan	*Q*	78	43	OLS
Netherlands	*A*	87	13	LIML and 2SLS
Sweden	*A*	133	75	OLS
United Kingdom	*Q*	226	106	OLS
United States	*Q*	207	70	OLS
Developing America	*A*	12	11	OLS
Developing South and East Asia	*A*	14	13	OLS
Developing Middle East and Libya	*A*	10	9	OLS
Developing Africa less Libya	*A*	11	10	OLS

†*Q*—quarterly data; *A*—annual data.
Source: J. Waelbroeck, *The Models of Project Link*, North-Holland, Amsterdam, 1976.

and so the logarithm of the likelihood in Eq. (11-83) may be written

$$L(\mathbf{A}, \mathbf{\Sigma}) = \text{constant} + n \ln|\det \mathbf{B}| - \frac{n}{2} \ln \det \mathbf{\Sigma} - \frac{n}{2} \operatorname{tr}(\mathbf{\Sigma}^{-1}\mathbf{AMA}') \qquad (11\text{-}84)$$

The FIML estimator results from the maximization of $L(\mathbf{A}, \mathbf{\Sigma})$ with respect to the elements of $\mathbf{A}$ and $\mathbf{\Sigma}$. The equations are nonlinear and computationally expensive, though less so with each advance in computer technology. The asymptotic variance matrix of the FIML estimator, however, turns out to be identical with that for 3SLS, thus indicating the asymptotic efficiency of the latter method.†

This feature, combined with its less severe computational problems, leads some authors to recommend 3SLS over FIML. Most practical applications of 3SLS or FIML occur, not surprisingly, with fairly small models. What is perhaps surprising is the continued dominance of OLS over all other methods, especially in the estimation of major econometric models. A recent study by Waelbroeck‡ documents the main features of the various countrywide econometric models in Project Link. Of the 17 models summarized, OLS is the estimating method in 15, FIML is used in only one model, and a combination of LIML and 2SLS in the remaining model. Details are given in Table 11-1.

† See H. Theil, *Principles of Econometrics*, Wiley, New York, 1971, pp. 524–527.
‡ J. Waelbroeck, *The Models of Project Link*, North-Holland, Amsterdam, 1976.

PROBLEMS

11-1 For the model defined by Eqs. (11-1) and (11-2) show that

$$\text{plim}(b) = \frac{\beta \overline{m}_{zz} + \sigma_u^2}{\overline{m}_{zz} + \sigma_u^2} > \beta$$

where b is the slope of OLS regression of C on Y and

$$\overline{m}_{zz} = \text{plim}\left[\frac{1}{n}\Sigma(Z_t - \overline{Z})^2\right]$$

11-2 Prove the equivalence between the alternative expressions for the 2SLS estimator in Eqs. (11-45) and (11-46).

11-3 The structure of the Klein model is

$$C = \alpha_0 + \alpha_1(W_p + W_G) + \alpha_2\Pi + \alpha_3\Pi_{-1} + u_1$$

$$I = \beta_0 + \beta_1\Pi + \beta_2\Pi_{-1} + \beta_3 K_{-1} + u_2$$

$$W_p = \gamma_0 + \gamma_1(Y + T - W_G) + \gamma_2(Y + T - W_G)_{-1} + \gamma_3 t + u_3$$

$$Y = C + I + G$$

$$\Pi = Y - W_P - T$$

$$K = K_{-1} + I$$

The six endogenous variables are Y (output), C (consumption), I (net investment), W_p (private wages), Π (profits), and K (capital stock at year-end). The four exogenous variables are G (government nonwage expenditure), W_G (public wages), T (business taxes), and t (time).

Examine the rank condition for the identifiability of the consumption function.

11-4 Tintner's model of the U.S. meat market is specified as follows:

$$y_1(t) = \alpha_0 + \alpha_1 y_2(t) + \alpha_2 x_1(t) + u_1(t) \qquad \text{demand}$$

$$y_1(t) = \beta_0 + \beta_1 y_2(t) + \beta_2 x_2(t) + \beta_3 x_3(t) + u_2(t) \qquad \text{supply}$$

(*a*) Determine the identification status of each equation.

(*b*) Suppose it is known a priori that $\beta_2/\beta_3 = k$ where k is a known number. Determine the identification status of each equation under *this* specification.

(*c*) Suppose the model stated at the outset is changed by specifying that $\alpha_2 = \beta_2 = \beta_3 = 0$. What prior restrictions (if any) on the disturbance variance-covariance matrix would lead to the identification of both equations?

(University of Michigan, 1981)

11-5 In the model

$$y_{1t} + \beta_{12} y_{2t} + \gamma_{11} x_{1t} = u_{1t}$$

$$y_{2t} + \beta_{21} y_{1t} + \gamma_{22} x_{2t} + \gamma_{23} x_{3t} = u_{2t}$$

the y's are endogenous, the x's exogenous, and $u_t' = [u_{1t} u_{2t}]$ is a vector of serially independent normal random disturbances with mean zero vector and the same nonsingular covariance matrix for each t. Given the following sample second moment matrix:

	y_1	y_2	x_1	x_2	x_3
y_1	14	6	2	3	0
y_2	6	10	2	1	0
x_1	2	2	1	0	0
x_2	3	1	0	1	0
x_3	0	0	0	0	1

calculate the LIML and 2SLS estimates of β_{12} and γ_{11}.

(University of Michigan, 1981)

11-6 An investigator has specified the following two models and proposes to use them in some empirical work with macroeconomic time series data.

Model 1:

$$c_t = \alpha_1 y_t + a_2 m_{t-1} + u_{1t}$$

$$i_t = \beta_1 y_t + \beta_2 r_t + u_{2t}$$

$$y_t = c_t + i_t$$

Jointly dependent variables: c_t, i_t, y_t

Predetermined variables: r_t, m_{t-1}

Model 2:

$$m_t = \gamma_1 r_t + \gamma_2 m_{t-1} + v_{1t}$$

$$r_t = \delta_1 m_t + \delta_2 m_{t-1} + \delta_3 y_t + v_{2t}$$

Jointly dependent variables: m_t, r_t

Predetermined variables: m_{t-1}, y_t

(*a*) Assess the identifiability of the parameters that appear as coefficients in the above two models (treating the two models separately).

(*b*) Obtain the reduced-form equation for y_t in model 1 and the reduced-form equation for r_t in model 2.

(*c*) Assess the identifiability of the two-equation model comprising the reduced-form equation for y_t in model 1 (an IS curve) and the reduced-form equation for r_t in model 2 (an LM curve).

(Yale University, 1980)

11-7 Suppose the following sample second moment matrix (based on 36 observations) has been obtained for the variables in the Tintner meat model of Problem 11-4:

	y_1	y_2	x_1	x_2	x_3
y_1	10	0	1	0	−1
y_2	0	10	−1	−1	0
x_1	1	−1	1	0	0
x_2	0	−1	0	1	0
x_3	−1	0	0	0	1

(*a*) Estimate the parameters α_1 and α_2 by 2SLS and test the hypothesis $\alpha_2 = 0$ against the alternative $\alpha_2 \neq 0$.

(*b*) Repeat part (*a*) using IV estimates of α_1 and α_2 obtained with x_{2t} as an instrument for y_{2t} and x_{1t} as its own instrument.

(Yale University, 1980)

11-8 (*a*) Assess the identification of the parameters of the following five-equation system:

$$y_{1t} + \beta_{12} y_{2t} + \beta_{14} y_{4t} + \gamma_{11} z_{1t} + \gamma_{14} z_{4t} = u_{1t}$$
$$y_{2t} + \beta_{23} y_{3t} + \beta_{25} y_{5t} + \gamma_{22} z_{2t} = u_{2t}$$
$$y_{3t} + \gamma_{31} z_{1t} + \gamma_{33} z_{3t} = u_{3t}$$
$$\beta_{41} y_{1t} + \beta_{43} y_{3t} + y_{4t} + \gamma_{42} z_{2t} + \gamma_{44} z_{4t} = u_{4t}$$
$$2 y_{3t} + y_{5t} - z_{2t} = 0$$

(*b*) How are your conclusions altered if $\gamma_{33} = 0$? Comment.

(*c*) Briefly explain how you would estimate the parameters of this model. What can be said about the parameters of the second equation?

(UL, 1979)

11-9 The model given by

$$y_{1t} = \beta_{12} y_{2t} + \gamma_{11} z_{1t} + \gamma_{12} z_{2t} + \varepsilon_{1t} \qquad (1)$$
$$y_{2t} = \beta_{21} y_{1t} + \gamma_{23} z_{3t} + \varepsilon_{2t} \qquad (2)$$

generates the following matrix of second moments:

	y_1	y_2	z_1	z_2	z_3
y_1	3.5	3	1	1	0
y_2		11.5	1	3	4
z_1			1	0	0
z_2				1	1
z_3					2

Calculate:

(*a*) Least-squares estimates of the unrestricted reduced-form parameters
(*b*) ILS estimates of the parameters of Eq. (1)
(*c*) 2SLS estimates of the parameters of Eq. (2)
(*d*) The restricted reduced form derived from parts (*b*) and (*c*)
(*e*) A consistent estimate of $E(\varepsilon_{12}\varepsilon_{2t}) = \sigma_{12}$

(UL, 1973)

11-10 Let the model be

$$y_{1t} + \beta_{12} y_{2t} + \gamma_{11} x_{1t} + \gamma_{13} x_{3t} = u_{1t}$$
$$\beta_{21} y_{1t} + y_{2t} + \gamma_{22} x_{2t} + \gamma_{23} x_{3t} = u_{2t} \qquad (1)$$

and suppose the observations on the variables are

$$\mathbf{X}' = \begin{bmatrix} 1 & 2 & 3 & 4 & 5 & 6 \\ 4 & 4 & 8 & 10 & 12 & 20 \\ 2 & 2 & 4 & 5 & 6 & 10 \end{bmatrix} \qquad \mathbf{Y}' = \begin{bmatrix} 4 & 7 & 8 & 9 & 10 & 11 \\ 3 & 6 & 2 & 5 & 7 & 9 \end{bmatrix} \qquad (2)$$

(*a*) Examine the rank and order conditions for identification on the basis of Eqs. (1) and suggest a suitable estimation procedure for both equations.

(*b*) In the light of Eqs. (2) investigate whether the answer under part (*a*) needs modification and, if so, in what way. Interpret by reformulating the model in Eqs. (1).

(UL, 1971)

11-11 Let the model be

$$y_{1t} + \beta_{12} y_{2t} + \gamma_{12} x_{2t} + \gamma_{13} x_{3t} = u_{1t}$$
$$\beta_{21} y_{1t} + y_{2t} + \gamma_{21} x_{1t} + \gamma_{24} x_{4t} = u_{2t}$$

If the second moment matrices of a sample of 100 observations are

$$\mathbf{Y'Y} = \begin{bmatrix} 80.0 & -4.0 \\ -4.0 & 5.0 \end{bmatrix} \qquad \mathbf{Y'X} = \begin{bmatrix} 2.0 & 1.0 & -3.0 & -5.0 \\ -0.5 & 1.5 & 0.5 & -1.0 \end{bmatrix}$$

$$\mathbf{X'X} = \begin{bmatrix} 3.0 & 0 & 0 & 0 \\ 0 & 2.0 & 0 & 0 \\ 0 & 0 & 1.0 & 0 \\ 0 & 0 & 0 & 0.5 \end{bmatrix}$$

find the 2SLS estimates of the coefficients of the first equation and their standard errors.

(UL, 1970)

11-12 In the following market model

$$\text{Supply} \qquad Q_t = \beta_{11}P_t + \gamma_{10} + u_{1t}$$

$$\text{Demand} \qquad Q_t = \beta_{21}P_t + \gamma_{20} + \gamma_{21}Z_{1t} + \gamma_{22}Z_{2t} + u_{2t}$$

quantity Q_t and price P_t are endogenous, while income Z_{1t} and the price of some other good Z_{2t} are exogenous. If the supply function is estimated directly by least squares, will the resulting estimate of β_{11} be biased? If so, in which direction will the bias occur?

(UL, 1972)

11-13 If

$$y_{1t} = \beta_{12}y_{2t} + \gamma_{11}x_{1t} + \gamma_{12}x_{2t} + u_{1t}$$

$$y_{2t} = \beta_{21}y_{1t} + \gamma_{23}x_{3t} + u_{2t}$$

and

$$\mathbf{X'X} = \begin{bmatrix} 10 & 0 & 0 \\ 0 & 5 & 0 \\ 0 & 0 & 10 \end{bmatrix} \qquad \mathbf{X'Y} = \begin{bmatrix} 10 & 20 \\ 20 & 10 \\ 30 & 20 \end{bmatrix}$$

estimate the parameters in the model and comment on your results. If β_{21} is known to be equal to 0.6, would you modify your estimation procedure, and if so how?

11-14 The **X'X** matrix for all the exogenous variables in a model is

$$\mathbf{X'X} = \begin{bmatrix} 7 & 0 & 3 & 1 \\ 0 & 2 & -2 & 0 \\ 3 & -2 & 5 & 1 \\ 1 & 0 & 1 & 1 \end{bmatrix}$$

Only the first of these exogenous variables has a nonzero coefficient in a structural equation to be estimated by 2SLS. This equation includes two endogenous variables, and the least-squares estimates of the reduced-form coefficients for these two variables are

$$\begin{bmatrix} 0 & 1 & 3 & 2 \\ 1 & -1 & 1 & -1 \end{bmatrix}$$

Taking the first endogenous variable as the dependent variable, state and solve the equation for the 2SLS estimates.

11-15 For the model

$$y_{1t} = \beta_{12}y_{2t} + \gamma_{11}x_{1t} + u_{1t}$$

$$y_{2t} = \beta_{21}y_{1t} + \gamma_{22}x_{2t} + \gamma_{23}x_{3t} + u_t$$

you are given the following information:

1. The least-squares estimates of the reduced-form coefficients are

$$\begin{bmatrix} 5 & 10 & 2 \\ 10 & 10 & 5 \end{bmatrix}$$

2. The estimates of variance of the errors of the coefficients in the first reduced-form equation are 1, 0.5, 0.1.
3. The corresponding covariances are estimated to be all zero.
4. The estimated variance of the error on the first reduced-form equation is 2.0.

Use this information to reconstruct the 2SLS equations for the estimates of the coefficients of the first structural equation, and compute these estimates.

(UL, 1969)

11-16

$$y_{1t} = \beta_{12}y_{2t} + \beta_{13}y_{3t} + \gamma_{11}x_{1t} + u_{1t}$$

is one equation in a three-equation model which contains three other exogenous variables x_{2t}, x_{3t}, and x_{4t}. Observations give the following matrices:

$$\mathbf{Y'Y} = \begin{bmatrix} 20 & 15 & -5 \\ 15 & 60 & -45 \\ -5 & -45 & 70 \end{bmatrix} \quad \mathbf{Y'X} = \begin{bmatrix} 2 & 2 & 4 & 5 \\ 0 & 4 & 12 & -5 \\ 0 & -2 & -12 & 10 \end{bmatrix} \quad \mathbf{X'X} = \begin{bmatrix} 1 & 0 & 0 & 0 \\ 0 & 2 & 0 & 0 \\ 0 & 0 & 4 & 0 \\ 0 & 0 & 0 & 5 \end{bmatrix}$$

Obtain 2SLS estimates of the parameters of the equation and estimate their standard errors (on the assumption that the sample consisted of 30 observation points).

(UL, 1968)

CHAPTER
TWELVE

ECONOMETRICS IN PRACTICE: PROBLEMS AND PERSPECTIVES

A careful study of the material covered in the previous eleven chapters would not, unfortunately, equip the reader to conduct a successful piece of applied econometric research, since that involves many more problems than those already discussed. We will tentatively explore some of these issues in the present chapter, but the reality should be faced at the outset that it is not feasible to write a comprehensive manual that would prepare applied econometricians for all the problems that can arise in a wide variety of research projects. Successful econometric modeling is not a collection of mechanistic and routine procedures but more of an art requiring wide-ranging knowledge and judgment. Such an art is best learned by practice, hopefully with talented supervisors and colleagues, and by study of "best practice" examples. It is, however, not always easy to find the latter. Indeed a very instructive book might be written under the title, *How NOT to Do Econometrics*, with every chapter illustrated by one or more published articles. The author of such a book would have to time its publication carefully in relation to his own impending demise or retirement from contact with his professional colleagues: he might also face the difficult problem of choosing some of his own previous work for inclusion.

There is a widespread view that econometrics has in some sense not lived up to its early promise, and there is much scepticism about the value of the plethora of empirical results embedded in the literature. This state of affairs should not be too surprising. There is, after all, a sound proposition in economics that the use of a good or service tends to expand to the point at which price and marginal utility are equated. If computers are essentially free goods, if "researchers" can plug into a data bank without any understanding of where the series come from or how they were constructed, if they can press buttons to implement computer programs whose contents they dimly comprehend, it then follows, as night follows the day, that some work of zero worth will emerge. Indeed, given the uncertainty inherent in the research process, compounded by the fallibility of the researcher, some outputs may err on the wrong side of zero and be positively dangerous. Our twin defenses against further encroachments by a flow of dubious work lie in improving still further the quality of the editorial screening process and raising also the quality of the training given to would-be practitioners.

The Origins and Objectives of an Econometric Research Project

The origins and objectives of econometric research projects are as many and various as the persons and groups who undertake them. It may be a lone graduate student scratching his head or rummaging in his supervisor's "bottom drawer" for a thesis project; it may be an academic intrigued by a theoretical debate in the literature or impelled by some idea of her own; it may be a public or commercial research group building or expanding an econometric model to be used for short-term forecasting. In my own experience the writing of this book was delayed for several years by two separate phone calls. One led to a year's work estimating demand functions for oil for the major industrial countries of the world. A subsequent, but not unrelated, call led to two years' intense activity as the econometric consultant on the construction of a world model of energy demands and supplies. It is platitudinous but important to say that in all cases one should be as clear and precise as possible about the objectives of the research, since these condition the design and layout of the project, though of course they may have to be revised as the project proceeds.

Data and Model Specification

These two topics are inextricably linked. The model specification will have strong implications for the data required and, conversely, data limitations may constrain the feasible specification. As an illustration suppose an objective is the estimation of a demand function for crude oil in the United Kingdom that might then be used to forecast demand, conditional on various assumptions about the future paths of income and relative prices. The first step is to investigate the range of possible strategies. Should one estimate an aggregative demand function for crude, using some measure of "income" and some relative price? If so, should the income measure be real GDP, or an index of industrial production, or what? What, in turn, are the appropriate price series from which an index of relative prices should be constructed? Or, alternatively, should one use a more disaggregated approach looking at the final demands for specific products from the refining process, such as gasoline, jet fuel, heating oil, and so on, and should one disaggregate also by consuming sector, whether residential, commercial, industrial, public utilities, and so forth? The disaggregated approach would also require the modeling of the refining decision and of the relationship between the price of crude and the prices of refined products. In this decision process it is of great importance to have as much knowledge as possible of what may be called the "institutional realities" of the situation, specifically in this case such things as the nature of the refining process and the constraints on the refining decision, the quantitative importance of various groups of consumers, and the crucial factors in their decision processes. An econometrician coming cold to the study would run the risk of very slow progress with much searching through inappropriate formulations. In my own experience collaboration with an experienced oil specialist greatly improved the research efficiency.

Knowledge of the "institutional realities" is, of course, valuable in all areas. In a study of cost-output relationships in coal mining this author felt it necessary to don a safety helmet and get to the coal face in the narrow and twisting seams of the Lancashire coal field in order to see at first hand the nature of the production process before sitting down to peruse the statistics at the regional headquarters of the National Coal Board. Similarly in studies of scale, costs, and profitability in road passenger transport and of cost-output variations in a multiple-product firm the author spent time at each firm talking to accountants and managers to study their accounting and decision processes before extracting the relevant data by hand from the firm's records.† To take a final data problem, monetary theory postulates the demand for money to be positively related to income and negatively related to the rate of interest. Each of the three nouns in this proposition raises formidable problems of definition and measurement. There are numerous definitions of money and almost continual evolution of payments technology, there are many interest rates, and even income is not unambiguous.

When appropriate data series have been identified, the next decision in time-series contexts is what data period (hourly, weekly, monthly, quarterly, annual, or whatever) to use. Again if we had institutional information about decision processes (*who* decides *when* about *what*) we could make the appropriate choice. If, for example, production decisions are revised at the start of each month, a model of the production decision employing monthly data would have the best chance of capturing the essential features of the process. Quarterly or annual data would in this case involve an inappropriate aggregation over time, thus making it difficult, if not impossible, to determine the lag structure. Often, however, there is little firm information about decision procedures, and the main choice between quarterly and annual data is based largely on a mixture of empirical considerations and the objectives of the modeling process. As Table 11-1 shows, the macroeconometric models for the developed economies are split roughly evenly between those based on quarterly and those based on annual data.

By far the most difficult problem of all is the initial specification of the model, be it a single equation or a set of equations. By specification we mean the

† For these and other studies see J. Johnston, *Statistical Cost Analysis*, McGraw-Hill, New York, 1960.

following:

1. The listing of explanatory variables, including lagged values, in each equation
2. The functional form relating these variables to the dependent variable
3. The stochastic properties of the disturbance term or terms

Economic theory is mostly about *equilibrium* situations and contains little in the way of systematically developed dynamic theory. Thus it cannot be expected to yield strong insights about lag structure. Nor can it be expected to indicate the correct functional form. Thus items 1 and 2 inevitably lead to a certain amount of interaction between theory and data. This interaction also impinges on item 3, which essentially consists of assumptions about *unobservable* variables. However, each specification under items 1 and 2 provides estimates of the unobservables, and the interaction between specification and data usually continues until the researcher feels that a "reasonable" set of results under items 1, 2, and 3 has been obtained.

Data Mining and Specification Searches†

This interactive process has been labeled *data mining* or, more recently and less pejoratively, *specification searches*. At one extreme it is alleged that data mining invalidates all the conventional significance levels or, even more strongly, that the final results are quite valueless, since the researcher has gone on a "fishing expedition" or beaten the data set into submission until they finally yielded the desired conclusion. At the other extreme it is suggested that if the set of models includes the "true" model, that model will have the smallest residual variance and hence the highest true $\bar{R}^2$, so that searching for the best fit to the sample data is a reasonable and sensible procedure.

Let us take a look at the data mining problem by means of two hypothetical examples.

Example 1. A researcher's objective is to explain the variation in a variable y. He has 10 candidate explanatory variables $x_1, \ldots, x_{10}$ on the basis of his a priori theory. The underlying theory can only be characterized as "lousy" for

1. It specifies that only three of the possible 10 variables actually influence y, but it does not know which three, and, more seriously,
2. The theory is totally in error for, in fact, none of the 10 variables has any effect on y.

The first defect of the theory actually appears as an advantage to our researcher for his computer cannot handle more than three explanatory variables

† Our brief discussion cannot hope to do adequate justice to this topic. The interested reader will find much nourishment in the elegant, entertaining, and enlightening E. E. Leamer, *Specification Searches*, Wiley, New York, 1978.

at a time. Thus he computes all ${}^{10}C_3 = 120$ possible multiple regressions and the attendant F statistics for the overall fit. The true value of all 120 population F statistics is of course zero, but the reader would not be surprised to find that our researcher discovers some significant sample regressions.† His theoretical and institutional knowledge enables him to write a plausible commentary on these regressions and perhaps select one as the seemingly best theory for the explanation of y. Sending the write-up to an editor, who likes to publish "significant" results, guarantees another "scientific" paper and a further small step by the author up the academic ladder.

Another variant of Example 12-1 is a theory that only identifies the three candidate variables, none of which, in fact, has any relevance to y. A series of investigators drawing different sets of sample data from y, x_1, x_2, x_3 fail to find a significant regression, consigning their computer printout to the waste paper basket or filing cabinet, according to temperament. In either case their professional colleagues are unaware of this accumulation of "negative" results, and so testing of the theory continues. Working at any conventional level of significance, it is only a matter of time until a set of sample data is drawn that yields a "significant" result, which will, of course, have a good chance of being published.

The moral of Example 12-1 is clear. In an area where theory is poor and provides little guidance on specification to the researcher, data mining is a highly dangerous activity. Combined with the propensity of editors to publish only significant results, it can in extreme cases result in the publication of falsehoods and the suppression of truth.‡ However, take heart, faint reader, the above surely cannot be a description of economics, the queen of the social sciences, richly endowed with well articulated theory. Consider then Example 12-2.

Example 2. The minister of petroleum in the mythical oil-rich country of Sandia desires to know the demand function for crude oil so that he may better inject some good sense and realism into the next round of cartel discussions. Having

† The 120 models may be represented by

$$y = \text{constant} + \beta_i x_i + \beta_j x_j + \beta_k x_k + u \qquad \text{for all } i, j, k;\ i \neq j \neq k$$

In each case the null hypothesis is

$$H_0\colon\ \beta_i = \beta_j = \beta_k$$

Working at the 5 percent level of significance, the probability of accepting the null hypothesis for any specific model is 0.95. Assuming independence of the models, the probability of accepting the null hypothesis for all the models considered is $(0.95)^{120} = 0.0021$. Thus the chance that the researcher finds *at least one* "significant" regression is 0.998. Working at the more stringent 1 percent level of significance, the probability of finding at least one significant regression is still as high as 0.70. The models will not all be independent of each other because of overlapping explanatory variables, so these startling probabilities need not be taken too seriously, but they do indicate the nature of the potential problem associated with data mining.

‡ A small but constructive step toward addressing this problem was taken a few years ago by the editors of the *Journal of Political Economy*, who initiated a section for the publication of "confirmations and contradictions."

ample resources at his disposal, he commissions four separate econometricians to estimate and deliver such a demand function. All four have access to the same data base, namely, all the statistics ever published in the world plus the internal files of the Sandia ministry of petroleum, but they are to work completely independently.

Econometrician A is an able econometrician, trained in a good graduate school and already prewarned of the sin of data mining. After much cogitation, research, and study of the institutional realities, he specifies his demand function, estimates it by the appropriate procedures, and sends off the results to Sandia. Econometrician B is a better econometrician, who went to a better graduate school than A. He too is not about to engage in data mining, so he formulates his specification, which happens to differ somewhat from that of A, estimates the equation, and dispatches the results. Econometrician C is a clever chap from Cambridge (either one). He follows the same procedure as A and B, but as one might expect, his a priori specification is, in truth, superior to theirs. Econometrician D is a data miner from Dublin, who unhappily never had the good fortune to go to graduate school nor even to attend a lecture on statistics, but nonetheless has a certain degree of native intelligence. As benefits an Irishman, he has been warned about so many sins that he has completely forgotten the sin of data mining. His first attempt at the problem just happens to be the specification used by A. However, D does not much like the results and respecifies, just happening now to arrive at the specification used by B. The results of that are still not quite to his pleasing, so he respecifies once more and now happens to hit on the specification used by C. The results of that please him and are sent off to Sandia, but he does not confuse the minister by including the results of his earlier and, to him, unsatisfactory specifications.

Suppose we are privileged to have one further piece of information, which is that the C/D specification is the true and correct one. The statistical purist would presumably congratulate C and criticize D. However, their standard errors, confidence intervals, and associated F statistics are identical. Classical inference establishes the properties of estimators and tests of hypotheses by examining what might be expected to happen in *repeated sampling* from a given population or model. If the model has not been correctly specified, the tests are strictly invalid and the various probability statements are not correct. In the present hypothetical example inferences based on the A or B specifications would, strictly speaking, not be correct, while those based on the C/D specification are. Data mining has only enabled D to make good the defects in his education and has been beneficial rather than damaging. Finally we may observe that most classical procedures are fairly robust to specification errors, and in practice, probably no finite model will ever be the "true and correct" model so we should not be slavish devotees of spuriously precise significance levels.†

† The development of econometric theory has been heavily influenced by the early work of the Cowles Commission, which emphasized problems of *equation error* to the almost total exclusion of problems of *measurement error*. Little is known about significance levels or the relative properties of different estimators when these problems jointly coexist, as indeed they do in practice.

We conclude that the circumstances of Example 12-2 are closer to those of real economic research than those of Example 12-1, that interaction between theory and data is both inevitable and, indeed, desirable, and we turn now to a discussion of some specific guides to that respecification.

Criteria for Model Selection

Residual variance ($\bar{R}^2$) criterion. Most of the operational criteria have been developed in the context of a single equation model. The first is the residual variance, or $\bar{R}^2$, criterion. Suppose there are just two competing models for the explanation of **y**, namely,

$$\mathbf{y} = \mathbf{X}_1\boldsymbol{\beta}_1 + \mathbf{u}_1 \qquad \text{and} \qquad \mathbf{y} = \mathbf{X}_2\boldsymbol{\beta}_2 + \mathbf{u}_2$$

where $\mathbf{X}_i$ is nonstochastic, of order $n \times k_i$, and of full column rank. Suppose that, in fact, the first model is correct. If the second model is fitted, the vector of OLS residuals is

$$\begin{aligned} \mathbf{e}_2 &= \mathbf{M}_2\mathbf{y} \\ &= \mathbf{M}_2(\mathbf{X}_1\boldsymbol{\beta}_1 + \mathbf{u}_1) \end{aligned}$$

where $$\mathbf{M}_2 = \mathbf{I} - \mathbf{X}_2(\mathbf{X}_2'\mathbf{X}_2)^{-1}\mathbf{X}_2'$$

Thus the residual sum of squares is

$$\mathbf{e}_2'\mathbf{e}_2 = \boldsymbol{\beta}_1'\mathbf{X}_1'\mathbf{M}_2\mathbf{X}_1\boldsymbol{\beta}_1 + 2\boldsymbol{\beta}_1'\mathbf{X}_1'\mathbf{M}_2\mathbf{u}_1 + \mathbf{u}_1'\mathbf{M}_2\mathbf{u}_1$$

Taking expectations

$$E(\mathbf{e}_2'\mathbf{e}_2) = \boldsymbol{\beta}_1'\mathbf{X}_1'\mathbf{M}_2\mathbf{X}_1\boldsymbol{\beta}_1 + (n - k_2)\sigma_1^2 \tag{12-1}$$

Since $\mathbf{M}_2$ is idempotent, the quadratic form on the right-hand side of Eq. (12-1) is positive semidefinite. Defining $s_2^2 = \mathbf{e}_2'\mathbf{e}_2/(n - k_2)$, it then follows that

$$E(s_2^2) \geq \sigma_1^2$$

If the first (and correct) model is fitted, we know from Sec. 5-3 that

$$E(s_1^2) = \sigma_1^2$$

where

$$(n - k_1)s_1^2 = \mathbf{e}_1'\mathbf{e}_1 = \mathbf{y}'\mathbf{y} - \mathbf{y}'\mathbf{X}_1(\mathbf{X}_1'\mathbf{X}_1)^{-1}\mathbf{X}_1'\mathbf{y}$$

Thus†

$$E(s_1^2) \leq E(s_2^2) \tag{12-2}$$

Notice that the inequality is in terms of the *expected* values of the residual variances. In practice we can only compare the *estimated* residual variances. It is, of course, possible for s_2^2 to be less than s_1^2, even though, in fact, $E(s_1^2) < E(s_2^2)$. Thus minimum residual variance cannot be taken as a single overriding criterion

† This argument is due to H. Theil, *Principles of Econometrics*, Wiley, New York, 1971, p. 543.

for equation selection. Since there is a monotonic negative relationship between $\overline{R}^2$ and s^2, the same comments apply to a maximum $\overline{R}^2$ criterion, but the fact that the degree of fit does not discriminate perfectly between the true and competing models does not mean that evidence on fit is to be ignored.

Criteria for individual coefficients. There are two important criteria under this heading. Economic theory is rich in *qualitative* predictions about the direction of various effects. Thus one looks for agreement between a priori expectation and the signs of estimated coefficients. Second, one looks for correctly signed coefficients which have reasonable statistical significance. The latter criterion should not be applied too stringently since we have seen, for example, that collinearity among the regressors can inflate estimated standard errors. The $\overline{R}^2$ criterion also has implications for the significance level of individual coefficients. As shown in Problem 5-12, $\overline{R}^2$ only increases with the addition of an extra regressor if the F or, equivalently, the t statistic for that variable exceeds unity, which corresponds to the use of a significance level of about 30 percent rather than the conventional 5 or 1 percent level.†

The previous remark is in the context of a fixed sample size. However, any substantial increase in sample size has implications for significance levels. As seen in Chap. 5, the test of the hypothesis that a subvector of q elements in $\boldsymbol{\beta}$ is the zero vector is given by

$$F = \frac{(\mathbf{e}_*'\mathbf{e}_* - \mathbf{e}'\mathbf{e})/q}{\mathbf{e}'\mathbf{e}/(n-k)} \sim F(q, n-k)$$

where $\mathbf{e}'\mathbf{e}$ is the residual sum of squares from the unrestricted model and $\mathbf{e}_*'\mathbf{e}_*$ that from the restricted model, the relevant q variables having been omitted. This statistic is written equivalently as

$$F = \frac{R^2 - R_*^2}{1 - R^2} \cdot \frac{n-k}{q}$$

Thus even though $R^2 - R_*^2$ may be very small, the test statistic can become arbitrarily large with increasing sample size. Using a given significance level, the null hypothesis is more and more likely to be rejected as n increases. This point has been emphasized by Leamer, who, along with others, argues that the significance level for this kind of test should be adjusted downward for larger samples.‡

Well-behaved disturbances. As seen in earlier chapters, a homoscedastic nonautocorrelated disturbance term is a wonderfully powerful assumption from a *statistical* point of view. Its presence underlies the derivation of a battery of statistical tests, while its absence seriously distorts some of these tests and calls for revised procedures. Thus it is essential to examine the properties of the disturbance term in order to assess the validity of the statistical tests being applied. However, the

† Recall that $t(r) = \sqrt{F(1, r)}$. See App. A-7.

‡ E. E. Leamer, *Specification Searches*, Wiley, New York, 1978, pp. 88–89.

same property is often implicitly, and occasionally explicitly, taken as a desirable feature of a well-specified economic relationship. The purpose of such a relation is to model the behavior of some group of economic agents. Can it be a good model if the net effect of the omitted variables displays some systematic autocorrelated pattern? A misspecification of functional form can also lead to nonrandom disturbances. Thus statistical and economic considerations alike lead one to look for relations with well-behaved disturbances. However, as noted in Chap. 8, discrepancies between decision periods and data periods may well produce autocorrelated disturbances in a properly specified economic model. It is also the case that *efficient* estimation of fairly complex dynamic regressions may require an autoregressive specification for the disturbance term, but this is a by-product of considerations of statistical efficiency: the original relationship is desired to have a nonautocorrelated disturbance term. This point is emphasized by Hendry and Mizon.† Suppose one-period lags on both variables are sufficient to give a white noise disturbance. The original (general) dynamic relationship between y and x may then be written as

$$y_t = \beta_1 y_{t-1} + \gamma_0 x_t + \gamma_1 x_{t-1} + v_t \tag{12-3}$$

where $|\beta_1| < 1$ and $\{v_t\}$ is white noise. Using the lag operator, this may be rewritten as

$$(1 - \beta_1 L) y_t = (\gamma_0 + \gamma_1 L) x_t + v_t$$

If it then were true that the parameters satisfied a restriction

$$\gamma_1 = -\beta_1 \gamma_0$$

the relation would become

$$(1 - \beta_1 L) y_t = \gamma_0 (1 - \beta_1 L) x_t + v_t \tag{12-4}$$

which gives

$$\begin{aligned} y_t &= \gamma_0 x_t + u_t \\ \text{with} \qquad u_t &= \beta_1 u_{t-1} + v_t \end{aligned} \tag{12-5}$$

If the restriction were valid, estimation of Eqs. (12-5) would involve just three parameters, namely β_1, γ_0, and σ_v^2, whereas estimation of Eq. (12-3) involves four parameters. However, Eq. (12-3) has, in fact, to be estimated to test the restriction. The payoff is improved statistical efficiency of the parameter estimates if the restriction is upheld. Comparing Eqs. (12-3) and (12-4) the restriction implies that $\{y_t\}$ and $\{x_t\}$ have a *common factor* with root β_1.‡ There may be no economic rationale for the restriction or common factor. If so, it is likely to be rejected and the "general" equation (12-3) cannot then legitimately be reduced to the "simpler" form in Eq. (12-5). Sargan's COMFAC program tests for the existence of

† D. F. Hendry and G. E. Mizon, "Serial Correlation as a Convenient Simplification, Not a Nuisance: A Comment on a Study of the Demand for Money by the Bank of England," *Economic Journal*, vol. 88, 1978, pp. 549–563.

‡ Strictly speaking the root of the polynomial $1 - \beta_1 L = 0$ is $1/\beta_1$.

common factors in dynamic regressions.† Suppose a general dynamic relation

$$\beta(L)y_t = \gamma(L)x_t + v_t \tag{12-6}$$

can be found where $\{v_t\}$ is white noise. If $\beta(L)$ and $\gamma(L)$ have, say, two common roots, there exists a quadratic in L, say $\delta(L)$, which is common to both $\beta(L)$ and $\gamma(L)$. Thus we can write

$$\beta(L) = \delta(L)\beta^*(L) \qquad \text{and} \qquad \gamma(L) = \delta(L)\gamma^*(L)$$

so that Eq. (12-6) becomes

$$\begin{aligned} \beta^*(L)y_t &= \gamma^*(L)x_t + u_t \\ \delta(L)u_t &= v_t \end{aligned} \tag{12-7}$$

which involves considerably fewer parameters than Eq. (12-6). Suppose, for example, that a relationship

$$y_t = \beta_1 y_{t-1} + \beta_2 y_{t-2} + \gamma_0 x_t + \gamma_1 x_{t-1} + \gamma_2 x_{t-2} + \gamma_3 x_{t-3} + v_t \tag{12-8}$$

was estimated and a common polynomial $\delta(L) = (1 - L)(1 - \rho L)$ found. The relation (12-8) may then be written

$$(1 - L)(1 - \rho L)y_t = (1 - L)(1 - \rho L)(\gamma_0^* + \gamma_1^* L)x_t + v_t$$

which only involves three parameters instead of six. For estimation purposes it may be put in the form

$$\begin{aligned} \Delta y_t &= \gamma_0^* \Delta x_t + \gamma_1^* \Delta x_{t-1} + u_t \\ \text{with} \qquad (1 - \rho L)u_t &= v_t \end{aligned} \tag{12-9}$$

that is, a simple relationship between first differences with an AR(1) process in the disturbance. The Sargan-Hendry message is that researchers should not begin with simplified specifications such as Eqs. (12-5) or Eqs. (12-9), but should instead commence with a general model containing sufficient lags to yield a white noise disturbance and then test to see how far it can be legitimately simplified.

Stability of the relationship. A very important indicator of the quality of a functional specification is the stability of the parameters over various data sets. This may be examined in two alternative fashions. One is a straightforward test for structural change as outlined in some detail in Chap. 6. This presupposes sufficient observations in each subset of data to permit estimation of all parameters. When that is not the case, the Chow forecasting test may be applied. This has already been set out in Example 6-5 of Sec. 6-2 and was derived in Sec. 10-1 by using recursive residuals. However, it is often derived in an alternative fashion as follows.

Suppose the usual linear model has been fitted to n observations of k variables. The OLS coefficient vector is

$$\mathbf{b} = \boldsymbol{\beta} + (\mathbf{X}'\mathbf{X})^{-1}\mathbf{X}'\mathbf{u}$$

† J. D. Sargan and J. D. Sylwestrowicz, "COMFAC: Algorithm for Wald Tests of Common Factors in Lag Polynomials," *User's Manual*, London School of Economics, London, 1976.

and it is assumed, as usual, that $\mathbf{u} \sim N(\mathbf{0}, \sigma^2 \mathbf{I}_n)$. Now suppose a new set of m $(< k)$ observations on these same variables becomes available. On the assumption that the original model still holds, the new observations may be characterized by

$$\mathbf{y}_0 = \mathbf{X}_0 \boldsymbol{\beta} + \mathbf{u}_0$$

where $E(\mathbf{u}_0 \mathbf{u}_0') = \sigma^2 \mathbf{I}_m$. The m observations are insufficient to allow reestimation of the model, but one may forecast the $\mathbf{y}_0$ vector by

$$\hat{\mathbf{y}}_0 = \mathbf{X}_0 \mathbf{b}$$

The vector of forecast errors is

$$\begin{aligned} \mathbf{e}_0 = \mathbf{y}_0 - \hat{\mathbf{y}}_0 &= \mathbf{X}_0 \boldsymbol{\beta} + \mathbf{u}_0 - \mathbf{X}_0 \left[\boldsymbol{\beta} + (\mathbf{X}'\mathbf{X})^{-1} \mathbf{X}'\mathbf{u} \right] \\ &= \mathbf{u}_0 - \mathbf{X}_0 (\mathbf{X}'\mathbf{X})^{-1} \mathbf{X}'\mathbf{u} \end{aligned}$$

It then follows directly that

$$\mathbf{e}_0 \sim N(\mathbf{0}, \sigma^2 \mathbf{V})$$

where
$$\mathbf{V} = \mathbf{I}_m + \mathbf{X}_0 (\mathbf{X}'\mathbf{X})^{-1} \mathbf{X}_0'$$

Thus
$$\frac{\mathbf{e}_0' \mathbf{V}^{-1} \mathbf{e}_0}{\sigma^2} \sim \chi^2(m)$$

Since $\mathbf{e}'\mathbf{e}/\sigma^2$ has an independent $\chi^2(n-k)$ distribution, it follows that under the hypothesis of parameter constancy

$$F = \frac{\mathbf{e}_0' \left[\mathbf{I}_m + \mathbf{X}_0 (\mathbf{X}'\mathbf{X})^{-1} \mathbf{X}_0' \right]^{-1} \mathbf{e}_0 / m}{\mathbf{e}'\mathbf{e}/(n-k)} \sim F(m, n-k) \tag{12-10}$$

The hypothesis of a stable relationship would be rejected if the F statistic in Eq. (12-10) exceeded some preselected critical value. Chow demonstrates the equality of Eq. (12-10) with the alternative expression in Eq. (6-27).† In an interesting and important study Jorgenson, Hunter, and Nadiri have used measures of fit, Durbin-Watson statistics, and tests of structural change to assess and compare different investment equations.‡ When the regressors are stochastic, the test statistic in Eq. (12-10) will only be approximately distributed as F. Hendry suggests using an asymptotically equivalent test which neglects the variation due to estimating the $\boldsymbol{\beta}$ vector. Under the hypothesis of parameter constancy§

$$\frac{\mathbf{e}_0' \mathbf{e}_0}{s^2} \xrightarrow{D} \chi^2(m) \tag{12-11}$$

† G. C. Chow, "Tests of Equality between Sets of Coefficients in Two Linear Regressions," *Econometrica*, vol. 28, 1960, pp. 591–605.

‡ D. W. Jorgenson, J. Hunter, and M. I. Nadiri, "A Comparison of Alternative Econometric Models of Quarterly Investment Behavior," and "The Predictive Performance of Econometric Models of Quarterly Investment Behavior," *Econometrica*, vol. 38, 1970, pp. 187–224.

§ D. F. Hendry, "Predictive Failure and Econometric Modelling in Macro-Economics: The Transactions Demand for Money," London School of Economics, London, September 1978.

where

$$s^2 = \frac{\mathbf{e}'\mathbf{e}}{n - k}$$

The test of forecast errors in Eq. (12-10) may be extended to deal with joint forecasts from the reduced form of a simultaneous equation model.†

An aspect of prediction which is frequently ignored, and unjustly so, is the longer-term implications of the dynamic regression that has been estimated. For example, return again to our hypothetical demand function for oil, and ask questions such as:

- What does it imply about the long-run elasticities?
- What does it imply about the length of the long run, how long is it estimated to take for a full adjustment to a "shock"?
- Is the reaction path plausible or is it the result of a statistical straitjacket imposed on the data?

The model's answers to questions such as these have to be put up against the intuition and good sense of the researchers themselves and, more importantly, the intuition and good sense of informed critics. This may seem very "unscientific" and perhaps it is, but it is nonetheless very important and in the next two sections we present a brief discussion of some ways in which it is attempted.

The Cairncross Test

We have suggested that there are various aspects of any specification which are important, namely,

1. Residual variance (or fit)
2. Signs and precision of specific coefficients
3. Properties of the disturbance
4. Parameter stability (predictive performance)

In comparing different specifications there is no serious problem if the indicators more or less all point in the same direction, as was the case in the Jorgenson, Hunter, and Nadiri study of the investment equation. Where contrary indicators emerge, the choice between specifications has to rest on the relative importance of various factors to the decision maker. As in the choice of a husband or a place to live, a specification is a "package deal." No one has yet found a way to piece together the perfect package, though we continually try to improve, as is evidenced by the statistics on divorce, population mobility, and the flood of computer printout. In the case of economic specifications the choice can be based less on purely subjective personal considerations and more on the accumulated knowledge and experience of the critic.

† See P. H. Dhrymes et al., "Criteria for Evaluation of Econometric Models," *Annals of Economic and Social Measurement*, vol. 1, 1972, pp. 307–308.

This point was brought home to me forcefully and convincingly a few years ago when I was working on an energy research project. Each month a report on the econometric activity had to be presented to a steering committee in London, presided over by Sir Alex Cairncross.† Cairncross had (and still has) a healthy scepticism of econometrics, no doubt partly due to his days at the U.K. Treasury when, to quote, "the young men might present me with thirty different equations to 'explain' British imports, so that, at the end of the day, neither they nor I knew what determined British imports." Each month the econometric output was subjected to his shrewd, informed, and penetrating scrutiny. Eventually, however, there came a monthly report which secured the approbation, "I wouldn't mind getting on a plane and taking this to Riyadh." Presumably I had been engaged in some successful data mining or, perhaps, had been "learning by doing," so I suggested to him jokingly that the Cairncross test would appear in the next edition of *Econometric Methods*. The two-step Cairncross test is thus as follows.

1. Compute your $\bar{R}^2$, Durbin-Watson statistic, assorted t, F, and χ^2 statistics for the best specification you can manage.
2. Send the resultant report to Sir Alex Cairncross with the question "Would you be prepared to take this to Riyadh?"

The suggestion is, of course, not entirely frivolous. Researchers circulating their discussion papers are carrying out informal Cairncross tests. For Cairncross substitute the expert of your choice and for Riyadh substitute Washington, the editorial offices of the *American Economic Review*, or some other preferred location.

Economists, however, are not alone in facing difficult choice problems in which all the elements cannot be fully quantified and brought together in a single equation. Circumstances comparable to those of the Cairncross test arise in a broad spectrum of commercial, industrial, and governmental decisions, where the best possible research still does not eliminate the need for some personal element based on judgment and experience.

The Bayesian Approach‡

A Bayesian would criticize the Cairncross test on the grounds that the opinions, judgment, and, possibly, prejudices of the expert have only been introduced in some implicit, informal, and nonreproducible fashion. Bayesians also tend to make a more general criticism of classical inference in that its procedures are

† Sir Alex Cairncross, a very distinguished British economist, was for many years economic advisor to Her Majesty's Government and subsequently Master of an Oxford College. I hesitate to give his present address lest he be deluged with manuscripts from aspiring econometricians, but I suspect he is mostly to be found in his Scottish retreat north of the Solway Firth, enjoying the Scotsman's favorite view "looking down upon England."

‡ The Bayesian approach requires a book of its own. The premier references are A. Zellner, *An Introduction to Bayesian Inference in Econometrics*, Wiley, New York, 1971; and E. E. Leamer, *Specification Searches*, Wiley, New York, 1978.

justified in terms of sampling distributions, which picture the behavior of estimators in repeated sets of sample data. Such repeated samples are never drawn. We typically have one sample and have to do the best we can with that. Moreover the possible losses from incorrect conclusions are not usually considered in the choice of inference procedures.

In principle the Bayesian approach can cope with these problems in one integrated framework. The underlying principle is both simple and beautiful, but there are problems in the way of practical applications, especially in the area of large and complex models. The approach may be illustrated in two steps. Suppose, first of all, that there is no uncertainty about the form of the relevant model but only about its parameters. To be more specific, let us assume that we have n observations drawn at random from

$$p(y) = \left(2\pi\sigma_0^2\right)^{-1/2}\exp\left[-\frac{1}{2\sigma_0^2}(y-\mu)^2\right]$$

where σ_0 is known, but the mean μ is unknown. This gives the vector

$$\mathbf{y} = [y_1 \quad y_2 \quad \cdots \quad y_n]'$$

The probability density function (pdf) for $\mathbf{y}$ is then

$$p(\mathbf{y}|\mu) = \left(2\pi\sigma_0^2\right)^{-n/2}\exp\left[-\frac{1}{2\sigma_0^2}\sum_{i=1}^{n}(y_i-\mu)^2\right] \tag{12-12}$$

This is the likelihood for the sample observations, conditional on the parameters μ and σ_0^2, but the latter has been omitted from the left-hand side since it is assumed known.

The first crucial element in the Bayesian approach is to postulate the existence of *prior* information about μ. This may come from theoretical sources, from previous empirical studies, hunch, judgment, or what have you. Such information cannot be exact, so it is formulated in a stochastic fashion. It is theoretically convenient to model this information in a way that is compatible with the likelihood in Eq. (12-12). This leads to the concept of the *conjugate prior*. The prior pdf for μ is thus taken to be normal and written

$$\pi(\mu) = (2\pi\sigma^2)^{-1/2}\exp\left[-\frac{1}{2\sigma^2}(\mu-m)^2\right] \tag{12-13}$$

where m and σ^2 are specified *numerically*.†

From elementary probability theory for any two events A and B we can write

$$\Pr(A, B) = \Pr(A)\cdot\Pr(B|A) = \Pr(B)\cdot\Pr(A|B)$$

† We are using $p(\cdot)$ to indicate a pdf for sample data and $\pi(\cdot)$ to indicate a pdf for parameters. This practice was suggested in K. M. Gaver and M. S. Geisel, "Discriminating Among Alternative Models: Bayesian and non-Bayesian Methods," in P. Zarembka, Ed., *Frontiers in Econometrics*, Academic Press, New York, 1974, Chap. 2.

from which

$$\Pr(B|A) = \frac{\Pr(B) \cdot \Pr(A|B)}{\Pr(A)} \tag{12-14}$$

Letting A represent the sample vector $\mathbf{y}$, B the unknown parameter μ, and replacing probabilities by pdf's, we have

$$\pi(\mu|\mathbf{y}) = \frac{\pi(\mu) \cdot p(\mathbf{y}|\mu)}{p(\mathbf{y})} \tag{12-15}$$

In Eq. (12-15) the expression $\pi(\mu|\mathbf{y})$ represents the *posterior* pdf for μ, and comparison with $\pi(\mu)$ indicates the change in the researcher's beliefs about μ brought about by the sample information in $\mathbf{y}$. The denominator in Eq. (12-15) is given by

$$p(\mathbf{y}) = \int p(\mathbf{y}|\mu)\pi(\mu)\, d\mu$$

For given $\mathbf{y}$, m, σ_0^2, and σ^2 this reduces to a constant. Thus Eq. (12-15) can be rewritten as

$$\pi(\mu|\mathbf{y}) \propto \pi(\mu) \cdot p(\mathbf{y}|\mu)$$

Substituting from Eqs. (12-12) and (12-13),

$$\pi(\mu|\mathbf{y}) \propto \exp\left\{ -\frac{1}{2}\left[\frac{(\mu - m)^2}{\sigma^2} + \frac{\Sigma(y_i - \mu)^2}{\sigma_0^2} \right]\right\}$$

As shown by Zellner, this pdf can be simplified to†

$$\pi(\mu|\mathbf{y}) \propto \exp\left[- \left(\frac{\sigma^2 + \sigma_0^2/n}{2\sigma^2\sigma_0^2/n} \right)\left(\mu - \frac{\hat{\mu}\sigma^2 + m\sigma_0^2/n}{\sigma^2 + \sigma_0^2/n} \right) \right]$$

where $\hat{\mu} = \Sigma y_i/n$. Thus the posterior pdf for μ is also normal with mean

$$E(\mu) = \frac{\hat{\mu}(\sigma_0^2/n)^{-1} + m(\sigma^2)^{-1}}{(\sigma_0^2/n)^{-1} + (\sigma^2)^{-1}} \tag{12-16}$$

and

$$\operatorname{var}(\mu) = \frac{1}{(\sigma_0^2/n)^{-1} + (\sigma^2)^{-1}}$$

Formula (12-16) shows that the posterior mean is a weighted average of the sample mean and the prior mean, the weights being the reciprocals of the respective variances. Strong prior information (low σ^2) gives the prior mean a large role to play in determining the posterior mean, and conversely, strong sample information (large n and/or low σ_0^2) gives the sample mean a dominating role. The importance of the posterior mean rests on a basic result in Bayesian

† A. Zellner, *An Introduction to Bayesian Inference in Econometrics*, Wiley, New York, 1971, p. 150.

statistics that if one assumes a quadratic loss function for errors in estimating μ, the estimate which minimizes the expected loss is the posterior mean.†

A parallel result holds in the linear regression case when the form of the model is assumed known, but a multivariate Bayesian prior distribution is specified for the $\boldsymbol{\beta}$ vector.‡ Assuming a multivariate normal prior, this involves specifying the mean vector $\mathbf{b}_*$ and all the elements in the variance-covariance matrix, indicated, say, by $\sigma_u^2\mathbf{N}_*^{-1}$. Assuming the usual linear model

$$\mathbf{y} = \mathbf{X}\boldsymbol{\beta} + \mathbf{u} \qquad \text{with} \qquad \mathbf{u} \sim N(\mathbf{0}, \sigma_u^2\mathbf{I})$$

the mean of the posterior distribution is§

$$\mathbf{b}_{**} = (\mathbf{N}_* + \mathbf{X}'\mathbf{X})^{-1}(\mathbf{N}_*\mathbf{b}_* + \mathbf{X}'\mathbf{X}\mathbf{b}) \tag{12-17}$$

where $\mathbf{b} = (\mathbf{X}'\mathbf{X})^{-1}\mathbf{X}'\mathbf{y}$ is the OLS estimate of $\boldsymbol{\beta}$ from the sample data. This is the linear regression equivalent of Eq. (12-16). The posterior mean vector is seen to be a matrix weighted combination of the prior vector $\mathbf{b}_*$ and the OLS vector $\mathbf{b}$, with weights proportional to the inverses of the respective variance matrices. Two immediate problems arise with any attempt to implement Eq. (12-17) in practice. The first relates to the problem of specifying numerically the elements of the variance matrix $\mathbf{N}_*^{-1}$. One may have some intuition about the mean vector $\mathbf{b}_*$, but it is difficult to see the source of numerical information about variances and covariances. The second problem, as Leamer emphasizes, is that if $\mathbf{b}_*$ and $\mathbf{N}_*$ are specified, the posterior is then a function of these specific values. Other investigators might specify different parameters for the prior distribution with different implications for the posterior distribution. What is important is to make clear the *mapping* from priors to posteriors and to investigate, if possible, the implications of various *classes* of prior distribution for posterior distributions.

The second step in the Bayesian approach relaxes the assumption that the form of the model is known and that the only uncertainty relates to the parameter values. The extension allows uncertainty about both models and parameters. To simplify the exposition let us suppose that there are just two competing models, both in the linear regression format. They are specified as

$$M_1: \quad \mathbf{y} = \mathbf{X}_1\boldsymbol{\beta}_1 + \mathbf{u}_1$$

$$M_2: \quad \mathbf{y} = \mathbf{X}_2\boldsymbol{\beta}_2 + \mathbf{u}_2$$

where $\mathbf{X}_i$ is nonstochastic of order $n \times k_i$, of full column rank, $\mathbf{u}_i \sim N(\mathbf{0}, \sigma_i^2\mathbf{I}_n)$, and there are n sample observations. There are two possible situations. One is where the models (or hypotheses) are *nested*, which is the case when $\mathbf{X}_2$, say, includes all the variables in $\mathbf{X}_1$ plus some others. The *nonnested* case occurs when some (or all) variables in $\mathbf{X}_1$ do not appear in $\mathbf{X}_2$ and vice versa. Classical inference procedures apply in a straightforward fashion to the nested case, but

† A. Zellner, op. cit., p. 24.

‡ In practice, there is no justification for assuming the disturbance variance σ_u^2 to be known. Thus the prior distribution should incorporate $\boldsymbol{\beta}$ and σ_u^2.

§ E. E. Leamer, *Specification Searches*, Wiley, New York, 1978, p. 78.

have no simple treatment for the nonnested case, where Bayesian procedures admit, in principle, of a very simple solution.

For any model the marginal density of the observations M_i, sometimes referred to as the predictive pdf, is given by†

$$p(\mathbf{y}|M_i) = \int p(\mathbf{y}|\boldsymbol{\beta}_i, M_i)\pi(\boldsymbol{\beta}_i|M_i)\, d\boldsymbol{\beta}_i \tag{12-18}$$

In Eq. (12-18) $p(\mathbf{y}|\boldsymbol{\beta}_i, M_i)$ is the likelihood for the sample observations, conditional on the model M_i and its parameters $\boldsymbol{\beta}_i$, and $\pi(\boldsymbol{\beta}_i|M_i)$ is the prior density for the parameters, given that the model is M_i. Equation (12-18) says that *if M_i is the true model*, the marginal pdf for the sample observations is found by taking a *weighted average* of the sample likelihoods, where the weights are the elements of the prior distribution for the parameters, given the model. Now suppose that associated with each model there is a nonnegative fraction $P(M_i)$ indicating the prior subjective probability that M_i is the true model and, in this case, such that

$$P(M_1) + P(M_2) = 1$$

The *unconditional* pdf for the sample observations is then

$$p(\mathbf{y}) = P(M_1)p(\mathbf{y}|M_1) + P(M_2)p(\mathbf{y}|M_2)$$

and the application of Bayes's rule to revise the prior probabilities of the models gives

$$P(M_i|\mathbf{y}) = \frac{P(M_i)p(\mathbf{y}|M_i)}{p(\mathbf{y})} \tag{12-19}$$

In comparing two models there are just two possible losses, one if M_1 is chosen when M_2 is the true model and the other if M_2 is chosen when M_1 applies. If these losses were equal, the decision rule that minimizes the posterior expected loss is as follows. Choose M_1 if

$$\frac{P(M_1|\mathbf{y})}{P(M_2|\mathbf{y})} = \frac{P(M_1)p(\mathbf{y}|M_1)}{P(M_2)p(\mathbf{y}|M_2)} \tag{12-20}$$

is greater than 1. Equation (12-20) defines the *posterior odds* ratio, which is seen to be equal to the prior odds ratio multiplied by the ratio of the marginal densities (weighted likelihood functions). If there are more than two models, posterior odds as defined in Eq. (12-20) can be computed for any pair.

It is clear from Eq. (12-18) that the formidable task in the computation of Eq. (12-20) is the evaluation of the marginal pdf's. If a multivariate normal prior is assumed for $\boldsymbol{\beta}_i$, given M_i, that is,

$$\pi(\mathbf{b}_i|M_i) \qquad \text{is} \qquad N(\mathbf{b}_{i*}, \mathbf{N}_{i*}^{-1})$$

then Leamer has shown that $p(\mathbf{y}|M_i)$ varies inversely with a quadratic form Q,

† We are assuming unrealistically, but for simplicity, that there is no uncertainty about the disturbance variances.

which may be expressed in alternative ways as†

$$Q_i = (\mathbf{y} - \mathbf{X}_i\mathbf{b}_i)'(\mathbf{y} - \mathbf{X}_i\mathbf{b}_i) + (\mathbf{b}_i - \mathbf{b}_{i*})'(\mathbf{N}_{i*}^{-1} + \mathbf{N}_i^{-1})(\mathbf{b}_i - \mathbf{b}_{i*}) \qquad (12\text{-}21)$$

or

$$Q_i = (\mathbf{y} - \mathbf{X}_i\mathbf{b}_{i*})'(\mathbf{y} - \mathbf{X}_i\mathbf{b}_{i*}) - (\mathbf{b}_i - \mathbf{b}_{i*})'\mathbf{N}_i(\mathbf{N}_i^* + \mathbf{N}_i)^{-1}\mathbf{N}_i(\mathbf{b}_i - \mathbf{b}_{i*}) \qquad (12\text{-}22)$$

where $\mathbf{N}_i = \mathbf{X}_i'\mathbf{X}_i$ and $\mathbf{b}_i = (\mathbf{X}_i'\mathbf{X}_i)^{-1}\mathbf{X}_i'\mathbf{y}_i$. The first term in Eq. (12-21) is the residual sum of squares from the OLS fit of model M_i. This has to be increased by a factor depending on the discrepancy between the OLS vector and the prior mean vector. Alternatively, the first term in Eq. (12-22) is the error sum of squares if the coefficient vector were set equal to the prior mean vector. This is adjusted downward by a term which is again dependent on the discrepancy between the sample and the prior coefficient vectors. Thus apart from the prior odds ratio, the choice between models would depend on these adjusted sums of squares, which are a mixture of sample and prior information.

Readers must judge for themselves whether a criterion such as Eq. (12-20), for all its elegance and simplicity, is a valid guide for choice. Suppose that just two crude and simple models are being compared. M_1, say, is a "Keynesian" reduced-form equation relating GNP to "exogenous expenditures," while M_2 is a "Friedmanian" equation relating GNP to "money." If the Ghost of Keynes could be contacted, he would presumably offer a prior-odds ratio $P(M_1)/P(M_2)$, dramatically different from that forthcoming from Professor Friedman. How can the protagonist of one theory begin to specify the prior pdf's for the parameters of the opposing theory, which he basically regards as false? Must then a Bayesian researcher be certified ideologically pure and unbiased before being allowed to specify prior odds and prior densities for model parameters?

A partial resolution to the problem of excessive dependence on priors, which are, perhaps, spuriously precise, idiosyncratic, or just personal to one investigator, is provided by some recent work by Chamberlin and Leamer.‡ It is assumed that in a single equation there are one or more "focus" variables, whose coefficients are of crucial interest. The equation may also contain other "doubtful" variables. The investigator specifies a prior zero mean vector for the doubtful variables. However, he does not have to specify the elements of the prior variance matrix, merely that it belongs to the class of positive definite or semidefinite matrices. Leamer's SEARCH program computes bounds on the focus coefficients, so that the researcher can study the robustness of these coefficients under a variety of specifications. This approach is appealing and seems likely to be developed and considerably extended. It adds yet another dimension to the array of information that we can obtain on any specific problem. How to weigh and interpret the

† E. E. Leamer, op. cit., p. 109.

‡ E. E. Leamer, op. cit., pp. 182–201. See also T. F. Cooley and S. F. LeRoy, "Identification and Estimation of Money Demand," *American Economic Review*, vol. 71, 1981, pp. 825–844, for a very interesting detailed application of the procedure.

jigsaw of computation and information will still depend on the vital spark of human imagination and powers of judgment.

The position can best be summarized by a quotation from the late Jacob Bronowski.† Though writing of the physical world, his comments are very apposite to the economic and social world that we study.

> The world is not a fixed, solid array of objects, out there, for it cannot be fully separated from our perception of it. It shifts under our gaze, it interacts with us, and the knowledge that it yields has to be interpreted by us. There is no way of exchanging information that does not demand an act of judgment.
>
> Science is a very human form of knowledge. We are always at the brink of the known, we always feel forward for what is to be hoped. Every judgment in science stands on the edge of error, and is personal.

† J. Bronowski, *The Ascent of Man*, Little, Brown, Boston, 1973, pp. 364 and 374.

APPENDIX

A

MATHEMATICAL AND STATISTICAL APPENDICES

A-1 FUNCTIONS AND DERIVATIVES

The purpose of this section is merely to remind the reader of various notational conventions for functions and derivatives. It is not intended to review the basic rules of differentiation.† If y is a function of x, the relationship may be denoted variously as

$$y = y(x) \qquad y = f(x) \qquad y = g(x) \qquad y = F(x)$$

and so on. Once a specific *functional form* for the relationship has been assumed, one can determine the shape of the function by studying the behavior of y in response to variation in x. Starting from an initial value, say, x_0, and moving to $x_1 = x_0 + \Delta x$ will trace a movement in the dependent variable from y_0 to y_1. The ratio

$$\frac{\Delta y}{\Delta x} = \frac{y_1 - y_0}{x_1 - x_0}$$

measures the change in y per unit change in x. Taking the limit of this ratio as $\Delta x \to 0$ gives the *derivative* of y with respect to x, written variously as

$$\frac{dy}{dx} \equiv f'(x) \equiv \lim_{\Delta x \to 0} \left(\frac{\Delta y}{\Delta x} \right)$$

The derivative measures the slope of the function at a specific point and is, in general, a function of x, as is emphasized by the $f'(x)$ notation. Thus it may itself

† For a lucid introduction to the calculus and other mathematical topics of special relevance to economists see A. C. Chiang, *Fundamental Methods of Mathematical Economics*, 2d edition, McGraw-Hill, 1974.

be differentiated with respect to x, giving the *second-order* derivative, denoted by

$$\frac{d^2y}{dx^2} \qquad \text{or} \qquad f''(x)$$

When y is a function of several variables, say,

$$y = f(x_1, x_2, \ldots, x_n)$$

where the x's are capable of moving independently of one another, then one may study the change in y in response to the change in any one of the independent variables (or *arguments*) of the function, the other independent variables being held constant at any arbitrary set of values. This gives rise to the *partial derivatives*, denoted by

$$\frac{\partial y}{\partial x_i} \equiv \frac{\partial f}{\partial x_i} \equiv f_i \equiv \lim_{\Delta x_i \to 0} \left(\frac{\Delta y}{\Delta x_i} \right) \qquad i = 1, \ldots, n$$

In this notation f_2, for example, would indicate the rate of change of y with respect to x_2. Once again further partial differentiation may be carried out, yielding the second-order partial derivatives

$$\frac{\partial^2 y}{\partial x_i \partial x_j} \equiv \frac{\partial^2 f}{\partial x_i \partial x_j} \equiv f_{ij}$$

Alternatively, if the independent variables are given separate labels, as in

$$y = f(u, v)$$

the partial derivatives may be denoted by

$$\frac{\partial y}{\partial u} \equiv f_u \qquad \frac{\partial y}{\partial v} \equiv f_v \qquad \frac{\partial^2 y}{\partial u \partial v} = f_{uv}$$

though, even here, one may see f_1 used for f_u and f_2 for f_v.

A-2 EXPONENTIAL AND LOGARITHMIC FUNCTIONS

Consider the function

$$y = b^x \qquad b > 0 \tag{A-1}$$

This is called an exponential function since the variable x appears as the *exponent* of the constant, or base, b. We rule out negative values for b, since if x were, say, one-half, y would be the square root of a negative number, which is imaginary. If x denoted time t measured at equal intervals, then

$$y_t = b^t \qquad \text{and} \qquad \frac{y_t}{y_{t-1}} = b$$

Thus y_t denotes a series which is growing ($b > 1$) or declining ($0 < b < 1$) at a constant rate. If we set $b = 1 + r$, then r denotes the proportionate rate of change in y per unit period of time.

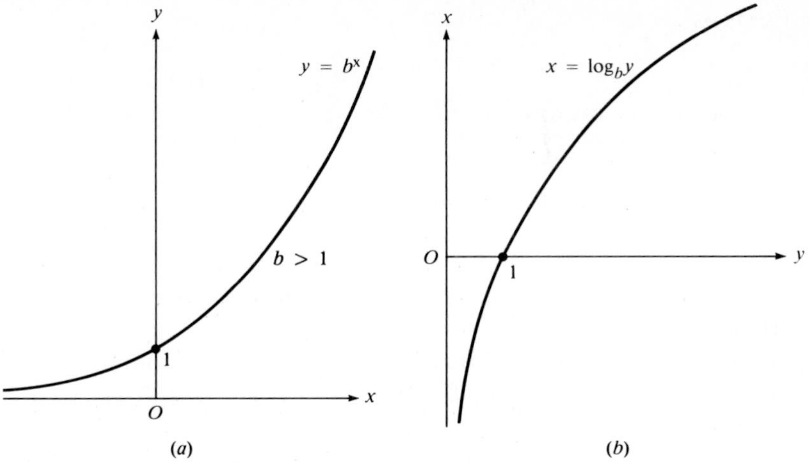

Figure A-1 (*a*) Exponential function; (*b*) logarithmic function.

The logarithm of a number to a given base is defined as the power to which the base must be raised to give the number. Thus in Eq. (A-1) x is the logarithm of y to base b, written

$$x = \log_b y \tag{A-2}$$

This is the *inverse* of the exponential function. The first expresses y as a function of x and the second expresses x as a function of y. Typical graphs for $b > 1$ are shown in Fig. A-1. If the graph in Fig. A-1b were superimposed on Fig. A-1a with the y axis on the y axis and the x axis on the x axis, the curves would coincide. Numerical calculations are facilitated by the tables of *common* logarithms, which are taken to the base 10. Thus, for example, $\log_{10} 100 = 2$ since $100 = (10)^2$. In practice the subscript 10 is rarely shown explicitly. For mathematical purposes it is usually much more convenient to work with *natural* logarithms, which are taken to base e. This is the mathematical constant defined by†

$$e = \lim_{n \to \infty} \left(1 + \frac{1}{n}\right)^n \cong 2.41828$$

This has the remarkable property that if

$$y = e^x$$

then

$$\frac{dy}{dx} = \frac{d^2y}{dx^2} = \cdots = e^x$$

that is, all derivatives are equal to the original function. The function is written in

† See also the footnote on p. 68.

alternative forms as

$$y = e^x \qquad \text{or} \qquad y = \exp\{x\}$$

and the inverse logarithmic function is written as†

$$x = \log_e y \qquad \text{or} \qquad x = \ln y$$

The general exponential function is written as

$$y = Ae^{cx} \qquad \text{or} \qquad y = A\exp\{cx\}$$

which has the effect of stretching or contracting the typical exponential shape in Fig. A-1*a* vertically and horizontally.

If the inverse function exists, as it does when $y = f(x)$ is monotonic (that is, to each value of x there corresponds a unique value of y and vice versa), then

$$\frac{dx}{dy} = \frac{1}{dy/dx}$$

If $y = e^x$, then $dy/dx = e^x = y$, and so for the inverse function, $x = \ln y$, $dx/dy = 1/y$. Thus we have the two standard forms:

$$y = e^x \qquad \frac{dy}{dx} = e^x$$

$$y = \ln x \qquad \frac{dy}{dx} = \frac{1}{x}$$

Suppose we have $y = \log x$. What then is dy/dx? We may write

$$x = 10^y$$

Thus

$$y = \frac{\ln x}{\ln 10} = \ln x \cdot \log e$$

since it may easily be shown that $\ln 10 \cdot \log e = 1$. It then follows that

$$\frac{d(\log x)}{dx} = \frac{1}{x}\log e \tag{A-3}$$

Finally we may note a frequently used connection between logarithms and elasticities. If $y = f(x)$ and a change Δx is imposed leading to a change Δy, then

$$\frac{\Delta y}{y} \div \frac{\Delta x}{x} = \frac{\Delta y}{\Delta x} \cdot \frac{x}{y}$$

measures the proportionate change in y per unit proportionate change in x. The *elasticity* of y with respect to x is defined as the limiting value of this ratio as $\Delta x \to 0$, that is,

$$\text{(Point) elasticity of } y \text{ with respect to } x = \frac{dy}{dx} \cdot \frac{x}{y}$$

† In general ln denotes a logarithm to base e and log a logarithm to base 10.

It may be shown that

$$\frac{dy}{dx}\cdot\frac{x}{y} \equiv \frac{d(\ln y)}{d(\ln x)} \equiv \frac{d(\log y)}{d(\log x)} \qquad \text{(A-4)}$$

To show the first part of the identity let

$$z = \ln y \qquad y = f(x) \qquad \text{and} \qquad x = e^w \qquad \text{so that } w = \ln x$$

Then

$$\begin{aligned}\frac{dz}{dw} &= \frac{dz}{dy}\cdot\frac{dy}{dx}\cdot\frac{dx}{dw} \\ &= \frac{1}{y}\cdot\frac{dy}{dx}\cdot x \qquad \text{using } \frac{dx}{dw} = \frac{1}{dw/dx} = x \\ &= \text{elasticity of } y \text{ with respect to } x\end{aligned}$$

The second part of the identity shows that the same relation holds if logarithms are taken to base 10, since there is a proportionate relationship between logarithms to the two bases.

It follows from Eq. (A-4) that a functional form which implies a linear relation between the logs of the variables is a constant elasticity function. For instance,

$$y = Ax^{\alpha}$$

gives

$$\log y = \log A + \alpha(\log x)$$

so that α is the elasticity of y with respect to x. A simple way to fix the meaning of an elasticity is that it measures the percentage change in y produced by a *1 percent* change in x.

The elasticity concept extends to functions of several variables. Thus

$$y = Ax^{\alpha}v^{\beta}z^{\gamma}$$

is a constant elasticity function, where α, β, and γ are the *partial elasticities* with respect to the arguments x, v, and z.

A-3 OPERATIONS WITH SUMMATION SIGNS

The Greek capital sigma is used to indicate summation. Thus

$$\sum_{i=1}^{n} X_i = (X_1 + X_2 + \cdots + X_n)$$

This sum is variously denoted by

$$\sum_{i=1}^{i=n} X_i \qquad \sum_{i=1}^{n} X_i \qquad \sum_{1}^{n} X_i \qquad \sum X_i \qquad \text{or just} \qquad \sum X$$

so long as no ambiguity is involved in any particular application.

If each value of X is multiplied by a constant a, the sum is

$$(aX_1 + aX_2 + \cdots + aX_n) = \sum_{i=1}^{n} aX_i = a\sum_{i=1}^{n} X_i \qquad \text{(A-5)}$$

Thus a constant appearing after a summation sign may be moved in front of it to multiply the sum. If each X_i in Eq. (A-5) were equal to unity, $\Sigma X_i = n$ and

$$\sum_{i=1}^{n} aX_i = \sum_{i=1}^{n} a = na$$

Thus the summation of a constant over n points is n times the constant.

The arithmetic mean of the X's is

$$\bar{X} = \frac{\Sigma X_i}{n}$$

It follows directly from the definition that

$$\sum_{i=1}^{n} (X_i - \bar{X}) = \Sigma X_i - n\bar{X}$$

so that the algebraic sum of deviations around an arithmetic mean is zero. The sum of squared deviations from the arithmetic mean is

$$\begin{aligned} \sum_{i=1}^{n} (X_i - \bar{X})^2 &= \sum_{i=1}^{n} (X_i^2 - 2\bar{X}X_i + \bar{X})^2 \\ &= \sum X_i^2 - 2\bar{X}\sum X_i + n\bar{X}^2 \\ &= \sum X_i^2 - \frac{1}{n}\left(\sum X_i\right)^2 \end{aligned}$$

or alternatively,

$$\sum_{i=1}^{n} (X_i - \bar{X})^2 = \sum X_i^2 - n\bar{X}^2$$

that is, the sum of squared deviations about the sample mean can be expressed as the sum of the squared values of the original variables less a correction factor for the mean. Similarly, one may derive

$$\begin{aligned} \sum_{i=1}^{n} (X_i - \bar{X})(Y_i - \bar{Y}) &= \sum (X_i Y_i) - n\overline{XY} \\ &= \sum (X_i Y_i) - \frac{1}{n}\left(\sum X_i\right)\left(\sum Y_i\right) \end{aligned}$$

Suppose a variable has *two* subscripts, say,

$$X_{ij} \qquad i = 1, 2, \ldots, p; j = 1, 2, \ldots, n_i$$

This is illustrated in the following table:

Class	1	$X_{11}, X_{12}, \ldots, X_{1n_1}$
	2	$X_{21}, X_{22}, \ldots, X_{2n_2}$
	$\vdots$	$\vdots \quad \vdots \quad \vdots$
	p	$X_{p1}, X_{p2}, \ldots, X_{pn_p}$

As an example, X might measure personal income and the sample data consist of n_1 observations from social group 1, n_2 observations from social group 2, and so forth. Total income in the sample is defined by

$$\sum_{i=1}^{p} \sum_{j=1}^{n_i} X_{ij} \qquad \text{or, more simply,} \qquad \sum_{i,j} X_{ij}$$

The total number of sample observations is

$$n = \sum_{i=1}^{p} n_i$$

and the *overall* mean income is then

$$\bar{\bar{X}} = \frac{\Sigma_{i,j} X_{ij}}{n}$$

The mean income for the ith group, or class, is

$$\bar{X}_i = \frac{\Sigma_{j=1}^{n_i} X_{ij}}{n_i}$$

The sum of squared deviations about the overall mean is

$$\sum_{i,j} \left(X_{ij} - \bar{\bar{X}} \right)^2 = \sum_{i,j} \left[\left(X_{ij} - \bar{X}_i \right) + \left(\bar{X}_i - \bar{\bar{X}} \right) \right]^2$$

$$= \sum_{i,j} \left(X_{ij} - \bar{X}_i \right)^2 + \sum_{i,j} \left(\bar{X}_i - \bar{\bar{X}} \right)^2 + 2 \sum_{i,j} \left(X_{ij} - \bar{X}_i \right)\left(\bar{X}_i - \bar{\bar{X}} \right)$$

The last term may be written

$$\sum_{i=1}^{p} \sum_{j=1}^{n_i} \left(X_{ij} - \bar{X}_i \right)\left(\bar{X}_i - \bar{\bar{X}} \right) = \sum_{i=1}^{p} \left(\bar{X}_i - \bar{\bar{X}} \right) \sum_{j=1}^{n_i} \left(X_{ij} - \bar{X}_i \right)$$

since the factor $(\bar{X}_i - \bar{\bar{X}})$ does not involve the j subscript and so may be moved in front of the summation over j. But

$$\sum_{j=1}^{n_i} \left(X_{ij} - \bar{X}_i \right) = 0$$

for each i, and so the whole term vanishes. The middle term may be written

$$\sum_{i,j}\left(\bar{X}_i - \bar{\bar{X}}\right)^2 = \sum_{i=1}^{p}\sum_{j=1}^{n_i}\left(\bar{X}_i - \bar{\bar{X}}\right)^2$$

$$= \sum_{i=1}^{p} n_i\left(\bar{X}_i - \bar{\bar{X}}\right)^2$$

since $(\bar{X}_i - \bar{\bar{X}})^2$ is a constant for each element in the ith group, so that the sum over j is simply $n_i(\bar{X}_i - \bar{\bar{X}})$. Thus

$$\sum_{i,j}\left(X_{ij} - \bar{\bar{X}}\right)^2 = \sum_{i,j}\left(X_{ij} - \bar{X}_i\right)^2 + \sum_{i} n_i\left(\bar{X}_i - \bar{\bar{X}}\right)^2$$

This decomposition is often written as

Total sum of squares = *within*-group sum of squares
+ *between*-group sum of squares

A-4 RANDOM VARIABLES AND PROBABILITY DISTRIBUTIONS†

A discrete random variable X consists of a set of possible values $x_1, x_2, \ldots, x_k$ and associated positive fractions (probabilities) $p_1, p_2, \ldots, p_k$ such that

$$\sum_{i=1}^{k} p_i = 1$$

The two most important features of the probability distribution are the mean and the variance. The mean, often denoted by μ, is defined as

$$\mu = E(X) = \sum_{i=1}^{k} x_i p_i \tag{A-6}$$

which is just a weighted average of the x values, the weights being the respective probabilities. E is the expectation operator, and it may also be applied to various functions of X. For example, $E(X^2)$ indicates the expected value of X^2. The possible values for X^2 are $x_1^2, x_2^2, \ldots, x_k^2$, which occur with probabilities $p_1, p_2, \ldots, p_k$. Thus

$$E(X^2) = \sum_{i=1}^{k} x_i^2 p_i$$

The second most important feature of the probability distribution is the variance

† For the statistical paragraphs in this appendix, two of the most lucid texts at an introductory level are P. J. Hoel, *Introduction to Mathematical Statistics*, 4th edition, Wiley, New York, 1971, and L. D. Taylor, *Probability and Mathematical Statistics*, Harper and Row, New York, 1974.

or *expected squared deviation* about the mean. This is usually denoted by σ^2. Thus

$$\sigma^2 = E\{(X - \mu)^2\} \tag{A-7}$$

Evaluating this from first principles,

$$\begin{aligned} E\{(X-\mu)^2\} &= \sum_{i=1}^{k} (x_i - \mu)^2 p_i \\ &= \Sigma x_i^2 p_i - 2\mu \Sigma x_i p_i + \mu^2 \Sigma p_i \\ &= \Sigma x_i^2 p_i - (\Sigma x_i p_i)^2 \\ &= E(X^2) - [E(X)]^2 \end{aligned}$$

This result may also be obtained by squaring the expression in Eq. (A-7) and applying the expectation operator to each term in turn. Thus

$$\begin{aligned} E\{(X-\mu)^2\} &= E\{X^2 - 2\mu X + \mu^2\} \\ &= E(X^2) - 2\mu E(X) + E(\mu^2) \\ &= E(X^2) - [E(X)]^2 \end{aligned}$$

since $E(\mu^2)$ indicates the expectation of a constant, which is simply the constant.

When the random variable is continuous, the discrete probabilities are replaced by a continuous *probability density function* (pdf), usually denoted by $p(x)$ or $f(x)$. An example is shown in Fig. A-2.

The pdf has the properties that

$$f(x) \geq 0 \qquad \text{for all } x$$

$$\int f(x)\, dx = 1$$

and

$$\int_a^b f(x)\, dx = \Pr[a < x < b]$$

The mean and the variance are defined as before, but integrals now replace summation signs.

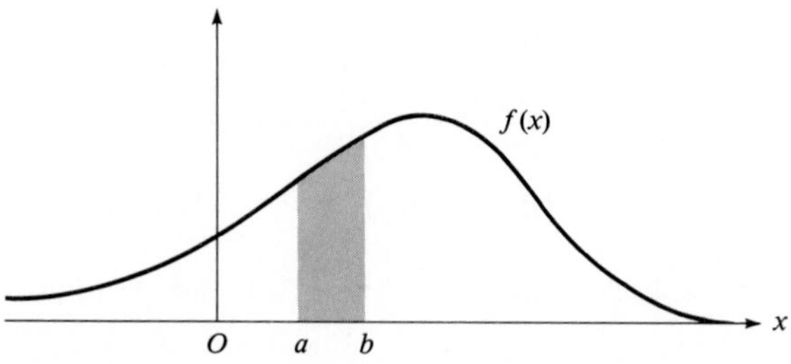

Figure A-2

We are often interested in the *joint variation* of a pair of random variables. Let the variables X, Y have a bivariate pdf denoted by $f(x, y)$. Then

$$f(x, y) \geq 0 \qquad \text{for all } x, y$$

$$\iint f(x, y)\, dx\, dy = 1$$

and

$$\int_c^d \int_a^b f(x, y)\, dx\, dy = \Pr[a < X < b, c < y < d]$$

Given the joint density, a *marginal* density is obtained for each variable by integrating over the range of the other variable. Thus

$$\text{Marginal pdf for } X = \int_{-\infty}^{\infty} f(x, y)\, dy = f(x)$$

and

$$\text{Marginal pdf for } Y = \int_{-\infty}^{\infty} f(x, y)\, dx = f(y)$$

A *conditional* pdf for Y, *given* X, is defined as

$$f(y|x) = \frac{f(x, y)}{f(x)} \tag{A-8}$$

and similarly, a conditional pdf for X, given Y, is defined as

$$f(x|y) = \frac{f(x, y)}{f(y)}$$

Two variables are said to be *statistically independent*, or independently distributed, if the marginal and conditional densities are the same. Thus the joint density can be written as the product of the marginal densities

$$f(x, y) = f(x) \cdot f(y) \tag{A-9}$$

The mean and variance for each variable may be obtained from the marginal densities. Thus

$$\mu_x = E(X) = \iint x f(x, y)\, dx\, dy = \int x f(x)\, dx$$

$$\sigma_x^2 = \operatorname{var}(X) = \int (x - \mu_x)^2 f(x)\, dx$$

and similarly for the mean and the variance of Y. A new statistic for the bivariate case is the *covariance*. It is defined as

$$\sigma_{xy} = \operatorname{cov}(X, Y) = E\{(x - \mu_x)(y - \mu_y)\} = \iint (x - \mu_x)(y - \mu_y) f(x, y)\, dx\, dy$$

and measures the linear association between the two variables. For independently distributed variables the covariance is zero since

$$\iint (x-\mu_x)(y-\mu_y)f(x,y)\,dx\,dy = \int (x-\mu_x)f(x)\,dx \int (y-\mu_y)f(y)\,dy$$
$$= 0$$

In general, the converse of this proposition is not true, that is, a zero covariance does not necessarily imply independence. An important exception to the proposition, however, exists in the case of normally distributed variables, as is shown in App. A-5.

A-5 NORMAL PROBABILITY DISTRIBUTION

The pdf for the univariate normal distribution is

$$f(x) = \frac{1}{\sigma\sqrt{2\pi}} \exp\left[-\frac{1}{2\sigma^2}(x-\mu)^2\right] \tag{A-10}$$

This defines a two-parameter family of distributions, the parameters being the mean μ and the variance σ^2. The bell-shaped curve reaches its maximum at $x = \mu$ and is symmetrical about that point. A special member of the family is the *standard* normal distribution, which has zero mean and unit variance. An area under any specific normal distribution may be expressed as an equivalent area under the standard distribution by defining

$$z = \frac{x-\mu}{\sigma}$$

Clearly, $E(z) = 0$ and $\text{var}(z) = 1$, so that

$$f(z) = \frac{1}{\sqrt{2\pi}} e^{-z^2/2} \tag{A-11}$$

Then
$$\int_{x_1}^{x_2} f(x)\,dx = \int_{z_1}^{z_2} f(z)\,dz$$

where $z_i = (x_i - \mu)/\sigma$. The areas under Eq. (A-11) are tabulated in App. B-1.

Three very important results about the normal distribution are as follows.

1. *Linear combinations of normally distributed variables are themselves normally distributed.*† For example, if $\mathbf{x}$ denotes an $n \times 1$ vector of variables, which follow the multivariate normal distribution

$$\mathbf{x} \sim N(\boldsymbol{\mu}, \boldsymbol{\Sigma})$$

and if a vector $\mathbf{y}$ is defined by $\mathbf{y} = \mathbf{Dx}$ where $\mathbf{D}$ is an $m \times n$ matrix of rank

† See L. D. Taylor, *Probability and Mathematical Statistics*, Harper and Row, New York, 1974, pp. 154–160.

$m \leq n$, then

$$\mathbf{y} \sim N(\mathbf{D}\boldsymbol{\mu}, \mathbf{D}\boldsymbol{\Sigma}\mathbf{D}')$$

2. *Central limit theorem.*† If $(x_1, x_2, \ldots)$ is a sequence of independent random variables with means $(\mu_1, \mu_2, \ldots)$ and variances $(\sigma_1^2, \sigma_2^2, \ldots)$, then

$$\lim_{n \to \infty} \Pr\left[\frac{\sum_{i=1}^{n}(x_i - \mu_i)}{\sqrt{\sum_{i=1}^{n}\sigma_i^2}} \leq y\right] = \frac{1}{\sqrt{2\pi}}\int_{-\infty}^{y} e^{-(1/2)z^2}\,dz \qquad \text{(A-12)}$$

Notice first of all that nothing is assumed about the specific forms of the various pdf's other than the existence of means and variances. The remarkable result embodied in Eq. (A-12) is that the limiting or asymptotic distribution of the quantity $\Sigma(x_i - \mu_i)/\sqrt{\Sigma\sigma_i^2}$ is the standard normal distribution. A special case of the result may help to make its meaning clearer. Suppose the means and variances are all identical. The statistic in Eq. (A-12) then reduces to

$$\sum_{i=1}^{n}(x_i - n\mu) = \frac{\bar{x} - \mu}{\sigma/\sqrt{n}}$$

and the theorem states that $\bar{x}$ is asymptotically normally distributed with mean μ and variance σ^2/n.

3. *Zero covariance between two normally distributed variables implies statistical independence.* The bivariate normal distribution is

$$f(x, y) = \frac{1}{2\pi\sigma_x\sigma_y\sqrt{1 - \rho^2}}\exp\left\{-\frac{1}{2(1 - \rho^2)}\left[\left(\frac{x - \mu_x}{\sigma_x}\right)^2 - 2\rho\left(\frac{x - \mu_x}{\sigma_x}\right)\left(\frac{y - \mu_y}{\sigma_y}\right) + \left(\frac{y - \mu_y}{\sigma_y}\right)^2\right]\right\}$$

where $\rho = \sigma_{xy}/\sigma_x\sigma_y$. When the covariance σ_{xy} is zero, the joint pdf simplifies to

$$f(x, y) = \left[\frac{1}{\sqrt{2\pi}\,\sigma_x}\exp\left[-\frac{1}{2}\left(\frac{x - \mu_x}{\sigma_x}\right)^2\right]\right]\left[\frac{1}{\sqrt{2\pi}\,\sigma_y}\exp\left[-\frac{1}{2}\left(\frac{y - \mu_y}{\sigma_y}\right)^2\right]\right]$$

which is the product of two separate normal pdf's. Thus X and Y are independently distributed.

† S. S. Wilks, *Mathematical Statistics*, Wiley, New York, 1962, pp. 257–258.

A-6 LAGRANGE MULTIPLIERS AND CONSTRAINED OPTIMIZATION

Frequently in economics one has to find the maximum or minimum of a function subject to some constraint, or set of constraints, on the independent variables. Thus one may have to maximize profits subject to the constraint of the production function, or maximize utility subject to the constraint of the budget equation. In the context of the regression model, as in Chap. 6, one may need to minimize a residual sum of squares subject to a set of constraints on the regression coefficients. Such constrained optimization problems may be tackled in two alternative fashions. The first is to substitute the constraints into the objective function, thus reducing the number of independent variables and find the stationary values of the resultant, unrestricted function. The second is to use the method of Lagrange multipliers. We will illustrate with a simple example.

Suppose the problem is to find the minimum value of $y = f(x, z) = x^2 + z^2$ subject to $x + 2z = 10$. Substituting the constraint in the objective function means that the latter may be expressed as a function of just a single variable, either x or z. For example, replacing x by $10 - 2z$ gives

$$y = (10 - 2z)^2 + z^2 = 100 - 40z + 5z^2$$

Differentiating

$$\frac{dy}{dz} = -40 + 10z \qquad \frac{d^2y}{dz^2} = 10$$

Thus a minimum value occurs at $z = 4$ ($x = 2$), and that minimum value is $y = 20$.

Alternatively, define a new, or augmented, objective function as

$$\phi = x^2 + z^2 - \lambda(x + 2z - 10)$$

where λ is a Lagrange multiplier, whose value is as yet unknown. So long as the constraint is satisfied, the term $\lambda(x + 2z - 10)$ vanishes, irrespective of the value of λ, and ϕ will have the same stationary value as y. To find the stationary value of ϕ we must take the *three* partial derivatives and equate to zero. Thus

$$\frac{\partial \phi}{\partial x} = 2x - \lambda = 0$$

$$\frac{\partial \phi}{\partial z} = 2z - 2\lambda = 0$$

$$\frac{\partial \phi}{\partial \lambda} = x + 2z - 10 = 0$$

The third equation ensures that the constraint is satisfied. Eliminating λ from the first two gives $2x = z$, which on substitution in the third gives $x = 2 (z = 4)$ and, as before,

$$\phi_{\min} = y_{\min} = 20$$

The solution value for λ is $\lambda = 2x = z = 4$, which in this case has no specific significance. There are problems, however, where λ may have a meaningful economic interpretation.

The technique extends to handle more than one constraint, as is evidenced by the examples in Chaps. 2 and 6.

A-7 RELATIONS BETWEEN THE NORMAL, χ^2, t AND F DISTRIBUTIONS

Let $z \sim N(0, 1)$ be a standard normal variable. If n random values $z_1, z_2, \ldots, z_n$ are drawn from this distribution, squared, and summed, the resultant statistic is said to have a χ^2 distribution with n degrees of freedom,

$$\left(z_1^2 + z_2^2 + \cdots + z_n^2\right) \sim \chi^2(n)$$

The precise mathematical form of the χ^2 distribution need not concern us here. The important point is that it constitutes a *one-parameter* family of distributions, and the parameter is conventionally labeled the degrees of freedom of the distribution. As the degrees of freedom tend to infinity, the χ^2 distribution approaches the normal density. Critical values of the χ^2 distribution are given in App. B-3.

The t distribution may be defined in terms of a normal and an independent χ^2 variable. Let

$$z \sim N(0, 1) \qquad \text{and} \qquad v \sim \chi^2(\nu)$$

where z and v are independently distributed. Then

$$t = \frac{z\sqrt{\nu}}{\sqrt{v}} \tag{A-13}$$

has Student's t distribution with ν degrees of freedom. The t distribution, like χ^2, is a one-parameter family. It is symmetrical about zero and tends asymptotically to the standard normal distribution. Its critical values are given in App. B-2.

The F distribution is defined in terms of two independent χ^2 variables. Let u and v be independently distributed χ^2 variables with ν_1 and ν_2 degrees of freedom, respectively. Then the statistic

$$F = \frac{u/\nu_1}{v/\nu_2} \tag{A-14}$$

has the F distribution with (ν_1, ν_2) degrees of freedom. Critical values are given in App. B-4. In using the table note carefully that ν_1 refers to the degrees of freedom attaching to the expression in the numerator and ν_2 to the expression in the denominator.

If we square the expression for t, the result may be written

$$t^2 = \frac{z^2/1}{v/\nu}$$

where z^2, being the square of a standard normal variable, has the $\chi^2(1)$ distribution. Thus $t^2 = F(1, \nu)$, that is, the square of a t variable with ν degrees of freedom is an F variable with $(1, \nu)$ degrees of freedom.

The χ^2 variable was formed from the sum of squares of a standard normal variable. Suppose, however, that the z variables are still independent but distributed as

$$z_i \sim N(\mu_i, 1)$$

The statistic $z_1^2 + z_2^2 + \cdots + z_n^2$ now has the *noncentral* χ^2 distribution with n degrees of freedom. The previous distribution is sometimes referred to as the *central* χ^2 distribution. Corresponding to a noncentral χ^2 distribution, there are noncentral t and F distributions, the former arising when the v variable in Eq. (A-13) is noncentral and the latter when u in Eq. (A-14) is noncentral, but v is central.†

A-8 EXPECTATIONS IN BIVARIATE DISTRIBUTIONS

Let X and Y be two variables with a bivariate pdf denoted by $f(x, y)$. Let $g(x, y)$ be some function of the variables.‡ The problem is to evaluate $E\{g(x, y)\}$. By definition

$$\begin{aligned} E\{g(x, y)\} &= \iint g(x, y) f(x, y)\, dx\, dy \\ &= \iint g(x, y) f(x|y) f(y)\, dx\, dy \end{aligned} \tag{A-15}$$

where $f(x|y)$ denotes the conditional distribution of X given Y and $f(y)$ denotes the marginal distribution of Y. Rearranging

$$E\{g(x, y)\} = \int \left[\int g(x, y) f(x|y)\, dx \right] f(y)\, dy \tag{A-16}$$

The term inside the square brackets gives the expected value of $g(x, y)$ in the conditional distribution $f(x|y)$, and we will denote the operation by $E_{x|y}$. This conditional expectation is a function of Y, and it is then averaged over the

† For references to some tables for noncentral distributions see B. W. Lindgren, *Statistical Theory*, 2d edition, Macmillan, New York, 1968, p. 383.

‡ We exclude functions $g(\cdot)$ which may have some values undefined such as $x/0$ or $0/0$.

marginal distribution $f(y)$. Thus we may write

$$E\{g(x, y)\} = E_y\{E_{x|y}g(x, y)\}$$

Example Consider the simple bivariate distribution

$f(x, y)$

	$y = 2$	$y = 4$	$f(x)$
$x = 1$	0.2	0.4	0.6
$x = 2$	0.3	0.1	0.4
$f(y)$	0.5	0.5	1.0

Let $g(x, y) = x/y$. The straightforward application of Eq. (A-15) would then give

$$E\left(\frac{x}{y}\right) = \tfrac{1}{2}(0.2) + \tfrac{1}{4}(0.4) + \tfrac{2}{2}(0.3) + \tfrac{2}{4}(0.1) = 0.55$$

Using Eq. (A-16) we would first find $E(x/y)$ within each of the two columns of the table, which contain the conditional distributions $f(x|y)$. Thus

$$E\left(\frac{x}{y}\middle| y = 2\right) = \frac{1}{2}\left(\frac{0.2}{0.5}\right) + \frac{2}{2}\left(\frac{0.3}{0.5}\right) = 0.8$$

and

$$E\left(\frac{x}{y}\middle| y = 4\right) = \frac{1}{4}\left(\frac{0.4}{0.5}\right) + \frac{2}{4}\left(\frac{0.1}{0.5}\right) = 0.3$$

Then averaging these expectations over $f(y)$ gives, as before,

$$E\left(\frac{x}{y}\right) = 0.8(0.5) + 0.3(0.5) = 0.55$$

Clearly the process is symmetrical and we could average first of all over each conditional distribution $f(y|x)$ and then average the results over $f(x)$. The procedure, however, would break down for the function $g(x, y) = x/y$ if zero is a possible value for y.

This result has useful applications in regression theory, but it has to be handled carefully. As a simple illustration consider the model

$$y_t = \beta x_t + u_t$$

where the u's are well-behaved, the x's are stochastic and distributed independently of the u's so that, in particular,

$$E(x_t u_t) = E(x_t)E(u_t) = 0 \qquad \text{for all } t$$

The OLS estimator of β is

$$b = \frac{\Sigma x_t y_t}{\Sigma x_t^2} = \beta + \frac{\Sigma x_t u_t}{\Sigma x_t^2}$$

To examine the bias of b we need to evaluate $E(\Sigma x_t u_t / \Sigma x_t^2)$. Applying the theorem

$$E\left\{\frac{\Sigma x_t u_t}{\Sigma x_t^2}\right\} = E_x\left\{E_{u|x}\left(\frac{\Sigma x_t u_t}{\Sigma x_t^2}\right)\right\} = 0$$

so that b is still unbiased when x is stochastic, provided it is independent of u. The sampling avariance is given by

$$\text{var}(b) = E\{(b - \beta)^2\} = E\left\{\left(\frac{\Sigma x_t u_t}{\Sigma x_t^2}\right)^2\right\}$$

Now

$$E_{u|x}\left\{\left(\frac{\Sigma x_t u_t}{\Sigma x_t^2}\right)^2\right\} = \frac{\sigma_u^2}{\Sigma x_t^2}$$

Thus

$$\text{var}(b) = \sigma_u^2 E\left\{\frac{1}{\Sigma x_t^2}\right\}$$

which is the one-dimensional version of the general result given in Eq. (7-26).

Now consider the case where x is stochastic but no longer independent of u. Suppose, for example, that x, u follow a bivariate normal distribution

$$f(x, u) = \frac{1}{2\pi\sigma_x\sigma_u\sqrt{1-\rho^2}} \exp\left\{-\frac{1}{2(1-\rho^2)}\left[\left(\frac{x-\mu_x}{\sigma_x}\right)^2 - 2\rho\left(\frac{x-\mu_x}{\sigma_x}\right)\left(\frac{u}{\sigma_u}\right) + \left(\frac{u}{\sigma_u}\right)^2\right]\right\}$$

with marginal densities

$$f(x) = \frac{1}{\sqrt{2\pi}\cdot\sigma_x} \exp\left[-\frac{1}{2}\left(\frac{x-\mu_x}{\sigma_x}\right)^2\right]$$

and

$$f(u) = \frac{1}{\sqrt{2\pi}\cdot\sigma_u} \exp\left[-\frac{1}{2}\left(\frac{u}{\sigma_u}\right)^2\right]$$

The conditional density for u, given x, is

$$f(u|x) = \frac{1}{\sqrt{2\pi}\cdot\sigma_u\cdot\sqrt{1-\rho^2}} \exp\left\{-\frac{1}{2\sigma_u^2(1-\rho^2)}\left[u - \frac{\rho\sigma_u}{\sigma_x}(x-\mu_x)\right]^2\right\} \tag{A-17}$$

Thus

$$E(xu|x) = xE(u|x) = x\cdot\frac{\rho\sigma_u}{\sigma_x}(x-\mu_x)$$

since Eq. (A-17) shows $f(u|x)$ to be normal about mean $\rho\sigma_u(x - \mu_x)/\sigma_x$. It then follows that

$$E\left\{\frac{\Sigma x_t u_t}{\Sigma x_t^2}\right\} = E_x\left\{E_{u|x}\left(\frac{\Sigma x_t u_t}{\Sigma x_t^2}\right)\right\}$$

$$= E_x\left\{\frac{\rho\sigma_u}{\sigma_x}\cdot\frac{1}{\Sigma x_t^2}\cdot\Sigma x_t(x_t - \mu_x)\right\}$$

$$= \frac{\rho\sigma_u}{\sigma_x}\cdot E\left\{\frac{\Sigma x_t^2 - \mu_x\Sigma x_t}{\Sigma x_t^2}\right\}$$

On dividing the top and bottom by n, the term in brackets is approximately the ratio of the sample variance of the x observations to their sum of squares. This expectation does not vanish, and so b is a biased estimator, both for finite samples and also asymptotically. This example is a legitimate application of Eq. (A-16) since $f(x, u)$ is a well-defined bivariate distribution.

Now consider the model

$$y_t = \beta y_{t-1} + u_t \tag{A-18}$$

The OLS estimator is

$$b = \beta + \frac{\Sigma y_{t-1}u_t}{\Sigma y_{t-1}^2}$$

With the u's well-behaved there is no problem about assuming

$$E(y_{t-1}u_t) = 0 \qquad \text{for all } t$$

An application of Eq. (A-16) would then appear to give

$$E\left\{\frac{\Sigma y_{t-1}u_t}{\Sigma y_{t-1}^2}\right\} = E_y\left\{E_{u|y}\left(\frac{\Sigma y_{t-1}u_t}{\Sigma y_{t-1}^2}\right)\right\} = 0$$

However, the OLS b is well known to be biased in finite samples.† The source of the error is that (y_{t-1}, u_t) does not have a well-defined *bivariate* pdf, which renders the application of Eq. (A-16) invalid. Given some starting value y_0, once a **u** vector is drawn, the **y** vector is exactly determined by Eq. (A-18). The stochastic behavior of y is completely determined by u, so there is, in effect, only one stochastic variable. Thus $E\{\Sigma y_{t-1}u_t/\Sigma y_{t-1}^2\}$ has to be evaluated solely over the u distribution, and the two-step procedure of Eq. (A-16) does not apply.

A more complicated version of the same error can arise in IV estimation. Consider

$$y_t = \beta y_{t-1} + \gamma x_t + u_t$$

Suppose $\{x_t\}$ is taken to be nonstochastic and x_{t-1} is used as an instrument for

† J. S. White, "Asymptotic Expansions for the Mean and Variance of the Serial Correlation Coefficient," *Biometrika*, vol. 48, 1961, pp. 85–94.

y_{t-1}. The $\mathbf{W'Z}$ matrix of Sec. 9-2 will then include terms in $\Sigma x_t y_{t-1}$ and $\Sigma x_{t-1} y_{t-1}$. These are stochastic simply because u is stochastic and, as in the simple example given above, a two-stage evaluation via $E_{u|y}$ followed by E_y is invalid.

A-9 CHANGE OF VARIABLES IN DENSITY FUNCTIONS†

The basic idea may be simply illustrated for the univariate case. Suppose u is a random variable with density function $p(u)$, and suppose that a new variable y is defined by the relation $y = f(u)$. The y variable must then also have a density function for y in terms of the density function for u and the relation $y = f(u)$. Suppose the relation between y and u is monotonically increasing, as shown in Fig. A-3. Whenever u lies in the interval Δu, y will be in the corresponding interval Δy. Thus

$$\Pr\{y \text{ lies in } \Delta y\} = \Pr\{u \text{ lies in } \Delta u\}$$

or

$$p(y')\,\Delta y = p(u')\,\Delta u$$

where u' and y' denote appropriate values of u and y in the intervals Δu and Δy, and $p(y)$ indicates the postulated density function for y. Taking limits as Δu goes to zero gives

$$p(y) = p(u)\frac{du}{dy} \qquad \text{(A-19)}$$

If y were a decreasing function of u, the derivative in Eq. (A-19) would be negative, thus giving an impossible negative value for the density function. Thus the *absolute* value of the derivative must be taken and the result reformulated to

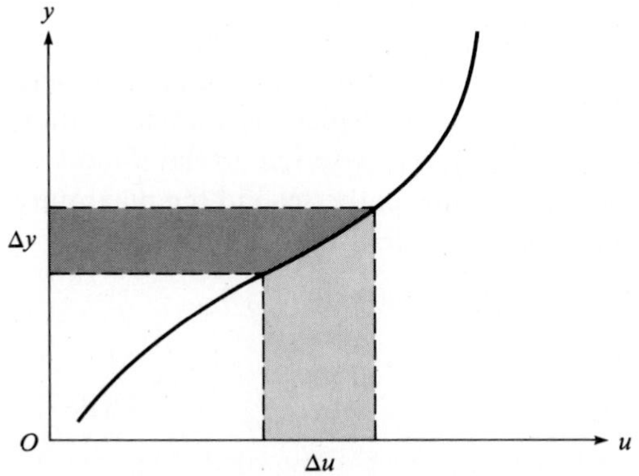

Figure A-3

† A detailed treatment of this topic is given in L. D. Taylor, *Probability and Mathematical Statistics*, Harper and Row, New York, 1974, Chap. 10.

read

$$p(y) = p(u) \cdot \left| \frac{du}{dy} \right| \tag{A-20}$$

If $y = f(u)$ were not a monotonic function, Eq. (A-20) would require amendment, but we are only concerned here with monotonic functions.

In the multivariate case **u** and **y** now indicate vectors of, say, n variables each. Under suitable conditions a result similar to Eq. (A-20) still holds, namely,

$$p(\mathbf{y}) = p(\mathbf{u}) \left| \frac{\partial \mathbf{u}}{\partial \mathbf{y}} \right| \tag{A-21}$$

where $|\partial\mathbf{u}/\partial\mathbf{y}|$ indicates the absolute value of the determinant formed from the matrix of partial derivatives

$$\begin{bmatrix} \dfrac{\partial u_1}{\partial y_1} & \dfrac{\partial u_1}{\partial y_2} & \cdots & \dfrac{\partial u_1}{\partial y_n} \\ \dfrac{\partial u_2}{\partial y_1} & \dfrac{\partial u_2}{\partial y_2} & \cdots & \dfrac{\partial u_2}{\partial y_n} \\ \cdots & \cdots & \cdots & \cdots \\ \dfrac{\partial u_n}{\partial y_1} & \dfrac{\partial u_n}{\partial y_2} & \cdots & \dfrac{\partial u_n}{\partial y_n} \end{bmatrix}$$

A-10 PRINCIPAL COMPONENTS

Suppose we have a matrix **X** of n observations on k variables,

$$\mathbf{X} = \begin{bmatrix} x_{11} & \cdots & x_{k1} \\ \cdots & \cdots & \cdots \\ x_{1n} & \cdots & x_{kn} \end{bmatrix}$$

where the observations have been expressed as deviations from the sample means, for we are concerned with studying the variation in the data.

The nature of principal components may be approached in a number of ways. One is to ask how many dimensions there are or how much independence there really is in the set of k variables. More explicitly we consider the transformation of the X's to a new set of variables which will be pairwise uncorrelated and of which the first will have the maximum possible variance, the second the maximum possible variance among those uncorrelated with the first, and so forth. Let

$$z_{1t} = a_{11}x_{1t} + a_{21}x_{2t} + \cdots + a_{k1}x_{kt} \qquad t = 1, \ldots, n$$

denote the first new variable. In matrix form

$$\mathbf{z}_1 = \mathbf{X}\mathbf{a}_1 \tag{A-22}$$

where $\mathbf{z}_1$ is an n-element vector and $\mathbf{a}_1$ a k-element vector. The sum of squares of z_1 is

$$\mathbf{z}_1'\mathbf{z}_1 = \mathbf{a}_1'\mathbf{X}'\mathbf{X}\mathbf{a}_1 \tag{A-23}$$

We wish to choose $\mathbf{a}_1$ to maximize $\mathbf{z}_1'\mathbf{z}_1$, but clearly some constraint must be imposed on $\mathbf{a}_1$, otherwise $\mathbf{z}_1'\mathbf{z}_1$ could be made infinitely large. So let us normalize by setting

$$\mathbf{a}_1'\mathbf{a}_1 = 1 \tag{A-24}$$

The problem now is to maximize Eq. (A-23) subject Eq. (A-24). Define

$$\phi = \mathbf{a}_1'\mathbf{X}'\mathbf{X}\mathbf{a}_1 - \lambda_1(\mathbf{a}_1'\mathbf{a}_1 - 1)$$

where λ_1 is a Lagrange multiplier. Thus

$$\frac{\partial\phi}{\partial\mathbf{a}_1} = 2\mathbf{X}'\mathbf{X}\mathbf{a}_1 - 2\lambda_1\mathbf{a}_1$$

Setting

$$\frac{\partial\phi}{\partial\mathbf{a}_1} = \mathbf{0}$$

gives

$$(\mathbf{X}'\mathbf{X})\mathbf{a}_1 = \lambda_1\mathbf{a}_1 \tag{A-25}$$

Thus $\mathbf{a}_1$ is an eigenvector of $\mathbf{X}'\mathbf{X}$ corresponding to the root λ_1. From Eqs. (A-23) and (A-25) we see that

$$\mathbf{z}_1'\mathbf{z}_1 = \lambda_1\mathbf{a}_1'\mathbf{a}_1 = \lambda_1$$

and so we must choose λ_1 as the largest eigenvalue of $\mathbf{X}'\mathbf{X}$. The $\mathbf{X}'\mathbf{X}$ matrix, in the absence of perfect collinearity, will be positive definite and thus have positive eigenvalues. The first principal component of $\mathbf{X}$ is then $\mathbf{z}_1$.

Now define $\mathbf{z}_2 = \mathbf{X}\mathbf{a}_2$. We wish to choose $\mathbf{a}_2$ to maximize $\mathbf{a}_2'\mathbf{X}'\mathbf{X}\mathbf{a}_2$ subject to $\mathbf{a}_2'\mathbf{a}_2 = 1$ and $\mathbf{a}_1'\mathbf{a}_2 = 0$. The reason for the second condition is that $\mathbf{z}_2$ is to be uncorrelated with $\mathbf{z}_1$. The covariation between them is given by

$$\begin{aligned}\mathbf{a}_1'\mathbf{X}'\mathbf{X}\mathbf{a}_2 &= \lambda_1\mathbf{a}_1'\mathbf{a}_2 \\ &= 0 \qquad \text{if and only if } \mathbf{a}_1'\mathbf{a}_2 = 0\end{aligned}$$

Define

$$\phi = \mathbf{a}_2'\mathbf{X}'\mathbf{X}\mathbf{a}_2 - \lambda_2(\mathbf{a}_2'\mathbf{a}_2 - 1) - \mu(\mathbf{a}_1'\mathbf{a}_2)$$

where λ_2 and μ are Lagrange multipliers.

$$\frac{\partial\phi}{\partial\mathbf{a}_2} = 2\mathbf{X}'\mathbf{X}\mathbf{a}_2 - 2\lambda_2\mathbf{a}_2 - \mu\mathbf{a}_1 = 0$$

Premultiply by $\mathbf{a}_1'$

$$2\mathbf{a}_1'\mathbf{X}'\mathbf{X}\mathbf{a}_2 - \mu = 0$$

But from

$$\begin{aligned}(\mathbf{X}'\mathbf{X})\mathbf{a}_1 &= \lambda_1\mathbf{a}_1 \\ \mathbf{a}_2'(\mathbf{X}'\mathbf{X})\mathbf{a}_1 &= \lambda_1\mathbf{a}_2'\mathbf{a}_1 = 0\end{aligned}$$

Thus

$$\mu = 0$$

and we have

$$(\mathbf{X}'\mathbf{X})\mathbf{a}_2 = \lambda_2 \mathbf{a}_2 \tag{A-26}$$

and λ_2 should obviously be chosen as the second largest latent root of $\mathbf{X}'\mathbf{X}$.

We can proceed in this way for each of the k roots of $\mathbf{X}'\mathbf{X}$ and assemble the resultant vectors in the orthogonal matrix

$$\mathbf{A} = [\mathbf{a}_1 \quad \mathbf{a}_2 \quad \cdots \quad \mathbf{a}_k] \tag{A-27}$$

The k principal components of $\mathbf{X}$ are then given by the $n \times k$ matrix $\mathbf{Z}$,

$$\mathbf{Z} = \mathbf{XA} \tag{A-28}$$

Moreover,

$$\mathbf{Z}'\mathbf{Z} = \mathbf{A}'\mathbf{X}'\mathbf{XA} = \mathbf{\Lambda} = \begin{bmatrix} \lambda_1 & 0 & \cdots & 0 \\ 0 & \lambda_2 & \cdots & 0 \\ \cdots & \cdots & \cdots & \cdots \\ 0 & 0 & \cdots & \lambda_k \end{bmatrix} \tag{A-29}$$

showing that the principal components are indeed pairwise uncorrelated and that their variances are given by

$$\mathbf{z}_i'\mathbf{z}_i = \lambda_i \qquad i = 1, \ldots, k \tag{A-30}$$

If the rank of $\mathbf{X}$ were $r < k$, $k - r$ eigenvalues would be zero and the variation in the X's could be completely expressed in terms of r independent variables. Even if $\mathbf{X}$ has full column rank, some of the λ's may be fairly close to zero so that a small number of principal components account for a substantial proportion of the variance of the X's. The total variation in the X's is given by

$$\sum_t x_{1t}^2 + \sum_t x_{2t}^2 + \cdots + \sum_t x_{kt}^2 = \mathrm{tr}(\mathbf{X}'\mathbf{X})$$

but

$$\begin{aligned} \mathrm{tr}(\mathbf{A}'\mathbf{X}'\mathbf{XA}) &= \mathrm{tr}(\mathbf{X}'\mathbf{XAA}') \\ &= \mathrm{tr}(\mathbf{X}'\mathbf{X}) \end{aligned}$$

since $\mathbf{AA}' = \mathbf{I}$, and so from Eq. (A-29)

$$\sum_{i=1}^{k} \sum_{t=1}^{n} x_{it}^2 = \mathrm{tr}(\mathbf{X}'\mathbf{X}) = \sum_{i=1}^{k} \lambda_i = \mathbf{z}_1'\mathbf{z}_1 + \cdots + \mathbf{z}_k'\mathbf{z}_k$$

Thus

$$\frac{\lambda_1}{\Sigma\lambda}, \frac{\lambda_2}{\Sigma\lambda}, \ldots, \frac{\lambda_k}{\Sigma\lambda}$$

represent the proportionate contributions of each principal component to the total variation of the X's, and since the components are orthogonal, these contributions sum to unity.

It is sometimes difficult to attach a concrete meaning to specific principal components. Occasionally a suggestion may be found in the correlations of a component with various X's. To find the correlation between, say, the first principal component and the X variables, we proceed as follows. The vector $\mathbf{X}'\mathbf{z}_1$ gives the cross products between z_1 and each X variable. But

$$\mathbf{X}'\mathbf{z}_1 = \mathbf{X}'\mathbf{X}\mathbf{a}_1 = \lambda_1 \mathbf{a}_1$$

Thus the correlation between X_i and z_i is

$$r_{i1} = \frac{\lambda_1 a_{i1}}{\sqrt{\lambda_1}\sqrt{\sum_{t=1}^{n} x_{it}^2}}$$

$$= \frac{a_{i1}\sqrt{\lambda_1}}{\sqrt{\sum_{t=1}^{n} x_{it}^2}} \qquad i = 1, \ldots, k \tag{A-31}$$

where a_{i1} is the ith element in the vector $\mathbf{a}_1$. In general, the correlation between X_i and z_j is

$$r_{ij} = \frac{a_{ij}\sqrt{\lambda_j}}{\sqrt{\sum_t x_{it}^2}} \qquad i, j = 1, \ldots, k \tag{A-32}$$

These correlation coefficients may also be used to show how the variations in *each* X variable may be decomposed into the contribution due to each component. From

$$\mathbf{Z} = \mathbf{XA}$$

we have

$$\mathbf{Z}' = \mathbf{A}'\mathbf{X}'$$

and

$$\mathbf{X}' = \mathbf{AZ}'$$

since $\mathbf{A}$ is orthogonal.

So

$$\mathbf{X}'\mathbf{X} = \mathbf{AZ}'\mathbf{ZA}' = \mathbf{A}\boldsymbol{\Lambda}\mathbf{A}'$$

from Eq. (A-29), and so

$$\sum_{t=1}^{n} x_{it}^2 = \sum_{j=1}^{k} a_{ij}^2 \lambda_j \qquad i = 1, \ldots, k \tag{A-33}$$

Dividing both sides of Eq. (A-33) by $\Sigma_t x_{it}^2$ gives

$$1 = \frac{a_{i1}^2 \lambda_1}{\Sigma_t x_{it}^2} + \frac{a_{i2}^2 \lambda_2}{\Sigma_t x_{it}^2} + \cdots + \frac{a_{ik}^2 \lambda_k}{\Sigma_t x_{it}^2} \tag{A-34}$$

where the terms on the right-hand side are the squares of the correlation coefficients defined in Eq. (A-32). Thus the proportions of the variation in X_i associated with the various principal components are given by

$$r_{i1}^2, r_{i2}^2, \ldots, r_{ik}^2$$

and since the components are uncorrelated, these proportions sum to unity, as is shown by Eq. (A-34).

A note of warning should be inserted here. The development so far has proceeded on the implicit assumption that the X variables are all measured in the same units. If not, it is difficult to attach a meaning to concepts such as the total variation of the X's and the partitioning of that total variation into the contribution due to each component. It is still, of course, possible to compute the eigenvalues and eigenvectors of $\mathbf{X'X}$ even if the dimensions of the variables are not all the same and the correlations in Eq. (A-32) and the partitioning in Eq. (A-34) would still be meaningful even though the partitioning of the *total* variation in the X's would not. As an alternative, analyses are sometimes carried out after all the X variables have been *standardized*, that is, each deviation from the sample mean is divided by $\sqrt{n}$ times the sample standard deviation of that variable. $\mathbf{X'X}$ is now the matrix of zero-order correlation coefficients of the X variables. The analysis can proceed from $\mathbf{X'X}$ as before. Now $\text{tr}(\mathbf{X'X}) = k$, and from the development following Eq. (A-29),

$$\lambda_1 + \lambda_2 + \cdots + \lambda_k = k$$

The eigenvalues and eigenvectors will in general be different from those yielded by unstandardized variables. We leave it as an exercise for the reader to establish whether the correlation coefficients in Eq. (A-32) are affected by the standardization of the X variables.

Empirically, then, one may compute the principal components for a given $\mathbf{X}$ matrix and see how much of the variation of the X's is accounted for by various components. Frequently the intercorrelation of economic and social data means that a small number of components will account for a large proportion of the total variation, and it is desirable to have a test for judging the number of components to retain for further analysis. Suppose that we have computed the roots $\lambda_1, \lambda_2, \ldots, \lambda_k$ and that the first r roots $\lambda_1, \lambda_2, \ldots, \lambda_r$ $(r < k)$ seem both sufficiently large and sufficiently different to be retained. The question then is whether the remaining $k - r$ roots and their associated vectors and the components are sufficiently alike for one to conclude that the true values are equal. A very approximate test is based on

$$\rho = (\lambda_{r+1}\lambda_{r+2}\cdots\lambda_k)^{-1}\left(\frac{\lambda_{r+1} + \lambda_{r+2} + \cdots + \lambda_k}{k - r}\right)^{k-r} \tag{A-35}$$

The proposed test is to consider $n \log_e \rho$ to follow a χ^2 distribution with $\frac{1}{2}(k - r - 1)(k - r + 2)$ degrees of freedom, if the null hypothesis of equality of the remaining latent roots is true.† One hopes in practical applications that the number r of significantly different components to be retained is substantially less than the number of variables k from which the components have been computed.

† See M. G. Kendall and A. Stuart, *The Advanced Theory of Statistics*, vol. 3, Griffin, London, 1966, pp. 292–293, for details and qualifications.

A somewhat similar result is achieved by factor analysis in which the X variables are specified ab initio to be linear combinations of a small number of independent standard normal variables (factors) plus an independent normal error term. From the principal component analysis we have

$$\mathbf{Z} = \mathbf{XA}$$

and hence

$$\mathbf{X} = \mathbf{ZA}' \tag{A-36}$$

Equations (A-36) express the X's as exact linear combinations of the components with coefficients given by the elements of **A**. If, however, we retain less than k principal components, Eqs. (A-36) would have to be replaced by

$$\mathbf{X} = \mathbf{Z}^*\mathbf{A}^{*\prime} + \mathbf{U} \tag{A-37}$$

where $\mathbf{Z}^*$ and $\mathbf{A}^*$ denote the submatrices of **Z** and **A** giving the retained components and the corresponding eigenvectors, and **U** is a matrix of errors. Principal components is obviously a possible estimation method in factor analysis, but slight modifications are required to the $\mathbf{A}^*$ coefficients to conform to the imposed assumption that the factors should have unit variance. Without additional restrictions $\mathbf{z}_i'\mathbf{z}_i = \lambda_i$, as we have seen in Eq. (A-29). When the $\mathbf{A}^*$ coefficients have been adjusted, they are referred to as factor loadings. However, several other estimation methods are used in factor analysis, and we do not propose to discuss them here.† An interesting application of factor analysis is given by Adelman and Morris, who find that 66 percent of the variance of the GNP per capita in 74 underdeveloped countries associated with just four factors, which have in turn been based on a complex of more than 20 social and political variables.‡

Table A-1 shows another example in which a small number of components effectively account for the variation in a set of data. The basic data are 11 series of average quarterly interest rates in the United Kingdom from the first quarter of 1963 to the first quarter of 1969. They include various national and local government rates as well as commercial rates, such as those on Building Society deposits. The series were standardized and the second row of the table gives the values of $\lambda_i/\Sigma\lambda$ for the first four principal components. The first principal component, which turned out to be effectively a simple arithmetic average of the standardized series, accounts for over 83 percent of the total variance and the first three components account for almost 97 percent. The last seven components account for less than 2 percent of the total variation.

† See J. T. Scott, Jr., "Factor Analysis and Regression," *Econometrica*, vol. 34, 1966, pp. 552–562; M. G. Kendall and A. Stuart, op. cit., pp. 306–311; and H. H. Hyman, *Modern Factor Analysis*, University of Chicago Press, Chicago, 1960.

‡ Adelman and C. T. Morris, "Factor Analysis of the Interrelationship between Social and Political Variables and Per Capita Gross National Product," *Quarterly Journal of Economics*, vol. 79, 1965, pp. 555–578.

Table A-1 Contribution of principal components to the total variation of 11 interest rates†

Component	1	2	3	4
Contribution	0.8368	0.0831	0.0482	0.0156
Cumulative contribution	0.8368	0.9199	0.9681	0.9837

Source: L. D. D. Price and P. Burman, Bank of England.

An important but as yet unresolved question concerns the use of principal components in conventional econometric regression problems. There appear to be at least two possibilities that are worth distinguishing. In both we are still assuming that some Y variable is to be explained in terms of a set of X variables. In the first problem, however, the number of variables that might possibly be included in the **X** matrix on theoretical or other grounds is so large and possibly so intercorrelated that conventional estimation procedures would be dubious for lack of degrees of freedom aggravated by multicollinearity. An obvious approach is then to apply principal component analysis *to the* X *variables* to see whether a small number of components might account for a sufficiently large proportion of the total variation of the X's and then to use these components as explanatory variables in a conventional regression with Y as the dependent variable. Some discussion of this topic is given in the treatment of 2SLS in Chap. 11. A possible variant on this approach is to retain a small number of specific important X variables in the final regression along with principal components determined from the other X variables.† This seems valid and useful, as far as it goes, and if some economic or social significance can be attached to specific components, so much the better. The second suggested use is more doubtful and requires more examination than it has yet received.‡ It concerns the case where multicollinearity rather than an excessive number of the X variables is the problem. As is well known, least-squares estimation of the coefficients of the X variables becomes very imprecise. Kendall's suggestion is to compute the principal components of the X variables, discard those with low eigenvalues, regress Y on the retained principal components, and transform back from the regression coefficients on the principal components to obtain estimates of the coefficients of the X variables. Suppose, for example, that there are five X variables and we retain just two principal components,

$$z_1 = a_{11}x_1 + a_{21}x_2 + \cdots + a_{51}x_5$$

$$z_2 = a_{12}x_1 + a_{22}x_2 + \cdots + a_{52}x_5$$

† For an illustration see G. B. Pidot, Jr., "A Principal Components Analysis of the Determinants of Local Government Fiscal Patterns," *Review of Economics and Statistics*, vol. 51, 1969, pp. 176–188.

‡ See M. G. Kendall, *A Course in Multivariate Analysis*, Griffin, London, 1957, pp. 70–74.

The regression of Y on z_1, z_2 is then

$$\begin{aligned} Y &= b_1 z_1 + b_2 z_2 + e \\ &= b_1(a_{11}x_1 + \cdots + a_{51}x_5) + b_2(a_{12}x_1 + \cdots + a_{52}x_{55}) + e \\ &= (b_1 a_{11} + b_2 a_{12})x_1 + \cdots + (b_1 a_{51} + b_2 a_{52})x_5 + e \end{aligned} \tag{A-38}$$

If one retained all five principal components, the coefficients of the x's in Eq. (A-38) would be identical with those given by a direct regression of Y on the x's. How should we decide on the number of components to retain? Purely subjective decision on the size of the latent roots, as in Kendall's illustrative example, is hardly satisfactory. Should one use the test based on Eq. (A-35) or a conventional analysis of variance test on the regression? The procedure would give a nonsense result in the case of perfectly collinear x variables. For example, suppose $x_2 = 2x_1$ and let

$$\mathbf{X'X} = \begin{bmatrix} 1 & 2 \\ 2 & 4 \end{bmatrix}$$

The eigenvalues are $\lambda_1 = 5$ and $\lambda_2 = 0$. For $\lambda_1 = 5$,

$$\mathbf{a}_1' = \begin{bmatrix} \dfrac{1}{\sqrt{5}} & \dfrac{2}{\sqrt{5}} \end{bmatrix}$$

and for $\lambda_2 = 0$,

$$\mathbf{a}_2' = \begin{bmatrix} \dfrac{2}{\sqrt{5}} & -\dfrac{1}{\sqrt{5}} \end{bmatrix}$$

The second principal component does not exist, for

$$z_2 = \frac{2}{\sqrt{5}}x_1 - \frac{1}{\sqrt{5}}x_2 = 0$$

since $x_2 = 2x_1$. However, the first component does exist, for

$$z_1 = \frac{1}{\sqrt{5}}x_1 + \frac{2}{\sqrt{5}}x_2 = \sqrt{5}\,x_1$$

and so the coefficient of z_1 in the regression with Y as the dependent variable can be computed as

$$b_1 = \frac{\Sigma z_1 y}{\Sigma z_1^2} = \frac{\Sigma z_1 y}{\lambda_1} = \frac{1}{\sqrt{5}}\Sigma x_1 y$$

Substituting in Eq. (A-38) gives

$$\begin{aligned} Y &= b_1 z_1 + e \\ &= \left(\frac{b_1}{\sqrt{5}}\right)x_1 + 2\left(\frac{b_1}{\sqrt{5}}\right)x_2 + e \end{aligned}$$

and apparently the relative influence of x_1 and x_2 has been determined in a perfectly collinear case where such a determination is impossible. The coefficients on x_1 and x_2 from the principal component regression are seen to reflect simply the fact that $x_2 = 2x_1$ and are unrelated to the true but unknown parameters. Nevertheless the question remains whether or not the approach might work reasonably well in a less than perfectly collinear case.†

† For a further contribution which shows that the principal component approach can be an improvement over OLS in certain circumstances see B. T. McCallum, "Artificial Orthogonalization in Regression Analysis," *Review of Economics and Statistics*, vol. 52, 1970, pp. 110–113. The basic point is that the principal component estimators will be biased but will have smaller variances than the unbiased OLS estimators. Thus under certain conditions, the principal components estimators may have smaller mean-square errors than OLS estimators.

APPENDIX

B

STATISTICAL TABLES

Table B-1 Areas of a standard normal distribution

An entry in the table is the proportion under the entire curve which is between $z = 0$ and a positive value of z. Areas for negative values of z are obtained by symmetry.

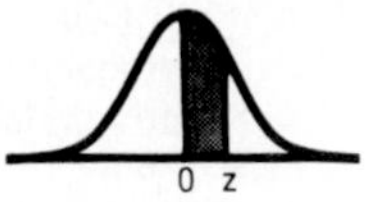

z	.00	.01	.02	.03	.04	.05	.06	.07	.08	.09
0.0	.0000	.0040	.0080	.0120	.0160	.0199	.0239	.0279	.0319	.0359
0.1	.0398	.0438	.0478	.0517	.0557	.0596	.0636	.0675	.0714	.0753
0.2	.0793	.0832	.0871	.0910	.0948	.0987	.1026	.1064	.1103	.1141
0.3	.1179	.1217	.1255	.1293	.1331	.1368	.1406	.1443	.1480	.1517
0.4	.1554	.1591	.1628	.1664	.1700	.1736	.1772	.1808	.1844	.1879
0.5	.1915	.1950	.1985	.2019	.2054	.2088	.2123	.2157	.2190	.2224
0.6	.2257	.2291	.2324	.2357	.2389	.2422	.2454	.2486	.2517	.2549
0.7	.2580	.2611	.2642	.2673	.2703	.2734	.2764	.2794	.2823	.2852
0.8	.2881	.2910	.2939	.2967	.2995	.3023	.3051	.3078	.3106	.3133
0.9	.3159	.3186	.3212	.3238	.3264	.3289	.3315	.3340	.3365	.3389
1.0	.3413	.3438	.3461	.3485	.3508	.3531	.3554	.3577	.3599	.3621
1.1	.3643	.3665	.3686	.3708	.3729	.3749	.3770	.3790	.3810	.3830
1.2	.3849	.3869	.3888	.3907	.3925	.3944	.3962	.3980	.3997	.4015
1.3	.4032	.4049	.4066	.4082	.4099	.4115	.4131	.4147	.4162	.4177
1.4	.4192	.4207	.4222	.4236	.4251	.4265	.4279	.4292	.4306	.4319
1.5	.4332	.4345	.4357	.4370	.4382	.4394	.4406	.4418	.4429	.4441
1.6	.4452	.4463	.4474	.4484	.4495	.4505	.4515	.4525	.4535	.4545
1.7	.4554	.4564	.4573	.4582	.4591	.4599	.4608	.4616	.4625	.4633
1.8	.4641	.4649	.4656	.4664	.4671	.4678	.4686	.4693	.4699	.4706
1.9	.4713	.4719	.4726	.4732	.4738	.4744	.4750	.4756	.4761	.4767
2.0	.4772	.4778	.4783	.4788	.4793	.4798	.4803	.4808	.4812	.4817
2.1	.4821	.4826	.4830	.4834	.4838	.4842	.4846	.4850	.4854	.4857
2.2	.4861	.4864	.4868	.4871	.4875	.4878	.4881	.4884	.4887	.4890
2.3	.4893	.4896	.4898	.4901	.4904	.4906	.4909	.4911	.4913	.4916
2.4	.4918	.4920	.4922	.4925	.4927	.4929	.4931	.4932	.4934	.4936
2.5	.4938	.4940	.4941	.4943	.4945	.4946	.4948	.4949	.4951	.4952
2.6	.4953	.4955	.4956	.4957	.4959	.4960	.4961	.4962	.4963	.4964
2.7	.4965	.4966	.4967	.4968	.4969	.4970	.4971	.4972	.4973	.4974
2.8	.4974	.4975	.4976	.4977	.4977	.4978	.4979	.4979	.4980	.4981
2.9	.4981	.4982	.4982	.4983	.4984	.4984	.4985	.4985	.4986	.4986
3.0	.4987	.4987	.4987	.4988	.4988	.4989	.4989	.4989	.4990	.4990

Reprinted from P. G. Hoel, *Introduction to Mathematical Statistics*, 4th ed., New York, Wiley, 1971, by permission of the publishers.

Table B-2 Student's *t* distribution

The first column lists the number of degrees of freedom (ν). The headings of the other columns give probabilities (P) for t to exceed the entry value. Use symmetry for negative t values.

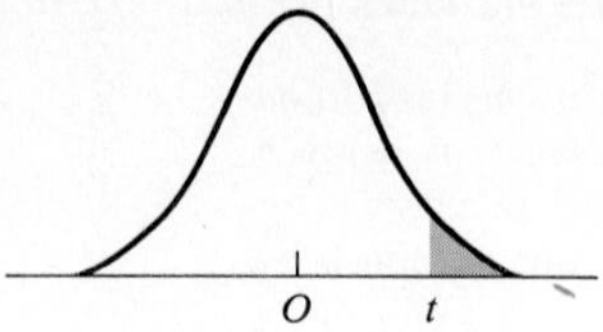

v \ P	.10	.05	.025	.01	.005
1	3.078	6.314	12.706	31.821	63.657
2	1.886	2.920	4.303	6.965	9.925
3	1.638	2.353	3.182	4.541	5.841
4	1.533	2.132	2.776	3.747	4.604
5	1.476	2.015	2.571	3.365	4.032
6	1.440	1.943	2.447	3.143	3.707
7	1.415	1.895	2.365	2.998	3.499
8	1.397	1.860	2.306	2.896	3.355
9	1.383	1.833	2.262	2.821	3.250
10	1.372	1.812	2.228	2.764	3.169
11	1.363	1.796	2.201	2.718	3.106
12	1.356	1.782	2.179	2.681	3.055
13	1.350	1.771	2.160	2.650	3.012
14	1.345	1.761	2.145	2.624	2.977
15	1.341	1.753	2.131	2.602	2.947
16	1.337	1.746	2.120	2.583	2.921
17	1.333	1.740	2.110	2.567	2.898
18	1.330	1.734	2.101	2.552	2.878
19	1.328	1.729	2.093	2.539	2.861
20	1.325	1.725	2.086	2.528	2.845
21	1.323	1.721	2.080	2.518	2.831
22	1.321	1.717	2.074	2.508	2.819
23	1.319	1.714	2.069	2.500	2.807
24	1.318	1.711	2.064	2.492	2.797
25	1.316	1.708	2.060	2.485	2.787
26	1.315	1.706	2.056	2.479	2.779
27	1.314	1.703	2.052	2.473	2.771
28	1.313	1.701	2.048	2.467	2.763
29	1.311	1.699	2.045	2.462	2.756
30	1.310	1.697	2.042	2.457	2.750
40	1.303	1.684	2.021	2.423	2.704
60	1.296	1.671	2.000	2.390	2.660
120	1.289	1.658	1.980	2.358	2.617
∞	1.282	1.645	1.960	2.326	2.576

Table B-3 χ^2 distribution

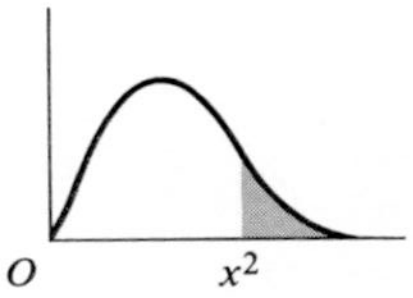

Degrees of freedom	P = 0.99	0.98	0.95	0.90	0.80	0.70	0.50	0.30	0.20	0.10	0.05	0.02	0.01
1	0.000157	0.000628	0.00393	0.0158	0.0642	0.148	0.455	1.074	1.642	2.706	3.841	5.412	6.635
2	0.0201	0.0404	0.103	0.211	0.446	0.713	1.386	2.408	3.219	4.605	5.991	7.824	9.210
3	0.115	0.185	0.352	0.584	1.005	1.424	2.366	3.665	4.642	6.251	7.815	9.837	11.341
4	0.297	0.429	0.711	1.064	1.649	2.195	3.357	4.878	5.989	7.779	9.488	11.668	13.277
5	0.554	0.752	1.145	1.610	2.343	3.000	4.351	6.064	7.289	9.236	11.070	13.388	15.086
6	0.872	1.134	1.635	2.204	3.070	3.828	5.348	7.231	8.558	10.645	12.592	15.033	16.812
7	1.239	1.564	2.167	2.833	3.822	4.671	6.346	8.383	9.803	12.017	14.067	16.622	18.475
8	1.646	2.032	2.733	3.490	4.594	5.527	7.344	9.524	11.030	13.362	15.507	18.168	20.090
9	2.088	2.532	3.325	4.168	5.380	6.393	8.343	10.656	12.242	14.684	16.919	19.679	21.666
10	2.558	3.059	3.940	4.865	6.179	7.267	9.342	11.781	13.442	15.987	18.307	21.161	23.209
11	3.053	3.609	4.575	5.578	6.989	8.148	10.341	12.899	14.631	17.275	19.675	22.618	24.725
12	3.571	4.178	5.226	6.304	7.807	9.034	11.340	14.011	15.812	18.549	21.026	24.054	26.217
13	4.107	4.765	5.892	7.042	8.634	9.926	12.340	15.119	16.985	19.812	22.362	25.472	27.688
14	4.660	5.368	6.571	7.790	9.467	10.821	13.339	16.222	18.151	21.064	23.685	26.873	29.141
15	5.229	5.985	7.261	8.547	10.307	11.721	14.339	17.322	19.311	22.307	24.996	28.259	30.578
16	5.812	6.614	7.962	9.312	11.152	12.624	15.338	18.418	20.465	23.542	26.296	29.633	32.000
17	6.408	7.255	8.672	10.085	12.002	13.531	16.338	19.511	21.615	24.769	27.587	30.995	33.409
18	7.015	7.906	9.390	10.865	12.857	14.440	17.338	20.601	22.760	25.989	28.869	32.346	34.805
19	7.633	8.567	10.117	11.651	13.716	15.352	18.338	21.689	23.900	27.204	30.144	33.687	36.191
20	8.260	9.237	10.851	12.443	14.578	16.266	19.337	22.775	25.038	28.412	31.410	35.020	37.566
21	8.897	9.915	11.591	13.240	15.445	17.182	20.337	23.858	26.171	29.615	32.671	36.343	38.932
22	9.542	10.600	12.338	14.041	16.314	18.101	21.337	24.939	27.301	30.813	33.924	37.659	40.289
23	10.196	11.293	13.091	14.848	17.187	19.021	22.337	26.018	28.429	32.007	35.172	38.968	41.638
24	10.856	11.992	13.848	15.659	18.062	19.943	23.337	27.096	29.553	33.196	36.415	40.270	42.980
25	11.524	12.697	14.611	16.473	18.940	20.867	24.337	28.172	30.675	34.382	37.652	41.566	44.314
26	12.198	13.409	15.379	17.292	19.820	21.792	25.336	29.246	31.795	35.563	38.885	42.856	45.642
27	12.879	14.125	16.151	18.114	20.703	22.719	26.336	30.319	32.912	36.741	40.113	44.140	46.963
28	13.565	14.847	16.928	18.939	21.588	23.647	27.336	31.391	34.027	37.916	41.337	45.419	48.278
29	14.256	15.574	17.708	19.768	22.475	24.577	28.336	32.461	35.139	39.087	42.557	46.693	49.588
30	14.953	16.306	18.493	20.599	23.364	25.508	29.336	33.530	36.250	40.256	43.773	47.962	50.892

For degrees of freedom greater than 30, the expression $\sqrt{2x^2} - \sqrt{2n-1}$ may be used as normal deviate with unit variance, where n is the number of degrees of freedom.

Reprinted from R. A. Fisher, *Statistical Methods for Research Workers*, 14th ed., New York, Macmillan Publishing Co., Inc.

Table B-4 *F* distribution

5 percent (Roman type) and 1 percent (*italic type*) points for the distribution of *F*

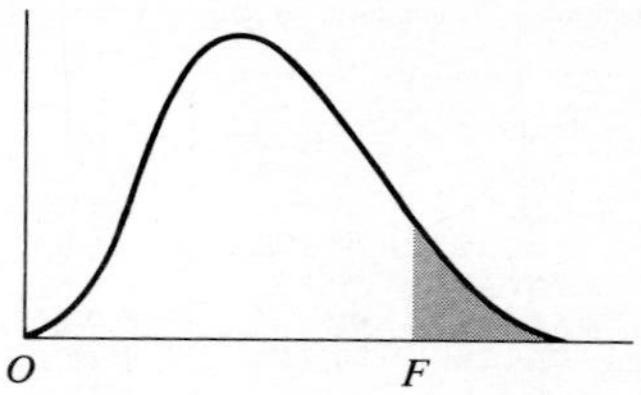

Degrees of freedom for denominator (ν_2)	Degrees of freedom for numerator (ν_1) 1	2	3	4	5	6	7	8	9	10	11	12	14	16	20	24	30	40	50	75	100	200	500	∞
1	161	200	216	225	230	234	237	239	241	242	243	244	245	246	248	249	250	251	252	253	253	254	254	254
	4052	*4999*	*5403*	*5625*	*5764*	*5859*	*5928*	*5981*	*6022*	*6056*	*6082*	*6106*	*6142*	*6169*	*6208*	*6234*	*6258*	*6286*	*6302*	*6323*	*6334*	*6352*	*6361*	*6366*
2	18.51	19.00	19.16	19.25	19.30	19.33	19.36	19.37	19.38	19.39	19.40	19.41	19.42	19.43	19.44	19.45	19.46	19.47	19.47	19.48	19.49	19.49	19.50	19.50
	98.49	*99.01*	*99.17*	*99.25*	*99.30*	*99.33*	*99.34*	*99.36*	*99.38*	*99.40*	*99.41*	*99.42*	*99.43*	*99.44*	*99.45*	*99.46*	*99.47*	*99.48*	*99.48*	*99.49*	*99.49*	*99.49*	*99.50*	*99.50*
3	10.13	9.55	9.28	9.12	9.01	8.94	8.88	8.84	8.81	8.78	8.76	8.74	8.71	8.69	8.66	8.64	8.62	8.60	8.58	8.57	8.56	8.54	8.54	8.53
	34.12	*30.81*	*29.46*	*28.71*	*28.24*	*27.91*	*27.67*	*27.49*	*27.34*	*27.23*	*27.13*	*27.05*	*26.92*	*26.83*	*26.69*	*26.60*	*26.50*	*26.41*	*26.30*	*26.27*	*26.23*	*26.18*	*26.14*	*26.12*
4	7.71	6.94	6.59	6.39	6.26	6.16	6.09	6.04	6.00	5.96	5.93	5.91	5.87	5.84	5.80	5.77	5.74	5.71	5.70	5.68	5.66	5.65	5.64	5.63
	21.20	*18.00*	*16.69*	*15.98*	*15.52*	*15.21*	*14.98*	*14.80*	*14.66*	*14.54*	*14.45*	*14.37*	*14.24*	*14.15*	*14.02*	*13.93*	*13.83*	*13.74*	*13.69*	*13.61*	*13.57*	*13.52*	*13.48*	*13.46*
5	6.61	5.79	5.41	5.19	5.05	4.95	4.88	4.82	4.78	4.74	4.70	4.68	4.64	4.60	4.56	4.53	4.50	4.46	4.44	4.42	4.40	4.38	4.37	4.36
	16.26	*13.27*	*12.06*	*11.39*	*10.97*	*10.67*	*10.45*	*10.27*	*10.15*	*10.05*	*9.96*	*9.89*	*9.77*	*9.68*	*9.55*	*9.47*	*9.38*	*9.29*	*9.24*	*9.17*	*9.13*	*9.07*	*9.04*	*9.02*
6	5.99	5.14	4.76	4.53	4.39	4.28	4.21	4.15	4.10	4.06	4.03	4.00	3.96	3.92	3.87	3.84	3.81	3.77	3.75	3.72	3.71	3.69	3.68	3.67
	13.74	*10.92*	*9.78*	*9.15*	*8.75*	*8.47*	*8.26*	*8.10*	*7.98*	*7.87*	*7.79*	*7.72*	*7.60*	*7.52*	*7.39*	*7.31*	*7.23*	*7.14*	*7.09*	*7.02*	*6.99*	*6.94*	*6.90*	*6.88*
7	5.59	4.74	4.35	4.12	3.97	3.87	3.79	3.73	3.68	3.63	3.60	3.57	3.52	3.49	3.44	3.41	3.38	3.34	3.32	3.29	3.28	3.25	3.24	3.23
	12.25	*9.55*	*8.45*	*7.85*	*7.46*	*7.19*	*7.00*	*6.84*	*6.71*	*6.62*	*6.54*	*6.47*	*6.35*	*6.27*	*6.15*	*6.07*	*5.98*	*5.90*	*5.85*	*5.78*	*5.75*	*5.70*	*5.67*	*5.65*
8	5.32	4.46	4.07	3.84	3.69	3.58	3.50	3.44	3.39	3.34	3.31	3.28	3.23	3.20	3.15	3.12	3.08	3.05	3.03	3.00	2.98	2.96	2.94	2.93
	11.26	*8.65*	*7.59*	*7.01*	*6.63*	*6.37*	*6.19*	*6.03*	*5.91*	*5.82*	*5.74*	*5.67*	*5.56*	*5.48*	*5.36*	*5.28*	*5.20*	*5.11*	*5.06*	*5.00*	*4.96*	*4.91*	*4.88*	*4.86*
9	5.12	4.26	3.86	3.63	3.48	3.37	3.29	3.23	3.18	3.13	3.10	3.07	3.02	2.98	2.93	2.90	2.86	2.82	2.80	2.77	2.76	2.73	2.72	2.71
	10.56	*8.02*	*6.99*	*6.42*	*6.06*	*5.80*	*5.62*	*5.47*	*5.35*	*5.26*	*5.18*	*5.11*	*5.00*	*4.92*	*4.80*	*4.73*	*4.64*	*4.56*	*4.51*	*4.45*	*4.41*	*4.36*	*4.33*	*4.31*
10	4.96	4.10	3.71	3.48	3.33	3.22	3.14	3.07	3.02	2.97	2.94	2.91	2.86	2.82	2.77	2.74	2.70	2.67	2.64	2.61	2.59	2.56	2.55	2.54
	10.04	*7.56*	*6.55*	*5.99*	*5.64*	*5.39*	*5.21*	*5.06*	*4.95*	*4.85*	*4.78*	*4.71*	*4.60*	*4.52*	*4.41*	*4.33*	*4.25*	*4.17*	*4.12*	*4.05*	*4.01*	*3.96*	*3.93*	*3.91*

11	4.84	3.98	3.59	3.36	3.20	3.09	3.01	2.95	2.90	2.96	2.82	2.79	2.74	2.70	2.65	2.61	2.57	2.53	2.50	2.47	2.45	2.42	2.41	2.40
	9.65	**7.20**	**6.22**	**5.67**	**5.32**	**5.07**	**4.88**	**4.74**	**4.63**	**4.54**	**4.46**	**4.40**	**4.29**	**4.21**	**4.10**	**4.02**	**3.94**	**3.86**	**3.80**	**3.74**	**3.70**	**3.66**	**3.62**	**3.60**
12	4.75	3.88	3.49	3.26	3.11	3.00	2.92	2.85	2.80	2.76	2.72	2.69	2.64	2.60	2.54	2.50	2.46	2.42	2.40	2.36	2.35	2.32	2.31	2.30
	9.33	**6.93**	**5.95**	**5.41**	**5.06**	**4.82**	**4.65**	**4.50**	**4.39**	**4.30**	**4.22**	**4.16**	**4.05**	**3.98**	**3.86**	**3.78**	**3.70**	**3.61**	**3.56**	**3.49**	**3.46**	**3.41**	**3.38**	**3.36**
13	4.67	3.80	3.41	3.18	3.02	2.92	2.84	2.77	2.72	2.67	2.63	2.60	2.55	2.51	2.46	2.42	2.38	2.34	2.32	2.28	2.26	2.24	2.22	2.21
	9.07	**6.70**	**5.74**	**5.20**	**4.86**	**4.62**	**4.44**	**4.30**	**4.19**	**4.10**	**4.02**	**3.96**	**3.85**	**3.78**	**3.67**	**3.59**	**3.51**	**3.42**	**3.37**	**3.30**	**3.27**	**3.21**	**3.18**	**3.16**
14	4.60	3.74	3.34	3.11	2.96	2.85	2.77	2.70	2.65	2.60	2.56	2.53	2.48	2.44	2.39	2.35	2.31	2.27	2.24	2.21	2.19	2.16	2.14	2.13
	8.86	**6.51**	**5.56**	**5.03**	**4.69**	**4.46**	**4.28**	**4.14**	**4.03**	**3.94**	**3.86**	**3.80**	**3.70**	**3.62**	**3.51**	**3.43**	**3.34**	**3.26**	**3.21**	**3.14**	**3.11**	**3.06**	**3.02**	**3.00**
15	4.54	3.68	3.29	3.06	2.90	2.79	2.70	2.64	2.59	2.55	2.51	2.48	2.43	2.39	2.33	2.29	2.25	2.21	2.18	2.15	2.12	2.10	2.08	2.07
	8.68	**6.36**	**5.42**	**4.89**	**4.56**	**4.32**	**4.14**	**4.00**	**3.89**	**3.80**	**3.73**	**3.67**	**3.56**	**3.48**	**3.36**	**2.39**	**3.20**	**3.12**	**3.07**	**3.00**	**2.97**	**2.92**	**2.89**	**2.87**
16	4.49	3.63	3.24	3.01	2.85	2.74	2.66	2.59	2.54	2.49	2.45	2.42	2.37	2.33	2.28	2.24	2.20	2.16	2.13	2.09	2.07	2.04	2.02	2.01
	8.53	**6.23**	**5.29**	**4.77**	**4.44**	**4.20**	**4.03**	**3.89**	**3.78**	**3.69**	**3.61**	**3.55**	**3.45**	**3.37**	**3.25**	**3.18**	**3.10**	**3.01**	**2.96**	**2.89**	**2.86**	**2.80**	**2.77**	**2.75**
17	4.45	3.59	3.20	2.96	2.81	2.70	2.62	2.55	2.50	2.45	2.41	2.38	2.33	2.29	2.23	2.19	2.15	2.11	2.08	2.04	2.02	1.99	1.97	1.96
	8.40	**6.11**	**5.18**	**4.67**	**4.34**	**4.10**	**3.93**	**3.79**	**3.68**	**3.59**	**3.52**	**3.45**	**3.35**	**3.27**	**3.16**	**3.08**	**3.00**	**2.92**	**2.86**	**2.79**	**2.76**	**2.70**	**2.67**	**2.65**
18	4.41	3.55	3.16	2.93	2.77	2.66	2.58	2.51	2.46	2.41	2.37	2.34	2.29	2.25	2.19	2.15	2.11	2.07	2.04	2.00	1.98	1.95	1.93	1.92
	8.28	**6.01**	**5.09**	**4.58**	**4.25**	**4.01**	**3.85**	**3.71**	**3.60**	**3.51**	**3.44**	**3.37**	**3.27**	**3.19**	**3.07**	**3.00**	**2.91**	**2.83**	**2.78**	**2.71**	**2.68**	**2.62**	**2.59**	**2.57**
19	4.38	3.52	3.13	2.90	2.74	2.63	2.55	2.48	2.43	2.38	2.34	2.31	2.26	2.21	2.15	2.11	2.07	2.02	2.00	1.96	1.94	1.91	1.90	1.88
	8.18	**5.93**	**5.01**	**4.50**	**4.17**	**3.94**	**3.77**	**3.63**	**3.52**	**3.43**	**3.36**	**3.30**	**3.19**	**3.12**	**3.00**	**2.92**	**2.84**	**2.76**	**2.70**	**2.63**	**2.60**	**2.54**	**2.51**	**2.49**
20	4.35	3.49	3.10	2.87	2.71	2.60	2.52	2.45	2.40	2.35	2.31	2.28	2.23	2.18	2.12	2.08	2.04	1.99	1.96	1.92	1.90	1.87	1.85	1.84
	8.10	**5.85**	**4.94**	**4.43**	**4.10**	**3.87**	**3.71**	**3.56**	**3.45**	**3.37**	**3.30**	**3.23**	**3.13**	**3.05**	**2.94**	**2.86**	**2.77**	**2.69**	**2.63**	**2.56**	**2.53**	**2.47**	**2.44**	**2.42**
21	4.32	3.47	3.07	2.84	2.68	2.57	2.49	2.42	2.37	2.32	2.28	2.25	2.20	2.15	2.09	2.05	2.00	1.96	1.93	1.89	1.87	1.84	1.82	1.81
	8.02	**5.78**	**4.87**	**4.37**	**4.04**	**3.81**	**3.65**	**3.51**	**3.40**	**3.31**	**3.24**	**3.17**	**3.07**	**2.99**	**2.88**	**2.80**	**2.72**	**2.63**	**2.58**	**2.51**	**2.47**	**2.42**	**2.38**	**2.36**
22	4.30	3.44	3.05	2.82	2.66	2.55	2.47	2.40	2.35	2.30	2.26	2.23	2.18	2.13	2.07	2.03	1.98	1.93	1.91	1.87	1.84	1.81	1.80	1.78
	7.94	**5.72**	**4.82**	**4.31**	**3.99**	**3.76**	**3.59**	**3.45**	**3.35**	**3.26**	**3.18**	**3.12**	**3.02**	**2.94**	**2.83**	**2.75**	**2.67**	**2.58**	**2.53**	**2.46**	**2.42**	**2.37**	**2.33**	**2.31**
23	4.28	3.42	3.03	2.80	2.64	2.53	2.45	2.38	2.32	2.28	2.24	2.20	2.14	2.10	2.04	2.00	1.96	1.91	1.88	1.84	1.82	1.79	1.77	1.76
	7.88	**5.66**	**4.76**	**4.26**	**3.94**	**3.71**	**3.54**	**3.41**	**3.30**	**3.21**	**3.14**	**3.07**	**2.97**	**2.89**	**2.78**	**2.70**	**2.62**	**2.53**	**2.48**	**2.41**	**2.37**	**2.32**	**2.28**	**2.26**
24	4.26	3.40	3.01	2.78	2.62	2.51	2.43	2.36	2.30	2.26	2.22	2.18	2.13	2.09	2.02	1.98	1.94	1.89	1.86	1.82	1.80	1.76	1.74	1.73
	7.82	**5.61**	**4.72**	**4.22**	**3.90**	**3.67**	**3.50**	**3.36**	**3.25**	**3.17**	**3.09**	**3.03**	**2.93**	**2.85**	**2.74**	**2.66**	**2.58**	**2.49**	**2.44**	**2.36**	**2.33**	**2.27**	**2.23**	**2.21**
25	4.24	3.38	2.99	2.76	2.60	2.49	2.41	2.34	2.28	2.24	2.20	2.16	2.11	2.06	2.00	1.96	1.92	1.87	1.84	1.80	1.77	1.74	1.72	1.71
	7.77	**5.57**	**4.68**	**4.18**	**3.86**	**3.63**	**3.46**	**3.32**	**3.21**	**3.13**	**3.05**	**2.99**	**2.89**	**2.81**	**2.70**	**2.62**	**2.54**	**2.45**	**2.40**	**2.32**	**2.29**	**2.23**	**2.19**	**2.17**

Table B-4 (*Continued*)

5 percent (Roman type) and 1 percent (italic type) points for the distribution of F

Degrees of freedom for denominator (ν_2)	Degrees of freedom for numerator (ν_1)																						
	1	2	3	4	5	6	7	8	9	10	11	12	14	16	20	24	30	40	50	75	100	200	500	∞
26	4.22	3.37	2.89	2.74	2.59	2.47	2.39	2.32	2.27	2.22	2.18	2.15	2.10	2.05	1.99	1.95	1.90	1.85	1.82	1.78	1.76	1.72	1.70	1.69
	7.72	*5.53*	*4.64*	*4.14*	*3.82*	*3.59*	*3.42*	*3.29*	*3.17*	*3.09*	*3.02*	*2.96*	*2.86*	*2.77*	*2.66*	*2.58*	*2.50*	*2.41*	*2.36*	*2.28*	*2.25*	*2.19*	*2.15*	*2.13*
27	4.21	3.35	2.96	2.73	2.57	2.46	2.37	2.30	2.25	2.20	2.16	2.13	2.08	2.03	1.97	1.93	1.88	1.84	1.80	1.76	1.74	1.71	1.68	1.67
	7.68	*5.49*	*4.60*	*4.11*	*3.79*	*3.56*	*3.39*	*3.26*	*3.14*	*3.06*	*2.98*	*2.93*	*2.83*	*2.74*	*2.63*	*2.55*	*2.47*	*2.38*	*2.33*	*2.25*	*2.21*	*2.16*	*2.12*	*2.10*
28	4.20	3.34	2.95	2.71	2.56	2.44	2.36	2.29	3.24	2.19	2.15	2.12	2.06	2.02	1.96	1.91	1.87	1.81	1.78	1.75	1.72	1.69	1.67	1.65
	7.64	*5.45*	*4.57*	*4.07*	*3.76*	*3.53*	*3.36*	*3.23*	*3.11*	*3.03*	*2.95*	*2.90*	*2.80*	*2.71*	*2.60*	*2.52*	*2.44*	*2.35*	*2.30*	*2.22*	*2.18*	*2.13*	*2.09*	*2.06*
29	4.18	3.33	2.93	2.70	2.54	2.43	2.35	2.28	2.22	2.18	2.14	2.10	2.05	2.00	1.94	1.90	1.85	1.80	1.77	1.73	1.71	1.68	1.65	1.64
	7.60	*5.52*	*4.54*	*4.04*	*3.73*	*3.50*	*3.33*	*3.20*	*3.08*	*3.00*	*2.92*	*2.87*	*2.77*	*2.68*	*2.57*	*2.49*	*2.41*	*2.32*	*2.27*	*2.19*	*2.15*	*2.10*	*2.06*	*2.03*
30	4.17	3.32	2.92	2.69	2.53	2.42	2.34	2.27	2.21	2.16	2.12	2.09	2.04	1.99	1.93	1.89	1.84	1.79	1.76	1.72	1.69	1.66	1.64	1.62
	7.56	*5.39*	*4.51*	*4.02*	*3.70*	*3.47*	*3.30*	*3.17*	*3.06*	*2.98*	*2.90*	*2.84*	*2.74*	*2.66*	*2.55*	*2.47*	*2.38*	*2.29*	*2.24*	*2.16*	*2.13*	*2.07*	*2.03*	*2.01*
32	4.15	3.30	2.90	2.67	2.51	2.40	2.32	2.25	2.19	2.14	2.10	2.07	2.02	1.97	1.91	1.86	1.82	1.76	1.74	1.69	1.67	1.64	1.61	1.59
	7.50	*5.34*	*4.46*	*3.97*	*3.66*	*3.42*	*3.25*	*3.12*	*3.01*	*2.94*	*2.86*	*2.80*	*2.70*	*2.62*	*2.51*	*2.42*	*2.34*	*2.25*	*2.20*	*2.12*	*2.08*	*2.02*	*1.98*	*1.96*
34	4.13	3.28	2.88	2.65	2.49	2.38	2.30	2.23	2.17	2.12	2.08	2.05	2.00	1.95	1.89	1.84	1.80	1.74	1.71	1.67	1.64	1.61	1.59	1.57
	7.44	*5.29*	*4.42*	*3.93*	*3.61*	*3.38*	*3.21*	*3.08*	*2.97*	*2.89*	*2.82*	*2.76*	*2.66*	*2.58*	*2.47*	*2.38*	*2.30*	*2.21*	*2.15*	*2.08*	*2.04*	*1.98*	*1.94*	*1.91*
36	4.11	3.26	2.86	2.63	2.48	2.36	2.28	2.21	2.15	2.10	2.06	2.03	1.89	1.93	1.87	1.82	1.78	1.72	1.69	1.65	1.62	1.59	1.56	1.55
	7.39	*5.25*	*4.38*	*3.89*	*3.58*	*3.35*	*3.18*	*3.04*	*2.94*	*2.86*	*2.78*	*2.72*	*2.62*	*2.54*	*2.43*	*2.35*	*2.26*	*2.17*	*2.12*	*2.04*	*2.00*	*1.94*	*1.90*	*1.87*
38	4.10	3.25	2.85	2.62	2.46	2.35	2.26	2.19	2.14	2.09	2.05	2.02	1.96	1.92	1.85	1.80	1.76	1.71	1.67	1.63	1.60	1.57	1.54	1.53
	7.35	*5.21*	*4.34*	*3.86*	*3.54*	*3.32*	*3.15*	*3.02*	*2.91*	*2.82*	*2.75*	*2.69*	*2.59*	*2.51*	*2.30*	*2.32*	*2.22*	*2.14*	*2.08*	*2.00*	*1.97*	*1.90*	*1.86*	*1.84*
40	4.08	3.23	2.84	2.61	2.45	2.34	2.25	2.18	2.12	2.07	2.04	2.00	1.95	1.90	1.84	1.79	1.74	1.69	1.66	1.61	1.59	1.55	1.53	1.51
	7.31	*5.18*	*4.31*	*3.83*	*3.51*	*3.29*	*3.12*	*2.99*	*2.88*	*2.80*	*2.73*	*2.66*	*2.56*	*2.49*	*2.37*	*2.29*	*2.20*	*2.11*	*2.05*	*1.97*	*1.94*	*1.88*	*1.84*	*1.81*
42	4.07	3.22	2.83	2.59	2.44	2.32	2.24	2.17	2.11	2.06	2.02	1.99	1.94	1.89	1.82	1.78	1.73	1.68	1.64	1.60	1.57	1.54	1.51	1.49
	7.27	*5.15*	*4.29*	*3.80*	*3.49*	*3.26*	*3.10*	*2.96*	*2.86*	*2.77*	*2.70*	*2.64*	*2.54*	*2.46*	*2.35*	*2.26*	*2.17*	*2.08*	*2.02*	*1.94*	*1.91*	*1.85*	*1.80*	*1.78*
44	4.06	3.21	2.82	2.58	2.43	2.31	2.23	2.16	2.10	2.05	2.01	1.98	1.92	1.88	1.81	1.76	1.72	1.66	1.63	1.58	1.56	1.52	1.50	1.48
	7.24	*5.12*	*4.26*	*3.78*	*3.46*	*3.24*	*3.07*	*2.94*	*2.84*	*2.75*	*2.68*	*2.62*	*2.52*	*2.44*	*2.32*	*2.24*	*2.15*	*2.06*	*2.00*	*1.92*	*1.88*	*1.82*	*1.78*	*1.75*
46	4.05	3.20	2.81	2.57	2.42	2.30	2.22	2.14	2.09	2.04	2.00	1.97	1.91	1.87	1.80	1.75	1.71	1.65	1.62	1.57	1.54	1.51	1.48	1.46
	7.21	*5.10*	*4.24*	*3.76*	*3.44*	*3.22*	*3.05*	*2.92*	*2.82*	*2.73*	*2.66*	*2.60*	*2.50*	*2.42*	*2.40*	*2.22*	*2.13*	*2.04*	*1.98*	*1.90*	*1.86*	*1.80*	*1.76*	*1.72*

48	4.04	3.19	2.80	2.56	2.41	2.30	2.21	2.14	2.08	2.03	1.99	1.96	1.90	1.86	1.79	1.74	1.70	1.64	1.61	1.56	1.53	1.50	1.47	1.45
	7.19	5.08	4.22	3.74	3.42	3.20	3.04	2.90	2.80	2.71	2.64	2.58	2.48	2.40	2.28	2.20	2.11	2.02	1.96	1.88	1.84	1.78	1.73	1.70
50	4.03	3.18	2.79	2.56	2.40	2.29	2.20	2.13	2.07	2.02	1.98	1.95	1.90	1.85	1.78	1.74	1.69	1.63	1.60	1.55	1.52	1.48	1.46	1.44
	7.17	5.06	4.20	3.72	3.41	3.18	3.02	2.88	2.78	2.70	2.62	2.56	2.46	2.39	2.26	2.18	2.10	2.00	1.94	1.86	1.82	1.76	1.71	1.68
55	4.02	3.17	2.78	2.54	2.38	2.27	2.18	2.11	2.05	2.00	1.97	1.93	1.88	1.83	1.76	1.72	1.67	1.61	1.58	1.52	1.50	1.46	1.43	1.41
	7.12	5.01	4.16	3.68	3.37	3.15	2.98	2.85	2.75	2.66	2.59	2.53	2.43	2.35	2.23	2.15	2.06	1.96	1.90	1.82	1.78	1.71	1.66	1.64
60	4.00	3.15	2.76	2.52	2.37	2.25	2.17	2.10	2.04	1.99	1.95	1.92	1.86	1.81	1.75	1.70	1.65	1.59	1.56	1.50	1.48	1.44	1.41	1.39
	7.08	4.98	4.13	3.65	3.34	3.12	2.95	2.82	2.72	2.63	2.56	2.50	2.40	2.32	2.20	2.12	2.03	1.93	1.87	1.79	1.74	1.68	1.63	1.60
65	3.99	3.14	2.75	2.51	2.36	2.24	2.15	2.08	2.02	1.98	1.94	1.90	1.85	1.80	1.73	1.68	1.63	1.57	1.54	1.49	1.46	1.42	1.39	1.37
	7.04	4.95	4.10	3.62	3.31	3.09	2.93	2.79	2.70	2.61	2.54	2.47	2.30	2.37	2.18	2.09	2.00	1.90	1.84	1.76	1.71	1.64	1.60	1.56
70	3.98	3.13	2.74	2.50	2.35	2.32	2.14	2.07	2.01	1.97	1.93	1.89	1.84	1.79	1.72	1.67	1.62	1.56	1.53	1.47	1.45	1.40	1.37	1.35
	7.01	4.92	4.08	3.60	3.29	3.07	2.91	2.77	2.67	2.59	2.51	2.45	2.35	2.28	2.15	2.07	1.98	1.88	1.82	1.74	1.69	1.63	1.56	1.53
80	3.96	3.11	2.72	2.48	2.33	2.21	2.12	2.05	1.99	1.95	1.91	1.88	1.82	1.77	1.70	1.65	1.60	1.54	1.51	1.45	1.42	1.38	1.35	1.32
	6.96	4.88	4.04	3.56	3.25	3.04	2.87	2.74	2.64	2.55	2.48	2.41	2.32	2.24	2.11	2.03	1.94	1.84	1.78	1.70	1.65	1.57	1.52	1.49
100	3.94	3.09	2.70	2.46	2.30	2.19	2.10	2.03	1.97	1.92	1.88	1.85	1.79	1.75	1.68	1.63	1.57	1.51	1.48	1.42	1.39	1.34	1.30	1.28
	6.90	4.82	3.98	3.51	3.20	2.99	2.82	2.69	2.59	2.51	2.43	2.36	2.26	2.19	2.06	1.98	1.89	1.79	1.73	1.64	1.59	1.51	1.46	1.43
125	3.92	3.07	2.68	2.44	2.29	2.17	2.08	2.01	1.95	1.90	1.86	1.83	1.77	1.72	1.65	1.60	1.55	1.49	1.45	1.39	1.36	1.31	1.27	1.25
	6.84	4.78	3.94	3.47	3.17	2.95	2.79	2.65	2.56	2.47	2.40	2.33	2.23	2.15	2.03	1.94	1.85	1.75	1.68	1.59	1.54	1.46	1.40	1.37
150	3.91	3.06	2.67	2.43	2.27	2.16	2.07	2.00	1.94	1.89	1.85	1.82	1.76	1.71	1.64	1.59	1.54	1.47	1.44	1.37	1.34	1.29	1.25	1.22
	6.81	4.75	3.91	3.44	3.13	2.92	2.76	2.62	2.53	2.44	2.37	2.30	2.20	2.12	2.00	1.91	1.83	1.72	1.66	1.56	1.51	1.43	1.37	1.33
200	3.89	3.04	2.65	2.41	2.26	2.14	2.05	1.98	1.92	1.87	1.83	1.80	1.74	1.69	1.62	1.57	1.52	1.45	1.42	1.35	1.32	1.26	1.22	1.19
	6.76	4.71	3.88	3.41	3.11	2.90	2.73	2.60	2.50	2.41	2.34	2.28	1.17	2.09	1.97	1.88	1.79	1.69	1.62	1.53	1.48	1.39	1.33	1.28
400	3.86	3.02	2.62	2.39	2.23	2.12	2.03	1.96	1.90	1.85	1.81	1.78	1.72	1.67	1.60	1.54	1.49	1.42	1.38	1.32	1.28	1.22	1.16	1.13
	6.70	4.66	3.83	3.36	3.06	2.85	2.69	2.55	2.46	2.37	2.29	2.23	2.12	2.04	1.92	1.84	1.74	1.64	1.57	1.47	1.42	1.32	1.24	1.19
1000	3.85	3.00	2.61	2.38	2.22	2.10	2.02	1.95	1.89	1.84	1.80	1.76	1.70	1.65	1.58	1.53	1.47	1.41	1.36	1.30	1.26	1.19	1.13	1.08
	6.66	4.62	3.80	3.34	3.04	2.82	2.66	2.53	2.43	2.34	2.26	2.20	2.09	2.01	1.89	1.81	1.71	1.61	1.54	1.44	1.38	1.28	1.19	1.11
	3.84	2.99	2.60	2.37	2.21	2.09	2.01	1.94	1.88	1.83	1.79	1.75	1.69	1.64	1.57	1.52	1.46	1.40	1.35	1.28	1.24	1.17	1.11	1.00
	6.64	4.60	3.78	3.32	3.02	2.80	2.64	2.51	2.41	2.32	2.24	2.18	2.07	1.99	1.87	1.79	1.69	1.59	1.52	1.41	1.36	1.25	1.15	1.00

Reprinted by permission from *Statistical Methods* by George W. Snedecor and William G. Cochran, Seventh Edition, © 1980 by The Iowa State University Press, Ames, Iowa.

Table B-5 Durbin-Watson statistic (Savin-White tables) Durbin-Watson statistic: 1 percent significance points of d_L and d_U[a]

n	k'=1		k'=2		k'=3		k'=4		k'=5		k'=6		k'=7		k'=8		k'=9		k'=10	
	d_L	d_U	d_L	d_U	d_L	d_U	d_L	d_U	d_L	d_U	d_L	d_U	d_L	d_U	d_L	d_U	d_L	d_U	d_L	d_U
6	0.390	1.142	----	----	----	----	----	----	----	----	----	----	----	----	----	----	----	----	----	----
7	0.435	1.036	0.294	1.676	----	----	----	----	----	----	----	----	----	----	----	----	----	----	----	----
8	0.497	1.003	0.345	1.489	0.229	2.102	----	----	----	----	----	----	----	----	----	----	----	----	----	----
9	0.554	0.998	0.408	1.389	0.279	1.875	0.183	2.433	----	----	----	----	----	----	----	----	----	----	----	----
10	0.604	1.001	0.466	1.333	0.340	1.733	0.230	2.193	0.150	2.690	----	----	----	----	----	----	----	----	----	----
11	0.653	1.010	0.519	1.297	0.396	1.640	0.286	2.030	0.193	2.453	0.124	2.892	----	----	----	----	----	----	----	----
12	0.697	1.023	0.569	1.274	0.449	1.575	0.339	1.913	0.244	2.280	0.164	2.665	0.105	3.053	----	----	----	----	----	----
13	0.738	1.038	0.616	1.261	0.499	1.526	0.391	1.826	0.294	2.150	0.211	2.490	0.140	2.838	0.090	3.182	----	----	----	----
14	0.776	1.054	0.660	1.254	0.547	1.490	0.441	1.757	0.343	2.049	0.257	2.354	0.183	2.667	0.122	2.981	0.078	3.287	----	----
15	0.811	1.070	0.700	1.252	0.591	1.464	0.488	1.704	0.391	1.967	0.303	2.244	0.226	2.530	0.161	2.817	0.107	3.101	0.068	3.374
16	0.844	1.086	0.737	1.252	0.633	1.446	0.532	1.663	0.437	1.900	0.349	2.153	0.269	2.416	0.200	2.681	0.142	2.944	0.094	3.201
17	0.874	1.102	0.772	1.255	0.672	1.432	0.574	1.630	0.480	1.847	0.393	2.078	0.313	2.319	0.241	2.566	0.179	2.811	0.127	3.053
18	0.902	1.118	0.805	1.259	0.708	1.422	0.613	1.604	0.522	1.803	0.435	2.015	0.355	2.238	0.282	2.467	0.216	2.697	0.160	2.925
19	0.928	1.132	0.835	1.265	0.742	1.415	0.650	1.584	0.561	1.767	0.476	1.963	0.396	2.169	0.322	2.381	0.255	2.597	0.196	2.813
20	0.952	1.147	0.863	1.271	0.773	1.411	0.685	1.567	0.598	1.737	0.515	1.918	0.436	2.110	0.362	2.308	0.294	2.510	0.232	2.714
21	0.975	1.161	0.890	1.277	0.803	1.408	0.718	1.554	0.633	1.712	0.552	1.881	0.474	2.059	0.400	2.244	0.331	2.434	0.268	2.625
22	0.997	1.174	0.914	1.284	0.831	1.407	0.748	1.543	0.667	1.691	0.587	1.849	0.510	2.015	0.437	2.188	0.368	2.367	0.304	2.548
23	1.018	1.187	0.938	1.291	0.858	1.407	0.777	1.534	0.698	1.673	0.620	1.821	0.545	1.977	0.473	2.140	0.404	2.308	0.340	2.479
24	1.037	1.199	0.960	1.298	0.882	1.407	0.805	1.528	0.728	1.658	0.652	1.797	0.578	1.944	0.507	2.097	0.439	2.255	0.375	2.417
25	1.055	1.211	0.981	1.305	0.906	1.409	0.831	1.523	0.756	1.645	0.682	1.766	0.610	1.915	0.540	2.059	0.473	2.209	0.409	2.362
26	1.072	1.222	1.001	1.312	0.928	1.411	0.855	1.518	0.783	1.635	0.711	1.759	0.640	1.889	0.572	2.026	0.505	2.168	0.441	2.313
27	1.089	1.233	1.019	1.319	0.949	1.413	0.878	1.515	0.808	1.626	0.738	1.743	0.669	1.867	0.602	1.997	0.536	2.131	0.473	2.269
28	1.104	1.244	1.037	1.325	0.969	1.415	0.900	1.513	0.832	1.618	0.764	1.729	0.696	1.847	0.630	1.970	0.566	2.098	0.504	2.229
29	1.119	1.254	1.054	1.332	0.988	1.418	0.921	1.512	0.855	1.611	0.788	1.718	0.723	1.830	0.658	1.947	0.595	2.068	0.533	2.193
30	1.133	1.263	1.070	1.339	1.006	1.421	0.941	1.511	0.877	1.606	0.812	1.707	0.748	1.814	0.684	1.925	0.622	2.041	0.562	2.160
31	1.147	1.273	1.085	1.345	1.023	1.425	0.960	1.510	0.897	1.601	0.834	1.698	0.772	1.800	0.710	1.906	0.649	2.017	0.589	2.131
32	1.160	1.282	1.100	1.352	1.040	1.428	0.979	1.510	0.917	1.597	0.856	1.690	0.794	1.788	0.734	1.889	0.674	1.995	0.615	2.104
33	1.172	1.291	1.114	1.358	1.055	1.432	0.996	1.510	0.936	1.594	0.876	1.683	0.816	1.776	0.757	1.874	0.698	1.975	0.641	2.080
34	1.184	1.299	1.128	1.364	1.070	1.435	1.012	1.511	0.954	1.591	0.896	1.677	0.837	1.766	0.779	1.860	0.722	1.957	0.665	2.057
35	1.195	1.307	1.140	1.370	1.085	1.439	1.028	1.512	0.971	1.589	0.914	1.671	0.857	1.757	0.800	1.847	0.744	1.940	0.689	2.037
36	1.206	1.315	1.153	1.376	1.098	1.442	1.043	1.513	0.988	1.588	0.932	1.666	0.877	1.749	0.821	1.836	0.766	1.925	0.711	2.018
37	1.217	1.323	1.165	1.382	1.112	1.446	1.058	1.514	1.004	1.586	0.950	1.662	0.895	1.742	0.841	1.825	0.787	1.911	0.733	2.001
38	1.227	1.330	1.176	1.388	1.124	1.449	1.072	1.515	1.019	1.585	0.966	1.658	0.913	1.735	0.860	1.816	0.807	1.899	0.754	1.985
39	1.237	1.337	1.187	1.393	1.137	1.453	1.085	1.517	1.034	1.584	0.982	1.655	0.930	1.729	0.878	1.807	0.826	1.887	0.774	1.970
40	1.246	1.344	1.198	1.398	1.148	1.457	1.098	1.518	1.048	1.584	0.997	1.652	0.946	1.724	0.895	1.799	0.844	1.876	0.789	1.956
45	1.288	1.376	1.245	1.423	1.201	1.474	1.156	1.528	1.111	1.584	1.065	1.643	1.019	1.704	0.974	1.768	0.927	1.834	0.881	1.902
50	1.324	1.403	1.285	1.446	1.245	1.491	1.205	1.538	1.164	1.587	1.123	1.639	1.081	1.692	1.039	1.748	0.997	1.805	0.955	1.864
55	1.356	1.427	1.320	1.466	1.284	1.506	1.247	1.548	1.209	1.592	1.172	1.638	1.134	1.685	1.095	1.734	1.057	1.785	1.018	1.837
60	1.383	1.449	1.350	1.484	1.317	1.520	1.283	1.558	1.249	1.598	1.214	1.639	1.179	1.682	1.144	1.726	1.108	1.771	1.072	1.817
65	1.407	1.468	1.377	1.500	1.346	1.534	1.315	1.568	1.283	1.604	1.251	1.642	1.218	1.680	1.186	1.720	1.153	1.761	1.120	1.802
70	1.429	1.485	1.400	1.515	1.372	1.546	1.343	1.578	1.313	1.611	1.283	1.645	1.253	1.680	1.223	1.716	1.192	1.754	1.162	1.792
75	1.448	1.501	1.422	1.529	1.395	1.557	1.368	1.587	1.340	1.617	1.313	1.646	1.284	1.682	1.256	1.716	1.227	1.746	1.199	1.785
80	1.466	1.515	1.441	1.541	1.416	1.568	1.390	1.595	1.364	1.624	1.338	1.653	1.312	1.683	1.285	1.714	1.259	1.745	1.232	1.777
85	1.482	1.528	1.458	1.553	1.435	1.578	1.411	1.603	1.386	1.630	1.362	1.657	1.337	1.685	1.312	1.714	1.287	1.743	1.262	1.773
90	1.496	1.540	1.474	1.563	1.452	1.587	1.429	1.611	1.406	1.636	1.383	1.661	1.360	1.687	1.336	1.714	1.312	1.741	1.288	1.769
95	1.510	1.552	1.489	1.573	1.468	1.596	1.446	1.618	1.425	1.642	1.403	1.666	1.381	1.690	1.358	1.715	1.336	1.741	1.313	1.767
100	1.522	1.562	1.503	1.583	1.482	1.604	1.462	1.625	1.441	1.647	1.421	1.670	1.400	1.693	1.378	1.717	1.357	1.741	1.335	1.765
150	1.611	1.637	1.598	1.651	1.584	1.665	1.571	1.679	1.557	1.693	1.543	1.708	1.530	1.722	1.515	1.737	1.501	1.752	1.486	1.767
200	1.664	1.684	1.653	1.693	1.643	1.704	1.633	1.715	1.623	1.725	1.613	1.735	1.603	1.746	1.592	1.757	1.582	1.768	1.571	1.779

Table B-5 (*Continued*)

n	k'=11		k'=12		k'=13		k'=14		k'=15		k'=16		k'=17		k'=18		k'=19		k'=20	
	d_L	d_U	d_L	d_U	d_L	d_U	d_L	d_U	d_L	d_U	d_L	d_U	d_L	d_U	d_L	d_U	d_L	d_U	d_L	d_U
16	0.060	3.446	----	----	----	----	----	----	----	----	----	----	----	----	----	----	----	----	----	----
17	0.084	3.286	0.053	3.506	----	----	----	----	----	----	----	----	----	----	----	----	----	----	----	----
18	0.113	3.146	0.075	3.358	0.047	3.557	----	----	----	----	----	----	----	----	----	----	----	----	----	----
19	0.145	3.023	0.102	3.227	0.067	3.420	0.043	3.601	----	----	----	----	----	----	----	----	----	----	----	----
20	0.178	2.914	0.131	3.109	0.092	3.297	0.061	3.474	0.038	3.639	----	----	----	----	----	----	----	----	----	----
21	0.212	2.817	0.162	3.004	0.119	3.185	0.084	3.358	0.055	3.521	0.035	3.671	----	----	----	----	----	----	----	----
22	0.246	2.729	0.194	2.909	0.148	3.084	0.109	3.252	0.077	3.412	0.050	3.562	0.032	3.700	----	----	----	----	----	----
23	0.281	2.651	0.227	2.822	0.178	2.991	0.136	3.155	0.100	3.311	0.070	3.459	0.046	3.597	0.029	3.725	----	----	----	----
24	0.315	2.580	0.260	2.744	0.209	2.906	0.165	3.065	0.125	3.218	0.092	3.363	0.065	3.501	0.043	3.629	0.027	3.747	----	----
25	0.348	2.517	0.292	2.674	0.240	2.829	0.194	2.982	0.152	3.131	0.116	3.274	0.085	3.410	0.060	3.538	0.039	3.657	0.025	3.766
26	0.381	2.460	0.324	2.610	0.272	2.758	0.224	2.906	0.180	3.050	0.141	3.191	0.107	3.325	0.079	3.452	0.055	3.572	0.036	3.682
27	0.413	2.409	0.356	2.552	0.303	2.694	0.253	2.836	0.208	2.976	0.167	3.113	0.131	3.245	0.100	3.371	0.073	3.490	0.051	3.602
28	0.444	2.363	0.387	2.499	0.333	2.635	0.283	2.772	0.237	2.907	0.194	3.040	0.156	3.169	0.122	3.294	0.093	3.412	0.068	3.524
29	0.474	2.321	0.417	2.451	0.363	2.582	0.313	2.713	0.266	2.843	0.222	2.972	0.182	3.098	0.146	3.220	0.114	3.338	0.087	3.450
30	0.503	2.283	0.447	2.407	0.393	2.533	0.342	2.659	0.294	2.785	0.249	2.909	0.208	3.032	0.171	3.152	0.137	3.267	0.107	3.379
31	0.531	2.248	0.475	2.367	0.422	2.487	0.371	2.609	0.322	2.730	0.277	2.851	0.234	2.970	0.196	3.087	0.160	3.201	0.128	3.311
32	0.558	2.216	0.503	2.330	0.450	2.446	0.399	2.563	0.350	2.680	0.304	2.797	0.261	2.912	0.221	3.026	0.184	3.137	0.151	3.246
33	0.585	2.187	0.530	2.296	0.477	2.408	0.426	2.520	0.377	2.633	0.331	2.746	0.287	2.858	0.246	2.969	0.209	3.078	0.174	3.184
34	0.610	2.160	0.556	2.266	0.503	2.373	0.452	2.481	0.404	2.590	0.357	2.699	0.313	2.808	0.272	2.915	0.233	3.022	0.197	3.126
35	0.634	2.136	0.581	2.237	0.529	2.340	0.478	2.444	0.430	2.550	0.383	2.655	0.339	2.761	0.297	2.865	0.257	2.969	0.221	3.071
36	0.658	2.113	0.605	2.210	0.554	2.310	0.504	2.410	0.455	2.512	0.409	2.614	0.364	2.717	0.322	2.818	0.282	2.919	0.244	3.019
37	0.680	2.092	0.628	2.186	0.578	2.282	0.528	2.379	0.480	2.477	0.434	2.576	0.389	2.675	0.347	2.774	0.306	2.872	0.268	2.969
38	0.702	2.073	0.651	2.164	0.601	2.256	0.552	2.350	0.504	2.445	0.458	2.540	0.414	2.637	0.371	2.733	0.330	2.828	0.291	2.923
39	0.723	2.055	0.673	2.143	0.623	2.232	0.575	2.323	0.528	2.414	0.482	2.507	0.438	2.600	0.395	2.694	0.354	2.787	0.315	2.879
40	0.744	2.039	0.694	2.123	0.645	2.210	0.597	2.297	0.551	2.386	0.505	2.476	0.461	2.566	0.418	2.657	0.377	2.748	0.338	2.838
45	0.835	1.972	0.790	2.044	0.744	2.118	0.700	2.193	0.655	2.269	0.612	2.346	0.570	2.424	0.528	2.503	0.488	2.582	0.448	2.661
50	0.913	1.925	0.871	1.987	0.829	2.051	0.787	2.116	0.746	2.182	0.705	2.250	0.665	2.318	0.625	2.387	0.586	2.456	0.548	2.526
55	0.979	1.891	0.940	1.945	0.902	2.002	0.863	2.059	0.825	2.117	0.786	2.176	0.748	2.237	0.711	2.298	0.674	2.359	0.637	2.421
60	1.037	1.865	1.001	1.914	0.965	1.964	0.929	2.015	0.893	2.067	0.857	2.120	0.822	2.173	0.786	2.227	0.751	2.283	0.716	2.338
65	1.087	1.845	1.053	1.889	1.020	1.934	0.986	1.980	0.953	2.027	0.919	2.075	0.886	2.123	0.852	2.172	0.819	2.221	0.786	2.272
70	1.131	1.831	1.099	1.870	1.068	1.911	1.037	1.953	1.005	1.995	0.974	2.038	0.943	2.082	0.911	2.127	0.880	2.172	0.849	2.217
75	1.170	1.819	1.141	1.856	1.111	1.893	1.082	1.931	1.052	1.970	1.023	2.009	0.993	2.049	0.964	2.090	0.934	2.131	0.905	2.172
80	1.205	1.810	1.777	1.844	1.150	1.878	1.122	1.913	1.094	1.949	1.066	1.984	1.039	2.022	1.011	2.057	0.983	2.097	0.955	2.135
85	1.236	1.803	1.210	1.834	1.184	1.866	1.158	1.898	1.132	1.931	1.106	1.965	1.080	1.999	1.053	2.033	1.027	2.068	1.000	2.104
90	1.264	1.798	1.240	1.827	1.215	1.856	1.191	1.886	1.166	1.917	1.141	1.948	1.116	1.979	1.091	2.012	1.066	2.044	1.041	2.077
95	1.290	1.793	1.267	1.821	1.244	1.848	1.221	1.876	1.197	1.905	1.174	1.934	1.150	1.963	1.126	1.993	1.102	2.023	1.079	2.054
100	1.314	1.790	1.292	1.816	1.270	1.841	1.248	1.868	1.225	1.895	1.203	1.922	1.181	1.949	1.158	1.977	1.136	2.006	1.113	2.034
150	1.473	1.783	1.458	1.799	1.444	1.814	1.429	1.830	1.414	1.847	1.400	1.863	1.385	1.880	1.370	1.897	1.355	1.913	1.340	1.931
200	1.561	1.791	1.550	1.801	1.539	1.813	1.528	1.824	1.518	1.836	1.507	1.847	1.495	1.860	1.484	1.871	1.474	1.883	1.462	1.896

[a] k' is the number of regressors excluding the intercept.

Table B-5 (*Continued*) Durbin-Watson statistic: 5 percent significance points of d_L and d_U[a]

n	k'=1		k'=2		k'=3		k'=4		k'=5		k'=6		k'=7		k'=8		k'=9		k'=10	
	d_L	d_U	d_L	d_U	d_L	d_U	d_L	d_U	d_L	d_U	d_L	d_U	d_L	d_U	d_L	d_U	d_L	d_U	d_L	d_U
6	0.610	1.400	----	----	----	----	----	----	----	----	----	----	----	----	----	----	----	----	----	----
7	0.700	1.356	0.467	1.896	----	----	----	----	----	----	----	----	----	----	----	----	----	----	----	----
8	0.763	1.332	0.559	1.777	0.368	2.287	----	----	----	----	----	----	----	----	----	----	----	----	----	----
9	0.824	1.320	0.629	1.699	0.455	2.128	0.296	2.588	----	----	----	----	----	----	----	----	----	----	----	----
10	0.879	1.320	0.697	1.641	0.525	2.016	0.376	2.414	0.243	2.822	----	----	----	----	----	----	----	----	----	----
11	0.927	1.324	0.758	1.604	0.595	1.928	0.444	2.283	0.316	2.645	0.203	3.005	----	----	----	----	----	----	----	----
12	0.971	1.331	0.812	1.579	0.658	1.864	0.512	2.177	0.379	2.506	0.268	2.832	0.171	3.149	----	----	----	----	----	----
13	1.010	1.340	0.861	1.562	0.715	1.816	0.574	2.094	0.445	2.390	0.328	2.692	0.230	2.985	0.147	3.266	----	----	----	----
14	1.045	1.350	0.905	1.551	0.767	1.779	0.632	2.030	0.505	2.296	0.389	2.572	0.286	2.848	0.200	3.111	0.127	3.360	----	----
15	1.077	1.361	0.946	1.543	0.814	1.750	0.685	1.977	0.562	2.220	0.447	2.472	0.343	2.727	0.251	2.979	0.175	3.216	0.111	3.438
16	1.106	1.371	0.982	1.539	0.857	1.728	0.734	1.935	0.615	2.157	0.502	2.388	0.398	2.624	0.304	2.860	0.222	3.090	0.155	3.304
17	1.133	1.381	1.015	1.536	0.897	1.710	0.779	1.900	0.664	2.104	0.554	2.318	0.451	2.537	0.356	2.757	0.272	2.975	0.198	3.184
18	1.158	1.391	1.046	1.535	0.933	1.696	0.820	1.872	0.710	2.060	0.603	2.257	0.502	2.461	0.407	2.667	0.321	2.873	0.244	3.073
19	1.180	1.401	1.074	1.536	0.967	1.685	0.859	1.848	0.752	2.023	0.649	2.206	0.459	2.396	0.456	2.589	0.369	2.783	0.290	2.974
20	1.201	1.411	1.100	1.537	0.998	1.676	0.894	1.828	0.792	1.991	0.692	2.162	0.595	2.339	0.502	2.521	0.416	2.704	0.336	2.885
21	1.221	1.420	1.125	1.538	1.026	1.669	0.927	1.812	0.829	1.964	0.732	2.124	0.637	2.290	0.547	2.460	0.461	2.633	0.380	2.806
22	1.239	1.429	1.147	1.541	1.053	1.664	0.958	1.797	0.863	1.940	0.769	2.090	0.677	2.246	0.588	2.407	0.504	2.571	0.424	2.734
23	1.257	1.437	1.168	1.543	1.078	1.660	0.986	1.785	0.895	1.920	0.804	2.061	0.715	2.208	0.628	2.360	0.545	2.514	0.465	2.670
24	1.273	1.446	1.188	1.546	1.101	1.656	1.013	1.775	0.925	1.902	0.837	2.035	0.751	2.174	0.666	2.318	0.584	2.464	0.506	2.613
25	1.288	1.454	1.206	1.550	1.123	1.654	1.038	1.767	0.953	1.886	0.868	2.012	0.784	2.144	0.702	2.280	0.621	2.419	0.544	2.560
26	1.302	1.461	1.224	1.553	1.143	1.652	1.062	1.759	0.979	1.873	0.897	1.992	0.816	2.117	0.735	2.246	0.657	2.379	0.581	2.513
27	1.316	1.469	1.240	1.556	1.162	1.651	1.084	1.753	1.004	1.861	0.925	1.974	0.845	2.093	0.767	2.216	0.691	2.342	0.616	2.470
28	1.328	1.476	1.255	1.560	1.181	1.650	1.104	1.747	1.028	1.850	0.951	1.958	0.874	2.071	0.798	2.188	0.723	2.309	0.650	2.431
29	1.341	1.483	1.270	1.563	1.198	1.650	1.124	1.743	1.050	1.841	0.975	1.944	0.900	2.052	0.826	2.164	0.753	2.278	0.682	2.396
30	1.352	1.489	1.284	1.567	1.214	1.650	1.143	1.739	1.071	1.833	0.998	1.931	0.926	2.034	0.854	2.141	0.782	2.251	0.712	2.363
31	1.363	1.496	1.297	1.570	1.229	1.650	1.160	1.735	1.090	1.825	1.020	1.920	0.950	2.018	0.879	2.120	0.810	2.226	0.741	2.333
32	1.373	1.502	1.309	1.574	1.244	1.650	1.177	1.732	1.109	1.819	1.041	1.909	0.972	2.004	0.904	2.102	0.836	2.203	0.769	2.306
33	1.383	1.508	1.321	1.577	1.258	1.651	1.193	1.730	1.127	1.813	1.061	1.900	0.994	1.991	0.927	2.085	0.861	2.181	0.795	2.281
34	1.393	1.514	1.333	1.580	1.271	1.652	1.208	1.728	1.144	1.808	1.080	1.891	1.015	1.979	0.950	2.069	0.885	2.162	0.821	2.257
35	1.402	1.519	1.343	1.584	1.283	1.653	1.222	1.726	1.160	1.803	1.097	1.884	1.034	1.967	0.971	2.054	0.908	2.144	0.845	2.236
36	1.411	1.525	1.354	1.587	1.295	1.654	1.236	1.724	1.175	1.799	1.114	1.877	1.053	1.957	0.991	2.041	0.930	2.127	0.868	2.216
37	1.419	1.530	1.364	1.590	1.307	1.655	1.249	1.723	1.190	1.795	1.131	1.870	1.071	1.948	1.011	2.029	0.951	2.112	0.891	2.198
38	1.427	1.535	1.373	1.594	1.318	1.656	1.261	1.722	1.204	1.792	1.146	1.864	1.088	1.939	1.029	2.017	0.970	2.098	0.912	2.180
39	1.435	1.540	1.382	1.597	1.328	1.658	1.273	1.722	1.218	1.789	1.161	1.859	1.104	1.932	1.047	2.007	0.990	2.085	0.932	2.164
40	1.442	1.544	1.391	1.600	1.338	1.659	1.285	1.721	1.230	1.786	1.175	1.854	1.120	1.924	1.064	1.997	1.008	2.072	0.945	2.149
45	1.475	1.566	1.430	1.615	1.383	1.666	1.336	1.720	1.287	1.776	1.238	1.835	1.189	1.895	1.139	1.958	1.089	2.002	1.038	2.088
50	1.503	1.585	1.462	1.628	1.421	1.674	1.378	1.721	1.335	1.771	1.291	1.822	1.246	1.875	1.201	1.930	1.156	1.986	1.110	2.044
55	1.528	1.601	1.490	1.641	1.452	1.681	1.414	1.724	1.374	1.768	1.334	1.814	1.294	1.861	1.253	1.909	1.212	1.959	1.170	2.010
60	1.549	1.616	1.514	1.652	1.480	1.689	1.444	1.727	1.408	1.767	1.372	1.808	1.335	1.850	1.298	1.894	1.260	1.939	1.222	1.984
65	1.567	1.629	1.536	1.662	1.503	1.696	1.471	1.731	1.438	1.767	1.404	1.805	1.370	1.843	1.336	1.882	1.301	1.923	1.266	1.964
70	1.583	1.641	1.554	1.672	1.525	1.703	1.494	1.735	1.464	1.768	1.433	1.802	1.401	1.837	1.369	1.873	1.337	1.910	1.305	1.948
75	1.598	1.652	1.571	1.680	1.543	1.709	1.515	1.739	1.487	1.770	1.458	1.801	1.428	1.834	1.399	1.867	1.369	1.901	1.339	1.935
80	1.611	1.662	1.586	1.688	1.560	1.715	1.534	1.743	1.507	1.772	1.480	1.801	1.453	1.831	1.425	1.861	1.397	1.893	1.369	1.925
85	1.624	1.671	1.600	1.696	1.575	1.721	1.550	1.747	1.525	1.774	1.500	1.801	1.474	1.829	1.448	1.857	1.422	1.886	1.396	1.916
90	1.635	1.679	1.612	1.703	1.589	1.726	1.566	1.751	1.542	1.776	1.518	1.801	1.494	1.827	1.469	1.854	1.445	1.881	1.420	1.909
95	1.645	1.687	1.623	1.709	1.602	1.732	1.579	1.755	1.557	1.778	1.535	1.802	1.512	1.827	1.489	1.852	1.465	1.877	1.442	1.903
100	1.654	1.694	1.634	1.715	1.613	1.736	1.592	1.758	1.571	1.780	1.550	1.803	1.528	1.826	1.506	1.850	1.484	1.874	1.462	1.898
150	1.720	1.746	1.706	1.760	1.693	1.774	1.679	1.788	1.665	1.802	1.651	1.817	1.637	1.832	1.622	1.847	1.608	1.862	1.594	1.877
200	1.758	1.778	1.748	1.789	1.738	1.799	1.728	1.810	1.718	1.820	1.707	1.831	1.697	1.841	1.686	1.852	1.675	1.863	1.665	1.874

Table B-5 (*Continued*)

n	k'=11		k'=12		k'=13		k'=14		k'=15		k'=16		k'=17		k'=18		k'=19		k'=20	
	d_L	d_U	d_L	d_U	d_L	d_U	d_L	d_U	d_L	d_U	d_L	d_U	d_L	d_U	d_L	d_U	d_L	d_U	d_L	d_U
16	0.098	3.503	----	----	----	----	----	----	----	----	----	----	----	----	----	----	----	----	----	----
17	0.138	3.378	0.087	3.557	----	----	----	----	----	----	----	----	----	----	----	----	----	----	----	----
18	0.177	3.265	0.123	3.441	0.078	3.603	----	----	----	----	----	----	----	----	----	----	----	----	----	----
19	0.220	3.159	0.160	3.335	0.111	3.496	0.070	3.642	----	----	----	----	----	----	----	----	----	----	----	----
20	0.263	3.063	0.200	3.234	0.145	3.395	0.100	3.542	0.063	3.676	----	----	----	----	----	----	----	----	----	----
21	0.307	2.976	0.240	3.141	0.182	3.300	0.132	3.448	0.091	3.583	0.058	3.705	----	----	----	----	----	----	----	----
22	0.349	2.897	0.281	3.057	0.220	3.211	0.166	3.358	0.120	3.495	0.083	3.619	0.052	3.731	----	----	----	----	----	----
23	0.391	2.826	0.322	2.979	0.259	3.128	0.202	3.272	0.153	3.409	0.110	3.535	0.076	3.650	0.048	3.753	----	----	----	----
24	0.431	2.761	0.362	2.908	0.297	3.053	0.239	3.193	0.186	3.327	0.141	3.454	0.101	3.572	0.070	3.678	0.044	3.773	----	----
25	0.470	2.702	0.400	2.844	0.335	2.983	0.275	3.119	0.221	3.251	0.172	3.376	0.130	3.494	0.094	3.604	0.065	3.702	0.041	3.790
26	0.508	2.649	0.438	2.784	0.373	2.919	0.312	3.051	0.256	3.179	0.205	3.303	0.160	3.420	0.120	3.531	0.087	3.632	0.060	3.724
27	0.544	2.600	0.475	2.730	0.409	2.859	0.348	2.987	0.291	3.112	0.238	3.233	0.191	3.349	0.149	3.460	0.112	3.563	0.081	3.658
28	0.578	2.555	0.510	2.680	0.445	2.805	0.383	2.928	0.325	3.050	0.271	3.168	0.222	3.283	0.178	3.392	0.138	3.495	0.104	3.592
29	0.612	2.515	0.544	2.634	0.479	2.755	0.418	2.874	0.359	2.992	0.305	3.107	0.254	3.219	0.208	3.327	0.166	3.431	0.129	3.528
30	0.643	2.477	0.577	2.592	0.512	2.708	0.451	2.823	0.392	2.937	0.337	3.050	0.286	3.160	0.238	3.266	0.195	3.368	0.156	3.465
31	0.674	2.443	0.608	2.553	0.545	2.665	0.484	2.776	0.425	2.987	0.370	2.996	0.317	3.103	0.269	3.208	0.224	3.309	0.183	3.406
32	0.703	2.411	0.638	2.517	0.576	2.625	0.515	2.733	0.457	2.840	0.401	2.946	0.349	3.050	0.299	3.153	0.253	3.252	0.211	3.348
33	0.731	2.382	0.668	2.484	0.606	2.588	0.546	2.692	0.488	2.796	0.432	2.899	0.379	3.000	0.329	3.100	0.283	3.198	0.239	3.293
34	0.758	2.355	0.695	2.454	0.634	2.554	0.575	2.654	0.518	2.754	0.462	2.854	0.409	2.954	0.359	3.051	0.312	3.147	0.267	3.240
35	0.783	2.330	0.722	2.425	0.662	2.521	0.604	2.619	0.547	2.716	0.492	2.813	0.439	2.910	0.388	3.005	0.340	3.099	0.295	3.190
36	0.808	2.306	0.748	2.398	0.689	2.492	0.631	2.586	0.575	2.680	0.520	2.774	0.467	2.868	0.417	2.961	0.369	3.053	0.323	3.142
37	0.831	2.285	0.772	2.374	0.714	2.464	0.657	2.555	0.602	2.646	0.548	2.738	0.495	2.829	0.445	2.920	0.397	3.009	0.351	3.097
38	0.854	2.265	0.796	2.351	0.739	2.438	0.683	2.526	0.628	2.614	0.575	2.703	0.522	2.792	0.472	2.880	0.424	2.968	0.378	3.054
39	0.875	2.246	0.819	2.329	0.763	2.413	0.707	2.499	0.653	2.585	0.600	2.671	0.549	2.757	0.499	2.843	0.451	2.929	0.404	3.013
40	0.896	2.228	0.840	2.309	0.785	2.391	0.731	2.473	0.678	2.557	0.626	2.641	0.575	2.724	0.525	2.808	0.477	2.892	0.430	2.974
45	0.988	2.156	0.938	2.225	0.887	2.296	0.838	2.367	0.788	2.439	0.740	2.512	0.692	2.586	0.644	2.659	0.598	2.733	0.553	2.807
50	1.064	2.103	1.019	2.163	0.973	2.225	0.927	2.287	0.882	2.350	0.836	2.414	0.792	2.479	0.747	2.544	0.703	2.610	0.660	2.675
55	1.129	2.062	1.087	2.116	1.045	2.170	1.003	2.225	0.961	2.281	0.919	2.338	0.877	2.396	0.836	2.454	0.795	2.512	0.754	2.571
60	1.184	2.031	1.145	2.079	1.106	2.127	1.068	2.177	1.029	2.227	0.990	2.278	0.951	2.330	0.913	2.382	0.874	2.434	0.836	2.487
65	1.231	2.006	1.195	2.049	1.160	2.093	1.124	2.138	1.088	2.183	1.052	2.229	1.016	2.276	0.980	2.323	0.944	2.371	0.908	2.419
70	1.272	1.986	1.239	2.026	1.206	2.066	1.172	2.106	1.139	2.148	1.105	2.189	1.072	2.232	1.038	2.275	1.005	2.318	0.971	2.362
75	1.308	1.970	1.277	2.006	1.247	2.043	1.215	2.080	1.184	2.118	1.153	2.156	1.121	2.195	1.090	2.235	1.058	2.275	1.027	2.315
80	1.340	1.957	1.311	1.991	1.283	2.024	1.253	2.059	1.224	2.093	1.195	2.129	1.165	2.165	1.136	2.201	1.106	2.238	1.076	2.275
85	1.369	1.946	1.342	1.977	1.315	2.009	1.287	2.040	1.260	2.073	1.232	2.105	1.205	2.139	1.177	2.172	1.149	2.206	1.121	2.241
90	1.395	1.937	1.369	1.966	1.344	1.995	1.318	2.025	1.292	2.055	1.266	2.085	1.240	2.116	1.213	2.148	1.187	2.179	1.160	2.211
95	1.418	1.929	1.394	1.956	1.370	1.984	1.345	2.012	1.321	2.040	1.296	2.068	1.271	2.097	1.247	2.126	1.222	2.156	1.197	2.186
100	1.434	1.923	1.416	1.948	1.393	1.974	1.371	2.000	1.347	2.026	1.324	2.053	1.301	2.080	1.277	2.108	1.253	2.135	1.229	2.164
150	1.579	1.892	1.564	1.908	1.550	1.924	1.535	1.940	1.519	1.956	1.504	1.972	1.489	1.989	1.474	2.006	1.458	2.023	1.443	2.040
200	1.654	1.885	1.643	1.896	1.632	1.908	1.621	1.919	1.610	1.931	1.599	1.943	1.588	1.955	1.576	1.967	1.565	1.979	1.554	1.991

[a] k' is the number of regressors excluding the intercept.

Reprinted by permission from *Econometrica*, vol. 45, no. 8, 1977, pp. 1992–1995.

Table B-6 Wallis statistic for fourth-order autocorrelation

5 percent significance points of $d_{4,L}$ and $d_{4,U}$ for regressions without quarterly dummy variables ($k = k' + 1$)

	$k'=1$		$k'=2$		$k'=3$		$k'=4$		$k'=5$	
n	$d_{4,L}$	$d_{4,U}$	$d_{4,L}$	$d_{4,U}$	$d_{4,L}$	$d_{4,U}$	$d_{4,L}$	$d_{4,U}$	$d_{4,L}$	$d_{4,U}$
16	0.774	0.982	0.662	1.109	0.549	1.275	0.435	1.381	0.350	1.532
20	0.924	1.102	0.827	1.203	0.728	1.327	0.626	1.428	0.544	1.556
24	1.036	1.189	0.953	1.273	0.867	1.371	0.779	1.459	0.702	1.565
28	1.123	1.257	1.050	1.328	0.975	1.410	0.898	1.487	0.828	1.576
32	1.192	1.311	1.127	1.373	1.061	1.443	0.993	1.511	0.929	1.587
36	1.248	1.355	1.191	1.410	1.131	1.471	1.070	1.532	1.013	1.598
40	1.295	1.392	1.243	1.442	1.190	1.496	1.135	1.550	1.082	1.609
44	1.335	1.423	1.288	1.469	1.239	1.518	1.189	1.567	1.141	1.620
48	1.369	1.451	1.326	1.493	1.281	1.537	1.236	1.582	1.191	1.630
52	1.399	1.475	1.359	1.513	1.318	1.554	1.276	1.595	1.235	1.639
56	1.426	1.496	1.389	1.532	1.351	1.569	1.312	1.608	1.273	1.648
60	1.449	1.515	1.415	1.548	1.379	1.583	1.343	1.619	1.307	1.656
64	1.470	1.532	1.438	1.563	1.405	1.596	1.371	1.629	1.337	1.664
68	1.489	1.548	1.459	1.577	1.427	1.608	1.396	1.639	1.364	1.671
72	1.507	1.562	1.478	1.589	1.448	1.618	1.418	1.648	1.388	1.678
76	1.522	1.574	1.495	1.601	1.467	1.628	1.439	1.656	1.411	1.685
80	1.537	1.586	1.511	1.611	1.484	1.637	1.457	1.663	1.431	1.691
84	1.550	1.597	1.525	1.621	1.500	1.646	1.475	1.671	1.449	1.696
88	1.562	1.607	1.539	1.630	1.515	1.654	1.490	1.677	1.466	1.702
92	1.574	1.617	1.551	1.639	1.528	1.661	1.505	1.684	1.482	1.707
96	1.584	1.626	1.563	1.647	1.541	1.668	1.519	1.690	1.496	1.712
100	1.594	1.634	1.573	1.654	1.552	1.674	1.531	1.695	1.510	1.717

5 percent significance points of $d_{4,L}$ and $d_{4,U}$ for regressions including a constant term and quarterly dummy variables ($k = k'' + 4$)

	$k''=1$		$k''=2$		$k''=3$		$k''=4$		$k''=5$	
n	$d_{4,L}$	$d_{4,U}$	$d_{4,L}$	$d_{4,U}$	$d_{4,L}$	$d_{4,U}$	$d_{4,L}$	$d_{4,U}$	$d_{4,L}$	$d_{4,U}$
16	1.156	1.381	1.031	1.532	0.902	1.776	0.777	2.191	0.693	2.238
20	1.228	1.428	1.123	1.556	1.013	1.726	0.899	1.954	0.806	2.042
24	1.287	1.459	1.199	1.565	1.107	1.694	1.011	1.856	0.928	1.949
28	1.337	1.487	1.261	1.576	1.181	1.679	1.099	1.803	1.025	1.889
32	1.379	1.511	1.312	1.587	1.243	1.673	1.171	1.773	1.104	1.850
36	1.414	1.532	1.355	1.598	1.293	1.672	1.230	1.755	1.170	1.824
40	1.445	1.550	1.391	1.609	1.336	1.674	1.279	1.745	1.225	1.807
44	1.471	1.567	1.422	1.620	1.373	1.677	1.321	1.739	1.272	1.795
48	1.494	1.582	1.450	1.630	1.404	1.681	1.357	1.737	1.312	1.788
52	1.514	1.595	1.474	1.639	1.432	1.686	1.389	1.736	1.347	1.782
56	1.533	1.608	1.495	1.648	1.456	1.691	1.416	1.736	1.377	1.779
60	1.549	1.619	1.514	1.656	1.478	1.696	1.441	1.737	1.404	1.777
64	1.564	1.629	1.531	1.664	1.497	1.700	1.463	1.739	1.429	1.776
68	1.577	1.639	1.546	1.671	1.515	1.705	1.482	1.741	1.450	1.775
72	1.590	1.648	1.560	1.678	1.531	1.710	1.500	1.743	1.470	1.776
76	1.601	1.656	1.573	1.685	1.545	1.714	1.517	1.746	1.488	1.776
80	1.611	1.663	1.585	1.691	1.559	1.719	1.531	1.748	1.504	1.777
84	1.621	1.671	1.596	1.696	1.571	1.723	1.545	1.751	1.519	1.778
88	1.630	1.677	1.607	1.702	1.582	1.727	1.558	1.753	1.533	1.779
92	1.639	1.684	1.616	1.707	1.593	1.731	1.570	1.756	1.546	1.781
96	1.647	1.690	1.625	1.712	1.603	1.735	1.580	1.759	1.558	1.782
100	1.654	1.695	1.633	1.717	1.612	1.739	1.591	1.761	1.569	1.784

Table B-7 The modified Von Neumann ratio

5 percent, 1 percent, and .1 percent points of the modified Von Neumann ratio

Degrees of Freedom	5%	1%	.1%	5%	1%	.1%	Degrees of Freedom	5%	1%	.1%	5%	1%	.1%
	One-tailed test against positive autocorrelation			One-tailed test against negative autocorrelation				One-tailed test against positive autocorrelation			One-tailed test against negative autocorrelation		
							31	1.410	1.186	.955	2.595	2.826	3.066
2	.025	.001	.000	3.975	3.999	4.000	32	1.419	1.198	.970	2.585	2.813	3.051
3	.252	.052	.005	4.142	4.427	4.493	33	1.428	1.209	.984	2.576	2.801	3.036
4	.474	.170	.037	3.827	4.295	4.496	34	1.437	1.221	.997	2.567	2.789	3.021
5	.598	.292	.095	3.571	4.076	4.378	35	1.445	1.231	1.010	2.559	2.778	3.007
6	.701	.386	.163	3.413	3.881	4.233	36	1.452	1.241	1.022	2.551	2.767	2.994
7	.790	.464	.228	3.299	3.731	4.095	37	1.460	1.251	1.034	2.544	2.757	2.982
8	.861	.537	.285	3.206	3.618	3.973	38	1.467	1.261	1.045	2.536	2.747	2.969
9	.922	.601	.339	3.131	3.524	3.871	39	1.474	1.270	1.057	2.529	2.738	2.957
10	.975	.657	.390	3.069	3.445	3.784	40	1.480	1.279	1.067	2.522	2.729	2.946
11	1.020	.708	.438	3.016	3.378	3.710	41	1.487	1.287	1.078	2.516	2.720	2.935
12	1.060	.753	.482	2.970	3.319	3.645	42	1.493	1.295	1.088	2.510	2.711	2.925
13	1.096	.795	.523	2.930	3.268	3.587	43	1.499	1.303	1.097	2.504	2.703	2.914
14	1.128	.832	.561	2.895	3.222	3.535	44	1.504	1.311	1.107	2.498	2.695	2.904
15	1.157	.866	.597	2.863	3.181	3.488	45	1.510	1.318	1.116	2.492	2.687	2.895
16	1.183	.898	.630	2.835	3.144	3.445	46	1.515	1.325	1.125	2.487	2.680	2.885
17	1.207	.927	.661	2.809	3.110	3.406	47	1.520	1.332	1.133	2.482	2.673	2.876
18	1.228	.954	.691	2.785	3.079	3.370	48	1.525	1.339	1.142	2.477	2.666	2.868
19	1.249	.979	.718	2.764	3.051	3.337	49	1.530	1.346	1.150	2.472	2.659	2.859
20	1.267	1.003	.744	2.744	3.025	3.306	50	1.535	1.352	1.158	2.467	2.653	2.851
21	1.285	1.024	.769	2.725	3.000	3.277	51	1.540	1.358	1.165	2.462	2.646	2.843
22	1.301	1.045	.792	2.708	2.978	3.250	52	1.544	1.364	1.173	2.458	2.640	2.835
23	1.316	1.064	.814	2.692	2.957	3.225	53	1.548	1.370	1.180	2.453	2.634	2.828
24	1.330	1.082	.834	2.677	2.937	3.201	54	1.552	1.376	1.187	2.449	2.628	2.820
25	1.344	1.100	.854	2.663	2.918	3.179	55	1.557	1.381	1.194	2.445	2.623	2.813
26	1.356	1.116	.873	2.650	2.901	3.157	56	1.561	1.387	1.201	2.441	2.617	2.806
27	1.368	1.131	.891	2.638	2.884	3.137	57	1.564	1.392	1.207	2.437	2.612	2.799
28	1.380	1.146	.908	2.626	2.868	3.118	58	1.568	1.397	1.214	2.433	2.606	2.793
29	1.390	1.160	.925	2.615	2.854	3.100	59	1.572	1.402	1.220	2.429	2.601	2.786
30	1.400	1.173	.940	2.605	2.839	3.083	60	1.575	1.407	1.226	2.426	2.596	2.780

Reprinted by permission of S. J. Press and R. B. Brooks from Report No. 6911, Center for Mathematical Studies in Business and Economics, University of Chicago, Chicago, 1969.

Table B-8 Significance values for c_0 in the cusum of squares test

	α						α				
m	0-10	0-05	0-025	0-01	0-005	m	0-10	0-05	0-025	0-01	0-005
1	0.40000	0.45000	0.47500	0.49000	0.49500	41	0.14916	0.17215	0.19254	0.21667	.233310
2	.35044	.44306	.50855	.56667	.59596	42	.14761	.17034	.19050	.21436	.23081
3	.35477	.41811	.46702	.53456	.57900	43	.14611	.16858	.18852	.21212	.22839
4	.33435	.39075	.44641	.50495	.54210	44	.14466	.16688	.18661	.20995	.22605
5	.31556	.37359	.42174	.47692	.51576	45	.14325	.16524	.18475	.20785	.22377
6	.30244	.35522	.40045	.45440	.48988	46	.14188	.16364	.18295	.20581	.22157
7	.28991	.33905	.38294	.43337	.46761	47	.14055	.16208	.18120	.20383	.21943
8	.27828	.32538	.36697	.41522	.44819	48	.13926	.16058	.17950	.20190	.21735
9	.26794	.31325	.35277	.39922	.43071	49	.13800	.15911	.17785	.20003	.21534
10	.25884	.30221	.34022	.38481	.41517	50	.13678	.15769	.17624	.19822	.21337
11	.25071	.29227	.32894	.37187	.40122	51	.13559	.15630	.17468	.19645	.21146
12	.24325	.28330	.31869	.36019	.38856	52	.13443	.15495	.17316	.19473	.20961
13	.23639	.27515	.30935	.34954	.37703	53	.13330	.15363	.17168	.19305	.20780
14	.23010	.26767	.30081	.33980	.36649	54	.13221	.15235	.17024	.19142	.20604
15	.22430	.26077	.29296	.33083	.35679	55	.13113	.15110	.16884	.18983	.20432
16	.21895	.25439	.28570	.32256	.34784	56	.13009	.14989	.16746	.18828	.20265
17	.21397	.24847	.27897	.31489	.33953	57	.12907	.14870	.16613	.18677	.20101
18	.20933	.24296	.27270	.30775	.33181	58	.12807	.14754	.16482	.18529	.19942
19	.20498	.23781	.26685	.30108	.32459	59	.12710	.14641	.16355	.18385	.19786
20	.20089	.23298	.26137	.29484	.31784	60	.12615	.14530	.16230	.18245	.19635
21	.19705	.22844	.25622	.28898	.31149	62	.12431	.14316	.15990	.17973	.19341
22	.19343	.22416	.25136	.28346	.30552	64	.12255	.14112	.15760	.17713	.19061
23	.19001	.22012	.24679	.27825	.29989	66	.12087	.13916	.15540	.17464	.18792
24	.18677	.21630	.24245	.27333	.29456	68	.11926	.13728	.15329	.17226	.18535
25	.18370	.21268	.23835	.26866	.28951	70	.11771	.13548	.15127	.16997	.18288
26	.18077	.20924	.23445	.26423	.28472	72	.11622	.13375	.14932	.16777	.18051
27	.17799	.20596	.23074	.26001	.28016	74	.11479	.13208	.14745	.16566	.17823
28	.17533	.20283	.22721	.25600	.27582	76	.11341	.13048	.14565	.16363	.17604
29	.17280	.19985	.22383	.25217	.27168	78	.11208	.12894	.14392	.16167	.17392
30	.17037	.19700	.22061	.24851	.26772	80	.11079	.12745	.14224	.15978	.17188
31	.16805	.19427	.21752	.24501	.26393	82	.10955	.12601	.14063	.15795	.16992
32	.16582	.19166	.21457	.24165	.26030	84	.10835	.12462	.13907	.15619	.16802
33	.16368	.18915	.21173	.23843	.25683	86	.10719	.12327	.13756	.15449	.16618
34	.16162	.18674	.20901	.23534	.25348	88	.10607	.12197	.13610	.15284	.16440
35	.15964	.18442	.20639	.23237	.25027	90	.10499	.12071	.13468	.15124	.16268
36	.15774	.18218	.20387	.22951	.24718	92	.10393	.11949	.13331	.14970	.16101
37	.15590	.18003	.20144	.22676	.24421	94	.10291	.11831	.13198	.14820	.15940
38	.15413	.17796	.19910	.22410	.24134	96	.10192	.11716	.13070	.14674	.15783
39	.15242	.17595	.19684	.22154	.23857	98	.10096	.11604	.12944	.14533	.15631
40	.15076	.17402	.19465	.21906	.23589	100	.10002	.11496	.12823	.14396	.15483

Values for odd n greater than 650 are available from the author on request.

The values of c_0 are used to determine the pair of lines, $s_r = \pm c_0 + (r-k)/(n-k)$. For n observations, k explanatory variables (including the intercept, if there is one) and a given significance level α, c_0 is found by entering the table at $m = \frac{1}{2}(n-k) - 1$ and $\frac{1}{2}\alpha$. For a one-sided test, enter at $m = \frac{1}{2}(n-k) - 1$ and α. When $(n-k)$ is odd, the procedure suggested is to interpolate linearly between $m = \frac{1}{2}(n-k) - \frac{3}{2}$ and $m = \frac{1}{2}(n-k) - \frac{1}{2}$.

INDEX